THE STATISTICAL ACCOUNT OF SCOTLAND

General Editors: Donald J. Withrington and Ian R. Grant

VOLUME XIII

ANGUS

THE
STATISTICAL ACCOUNT OF SCOTLAND

GENERAL EDITORS' INTRODUCTION

The *Statistical Account of Scotland* has been used by generation after generation of social historians enquiring into the local or national affairs of Scotland in the later 18th century. It is an unrivalled source, and historians of other countries, as well as their sociologists, geographers and natural scientists, have long regretted having no similar body of evidence available to them. Sir John Sinclair, determinedly cajoling the parish ministers of the Established Church to respond to his long list of over 160 queries, intended his statistical enquiry to enable the country, and its government, not only to assess its current state but to prepare better for a better future— "ascertaining the quantum of happiness enjoyed by its inhabitants and the means of its future improvement", moral as well as economic or political. The quality of the returns he received was generally good and was often excellent, and the parochial reports provided the Scots of the 1790s with a uniquely valuable analysis of their own times: the same reports provide us today with an incomparable view of Scotland two centuries ago, through the sharp eyes and the often sharp words of men who knew their localities very well indeed.

However, the original *Account*, printed in twenty-one volumes in the course of the 1790s, is difficult and often exasperating to use. Sinclair published the parish returns just as they came in to him; therefore the reports for one county or for part of one county may be scattered throughout a dozen volumes or more. Readers of the original printing must have the index in volume xx in order to search out easily the particular returns they want, and even then they may overlook the supplementary replies eventually published in volume xxi. Furthermore, Sinclair's indexes of subjects and persons in volume xxi are woefully inadequate.

In this new edition we have brought together the parish returns in groupings by county and have printed them in alphabetical order, thus avoiding a major difficulty in using the earlier compilation. This new arrangement will not only assist those who wish to use the *Account* as a whole, it will also be especially useful to local historians and to others engaged in local or regional researches with an historical basis: and the new format makes much easier a direct comparison of the Sinclair *Account* with the *New Statistical Account*, published by counties in 1845. So large is the volume of material for Aberdeenshire and Perthshire, however, that these counties have required two volumes each in this reissue. And we have decided to gather together in one volume all the returns from western island parishes, in the Inner and Outer Hebrides and in Bute, rather than leave them scattered among the returns from mainland Ross-shire, Inverness-shire and Argyll: these have a coherence in themselves which would be lost if placed with their respective counties.

Each of the twenty volumes in this reissue is being edited by a scholar who contributes an introduction showing the significance of the *Statistical Account* reports for the region and assessing their importance for modern historical and other social studies. Each volume will also contain an index (of the more important topics discussed in the returns, but not of persons or places) which will make the *Account* more accessible to and more immediately useful to all students, not least to pupils in schools where Scottish local studies are being introduced or extended. We are grateful to James Hamilton for his help in preparing the indexes.

We believe that the significantly improved format of this reissue will make more widely useful, and more widely used, an already acknowledged vital work of standard reference.

Ian R. Grant   Donald J. Withrington

THE

STATISTICAL ACCOUNT

OF

SCOTLAND
1791–1799

EDITED BY SIR JOHN SINCLAIR

VOLUME XIII

ANGUS

With a new introduction by
BRUCE LENMAN

EP Publishing Limited
1976

This is volume XIII of a reissue in twenty volumes of *The Statistical Account of Scotland*, originally published between 1791 and 1799. In this reissue all the parish accounts for individual counties are printed together for the first time, with a new introduction and index in each volume.

Volume I of this reissue carries a general introduction by Donald J. Withrington.

ISBN 0 7158 1000 6 (set)
0 7158 1013 8 (vol. XIII)

Errata   PARISH OF RESCOBIE (pages 587–597)

The publisher apologises for the confusion in pages 587–592 of this volume, caused by the fact that two printed versions of the original are in existence. The correct version of these pages is included at the end of the book, together with details of the resultant amendments to the index.

Printed in Great Britain by
The Scolar Press Limited, Ilkley, Yorkshire

CONTENTS

INTRODUCTION

T HE county which is the subject of this volume has two distinct names, Angus and Forfarshire. Of these Angus is much the older, but is still not the oldest name which has been applied to the county for it is clear that Angus and Mearns together correspond to the dark-age Pictish province of Circhenn. The name Angus may derive from the Gaelic take-over of this southern Pictish region and may well embody the name of the Cenel nOengusa, one of the three main kinship groups in the Gaelic population moving into this area after 843 A.D.[1] The county in modern times was usually referred to as Forfarshire (following the name of the county town), but since the Local Government (Scotland) Act of 1929 Angus has been both the official and the popular term.

Despite a long history of administrative separation Angus and the neighbouring county of Kincardine or Mearns still form what is recognisably one geographical unit. In its own right, however, Angus is a substantial and significant county with strongly-marked internal geographical divisions. Its area is 559,171 acres or roughly 807 square miles, which makes it the eleventh biggest county in Scotland. Being nearly circular in shape, it is a very compact county and of its 190 miles or so of boundary some forty-four are washed by the North Sea or by the waters of the Firth of Tay. Its land surface is extremely varied – highland, lowland and maritime – and divided into sharply-marked zones by its under-lying geology. The most northerly zone is the highland one, a substantial tract of country some nine to fifteen miles wide and containing in the north-west the peak of Glas Maol (3,502 feet). The mountains in this zone are composed of old, durable, metamorphic rocks and its limit is marked

---

1. W. J. Watson, *The History of the Celtic Place-Names of Scotland* (Edinburgh, 1926), 107–110; J. Bannerman, *Studies in the History of Dalriada* (Edinburgh, 1974), 108–9; M. O. Anderson, *Kings and Kingship in Early Scotland* (Edinburgh, 1973), 142.

Introduction

out by the Highland Boundary Fault, which runs south-westward across Scotland from Stonehaven to the Clyde at Helensburgh. These mountain rocks are predominantly mica, schists, gneisses and grits, and do not break down into fertile soils: as a result this highland zone is mainly a heather-covered plateau cut into by a series of impressive glens – Glen Isla to the west, Glen Prosen, Glen Clova and Glenesk to the east, with a couple of minor glens, Glen Ogil and Glen Lethnot, lying between Clova and Glenesk.

Parallel with the foothills (or braes) of the highland zone, lies the broad expanse of the Howe of Angus, a portion of the great valley of Strathmore which stretches through Kincardine, Angus and the eastern part of Perthshire. Nothing more clearly demonstrates geological influence in Angus topography than the contrast of this fertile corridor (some 32 miles long and 4 to 6 miles wide) with the highland zone which covers some two-fifths of the entire county, for the Lower Old Red Sandstone rocks underlying the Howe have produced fertile soils capable of sustaining a productive agriculture. Well drained by rivers like the South Esk, this region contrasts sharply with the next zone which takes its character from the Sidlaw Hills, dry volcanic outcrops of predominantly black andesite rocks with their highest point in Craigowal (1,493 feet), north of Dundee. Beyond the south-facing slopes of these hills lies the maritime fringe of Angus: it stretches for some forty miles from west to east, and its southern slopes and raised beaches, with their light, easily-drained soils, had an early and continuing importance in the development of arable farming in the county. Between Broughty Ferry and Arbroath, and between the mouths of the North and the South Esk, there are considerable areas of consolidated sand dunes or links, which have been valued by man for a variety of purposes ranging from grazing and rabbit warrens to golf.[1]

1. A. R. MacGregor, *Fife and Angus Geology* (Edinburgh, 1968); F. Walker, *Tayside Geology* (Dundee: Museum and Art Gallery, 1961); E. S. Valentine, *Forfarshire* (Cambridge, 1912).

Introduction

We are fortunate in possessing a late seventeenth-century survey of Angus which, if far briefer than the Angus entries in the *Statistical Account*, is still an instructive contrast to it. This earlier account was originally written in Latin by Robert Edward, minister of Murroes, and published in 1678 with a fairly big map of the county executed by the same hand: until a translation into English was produced and printed in 1793 in Dundee by Thomas Colville,[1] this was a very rare item. Edward described the great central valley of Strathmore as "the most plain, pleasant and fruitful" part of the county and remarked that anyone climbing to the top of Turin Hill "will have a view of almost numberless castles and houses of the great, lying between Cupar and Montrose, and which are ornamented with fine woods and gardens. He may also see four of the royal burghs of Angus, viz. Forfar, Brechin, Montrose and Abrinca (commonly called Arbroath, or Aberbrothock), likewise the little towns of Glammis and Kirriemuir: and behind, in the valley of Lunan, there are many elegant seats of gentry." This extract is typical of the Angus that Edward saw – a society dominated by its aristocracy. That same aristocracy and the episcopalian clergy associated with it were, especially after the Revolution of 1688–90, very self-conscious about the idea of gentility.

Nevertheless, Edward does not fail to give an account of the economic basis of his county. The land south of the Grampians, he wrote, grew an abundance of grain: "wheat, barley, pease, oats and beans, in such plenty as to suffice not only for home consumption, but for a supply to the inhabitants of other countries." In the glens a little barley and oats were cultivated but the real wealth of the Angus glens lay in the hill pastures "where oxen, sheep, goats, and thousands of unbroken horses are fed, until sold in the fairs at the foot of the mountains." After the

1. This enterprising man was for many years the only printer in Dundee, but his attempts to establish periodicals and his own newspaper, the *Dundee Mercury*, were not in the long run successful. The translation of Edward's account was reprinted in 1967 by the Forfar and District Historical Society. The quotations from Colville in this introduction are taken from the 1967 reprint.

spring-ploughing, oxen were driven in herds to the Grampian pastures where they remained until the harvest. Cattle, sheep and horses could, of course be walked considerable distances in favourable weather in a countryside devoid of good roads. But lack of roads restricted the value of the extensive timber reserves which existed in the Grampians: as Edward remarked, "Here is abundance of timber for labouring utensils, and for the houses of the common people: but for the houses in towns, and those of gentlemen in the country, timber is brought from Norway, not because Scotland does not afford wood sufficient to supply the whole kingdom but because rugged and impassable rocks prevent its being transported from these places where it grows." For fuel in a county with no coal, the people made use of peat, bog oak and broom (which was extensively sown as a means of providing a quick fire). Near sea or firth, which afforded good water transport, there was extensive quarrying of freestone and millstones, the latter being exported as far away as to Holland and North America. Edward also remarked on the lead and silver mining activities in which the Lindsay lairds of Glenesk had indulged since the sixteenth century but without any lasting success.[1] Finally, it is worth glancing at what Edward said about the towns of Angus. He remarked that, in all, there were five royal burghs in Angus

"viz. Forfar, almost in the centre of the county; Brechin, on the north bank of South Esk; at the mouth of which is situated Montrose, where there is a convenient harbour; that of Arbroath (another of the royal burghs), is not so much liked by mariners. But at Dundee (the last of the five), the harbour, by great labour and expence, has been rendered a very safe and agreeable station for vessels; and from this circumstance, the town has become the chief emporium not only of Angus, but of Perthshire. The citizens here (whose houses resemble palaces) are so eminent in

---

1. For a fuller account of the Lindsays' mining schemes, see G. Michie and B. Lenman, "The miners of Glenesk", *Scots Magazine*, n.s., 98 (Nov. 1972), 104–113.

regard to their skill and industry in business, that they
have got more rivals than equals in the kingdom."
It is perhaps surprising after reading this description to
recall that all the harbours referred to were purely tidal.
And, without believing to the letter the statements
about Dundee, it is nonetheless clear that the town had,
by 1678, greatly recovered from its terrible experiences of
the Civil War when it had been twice sacked, once by the
royalist army of Montrose and once by the English
parliamentary forces under General Monk. As we know,
in the late 1650s the commercial life of Dundee had been
at a low ebb,[1] but a generation of peace had, so it appears,
enabled its merchants to re-establish their old regional
primacy.

That primacy was, however, essentially in the import
and distribution of luxuries like wine and silks, and
expensive consumer or construction goods such as cut
timbers, for the benefit of the aristocracy and gentry of a
still overwhelmingly agricultural and relatively under-
developed hinterland. Their importance is obvious:
indeed, another account of the shire, written by John
Ochterlony of Guynd about 1682 for Sir Robert Sibbald,
is little more than a catalogue of the seats of the gentry.[2]
What is so exciting about the accounts produced for Sir
John Sinclair a century later is that they demonstrate how
far Angus had changed, in the course of the eighteenth
century, into a county with rapidly expanding burghs,
substantial areas of advanced agriculture and a formidable
textile industry. Between the rapidly-changing Angus of
the late eighteenth century and the more static Angus of
c.1700, however, the old aristocracy had been notably
active in the Jacobite rebellions.

Angus was heavily involved in the Jacobite risings. The
magistrates of Dundee became more, rather than less,
Jacobite in sentiment after the parliamentary union with
England in 1707. Indeed, in May 1715, long before the

1. S. G. E. Lythe, *Life and Labour in Dundee from the Reformation to the Civil
    War* (Dundee: Abertay Historical Society, 1958).
2. *Account of the Shire of Forfar circa 1682 by John Ochterlony, Esq. of Guynd*,
    reprinted in a limited edition of 300 copies for the Forfar and District
    Historical Society, 1969.

earl of Mar raised the standard of rebellion at Braemar on 6 September, the magistrates in Dundee had forbidden public celebration of George I's birthday and local Hanoverians had to gather, in arms, within Dudhope Castle in order to defy the proclamation. Predictably, the Dundee authorities rallied enthusiastically to the rebellion, sending men and cannon into Mar's camp at Perth; and, when in January 1716 the Old Pretender rode into Dundee, he did so accompanied by three hundred gentlemen (including the great majority of the Angus gentry) and was given the warmest of welcomes. Thirty years later, however, the '45 roused much less enthusiasm in Dundee, although some 600 troops under an Angus laird – Sir James Kinloch – took and held Dundee for Prince Charles between 7 September 1745 and 14 January 1746. Nevertheless, as soon as the Jacobite army retreated towards defeat at Culloden, the town reverted to the Hanoverian allegiance and even offered the duke of Cumberland the freedom of the burgh.[1] In the landward areas, Jacobite support ebbed more slowly after 1715. The noble families of Strathmore and Airlie were bitterly hostile to the union of 1707, seeing it as a betrayal of that Scottish independence which both houses had stoutly upheld for six centuries: both families came out for the Pretender in 1715, and the '45 saw the heir to the Airlie earldom, David Lord Ogilvy, in the forefront of the Jacobite army. While the Airlies eventually recovered from the attainder and exile which followed the '45, the experience certainly relegated them to the background of Scottish social and political life.[2]

Scotland could scarcely hope to make rapid economic progress until it had turned its back upon the political turmoil and underlying economic depression of the Jacobite era. The transition from stagnation to growth is well illustrated by Mr George Gleig, minister of Arbroath in his account of the burgh:

"Before the year 1736, Arbroath had little or no commerce, unless a little traffic in fish, and a kind of contra-

1. J. Thomson, *The History of Dundee* (Dundee, 1847), 91–99.
2. W. Wilson, *The House of Airlie*, 2 vols. (London, 1924).

band or smuggling trade deserve the name. It had no manufactures; and any piece of cloth that was made was carried to Montrose, and sold there."

At this period, too, he states, Arbroath had no regular imports apart from an occasional small cargo of wood from Norway: flax, iron and other commodities had to be bought from merchants in Montrose and Dundee. But then came a deliberate stimulus to industrial growth[1] –

"A few years subsequent to that mentioned above, several gentlemen of property jointly undertook to establish the manufacture of Oznaburghs, and other brown linens here, and to import their own materials. They laid out considerable sums of money on different kinds of machinery, which were executed on a very complete and extensive scale. Success attended their spirited exertions."

Arbroath harbour, still tidal, had been reconstructed in 1725 with a mouth which could be secured by a barrier of beams slipped into slots on either side of a stone-walled entrance – which sounds and no doubt looked like the even older harbour that the Fife burgh of Crail managed to preserve into the twentieth century. This was scarcely adequate for more than a very modest volume of trade and, indeed, it looks as if the truly significant spurt in the quantity of Arbroath sea-trade really came later. In the middle years of the eighteenth century the Wallaces, a family of North Sea merchants, had sponsored the intro-duction of coarse German-style linens into the local tex-tile industry,[2] and by the 1790s Arbroath had become a modest but busy port, serving the expanding industries of the town and its hinterland: "In the year 1781, there belonged to this harbour no more than 17 or 18 vessels, making altogether only about 900 tons; now [1792] there are 32 vessels, making 1,704 tons, which employ about 160 seamen. There are besides two vessels on the stocks,

---

1. Arbroath, 25–26.
2. B. Lenman and E. Gauldie, "The industrial history of the Dundee region from the eighteenth to the early twentieth century", *Dundee and District*, ed. S. J. Jones (Dundee: British Association, 1968), 163. John Wallace, greatest of his dynasty, became provost of Arbroath for the first time in 1738, a year in which all the other magistrates of the burgh were also members of the Wallace family.

together above 150 tons."[1] Gleig's comments on the foundations of a new industrial society in Arbroath are invaluable: indeed, it is the particular merit of the accounts of Angus parishes that they were written very close to the most significant period in the process of industrialisation. Not all accounts are equally valuable in this respect, of course, for they vary in quality and necessarily reflect the interests and personalities of their authors. For this reason, it is worth our taking a look at them, to discover what sort of people they were.

The great majority were parish ministers, but there were exceptions. In the case of Arbroath we actually have two accounts and two authors. As we have seen the main report was prepared by the minister, George Gleig, born at Brechin in 1757, the son of a blacksmith, and brought up as an episcopalian. He was assistant at Garvock before obtaining a presentation from the Crown at Arbroath in 1788. Objection was taken to his settlement in the parish on the ground that nobody had signed his call. Presbytery proceeded to ordination regardless but was rebuked by the General Assembly and urged to avoid such irregularities in future. Gleig's daughter Anne later married the town clerk of Arbroath.[2] The other and earlier account of Arbroath, giving a brief survey of the burgh in 1742, was written by the then town clerk, David Mudie: it was included as an appendix to Gleig's report in vol. xxi of Sinclair's edition of the *Account*. Mudie writes there that quarrying and shoemaking were important export industries in Arbroath and its neighbourhood in the 1740s but adds that the weavers were as numerous as all other trades put together with the bulk of their brown linens being sent to London.[3]

1. Arbroath, 28.
2. Hew Scott, *Fasti Ecclesiae Scoticanae,* vol. v (Edinburgh 1925). This work is the source of all unascribed ministerial biography in this introduction.
3. By 1772 sailcloth was being made as well as osnaburgs, and by 1790 Arbroath had become the principal producer of sailcloth in Scotland: in 1793 the first water-powered flax-spinning mill was built at Letham just north of the town, so Mudie and Gleig between them span a half-century of rapid change in this industry – see W. H. K. Turner, *The Textile Industry of Arbroath since the early 18th Century* (Dundee: Abertay Historical Society, 1954), 4–5.

Gleig was reasonably typical of the ministers in Angus parishes who, in the 1790s, might be loosely described as Moderates – that is to say, they belonged to that school of Church of Scotland ministers who regarded lay patronage as a good rather than as an undesirable phenomenon, and who were less interested in the finer points of theology than in the inculcation of social virtues conducive to tolerant and civilised existence. On the whole, Angus ministers tended to have been mainly educated at St Andrews University or, rather less frequently, at one of the two Aberdeen universities – King's College and Marischal College. James Paton, minister of Craig (directly south of Montrose across the South Esk), educated at both St Andrews and Edinburgh, was another very typical Moderate who had served as a tutor in the families of James, Earl of Moray, and John Balfour of Fernie before obtaining his presentation from St Mary's College, St Andrews.

Although they were very dependent on the gentry or the Crown for presentations to parishes, the rural Angus clergy were only in quite exceptional circumstances able to marry into the gentry class. A town minister, however, was more likely to form family alliances with the rising manufacturer group. It was even more natural for a minister to solve a social dilemma by marrying a minister's daughter and ministerial families tended to be self-perpetuating. Thus, in the parish of Panbride, Robert Trail founded a local clerical dynasty which ministered to the same parish for some 133 years. Very few ministers indeed, by the 1790s, maintained the older, seventeenth-century tradition of close blood links between clergy and gentry. We have a good example, however, in the author of the account of the parish of Glamis, James Lyon: but he was a Lyon of Wester Ogil, a cadet branch of the mighty house of Strathmore. His father was minister of Long-forgan, a village which was an appanage of Castle Lyon (later Castle Huntly), one of the two main seats of the earl of Strathmore: James obtained the living at Glamis, at the gates of Glamis Castle, the principal seat of Strathmore.[1] Notwithstanding their conservatism and Moderatism, these Angus ministers frequently had to struggle to obtain increased stipends in the later eighteenth century, a period of high inflation. William Milligan, minister of Kirkden and described by George Dempster of Dunnichen as "the best informed man in the presbytery", is more notable than some since he had to fight his heritors all the way to the House of Lords in 1789 before securing his augmentation. The career of the author of the account of the parish of Monifieth, James Roger, "preacher of the gospel" and later to be minister of Dunino in Fife, is more typical of the style of advancement of the eighteenth century. Educated at the universities of Aberdeen and St Andrews, he was an assistant minister in the parishes of Cortachy and Monifieth before he became schoolmaster at Monikie. From that post he elevated himself to be secretary to George Dempster of Dunnichen, politician, laird, and ardent improver of both industry and agriculture. This was followed by a spell in journalism, first in Dundee and then in London, before he gained the living of Dunino, in the patronage of the United College, St Andrews. In addition to the statistical accounts of the parishes of Monikie and Dunino, he also compiled for Sir John Sinclair in 1794 the *General View of the Agriculture of the County of Angus or Forfar* (which included observations by George Dempster of Dunnichen), and in 1797 published an *Essay on Government*. Here, indeed, was one type of Moderate clergyman. Of another kind perhaps was the author of the account of Oathlaw, Thomas Raiker, of whom it was remarked that he was "a singular and zealous servant of his divine Master, while he was not inattentive to his own concerns": to be more precise, he managed at the age of 92 to leave £5,000 though his annual stipend as a minister had never apparently exceeded £70.

1. James Lyon was described as "A severe, determined-looking figure who ruled the people with a rod of iron, and was a strict disciplinarian". Curiously enough, his wife Agnes was a poetess and author of words set to the tune "Farewell to Whisky" by the great fiddler, Neil Gow.

Introduction

The single most informative account in this collection is almost certainly by Robert Small of Dundee, for it demonstrates how an active Moderate clergyman could feel very sensitively the pulse of the developing society in which he lived. Small was born in 1732, the son of the minister of Carmylie, another Angus parish. Educated at Dundee Grammar School and at the University of St Andrews, he was called to the first charge of St Mary's, the burgh kirk, in 1761, and began an ecclesiastical career laced with distinctions, ranging from a doctorate in Divinity from St Andrews in 1778 to the moderatorship of the General Assembly of the Church of Scotland in 1791. It was said of him that "he was an excellent classical scholar and a highly interesting preacher, deeply versed in mathematics, natural philosophy and astronomy, and a patron of literature." He was also a practical philanthropist. A voluntary dispensary, giving medical aid to the poor, had been organised in Dundee as early as 1735, but in 1782 Small and Robert Stewart, surgeon, opened a fresh subscription to meet the growing needs of both the town and its surrounding area – an enterprise which, in due course, developed into the Dundee Infirmary some ten years later.[1]

There was, however, a troubled side to Small's life. He was to appear before the General Assembly in 1800, charged with using different questions to elders of St Mary's at their ordination from those laid down in the official formularies and with omitting to require his elders to subscribe the Confession of Faith. Much more hurtful, however, was the trouble brought upon him by the career of his son, James, who became a manufacturer in Dundee and whose failure in business ruined his father. Thus Small's account of the industrial and commercial life of Dundee in the early 1790s is no outsider's survey, but a picture drawn by a man deeply involved in many aspects of the life of the burgh.

1. H. J. C. Gibson, *Dundee Royal Infirmary 1798 to 1948* (Dundee, 1948), 7–9: merchants from the town and gentlemen from the landward area were alike represented at the general meeting of subscribers in 1793, presided over by Robert Small.

Introduction

It is a picture of rapid development, not least in respect of population. In 1766 there were 12,426 inhabitants in Dundee; in 1781 the figure was 15,700; and in 1788 it had risen to 19,329.[1] And Small, writing in 1791–2, reckoned that the population was then of the order of 23,500.[2] Of course these figures are not impressive in absolute terms compared with a population of 78,931 in 1851 or 120,724 in 1871 or 160,836 in 1901. Nevertheless, the spectacular growth recorded by these census figures from the Victorian period was founded on the achievements of the eighteenth century. Small leaves no doubt that textiles formed the heart of Dundee's industrial dynamic – "The principal and staple manufacture of Dundee is linen of various kinds; viz. Osnaburghs, and other similar coarse fabrics of different names, for exportation, and which alone, till lately, were subjected to the national stamps". The reference to the stamps is to the passing of the cloth (as having reached a certain quality) by the Board of Trustees for Manufactures, a body set up in 1727 with the task of stimulating manufactures and fisheries in Scotland with the aid of a small amount of state funds. A good deal of domestic linen was never submitted to the stamp-masters, as Small noted, but their returns still give us a very good indication of the prevailing levels of commercial production: and they were high.

The account records that the quantity of linen stamped in Dundee between November 1788 and November 1789 amounted to 4,242,653 yards valued at £108,782 14s 2d, of which only a quarter was brought from neighbouring parishes to the Dundee stamp offices. The manufacture of all sorts of canvas for shipping, confined to the town itself, produced in the same period 704,000 yards valued at £32,000. Dundee also produced significant quantities of bagging for cotton wool. Also, for fifty years at least, the manufacture of coloured thread had been a Dundee speciality: and Small reported the existence of seven different companies or masters in this trade, employing

1. Dundee, 156.
2. Ibid., 163–4.

over 1,700 people, but added significantly that "the spinners live in distant parts of Scotland, where labour is cheaper than in Dundee." Dundee also had a thriving tanning trade which was, however, more remarkable for the oak-bark it consumed than for the number of hands it employed, although it did lead to a rapidly-expanding manufacture of boots and shoes.

Not all attempts in the later eighteenth century to diversify the Dundee economy were successful. Small, for instance, had high hopes for the future of the cotton manufacture which had been recently introduced into a Dundee that in 1791–2 had seven companies employing several hundred people, both in spinning yarn and also in "working up" such products as "callicoes, handkerchiefs, and coarse waistcoats". But by 1820 the expansion of the Scottish cotton industry, spreading eastwards from Glasgow, was virtually over, and by 1839 no fewer than 175 of the 192 cotton mills in Scotland were sited in Lanarkshire and Renfrewshire.[1] Nor was cotton the only manufacture proudly mentioned by Small in his account which was, in the end, to have very little future in Dundee. A hundred people were then employed by a company with two "glass-houses", manufacturing bottle glass and window glass, but the enterprise never paid well enough to survive to grow into a major industry.[2] Sugar-refining, though it involved a member of the Baxter textile family, had only a brief life in Dundee and has left to us only the name of Sugar House Wynd.

Small is an accurate and a fair-minded commentator on contemporary Dundee – his description of the harbour, for instance, should be compared with the vague but complementary account by Edward in 1678. Small points out that Dundee harbour was not naturally a good one, for the main navigation channel was on the Fife side of the Firth of Tay: siltation was a continual problem. He was

1. J. Butt, *The Industrial Archaeology of Scotland* (Newton Abbot, 1967), 72.
2. P. Mathias, *English Trade Tokens* (London, 1962), plate xvi, despite its title, includes a Dundee halfpenny token of 1797 which shows the "cones" of these glass-houses.

ready to admit, however, that the town council, a self-perpetuating closed corporation as were those in other Scottish burghs of the time, had done its very best over the previous ten or twelve years to improve matters. (Small made no secret of his sympathy with demands for town council reform, though one must not assume that this indicated "popular" or "radical" sympathies, since his chief complaint about the old council was that "no appeal whatever is made to the guildry, or great body of merchants, who may be considered as the aristocracy of the place."[1]) The harbour was in fact crucially important to the merchants in an age when coastal shipping was vastly superior to land transport for bulk commodities. Equally, the harbour, with its rising revenue, seemed to the unreformed council their one hope of reducing their chronic financial deficit. Indeed the growing weakness of the old oligarchy is seen in the fact that, long before the municipal reforms of 1833, it had been forced to concede control of Dundee's harbour to independent bodies on which the merchant interest was well-represented.[2]

From Small's thriving Dundee, expanding in area and enjoying rising land-values,[3] it is interesting to turn to some of the landward towns lying across the Sidlaws. Kirriemuir was a burgh of barony rather than a royal burgh, but by 1790 that hardly mattered. According to the account of its minister, Thomas Ogilvy, the town, situated at the foot of the Braes of Angus in a fertile and well-populated district, was

"the mart to which the inhabitants of the neighbouring parishes chiefly resort. Hence no town in the county has a better weekly market; in none of its size is more trade carried on. Nine carriers go regularly to Dundee twice, and often thrice a-week, loaded with the produce or manufactures of the district, and bring from thence flax, sugar, tea, porter, rum, and all kinds of merchant goods."[4]

1. Dundee, 150–1, 172–7.
2. B. Lenman, *From Esk to Tweed* (Glasgow, 1975), chaps. 1 and 2.
3. Dundee, 170–1.
4. Kirriemuir, 360–1.

The significance of this ease in transportation between Kirriemuir and Dundee can hardly be exaggerated. The development of the linen industry together with the creation of a turnpike road system over the Sidlaw Hills were instrumental in making landward burghs like Kirriemuir part of a Dundee-centred industrial and commercial complex. In this matter, Small's account wisely remarks that Dundee

"must draw the most signal benefits from the excellent turnpike roads lately constructed and continuing to be extended through all the principal districts of Angus, and the neighbouring parts of Perthshire. For these the town is entirely indebted to the exertions of a few country gentlemen; and though its inhabitants have had no share, either in the trouble or the risk of the undertaking, they will be probably the principal sharers in the profits; for their markets instead of being often shut up, and becoming inaccessible, will now be open at all seasons of the year, for the heaviest goods".[1]

Linen woven in Kirriemuir for a Dundee merchant was most probably shipped direct to London, whence it might well be re-exported to the West Indies. The coastal trade from Dundee was a substantial one: thus, of 116 vessels recorded as belonging to the port of Dundee in January 1792, four were in the whale fishery, 34 in foreign trade and the remainder, 78, in the coasting trade. Since Small obtained this information from "Mr Hunter, clerk of the customs" there is every reason to regard it as substantially correct.[2] Nor were coarse linens the only major product available from Kirriemuir, for the local account mentions that about 1,200 pairs of shoes were made annually "for exportation".[3]

The account of Forfar by the Reverend John Bruce tells a very similar tale, stressing the importance of new turnpike roads, then nearing completion, to Arbroath, Dundee and Perth. The manufacture of shoes, once Forfar's biggest trade, still flourished but it had lost its

1. Dundee, 191.
2. Dundee, 169.
3. Kirriemuir, 161.

primacy to linen manufacture – introduced by way of an Arbroath connection about 1745. By 1750 upwards of 150 looms were active in Forfar, and by the early 1790s that number had grown to between 400 and 500. Many achieved prosperity through weaving, and Bruce tells us that one sign of it in Forfar was the way in which the humble thatched dwellings of 1745 had given way to substantial houses with slate roofs.[1] There was, however, a price to be paid for such industrial growth: although, despite a steady upward trend in prices, especially the prices of foodstuffs, the humbler classes could afford to buy more food and more of what we would call consumer goods (such as tea-kettles, hand-bellows and watches), this was only true of those in employment – and there were many poor in the town dependent upon charitable funds. Forfar, like Kirriemuir, was becoming a peripheral part of the Dundee textile complex, and was peculiarly susceptible to the effects of trade slumps when Dundee merchants were liable to cut their contracts in the Strathmore burghs as the first measure of economy. Even Bruce had to admit that "the Osnaburgh trade is indeed a fluctuating one, and when the demand for that fabric slackens at any time, it brings many of the young and unprovident into difficulties, and often times adds to the number of the poor."[2]

In the 1790s Brechin, the most northerly of the Strathmore burghs in Angus, was at an earlier stage of industrial development than burghs closer to Dundee. We have, as it happens, two accounts of Brechin, one drawn up from materials submitted by the Reverend Andrew Bruce clearly earlier than that written by John Bisset, minister of the first charge in the town. Even in Bisset's account it is the rôle of Brechin as a market town and a centre for the processing of agricultural produce that is stressed: there was "a constant traffic of horses and cattle at Brechin through a great part of the year," and at the four major markets of the year "a vast resort of people from the neighbouring parishes, expecting to purchase a

1. Forfar, 253–5.
2. Forfar, 254.

variety of articles from the stands or tents of the chapmen at a cheaper rate than from the merchants' shops." But there was some industry. In 1785 a new brewery opened near the bridge over the River South Esk, an addition no doubt to the several breweries noted by Andrew Bruce at an earlier date: a distillery opened in 1786 received judicious clerical praise for the quality of the drams it produced.[1] Bruce reported that most merchants dealt in "the linen and yarn" trade, buying at all the markets vast quantities of yarn produced by "most of the women in this and the adjoining parishes" who, it is said, used the saxon or treadle-operated spinning-wheel and were "well paid".[2] Linen yarn from the rural areas was bleached at a local bleachfield. Of factory industry using advanced machinery there was one precocious example in the shape of a "cotton manufactory" which employed 100 hands between its establishment in 1786 and its first closure in 1790: its reopening in 1792 was not a prelude to the stable expansion of the cotton trade in Brechin, despite the fact that the enterprise was controlled by John Smith, the provost of Brechin, in conjunction with Colin Gillies, a merchant.[3] Brechin in 1792 was still essentially a market for agricultural produce.

Turning now to rural Angus, the changing face of the countryside in the early 1790s is well reflected in these accounts, with the pace and scale of change different in the well-favoured lowland parts of the county from that in the county beyond the Highland Line. The parish of Auchterhouse, lying some seven miles north-west of Dundee, provided a good illustration of lowland change, the minister writing that "great improvements in agriculture have been made in this parish since the year 1776."[4] Note the lateness of this date. Agricultural improvement tended to come later than the rise of the linen trade, already impressive by 1745. Improvement in the countryside, indeed, tended to owe everything to

1. Brechin, 96–8.
2. Brechin 76.
3. Brechin, 98.
4. Auchterhouse, 46.

aristocratic initiative: in Auchterhouse "Lord Airly gave the example of enclosing, draining, and otherwise improving the soil." The local account includes a detailed eulogy of the stout dry-stane dykes surrounding his lordship's enclosures and we are told that, "such is the present prevailing spirit of improvement in all the branches of agriculture, that it is thought, within a few years hence, the whole arable land of the parish will be enclosed."[1] Yet Auchterhouse was clearly not completely enclosed even in the early 1790s: enclosure meant enlargement as well as consolidation of holdings, and that implied a depopulation of the parish which was disliked by the dominant economic theorists of the day. The minister of Essie and Nevay, Dr James Playfair, later to become principal of the United College at St Andrews, reflected this, reporting on the whole process of improvement with a salutary if restrained radicalism. Although farms were now larger than they had been forty years before the beginnings of consolidation, Playfair remarked, all was not gain, for

"When cottages are demolished, their inhabitants are constrained to retire to towns in quest of lodging and subsistence. When these nurseries of population fail, a sufficient number of working people cannot be easily procured".

He reported too that some farmers had found it necessary to employ "bands of shearers from the north country, who cut down the corn at the rate of 6s or 7s per acre, and as soon as this work is finished, retire to the mountains". Playfair clearly held a high opinion of James Stuart Mackenzie, Lord Privy Seal of Scotland and the proprietor of Nevay, who had just granted new leases to all his tenants, in exchange for a very small rise in rent; otherwise, "had the usual methods of screwing and racking tenants been adopted, the landlord might have greatly increased his revenue."[2] In short, landed proprietors were re-structuring their estates so as to increase their incomes, but usually at the cost of extensive removals of tenants

1. Ibid., 47.
2. Essie and Nevay, 231–2.

whom they were fortunate enough to be able to dump in the expanding towns of Angus. Yet such a brief statement of the underlying reality greatly over-simplifies what was a very complex situation.

Even in lowland Angus in the 1790s, agricultural improvement was far from universal or complete. In the parish of Craig, just south of Montrose, two lairds, Scot of Duninald and Scot of Rossie, had begun to enclose their property about 1730, and initiated significant agricultural change in the area. However, there were all sorts of problems with respect to the techniques of enclosure. Thorn hedges were first tried as boundary markers, followed by lengthy experiments with whin and furze-topped earthen banks, before dry-stane dykes were accepted as the only satisfactory method. The statement that "in a few years, the whole fields of the parish will be inclosed in that manner"[1] implies that, even in Craig, the process was not yet complete. Improvement was in fact patchy. In the *Account* there are instances of landlords granting leases which obliged tenants to follow up-to-date rotations of crops.[2] Yet we find that the house of Airlie did not believe in leases on its great estates, and find too an enlightened minister who was prepared to defend this, pointing out that rents were moderate and that in practice tenants enjoyed security of tenure from generation to generation. Here at least was an old, patriarchal world, still intact.[3]

One reason for the comparative lack of urgency in agricultural improvement was undoubtedly the fact that even lowland Angus had a very strong pastoral tradition. Arable agriculture existed on a substantial scale, but the biggest returns were gained from black cattle. Horses were also bred on a large scale, but not sheep. It was easy and profitable to buy in black cattle from the highland glens and fatten them on the lowland pastures of Angus,[4]

1. Craig, 129.
2. Kirkden, 350.
3. Lintrathen, 421–2.
4. Kinnettles, 326.

and the growing of turnips as winter feed for cattle was therefore a significant and important innovation, widely adopted.[1] The black cattle trade, indeed, was big business: in the parish of Glamis, for instance, one grazier often held at the one time as much as £10,000 worth of cattle destined for the English market.[2] But in many ways the "agricultural revolution" in eighteenth-century Angus represented an intensification of a long-standing pattern. Thus the minister of Kirriemuir tells us that his parish produced insufficient grain to feed itself, but exported very large quantities of pastoral products.[3] Not all of these accounts go into great detail about arable farming: but it would appear that in the lowland parts it had become normal to replace the old Scots plough with a new light iron plough with mould board, and also that the practices of marling and liming land had become standard in lowland Angus by about 1790.[4]

The other vital growth sector in the Angus economy – the linen trade – was still in the 1790s a dispersed rural industry, despite a significant trend (as we have seen already) towards concentration in the towns. In its early development it was able to surmount poor transport facilities since a web of cloth could be carried to market on a weaver's shoulders or loaded on a pack horse. Indeed, minister after minister records for us the lack of enthusiasm for road improvement which lingered on in the countryside. In 1790, however, an act substituted a money payment for the labour service previously required for repairing the old parochial roads. Thereafter, the major roads could be turnpiked and proprietors enabled to recoup their expenditure on their improvement by taking tolls from users. As the author of the account of Dunnichen remarked, "turnpike roads between Cupar of Angus, Forfar, Arbroath, Dundee, Cupar of Angus, and Meigle, and from Dundee to Montrose" were all near completion despite "antient prejudices".[5]

1. Monikie, 531.
2. Glammiss, 277.
3. Kirriemuir, 359–60.
4. Rescobie, 588–9; Strathmartin, 438; Arbirlot, 13.
5. Dunnichen, 210.

Introduction

Beyond the area directly affected by these new turn-pikes lay the Angus glens, which form an instructive contrast with the lowland Angus of the 1790s. The parish of Lochlee, for instance, comprising the north-western parts of Glen Esk, was in many ways still a self-sufficient world, with its own weavers producing woollen clothing for the local inhabitants and its own shoemakers producing the coarse leather brogues which everyone wore. Whereas, before 1764, there had been no road suitable for cart traffic in the glen, and indeed no carts, by 1790 statute and privately-organized labour had so improved the situation that carts were in common use. We are told that the people were much attached to the glen and that the population had been very stable, but by 1790 the increasing wages available from work in the low country were beginning to tempt the men away to seasonal work there. It was also noted that the economy of the glen, as distinct from its infra-structure, had not escaped a substantial change. The numbers of black cattle which had once been pastured at the head of Glen Esk, had been reduced by two-thirds and replaced by black-faced sheep: in the early 1790s there were 9,200 sheep in the parish, compared with 600 black cattle. The glen was becoming a huge sheep-run.[1] In Glenisla, however, where many of the tenants owned their own feus, improvement was virtually unknown. Enclosure was rare; and, while there were sheep on the hill grazings, black cattle were still the principal product of the glen; and the terrain at the head of the glen was so difficult that the cumbrous "old Scotch plough" drawn by up to six horses was still in use. Improvement seems to have been a landlord's affair in Angus, even in the 1790s: where there were many owner-occupiers, as in Glenisla, improvement was hardly noticeable.[2] Not that every landlord was himself an agricultural innovator. But virtually every parish account in our group states that the landlords had at least doubled rents within the previous thirty years: and increased rents forced tenant farmers to improve or perish. Thus the minister of St Vigeans, a parish adjacent to Arbroath, was

1. Lochlee, 428–34.
2. Glenisla, 285–6.

not alone in believing that "the raising of the rents in this district, has, among other causes, contributed to the activity, attention, and industry of the farmers".[1] Here we have the central mechanism of agricultural change in late eighteenth-century Angus.

Quantitative evidence given by these accounts varies a great deal in quality. The least reliable is undoubtedly to be found in the sections on population. Where the ministers quote the mid-century enumeration by the learned and judicious Dr Alexander Webster, they are on solid ground. Too often their attempts to guess their way towards earlier or later figures, from fragmentary material, are of doubtful value, and may be epitomised by the minister of Careston's rather desperate use of the number of communion tokens struck in the parish in 1709 to judge the number of inhabitants at that time.[2] Such accounts do not easily fill the gap between Webster's census and the first government census of 1801,[3] but it is possible (see Appendix) to construct from the information given in the *Account* and elsewhere some picture of the demographic changes that were occurring.

The material in the accounts on wages is a good deal more accessible and reliable, and can be checked in some degree by comparing one account with another. Scotland was a very regionally-varied society in the 1790s, but there would be comparatively little variation in wages in a compact and similar grouping of parishes such as those of lowland rural Angus. In fact the reports all yield similar reports. Wages had roughly trebled in the forty years between 1750 and 1790, with a sharp acceleration in the rate of increase in the 1780s and farmers had reacted to this by such a scale of re-organisation and improvement as enabled them to produce more with fewer men.[4] To hire "a stout man" for harvest, for instance, cost £1 10s to £2, while a woman worker for the harvest cost £1 to £1 5s, and it was alleged that most of this increased income was

1. St Vigeans, 618.
2. Careston, 108.
3. T. C. Smout, *A History of the Scottish People* (London, 1969), 259.
4. Kingoldrum, 317–8.

spent "upon the back and the belly". The wearing of manufactured cloth from "Manchester, Glasgow and Paisley" and the abandonment of the woollen Scotch bonnet for the fancy hat were regarded, apart from the money spent on alcohol, as symptoms of decadence.[1] In fact inflation had absorbed a good deal of these wage increases: but, even so, when the wages of a male farm servant had risen from £2 per annum to £7 or more per annum, and those of a woman servant from £1 to £3 or more, both with food and bed in addition, the forty-year period had still seen a real increase in earnings, if for a reduced workforce.[2]

The fate of the poor in an economy where grain prices had doubled and meat prices trebled in forty years (and during which, as has been noted, the wages of those who could find secure employment had roughly trebled) could be harsh. In fact, how they fared depended very much on where they lived. In rural areas, lowland or highland, the funds available seem generally to have been adequate for a limited number of poor, and there was rarely a need for additional taxation in legal assessments. Church collections, plus the income from charitable bequests, were enough to cope with, say, a dozen poor in the parish of Edzell "in such a way as not only to be free of complaint, but to give full satisfaction to themselves, and to those who live around them". The disabled and otherwise helpless would have allowances for boarding them paid to relatives, or might have someone paid to care for them if they had no relatives.[3] In the lowland and coastal parish of Lunan the registered poor numbered from four to six persons for whom ample funds were said to be available, although the minister added that in a small parish with no resident heritors the weekly church collections could not feed the poor and they depended on "the annual rent arising from the accumulated stock" from charitable legacies.[4] The apparently comfortable relationship between the numbers of poor and the amount of available

1. Maryton, 496–7.
2. Fernell, 247.
3. Edzell, 224–7.
4. Lunan, 468–9.

funds in the landward areas was the result of substantial movements of population into the towns. And in the towns there were grave problems of social welfare, allied to much controversy over general policy in respect of poor relief. In Forfar, lands which had been purchased with seventeenth-century bequests to the poor yielded £96 per annum and church door collections produced another £100. These sums were dispensed not only as cash but as food, shoes, clothing and rent-money. But the minister of Forfar makes it clear that, with the sharp rises in food and other prices and in the numbers of the Forfar poor, the old system was on the verge of collapse. In the stress of this situation, he showed no particular sympathy for the poor – "The fact seems to be, that over-grown charity funds, are enemies to industry, as they encourage the idle and improvident to depend upon them as a security against want in the evening of life. And so they will neither work nor save."[1] But not all the Angus ministers took this line, and the incumbent at Kinnettles for one was ready to face up to the fact that legal assessment for the support of increasing numbers of poor might be unavoidable.[2]

The quality of life in late eighteenth-century Angus is difficult to assess, but the accounts do provide some pointers to it. Education was theoretically provided for in rural areas by a parish school. Every rural parish had one, but it was not always convenient and virtually never adequately financed. Ministers could compel heritors by law to augment their inadequate stipends: schoolmasters could not. In Glenisla the parish school, with a miserable salary for the master, was supplemented by a school erected by the Society for Propagating Christian Knowledge, but the account records that "both schools just now are in bad repair, and truly it is difficult to get these matters properly adjusted among such a number of heritors".[3] In Eassie and Nevay the number of scholars "for some years past has been inconsiderable" – the school

1. Forfar, 263–4.
2. Kinnettles, 339.
3. Glenisla, 287.

was situated "in a barren spot", geographically central but not near areas of habitation and, secondly, although the master had a house, his income including the usual emoluments from the salaries attached to the posts of precentor and session clerk was a mere £12 per annum.[1] In Liff and Benvie, again, the school was poorly sited and virtually inaccessible in winter, so that five private schools existed ("for the most part indifferently taught"): the emoluments of the parish school were "too inconsiderable for a teacher of any merit and capacity".[2]

The burghs were outwith the parochial school system, and the ministers say little of the schools which their wealth made it possible to sustain; but the account for Forfar proudly records that a spirit of reading and enquiry was springing up among his parishioners, that subscriptions to the *Encyclopedia Britannica*, the *Bee*, and scientific, political, and religious periodicals were surprisingly common and that "they already shed an evident lustre on the conversation of many".[3] The rising class of manufacturers was by no means bereft of the polite culture of their day.[4]

Another interesting aspect of contemporary society reflected in these accounts is to be found in the comments on the relations between the various religious groups. It is, of course, possible to find an Established Church minister here and there who equated the growth of the number of seceders in his parish with the growth of profanity and general wickedness, but this was unusual.[5] In the landward parishes, indeed, the Established Church was overwhelmingly ascendant and even in Cortachy and Clova, with a strong Jacobite tradition, episcopalians had shrunk to a mere handful.[6] The Moderate ministers were genuinely convinced of the desirability of a tolerant

1. Essie and Nevay, 236.
2. Liff and Bervie, 409–10.
3. Forfar, 273.
4. Bisset's account of Brechin describes one merchant's son there, John Gillies, LL.D., F.R.S., as "the brightest literary ornament" of the burgh and a considerable figure in the "republic" of classical letters: Brechin, 102.
5. Mains of Fintry, 491.
6. Cortachy and Clova, 124.

attitude, and hard words towards other denominations are rare. Even if we take a parish like Dundee, which contained a very large number of dissenters of many different sects, the account shows an extraordinarily charitable viewpoint, perhaps assisted by the fact that most dissenting congregations appear to have accepted responsibility for their own poor. Small's comment, apropos Dundee, that the sects "give very little disturbance to the general harmony and instead of increasing bigotry they seem to weaken it", is a notable one.[1] One parish account, that for Tannadice, while otherwise unremarkable, is notable for having been written by an Anti-Burgher secession minister. The author was Dr John Jamieson, described by Sir Walter Scott as "an excellent good man, and full of auld Scottish cracks": and the scholar who, while ministering to a Secession congregation in Forfar, was inspired by the suggestion of the Danish scholar Thorkelin to embark on researches which culminated in his epoch-making *Etymological Dictionary of the Scottish Language*, published in two volumes in 1808.[2]

To concentrate, in such a survey as this, on the main themes is to omit much that is interesting. Why, for example, when sheep are not extensively discussed in these accounts, is the report for Barrie, a parish composed largely of sand dune, a rather surprising exception? Yet it is in the main themes that the significance of these remarkable and perceptive accounts is to be found. We have here a priceless opportunity to observe Angus at a time when it had left behind the restrictive pattern of recurring economic disasters (such as famines) common to pre-industrial society and before the accelerating pace of change had shattered its pre-industrial social framework.

BRUCE LENMAN

Department of Modern History
University of St Andrews

1. Dundee, 186.
2. *Dictionary of National Biography*, xxix, 237–8.

APPENDIX

ANGUS

† The dates given in this first column indicate, as nearly as possible, the actual year in which the count of population was made.

†OSA date	Parish	Population in 1755	Population in 1790s	Population in 1801	Percentage Change 1755/1790s	Percentage Change 1755/1801
1790–1	Aberlemno	943	1033	945	+10	0
1792	Airlie	1013	865	1041	−15	+3
1790	Arbirlot	865	1055	1062	+22	+23
1792	Arbroath	2098	4676	4943	+123	+136
1793	Auchterhouse	600	600	653	0	+9
1790–1	Barry	689	796	886	+16	+29
1790–1	Brechin	3181	5000	5559	+57	+78
1790–1	Careston	269	260	229	−3	−15
1790–1	Carmyllie	745	700	892	−6	+20
1792–3	Cortachy and Clova	1233	1020	906	−17	−27
1791	Craig	935	1314	1328	+41	+42
1790–1	Dun	657	500	651	−21	−1
1792–3	Dundee	12477	23500	26804	+88	+115
1790–1	Dunnichen	653	872	1049	+34	+61
1793	Eassie and Nevay	500	630	638	+26	+28
1791–2	Edzell	862	963	1012	+12	+17
1790–1	Fearn	500	490	448	−2	−1
1791	Fernell	509	620	576	+22	+13
1792	Forfar	2450	4756	5161	+94	+111
1783	Glamis	1781	2040	1931	+15	+8
1791	Glenisla	1852	1018	996	−45	−46
1792	Guthrie	584	571	501	−2	−14
1790–1	Inverarity	996	929	820	−7	−18
1790–1	Inverkeilor	1286	1747	1704	−36	−33
1794–5	Kettins	1475	1100	1207	−25	−18
1792–3	Kingoldrum	780	600	577	−23	−26
1790–1	Kinnell	761[1]	830	783	+9	+3
1790	Kinnettles	616	622	567	+1	−8
1790	Kirkden	585	727	674	+24	+15
1792	Kirriemuir	3409	4358	4421	+28	+30
1790	Lethnot	635	505	489	−20	−23
1793	Liff and Bervie	1311	1790	2194	+37	+67
1793	Lintrathen	1165	900	919	−25	−21
1792	Lochlee	686	608	541	−11	−21
1791	Logie Pert	696	999	908	+44	+30
1790–1	Lunan	208	291	318	+40	+53
1790	Lundie and Fowlis	586	648	693	+11	+18
1780	Mains of Fintry	709	878	1442	+24	+103

† The dates given in this first column indicate, as nearly as possible, the actual year in which the count of population was made. The parish account itself often gives this information: failing that, the date is either that indicated by Sinclair at the start of each volume of the published *Account* or is the date of publication of the appropriate volume in the 1790s.

1. "Supposed to be a mistake", says the account in 1790–1, "as, till within these 25 years, they never exceeded 600".

Appendix

ANGUS

OSA date	Parish	Population in 1755	Population in 1790s	Population in 1801	Percentage Change 1755/1790s	Percentage Change 1755/1801
1793	Maryton	633	529	596	−16	−6
1791	Menmuir	743	900	949	+21	+28
1793	Monifieth	1421	1218	1407	−14	−1
1790–1	Monikie	1345	1278	1236	−5	−8
1790	Montrose	4150	6194	7974	+49	+92
1792	Murroes	623	462	591	−26	−5
1791	Newtyle	913	594	781	−35	−14
1790–1	Oathlaw	435	430	384	−1	−12
1790	Panbride	1259	1460	1583	+16	+26
1790–1	Rescobie	798	934	870	+17	+9
1792	Ruthven	280	220	211	−21	−25
1793	St Vigeans	1592	3336	4243	+110	+167
1790	Stracathro	529	672	583	+27	+10
1793	Strathmartine	368	340	503	−8	+37
1794	Tannadice	1470	1421[2]	1373	−3	−7
1790–1	Tealing	735	802	755	+9	+3
		68593	91601	100507	+34	+47

2. No figure is given in the *Account*: the mid-point between the figures for 1755 and 1801 has been entered.

ANGUS

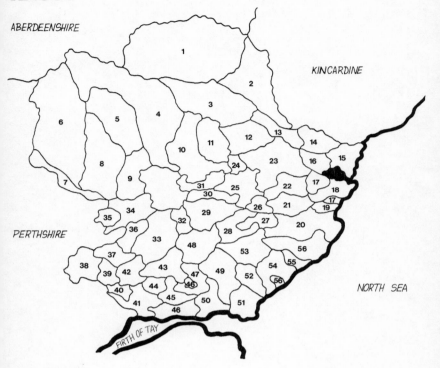

ABERDEENSHIRE

KINCARDINE

PERTHSHIRE

NORTH SEA

FIRTH OF TAY

Parishes

1. Lochlee
2. Edzell
3. Lethnot
4. Cortachy and Clova
5. Kirriemuir
6. Glenisla
7. Part of Alyth (Perthshire)
8. Lintrathen
9. Kingoldrum
10. Tannadice
11. Fearn
12. Menmuir
13. Stracathro
14. Logie Pert
15. Montrose
16. Dun
17. Maryton
18. Craig
19. Lunan
20. Inverkeilor
21. Kinkell
22. Fernell
23. Brechin

24. Careston
25. Aberlemno
26. Guthrie
27. Kirkden
28. Dunnichen
29. Forfar
30. Rescobie
31. Oathlaw
32. Kinnettles
33. Glamis
34. Airlie
35. Ruthven
36. Eassie and Nevay
37. Newtyle
38. Kettins
39. Lundie, with
40. Fowlis Easter (Perthshire)
41. Liff and Benvie
42. Auchterhouse
43. Tealing
44. Strathmartin
45. Mains
46. Dundee

47. Murroes
48. Inverarity
49. Monikie
50. Monifieth
51. Barry
52. Panbride
53. Carmylie
54. Arbirlot
55. Arbroath
56. St. Vigeans

PARISH OF ABERLEMNO.

(County of Forfar.)

By the Rev. Mr Andrew Mitchel.

Name, Situation, &c.

ABERLEMNO is said to derive its etymology from *aber* in the Gaelic language, signifying the " mouth of " or " above," and from the small river of Lemno, which takes its rise in this parish, and falls into the river South-Esk, about a mile N. from the church. The names of most places are said to be derived from the Gaelic language. This parish is situated 12 or 13 miles from the sea-coast, in the county and presbytery of Forfar, and Synod of Angus and Mearns. Its form somewhat resembles an oblique triangle. The extent of it from E. to W. is about 6 miles; and from N. to S. about 5. It is bounded on the N. by the parishes of Carrarton and Tannadice; on the N. W. by the parish of Oathlaw; on the W. and S. by the parish of Rescobie; on the S. E. by Guthrie, and on the E. by Brechin. The soil, in general, is fertile, the low grounds deep, the high grounds shallow and rocky. The appearance of the country, in this parish, is various; in some places flat, in others hilly; the hills are covered with heath. A large tract of ground upon the
banks

banks of the river South-Eſk, is ſometimes ſubjeƈt to in-undations ; the moſt remarkable of which happened in har-veſt 1774.

Population.—The population of this pariſh is ſuppoſed not to be materially different from what it was former-ly. The return to Dr Webſter was 943. The preſent amount of the population is 1033.

Males,	-	-	514	Between 20 and 50, - 431
Females,	-	-	519	———50 and 70, - 123
Aged below 10,	-	245	———70 and 100, - 17
Between 10 and 20,	217		

The annual average of births,   - - - 28
————————— deaths,   - - - 20
————————— marriages,   - - - 12
Average of children from each marriage, from - 5 to 7
Heritors, (four reſide in the pariſh.)   - - 10
Great farmers, about   - - - 30
Inhabited houſes, about   - - - 170
Poor receiving alms,   - - - 16
Expence of their yearly ſupply, at an average, - L. 25
Epiſcopalian families,   - - - 2
Weavers employed in the manufaƈture of brown linen
   or Oſnaburg,   - - - - 74

Smiths,	-	-	5	Merchants, - 4
Carpenters,	-	7	Gardeners, - 3
Tailors,	-	-	11	Flax-dreſſers, - 4
Shoemakers,	-	10	Male labouring ſervants, 47
Millers,	-	-	6	Female ditto, - 33
Maſons,	-	-	2	

Church, Stipend and School.—The church was repaired in 1774, and the manſe built in 1782. The ſtipend, in-cluding the glebe, is between L. 86 and L. 96 Sterling.

The

The fchoolmafter's falary is 200 merks; the number of fcholars generally about 40. Englifh and writing are taught for 1 s. 6 d. the quarter; arithmetic and Latin, for 2 s. 6 d. The emoluments of feffion-clerkfhip may be a-bout L. 4 or L. 5 Sterling, yearly.

Price of Labour and Provifions.—The wages of a day-labourer in hufbandry are 1 s. without victuals, and 8 d. with them. A male labouring fervant's wages are from L. 5 to L. 8 a-year; a female's, L. 3; a good labouring married fervant receives as wages about L. 6 Sterling in money, a houfe and yard, the value of which is between 20 s. and 30 s.; he gets a cow maintained through the year, and his fuel brought home: All which generally enable him to bring up a family. A carpenter's wages are 10 d. or 1 s. and his victuals; a mafon's 1 s. 4 d. or 1 s. 6 d. without victuals; a tailor's 8 d. with victuals.—The price of pro-vifions is doubled fince 1745: Butcher-meat is 4 d. the lb.; ducks and hens, 8 d. each; butter 8 d. the lb.; cheefe 6 s. or 7 s. the ftone.

Farms, &c.—The farms, in general, are from 50 to 250 or 300 acres; few are more extenfive, and fome are fmaller. Their number is not diminifhing. By a late re-gulation, the half of each farm fhould be in grafs. Oats and peafe are fown in March and April; barley in April and the beginning of May; and wheat generally in Sep-tember and October. The greatest part of the land is inclofed; the people being convinced of the advantage of inclofing. The loch of Balgavies has, for many years, fur-nifhed much marl for manure. The rent of the best ara-ble land may be about L. 1 the acre; but what the farmers chiefly ftudy is the bringing up of black cattle. The land-

rent

rent of the parish is fully L. 2000 Sterling. The number
of ploughs is 48, each of which is generally drawn by
four horses ; the number of horses 161 ; of carts 90.
There has been little sale of land from time immemorial.

Miscellaneous Observations.—The air, in most places is
healthy. There is plenty of moorstone, free-stone and
slates ; many of which last, are sent to London and o-
ther places. Coal, peat, turf, broom and furze, are used
for fuel. Coal from Fife costs 6 d. the boll, *i. e.* 7 stone
weight. Peat is got from a neighbouring parish, at about
2 s. the cart-load. There are 2 chaises in the parish.
Two obelisks remain, one in the church-yard, another
on the highway from Brechin to Forfar, about 8 or 9
feet high ; they were erected in memory of the total defeat of the Danes, and have some rude hieroglyphical
sculptures *. A few tumuli have been opened in this
neighbourhood, in one or two of which was found a
rude kind of stone coffin, containing a small quantity of
black earth, with some bones almost entirely consumed.
In 1777, there was a cut made the whole breadth of this
parish, from the church southward ; and a bridge built
by private subscription, to connect the road from Forfar
to Brechin with that to Arbroath. The statute-labour
has been, for the most part, commuted. The principal
manufacture is linen. Few inlist in the army. The people are industrious, œconomical, and, in general, humane
in their disposition. There is a great alteration for the
better, in the manners, dress and style of living within these
40 years. The parish always supplies itself with provisions
                                                          and

* See Pennant's Tour ; Gordon's Itinerary ; Buchanan's Hist. lib. 6.

and fometimes exports large quantities of grain. There are two inns on the great road between Brechin and Forfar, for the entertainment of travellers. Few fervices are performed by tenants or fubtenants, excepting the carriage of the landlord's coals.

PARISH OF AIRLY.

*(Preſbytery of Meigle—County of Forfar—Synod of Angus
and Mearns.*

By the Rev. Mr. JAMES STORMONTH, *Miniſter.*

Form, Extent, and Soil.

THE form of this pariſh is an irregular parallellogram. In
length it is between 5 and 6 miles; in breadth between
3 and 4, and in ſome places more. The ſoil is various, generally a light ſand, or deep black mould.

Situation, Climate and Diſeaſes.—The pariſh may be divided into 2 diſtricts. About two thirds of it lie in Strathmore,
and the other forms the higher ground, which ſeems to terminate the ſtrath on the N. In the former the climate is
mildeſt ; but the air is moſt pure and healthy in the latter,
and freeſt from the fogs. Rheumatiſms, ſlow fevers, and
ſometimes agues prevail, eſpecially in the neighbourhood of
the moſſy and ſwampy ground.

Surface

Surface and Cultivation.—The lower part of the parifh has the appearance of being flat; but in many places it is very unequal. About 26 years ago, it was almoft in a ftate of nature, with fcarcely an enclofure in it: Now, the greateft part is cultivated to a high degree, and about two thirds of it fubftantially enclofed, either with ftone dikes, ditch and hedge, or ditch and paling; which fences, with the ftripes and clumps of planting, well dreffed fields, and handfome farm fteadings, make a moft beautiful appearance.

	Acres.
Of arable land it is fuppofed there are about -	4300
Of moffy, fwampy, and wafte ground, about -	700
And in planting, about - - - - -	900
In all, - - -	5900

Produce and Cattle, &c.—The common returns from the arable ground, in oats and bear, are from 4 to 6 bolls per acre; and of wheat from 8 to 10. There is but little hay made, the farmer finding his account rather in fattening cattle.* Of thefe there may be reared in a feafon about 500, and fattened on turnips from 180 to 200. There are about 400 more cattle in the parifh. The mode of culture is much the fame with what has been defcribed in other improved parifhes. Farmers, who pay from 150l. to 300l. of rent, poffefs about one half. There is one farmer indeed who pays more; but he, with other two, does not refide. There is one threfhing machine in the parifh. There is only one flock of fheep. The ewes were brought from Northumberland about a year and a half ago, and thrive remarkably well. Their fleeces bring about 4s. each; and, when fat, they weigh about 22 lb. per leg.

---

* The prices of labour and provifions are much the fame as in the neighbouring parifhes of Meigle and Kingoldrum.

leg.   Their number, and that of the ploughs and mills, is as
follows :

SHEEP.			PLOUGHS.			MILLS.		
9 score ewes,	-	180	Two-horse ploughs,	-	33	Corn mills,	-	4
9 score lambs,	-	180	Three-horse ditto,	-	7	Flour ditto,	-	1
7 score hogs,	-	140	Four-horse ditto,	-	16	Lint ditto,	-	1
Total,	-	500	Total,	-	56	Total,	-	6

Heritors, Rent, and Fuel.—The heritors are 7 in number ;
none of whom reside, excepting one gentleman, a few months
in summer.   There is only one gentleman's seat in the parish;
but Airly Castle will soon make another.—The valued rent is
3310l. Scotch.   The real rent is about 2850l. Sterling, including what arises from mofs and marl.   The former will
bring for peats, the chief fuel of the lower clafs, near 100l.,
and the latter about 300l.

Church, School, and Poor.—The church was rebuilt in
1783, and the manse in 1792.   The living is 85 bolls 3 firlots 1 peck ⅓ lippie meal, and 43 bolls 3 firlots bear, with
about 9l. of vicarage tithes, a glebe and garden.   The Earl
of STRATHMORE is patron.—The schoolmafter's falary and
school fees amount to about 16l. or 17l.—The poor are fupplied by the weekly collections, mortcloth money, and the
interest of about 150l.   The number upon the roll, during
the laft 10 years, has been from 4 to 9, befides many who
have received occasional supplies.   In 1782, 20l. Sterling
were expended in purchasing meal for the moft neceffitous
families.

Population.—The number of parishioners has decreased
within these 40 years, owing to the improvements of land
and junction of farms, which have also greatly diminished the
number of inhabited houses.

POPU-

POPULATION TABLE of the Parish of AIRLY.

Number of fouls in 1755,	-	1012	Members of the Established	
Ditto in 1792,	-	865	Church, - -	854
		——	Seceders, - -	7
Decrease,	-	147	Episcopalians, -	4
				——
				865

—— houses uninhabited, or pulled			Persons under 10 years of age,	187
down,	- -	70	—— between 10 and 20, -	150
—— weavers,	-	49	—— —— 20 and 50, -	399
—— tailors,	- -	5	—— —— 50 and 70, -	110
—— shoemakers,	-	4	—— —— 70 and 80, -	16
—— smiths,	- -	5	—— —— 80 and 90, -	3
—— wrights,	- -	9		

MARRIAGES, BIRTHS, and BURIALS, for the last 10 years.

Years	Mar.	Births.		Bur.
		Mal.	Fem.	
1782	14	12	7	16
1783	11	21	8	11
1784	10	12	8	12
1785	10	14	18	14
1786	10	14	13	9
1787	7	10	17	15
1788	11	12	20	14
1789	8	13	12	14
1790	7	17	14	8
1791	13	9	10	24
Tot.	101	134	127	137

AIRLY CASTLE.——Airly Castle, which gave title to Ogilvy Earl of Airly, is situated in the N. W. corner of the parish, at the conflux of the Melgin and Isla. It is built on a promontory, formed by these two rivers, and elevated above their bed more than 100 feet. It has been a very large and strong fortress, seemingly inaccessible on every side but the South, on which it has been secured by a ditch and draw-bridge, more than 20, perhaps 30 feet wide, and a wall (the front of the

the caſtle), 10 feet thick, and 35 feet high[*]. For romantic ſituation, and natural beauties, (ſuch as the ſerpentine windings of rivers, trees and ſhrubs ſtarting from the brows of ſteep rocks, and lining the ſides of deep dens), it exceeds any thing in this part of the country. Till within theſe 3 years it has remained a ruin; but now an elegant modern houſe, built on the principal foundations of the caſtle, is juſt finiſhing.

Caſtle of Balrie.——The caſtle of Balrie, another ruin, ſituated in Strathmore, has been built upon a riſing ground, towards the W. end of the preſent moſs (formerly a large loch), containing about 120 acres, to the eaſtward of the caſtle, and 6 or 8 to the weſtward. The preſent proprietor, about 10 years ago, dug up a part of the cauſeway which led into the draw-bridge; ſo that there is little doubt of this place having been once very ſtrong, and almoſt impregnable. The walls, in general, are about 8 feet thick; but the houſe has been ſmall, and rather intended for a place of refuge in times of danger, than the conſtant reſidence of a family [†].

Moſs of Balrie.——The moſs of Balrie was begun to be drained about 40 years ago, and has, at various intervals, undergone different degrees of draining; the great object of which has no doubt been the immenſe quantity of fine ſhell marl found in it, as well as peats. The one has contributed

as

---

[*] At what time it was built, is not ſo certain, as that it was deſtroyed by the Marquis of Argyll in 1640; which was repaid in kind by the Marquis of Montrose and the royaliſts, a few years after, when they burnt Muckart and Dollar, and overthrew Lochow, Argyll's principal reſidence.

[†] The neighbouring lands, with the caſtle, were the property of the laſt Lord Viſcount Fenton, whoſe eldeſt daughter married into the family of Strathmore, and of which lands the Earl of Strathmore is ſtill ſuperior. It is ſaid to be more than 100 years ſince any part of the roof of the caſtle was ſtanding.

as much to the improvement of the neighbouring country, as
the other has to the comfort of the poor. Several thousand
bolls of marl are dug out of this mofs yearly, which in price
has arifen, from 4½d. to 10d. per boll, 8 cubical feet being
allowed to the boll. And there are ftill beds of marl in it
16 feet perpendicular, by the boring iron, and the bottom not
found; but impoffible to work out, without more water being
taken off, which will be as difficult as expenfive*. Confiderable quantities of marl have likewife been found in the moffes
of other proprietors.

* Several very large deer's horns have been found in the Mofs of Balrie;
one of which, prefented by the proprietor to the Antiquarian Society, weighed
about 24 lb. There are other two in his poffeffion, one of which weighs about
16lb. and the other about 14 lb. In the year 1775, the tufk of a wild boar was
dug up upon a marl fpade. The length of it, from the fuppofed feat in the jaw-
bone, is 4 inches; the greateft breadth near two. It refembles very much the
colour and fubftance of ivory, but is faid to be only bone.

PARISH OF ARBIRLOT.

(*County of Forfar.*)

By the Rev. Mr RICHARD WATSON.

—————

Name, Situation, Extent, &c.

ARBIRLOT is termed, in old writings, *Aberelliot*. The name seems to be of Gaelic original, in which language *aber* signifies *above*, and *Elliot* is the name of the water. Aberelliot, therefore, is expreffive of the local fituation of the village. The parifh of Arbirlot lies in the county of Forfar, in the prefbytery of Aberbrothock, and fynod of Angus and Mearns. It is about 4 miles in length, and 3 in breadth. The extent of fea coaft is about 3 miles, and, for the moft part, flat and fandy.

Soil and Climate.—The greater part of this parifh is hilly ; yet the hills are neither very high nor rocky. They are in general green, and capable of cultivation. The air is confidered as healthy, and there are no peculiar difeafes. The foil is various. Along the coaft there is a thin dry foil, which, in a wet feafon, yields a tolerable crop ; but in a dry feafon, a very fcanty one. The foil, contiguous to this, confifts of a light rich loam, on a gravelly bottom, which becomes fertile in proportion to the feafon, and the care beftowed on its cultivation. In fields adjoining to each other,

we

we have soils very different ; some shallow, others deep. The
deep soils have generally an under stratum of clay, which renders them hard to plough ; but when proper care is taken of
their culture, and the season favourable, they produce weighty crops. In the hilly parts of the parish, there are various
qualities of soil, some cold and wet, some moorish and spongy, some dry and gravelly. In a word, the variety of soil is
so great, that often, in the same field, different soils are to
be found. This inequality of soils, which, at first sight,
seems a defect, is in reality a remarkable proof of the wisdom
of providence ; for there is no soil so ungrateful, as not to
reward the labourer's toil, if he will only bestow proper care
on its culture, and each soil has a season, in which it is peculiarly productive. The ground, in this parish, has, for the most
part, a good exposure, and grows fruitful, in proportion to
its state of cultivation. This has encouraged the farmers of
late years to improve tracts of it, which formerly lay waste
and uncultivated.

Agriculture and Produce.—Such of the tenants as border
on the shore, use sea ware for manure. But the principal
manure here used is lime, which is brought partly from the
Frith of Forth, and partly from Sunderland in England, at
a very considerable expence ; yet the farmers value it so
much, that they look upon it as an essential requisite in carrying forward their improvements. The times of plowing,
sowing, and reaping, are determined by the seasons, and the
general rules laid down by the most experienced farmers.
The principal crops raised in this parish are oats and barley.
Of the former there is only a small quantity, but of the
latter a great deal is annually exported. Of late years, a considerable quantity of wheat and turnips has been sown, and,
in general, succeeded well. For some years past, the farmers
have paid due attention to the raising of flax ; and, from the
premiums

premiums they have received, it appears that their labour has not been in vain. In the year 1790, there were 97 acres of ground, within the bounds of this parish, sown with lint-seed, which in general succeeded well, and procured the pre-miums given by the Society for raising of flax in this county. There are from 40 to 50 ploughs in this parish, of different constructions. Some of them are drawn by 4 horses, and others by 2. When 4 horses are yoked, 2 servants are re-quisite; but when two do the work, one man is sufficient, as he both holds the plough, and drives the horses. This last mode of plowing has been introduced, partly from the im-proved state of the farm, and partly from the increase of servants wages. It will be admitted by the candid, that im-provements in husbandry, as in the fine arts, arrive at matu-rity by degrees. Encouraged by success, the farmers in this parish have, within these 20 years, made rapid progress in the cultivation of their lands. And as their farms are not over-rented, they are enabled to go on with their improve-ments.

Cattle.—It may not be improper to observe, that great at-tention is paid to the breeding of cattle; but little to the feeding of them. They are, for the most part, brought to the market about 3 years of age. There is only one grazier in the parish. It is remarkable, that there is not within the bounds of this parish one flock of sheep, especially when we consider, that the greater part of it is hilly. Perhaps the pe-riod is not far distant, when the farmers may see their interest in this particular, and take the benefit which their local situ-ation evidently points out.

Wages.—The yearly wages of men servants, in the diffe-rent branches of husbandry, are from 7 l. to 8 l. Sterling;
and

and of women fervants, from 3 l. to 4 l. Sterling, including the perquifites. The wages of a day labourer are 6 d. when the employer furnifhes him with provifions. But when the labourer victuals himfelf, his wages are from 1 s. to 15 d. *per* day.

Population.—The return to the inquiry made by Dr Web-fter, in 1755, refpecting the population of this parifh, was 865. No particular enumeration has been made fince that period, until about 12 months ago, (September 1790), when an exact lift of the inhabitants was made up; and their number amounted to 1055, of whom there were 550 males, and 505 females. By a regifter, well attefted, it appears, that the marriages, births, and deaths in this parifh, from the beginning of the year 1780, to the end of the year 1790, were as follows:

A. D.	Marriages.	Births.			Deaths.
		mal.	*fem.*	*in all.*	
1780	5	14	7	21	17
1781	3	17	13	30	4
1782	1	11	5	16	12
1783	5	11	11	22	11
1784	4	16	9	25	3
1785	11	8	7	15	12
1786	6	16	9	25	9
1787	3	18	9	27	10
1788	6	17	15	32	3
1789	5	11	10	21	6
1790	4	28	10	38	7
	53	167	105	272	94

The

The above account of births, corresponds with an observation made by the Baron de Montesquieu, in his Spirit of Laws, that there are born, in several parts of Europe, more boys than girls.

Manufactures.—The inhabitants of this parish enjoy the advantages of raising, watering, dressing, and spinning of flax, in a high degree, which might surely be an object of great importance, both to flax dealers and manufacturers; though, as yet, there is no established linen manufactory in the parish. For some years past, there has been a small brick-work carried on; but it does not appear, that this branch of manufacture has either enriched its proprietors, or much benefited the parishioners. Several houses have been built within these last 10 years for tradesmen, especially weavers, who have met with due encouragement from the farmers. They are allowed a piece of ground nigh to their houses, on reasonable terms; and are bound to perform no services, except a few day's labour, at different seasons of the year, during which time they receive, from their respective masters, 6 d. *per* day, and their victuals. It is probable that these persons, from their industry, economy, and attention to business, will increase the produce, the wealth, and the population of the parish. There is one brewer in this parish, and 4 persons who sell ale and spirituous liquors, and are known by the name of *tapsters*. These alehouses are rather for the accommodation of strangers, than for the use of the parishioners, who look upon idleness, debauchery, and intemperance, as the principal sources of human misery.

Fuel.—The fuel, commonly used by the inhabitants in the lower part of the parish, is coal, and by those in the higher part, peats and turf.

Roads and Bridges.—The bridges in the parish are good. The roads were exceeding bad, but have been altered for the better within the laſt two years; and at preſent there are ſeveral favourable circumſtances, which induce us to hope, that they will ſoon be repaired to our wiſhes. By a late act of Parliament, the ſtatute labour has been commuted; and the converſion money raiſed in this pariſh has been laid out by the gentlemen of the diſtrict to great advantage. Being furniſhed with every qualification requiſite for the improvement of the roads, we may juſtly be confident, that they will take the moſt effectual meaſures in order to complete a ſcheme, ſo conſonant to friendly intercourſe, ſympathetic aid, and ſound policy. A turnpike road is now making between Dundee and Arbroath, which runs through this pariſh; and though the tolls charged are conſiderable, yet the advantages are ſo viſible, both in ſpeculation and in fact, that very much good is expected from it.

River and Fiſh.—The water Elliot, which runs through this pariſh, from north to ſouth, hath its ſource in the pariſh of Carmylie, about the diſtance of 3 miles from the town of Arbirlot. It was noted, ſome time paſt, for trouts of a peculiar reliſh. At preſent there are very few in the water. It may be obſerved, that our young men, inſtead of uſing the well diſſembled fly to catch the finny race, have of late tried the gun to kill the ſpringing game. This new faſhion will, probably, ſoon be over. For ſome years paſt, there has been, at the mouth of the Elliot, a ſalmon fiſhery; but, either through the negligence of the perſon who has the management, or from the different run which that ſpecies of fiſh have taken, very few are caught. By the variety of trees and ſhrubs on the banks of Elliot, which invite the ſeveral kinds of ſinging birds, and the Caſtle of Kelly, built upon a rock, by the

water

water edge, though in a half ruined state, a very beautiful
and delightful romantic scene is formed, which is to be seen
to great advantage on the road betwixt Arbroath and Arbirlot. The Elliot is not only an object of beauty, but of utility. There are 5 mills upon it; one for cleaning flax, another for dressing yarn, and 3 for grinding corn. A few
years ago, the greatest part of this parish was under thirlage
to some of the corn mills in the neighbourhood, and payed
a very high multure. But the present tenants, desirous of
obtaining freedom from this thraldom, agreed among themselves to pay the rents of the several mills to which they
were thirled; and the late factor or steward on the estate of
Panmure accepted of their proposal; in consequence whereof,
they can carry their corn to any mill they please.

Heritor and Rent.—The whole parish of Arbirlot, at present, is the property of the Hon. William Maule, brother of
the Earl of Dalhousie, by a deed of the late William Maule,
Earl Panmure. The valued rent is 4266 l. 13 s. 4 d. Scotch.
The real rent is 22 bolls 2 pecks wheat, 454 bolls bear, 519
bolls 8 pecks meal, and 935 l. 11 s. 5 d. Sterling. The rent
paid by the tenants varies from 5 s. to 30 s. *per* acre. But
ground, in proper culture for flax, is frequently let for one
crop, by the farmer, at 5 guineas the acre. There are instances of individuals renting lands, formerly possessed by
several tenants, and of removing those people known by the
name of cottagers; but whether this has turned out to the
advantage or disadvantage of the farmer, is doubtful.

Church.—The living consists of 57 bolls 4 pecks meal,
Linlithgow measure, 44 bolls bear, 10 bolls 12 pecks wheat,
and 16 l. 6 s. 11¾ d. in money, with the addition of a manse,
a garden, and a glebe of 4 acres. The value of the living,

there-

therefore, cannot be eſtimated above 85 l. Sterling a year. The King is patron. The kirk was repaired in the year 1785, and the manſe in the year 1790. There are only a few Seceders in the pariſh, and no Roman Catholics.

School.—The parochial ſchoolmaſter has no legal ſalary paid him by the heritor. His income conſiſts of 8 bolls of meal, which was mortified in the year 1628, by Alexander Irvine of Drum, then proprietor of Kelly, in favour of the ſchoolmaſter of Arbirlot; and confirmed by his ſon, Sir Alexander Irvine, Knight, in the year 1637; and 5 bolls 8 pecks of oats, collected from the ſeveral tenants in the pariſh, at the rate of 2 pecks for each plough; which, together with a houſe, garden, ſeſſion-clerk's dues, and ſchool fees, may be eſtimated about 20 l. Sterling *per annum.* The number of children, educated at this ſchool, varies according to the different ſeaſons of the year. In winter, they may be reckoned from 40 to 50; in ſummer, from 30 to 40; in ſpring and autumn, from 20 to 30. The preſbytery have appointed every parochial ſchool, within their bounds, to be examined once a year, by a committee of their number.

Poor.—The poor, being few in number, are tolerably well provided for. In the year 1629, Alexander Irvine of Drum, a gentleman of fortune, then proprietor of Kelly, mortified 12 bolls of meal to the poor in the lands of Kelly, which have been of very great advantage to indigent perſons in that part of the pariſh, eſpecially in the years 1782 and 1783. There are, beſides, of certain annual income, 10 l. Sterling, belonging to the poor's fund, being the intereſt of 4000 merks, lent at $4\frac{1}{2}$ *per cent.* which, together with the collections in the church on Sundays, and at the celebration of the Lord's ſupper, produce about 35 l. Sterling a year.—The diſtribution

tion of this money is confidered as a branch of duty belonging to the minifter and kirk elders, who meet at various times in the year for that purpofe. Part of it is employed in buying coals, coats, and fhoes, for indigent perfons in the winter feafon; part in fupplying thofe who need a certain weekly, monthly, or quarterly allowance, according to their neceffities; part in teaching poor children of the parifh; and part, in relieving fuch other occafional objects of compaffion as make application to them. Of all thefe difburfements an exact account is kept, for the fatisfaction of every fair inquirer who is entitled to afk it. As the kirk feffion has advantages, both for knowing and fupplying the wants of the poor, fo its members are extremely attentive to diftribute to every one according to his exigencies, infomuch that there is not at prefent one beggar belonging to this parifh. Vagrants, however, to whom begging is fweet, infeft it from week to week, and from day to day, through the revolving year. It were to be wifhed, that work houfes, in every county, were erected for the diffolute and idle.

Longevity.—We have feveral inftances of great longevity. There was a man in this parifh, who died a few months ago, at the advanced age of 99. About eight days previous to his death, he feemed to have loft all his fenfes; he neither faw, heard, fpoke, felt, nor moved; but received food, when it was put into his mouth.

Mineral Waters.—Propitious nature has kindly provided feveral mineral fprings near Arbirlot, one of which had a high character fome years ago; and it is to be regreted, that for want of proper accommodation, perfons of high rank have declined coming to it. The well is about half a mile diftant from Arbirlot, and not exceeding 100 yards from the
high

high road betwixt Arbroath and Dundee. It is called *Wor-my-hills Well*, probably from the formation of the hills about it, which very much refemble worms, efpecially when they twift themfelves. The water of this well has been ufed with fuccefs, both in fcorbutic, and in rheumatic diforders. It is defervedly efteemed on account of its medicinal virtue; and being within 200 yards of the fea, perfons attending it have the benefit of fea bathing, which, of late years, has been much recommended by our beft phyficians.

Antiquities.—A few years ago, the remains of a religious houfe in the parifh, whofe ruins had been revered for ages, were taken down. And though we cannot fay at what time, or by what perfon, it was built, yet from the accounts given of it, we have reafon to believe, that it had been a Druidical temple. The province of the Druids, properly fo called, was religion; yet they managed matters fo dextroufly, that they engroffed all power, civil as well as religious; and under the character of either priefts, magiftrates, philofophers, or phy-ficians, took every thing under their cognizance. In this parifh, there are many heaps of ftones, which the people call *cairns*. But whether they were at firft defigned as monu-ments, raifed over the dead, or figns of memorable events, or altars of the druids, is uncertain.

Among the Greeks, there were many heaps of ftones, con-fecrated to Mercury; and among the Latins, there were num-berlefs rude pillars, confecrated to the fame divinity, under the denomination of Faunus. It is alfo certain, that in Gaul and Britain, there were many heaps and pillars exactly fimi-lar to thefe. But we cannot affirm, that the natives of this country performed any religious ceremonies on thefe cairns, or confidered them in any other point of view, than as objects of

grateful

grateful remembrance, of mutual confidence, and of future fame.

It is reported, with much confidence, that a crown of one of the kings of the Picts, was found in the Black-den of this parish, by a quarryman, about the beginning of the present century, who sold part of it in the neighbourhood, for 20 l. Scotch ; and sent the remainder to London, with a view to procure its real value. But by some unforeseen occurrence, he and his family were prevented from reaping that advantage, which might have been expected from so valuable a curiosity.—It is confidentially reported, that a road was made through part of this parish, by Hector Boethius, the Scotch historian, which still bears his name, though somewhat corrupted. It is called *Heckenbois-path.*

Castle of Kelly.—Neither the period when the Castle of Kelly was built, nor the proprietors, through a long series of ages, can now be traced. Tradition, however, has handed down a circumstance, which deserves notice, viz. that one Ouchterlony, laird of Kelly, was violently active in demolishing the Abbey at Aberbrothock. Nor is it unlikely that he considered every religious fabric as a relict of idolatry. And being remarkable for the activity of his zeal, he was appointed by the Convention to carry this barbarous deed into execution.—To describe, at large, the beauties of Kelly, and do justice to Nature's varied charms, would require uncommon descriptive powers. The soil does not refuse nourishment to trees of foreign birth. At present there is in the garden, a tree called the *Dall-hound-holly,* remarkable for its beauty. Then exposed to the sun, and sheltered from the chilly blast, it has grown up to full maturity.

Migratory

Migratory Birds.—The migratory birds are the ſwallow, the cuckoo, the lapwing, the dotterel, and corn-craick or rail. The ſea-gulls are conſidered as ominous. When they appear in the fields, a ſtorm from the ſouth-eaſt generally follows; and when the ſtorm begins to abate, they fly back to the ſhore.

General Character.—The inhabitants of this pariſh are ſober, induſtrious, and regular in their attendance on the ordinances of religion. Senſible of the advantages which they enjoy, both of a civil and religious nature, they wiſh to relieve the miſeries, and promote the happineſs of their fellow creatures. They are juſt in their dealings, true to their promiſes, liberal to the poor, and mutually helpful to one another.

PARISH OF ARBROATH.

(County of Forfar.—Presbytery of Arbroath.—Synod of
Angus and Mearns.)

By the Reverend Mr GEORGE GLEIG.

Town, &c.

ABERBROTHOCK, or Arbroath, is a royal burgh, situated on the discharge of the small river of Brothock into the sea, from whence it has its name, *Aber* implying such a situation. In conjunction with Aberdeen, Bervie, Montrose, and Brechin, it sends a member to Parliament. The post-road from Edinburgh to Aberdeen runs through it. It is distant 17 miles from Dundee, and 12 from Montrose. It is the general opinion, that it was erected into a royalty by King William the Lion about the year 1186; but this cannot be properly ascertained, owing to the loss of the original charter, which was taken away by force out of the Abbey of Arbroath, where it was lodged in the time of the civil wars, during the minority of James VI. by George Bishop of Moray, called Postulat of Arbroath. It was, however, confirmed in all the privileges of a royal burgh, which it had formerly enjoyed, by a *novodamus* granted by James VI. in the year 1599. The town is pleasantly situated within an amphitheatre of a ridge of small hills, enjoying a south exposure, and having a fair and extensive prospect of the Lothian

thian hills, the eaft coaft of Fife, and the entries into the
Frith of Forth, and the river Tay. The profpect towards
the north is bounded by the Grampian Hills. Few places
equal it in point of fituation. It is governed by a provoft,
two bailies, and 16 counfellors. The dean of guild and
deacon convener of the trades are members of council *ex
officio*. Befides the town-clerk, there are 5 writers, who are
notaries public, and 2 meffengers at arms. The revenue of
the town amounts to about 800 l. which arifes principally
from rents of land, harbour dues, town's mills, and 2 pennies
Scotch on each pint of ale fold within the royalty. There
are 7 trades incorporated; fmiths, glovers, taylors, weavers,
fhoemakers, wrights, and bakers.

Trade.—Before the year 1736, Arbroath had little or no
commerce, unlefs a little traffic in fifh, and a kind of contra-
band or fmuggling trade deferve the name. It had no manufactures; and any piece of cloth that was made was carried to Montrofe, and fold there. It imported nothing, except now and then a fmall cargo of wood from Norway.
Flax, iron, and other commodities, were purchafed by the
inhabitants from the merchants in Montrofe and Dundee.
A few years fubfequent to that mentioned above, feveral
gentlemen of property jointly undertook to eftablifh the
manufacture of Oznaburghs, and other brown linens here,
and to import their own materials. They laid out confiderable fums of money on different kinds of machinery, which
were executed on a very complete and extenfive fcale. Suc-
cefs attended their fpirited exertions; and, at that time, the
Arbroath fabrics procured a fuperiority, and commanded a
fale, in preference to any other of the kind, which they ftill
hold. From this eftablifhment, the rife and progrefs of the
trade and manufactures of Arbroath are to be dated. The
principal

principal manufactures are fail-cloth, Oznaburghs, and other
brown linens.   From November 1790, to November 1791,
1,055,303 yards of the two laft were manufactured in the
town and ftamp-office diftrict, which extends about 6 or 8
miles round the town, equal in value to 39,660 l. 6 s. 10 d.
There is likewife yearly manufactured in the town, fail-cloth
to the fame amount ; and nearly 500 looms are employed.
The greateft part of the linen and fail-cloth is fhipped for
London.   A fmall part is fent to Glafgow and Dundee.
The principal imports are flax and hemp from Ruffia, and
wood and iron from Norway and Sweden.   Of the two firft,
there were imported laft year from 700 to 800 tons ; and
wood and iron to the value of 4000 l.   A very confiderable
trade is likewife carried on in lime and coals.   Of the former, there are unloaded at the harbour about 18,000 bolls of
fhells ; and from 6000 to 8000 tons of the latter yearly.
This quantity will not feem fo great, when it is confidered
that this town not only fupplies its own neighbourhood, but
fends a great quantity of coals to Forfar, Brechin, and their
neighbourhood.   A repeal of the coal-tax would confiderably affect the revenue of this town, and be a lofs to individuals, who deal folely in the coal-trade ; yet the people are
not fo felfifh as to throw any obftacle in the way of a repeal,
fo ardently defired by their northern neighbours, nor fo
blind to their own intereft as to folicit its abolition.   About
18,000 bolls of barley are yearly fhipped here, and the trades
import about 3000 bolls of oat-meal.—There is a tan-yard,
which employs 6 men ; and hides are yearly dreffed, to the
value of 2500 l.   During the late war, and fome time prior
to it, a great number of fhoes were exported ; but, fince the
peace, that trade has almoft, if not entirely failed.   A fhort
time ago, a cotton manufactory was eftablifhed, which employs 18 men, women, and children.   Yarn is fpun to the
value

value of 1000 l. ; and 6 looms weave of calicoes to the amount of 500 l. yearly. There is also lately established here a manufacture of particular kinds of brown linens, never attempted in this part of the country. The number of looms employed is 18. The cloth is mostly used by coachmakers and upholsterers ; and the proprietor has a shop in London for selling it. One of the kinds is remarkable for its thinness, and more properly may be termed *gauze* than linen, of which a person will weave 40 yards a day, though it is yard wide. The common price of this last is 4 d. *per* yard.— In the year 1740, a thread manufactory was established, which was for many years carried on to a great extent, and turned out to good account. By it thousands of people gained a livelihood. For some time past it has been greatly on the decline, owing to the high prices of flax, the great rise on spinning, the high wages allowed to labourers in the Oznaburgh and linen manufactories, and more especially to the want of a proportionable rise of price for the thread in the London market. From these causes, the thread trade in this place may be said to be turned *thread bare*. But, though it has failed, trade goes briskly forward ; and, to show its increase, the increase of the imports and exports, it is only necessary to mention, that the harbour-dues were this year (1792) let at public roup for 293 l. exclusive of the guildry-dues, when 40 years ago they did not bring more than 70 l. guildry dues included.

Harbour.—The harbour was originally at the end of the East causeway, and built in the year 1194. There is yet extant an agreement between the abbot of Arbroath and the inhabitants, concerning the building of it, by which both parties were bound to contribute their proportions ; but the largest share fell to the abbot, for which he was to receive an
yearly

yearly tax, payable out of every rood of land lying within
the burgh. The pier was built of wood, and but ill constructed to defend the veſſels in ſtormy weather, from the
heavy ſurges which roll on ſhore. In the year 1725, a brief
was obtained for building a new one, which is ſituated a little
to the weſt of the old. It is ſtrongly built of ſtone all round,
ſmall, but very commodious, and ſo conſtructed that a veſſel
can lie to at any part of it, either to receive or diſcharge her
cargo. It is likewiſe perfectly ſafe, being contracted at the
entrance to the width of 31 feet, and defended by what is
called the *gates*, which are 14 or 15 ſtrong beams of wood,
let down in a groove on each ſide, and locked in on the top
by iron bars. Theſe beams, which are eaſily put in or taken
out in 15 minutes, by means of a crane made for the purpoſe,
completely break the force of the ſea, which runs into the
harbour, ſo that it is *fida ſtatio carinis*. It is always dry at low
water; but has a ſluice on the north ſide, by which the water
of Brothock is admitted, when it is thought neceſſary to clean
it. At ſpring tides there is, at its entrance, a depth of 15 or
16 feet; and at neep tides, of 9 or 10 feet water.

In the year 1781, there belonged to this harbour no more
than 17 or 18 veſſels, making all together only about 900
tons; now there are 32 veſſels, making 1704 tons, which
employ about 160 ſeamen. There are beſides two veſſels on
the ſtocks, together above 150 tons.

To this harbour belong alſo 3 fiſhing boats, beſides the pilot boats, which employ 14 fiſhermen; but theſe depend
upon a living more on what they make by pilotage, than on
what they can earn in the fiſhing trade, which has moſtly
failed *.

Soil

* During the late war, in the year 1781, the ſhipping on this
coaſt was much annoyed by a French privateer, named the
Fearnought of Dunkirk, commanded by one Fall. On the
evening

Soil and Produce.—The foil is various. On the northren extremity it is a thin muirifh foil, with a clay bottom; about the

evening of the 23d of May, he came to anchor in the Bay, and fired a few fhot into the town ; after which falute, he fent a flag of truce on fhore, with the following letter :

> " *At fea, May twenty third.*
>
> " Gentlemen, I fend thefe two words to inform you, that " I will have you to bring to the French colour, in lefs " than a quarter of an hour, or I fet the town on fire direftly ; " fuch is the order of my mafter the King of France I am fent " by. Send direftly the mair and chiefs of the town to make " fome agreement with me, or I'll make my duty. It is the " will of yours.
>
> " To Monffieurs Mair of the town called Arbrought, or in " his abfence, to the chief man after him in Scotland."

The Magiftrates, wifhing to gain time to arm the inhabitants, and fend expreffes to the neighbouring towns for military, gave an evafive anfwer to this letter, intimating, that he had mentioned no terms of ranfom, and begging he would do no injury to the town, till he fhould hear from them again. Upon this Fall wrote a fecond letter, which is as follows :

> " *At Sea, eigth o cloc in the afternoon.*
>
> " Gentlemen, I received juft now your anfwer, by which you " fay I afk no terms. I thought it was ufelefs, fince I afked you " to come aboard for agreement. But here are my terms ; I " will have 30,000l. Sterling at leaft, and 6 of the chiefs men " of the town for otage. Be fpeedy, or I fhoot your town away " direftly, and I fet fire to it. I am, Gentlemen, your fervant.
>
> " I fent fome of my crew to you ; but if fome harm happens " to them, you'll be fure will hang up the main-yard all the " prefeners we have aboard.
>
> " To Monfieurs the chiefs men of Arbrought in Scotland."

The magiftrates, before fending a return to this letter, having got fome of the inhabitants armed, and fome military from Montrofe, fet Fall at defiance, and ordered him to do his worft, for they would not give him a farthing Terribly enraged, and no doubt greatly difappointed, he began a heavy fire upon the town, and continued it for a long time ; but happily it did no harm, except knocking down fome chimney tops, and burning the fingers of thofe who took up his balls, which were heated. On the 24th he fent a third letter on fhore, by fome of our own people, whom he had captured at fea. It runs thus :

" A:

the middle it is black loam ; and hard on the fhore, the ground is light and fandy. The whole has been much improved of late, and it produces excellent crops of wheat, oats, barley, peafe, rye-grafs, turnip, potatoes, &c. About 27 years ago, the magiftrates planted 110 acres of muir with Scotch firs, which are thriving very well, and in a fhort time will bring a confiderable addition to the revenue of the town. —The coaft is flat and rocky, and, from the rocks, fea-weed is cut every third year, for the purpofe of making kelp. The quantity made is very inconfiderable, and the emolument thence arifing to the town not worth the mentioning.

Population.

At Sea, May 24th.

" Gentlemen, See whether you will come to fome terms with
" me, or I come in prefently with my cutter into the arbour,
" and I will caft down the town all over. Make hafte, becaufe
" I have no time to fpare. I give you a quarter of an hour for
" your decifion, and after I'll make my duty. I think it would
" be better for you, Gentlemen, to come fome you aboard pre-
" fently, to fettle the affairs of your town. You'll fure no to
" be hurt. I give you my parole of honor. I am your," &c.

To this letter the magiftrates fent a verbal meffage to Fall, that they would be glad to fee him on fhore, and hoifted a flag of defiance on the Ballaft Hill. Finding his threats to be in vain, after firing fome few ineffectual fhot, he weighed anchor, and failed in purfuit of fome floops which came into the offing, which he captured, but did not return.

To prevent all infults of this kind, from fo mean an enemy, for the future, a battery was propofed to be built. A fubfcription was opened for this purpofe, which was foon filled up. Government was applied to, and Captain Andrew Frafer was fent down to plan the work, which was quickly finifhed. The battery, mounting 6 12 pounders, is built fomewhat in the form of a half-moon, of ftone and lime, and faced with large banks of fods. The platform is paved with ftone, and below it there are vaults bomb-proof, for keeping powder and fhot, with other neceffaries. It is built on the Ballaft Hill, between the harbour and the fea, and has a compleat command of the Bay, fo that now no Fall, with his Fearnought, dare infult Arbroath with impunity.

Population, &c.—In the year 1755, the numbers were 2098. In the year 1776, the number of fouls in the parifh amounted to 3943 ; the total amount this year, (1792), in town and country, is 4676, of which there are, in the coun- try, 131, and 4545 in town. But to gain a complete lift of the number of people in the town of Arbroath, we muft add the number of fouls in that part of it belonging to the parifh of St. Vigeans, which is 638, and then the number of fouls in the town is exactly 5183.

In this parifh there are 517 females more than males. An exact regifter of births and deaths has not hitherto been kept : For the year 1791, it ftood as follows :

			Total.
Baptifms,	61 males.	53 females.	114
Deaths,	21	47	110
Marriages,	48 both parties in par.	20 one party out of parifh	68

For fome years paft the town has increafed confiderably. Laft year 30 houfes were built, many of them of confider- able value ; and this year there is much about the fame num- ber, though not of equal value. This increafe is no doubt owing to our manufactures ; and from the afpect which they at prefent wear, there is every reafon to look for a rapid in- creafe of population, and confequently of buildings.

Ecclefiaftical State.—Arbroath, which formerly belonged to the parifh of St Vigeans, was erected into a parochial charge about the year 1560. Befides the eftablifhed church there are meetings both of Englifh and Scotch Epifcopalians, Anti- burgher Seceders, and Independents ; and in the fuburbs be- longing to St Vigeans parifh there is a meeting-houfe, the property of the Methodifts. The church is built in the fouth-weft corner of the Abbey ground, and the tower ferves for a bell fteeple. It was repaired and enlarged about thirty

years

years ago, and fitted up in a very neat and commodious manner, capable to contain from 1800 to 2000 people. It is now rather fmall for the congregation, and it will be foon neceffary to have another, or a chapel of eafe. The right of patronage formerly belonged to the Earl of Panmure, but fell to the Crown by forfeiture in the year 1715. The ftipend is 6 bolls of wheat, 22 bolls 2 firlots 3 pecks and 1 lippie of barley, 23 bolls 2 firlots and 2 pecks of meal, and 54 l. 8 s. 10 d. including the rent for the church-yard grafs, 4 l. 3 s. 4 d. for communion elements, and 4 l. 8 s. 11 d. for houfe-rent. There is neither manfe nor glebe.—A forry ftipend for fo large a place. Arbroath is a fingle charge, but the minifter has an ordained affiftant who acts the part of a col-league. His ftipend arifes in part from the intereft of 565 l. mortified by a Convener Mill for that purpofe ; and fome gentlemen in the town have bound themfelves to make it at leaft equal to 50 l.

School.—There is only one eftablifhed fchool, which was built about 20 years ago. It is fpacious, and in every refpect well fituated, fit to accommodate with eafe 120 fcholars. There is only one mafter and an affiftant. The mafter's fa-lary which is paid by the town is 10 l. and the emoluments arifing to him from being feffion-clerk and precentor in the church may amount to about 12 l. The number of fcholars for 26 years paft has been between 70 and 80. The fchool-fees are 2 s. 6 d. for each fcholar *per* quarter, and have been the fame for more than 30 years ; of which the mafter re-ceives 1 s. 6 d. and the affiftant 1 s. The affiftant has 9 l. 2 s. 2 d. as falary, of which the town pays 5 l. and the reft is paid by the kirk-feffion. The branches of education taught are Englifh, writing, arithmetic, Euclid's elements, menfura-tion, geography, navigation, Latin, Greek, and French, but

the

the two laft are feldom required. There are likewife two or three private fchools, one of which is fupported by a number of the principal inhabitants of the town, who give the mafter 36 l. *per annum* for teaching 36 fcholars.

Poor.—The funds for the fupport of the poor arife from rents of land, mort-cloths, feats in the church, marriages, legacies, and collections at the church-door. There are diftributed yearly among them, about Martinmas, between 70 and 80 bolls of coals. The weekly penfioners receive among them 16 s. *per* week; and about 16 l. or 17 l. are divided among the poor at the facrament; befides, they receive occafionally as circumftances require. The diftribution, *communibus annis,* is about 130 l. The number of poor is about 120. There is alfo a fund for the fupport of feven poor widows of fhipmafters left by John Carmichael fhipmafter, about 60 years ago, in money, houfes, and land. This charity is not confined to Arbroath, but extends to Montrofe and Dundee. Widows of the names of Carmichael, Pearfon, and Strachan, have a preferable claim, and after them, widows whofe hufbands have been of any of the preceding names. None can be admitted upon this charity who do not live nine months in the year in Arbroath, or whofe yearly income amounts to a fum equal to that which they can receive from the fund.—An improper behaviour alfo excludes from the benefit of this charity.

This fund is under the direction of the magiftrates, minifter, kirk-treafurer, and boxmafter to the fraternity of feamen in Arbroath; and by the care and attention of the managers, it has increafed confiderably for fome years paft, fo that each of the widows inftead of 5 l. or 6 l. which they formerly received, now draw above 13 l. yearly.

Climate,

Climate, &c.—The air is dry and ſalubrious.—The people in general healthy. About 20 years ago, intermittent fevers were very prevalent, particularly during the ſpring months; but ſince the lands in the neighbourhood, in conſequence of a keen ſpirit for agriculture, have been drained of their exuberant latent moiſture, the diſeaſe has totally diſappeared. Continued fevers, which uſed rarely to occur, have been more frequent within theſe laſt two years; they are of a type between the nervous and inflammatory, and ſeldom prove fatal. They probably owe their exiſtence to our winters having been uncommonly open and moiſt. Comparatively ſpeaking, Arbroath is a remarkably healthy place, and the people live to a good old age. There are many of 70 and 80, and a few conſiderably above 90 years. I know five perſons whoſe ages added together make 476; one of theſe is an old woman aged 97, yet ſtrong and healthy, who never drank a dram. Another of them is an old man aged 96, whoſe wife, not included in the above number, is 85.—She is the man's third wife, and he is her third huſband. Prejudices againſt inoculation for the ſmall pox are almoſt entirely eradicated.

Mineral Spring.—About a quarter of a mile to the weſtward of the town, in a high ground called the Common, there is one of the ſtrongeſt Spaws, or Chalybeate ſprings, in Scotland. It is much frequented by people affected with ſcrophula, nervous, and ſtomachic diſorders, and other diſeaſes ariſing from relaxation of the habit; and in numberleſs caſes, the medical practitioners are obliged to acknowledge the ſuperior effect of the water, as a corroborant to any remedy they can preſcribe. Probably this ſpring would be more frequented, if there were ſome attention paid to the well, and proper accommodations for the reception of its viſitors. An inducement to the invalid to repair to this place,

is

is the opportunity of sea-bathing, which is the purest exercise of health, and perhaps does no less good, than the incredibly large gulps of water, which many in faith of its healing powers, force themselves to swallow.

Price of Labour and Provisions.—A common labourer receives from 1 s. to 1 s. 2 d. *per* day. The wages of a journeyman smith are from 5 l. to 7 l. a-year, with his victuals. A shoemaker will earn from 6 s. to 8 s.—a house-carpenter about 8 s.—a mason 10 s.—a slater 12 s.—and a weaver from 7 s. to 10 s. *per* week. A gardener has 1 s. 3 d. *per* day. The wages of a baker are much the same with the smiths; and a taylor receives from 6 d. to 8 d. *per* day, with his victuals. The common wages of a servant-maid is 3 l.; some receive 3 l. 10 s. and some 4 l. *per annum.*

Beef, mutton, lamb, veal, and pork, are sold at from 3½ d. to 5 d. *per lib.*—Butter from 8 d. to 11 d. *per lib.* which is 24 ounces.—Cheese, 5 s. *per* stone.—Eggs from 3½ to 4 d. *per* dozen.—Fowls from 1 s. 8 d. to 2 s. *per* pair.—Oat-meal sold this year for 15 s. 6 d.—Wheat for 1 l. 1 s.—and barley from 17 s. to 18 s. *per* boll.

Miscellaneous Observations.—The town is well supplied with butcher meat; and nearly 500 head of black cattle, and 350 calves, besides sheep, lambs, and swine, are slaughtered at the shambles. Formerly, fish were plenty, now they are scarce, and consequently very dear. The coast being rocky, we have plenty of crabs and lobsters, which find a ready market; but the greatest part of the latter is sent to London; and it is said, that the fishermen last year drew no less than 80 l. for lobsters sent thither. About the summer markets, boats loaded with dry fish, such as cod, ling, skate, &c.

come

come to us from Peterhead, and other small fishing towns in the north country. The country people buy the greatest part of them, and some of the Arbroath merchants buy of them to sell to their customers. It is supposed, that this year there was sold in the harbour, dry fish to the value of 1000l.

Parish of Aberbrothock.

Answers by the then minister of Arbroath, to the queries circulated by Mr. Maitland, when he was about to publish his History of Scotland; communicated by Dr. Lorimer.

The abbey of Aberbrothock was erected for the entertainment of the Tironensian monks by King William, in honour of Thomas O'Becket, falsely entitled saint and martyr. However, this dedication, it seems, obtained for the inhabitants of Aberbrothock a grant from John king of England, whereby they were to enjoy the several privileges of his own subjects in all parts of England, London excepted.——Pope Benedict granted the abbot and his successors a right to wear the mitre, rings, robes, and other pontifical ornaments.

The receipts of this monastery in 1562 were, in money, 2553l. 14s.; 30 chaldrons of coals; 3 bolls, 3 firlots, 2 pecks of wheat; 143 chaldrons, 9 bolls, 2 pecks of bear; 196 chaldrons, 9 bolls, 2 firlots of meal; 27 chaldrons, 11 bolls of oats; 3 lasts and 1 barrel of salmon;——the small receipts by fines, beasts, poultry, &c. being omitted. The last abbot, being John Hamilton, second son to the Duke of Chateauherault, becoming a protestant, he was created Marquis of Hamilton

the

the 19th of April 1599; and the abbey being erected into a temporal lordship, King James the Sixth, by his letters patent of about the 5th of May 1608, granted the same to James his son. But it afterwards coming to the Earl of Dysart, Patrick Maule of Panmure purchased the same, with the rights of patronage of 34 parishes, viz.

1. Arbroath,	14. Glamis,	25. Longlie,
2. Panbride,	15. Kirrymuir,	26. Guild,
3. Arbirlot.	16. Kingholdrum,	27. Kinginie,
4. Monikie,	17. Newtyle,	28. Banchory, or
5. Mairhouse,	18. Garvock,	Trinity,
6. Dunnichen,	19. Dinavig,	29. Bethlem, or
7. Mains,	20. Abernethy,	Bethelney,
8. Lunan.	in Fife,	30. Forgue,
9. Inverkeilor,	21. Inverness,	31. Tiree,
10. Ethie, or St.	22. Auchterarder,	32. Tarries,
Murdo, demol.	or Mornack,	33. Nigg,
11. Monyfieth,	23. Banff,	34. Fitter-Angus.
12. Clovoy,	24. Gamery, or	
13. Ruthven,	Gamesie,	

A Description of the Borough of Aberbrothock,
in the year 1742.

Aberbrothock is a royal borough, which, with the borough of Aberdeen, Montrose, Brechin, and Inverbervie, composeth a district that sends a member to the House of Commons of Great Britain. It is situated at the mouth and on the east side of the water or burn of Borthick, whence it hath its name; and very probably hath its rise from a monastery of that name, founded by King William the Lyon in honour of St. Thomas O'Becket, close by the town, which was one of the richest in the kingdom. It was certainly the abbot's borough before the Reformation; although the charter of erection

erection from King James the Sixth, in 1599, bears a *nova dona*, and affigns reafon, that their old evidences of royalty had been abftracted by the bifhop of Murray. Yet even before the Reformation the burgeffes had confiderable privileges; being under the immediate jurifdiction of two baillies, whereof one was chofen by themfelves, and the other named by the abbot: and there is an agreement between the abbot and them, an. 1394, about building a harbour, to the perfecting of which both were bound to contribute, but the abbot was to be at the greateft part of the charge, for which he was to have a certain yearly duty paid him out of every rood of land lying within the borough.

The town is compofed of one ftreet, running from north to fouth, about   geometrical paces in length; and another ftreet about 150 paces long, being parallel to the fouth end of the former, about 80 paces from it, and next to the water; with three or four bye lanes or wynds, and a fmall ftreet on the weft fide of the water. The whole lies on a flat almoft, only a little rifing on the north part; and the gardens interfperfed and adjoining to the town take up about three times more ground than what is built upon. On the water there are two bridges of ftone, one near the north end of the town, and the other near the fea. The town contains about 250 houfes, and 2,500 inhabitants.

The town council cannot exceed 19 in number; of whom the provoft, two baillies and a dean-of-guild are magiftrates, the deacon-convener being *ex officio* a counfellor and one of the number. Their offices are of the fame nature as in other royal boroughs in the kingdom.

The baillies' court, and that of the dean-of-guild, are courts of record. The convener and deacons of crafts make bye laws for regulating matters relating to the incorporations, but have no concomitant jurifdiction. There are feven trades incorporated,

corporated, viz. smiths, skinners, taylors, weavers, shoemakers, wrights, and bakers, each having their deacon; but these seem to have had no other foundation for their privileges than the charter before mentioned, erecting the borough, and empowering the community to incorporate the trades. The weavers are as numerous as all the other trades put together; and the greatest manufactory is coarse linen, which is commonly sold green, i. e. brown, and the greatest part sent to London. Of late, the most considerable merchants have set up a manufacture of white and check linens, which they are in good hopes to bring to perfection. Next to the weavers, the shoemakers are most numerous, and are much encouraged by the tanning of leather, which is here done to perfection; and they serve not only the town and adjacent country with boots and shoes, but furnish quantities of shoes to the merchants, who send them abroad.

The town had very little foreign trade till the year 1725, when they began to build a new harbour to the westward of the old, in which there was no safety for any vessels in winter storms. The work has been carrying on ever since at a vast expence for so small a town: and although it is not accessible for large ships, yet there are now belonging to the town about a dozen from about 120 to 50 tons burden, employed in trading to the northern colonies in America, the Baltic, France, Holland and Norway; besides vessels employed in the coal trade and coasting. The slate quarries, which lie within 4 miles of the town, afford outward carriage to the coal barges, who find a greater consumption for coals (as they are free of duty) than they are able to answer, so that great part of that article is bought here by strangers.

There are no remarkable public buildings or antiquities, except the ruins of the abbey or monastery; and these deserve a very particular description. The present church, of which

which the king, as come in place of the archbishop of St.
Andrews, is patron, has been built since the Reformation,
joining to a tower on the corner of the enclosure of the abbey, which serves it for a steeple, having nothing in it or
about it deserving notice. There are, besides the church,
two private meeting-houses for public worship; one of the
episcopal persuasion, and the other of the independants. The
tolbooth is an old, mean building.

There are 3 markets in the year. The first, on the 20th
of January, called St. Vigeans, in honour of the patron of
the parish church: for both the monastery and the town
were in the parish before the Reformation; and the parish
which has been erected since comprehends only what is within the town liberties. The second is called St. Ninian's, and
falls on the first Wednesday after Trinity-Sunday. He had
a chapel dedicated to him about half a mile east from the
town, near to the sea shore, adjoining to a fine spring. The
last is on the 7th July, called St. Thomas's, no doubt in honour of Thomas Becket, reckoned the patron of the town.
The weekly market was on Saturday, and ought by the charter to be so; but hath been changed to Thursday.

As to charitable foundations, there is an annual duty,
called the Elymosinary, extending to 5l. or 6l. sterling, paid
out of several houses and roads to the kirk session for the benefit of the poor; but how first constituted is uncertain. A
mortification was lately made of 1000l. sterling, in money,
lands, and tenements, for seven widows of shipmasters, (by
John Carmichael, shipmaster;) of which the magistrates, ministers and kirk-treasurer, together with the treasurer to the
fraternity of seamen, are patrons.

The first charter of the lands granted to the abbey by king
William under his seal is still extant, and contains large endowments. The nobility and great men at the same time

gave

gave many lands; and theſe, by poſterior endowments made by private perſons, and the patronage of about 30 churches, of which the abbot commonly drew the parſonage tithes, or ſet them in tacks, leaving only the ſmall tithes for the vicars, compoſed the abbot's eſtate.——In fixing the ſite of the abbey, the churchmen, who were good judges, pitched upon one of the moſt pleaſant and fertile ſpots of ground in the county. It ſtands on a ſmall eminence overlooking the town; with a fair proſpect of the county, of the Frith of Forth and the river Tay on the ſouth, and the country as far as the Grampian hills on the north.——There are many ſprings of fine water on the eaſt ſide of the incloſure. One of theſe was brought in lead pipes, parts of which have been lately diſcovered in digging, for the ſervice of the houſe; and the reſt formed a canal which ran through the garden, or cloſe, as the whole does now.

The ſoil is a brown clay of a great depth, covered in moſt places with a black mixed earth, which dries immediately after rain; ſo that it affords pleaſant walking in almoſt all ſeaſons.

The moſt valuable records of this abbey that eſcaped the fury of the reformers are preſerved in the Advocates' Library; but ſome are ſtill here.

To give ſome idea of the convent's manner of living, I ſhall tranſcribe from one of theſe volumes a part of the ordinary for the yearly proviſion of victuals to the houſe in 1530, or thereabout. There is appointed to be bought 800 wedders, 9 ſcore of marts or oxen, beſides kain marts and wedders paid by the tenants; 11 barrels of ſalmon, 1500 dried killings or cod; and to be conſumed and eaten in the houſe: 4 ſcore and 2 chaldrons of malt, 30 chaldrons of wheat, 40 chaldrons of meal; and other proviſions in proportion. This would appear ſurpriſing, for I hardly find there

there were above 20 or 25 religious at a time; but the ordinance bears, that fums appointed for buying provifions that year exceeded the appointments for the year 1528, notwithftanding the king's highnefs had been there twice, and the archbifhop thrice; fo that the great as well as the poor felt the fruits of their hofpitality.

The privileges of the convent were extended even to England; for there is ftill extant, although much fpoiled, an original charter of king John, under his feal, exempting them *a thelonio et confuetudine* in all parts of England, London excepted.

The abbey was all inclofed with a ftrong wall, the ground forming an oblong fquare, the length from north to fouth about 190 geometrical paces, and the mean breadth from eaft to weft 113, the breadth on the north end exceeding the fouth upwards of one third. On the S. W. corner is a tower, which is turned into a fteeple for the prefent church; and at the S. E. corner is the Darngate, which, from the name, appears to have been a private entry; over which was a houfe for catechifing, and bore that name. The greateft part of the walls were ftanding within the memory of the prefent generation, but are now in a great meafure demolifhed. On the N. of the fquare, and almoft in the middle betwixt the two corners, ftood the abbey church: a ftately Gothic fabric, having a crofs near the eaft end, and two rows of pillars, one on each fide, with the fide aifles without the pillars, from the entry to the crofs church. The length of the whole is about 275 feet; the breadth of the body and fide aifles 67; the length from the entry to the crofs church 150; the length of the crofs from N. to S. 165; the breadth of this laft 27. There were two fquare fteeples on each fide of the entry, furrounded by round pillars on the corners, one of which ftood entire until the great wind in January

1739.

1739. It is probable a great steeple stood in the middle of the cross: the view of the ruins seems to confirm this.

The floor of the body had been of tile, and the windows of baked glass. Pieces of both are yet dug up amongst the rubbish. The side aisles are paved with stone; yet seen, on digging. There is still so much standing of the edifice, as will shew the exact dimensions both as to the height, and form, and great variety of pilasters, carving, and other ornaments. Close by the church, near to the east end, stands the charter or chapter house. The lower part is a fine vault, entering from the church, and probably served for a vestry; above which there has been a square room, the roof long since taken off, where it may be supposed, from the name, the abbot and convent kept their chapterly meetings. This work is very strong, and closely built. To the west of the great entry of the church is the abbey gate, in form not unlike that at Edinburgh, but less; the walls above mostly standing: and west from that, on the south-west corner, are the walls of the regality prison, which have been very strong, having below two vaults, one above the other. Besides all these, there is now standing, and inhabited, but in bad repair, a part of the abbot's lodgings, with the vestiges of all the other buildings, which composed several square courts, close by.

The Earl of ⸺⸺ is heritable baillie of the regality. His deputes keep the head courts in the gate of the monastery, and their ordinary courts in the new church. He is not in use of exercising any civil jurisdiction, nor of judging of riots within the town; although, in crimes of moment, that are tried by juries, or that subject the criminals to great fines, he doth.

N. B. The above description was wrote by David Mudie, town-clerk town-clerk of Aberbrothock, at the defire of Mr Maitland, the hiftorian, in 1742.

———

The following is a copy of the charter referred to, as granted by king John of England to the abbot :

‘ John, by the grace of God, king of England, lord of Ireland, duke of Aquitane, earl of Anjou ; to the arch-bifhop, bifhops, abbots, earls, and barons, jufticiaries, fhe-riffs, minifters of ftate, baillies, and all faithful in our realm, happinefs.

‘ Wit ye, us, by the infpection and petition of William king of Scotland, and by this our charter, to have confirmed to the abbots, monks, and citizens of Aberbrothock, that they can fell their proper goods, and buy them for their own proper ufes, as they pleafe, through our whole territories, without moleftation from all public burdens, or any other cuftom which pertains to us, except within the liberty of the city of London. Wherefore, our will is, and we ftrictly command, that the forefaid abbots, monks, and citizens, may fell and buy their own proper goods, as they pleafe, through our whole territories aforefaid, freely and without mo-leftation.

‘ Given at Weftminfter the 4th of February, and of our reign the 7th year.’——Anfwers to the year 1204.

PARISH OF AUCHTERHOUSE.

(County of Forfar, Synod of Angus and Mearns, Presbytery of Dundee.)

By the Rev. Mr. James Scott.

Name, Situation, and Extent.

THE parish is supposed to derive its name from the situation of the church, which is placed upon the highest point of a considerable eminence, the ground declining in every direction. *Auchter* is from a Gaelic word that signifies *high*. Auchterhouse is 7 miles N. W. of Dundee. It lies in a gentle declivity to the S. of that range of hills called Sidlaw, which separates Strathmore from the Carse of Gowrie and the low part of Angus. It is of a triangular form, and contains (according to the best information I had access to), about 4160 acres; of which there are 3160 arable.

Soil, Agriculture, &c.—The soil is moorish. Below the heath, there is generally a bed of clay and sand, which,

when

when properly mixed by means of ſummer fallowing, make a good ſoil, called, in this place, light land. Great improvements in agriculture have been made in this pariſh ſince the year 1776, which took their riſe from the diſcovery and application of marl, of which there are 3 large fields and a ſmall one. The laſt mentioned, with 2 of the former, belong to the Earl of Airly; the other to Captain Laird of Strathmartine and Mr. Yeoman of Ballbeuchly. The ſurface of theſe fields conſiſts of 2 feet rich earth; below which are 6 feet of moſs; under the moſs, 4 or 5 feet of clay and ſand: then, the firſt bed of marl; in ſome places, 7 feet deep; in others, not above 3: Beneath this, there lies another ſtratum of clay of 5 feet; and next, the ſecond bed of marl, generally of the ſame depth with the firſt; which has ſeldom, if ever, been wrought, becauſe of the water which abounds, and which it would be extremely difficult and expenſive to draw off. In one of Lord Airly's moſſes, there is a rock of a peculiar ſpecies; hard as flint, and black as coal. Where it is neceſſary to open drains through it, it has always been found impracticable, without the aid of gunpowder, as no tool can make any impreſſion upon it. Yet, obdurate as it is found in its natural ſituation, when expoſed to the winter froſt and rain, it crumbles into pieces, and is good for no purpoſe.—Deers horns, of a great ſize, have often been found, at a conſiderable depth in the moſſes; as alſo oak trees, hazle, and other wood.—The marl is ſold at 9d. the boll; of which the digger has 3½d. Fifty or ſixty bolls are commonly allowed to each acre. And the effect of marl (together with the conſequent improvements), has been ſuch as to raiſe the rent of land from 5s. to 10s., 15s., 20s., and even to 40s. Sterling the acre.

Lord

Lord Airly gave the example of enclofing, draining, and otherwife improving the foil. His enclofures are all of the moft fubftantial kind : The walls are brought to a level at the height of 4 feet ; then covered with large flag ftones, projecting 2 or 3 inches on each fide ; and to bind and keep all faft, there is fet above thefe a capping of ftone, placed on edge, which ftands ftrong like an arch. The enclofures of Ballbeuchly are done after the fame manner : Thofe of Dronlaw and Scotfton are carrying on in a fimilar ftyle : The 2 Adamftons were enclofed many years ago ; but, from the want of good materials, the fences are not fo complete as thofe upon the other eftates in the parifh. Proprietors and tenants are now fo well convinced of the fuperior advantage of enclofed ground to open fields, and fuch is the prefent prevailing fpirit of improvement in all the branches of agriculture, that it is thought, within a few years hence, the whole arable land of the parifh will be enclofed. Thefe walls are built at 24s. the rood : 8s. for quarrying, 8s. for driving, and 8s. for building.

As to cropping, the farmers differ fomewhat in opinion, and vary in practice. Yet all are agreed, that their intereft lies in fowing out annually a large portion of their farm with grafs feeds, chiefly red and white clover, and rye-grafs ; and alfo in having a good deal of peafe, turnips, potatoes, and yams. Oats and barley are our principal crops. Some wheat is fown, but it does not often prove beneficial. Peafe meliorate the ground, and yield excellent fodder. It is for thefe reafons they are fown, and not for any other return they make ; the encreafe, in moft feafons, being rather fcanty. Turnips, potatoes, and yams, fucceed remarkably well. With the former, a great number of cattle are fed every winter for the butcher.

They

They are also given with great advantage to milch-cows and young cattle. Upon Lord Airly's farm, oxen have been reared and fattened to the weight of 80 stone.—Flax-seed is sown too, which generally yields from 3 to 4 or 5 stone the peck; the stone worth 11s. or 12s.—250 stone of hay an acre; 11 or 12 bolls of oats; 10 bolls of barley; 9 or 10 bolls of wheat; and 10 bolls of pease, are considered abundant crops; and not to be expected, if the fields are not in high cultivation, and the season favourable. In general, little more than the half of the above quantities are reaped; yet the produce is always more than what is necessary for the consumption of the inhabitants. The surplus is carried to the Dundee market, which is said to be about 2000 bolls of meal and barley.

The rent of farms is from 20l. to 200l. and upwards; their extent is from 50 to 500 acres. There are about 200 acres planted, including belts and clumps.

There are 40 ploughs in the parish; generally formed after Small's model, and drawn, some by 2, others by 4 horses, according as the soil is tender or rugged, and the fields level or steep. The number of horses may amount to 200; and milch-cows to 150.

The most deficient crop known in this country these 50 years past, was in the year 1792. Compared with it, crop 1782 was a great one. Still, no person suffered through scarcity, either in the one or other. In 1782, as meal was very dear (20s. the boll), and the price of labour not so high as now, the kirk-session purchased a quantity of meal, and sold it at a reduced price, according to the circumstances of the buyer *.

Heritors

* Wheat is sown in October; oats in March, and to the middle of April; barley and flax in May; turnips in June; potatoes and yams are planted in May; harvest, September, and to the middle or end of October.

Heritors and Rent.—Earl of Airly, proprietor of the barony of Auchterhouse; Colonel and Admiral Duncan, of Dronlaw, Templeton, E. and W. Adamstons; Mr. Maxwell of Scotston; Mr. Yeoman of Ballbeuchly; and George Christie of Templeland.—Valued rent 1691. 14s. 5d. Sterling. Real rent about 2000l. Sterling.

Population.—According to Dr. Webster's report, the population in 1755 was 600. The number of inhabitants, all ages included, at present is also 600. Ballbeuchly is in this parish only *quoad sacra;* otherwise, it is said, to be in the parish of Caputh, 20 miles distant. It pays no stipend to either; nor does it bear any part of the expense of building and repairing the church, manse, or offices.

There are here 12 farmers by profession; 40 weavers; 7 wrights; 2 smiths; 2 tailors; 8 dikers; 6 quarriers; 2 shoemakers, 3 merchants, having small retail shops; 3 retailers of ale and spirits; 1 clergyman; 1 schoolmaster. We have neither lawyer, writer, doctor, surgeon, nor apothecary; no butcher, baker, barber, brewer, distiller, nor exciseman.

Character of the People, &c.—The people are all of the Established Church; regular in their attendance upon publick worship; not mere formalists in religion, and yet free from enthusiasm; sober and diligent in their respective professions, contented with their situation, and well affected both to the civil and religious establishments of the country. In spite of the various wicked arts employed by the seditious in a neighbouring town to disseminate French doctrines, and to poison their honest minds, they remain unshaken in their loyalty, and think not they degrade themselves by paying honour to whom honour is due,

7

due, and tribute to whom tribute is due. From their fathers, they learned these principles, and their children are instructed in the same.——If the price of many of the neceffaries of life is greatly encreased, the price of labour is more than doubled fince the year 1774. Then, the wages of a man fervant were about 4l. Sterling; now they are 9l. or 10l., with victuals and lodging. The wages of female fervants and day-labourers have rifen in the fame proportion. The people of this country, in general, are happy, and will remain fo, if they fuffer not themfelves to fall under the influence of ambitious, difappointed, turbulent, and ill-defigning demagogues. The induftrious have ample encouragement, plenty of work, good payment, and full fecurity for their perfons, character, and property. Very few young men go from this parifh either to the army or navy : a fure proof of their not being addicted to idlenefs or vice. As to great crimes, they are not known here. No perfon recollects an inftance of fuicide or murder ; nor of any one who had been tried capitally. And fuch is their peaceable difpofition and integrity, that not many have been involved in law-fuits.

Climate.——The air of the parifh is keen, but not unhealthy. There are 2 men now alive between 80 and 90 years of age, and ftill ftrong and active ; and 16 perfons between 70 and 80.——The difeafes prevalent here are fuch as are common in the country. Not a few fuffer from rheumatifms and fcrofulous diforders : agues are fcarcely known : the fmall pox have frequently made fevere ravages among the children. By that fatal diforder, in 1775, no fewer than 20 were carried off in the fpace of 6 weeks. At that time, the prejudice of the people againft inoculation was inveterate *.

Baptifms,

* They employed one argument to juftify their obftinacy, upon which
they

Baptisms, Marriages, Burials.

Baptisms from 1st January 1782 to 1st January 1792, 172
————— for the same years in the last century, 205
Marriages from 1st October 1783 to 1st October 1792, 44
————— in 9 years last century, viz. from 1762 to 1678, 56
Burials from 1st January 1784 to 1st January 1791, 63

But as indigent persons were not registrated, they may be taken at 70, which make 10 annually.

Poor.—The number of poor upon the roll, who receive a weekly pension, seldom exceeds 5. These (and others, standing in need of occasional assistance), are supplied from the Sunday collections, and from the interest of 300l. Sterling, laid out upon bond, at 4½ per cent. The medium of the weekly collections, in the last century, from 10d. to 1s. Sterling. Of the first 30 years of the present century, about 1s. : of the year 1743, 1s. 6d. : and from March 1791 to March 1792, 50 Sundays, 5s. Sterling.

School.

they rested, viz. " To inflict a disease, is tempting Providence." The writer of this account exerted all his influence to inspire the people with more just and rational sentiments upon so very interesting a subject. He argued with them in private, and recommended inoculation from the pulpit. He told them, that many of the most pious and popular clergymen had adopted the scheme in their own families; and that, from the great success that attended it in every quarter of the globe, there was good reason to conclude, that it was a scheme highly favoured by Providence. But all in vain. Their prejudices remained, and their children continued to die. In 1782, he had a child of his own inoculated; and in the following year, by the advice of an eminent surgeon in Dundee, he performed the operation himself upon his second child ; and, at the same time, upon some other children in the village. They all did well. He continues the practice in his family ; and has prevailed with some to follow his example; that is, to inoculate their children without calling in either physician or surgeon. In short, it is believed, that by and bye the scheme will be generally adopted, and, in consequence thereof, many useful lives saved to the publick.

School.—The branches taught are, the principles of the Englifh and Latin languages ; the principles of the Chriftian religion ; writing, arithmetick, book-keeping, geometry, trigonometry, and menfuration. And in an evening fchool, kept in the winter months, for the accommodation of thofe who cannot attend the day fchool, all the above mentioned branches, except Latin, are taught, and alfo church mufick. The fchool fees are 1s. 6d. the quarter for reading Englifh ; 2s, for reading and writing ; and 2s. 6d. for reading, writing, and arithmetick : and no higher quarter fees have hitherto been charged for any branch taught at the fchool ; only thofe learning the Latin language pay 2s. 6d. the quarter, for 4 quarters in the year, no deduction being made for about 6 weeks of a vacation in the time of harveft. The number of fcholars fince 1788 (the time of the prefent fchoolmafter's fettlement), taking one year with another, have, in the middle of winter and the middle of fummer, exceeded 50. The number at the evening fchool about 18 *.

Stipend,

* All the parochial fchools, within the bounds of the prefbytery, are vifited and ftrictly examined annually by the prefbytery, and a report of the ftate of each fchool entered upon the record. The prefbytery is formed into three committees; the firft meeting of each committee fixed, who have power to fettle the fubfequent meetings. The examination of the feveral fchools is accomplifhed within three or four weeks. This plan, purfued for thefe fix years paft, has been productive of the very beft effects ; having acted as a ftimulus both upon mafters and fcholars, and proved highly gratifying to parents, and the inhabitants in general. In fome parifhes, there are heritors who attend the examination. And there is one gentleman (Mr. Paterfon of Caftle Huntly), who not only gives his countenance upon thefe occafions, but diftributes premiums to the fcholars who moft excel. The fchool of Auchterhoufe has given particular fatisfaction to the committee, which has been repeatedly expreffed, and inferted in the prefbytery record.—For fome years paft, a practice has been eftablifhed here, which, as it is not general, though

attended

Stipend, &c.—The church living, as augmented laſt ſeſſion, conſiſts of 104 bolls of meal and barley, and 36l. Sterling, with a glebe of 6 acres, a garden, manſe and offices.
The Earl of Airly is patron. The church was rebuilt in
1775; is very ſubſtantial and commodious, clean and neat,
with a ſteeple of cut ſtone on the W. end. Connected
with it, on the eaſtward, there is an aile, containing a
large vault, formerly a burying-place of the Buchan family, now belonging to the family of Airly. The old
church was an extenſive grand Gothick ſtructure, dedicated to the Virgin Mary. It bore no date. There is a
large fount ſtone remaining, with ſome images of angels,
or ſaints, in rude ſculpture, and but ill-ſuited to the elegance of the general building. The manſe was built in
1789, at the expenſe of 322l. 10s. Sterling, beſides the
materials of the old manſe and carriages. It is an excellent houſe, 39 feet by 25 within the walls; well finiſhed,
and covered with the beſt Eſdale ſlate. The offices were
built in 1784. A very handſome ſchool-houſe was alſo
built in 1789. And, to the honour of the gentlemen concerned

attended with very deſirable conſequences, deſerves, perhaps, to be mentioned. During the ſummer months, in the interval between forenoon
and afternoon worſhip, a few of the ſcholars are employed every Sunday
in the church, for half an hour at leaſt, in reading publickly a portion
of the Old and the New Teſtament; after which a catechetical exerciſe
follows. Theſe leſſons are duly prepared the preceding day in ſchool.
This practice inſpires a degree of emulation among the ſcholars, and affords the people an opportunity of marking the gradual improvement of
the childrens knowledge, while, at the ſame time, their own may be
advanced. At this ſchool, the manner of teaching the Engliſh language
is the ſame with that obſerved by the beſt Engliſh teachers in Edinburgh; and yet, notwithſtanding the abilities, the aſſiduity, and the
ſucceſs of the ſchoolmaſter, his preſent encouragement (including ſalary
paid by the heritors, ſalary as ſeſſion-clerk and precentor, ſchool-fees, and
perquiſites of office), does not exceed 25l. Sterling.

cerned, let it be mentioned, that, notwithstanding the heavy expense incurred by so many publick buildings within so short a period, the whole was done with the utmost cheerfulness, and without the interposition of the presbytery.

Minerals, Rivulets, &c.—The parish abounds with freestone, water, marl, and moss.—A fine rivulet, issuing from the lake of Lundie, runs along the S. border of the parish, which, at the village of Dronlaw, where it is joined by another stream, assumes the name of Dighty Water; and this it bears, till it empties itself into the frith of Tay, 4 miles E. of Dundee.

Roads and Bridges.—The turnpike road from Dundee to Meigle runs through the parish. Such as live near the turnpike, and have easy access to it, feel its great advantage, and readily acknowledge it; while those who live at a distance, derive but little benefit from it, owing to the wretched state of the bye-roads, which the commuted statute-labour will never render tolerable. There are in the parish 5 bridges, 2 corn mills, 1 lint mill, and 1 fulling-mill.

Antiquities.—Upon the summit of one of the Sidlaw hills, called the Whitesheets, about a mile N. of the church, there are evident traces of an ancient fortification. About 2 acres have been enclosed with deep ditches and stone walls. This fortification stands 1400 feet above the level of the sea. Both history and tradition are silent respecting its original design. Adjoining to the house of Auchterhouse, there stands a part of a very old building, that goes by the name of the Tower: the walls remaining

are

are still 10 feet in height, and about 8 in thickness, cemented in the strongest possible manner. It is said to have been very high ; and that the parish derived its name from hence.

Two of the subterraneous buildings, very common in this part of the country, called by the people *weems,* have been discovered : one, at a small distance from the church, and another not far from the house of Auchterhouse. This last was completely dug up. The space between the walls and covering was full of rich mould ; in which were found ashes of wood, some bones, hand mill-stones, about 14 inches diameter, and a brass ring without any inscription *.

Miscellaneous

* It is presumed, that a particular description of these buildings will be given in the account of the neighbouring parish, Liff, where a very extensive one, within a few yards of Lundie-house, was laid open by Colonel Duncan, the proprietor.

These are all the antiquities of this parish ; to which may be subjoined the following extracts from the old register, literally taken down : " On Sunday, the 25th of May 1645, Andrew Smith confeste that hee had carnal copulation with Jein Mores. Sicklick Jo. Williamsonne confessed, that he had adoe with Elspit Low ; therefore, they are ordained to mak ther repentance the Sabbath following.—On Sunday, the 1st of Junne, there was but anes preaching, because of the enemie lying so neir hand.—On Sunday, the 20th of July, there was no preaching, because of the enemie being so neir the towne.—On the 5th of July 1646, there was intimation made out of the pulpit, of a fast to be keept on the 9th of July. Also the minister told the people out of the pulpit, that the Earl of Seaforth was excommunicat.—Among many reasons assigned, for a fast, the following are two : 3d, Because of the desolate stat and cure of several congregations, which have been starved by dry-breasted ministers this long time bygone, and now are wandering like sheep but sheepherds, and witnesseth no sense of scanc. 4th, Because of the pregnant scandal of witches and charmers within this part of the land, we are to supplicat the Lord therefore, that he would enlighten and enclyne ministers and people, and enflame their hearts with more zeal to God and

Miscellaneous Observations.—The Kirktown of Auchter-house stands 100 feet above the level of the sea; and the prospect hence is very extensive and various. To the W., through an opening of Sidlaw, called the Glack of New-tyle, appear a considerable part of Strathmore, the Stor-mont, the Grampian mountains, and that famous hill Schihallian, at the distance of about 60 miles, rising in beautiful

and love to his truth; that the love of the Lord may constrain us all to walk more conscionably and closlie then before; that he would send forth more of his right hand unto the desolate congregations, &c.—On Sun-day, the 27th of September, the minister read, out of the pulpit, the names of those who were excommunicat bee Mr. Robert Blair in the kirk of Edinburgh, to wit, the Earl of Airly, Sir Alexander Makdonald, the Lord of ——, and some others.—On Sunday, the 7th of Januarie 1649, the minister and twa of the elders went through the church, after sermon, desiring the people to subscribe the covenant.—6th Januare 1650. On that day, the minister desired the session to make search every ane in their own quarter gave they knew of any witches or charmers in the paroch, and delate them to the next session.—On Sunday, the 18th of July 1652, Janet Fife made her publick repentance, before the pulpit, for learning M. Robertson to charm her child; and whereas M. Robertson should have done the like, it pleased the Lord before that time to call upon her by death.—March 21st 1658. The minister re-ported, that the presbytery had given comissione to Mr. William Gray and the minister, to speak my Lord and my Lady Buchane anent yr servant Mrs. Douglas, yt they would cause her attend God's service on the Lord's day, or else dismiss her; they promised.—Nov. — 1665. Mr. William Skeinner, minister and moderator of the presbyterie of Dundee, having preached, intimat to the congregation, Mr. James Campble, his suspension from serving the calling of the ministrie, till the synod assemblie of Dundee, for ane fornication committed betwixt him and dam Marjorie Ramsay, Countess of Buchanne: for the qlk, by the said presbyterie's order, he beganne his repentance on the pillare, and sat both sermons; and is exhorted to repentance.—December 24. Mr. James Campble, for ane fornication forsaid, being thryce in the pillare: upon evident signs of his repentance, was absolvit.—December 21. That day, the Countess of Buchanne, for ane fornication committed with Mr. James Campble her chaplain, beganne her repentance.—February 2. 1662. All kirk-sessions are discharged till farder orders."

beautiful and grand pre-eminence above all the neighbouring hills. Its figure is that of a perfect cone; and its common appellation the Maiden-pap. To the S., S. E. and E. we have the Lommond hills, Largo-law, the city and bay of St. Andrew's, the mouth of the frith of Tay, part of the German Ocean, and Law of Dundee, in full view. In the laſt mentioned quarter, and contiguous to the pariſh, the extenſive encloſures and valuable improvements of Captain Laird of Strathmartine greatly delight the eye. The ſame ardour and perſevering ſpirit, which diſtinguiſhed that gentleman in the whole of his naval purſuits, but eſpecially where dangers and difficulties occurred, has been conſpicuous in his land operations. By an unremitting activity, extraordinary perſonal exertion, and a judicious application of money, his eſtate, which, not many years ago, was purchaſed at 10,000l., has been raiſed to the value of between 30,000l. and 40,000l. Sterling. Such an example as this, cannot be without its due effect in the country. And it is here mentioned, not only becauſe theſe improvements beautify the proſpect, and tend to the general good, but becauſe Captain Laird poſſeſſes one part of this pariſh by an exchange, and another by purchaſe. But as neither of theſe is charged with any portion of the ſtipend, he is not included in the number of heritors.

The village of Dronlaw contains 112 perſons; Kirktown, 109; Newton, 57. Theſe, like all the other villages in the country, are built in the moſt irregular manner, and generally conſiſt of houſes of the meaneſt conſtruction. It is much to be regretted that the lower claſs of people, a numerous, uſeful, and virtuous body, are not more comfortably lodged. After toiling hard through the day, they come home to be involved in ſmoke and naſtineſs.

nefs. This evil will remain, till the proprietors of land refolve to build, at their own expenfe, all the houfes neceffary for the good accommodation of the people upon their eftates. And confidering that, by doing fo, they gain $2\frac{1}{2}$ *per cent.*, they beautify the country, and augment the happinefs of thofe perfons by whofe induftry and labour they enjoy eafe, affluence, and fplendour, it is not a little furprifing, that the gentlemen have been fo long inattentive to their own intereft, and the comfort of their fellow creatures.

From the tenants of one eftate in this parifh, no inconfiderable number of fervices and carriages are exacted; which, while they profit not the landlord, bear hard upon the tenant, and are hoftile to all improvement in agriculture. There is, however, reafon to believe, that a total abolition of this fpecies of flavery (the only thing meriting that odious name remaining in the country), will foon be accomplifhed: Already, much of it has been done away within thefe few years paft. It is true, thofe lands fubjected to the greateft weight of fervices, are comparatively low rented. The condition of cottagers is not the moft comfortable. Happy would it be for this order of men, were they to hold of the landlord, and not of the tenant. Few tenants prove gentle mafters.

PARISH of BARRIE,

(COUNTY OF FORFAR.)

By the Rev. Mr DAVID SIM.

Extent, Situation, Soil, Climate, &c.

THIS parish is computed to extend about 3 miles from
E. to W. and 4 from N. to S. Its figure resembles
the form of a long bow, with its string strained to the utmost pitch. The boldest side of the curve is bounded on
the W. and part of the S. by a quick bending of the banks
of the river Tay, and on the E. S. E. and part of the S.
by a low sandy shore of the German Sea. The flat side of
the curve is bounded by the parish of Panbride on the N.
E. and part of the N. and on part of the N. and N. W.
by the parish of Monikie.—The parish is in the presbytery of Aberbrothock, and the Synod of Angus and Mearns.
A high verdant bank, which seems once to have formed a
steep shore of the ocean, runs through the whole, from E.
to W. giving to the northern division the appearance of a
great regular terrace, elevated about 50 feet above the
southern part.—The soil is various. The lower division is
composed

compofed of a thirſty down, which barely ſuffices for the grazing of a few flocks of ſheep and of young cattle, interſperſed with ſome acres of arable land, which, in ſhowery ſeaſons, yield a moderate crop of grain. The upper diviſion is partly light loam, partly generous gravel, and a few fields approach to a deep black ſoil. The mould, though in no reſpeſt rich, favoured by incloſure in many parts, and aided in general by an enlightened huſbandry, produces crops of wheat, barley, oats, peas, turnip, flax, clover, potatoes, little inferior in quantity and quality to the growth of the ſame extent of land in diſtriſts diſtinguiſhed by a valuable ſoil.——Within the bounds of this ſmall pariſh, a diverſity of climate is experienced. The lower diviſion, from its ſandy nature, and the interpoſing banks which hide it from the ocean, though ſometimes covered with hazy fogs, is warm in ſummer, and enjoys a kindly temperature in the winter months. The upper diviſion, elevated above the level of the ſea, is ſenſibly cooler in the warmeſt weather, and in winter feels the almoſt unbroken ſeverity of the winds from the E. and the N. W. The climate is not uncommonly hoſtile to the conſtitution. The inhabitants paid an annual tribute to the ague, while the land continued undrained, and in rainy winters ſome complaints of rheumatiſm are ſtill heard of; but there are no diſtempers ſtriſtly local. It will readily be perceived, that a climate, circumſtanced as that of Barrie, muſt be friendly to vegetable productions. An early verdure covers the fields. The ſowing ſeaſon commences about the middle of March, and the corns are generally lodged in the barnyard before the ſecond week of Oſtober. Migratory birds viſit this place very early in the ſeaſon. The pariſh might perhaps claim the appellation of beautiful, did not the ſoil in ſome parts, and the vicinity to the ſea in others, deprive it of the verdure of thriving and copious wood.

Prices

Prices and Wages.—The parish is nearly supplied with provisions of its own produce. A few stones of butcher-meat are purchased from the Dundee market, by a family or two, during the summer; but oats, furnishing the meal, that is the principal article of food, are raised in sufficient quantities. A quantity of wheat and oat-meal is annually sold at Dundee, and several hundred bolls of barley are exported, to supply the exigencies of some of the northern and western counties of Scotland. A number of black cattle, reared and grazed within the parish, are yearly carried to England; and some oxen, stall-fed with turnip, are purchased by the butchers of the neighbouring towns. Wheat is generally sold at L. 1, 1 s. barley at 14 s. oat-meal at 14 s. the boll; beef, mutton, veal, pork, at 3¼ d. the pound, of 16 oz.; ducks at 10 d. a-piece; hens at 1 s.; butter at 8 d. the pound, of 22 oz.; cheese at 4 s. 6 d. the stone; eggs at 3 d. the dozen.—The hire of labourers is 1 s. a-day, from the 1st of March to the 1st of November, and 10 d. during the rest of the year, excepting the time of hay-mowing and harvest, when they are paid at the rate of 1 s. 6 d. a-day. The wages of a carpenter are 1 s. 3 d. of a mason 1 s. 8 d. of a tailor 1 s. In the above statement, the victuals of the labourers and tradesmen are included. The average hire of farm-servants, when they eat in the house, is L. 8 a-year for men, and L. 3 for women. Domestic servants form no distinct class. There is not a male or female servant in the parish, who is not employed sometime during the year in the work of the field.

Manufactures.—Every householder almost is a manufacturer of brown linen. In the foreign markets, the linen stamped at Aberbrothock has acquired a high reputation; and it will not be denied, that to the cloth made at Barrie, which has long been distinguished for the goodness of its materials,

materials, and the superiority of its workmanship, the stamp of Aberbrothock is indebted for part of its fame. By introducing honour as a prompter to excellence, the manufacture of Barrie has reached its present perfection. For more than 40 years, the inspection of the weaving, by the unanimous consent of the manufacturers, has been assigned to an annual officer, who is allowed to choose two assistant counsellors. The officer, with his assessors, are eagle-eyed to discover every blemish. A pecuniary fine, or what is more dreaded, the correction of ridicule, overtakes every one who is in fault. These circumstances have contributed to fix such habits of attention and accuracy, that instances occur of workmen whose cloth has not been cast at the stamp-office in a period of 20 years. Exclusive of considerable quantities of home-grown flax, the manufacturers use yearly of foreign flax, from Riga and Petersburg, several tons, amounting in value to more than L. 800. The manufacturers are in number 100. The condition of this useful class of men might be ameliorated, by insuring to them at all times abundance of flax at a reasonable rate, by continuing the encouragement on the linen branch, and by rescuing the manufactures from a twofold combination of the brown linen merchants, by which they enhance at pleasure the price of the foreign flax they sell, and depress the price of the cloth they buy.

Population.—At the time of Dr Webster's report, the numbers were 689. At present (1791) the population is 796.

Baptisms,

Baptisms, Marriages and Burials for the last 10 *Years.*

Years.	Baptisms.	Marriages.	Burials.
1781	21	4	11
1782	20	5	13
1783	22	5	13
1784	19	1	7
1785	21	3	12
1786	23	7	4
1787	24	5	8
1788	18	7	7
1789	23	7	10
1790	21	3	7
	212	47	92

Excepting 4 or 5 Antiburgher Seceders, and 3 Episcopalians, the people in the parish are all members of the Established Church. There are 3 students of divinity. There are 8 heritors, 3 only of whom reside.—It may not be entirely foreign to the present article, to notice, that by the late minister of Barrie, who lived in the parish not less than 50 years, it was frequently remarked, that dying persons expired during the ebbing of the tide. With this remark accords that observation in Pliny's Natural History, (Lib. ii. cap. 98.), quoted from Aristotle, who affirms, that ' no animal expires, unless during the going back of the ' tide.' To which Pliny adds, ' Observatum id multum ' in Gallico Oceano, et duntaxat in homine compertum.'

Stipend, School and Poor.—The living, including the glebe, is something more than L. 80 Sterling a-year. The King is patron. The manse, though repaired only 10 years ago, is hardly a tolerable house. The kirk is an old and sorry building.—The office of schoolmaster has, for many years past,

paſt, been diſcharged by young men of liberal education, who have ſucceſſively come forward to preach. to lecture in colleges, and to fill very reputable departments in ſocie-ty. The annual emoluments are inconſiderable. L. 5, 11 s. Sterling of ſalary, L. 2 as ſeſſion-clerk's fees, 5 s. for each proclamation of banns, 10 d. for regiſtering each baptiſm, 3 d. for the regiſtration of each burial, and 1 s. 6 d. a quar-ter, as the average fees for 40 ſcholars throughout the year, with ſome trifling gratuities, make up the total ſum of the annual income.—The ſum of L. 30 Sterling, ariſing partly from Sabbath day collections, partly from the rent of ſome ſeats in the church, is the only fund allotted for pious pur-poſes within the pariſh, and the annual ſupport of the poor. A ſmall portion of the money is yearly applied by the kirk-ſeſſion, to furniſh with neceſſary books a few of the children of indigent parents, who are unable to give them a ſchool education without this aid. The reverſion is di-ſtributed among the poor. The number on the roll is ge-nerally 11. The poor receive the public charity in their own cottages. A begging native has not been known in the pariſh for many years. Beggars from other places a-bound.

Sheep.—The late inſtitution of the Britiſh Wool Society, gives increaſed importance to the flocks of every diſtrict. The paſtures of Barrie may contain 1000 ſheep. In a country where ſheep are not the ſole object of the farmer's care, an unexceptionable breed can hardly be expected. The ſheep of Barrie have no diſtinct character. A few an-nual recruits imported partly from Fife, partly from the northern counties, lately formed the mixed race. It was ſuppoſed, that the union of the Fife ewe with the northern ram, would have produced a ſpecies hardy, and at the ſame time fine wool. Diſappointment, as to the latter quality in particular,

particular, has been the reſult of ſome experiments. An introduction of the Engliſh breed ſeemed to promiſe a ſpecies, valuable for wool, and of a large ſize. However, a paſture which affords but harſh graſs and ſcanty ſhelter, was found ill ſuited to ſuch ſheep. The ſmall Fife ſheep, weighing 32 pounds, unites in ſome meaſure the advantages of a profitable fleece and a pretty durable conſtitution, and at preſent appears beſt adapted to the ſoil. It were defirable, if a breed affording a greater weight of wool could be obtained. Not leſs than 12 fleeces, at an average, produce 1 ſtone of wool. Of the wool, which is generally ſold at 1 s. the pound, is manufactured almoſt every kind of cloth worn in the pariſh ; hodden, which is moſtly uſed for herds cloaks, and is ſold at 1 s. 8 d. the yard ; plaiding, which is ſometimes ſhaped into a coarſe kind of hoſe, and is ſold at 2 s. the yard ; ſey, the common cloth for mens apparel, ſold, when dyed, at 5 s. the yard ; timming, camblet for womens gowns, when in colours, are reſpectively ſold at 3 s. and 2 s. 1c d. the yard ; blankets ſold at 12 s. the pair, confiſting of 4 yards ; Sabbath day plaids for women, when dyed of 2 or 3 various colours, and containing about 4 yards, at 16 s. a-piece.——The ſcab, from accident, and the rot, from the nature of ſome of the ſheep-walks, are among the number of the diſeaſes to which the ſheep are liable. The preſcription of Dr Anderſon (tobacco oil) has been applied with ſome ſucceſs in the former diſeaſe. Another malady, againſt which no remedy has yet been deviſed, preys on the ſheep here. Among the ſhepherds, it is called the *Bracks*. The autumn is the ſeaſon of its attack. The moſt luſty, and apparently vigorous of the flock, are ſingled out as its victims. It kills in 2 hours from the time it is at firſt obſerved. From the deſcription which the writer has received, exceſs of blood appears to be the probable cauſe of the diſorder. The dead carcaſe is remarkably

markably bloated and difcoloured, and in a very fhort time becomes a carrion. The experience of an aged man, who for many years was a fheep-mafter in the parifh, affords fome prefumption, that a preventative may be found to the bracks. He let blood of his fheep uniformly in the fummer feafon, and he does not recolleƈ that the bracks at any time thinned his folds.

Remarkable Objeƈts and Antiquities.—In the fouthern extremity of the parifh, on the banks of the Tay, ftand 2 refleƈting light-houfes, reared to direƈt the veffels trading to Dundee and Perth through the perilous entrance of the Tay. The largeft, which is ftationary, is a circular ftone building ereƈted on piles; the other a moveable wooden fabric, raifed on rollers. When the two lights are feen in one, the pilot may navigate the river without fear. The expence of the lights is defrayed by a fmall tax on the tonnage of the veffels which enter the Tay.—The Danes feem to have been deftined, by their misfortunes, to furnifh the only memorable objeƈts of antiquity which Barrie affords. On the eaftern boundary of the parifh many tumuli appear. The traces of a camp in their immediate neighbourhood, Carnouftie, *i. e.* the Cairn of Heroes, the name of an adjoining eftate, the vicinity of a brook, which is faid to have run three days with blood, proclaim thefe tumuli the graves of thofe northern Marauders who fell in the defperate engagement, which, according to Buchanan, (B. 6. chap. 50.), took place near Panbride, between the Danifh troops commanded by Camus, and the Scotch army under King Malcolm II.

Roads and Bridges.—The roads have at no time been much indebted to the improvement of art. The poft-road between Dundee and Aberbrothock, which for a long period

riod ran through its bounds, was merely a line traced by
frequent paſſengers on the ſurface of the ſoil. A new poſt-
road, formed 20 years ſince to the northward of Barrie pariſh, has annually engroſſed nearly the ſtatute-labour of the
contiguous diſtrict. The ſmall reverſion allotted to Barrie,
has been faithfully and judiciouſly applied by a reſident Juſtice of the Peace ; but in a light ſandy track, where gravel cannot be obtained without great expence, it may well
be conceived, that the repairs effected by a trifling ſum,
can neither be permanent nor extenſive. Nature, however, has not been unkind ; the roads of Barrie, though
ſomewhat fatiguing, are at all ſeaſons dry. Voluntary contributions reared, and have hitherto ſupported, the bridges
within the pariſh. A detailed account of the bridges
would reflect no honour on the police of the diſtrict.

Advantages and Diſadvantages.—Vicinity to the ſea is
an obvious advantage to this pariſh. Though it has no
formed harbours, the ſurrounding beach affords a ſafe landing place to ſmall veſſels ; by which lime, the ſtaple manure, and coals, the chief article of fuel, are imported
from the frith of Forth, and ſold at a reaſonable rate.
Lime ſhells are delivered from the ſhip at 1 s. 6 d. the
boll. Coals, conveyed to the moſt diſtant parts of the
pariſh, are bought by the cottager at 6 s. 8 d. weighing
72 ſtones.—But amid the advantages which Providence
has already beſtowed, and human improvements promiſe
to confer, the pariſhioners of Barrie experience a rigorous
aſtriction to a barony mill ; a ſpecies of vaſſalage, which
they deem an inconvenience of no trivial kind. Legal applications for redreſs have hitherto produced a very partial relief ; while, from the unavoidable ambiguity of
old papers, the reciprocal ſervices of the millmaſter, and
the aſtricted farmer, furniſh a ſource of hourly diſcord ;
while

while dues are exacted by an unstamped measure, which is no part of the standard of the nation ; while a power is lodged with the renter of a hopper, to demand, by a solemn oath, an account of every pea, every barley-corn, every grain of oats, which is daily distributed to every labouring stead, perhaps dropped to every hen. Thus circumstanced, it will not appear strange, if the people of Barrie look forward to the abolition of thirlage, as a change much to be wished. They are sufficiently sensible, that an adequate compensation is due to the representatives of those men, who originally reared those accommodations, which have proved so eminently useful to the community. Keeping this in view, they find themselves strongly inclined to join in any legal, well-concerted plan, by which they may be relieved from a species of servitude, which has often produced the most bitter effects ; and has brought along with it, consequences not only hostile to improvements, but even to the best interests of morality and religion. The multiplicity of oaths introduced into processes relating to thirlage, tend in some degree to take off that respect to things sacred, which every true statesman would desire to preserve unviolated.

Miscellaneous Observations.—In general, the people are attached to the trades of their fathers. Farming and weaving are the professions which stand highest in their esteem. To other employments, hardly so many are inclined as supply the ordinary demands of the parish. The fine appearance of summer fleets on the smooth surface of the Tay, allures a few boys to a sea faring life. Dissipation is unknown ; though the short space of a quarter of a mile presents to the view of the traveller the whole inns and alehouses in the parish, amounting to no less than 4. This assemblage, principally designed for the accommodation of strangers

ſtrangers journeying between Dundee and Arbroath, muſt
not be interprèted to the diſadvantage of the pariſhioners,
who are induſtrious in a high degree, and in their money
engagements are punctual to a proverb. Vulgar report
has ſometimes involved, along with the inhabitants of the
ſurrounding country, the people of Barrie in a charge of
inhumanity to ſhipwrecked mariners; but more truly may
they be characteriſed as dupes, by their compaſſion to 100
pretendedly ſhipwrecked.—The oppreſſion muſt be grievous indeed, which can drive them from their native ſoil.
A ſort of *maladie de pais* rivets them to the place of their
birth.—Though the houſes, dreſs, ſtyle of living, &c. of the
pariſhioners, indicate nothing diſproportionate to their real
wealth, a conſiderable alteration in theſe different articles
has taken place within a period of 20 years. Inſtead of
the turf-built cottages of former days, the eyes of the ob-
ſerver are ſometimes pleaſed with manſions, neat, commodious, almoſt elegant. Leeds, Mancheſter, Spittalfields,
unite to furniſh the apparel of thoſe who were formerly
contented with clothing wholly manufactured on the north
ſide of the Tweed. The perſons, however, of this deſcription are not numerous. The bulk of the people are eaſily
diſtinguiſhed from thoſe of the ſurrounding pariſhes, by a
rejection of the fopperies of dreſs, and a becoming attachment to articles made in their own families. The improvement in the ſtyle of living may be characteriſed, not by a
rapid tranſition from ſordidneſs to luxury, but rather by a
gradual remove from meanneſs to a comfortable mode of
life. A ſtrict attention to œconomy, joined with a pride
of inheriting unimpaired their paternal acres, prevents, a-
mong the heritors of Barrie, that fluctuation of property
which has lately marked many parts of Scotland. Some
lands, however, have within theſe few years changed their
maſters. The price about 25 years purchaſe.—The ſize of
the

the farms can be reduced to no average meafure. The upper divifion of the parifh, which may be properly ftyled the arable part, is parcelled out among 10 or 11 landholders, 3 of whom are proprietors. Their farms contain refpectively from 30 to 300 acres a-piece. A happy adjuftment of things has prevented a monopoly of farms, many of the leafes prefently current having been granted before the all-engroffing fyftem began to extend its baneful influence. It cannot be denied, however, that when any tack happens to fall, this fyftem difcovers itfelf in miniature, by a marked avidity to join to the former poffeffion of a houfe and yard, the ground plot of a razed houfe, and the extent of its attached yard. Along with the mode of labouring with horfes, inftead of oxen, the number of cottagers in the fervice of the farmers has been diminifhed. There is no planned defign to deprefs cottagers; but fervants entertained in the houfe, are found more conveniently placed for every exigence, are perhaps lefs expenfive, not lefs active, not lefs difinterefted, than thofe who have families of their own. Befides 12 day-labourers, who have merely houfes and yards, the only clafs of men who fall under the defcription of cottagers, are thofe employed by the farmers for threfhing the corns. They receive as wages, the twenty-fifth boll of each kind of grain they feparate from the ftraw, with a dinner each working day. The plough of Small's conftruction, drawn generally by 4 horfes, and attended by a ftout lad and a boy, appears well a-dapted to every variety of foil in the parifh. In a fmall parifh, of which not a third part is arable land, the number of ploughs and carts is very inconfiderable. One waggon was made at Barrie in the year 1791. No waggon-road can reafonably be expected in the parifh fooner than the year 1793.

It was omitted to be mentioned that the valued rent of this parish in 1791, was L. 2255 : 8 : 4 Scotch ; and the real rent L. 900 sterling.

PARISH of BRECHIN,

(COUNTY OF FORFAR.)

*Drawn up from Materials communicated by the Rev.
Mr* ANDREW BRUCE,
One of the Ministers of that Parish.

Origin of the Name.

THE ancient and modern name of this parish is Brechin.   Some imagine it to be derived from the
Gaelic word *braechin*, which signifies fern ; but this
seems not very probable, as that plant is by no means a-
bundant in the parish.   Others, with more probability,
trace its origin from the Scotch word *brae*, which signifies,
the declivity of a hill, and is indeed very descriptive of
the local situation of the town of Brechin, whence the
name of the parish is derived.

Situation, Extent, Surface, Climate and Diseases.—This
parish is situated in the presbytery of Brechin, and
belongs

belongs to the Synod of Angus and Mearns. The town
is the ordinary ſeat of the preſbytery, and lies about 7¼
Engliſh miles N. W. from Montroſe. The pariſh extends
about 5 Scotch, or 7¼ Engliſh miles, from E. to W. in
length, and towards the weſt ſide, is nearly as broad from
N. to S. It riſes gradually on the north ſide of the river
South Eſk, and to a much greater height on the ſouth
ſide. To the weſt of the bridge on the ſouth ſide, there
is a large plantation of pines, birch and hard wood, which
decorates the north brow of the hill, fronting the town of
Brechin, and is a great ornament to the country in general. There is another in the moor of Dubtown, about an
Engliſh mile weſt from Brechin, but it lies low.—The climate is dry, and in general healthy, except in warm and
calm weather, when fogs ariſe from the river. The moſt
prevailing diſeaſes are fevers, conſumptions, and the king's
evil.

Soil, River, Fiſh and Minerals.—The greater part of the
ſoil is rich and fertile, eſpecially on the north ſide of the
river, and contiguous to it on the weſt. The river South
Eſk runs through the middle of the pariſh, all the way
from the bridge. It produces excellent trouts, and in the
ſpring, when the river is ſwelled, ſome ſalmon. The high
grounds on both ſides of the river, are rocky, but not extenſive, except where there is wood, and where the high
roads run.—There is a deal of freeſtone on both ſides of
the South Eſk, eſpecially on the ſouth ſide, to the eaſtward
of the bridge.

Animals.—There are no uncommon animals in the pariſh. There are a conſiderable number of horſes and black
cattle, but few ſheep, the ground being moſtly laid out in
grain. Cuckoos, lapwings, ſwallows, and other birds
of paſſage, viſit the pariſh in their ſeaſons.

Population.

Population.—The population of the town of Brechin is fuppofed to be doubled within thefe 100 years ; and, in confequence of the eftablifhment of feveral manufactures, within the laft 25 years, it has increafed a full third.

The return to Dr Webfter in 1755, of the number in the whole parifh, was,   -   -   -   -   3181
The number of fouls at prefent (1790-1) cannot be eftimated
under   -   -   -   -   5000
                                              ————
                       Increafe,   1819

Of thefe, there are, in the weft fide of the town, (the junior minifter's charge), examinable perfons, above 7 years of age, attending
the Eftablifhed Church,   -   -   1030
Examinable perfons contiguous to the town, but not within the
                         royalty,   -   14
———————————— in the country, about   -   -   697
Epifcopals in the town,   -   -   -   118
——— in the country,   -   -   -   12
Seceders in the town,   -   -   -   61
——— in the country,   -   -   -   6
                                              ————
                                              1956

There may be nearly about as many in the fenior mi-
nifter's (Mr BISSET's) charge : So that eftimating the number of children under 7 years of age, at the ufual proportion, there cannot be fewer than 5000 fouls in the pa-
rifh.

The following extract from the parifh regifter, for 6 years preceding 1790, will give fome idea of the proportion of the marriages, births and deaths in the parifh.

Years.

Years.	Baptiſms.	Burials.	Marriages.		
			Both parties pariſhioners.	One only.	Total.
1784	95	114	26	16	42
1785	115	89	23	13	36
1786	97	121	22	25	47
1787	105	88	32	17	49
1788	129	110	24	14	38
1789	121	104	39	12	51
	662	626	166	97	263
	626				

Majority, * 36, *of Baptiſms more than Burials.*

There are 3 ſurgeons, 1 of whom is alſo a phyſician, and 3 writers in the town of Brechin, beſides a number of merchants, ſhopkeepers, weavers, bakers, ſmiths, wrights, and the other neceſſary tradeſmen and mechanics.

Church, Burgh, Fuel, &c.—The church is collegiate. The King is patron. There are 5 clergymen, 3 of them Diſſenters. The livings are widely different in value. In the time of Epiſcopacy, the Biſhop filled the firſt charge.—Brechin is a royal burgh, and one of five that ſends a repreſentative to Parliament. The election is veſted in the town-council. It has a weekly market every Tueſday.—The fuel uſed is coals, wood and furze. Peats are alſo brought down from the Mearns. The coals coſt 8 s. *per* boll at Montroſe, ſometimes more, beſides the additional charges of carriage, &c. The duty on this neceſſary article, after paſſing the Redhead, has been long and juſtly complained of, as an unequal and partial tax, which

* This majority would be conſiderably greater, if all the births in the pariſh were regiſtered ; but the children of Diſſenters are not entered in the records, and even of thoſe who attend the Eſtabliſhed Church, ſome neglect to regiſter their children's names.

which is feverely felt by the poor; but although a redrefs of this grievance has been often talked of, nothing has as yet been done in the bufinefs.

Bridge, Antiquities, &c.—The bridge of Brechin is fuppofed to be one of the moft ancient ftone bridges in Scotland, but there is no tradition when, or by whom, it was built.—The monument in the church-yard is one of the moft remarkable pieces of antiquity, perhaps in Britain. It is a circular pillar, hollow within, clofe by the fteeple of the church, and confiderably higher; and, as tradition fays, was built by the Picts. It is undoubtedly a piece of very ancient architecture. The ftair-cafe within it is much decayed, and is now hardly paffable, though, within thefe few years, one could have afcended to the top of it without danger. The pillar is feen at a confiderable diftance from the E. and it is faid to bend like a willow in high winds, fo as almoft to touch the fteeple.

Commerce and Manufactures.—A confiderable quantity of oats and bear is exported by Meffrs Gillies and Company, and meal is fometimes imported. Moft of the merchants deal in the linen and yarn trade, of which great quantities are bought and fold every market day. This trade gives employment to moft of the women, in this and the adjoining parifhes, who all fpin on the two-handed wheel, and are well paid for their labour. There was alfo a cotton manufacture, which was lately given up, but is expected to be refumed foon; and there is a bleachfield, which gives employment to a number of people of both fexes; befides ftrong ale and porter breweries, which furnifh the town and neighbourhood with excellent liquor. The fpirited exertions of Mr Colin Gillies have been of great benefit to the population and commerce of Brechin.

Character.

Character.—The people, in general, are active and industrious, honest in their dealings, and by no means superstitious ; but cannot be said to be altogether free from those vices, which generally accompany an influx of wealth from trade and manufactures. They are also occasionally infected with a spirit of litigation, and spend considerable sums at the law, often about mere trifles.— In public spirit, they are inferior to none. They are, in general, of the ordinary stature, from 5 feet, to 5 feet 9 or 10 inches ; some near 6 feet, and there is one man several inches above it.

Miscellaneous Observations.—The low grounds on both sides of the river are occasionally overflowed by great inundations. The last memorable flood happened in the year 1774, when the whole bleachfield to the S. E. of the castle * was overflowed, and the people possessing the tenements, which lie along the E. side of the river, were obliged to go up to the highest apartments of their houses, the under stories being quite overflowed. There is an echo at the castle, and another at the cathedral.—There are neither Jews, Negroes, nor Roman Catholics in the parish, but some of those sturdy beggars, called gypsies, occasionally visit it. No person has been known to die for want. Indeed, there is work enough for all who are able and willing to work, and those who are not able, are provided for.—There have, therefore, been few or no instances of emigration ; only a few left the parish, upon the failing of the cotton manufactory.—None have been banished for a considerable time past. There are very few uninhabited

* The old mansion house on the side of the river, belonging to Lord Panmure, who resides in it, is commonly called the *Castle* of Brechin. It is pleasantly situated in the midst of a fine plantation of trees.

uninhabited houſes.—The language uſually ſpoken is the common Scotch dialeᵈ, but moſt of the names of places are derived from the Gaelic.—An event often related by tradition, but now almoſt forgot, which occurred in the reign of the unfortunate Queen Mary, deſerves to be recorded. On the 5th of July 1572, Sir Adam Gordon of Auchindown, who was of the Queen's party, and was beſieging the caſtle of Glenbervie, hearing that a party of the King's friends were in Brechin, came upon them by ſurpriſe in the morning, and cut off the whole party.—Another battle was fought in this neighbourhood, between the Earls of Crawford and Huntly, on the 18th May 1452, when the former was defeated, and the latter did King James II. very eſſential ſervice. This battle is called *The Battle of Brechin,* though the ſpot, on which it was fought, is not in the pariſh, but a little to the N. E. of it, on the road leading to the North Water Bridge.

Parish of Brechin.

By the Rev. John Bisset, minister of the first Charge.

Name and Etymology.——The city of Brechin is situated on the side of a small hill. After you enter the city from the north, you gradually descend all the way to the water of Southesk, which terminates the city and suburbs on the south. Thence Brechin probably receives its denomination; *Bruaichaun* signifying, in Gaelic, ' the top of a declivity.'

From the east of Brechin, you have a delightful prospect of the bay of Montrose, and of the rich and fertile country which lies betwixt Montrose and Brechin, containing a space of about eight English miles. I am not certain but from this circumstance Brechin may have derived its name; *Breaichuain* signifying, in Gaelic, ' a view of the frith.' As etymologies are uncertain, it is of no moment to investigate, in the present case, which of these ought to have the preference, because both of them perfectly agree with the situation of the place.

Royalty, Streets, Buildings, &c.——Brechin is a royal borough, which, with Aberdeen, Bervie, Montrose and Arbroath, sends a member to Parliament. The royalty or liberties

berties of the borough, northward, begin at a ſmall hill or eminence a ſhort way from the entrance of the city, called the Gallowhill. It ſeems Brechin had been in former times the county town, or at leaſt the ſheriff had frequently held his courts here. As malefactors, convicted of crimes which fell under the cognizance of the ſheriff, had been executed on this hill or eminence, it retains to this day the name of the Gallowhill.

There is a ſmall rivulet or burn which riſes to the weſt of Brechin, and runs directly eaſtward. Several houſes and lands on the north ſide of this rivulet are within the royalty. This burn ſoon alters its direction, and runs ſouthward through a large den, which is the property of the borough, and a common paſturage to the cows and cattle of the citizens in the ſummer ſeaſon. It is commonly called the Den-burn. This ſmall burn terminates the royalty on the eaſt. No part of the royalty is ſituated on the eaſt ſide of this burn, except a very few houſes on what is called the Cadger-brae. The eaſtern extremity of the borough, known by the name of the Cadger-wynd, lies wholly on the weſt ſide of the burn. This wynd had formerly been inhabited by fiſhmongers, whoſe buſineſs it was to furniſh the citizens of Brechin with a conſtant ſupply of fiſh from different parts of the coaſt. Hence probably it received its denomination.

The Den-burn, paſſing by the eaſt end of the Cadger-wynd, runs a conſiderable way ſouthward, till it falls into the Southeſk, at what is called the Ford-mouth. The houſes on the weſt ſide, all the way to the Ford-mouth, are within the royalty. Thoſe on the other ſide belong to Southeſk.

The whole length of the borough from north to ſouth, that is, from the Gallowhill to the Ford-mouth, is nearly an Engliſh mile.

The royalty of Brechin, to the weſt, extends half an Engliſh

lish mile from the Cross. It consists of upwards of 70 acres of burgage land, besides many acres which have lately been converted into garden ground. The extent eastward, to the end of the Cadger-wynd, is far from being so large, consisting only of 20 acres.

The city is bounded, on the north, by the lands of Cookstown; on the east, partly by the lands of Caldhame, and partly by the lands of Southesk; on the south, by the river Southesk, and the lands of Brechin Castle; and on the west, partly by the lands of Brechin Castle, and partly by the lands of Southesk.

The suburbs or entry to Brechin, from the east and south, consist of a row of houses independent of the borough, and built on ground held in feu from Sir David Carnegie of Southesk. They are called the tenements of Brechin; those on the east, the upper, and those on the south, the nether tenements.

At the end of the nether tenements, there is a convenient stone bridge over the river Southesk, of two large arches. The fords here are quite impassable in stormy weather; and the inhabitants here and in the neighbourhood, as well as all travellers, would be much incommoded, were it not for this bridge. It was repaired some years ago to great advantage. It is very remarkable that there is no record by whom, at whose expence, and at what time this useful and convenient bridge was erected; and there are no funds appropriated for its support: so that it must be repaired, when occasion requires, from the common money of the county.

The river Southesk takes its rise in the parish of Clova. Some miles from its source, it unites its stream with two rivers and a small rivulet. After this, it enters the parish of Brechin, and runs under the bridge at the end of the nether tenements, dividing the parish of Brechin into north and south.

fouth. From under the bridge, it continues its courfe directly eaftward till it falls into the fea at Montrofe. Efk, in Gaelic, fignifies an eel; whence it is probable that this and other rivers of the fame name in Scotland took their denomination, plainly alluding to their many turnings and windings.

Brechin is at no great diftance from the harbour of Montrofe, and the tide flows within two miles of our city. A canal would tend to increafe our trade. It would be of fervice in conveying down the corn of the country for exportation; and it would be particularly ufeful to the citizens here for carrying their coals from Montrofe to Brechin, the expence of carriage being very heavy on the poorer fort, who have no carts and horfes of their own. Something of this kind, I underftand, is at prefent in contemplation.

Brechin in former times had ports or gates at the different entries to the city. The places where they ftood are well known. Some veftiges of them are extant; and the names of north, fouth and weft port ftill remain.

Brechin, the city properly fo called, confifts of one large handfome ftreet, extending from the north to the fouth port, and two others which are called wynds, the upper and nether weft wynd.

Brechin was twice burnt. Firft by the Danes, about the year 1012, in the reign of Malcolm II. who had obtained a compleat victory over the Danes at Mortlich in Banffshire. This fo irritated Sweno, the Danifh king, that he ordered two fleets, one from England, and another from Norway, to make a defcent upon Scotland, under the command of Camus, one of his moft renowned generals. The Danes attempted to land at the mouth of the Forth; but finding every place there well fortified, they were obliged to move farther northward, and effected their purpofe at the Red-head in the county of

Angus,

Angus. They first attacked the castle of Brechin, and as they could make no impreſſion upon it, they wrecked their vengeance by laying the city and church of Brechin in aſhes.

In the month of March 1645, the Marquis of Montroſe, once a zealous covenanter, and afterwards as zealous a royaliſt, came to Fettercairn in his return from the north, where he had, in contradiction to his late ſolemn engagements, been promoting the intereſts of the king. He was on his way to Brechin: and as a ſavage and brutal cruelty had always marked the procedure of that unhappy nobleman, both when a covenanter and a royaliſt, the citizens of Brechin, alarmed at his approach, left their houſes and habitations, and depoſited their effects in the caſtle and church. This ſo enraged the Marquis, that he allowed his ſoldiers to plunder the town, and in the height of their fury they burnt ſixty houſes to the ground. Some of theſe houſes were to the north, but the moſt of them to the weſt. It ſeems, before this period, the houſes and buildings here had extended moſtly to the weſt.

There are at preſent very good houſes both on the eaſt and weſt ſide of the town.

In the year 1781, a very commodious Maſon-Lodge was built by the ſociety of Free-Maſons in Brechin, at their own expence. Here the maſter and different members of that reſpectable fraternity hold their meetings, as occaſions require.

In the year 1789, a very elegant town-houſe was built, with a ſecure and ſtrong priſon adjoining, at the expence of the town, aſſiſted by liberal contributions from ſeveral gentlemen both in town and country.

A very commodious gardener's lodge was built in the year 1791; and ſome years ago ſeveral gentlemen have built, at the end of the weſt wynd, very elegant and commodious houſes for the accommodation of themſelves and families: ſo that the city of Brechin makes a finer and more magnificent appearance

appearance to a ſtranger entering it from the weſt, than it did, or could do, many years before.

The ſtreets, which had been remarkably rugged, were new laid and paved in the year 1781.

Brechin is remarkably well watered; a very happy circumſtance. The waters from the wells or fountains in the lone of Cookſtown, diſtant about half an Engliſh mile from the middle of the town, were, in the year 1767, conveyed into the town by means of leaden pipes. There are ſix wells in the town, and one at Brechin Caſtle; to all which the water is conveyed in the manner already mentioned. The expence of this conveyance amounted nearly to L. 600 ſterling, which was generouſly complimented to the town by the late Earl of Panmure.

The revenue of Brechin ariſes from ſtreet and muir cuſtoms, fleſh-market, feus from muirs and property within the borough, graſs of the common den, bleachfield and common mills, and entry of burgeſſes; and will amount, one year with another, to L. 200 ſterling.

In the time of epiſcopacy, the biſhop was the chief magiſtrate; and ſince that period, there is a provoſt, two baillies, a dean-of-guild, a treaſurer and maſter of hoſpital. The council conſiſts of thirteen members, theſe office-bearers included.

There is likewiſe a guildry, and eight incorporated trades, viz. hammermen, glovers, bakers, ſhoemakers, weavers, taylors, wrights and butchers. Theſe trades have each of them a deacon of their own chooſing: but the guildry have no choice of their own dean, this being abſolutely in the power of the town-council.

In electing counſellors and magiſtrates, they proceed in the following manner. They meet on any lawful day within ten days preceding Michaelmas, for the purpoſe of electing counſellors

ſellors and leeting magiſtrates.   In this firſt election, the incorporated trades have nothing to ſay; but the deacons of the firſt ſix mentioned trades have a vote in chooſing the provoſt and the two bailies, which muſt be done on, or before Michaelmas day, and two days after the day of election and leeting; at leaſt there muſt be one day betwixt the two days. The convener of the trades is ſaid to be a member of the town council, *ex officio;* and as he does not continue in his office of convener above three years, he muſt in conſequence leave the council at the expiration of that period.   But it is competent for the remaining twelve members of the council to chooſe themſelves every year, if they think proper, as long as they live, which they commonly do; ſo that the town-council of Brechin is in the ſtricteſt ſenſe of the word, ſelf-elected.   A degraded counſellor is a rare phenomenon here. For the ſpace of 23 years bygone, I only recollect two inſtances of the kind.   The corporations and ſeveral of the burgeſſes here, look upon this ſet or conſtitution of the borough as not founded in equity, and for this reaſon have joined with others in an application to Parliament for what is called the Borough Reform, in order to bring back the Royal Boroughs in Scotland to their original conſtitution, according to which the body of burgeſſes were to chooſe every year, the members of the town council.

Eccleſiaſtical State.——Brechin was a rich and antient biſhoprick, founded about the year 1150 by David the I. ſurnamed the Saint, on account of his uncommon liberality to the church. The culdees had a convent here at that time. Their abbot Leod was witneſs to the grant made by King David to his new Abbey of Dunfermline: but where their convent ſtood I cannot ſay, nor do I find any mention of them in Brechin after this period.

The

The Red Friars, called alfo Mathurins, and Trinity Friars, had convents in different parts of the kingdom. Keith in his account of the religious houfes in Scotland is abfolutely certain from antient charters and records, that they had a convent in Brechin, but where it ftood, or by whom it was founded, he cannot fay. Maitland in his Hiftory of Scotland conjectures, that the convent of the Mathurins or Trinity Friars here, was founded by David the I. who erected the bifhoprick. The ruins of the abbey or convent, ftill called the College, are yet to be feen in the College or Chanonry Wynd, adjoining to the N. W. end of the grammar fchool, which was undoubtedly part of the faid college, and probably its fchool; and that this college or convent was of large dimenfion, is evident from its veftigia, or remains, which appear in the neighbouring gardens.

At the Reformation, the rents and revenues of all ecclefiaftical benefices were appointed to be given in to the Privy Council of Scotland. The revenue of the fee of Brechin in the year 1562, according to the account then given, was as follows:—In money, L. 410 : 5 Scots ; 138 capons, 208 fowls, 18 geefe, one chalder and two bolls of corn for horfes, three barrels of falmon; money in teinds, L. 24 : 6 : 8 Scots; teind wheat, 11 bolls; 14 chalders and 6 bolls of bear, and 25 chalders and 5 bolls of meal: a great revenue without all queftion.

At the time of the Reformation, Alexander Campbell, a fon of the family of Arkinglafs, by the recommendation of the Earl of Argyle, got a grant of the bifhopric of Brechin, while he was yet a boy, with a new and unheard-of power, to difpofe of, at his pleafure, all the revenues, which belonged either to the fpirituality or temporality of the benefice. Of this power he made a very liberal ufe, by alienating the moft of the lands and tithes of the bifhopric to his patron

the

the Earl of Argyle : fo that, from this period down to the Revolution, the revenue was among the fmalleft, if not the fmalleft, of any bifhopric in Scotland.

In the time of Popery, bifhops had both a civil and fpiritual jurifdiction ; and each of them had their official to judge in matters of tithes, marriages, orphans, and poor widows, and to confirm teftaments. At the Reformation, commiffaries were appointed in room of the officials ; accordingly there is a commiffariot in Brechin, the commiffary being nominated by the king, who is come in place of the bifhop.

It is not known by whom the cathedral church of Brechin was built. It is a Gothic pile fupported by 12 pillars. The whole length, including the chancel, which is now demolifhed, is about 166 feet, and the breadth 61. The weft end of one of the ailes is entire ; the door is gothic, and the arch confifts of many mouldings. It has a window of curious antique work ; on the fide of the wall there ftood a ftatue of the Virgin Mary, the niche in which it ftood ftill remains. The fteeple is a handfome tower, 120 feet high. The four lower windows are in form of a long narrow opening. The belfry windows are adorned with that fpecies of opening, called the quaterfoil, and the top battlemented, out of which rifes a handfome fpire.

The eaft part of the church, called the choir, or chancel, was deftroyed at the Reformation, and without all doubt by the reformers themfelves. It is to be obferved, that, in the time of Popery, cathedral churches, however different in their fize and dimenfions, were all fituated one way, and were all divided into the fame general parts in imitation of different parts of the temple of Jerufalem. There was the veftibule, or entry to the church, anfwering to the court of the temple, the nave, or body of the church, anfwering to the fanctuary or holy place ; and, the chancel, feparated from the body of
the

the church, by certain rails or lattices from which it took its name, anfwering to the *Sanctum Sanctorum*, or holy of holies. Here the altar ftood, and here mafs was faid. Our Reformers, moved with a laudable zeal againft the idolatries of the church of Rome, demolifhed that part of the cathedral, where the groffeft acts of idolatrous worfhip had been performed, and fpared the remainder; which is to this day the parifh church.

The round tower, adjoining to the church, well known by the name of the little fteeple of Brechin, is an object of attention and admiration to all ftrangers. It is hollow on the infide, and without a ftaircafe, two handfome bells are placed in it, which are got at by means of ladders, placed on wooden femicircular floors, each refting on the circular abutments withinfide of the tower. It confifts of fixty regular courfes of hewn free ftone, laid circularly and regularly, and tapering towards the top. It is covered at the top with a fpiral roof. In this fpire are four windows, placed alternate on the fides, refting on the top of the tower. Near the top of the tower are four others, facing the four cardinal points.

The perpendicular height of this famous tower or fteeple, and all its dimenfions within and without, have been fo accurately defcribed by Gordon in his Itinerarium, Pennant in his Tour, the authors of the Encyclopædia Britannica, and others, that I have no occafion to mention them. On the outfide is a crucifix, and below it the figure of two perfons on each hand, intended, I make no doubt, to reprefent our Saviour on the crofs, and the two thieves who were crucified along with him. It has been obferved fometimes to vibrate with a high wind.

I am of the commonly received opinion, notwithftanding all that has been faid of late to the contrary, that this famous tower or fteeple is a Pictifh monument. There is a tower or

fteeple

fteeple of the fame form, though far inferior in fize and dimenfions, at Abernethy, formerly the feat of the Pictifh kingdom. It is certain that Brechin, a city of great antiquity, was a part of that kingdom. When the church of Brechin was burnt down by the Danes in the reign of Malcolm II. in the manner already mentioned, this famous fteeple was ftanding, and efcaped the general conflagration. It is highly probable, that the church which was then burnt, and the fteeple to which it adjoined, as the church does at prefent, were both of them built during the continuance of the Pictifh kingdom.

It has been alledged that towers or fteeples of this kind could not be intended for belfries, becaufe they are placed near to churches, the fteeples of which are provided with bells of their own. Thofe who make this objection fhould advert, that the fine found of bells arifes in great meafure from their being rung together, or in concert. The large bell·in the fteeple of the church of Brechin is remarkably fine. It had fuffered fome hurt feveral years ago, and for that reafon was caft anew; and it is univerfally agreed, that its found at prefent is as melodious as formerly. When the large bell belonging to the church, and the two bells in the little fteeple are ringing together, the fweet and melodious found they produce cannot be exceeded by any bells in Scotland. A circumftance which every ftranger paffing through this city has had occafion to obferve.

There belonged to cathedrals certain chapels and altarages, inftituted for the devotions of the people, or for faying maffes for the fouls of their founders. There had been a chapel of this kind in the eafternmoft part of the country parifh, which having been dedicated to Saint Magdalene, ftill retains the name of Magdalene Chapel. Here is a burial ground, which is ftill ufed for this purpofe by feveral of the parifhioners,

ifhioners, it having been immemorially the place of interment for their anceftors.

There had been fome chapels and altarages at Caldhame,
part of the country parifh to the eaft of the town : of which
fome veftiges ftill remain. King James VI. in the year 1572,
mortified to the town of Brechin, for the ufes of their poor,
all the revenues belonging to any chaplainry or altarage within the cathedral church of Brechin. But, in a declarator at
the inftance of the Laird of Findowrie, againft the faid town,
for declaring the lands of the chapelry of Caldhame to belong
to him, as having right by progrefs from the chaplains of
Caldhame; the Lords declared in his favour, in regard he
was infeft upon the King's Confirmation Charter, before any
infeftment taken by the town upon their gift of mortification. Accordingly the heirs of Findowrie continued to poffefs the lands of Caldhame, till they were purchafed from
them feveral years ago, by the late Earl of Panmure.

Brechin is a collegiate church; one parifh under the care
of two minifters. The eaft part of the town, and the eaft
and north parts of the country parifh, with the upper and
nether tenements, are called the firft charge. The weft
part of the town, the upper and nether weft wynds, and
the whole country parifh to the weft and fouth, are called the fecond charge. When a minifter dies, or is tranflated, his fucceffor is admitted to the charge he had, whether it be the firft or fecond. The patronage of both is
in the gift of the crown.

The minifters in the firft charge were the immediate
fucceffors of the bifhop, after the year 1690, when Epifcopacy was abolifhed, and Prefbyterian government eftablifhed in Scotland. Mr. Willifon, afterwards minifter at
Dundee, was the firft. He was fucceeded by Mr. Gray,
who had been minifter at Cabrach, was tranflated to Edzel,

zel, and after that to the first charge in Brechin. He was
succeeded by Mr. David Blair, who had been minister at
Lochlee, was translated to the second, and after that to
the first charge in Brechin. He was succeeded by the present incumbent Mr. John Bisset, who had been minister at
Culsalmond, and was admitted minister of the first charge in
Brechin on the 9th of November 1769.

His stipend consisted at first of 85 bolls, 2 firlots, 2 lippies
of meal, 40 bolls 2 firlots of bear, and 3 bolls 2 firlots of
wheat, and L. 47 : 2 : 5 sterl. of money. It is to be observed, that the bishop's house and three gardens, which had belonged to the bishop, were allocated to the minister of the
first charge, by two different decreets of the Court of Teinds,
one in the year 1702, and the other in the year 1718, in lieu
of L. 3 : 6 : 8 sterl. of the above mentioned stipend.

In consequence of the suppression of the parish of Kinnaird
and the annexation of part of it to the parish of Brechin, the
minister of the first charge has enjoyed for three years past
L. 11 : 1 : 1$\frac{1}{2}$ sterling of additional stipend The church of
Kinnaird originally belonged to Brechin. It was disjoined
from it in the year 1597, and erected in a separate parson-
age ; and the patronage disponed to Sir David Carnegie.

The bishop's house was habitable at the Revolution, and
was actually possessed and inhabited by Messrs. Willison, Gray
and Blair for some time. In Mr. Blair's time it became un-
inhabitable, in consequence of which, he built a house of his
own. In the year 1770, the Barons of Exchequer, on an application from the magistrates and town council of Brechin,
granted the sum of L. 250 sterl. for repairing the bishop's
house. The magistrates of Brechin, to whom the management of the money was intrusted, finding the bishop's house
irreparable, laid out the money in building a new house, a
few

few yards diftant from the ftance of the old houfe, which the prefent incumbent poffeffes and inhabits.

The part of the country parifh which belongs to the firft charge, extends from the town eaftward about three Englifh miles, and about two Englifh miles northward; it goes no farther fouth than the extremity of the nether tenement at the bridge over the Southefk. It is bounded on the north by the parifh of Strickathrow, on the eaft by the parifh of Dun, and on the fouth by the parifh of Marytoun, and part of the fecond charge.

Population.——The number of people in the eaft fide of the town, and in the upper and nether tenements, counting the names from feven years of age and upwards, at which time they are entered on the catechifing rolls, and including all the different religious denominations, amount to 1500. The number of people in the north and eaft fide of the country parifh, amount fully to 500.

We have no Papifts, Independents, or Anabaptifts, in any part of the town or parifh of Brechin. There will be nearly of examinable perfons 243 Antiburgher Seceders. They have one minifter, his ftipend L. 60 fterling. His parifhioners, in the year 1790, built him a commodious houfe. He has a garden adjoining to his houfe; and his chapel, or meeting houfe, was of late very elegantly repaired. There will be of qualified Epifcopals about 500; one clergyman, his ftipend L. 50 fterling, with a neat houfe, garden, and office houfes. There are a few alfo of thofe Epifcopals, formerly called Nonjurants. Their minifters at prefent pray for King George and the royal family; and they are likewife obliged by a late act of Parliament, in order to enjoy the benefit of the toleration, to take the ufual oaths to govenment, and fub-fcribe the 39 articles of the Church of England. A Method-

ift

ift meeting houfe was built laft Summer on the eaft fide of the town. The methodifts have as yet been joined by very few, and as they had a footing here fo very lately, I cannot pretend to afcertain their numbers.

Schools.—There has been immemorially a refpectable fchool at Brechin, confifting of a rector and a doctor.

The rector has a falary of L. 8 : 6 : 8 fterling, paid from the town's revenue, and befides is preceptor of *Maifon Dieu*.

To underftand this matter fully, it muft be obferved, that, in the times of Popery, hofpitals inftituted for the maintenance of the poor, or the education of youth, as being of peculiar ufefulnefs to mankind, were honoured by the diftinguifhing epithet of *Maifons de Dieu*, fignifying, in French, ' Houfes of God.' There were houfes of this denomination in different parts of Scotland. One of this kind was founded in Brechin, as nearly as I can learn, in the year 1256, by William of Brechin, fon of Henry of Brechin, and grandfon to Earl David, for the benefit of the fouls of William and Alexander, kings of Scotland, John, Earl of Chefter and Huntington, his brother, Henry, his father, and Juliana, his mother. To his charter of foundation the fubfcribing witneffes are, Albin, bifhop of Brechin, and Robert de Monte Alto. The original is inferted in a confirmation charter of James the Third in the year 1477. It was fituated in a vennal or lane in the upper end of the town, on the weft fide of the ftreet. The fouth wall of the chapel is ftill ftanding pretty entire; and the houfe of the preceptor, who was the head of this religious foundation, was inhabited in the memory of fome perfons ftill alive, but is now quite demolifhed.

Here I am under the neceffity of making a digreffion to the honour of the antient and famous city of Brechin. Brechin gave name to the firft nobility of Scotland, and ma-

ny

ny of the royal family were called Lords of Brechin. King
James the Third's fecond fon, Alexander, was, in 1480, created Lord Brechin and Navar; a title which was afterwards
conferred upon the Maules of Panmure. David, 4th Lord
of Brechin, was in 1321 executed for high treafon. Um-
fraville, brother of the Earl of Angus, the moft antient title
in Scotland, was fo difgufted at the execution, that, after
giving David a decent burial, he repaired to King Robert
Bruce, and begged he might be allowed to fell his lands and
retire out of Scotland, as he could not live in a land where
fuch a man as David Lord Brechin had fuffered an ignomi-
nious death. This David was called The Flower of Chivalry.

The caftle of Brechin was built on a little eminence fouth
of the town, but no veftige of it is left. It underwent a
long fiege in the year 1303; was gallantly defended againft
the Englifh under Edward I.; and notwithftanding all the
efforts of that potent prince, the brave governor, Thomas
Maule, held out this fmall fortrefs for twenty days, till he
was flain by a ftone caft from an engine on the 20th of Auguft, when the place was inftantly furrendered. Patrick
Maule, defcendant of the governor, was, in 1646, created
Lord Maule of Brechin and Navar, and Earl of Panmure.

His family were patrons of the preceptory of Maifon Dieu,
which had for many ages been conferred on the fchoolmafter
of Brechin. A full fourth part of the town holds feu of
the preceptor of Maifon Dieu, who grants charters to his
vaffals; and, before the rebellion in 1715, thefe were granted
with the confent of the Earl of Panmure the patron, many
of which are ftill extant. Upon the forfeiture of the Panmure family in 1715, the right was vefted in the crown,
who, in cafe of vacancy, never fails to prefent to the precep-
torfhip of Maifon Dieu the perfon recommended by the magiftrates and town-council.

The

The income of the fchoolmaster, as preceptor of Maifon Dieu, confifts of gardens, rents, feu-duties from tenements within the town and from fome farms in the country, amounting to L. 8 : 18 : 7½ fterling, befides 17½ bolls of meal yearly. As fuperior of thefe lands, he is likewife entitled to the cafualties payable to vaffals at entry ; but the amount of thefe I cannot exactly afcertain : and to all this muft be added the fchool dues.

The doctor has a falary of L. 3 : 6 : 8 fterling from the town. He is always feffion-clerk ; for which he has a falary of L. 6 : 13 : 4 fterling from the kirk-feffion, befides the fchool dues and perquifites of his office as feffion-clerk.

The rector and doctor taught formerly together in one fchool ; but for feveral years paft they have taught in different fchools, which are under the fame roof, and feparated by a partition wall.

The rector or mafter is reftricted, by an act of the town-council, to the teaching Latin, and the doctor to the teaching Englifh, writing, arithmetic and book-keeping.

Poor, and Poor's Funds.——There is a confiderable number of poor in the town and parifh of Brechin. Some of them have weekly or monthly penfions, fuited to their particular exigencies. Others of them receive occafional charity, in confequence of precepts drawn by one or other of the minifters upon the kirk-treafurer. The funds for their maintenance are as yet very fufficient, and are,

Money lent on bond - - L. 295 11 0
Feu-duties, per annum - - 1 15 0
Weekly collections, at an average - 0 10 0

On occafion of the Sacrament, which is regularly difpenfed once a-year, L. 12 or L. 13 fterling.

There has been a great influx of people into the town and

tenements

tenements of late years, in confequence of the increafe of trade and manufactures; and as the number of people increafes, no doubt the number of poor will, at the fame time, through the various accidents of human life, increafe proportionally. It is however to be expected, that the collections at the church doors will increafe in the fame proportion; and therefore, if the poor's funds here are properly fecured and preferved, there is not the moft diftant profpect, that there will ever be occafion or neceffity for a legal affeffment.

Markets, Trade and Manufactures.—There is a conftant traffic of horfes and cattle at Brechin through a great part of the year. Trinity Fair, fo denominated from Trinity Muir, a little to the north of the town, where it is held, begins on the fecond Wednefday of June, and continues three days fucceffively. On Wednefday there is a fheep market, on Thurfday a cattle market, and on Friday the fineft horfe market in the north of Scotland. There is a market of the fame kind in the month of Auguft, on the fame muir, which, from the time of the year in which it is held, is called Lammas Fair: but it is in every refpect inferior to the former. A cattle market begins on the firft Tuefday after Michaelmas, and continues every Tuefday for fix weeks after Martinmas. A horfe market begins on the laft Tuefday of February, on the public ftreet, and is continued every Tuefday for fix weeks fucceffively. The weekly market in Brechin is on Tuefday. There is as good butcher meat here of every kind, beef, mutton, lamb, veal, pork and kid, as in any town in Scotland. One may likewife be provided with butcher meat on the Thurfday. The butchers here kill their beafts on Thurfday, and carry the flefh to Montrofe on Friday, which is the weekly market there.

There are four extraordinary markets in Brechin every
year,

year, which are called great Tuefdays, or muckle markets ; one on the firft Tuefday after Martinmas, another on Palm Tuefday, the third on the firft Tuefday after Trinity fair,· and the fourth on the firft Tuefday after Lammas fair. Thefe are foot markets, ftanding on the public ftreet, which is at that time crowded with merchants' ftands, expofing for fale many different commodities. This occafions a vaft refort of people from the neighbouring parifhes, expecting to purchafe a variety of articles from the ftands or tents of the chapmen at a cheaper rate than from the merchants' fhops.

There is a falmon fifhing on the Southefk, the property of the Hon. William Maule of Panmure. It is rented at prefent at L. 15 a-year ; and the average fale, as I am informed, will be from L. 60 to L. 100.

In the year 1785, a brewery was erected at the end of the nether tenements, near the bridge, with every apparatus neceffary for the purpofe. It has been very fuccefsful ; furnifhing ale and beer, not only to the people of Brechin, but to all the neighbouring parifhes, fome of them at a confiderable diftance.

In the year 1786, a diftillery was erected at the north port, for diftilling fpirits from malt. The whifky, or aquavitæ, diftilled here, is remarkably fine, and greatly run after, not only by the people here, but by the whole country round. Their yearly profits, I prefume, are very confiderable : but from any information I have as yet received, I am not able to afcertain them.

A diftillery of the fame kind was fet a-going very lately at the eaft end of the Cadger-wynd, and promifes to do well.

The yarn and the coarfe linen, commonly called Ofnaburgs, is a branch of trade in which moft of our merchants are at prefent engaged.

A cotton manufactory was eftablifhed here in March 1786.
Commodious

Commodious houfes were built, and very curious machinery, every way proper for the purpofe, was provided. It was given up in September 1790. It recommenced in April 1792: 100 hands, at an average, were employed in this manufactory from the year 1786 to 1790; and 80, at leaft, are employed at prefent. It is under the management of John Smith, Efq. prefent provoft of Brechin, and Colin Gillies, Efq. merchant here: two of our moft fubftantial merchants, and both of them diftinguifhed by prudence, induftry and unwearied attention to every branch of trade in which they happen to be engaged.

It is needlefs to mention the commodities retailed in the fhops, as they are well known. One thing however muft be noticed, that there is a greater number of fhop-keepers in Brechin at prefent than was ever known at any former period, owing to the great increafe of people, which occafions a greater demand for fhop commodities.

Soil, Produce and Agriculture.——The lands around Brechin are in general very good. There is not much wheat fown here. It is commonly fown in September or October, and from 3 firlots to 14 pecks an acre, and produces very often from 10 to 12 bolls per acre; is for ordinary ready to be cut down about the middle of Auguft. Barley fown in April will be ready to be cut down with the wheat, and commonly produces about 10 bolls per acre. The crops of oats have not been fo good within thefe twelve years paft: they produce, at an average, from 6 to 8 bolls per acre. There is a good deal of peafe fown in the parifh; and, after the peafe, barley, with grafs feeds, 12 pounds of clover and 2 bufhels of rye-grafs for an acre: and if cut the firft year; they will commonly produce from 200 to 300 ftones of hay, which fells, at a medium, from 4d. to 6d. per ftone.

The

The farmers here sow turnips, with which they fatten their cattle in winter. The inclosing with stone dykes goes on very rapidly; and in a few years the farmers will be enabled to fatten their cattle in summer. Some of our farmers who have inclosed fields, set them from 40s. to 50s. per acre.

Sir David Carnegie's tenants, who compose the greatest part of the country parish under the first charge, have good farm steadings, and are well lodged. Most of the leases were of late renewed, and the rents considerably raised: but still they have very good bargains. Little of their land is set above 15s. per acre; whereas other gentlemen, in this and the neighbouring parishes, have set their lands from 20s. to 30s. per acre. The tenants here are, generally speaking, good farmers, well acquainted with the proper methods of cultivation; and many of them are very substantial, so that they can afford to lay out a good deal of money in improving their farms: and there is every chance in the world, that what they have laid out, or may lay out, to this effect, will, in process of time, be repaid to great advantage.

Antiquities, and the Riding of the Muir.—There are the remains of a Danish camp near Keithoc, a part of the country parish northward. This camp lies west of the Battle-Dykes: the road leading from Brechin to the Grampian Hills passes through the middle of it. It is in the form of an oblong square. Its circumference is about one fourth of an English mile, that is to say, what is visible above ground. In the midst of this encampment is a well of water, generally known by the name of the Camp Well, and a mount, on the south side, about 8 or 10 feet high, and about 40 feet in circumference at the base. But from the best information I can learn, its original length was about one half of a Scots mile; the one point beginning at the north end of the Ward of Keithoc, going

in

in a ftraight line fouth-weft, and terminating at the Law of Keithoc, immediately at the top of the hill, and on the road leading from Brechin to Aberdeen. The Law of Keithoc is about 20 feet high above the furface of the ground, and about or 45 feet broad at the bafe, carried up or built in a round form, and gradually fmaller towards the top. To the fouth-weft of this camp, was a chapel, or temple, which is now ploughed down; and a large piece of land adjacent to this temple is ftill called the Temple or Kirk Shade.

At the time of Trinity and Lammas fairs, the youngeft baillie of Brechin, with a felect company, goes on horfeback to the North-water Bridge, which is about 5 meafured miles from the market, in order to prevent fore-ftalling; as no cattle, horfes or fheep can be fold within that diftance without being liable to the ufual cuftoms. At the fame time, the whole citizens proceed on foot with great pomp and folemnity, drums beating, pipes playing and colours flying, to the Law of Keithoc, alias the Hare-Cairn, which is about midway between Brechin and the North-water Bridge. In the days of club-law, the baillie of Brechin, and his company, often met with refiftance in the execution of their office. For this reafon, the citizens proceeded the length of the Law of Keithoc, or Hare-Cairn, in order to affift them, if there fhould be occafion for it, in preferving and maintaining the immemorial rights and privileges of the market, and this they were to do on the fhorteft notice. In thefe civilized times, no violence is offered: the old cuftom, however, is ftill kept up.

Learned Men who have been born, or refided in Brechin.— In the times of popery, any meafure of learning in the kingdom was moftly to be found among the clerical order. Hence clergymen were promoted to the higheft civil offices; few of

other

other denominations being ſufficiently qualified, at that period, to fill thoſe important ſtations.

Patrick de Leuchars, deſcended of an ancient family in
the ſhire of Fife, was inveſted in the ſee of Brechin in the
year 1354, and ſome time after was made Lord High Chancellor of the kingdom.

George Shoreſwood, of the family of Bedſhiel in the ſhire
of Berwick, was promoted to the biſhopric of Brechin in the
year 1454: he was alſo Royal Secretary, and laſt of all became Lord High Chancellor.

John Sinclair, a ſon of the houſe of Roſlin, a man well
learned in both laws, was dean of Reſtalrig, near Edinburgh,
and put into the ſee of Brechin by Queen Mary. He was likewiſe, for his ſingular knowledge of the law, firſt an ordinary
Lord of Seſſion, and then Lord Preſident. He joined Queen
Mary in marriage to Lord Darnley.

William Maitland, F. R. S. who publiſhed a hiſtory of
London in one folio volume, and alſo a hiſtory of Scotland
in two folios, was a native of Brechin. Some of his relations
are ſtill alive. He had ſtudied the hiſtory of his own country
with the utmoſt care and attention; and as he had occaſion to
travel through a great part of it, he deſcribes all its antiquities, which happened to fall under his perſonal obſervation,
with an uncommon degree of accuracy and preciſion.

Mr. Norman Sievewright, late miniſter of the qualified
epiſcopal chapel here, finiſhed, in the year 1764, what he
calls, ' The Hebrew Text conſidered ; being obſervations on
' the novelty and ſelf-inconſiſtency of the maſoretic ſcheme
' of pointing the ſacred Hebrew ſcriptures.' He had written
a grammar in order to ſhew, that the Hebrew may be taught
and learned without having recourſe to, or making any uſe of
the vowel points. It was never publiſhed : the manuſcript,
however, is ſtill extant. The opinions of the learned are
different

different on this fubject. Mr. Sievewright has advanced no new argument againft the antiquity of the vowel points. His publication, however, difcovers him to have ftudied the Hebrew with great care, and to have been no fmall proficient in that branch of literature.

John Gillies, LL.D. F.R.S. & S.A. fon of the deceafed Robert Gillies, late merchant here, is the brighteft literary ornament of Brechin. His tranflation of the orations of Lyfias and Ifocrates from the Greek, with his introductory difcourfe on the hiftory, manners and character of the Greeks from the conclufion of the Peloponnefian war to the battle of Chæronea, his firft publication, procured him no fmall degree of literary fame. It pointed him out as a thorough Greek fcholar; which I have ever confidered as the foundation of all real literature. His hiftory of Greece is the completeft and exacteft of the kind which has yet appeared. His view of the reign of the late king of Pruffia, and his parallel betwixt that prince and Philip the Second of Macedon, difcovers Dr. Gillies to have inveftigated the principles, genius and conftitution of the antient ftates of Greece, and the modern governments of Europe, with an equal degree of attention and accuracy. He makes a confiderable figure in the republic of letters, and does honour to the city which gave him birth.

Mr. William Guthrie, once minifter of Finwick, was born in the parifh of Brechin. He was eldeft fon of the laird of Pitforthie; and refigned his paternal eftate in favour of another brother, that he might be at more leifure to profecute the functions of the facred office. Mr. Guthrie had a fufficient meafure of learning; but was peculiarly eminent for his piety, and his fervent, indefatigable zeal in promoting the interefts of Chriftianity. He wrote a little treatife, entitled, ' The Trial of a Saving Intereft in Chrift.' This little treatife, however much it may be defpifed in an age of atheifm

and

and infidelity, was highly esteemed at the time it was published. It was translated into German, Dutch and French; and was circulated with amazing rapidity through all the Protestant churches abroad. It was translated, if my information be right, into one of the eastern languages, at the expence of the Hon. Robert Boyle, a promoter both of piety and learning. Dr. Owen, a divine of the last century, of extraordinary erudition, said of this little treatise, ' It is my ' vade-mecum : I carry it and the Sedan New Testament still ' about with me. I have written several folios, but there is ' more divinity in this than in them all.'

Ravages of the Plague.——In the year 1647, the plague made prodigious havock in Brechin. Six hundred persons died of the infection in the space of a few months. The most of them were buried in the little church-yard opposite to the porch door of the church; and the graves have not been opened to this day. A part of them were buried in the large church-yard; and the graves. there were opened, about 26 years ago, with no small apprehension of danger: however, through the goodness of Providence, no bad consequence ensued. The following inscription, on a monument in the little kirk-yard, sufficiently verifies the present narrative.——

1647.
Luna quater crescens
Sexcentos peste peremptos,
(Disce mori!) vidit.
Pulvis et umbra sumus.

SIR,

SIR,

In perufing the Statiftical Account of the parifh of Bre-chin, I was aftonifhed to find an affertion in my father's name, relating to the circular tower in that city, which, as it can hardly gain belief, even from the moft credulous, is like-ly to bring reproach either on his underftanding or veracity, or on both; and which, as equally falfe and impoffible to have been affirmed by him, I muft requeft that you will do him the juftice to have cancelled or contradicted in as public a manner as it has been circulated. He was not capable of fay-ing, that the tower in queftion, ' is faid to bend like a willow ' in high winds, fo as almoft to touch the fteeple;' nay, he affures me, that though many people have afferted its vibra-tion, and he was at pains to examine that circumftance often and moft attentively in fome of the moft violent gufts of wind, he never yet perceived it; and he is pofitive that fuch was the account he tranfmitted in his correfpondence with you. I am inclined, therefore, to believe that it muft have been in your abfence, and through the inattention of thofe whom you employed at Edinburgh, that fuch a mifreprefen-tation has crept into the prefs; or, perhaps the compiler has been mifled by the account of that matter in Pennant's Tour, though, if I rightly recollect, what Mr. Pennant fays is far from being fo unlikely and incredible as the language of the Statiftical Work; at any rate, it is not Mr. Pennant's, but Mr. Bruce's Account which it profeffes to exhibit to the public.

I am

I am sorry I should have occasion to trouble Sir John Sinclair on such a subject, but I feel it to be my duty; and I trust he will pay attention to it, as a just tribute of filial respect to a father's good name, and an expression of proper concern that the important work which owes its being to Sir John's patriotic exertions may be the vehicle only of truth.

I have the honour to be, Sir,

Your most obedient,

and humble Servant,

FORFAR,
25. *Dec.* 1794.

JOHN BRUCE.

To Sir John Sinclair, Baronet.

PARISH OF CARESTON.

(COUNTY OF ANGUS.)

By the Rev. MR. ANDREW GRAY.

Name, Situation, Extent, Soil, &c.

THE antient name of this parish was Caraldston, probably derived from a monument erected to the memory of Carril, a hero celebrated in the poems of Ossian; some
vestiges of which, (3 large stones standing on an'end, about a mile
and a half to the east of the church), still remain. It is now contracted into Careston.———It is situated in the county of
Angus, 9 miles north-east of Forfar the county town, 4 miles
from Brechin, and 12 from Montrose. It lies within the
bounds of the presbytery of Brechin, and the synod of Angus
and Mearns. Its form is very nearly an oblong square, 3
miles in length, and about 1 in breadth. The appearance of
the country is beautiful, well cultivated, lying with a gentle
slope from north to south. No part of it is rocky, hilly, or
mountainous.———The soil is generally deep and fertile, a-
bout one half on a gravelly bottom, and the other half on a
red clay, or mortar. The air is exceeding fine, free, and
healthful.———At present there are no prevailing distempers; it is said, however, that before the ground was drained

ed and cultivated, agues were very frequent, in so much, that in the spring, it was with difficulty the farmers could carry on their work. But now there is scarcely any such distemper known or felt in this place. Fevers were formerly pretty frequent, and carried off several. But they now occur but seldom.

Rivers.————There are two rivers which run through this parish : the South-Esk, and the Norin ; both of which run on a gravelly bottom. The water of Norin, in particular, is remarkable for its purity and clearness. The South-Esk rises to a great height, and at times overflows its banks to such a degree, that the greatest attention is requisite every year to raise bulwarks, in order to prevent it from covering the adjacent grounds on every side. The Norin, though considerably smaller than the Esk, frequently comes down with such impetuosity, that the low grounds, through which it runs, are often greatly hurt by it, which obliges the tenants to use every precaution to keep it within its banks. These two rivers join one another in the southern part of this parish. They have both their sources in the Grampian hills.———— There is no regular fishing with the net in this parish ; but there is, in the Esk, plenty of salmon, salmon-trout, and burn trout taken with the rod ; and, in the Norin, very fine burn trout.

Produce.————A variety of culinary plants, &c. are raised in this parish. There are likewise a vast variety of trees, such as ash, elm, plane, birch, beech, oak, chesnut, poplar, lime, &c. and a great number of firs of every kind. There are excellent fruit trees of different sorts ; and some very beautiful lime trees, not inferior, perhaps, to any in the island.

Considerable numbers of black cattle, (above 400), are

reared

reared every year, and also about 40 horses. The value of the horses may be reckoned, from L. 15 to L. 20, or L. 25 each. The price of cattle, when fattened, is generally from 5s to 5s 6d. per stone, and milk cows about the same. Other kinds of black cattle, are valued in proportion to the state they are in, when purchased,—to their age, and the particular purpose, for which they are bought. The weight of the black cattle, reared and fattened, generally runs from 18 to 40 stone a head; and some, which are highly fed, will be near 50 stone. The quality of the beef is exceeding good. Very few sheep are bred, except for family use.

Population.——It is difficult to ascertain the ancient state of the population of this parish, as no regular register was kept till the year 1714. The only conjecture, that can be formed, respecting the number of parishioners, arises from the number of tokens, struck for the use of communicants, in the year 1709, when this parish was under the care of an Episcopal clergyman, which number was 200 *. In the year 1716, the first presbyterian minister was settled : And there was, at the same time, a very numerous meeting of Episcopalians, or Nonjurors ; which meeting was made up of the disaffected in this, and the neighbouring parishes This meeting continued till the year 1746, when it was entirely dissolved. It appears from a note, in the session records, that, during the continuance of this Episcopal meeting, there were many parents in the parish, of that persuasion, who never applied to the session-clerk, to have their children's names registered, nor paid any dues to him. However, upon examining the list of baptisms,

* To double the number of tokens, would be too much, as it might be expected that many would come from other parishes, to the sacrament at Careston.

baptisms, recorded during that period, the number, at an a-
verage, may be reckoned at least nine ; which, by making
allowance for the disaffected, that sought no enrolment of
their children, will confirm the conjecture, that the number
of persons in the parish was formerly greater.   With respect
to the state of the population, for some time past, the number
has rather diminished ; there not being, at present, more than
260 persons, young and old, of which 132 are males, and 128
females ; whereas the return to Dr Webster was 269 souls.
The average of births annually does not exceed six.   The
average of burials may be estimated at six for these twenty
years back ; but exactness here cannot be expected, because
there are many, who die in this parish, that are buried in
other parishes ; and many, that die in other parishes, are buried
here.   For these twenty years past, it is supposed, that the
number of marriages, on an average, does not exceed five
annually.   The number of farmers amounts only to four, residing in the parish ; though there are one or two, not residing, who farm betwixt 100 and 140 acres in this district.
The diminution of the number of farmers, is owing to several
farms being turned into one, and also several farms taken into
the possession of the proprietor, for the purpose of improvement.   The number of trades people, in this parish, is
very small ; only one shoemaker, one house-carpenter or
wright, one weaver, one tailor, and one blacksmith.   There
is but one Seceder.   Of Episcopalians, there are about nine
or ten.   The diminution of the population of this parish, is
owing to the several farms, which the proprietor has in his
own hands, being all turned into grass ; and, as has been
mentioned, the other farms being held by fewer hands.
There is also no encouragement given here to manufacturers and small tenants ; so that there are, at least, an hundred,

dred, or an hundred and fifty or sixty persons, fewer in the parish, than there were 50 years ago.

Poor.——The number of poor, is fluctuating. At present, they do not exceed 4 or 5. The collections and funds for their relief, are amply sufficient to supply their wants liberally.

Church and Stipend.——The church was built in 1636, and has often been repaired. The stipend will not, including the glebe, exceed L. 60 *per annum,* when victual sells at 10s *per* boll. George Skene of Skene, Esq. is patron, and the only heritor. He commonly resides at Careston.

Farming.——The number of acres, in this parish, may be about 1500; above 200 of which, are planted with hard wood, and firs of various kinds. At an average, there are, at least, 350 acres employed in raising corn, flax, greens, cabbages, and turnips. The farms, in this parish, are all divided into ten equal parts, the one half in tillage, under crop, and the other half laid down with clover and rye-grass. The ordinary rotation observed, is five years in tillage, and five in grass. The first crop, after breaking up their fields, is oats; the second, barley; the third, oats; the fourth, turnips, potatoes, cabbage, and pease; and the fifth year, the field is laid down with barley and grass seeds. They sow sometimes wheat, and flax, as interim crops; but these are not reckoned in the ordinary course of cropping; though, it is observable, that the crop of flax is not allowed to stand in the room of a green crop, which can, by no means, be omitted. The lint is ordinarily sown the first crop in the rotation.

The parish is not only able to supply itself with the necessary provisions of meal malt, butter, and cheese, and poultry of all kinds, but there can be spared from it, annually, a very
considerable

considerable quantity of grain of all kinds; a number of fed cattle for the butcher; and some few fed sheep. Butter and cheese are also sold to a considerable amount. From 60 to near 70 acres are annually sown with flax. The ground in the possession of the proprietor, is mostly in clover and rye-grass, (about 20 acres excepted ;) and, as it is all inclosed and subdivided, it generally lets to graziers and others, at 20s, 25s, 30s, and 46s, per acre. The amount of grass fields in the proprietor's hand, and what the tenants have laid down in grass, on their farms, may be reckoned at least seven or eight hundred acres. The number of acres in natural grass does not exceed one hundred. Of boggy ground, there are not forty acres. There is no part of the parish in common ; and the number of acres of waste ground does not exceed thirty.

Antiquities.—There are two artificial mounts in the parish, about 200 yards distant from each other, which are commonly called *Laws;* and tradition says, that one of these mounts was the usual place where courts of justice were held, and judgement was given ; and that the other was the place, where the law was put in execution, when criminals were capitally convicted. Others imagine, that they were places of observation, on which fires were kindled, at the approach of an enemy.

School.—The schoolmaster has a salary of L. 10 yearly, exclusive of perquisites ; and he also officiates as session-clerk, for which he has a fee of 20 merks Scotch. The other emoluments are inconsiderable, on account of the small number of parishioners. He has likewise a good school-house and garden, with about two acres of ground, at a low rent, from Mr Skene. The number of scholars varies, as in other

places

places, seldom above thirty, and very often below 20. Engglish, writing, arithmetic, book-keeping, navigation, and astronomy, are the branches taught here; but no Latin.

Miscellaneous Observations—There are several disadvantages in this parish. A scarcity of fuel is one; as coal, the only fuel used here, cannot be got nearer than the port of Montrose, which is 12 miles distant; and there, coal is sold at a very high price, (8s and 8s 6d. per boll,) on account of the high duty laid on that article, at that and the other ports on the north coast of this island. Every boll, or 72 stones, costs 12s. to the consumer.——Montrose is also the nearest port for exporting grain, which, being a long carriage, is of considerable disadvantage to the farmer.——Lime and marle are the only means of improvement in this parish, and these are both to drive a considerable distance. Good lime cannot be had nearer than 12 miles, and marle 7 miles. There is indeed lime to be had nearer, but of an inferior quality.

This parish has also its advantages. The road to the port of Montrose, is very good, smooth, and level, without the interruption of hills, and is seldom interrupted by storms in the winter time; so that the communication is free and open at all seasons.——This parish being contiguous to Brechin, has a regular communication by post, every day of the week. In Brechin there is also a ready market for provisions of all kinds, which can be spared from this place. And, in return, may be had every other article, both for the necessity and conveniency of families.——The soil being good, and the climate temperate, give the advantage of good grain, which ordinarily comes to full maturity, without being hurt by the early frosts, or blasting storms in autumn; so that the farmer has the advantage of a true crop.——This parish has the advantage of being excellently well watered, not only from the two rivers already

already mentioned, but also by a number of fine springs, from which issue great abundance of exceeding fine water in almost every field.——There is plenty of freestone.——The number of ploughs will not exceed 9 or 10 ; some of which are made for 4, and some for 2 horses, as occasion requires. About 20 carts, or at most 24, are used for the purpose of husbandry. ——There is no inn, or even alehouse in the parish.—— The tenants have their leases on very reasonable terms ; are happy in their intercourse with one another, and enjoy in a considerable degree the blessings of social life.

PARISH OF CARMYLIE.

By the Rev. Mr PATRICK BRYCE.

Origin of the Name.

THE parish of Carmylie furnishes very little scope for statistical inquiry. The origin of the name cannot now be ascertained. In some antient records of the presbytery it is called Carmylie, probably from the high grounds which compose the greatest part of it: But this is merely conjectural. Previous to the period of the Reformation, the church was a chapel, built by the heritor of the estate of Carmylie, where the Monks from the Abbey of Aberbrothock, in its vicinity, performed divine service, according to the rites of the Church of Rome, in their courses. It was erected into a parochial charge, after the Reformation, by the Lords Commissioners for Plantation of Kirks.

Situation, Extent, and Productions.—The parish is situated in the county of Forfar, presbytery of Aberbrothock, and synod of Angus and Mearns. It is of an oblong form; surrounded by the parishes of Panbride, Guthrie, Monikie, Kirkden, Dunnichen, Inverkillor, St Vigians, and Arberlot. It is about 3 miles long, from east to west, and about 4 miles broad. It may be called a hilly and mountainous tract of ground,

ground, when compared with the conterminous parishes. The land is wet and spungy, and was thought, some years ago, to be better adapted for pasture than for grain. About 20 years ago, there were many farms in the parish occupied by farmers in the neighbourhood, who used them for grazing their cattle in the summer; but ever since that time, the proprietors have obliged the tenants to reside on them; who, by driving lime and marl to their respective farms, and by draining their lands by sunk fences, &c. have greatly meliorated the ground, and for several years have raised heavy crops; which, though they were not equal in quality, yet, in quantity, were not inferior to those produced on the grounds in the neighbourhood, that have been long in a proper state of cultivation. On a very moderate computation, there is four times the quantity of grain, especially of barley, raised in this parish than there was 20 years ago.

Rent.—The land rent is supposed to be about L. 1000 Sterling. It has risen about a third within these last 20 years. There are only 3 heritors in the parish, none of whom reside in it.

Church and Stipend, &c.—The walls of the church were repaired about 40 years ago, and a new roof was thrown over it last summer. It is decently fitted up within for the accommodation of the congregation, who are a sober and industrious people, and regular in their attendance on divine ordinances. The stipend amounts to about 400 merks Scots in money, and a little more than 5 chalders of victual. The manse was built about 18 years ago. There are very good funds for the poor; and they are liberally provided for without any assessment on the heritors.

Population.

Population.—The population of the parish, as returned to Dr Webster about 40 years ago, was 730 souls. It has since rather decreased. Some mechanics, especially weavers, have removed to the trading boroughs of Dundee and Aberbrothock, where they meet with good encouragement from the manufacturing companies in these towns. Its inhabitants may now amount to about 700. The number of burials do not exceed 15 or 18 yearly. The births are from 20 to 24 annually. There are very few dissenters in the parish; not exceeding 20. There is only 1 brewer; 4 persons retail ale.

School.—There is a parochial schoolmaster here. His salary is 100 merks Scots; a house, but no garden. The perquisites belonging to him are very inconsiderable. His whole income does not exceed L. 20 Sterling. He has about 50 scholars in winter, and 30 in summer. Much praise is due to the people for promoting and encouraging the education of the youth of both sexes. They have subscribed a certain sum for building a school-house; and are determined to give every support in their power to the person who is to have the charge of instructing the girls in the different branches of needlework.

Birds, &c.—The dotterels, birds of passage, alight on the rising grounds about the beginning of April, continue here about three weeks, remove to the Grampian Hills, about 12 miles to the northward, and revisit this parish about the beginning of August: After abiding here about three weeks, they fly off to the southward, and are not seen till the 1st of April following. There are quarries of grey-slate and pavement stones here, which have been wrought for some centuries. They supply the neighbourhood, and are exported to Fife, Perthshire, the Mearns, &c.

UNITED PARISHES OF CORTACHY AND CLOVA.

(County and Preſbytery of Forfar.—Synod of Angus and Mearns.)

By Mr WILLIAM HALDANE, *Preacher of the Goſpel.*

Name, Situation, and Extent.

CORTACHY, or *Quartachy*, is derived from the Gaelic word *chuartaich*, which ſignifies *encloſed* or *ſurrounded.* The name is deſcriptive of its local ſituation, as it lies in a ſmall valley, ſurrounded by riſing ground. The origin of the name CLOVA is uncertain. Theſe united pariſhes lie on the north ſide of the county of Angus. The river *Proſen* ſeparates them from the pariſhes of Kingoldrum and Kirriemuir, on the S. and S. W. The pariſh of Cortachy, from the extreme part on the ſouth to its northern boundary on the Grampian hills, is about 13 miles in length. Its breadth varies. The north and middle parts are about 8 miles broad. Towards the ſouth end, its breadth does not exceed two miles. The pariſh of Clova is ſituated on the north-weſt of Cortachy, and forms part of the Grampian mountains. It is about 10 miles long, from E. to W. and 7 broad. There is no map of the pariſh; nor has the number of acres been aſcertained.

Soil

Soil and Surface.—The soil of these united parishes is in general poor, upon a cold and wettish bottom. The haugh ground, on the banks of the Esk, is an open light soil, in many places interspersed with, or bordering on, peat moss. The greatest part of these parishes is mountainous, and calculated only for pasture. The hills in Cortachy are chiefly covered with heath, with a small mixture of rough grass along their sides. Those in Clova are, in general, green, producing excellent grass, and well adapted for sheep. In some places the hills are steep and rocky, and almost all of them abound with large whin-stone.

Climate and Diseases.—The air is sharp and piercing, particularly on the high grounds. That part of the united parishes, which is situated among the Grampian hills, is, in winter, generally covered with snow to a great depth, which often is not all dissolved before the months of June and July. The climate is favourable to health, and many of the inhabitants live to the age of 70 and 80 years. The most prevalent distempers are rheumatism and fevers, which are probably occasioned by the variations of the weather.

River, Lakes, and Fish.—The only river in the united parishes is the *Esk*. Originating among the Grampian hills, it passes through both parishes; and, after traversing a course of 16 miles to the eastward, empties itself into the sea at Montrose. It produces plenty of small trouts, but very few salmon; the latter being prevented from coming up by the number of cruives in the way. The only lakes deserving notice are *Loch Brandy* in the parish of Clova, and *Loch Churl* in the parish of Cortachy. They are situated on the north side of the Esk, nigh the summit of the Grampian hills, and are distant about 2 miles from each other. On the north side

they

they are bounded by a steep rock, and on the south they have outlets which communicate with the river below. Their form is circular, and they are about a mile and a half in circumference. These lakes abound with trouts of various sizes.

Hills.—The hills in these parishes are of a very considerable height, particularly those in Clova, which form part of the Grampians. They are partly conical, and partly almost perpendicular. The most romantic are those situated on the south-east end of the parish of Clova, and which, on the north and south side, encompass a beautiful valley about 4 miles in length, and half a mile in breadth. Here the stupenduous height of the mountain, contrasted with the delightful narrow plain below, exhibits a scene of grandeur and beauty united.

Quadrupeds and Birds.—The number of horses is about 400, and of black cattle 1200. The horses and cattle are generally of a small size. A horse of 5 years old brings, in the market, from 7 l. to 10 l. Sterling; a cow or ox, of 4 years old, from 4 l. to 6 l. The number of sheep may be about 8000 in summer, but fewer in winter. They are mostly of the black faced kind, bought, when a year old, in the Linton markets, in the months of June and July, and kept for four years. They are sold fat about Martinmas, to butchers, at the neighbouring markets. They bring from 12 s. to 16 s. a head. There are also white-faced sheep, but of a smaller size than the former. The number of swine in the parish is very small. The wild quadrupeds are deers, hares, and foxes. Of the winged tribe there are, besides tame fowl, muir fowl, wild ducks, partridges, and tarmacks.

Agriculture.

Agriculture.—Almost the only cultivated part of these united parishes, except what lies on the southern extremity, is that lying along the banks of the Esk, about 14 miles long and half a mile broad. The rest is hilly, or laid out for pasture. Considerable improvement of late has been made in agriculture, particularly in the lower part of the parish of Cortachy. Here the farmer observes a proper rotation in cropping; and the fields, after 3 years tillage, are sown out with grass seeds for 4 years. In the middle and upper districts of these united parishes, where sheep and cattle are the staple commodity, improvement in agriculture is not so much attended to; nor is the climate so favourable for raising corn as in the lower parts. If here the farmer can raise as much grain as will suffice for meal and seed, he seldom seeks farther, and trusts to his profits from sheep and cattle to pay his rents. The only manure on the parish is that which is made by the cattle on the farms. Some farmers, for the sake of improvement, drive marl from the loch of Kinordy, in the parish of Kirriemuir, which is about three miles distant from the southern boundary of the parish of Cortachy. Such of the farmers in the parish as can procure marl, are enabled to bring their farms into a state of high cultivation, and to raise excellent crops; but this species of manure can only be acquired by a few of them, by reason of their great distance from it.

The English plough has lately been introduced here; but that chiefly used is the Scotch plough. The harrow and cart used are of the common construction; the latter generally drawn by two horses. A good plough costs from 40 s. to 50 s.; a cart from 6 l. to 7 l.; and a harrow about 10 s. *

Crops,

---

* A ploughman, maintained in the family, receives, for wages, from 6 l. to 8 l. *per annum.* A labouring man, hired
per

Crops, Seed-time, & Harvest.—Thefe united parifhes produce oats, barley, peafe, flax, and potatoes. Turnips, white and red clover and rye-grafs, are feldom fown, except in the vicinity of Cortachy, which lies on the fouthern extremity of the parifh. The time of fowing oats generally commences about the 24th of March, and ends about the 24th of April. Barley fowing begins about the 8th of May, and ends about the 24th. Harveft is generally begun about the middle of September, and concluded by the firft of November. There is little grain exported from this parifh even in the moft fruitful feafons. The crops are feldom fufficient to fupport the inhabitants ; and often the farmers, in the upper diftricts, are under the neceffity of buying feed corn. Here the principal dependence of the farmer is on his fheep and cattle *.

Wood, Fuel, and Minerals.—The only natural wood in the parifh is allar, birch, hazel, and willow, which are to be found, in a few places, in fmall clumps along the banks of the Efk. There is only one fir plantation, deferving notice, lying near the

per day, receives from 8 d. to 10 d. with victuals ; and if hired during the harveft feafon, he earns from 20 s. to 25 s. A mafon, per day, gets from 18 d. to 20 d. and maintains himfelf. A taylor receives 8 d. with his maintainance ; a maid fervant, 3 l. *per annum;* and a carpenter, including victuals, 1 s. per day.

* The value of grain and provifions is very much regulated by the prices given in Kirriemuir, the neareft market town to this united parifh. Their value alfo is according to their plenty or fcarcity ; but, on an average, the following may be confidered as the prices of grain and provifions in this parifh. Hay brings from 5 d. to 7 d. per ftone, barley from 15 s. to 16 s. per boll, and oats from 13 s. to 15 s. A ftone of flax gives from 10 s. to 13 s. ; peafe, from 13 s. to 14 s. per boll ; potatoes, from 5 s. to 6 s. The average price of beef and mutton is 3 d. per lib. cheefe 4 d. butter 9 d. ; the laft two articles have 27 ounces to the pound weight. A hen is fold at 10 d. a chicken at 3 d. and a duck at 7 d.

the fouthern extremity of the parifh of Cortachy.   Around
the Caftle of Cortachy, one of the feats of the Earl of Airley,
there are various kinds of foreft trees, as afh, elm, larch,
plain, beech, &c. Adjoining the Caftle, there is a large garden, abounding with feveral fpecies of fruit trees, befides a
hot-houfe for peach, nectarine, and vine trees. There are
feveral moffes in the united parifhes, moft of them fituated
near the fummit of the hills.   Peats, turf, and heath, are the
principal fuel.   The only ftone here, found fit for building,
is whin-ftone; but it cannot be dreffed with an iron.

Population, &c.—The number of the inhabitants has decreafed nearly a fixth part, within thefe 40 years *.

The return to Dr Webfter, in 1755, was	1233
The number of fouls, at prefent, is - -	1020
Decreafe	213

Of thefe there are,

Males	490	Weavers	7
Females	530	Millers	3
Farmers	76	Shop-keepers	3
Sub-tenants	81	Shoemaker	1
Smiths	3	Gardeners	4
Carpenters	4	Ale & whifky fellers	10
Annual average of births - - -			22
————————— marriages - - -			7
————————— deaths - - -			15
Inhabited houfes - - - - -			218
Plough-gates - - - - - -			79

Pro-

* This decreafe has been chiefly owing to the thriving ftate
of manufactures in the feveral cities and villages of the county,
and to the higher wages given in the more inland parts.

Proprietors and Rent.—The Proprietors of the united pa‑ rishes are the Earl of Airley, and his brother the Hon. Wal‑ ter Ogilvy of Clova.

Ecclesiastical State.—There are two churches in the united parishes; the one in Clova, the other at Cortachy. The dis‑ tance between them is about 9 miles. Worship is performed in both on stated Sundays. The church in Clova was rebuilt in the year 1730, and is capable of containing 200 persons. The church of Cortachy was built about 300 years ago, and contains about 300 persons. The present state of the church of Cortachy, shews it to have undergone some reparation. One third of it is excellent workmanship, being of cut stone, nicely compacted; the remaining part is coarse, and seems to be of much later date. The value of the stipend, includ‑ ing a glebe of 6 acres, is 16 bolls of meal, 800 merks of mo‑ ney, and 20 merks for providing the communion elements. The manse was built about 50 years ago, and has been frequently repaired. Mr CHARLES GORDON, ordained in February 1774, is now minister of the united parishes. The family of Airley are patrons.

School and Poor.—The parochial school was rebuilt in the year 1785. The schoolmaster's salary is 100 merks, with a house and garden. The number of scholars in winter is be‑ tween 50 and 60, but much fewer in summer. The fees for teaching are 1 s. per quarter for English; 1 s. 6 d. for writing, and 2 s. for arithmetic. The Latin language is not taught. The value of the office, including the emoluments arising from the dues of baptisms, certificates of marriages, and session-clerk's fees, may be estimated at 17 l. Sterling. —Seven persons, on an average, receive aid from the paro‑ chial funds. The weekly collection in the church, amount‑ ing

ing to about 10 l. *per annum*, fines exacted from delinquents, dues paid for the use of the mort-cloth, the annual rent of two galleries, one in each church, together with the interest of 130 l laid out by the kirk-session, are the principal funds whence the poor are supplied.

General Character, &c.—The inhabitants are frugal and industrious, and enjoy, in a reasonable degree, the comforts and advantages of society. They are not fond of a military or sea-faring life. They seem contented with their situation and circumstances, and are regular in their attendance on the ordinances of public worship. There is no surgeon or law-yer in the united parish ; and the inhabitants are all of the established religion, except 4 families of Episcopalians.

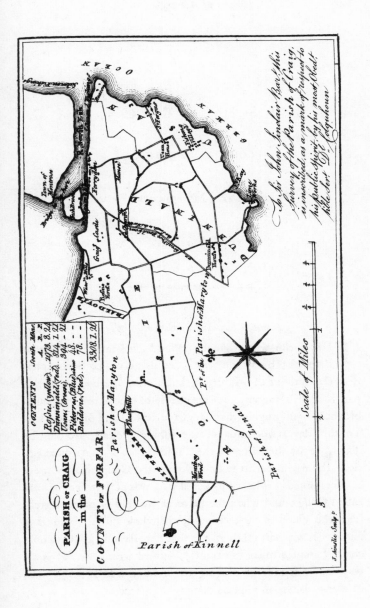

PARISH OF CRAIG
in the
COUNTY OF FORFAR

CONTENTS
Scotch Meas.
A. R. R.
Rosie (yellow)......... 2073. 8. 24
Dunninald (red)....... 824. 1. 22
Usan (green).......... 394. — 21
Pitterre (blue)....... 48. — —
Baldvie (red)......... 78. — —
                      ————————
                      3308. 1. 2½

To Sir John Sinclair Bar. this
Survey of the Parish of Craig,
is inscribed, as a mark of respect to
his public spirit, by his most Obed.t
hble. Serv.t D.r Colquhoun

Scale of Miles

Parish of Kinnell

Parish of Maryton

P.t of the Parish of Maryton

Parish of Lunan

J. Ainslie Sculp.t

GERMAN OCEAN

PARISH OF CRAIG.

(COUNTY OF ANGUS.)

By the Rev. MR. JAMES PATON.

With a MAP.

———————————

Name, Situation, Extent, &c.

THIS parish was originally called Inch-Brayoick, or Inch-Broyock; by which name, an island of 34 Scots acres, near the harbour of Montrose, but within the bounds of this parish, is still known. It is probably of Gaelic origin; Inch-broyock, signifying, in that language, the Island of Trouts.——To this day, two-thirds of the fishing ground, around the island, go by the name of the Trout-shot.———At what period, the parish began to be denominated Craig, cannot now be ascertained. The continental part was perhaps commonly called Craig; and when the place of worship was transferred, from the island to the continent, the whole might obtain that name. It was natural to give it that appellation, as the whole coast, (about 4 miles in extent,) is lined with rock. It is always to be found, by digging the ground a little way; and, in many places, in appears above the surface.

This

This parish is situated in the presbytery of Brechin, in the synod of Angus and Mearns, and shire of Forfar. It is between 5 and 6 miles long, and its greatest breadth is somewhat more than 2. To the south and west it is considerably elevated, being about 400 feet above the level of the sea. It contains, in all, 3308 : 1 : 26 acres, Scots measure ; the whole of which (a few hundred acres excepted) is arable. The soil is, in general, very good, and produces excellent crops.

Rivers, High Grounds.—The Southesk, after crossing a bason of water, about 8 or 9 miles in circumference, (which is filled by the tide twice every 24 hours) divides this parish from that of Montrose. It afterwards falls into the sea, at the eastern extremity of this parish.——On the coast, Dunninald is the highest ground, Govanhill in the middle, and Pittaris hill, and Mount-Bay to the West ; from all which there are very extensive and pleasant prospects. Mount-Bay was formerly called the King's seat, Red-castle, in the neighbourhood, having formerly been a royal residence.

Climate, Diseases, Mineral Springs, &c.—The air, in a situation so elevated, is pure ; the climate generally healthy.—The most common diseases are fevers and consumptions ; there are some instances of dysenteries, and rheumatisms ; agues are very rare, and there are some few cases of epilepsy and of lunacy. A singular kind of distemper, called the *louping ague,* has sometimes made its appearance in this parish. The patients, when seized, have all the appearances of madness ; their bodies are variously distorted ; they run, when they find an opportunity, with amazing swiftness, and over dangerous passes ; and, when confined to the house, they jump, and climb in an astonishing manner, till their strength be exhausted.— Cold bathing is found to be the most effectual remedy.——
There

There is a spring in Roffie, strongly impregnated with iron; which is drank, and, it is said, with good effect, by persons of relaxed habits.

Tides and Fisheries.——The course of the tide, on this coast, is north and south, the flood coming from the north. ——In this parish, there are two pretty large fishing villages, Ferryden and Usan; the first, contains about 38 families, and the other 20; all of whom are fishermen, or persons connected with them. Those of Ferryden employ six boats, 4 men to each boat; and, in the summer season, 3 barks for the coal trade. The fishermen of Usan have 3 boats, and 6 men to each boat. Last war, about 24 men from these villages, and the rest of the parish, served on board his Majesty's navy, and a few in the army.——The fish caught on the coast are cod, ling, haddocks, skate, flounders, and turbot. There is also great abundance of muscles, lobsters, and crabs. The common price of white fish here, may be calculated at 3 farthings per pound. The salmon fishings on the Southesk, belonging to two proprietors in this parish, were formerly very productive. Those of Roffie, some seasons, yielded 10,000 salmon, and grilses; but, since the year 1781, they have fallen off greatly. The barrel of salmon sold, 20 years ago, for about 3 guineas, and the fresh salmon for 2s. per Dutch stone; but, of late, the prices have increased to near double.——A few years ago, a quantity of oysters were brought from the Firth of Forth, and put down in a place where they were likely to breed. But, there is some reason to suspect, though the point is not yet ascertained, that oysters cannot thrive in the neighbourhood of muscles.

Progress of Improvement.——About 60 years ago, this parish was, in a great measure, open, scarcely a single field being inclosed.

inclosed. The late Mr Scott of Dunninald, and his brother, Mr Scott of Rossie, were the first who began to inclose their property, in 1730. Thorn hedges and hedge-row trees were first tried; but this mode being found tedious and expensive, earthen fences, with furze or whins on the top, were adopted. But these, after a trial of many years, being found insufficient, the gentlemen have begun to inclose with stone dykes, or walls; and, if they persevere, with the same spirit with which they have begun, (which there is every reason to believe will be the case,) in a few years, the whole fields of the parish will be inclosed in that manner.

Roads.——Formerly, the king's high-way, which passes through this parish, was very insufficient, and, in the winter season, almost impassable. But, about the year 1750, by the application of the statute labour, an excellent road betwixt Ferryden and Arbroath was begun, and in a few years completed. This year, a new turnpike road, a little to the west of the other, through this parish, was begun, (by a tract more circuitous indeed, but deemed to be more level, and commodious for travellers,) and will soon be finished. By means of the statute labour, now generally commuted, we begin to enjoy good private roads, of which we stood in great need.

Wood.—About the beginning of this century, there was little wood in this corner; but within these 70 or 80 years, a good deal has been planted, and the parish may now be said to be pretty well wooded; particularly in the waste part of it, where a great many acres have been inclosed and planted.

Agriculture.—About 60 years ago, Messrs. Scotts began gradually to make considerable improvements in the cultivation of their lands. They had plenty of lime within the parish;

rish; but several years elapsed, before the rest of the country began to follow their example. Of late, however, still farther improvements have been made, particularly by a quicker rotation of green crops: The lands are kept in better heart, and produce more plentiful crops than formerly.

Price of Land, and Rent.—Rather better than a century ago, Patrick Scott, Esq. bought, (with the exception of two small pieces of property,) the whole parish, for about L. 10,000 sterling; and, within these 8 years, that property, viz. Rossie, including Craig, and Dunninald, exclusive of the estate of Usan, was sold for L. 64,000.————About the year 1730, the average rent of land here, was about 4s 6d. whereas all the farms, let within these few years, give from L. 1 : 5 to L. 1 : 10, per acre.——The valued rent of the whole parish, is L. 4275 : 4 : 1 Scots. The real rent, including the produce of lime, and of salmon fishings, is above L. 4000 sterling.

Services.——The meagre look, the tattered garment, the wretched hovel, the ill-cultivated and unproductive field, with the other miserable effects of feudal tyranny, and the sure effects of personal services, are curses, from which this part of the country, has long since been generally delivered. The only relict of this kind here, is, the thirlage to a mill, to which the tenants, upon one of the estates are subjected; but which is soon to be removed.

Ferry Boats.—By the register of the kirk-session here, it appears, that, upon the sabbath day, especially in time of public worship, no boats were permitted to cross at Ferryden.—— Whereas now, they are more employed on that, than on any other day of the week;—the liberty of modern times having assumed, or being allowed, a slacker rein.

Castles

Castles and Forts.—There were, in this parish, two castles, that of Black Jack on the sea shore, formerly the residence of the family of Dunninald, of which, by the falling of the rock, there are hardly any remains ; and the castle of Craig, which was demolished not many years ago. At the extremity of the parish, to the east, where the Southesk falls into the sea, there are the remains of an earthen fort, in the form of a square ; each side of which was about 50 feet ; the walls 16 feet thick, and, formerly, as high, or higher than a man's head. With-in, there was a house for the purpose of affording shelter to the men, and holding stores or ammunition. Without the square, and facing the mouth of the river, there was a breast-work of earth, where cannon had been planted to defend the entrance of the river. Tradition reports, that it had been made use of in Oliver Cromwell's time ; but whether erected by him, or in more ancient times, cannot now be ascertained. At this fort some cannon were placed so late as the 1745.— About 20 years ago, the town of Montrose built within this square a quadrangular tower, between 20 and 30 feet high, for a land-mark, to direct vessels at sea ; and, along the south side of the river, at a small distance from one another, two conical towers, or pillars, were lately erected by that town, for directing vessels, when to take the river with safety.

Population.——There has been a regular and progressive in-crease, in the population of this parish, for these many years past. About a century ago, the number of souls was about 676. It rose, in 1738 to 806. The report to Dr Webster, in 1755, was 935. In 1768, the number was 1264, and, on the 24th of February 1791, it came to 1314. Of which there were,

Under

Under 10 years of age	-		-	359
Between 10 and 10	-	-	-	227
——— 20 and 30	-		-	214
——— 30 and 50	-		-	299
——— 50 and 70	-		-	170
——— 70 and 80	-	-	-	31
——— 80 and 90, and upwards			-	14

Total 1314

Excepting one man, who is about 91 years of age, no perfon, in this parifh, exceeds 86. The number of males is 639, of females, 675. The number of families, 302. Prior to 1693, the average of births was about 26; about 1738, they rofe to 31. More recently, the births, deaths, and marriages were as follows :

Years	Births	Deaths	Marriages.
1768	52	25	13
1778	50	16	13
1788	45	25	16
Average of thefe years 49		22	14

Poor.---The average amount of collections for the poor, from the year 1653 to 1758, inclufive, was about 2s 10d. per week. In the year 1760, when the prefent incumbent was fettled, there was only about L. 83 laid out at intereft. The collections have fince increafed confiderably, and, for fome years paft, have been, at a medium, 12s weekly.———Some years ago, the funds received, from Alexander Arbuthnot, Efq. Commiffioner of the cuftoms at Edinburgh, an addition of L. 100, and lately, from a proprietor of this parifh, L. 50. Thefe fums, together with former favings, amount now to L. 200, properly fecured at an intereft of 5 per cent.

The

The number of weekly pensioners is 12. The weekly pension is 12s. 9d. besides considerable sums given from time to time, to other poor, not upon the list, and the purchase of coals for all the poor annually. It may here be remarked, that, besides the private benefactions of residing heritors to the poor, they derive much benefit from the circumstance of such families being of our own communion, and attending the established church, which has generally been the case, for a century past. During 40 years, and upwards, no poor have had occasion or been allowed to beg; the parish being both able and willing to maintain its own poor. Many, however, are apt to give liberally to strolling vagrants, or sturdy beggars who infest this district and the neighbourhood; an evil severely felt, and which stands much in need of an effectual remedy.

Church, Patronage, &c.—The patrons are the masters of the new College of St. Andrew's. The manse was built about the year 1748; the offices in the year 1774; and an excellent garden wall, in 1788. The manse is inconveniently situated; being distant from the church about a mile. The stipend is L. 48 : 4 : 5$\frac{4}{12}$, with 3 chalders victual, half meal, and half bear. The glebe consists of 7 acres, including houses and garden. The church was repaired, and almost new built, in the year 1760. There were, in popish times, 4 burial places in the parish. The principal one, at present, is in the island of Inchbrayock.—The inhabitants belong, with very few exceptions, to the established church; in 1788, there were only 6 Seceders, and 16 Episcopalians.

School.—Very lately, a substantial and elegant house was built for the schoolmaster; and his yearly salary was raised, within these few years, from L. 8 to L. 20; the school fees, and other perquisites, may amount to L. 20 more. Adjoining

ing to his house, is a school-house, sufficiently large and commodious, with a small garden.

Manufactures.——In the manufacturing line, there is nothing carried on here to any great extent. The reasons may be, that the great object of pursuit, in this district, is agriculture, and that the situation of the parish, much elevated and remote from rivers, does not furnish the water that would be requisite for extensive bleachfields, and for the operations of mills. There are, however, 36 weavers including apprentices, 6 carpenters, 4 masons, 4 smiths, with a few servants of each class; 2 slaters; and one baker.

Miscellaneous Observations.—The good and justly celebrated Bishop Leighton was of the family of Usan, in this parish. Only one man, with his family, has emigrated from the district, for these some years past. The cause of this was, not oppression, nor want of employment, nor poverty unaided; (for none of these evils are felt here,) but the spirit, which prevailed at the time, and the delusive hope of gaining much with little labour.——There are, in this parish, in wheat, oats, barley, pease, flax, turnips, potatoes, and cabbages, about 2700 acres. Number of horses, 183; of black cattle, 804; of sheep, 1013.—There are 6 houses for vending ale and spirits, in one of which only ale is brewed. The practice of smuggling foreign spirits, from which this coast is not yet free, is productive of much loss to the public, and of many evils to individuals.

Advantages and Disadvantages.—One advantage arises from the nearness of the parish to Montrose, where the inhabitants can purchase what they want, and sell what they have to dispose of, with little loss of time; and, when the bridge is
built

built over the Southesk, (with the near prospect of which we are now flattered,) the communication will be much easier, and attended with many additional conveniences.——Another advantage is the easy access which the farmers have to lime. At Bodden, in this parish, there is a lime-work carried on to great extent ; and, to that spot, all the improvements in husbandry, made in this country, is, in a great measure owing. The greatest disadvantage, is the high price of coals, owing to the heavy duty, which takes place here. This tax is much complained of, as evidently partial, imoplitic, and unreasonable. A small duty laid at the pit, would yield much more to government than the present one ; and the burden being laid equally upon all, would be much more easily borne, and could scarcely be objected to, on any just and reasonable grounds.

PARISH OF DUN.

(*County of Forfar.*)

By the Rev. Mr JAMES LAUDER.

Situation, &c.

THE parish of Dun is situated in the county of Angus, sheriffdom of Forfar, and presbytery of Brechin. It is very near in the middle between the towns of Brechin and Montrose; is about 4 miles in length, and as much in breadth; is bounded on the west by the parish of Brechin, and on the east by that of Montrose. Between these two, there is an excellent high-road, kept in good repair by the gentlemen and tenants, so that at present it has no need of turnpikes. It is bounded on the south by the parishes of Maryton and Kinnaird, which last is now annexed to that of Farnel, and on the north by the parishes of Strickathrow and Logie.

Church, &c.—The kirk is within Mr Erskine's inclosures. It appears antiently to have been a chapel belonging to the family of Dun, the mansion-house of the family having been built very near to the church-yard. The glebe, I think, consists of little more than 5 acres, very good arable land. The stipend may amount to between 72 l. and 80 l. *communibus annis*, as a great part is paid in victual. The church is in

good

good repair ; it has two lofts, one to the eaſt, the other to the weſt. The eaſt end of the church is ſtiled the choir, and has a fount in the wall, intended, of old, for baptiſm.

Name, &c.—The name of *Dun* ſeems to be taken from the proprietor, who was called Dun of that ilk. It is ſaid that one of the name of Erſkine married the heireſs ; but when that happened, is difficult to ſay, as it is known only by family tradition. Others derive the name from the Gaelic *Dunis*, which ſignifies, in that language, a *hill* or riſing ground ; and it is indeed on a ground pretty much elevated above the river South Eſk, or ſouth water ; for *Eſk* is ſaid, in Gaelic, to ſignify *water*. There is a very elegant bridge over the river, conſiſting of three large arches, finely orna-mented. It was built in the 1787, and opens an eaſy and ſafe paſſage over the river, which was formerly very dange-rous ; and many lives were loſt, by venturing to croſs it when in flood, or covered with ice. There is a good ſalmon fiſhing upon the river, which abounds with trouts of various kinds, viz. ſmouts, which appear in the month of May, and continue till the end of June. They are thought by ſome to be ſalmon fry, the catching of which has been prohibited by thoſe who have the ſalmon fiſhings in leaſe. There are likewiſe plenty of ſea trouts, about 12, 18, or 20 inches in length ; beſides a trout called a finneck, which appears in the months of July and Auguſt, and diſappears towards the end of September. There are alſo many other kinds of trouts, which ſeem to be paſſengers, as they appear only at certain ſeaſons of the year.

Soil and Produce.—The lands upon the river ſide conſiſt of a clay ſoil, and produce excellent wheat and barley. There are about 30 bolls of wheat ſown in the pariſh, beſides

great

great quantities of barley, oats, and peafe. Potatoes are commonly planted about the middle of April, and turnips about the middle of June. Some farmers feed cattle with turnips, which turn out to very good account, as there is a great demand for butcher meat, the parifh being fituated in the neighbourhood of the two populous towns of Montrofe and Brechin. There are but few fheep kept in this diftrict, (as they are thought prejudicial to the fown grafs and hay), excepting fuch as are neceffary for the ufe of the inhabitants.

School.—There is one public fchool in the parifh. The legal falary of the fchoolmafter is only 100 merks, too fmall encouragement to obtain a properly qualified perfon for that office; and therefore the heritors, minifter, and principal tenants in the parifh, have fubfcribed a certain fum in addition to the legal falary, in order to make up a tolerable living for the fchoolmafter.

Population.—The number of parifhioners, in the year 1750, by the late incumbent's examination roll, amounted to 506. Afterwards they increafed greatly; for in the years 1760, and 1766, they amounted to 640. But after that period, when many fmall farms were converted into one, the numbers decreafed, and at prefent do not exceed 500 fouls. In Dr Webfter's lift, the number is 657. There is a regifter of marriages, births, and burials, kept, an extract of which, for ten years paft, is as follows:

Years.	Marriages.	Births.		Burials.
		mal.	fem.	
1781	4	9	7	31
1782	8	13	12	15
1783	4	5	10	18
1784	3	7	12	17
1785	3	8	5	23
1786	7	16	9	9
1787	5	3	5	18
1788	5	3	5	15
1789	4	8	7	18
1790	9	8	6	10
	—	—	—	——
	52	80	78	174

Antiquities.—On the height, to the weft of the manfe, there were two tumuli of earth, covered over with ftones. When the tenant cleared off the ftones, and digged to level his field, he found feveral urns of potter's clay figured, in which were afhes and pieces of bones. There is likewife, a little farther to the north weft, a pretty large tumulus, wherein there were alfo found feveral urns of the fame kind, with afhes and bones in them.

Poor.—None are allowed to beg in the parifh. The poor's funds, together with the weekly collections, are fufficient to fupply them.

TOWN AND PARISH OF DUNDEE.

(County of Forfar.—Preſbytery of Dundee.—Synod of Angus and Mearns.)

By the Rev. ROBERT SMALL, *D. D. one of the Miniſters of that City.*

Origin of the Name.

THE modern name of the pariſh is Dundee, from the large town ſituated in it. This name, formerly, and even ſo late as the beginning of the preſent century, was generally ſpelled *Dondè* or *Dondie* ; and in Queen Mary's charter *Dondei*, in law-Latin it is *Deidonum* ; and it has been affirmed by various Highlanders, that they conſider it as ſignifying, what this Latin imports, the Gift, or otherwiſe, the Hill of God. Theſe circumſtances give probability to the tradition, that it obtained the name, about the middle of the 12th century, from David Earl of Huntingdon, who landing here, after a dreadful ſtorm in his return from the holy wars, deſigned by it to expreſs his gratitude for his deliverance ; and, in conſequence of a vow, built the preſent pariſh church. Had the ſignification been the hill of Tay, as *Taodunum*, according to Buchanan, it would in Gaelic have been pronounced *Duntaw*. The ancient name was *Alec*, in Boece's Latin, *Alectum*

Alectum, and by this it is diftinguifhed in the highlands. The fignification of *Alec* is faid to be pleafant or beautiful. The language fpoken by the inhabitants, has. from time immemorial, been the broad Scotch ; that is Englifh or Saxon, with a peculiar provincial accent. The names of places in the parifh are partly in this language, and partly G elic. Of the former kind are *Blacknefs*, *Coldfide*, *Clepingtown* and *Claypots*. *Balgay*, *Dudhope*, *Drumgeith*, *Duntroon*, *Baldovie*, and various others are examples of the latter.

Situation, *Extent*, *&c.*—The parifh of Dundee is fituated in the county of Angus, now called, in writings, Forfarfhire, from the county town. The length from W. to E. is about 6 miles, but its breadth is various ; for, towards the weft end, it is nearly two miles, towards the middle, where the town ftands, not more than one, and towards the eaft end, between three and four *. The territory of the parifh belongs to a

great

* As there is no map of the parifh, it is hardly poffible to communicate an intelligible defcription of its form. The ridge of mountains, which runs from Perth to the eaft promontory of Angus, called the Red Head, feparating between this country and Strathmore, is well known, being a continuation of the Ochil Hills ; and in the parts where it approaches neareft to the parifh of Dundee, it is named the Siedlaw Hills, and Lorn's Hill. While thefe m untains run along the Carfe of Gowrie, no new range rifes between them and the Tay, and there the country is flat, and almoft level; but, where the Carfe terminates near Millfield, a new range rifes of lower hills, running from Balgay Hill on the weft, to the Knock-Hills near Arbroath on the eaft, where it forms the fouth boundary of a fort of vale or ftrath, contained between them and the ridge of Siedlaw and Lorn, &c. on the north. In this vale, no fingle great river runs, but it is watered by feveral ftreams, which defcend from the northern ridge, and, after traverfing various parts of the vale, make their way through the lower range into the ay. On part of this lower range of hills, and chiefly on their fouthern expofure, the parifh of Dundee is fituated ; towards the eaft end it is interfected by Dighty and Fiethy, the principal of all the ftreams which

run

great variety of proprietors. The valued rent of the whole
is, 7874 l. 3 s. 2 d. Scotch. The real rent abstracting from
the houses and gardens in the town, is probably between
8,000 l. and 9,000 l. Sterling. The number of Scottish acres,
under culture, is about 3,400, and in plantation, about 300.
The principal estates in the parish are those of Dudhope, with
the other lands belonging to Lord Douglas, Craigie, Drumgeith, Baldovie, Pitkerro, Duntroon, Clepingtown, Wallace,
Blackness, Upper Dudhope, Logie, and Balgay. None of
these except the Duntroon and Douglas estates, have been
above 100 years in possession of the family of its present proprietors. In most of the others, the property has been fluctuating ; and, the average term of possession is rated sufficiently high at 20 years. Logie, Blackness, and Balgay, are
said to be in the parish, only *quoad sacra*.

Situation of the Town.—From the south side of Balgay Hill,
a small stream springs, which, running eastward, is joined by
another on the west side of the Law ; and both together continue their course south east, through a narrow low ground,
till,

run from the higher ridge ; and on the north, and also partly on the east, another of them, the Burn of Murroes, is the boundary which separates it from
Murroes, and Moneyfieth. The parish however, is not mountainous, for the
Law of Dundee, the highest hill in the whole range, is only 525 feet above the
level of the Tay. Balgay Hill, to the west of the Law, is considerably lower ;
and the ground of Craigie, to the east of it, excepting at one point, is a gently
rising bank. The appearance of the country is beautiful, particularly the south
slope of all the grounds towards the Tay, the south slope of Duntroon Hill towards Fiethy, and the bottom where Dighty and Fiethy meet, and where they
are soon after joined by the Burn of Murroes. Balgay Hill, besides its beautiful
form, is covered with a thriving plantation of various trees ; and the Law of
Dundee, rising gently from some low grounds behind the town, is cultivated
through its whole ascent, till at last it shoots into a round, green, and uncommonly pleasing summit.

till, after dividing the town of Dundee, nearly in the middle, they fall into the Tay. Another small stream, called Wallace Burn, rises on the north of the Law, and running east, and then south, falls into the Tay at the east end of the royalty, and at the distance of a quarter of a mile from the mouth of the former. Between these two, on the sea-shore, and on a low flat ground, the ancient town of Dundee is said to have been situated. It seems to have consisted of two parallel streets, the Seagate, and on the north of it the Cowgate. In the broadest part of the Seagate, remains of the ancient cross were some years ago to be seen ; and, by marks in the present causeway, its situation is still distinguished. West from the mouth of the first stream, the ground rises into rocks, which are from 50 to 90 feet above the level of the Tay. On one of these, the ancient castle stood, and on the grounds lying among them, and declining towards the east and south from them, the more modern and largest part of the town is situated. When the great church was built by David Earl of Huntingdon, a great part of the grounds was probably in a state of cultivation, and the ordinary designation of the church was for a long time *the Kirk in the field*. From these rocks, the ground continues to rise all the way west to Balgay-Hill, and forms a sort of ridge, bounded on the south by the Tay, and on the north by the Balgay stream. The valley, where the stream runs, is exceedingly beautiful ; and few situations can be conceived more delightful, than those of the castle of Dudhope, and the house of Logie to the north of the valley; of the house of Balgay, at its western extremity; or of Blackness on the ridge on the south of it. On this ridge, the late additions to the town have chiefly been built, and they extend along the summit, and on both sides of it, near to Blackness itself. Other considerable additions have, however, been also made in other quarters, particularly at the east end of the royalty,

beyond

beyond the low ground, on the north of it, and on the east
of the ancient suburb known by the name of the *Bonnet-
Hill.* The point of the principal pier in the harbour, is in
56°. 27'. 23''. of latitude, and in 3°. 2'. 55''. of longitude, west
from Greenwich, or in time 12'. 11'. The latitude may be
considered as accurate, being the result of a great variety of
observations made with a good Hadley's Quadrant, both in
the meridian and other circles of altitude, at a place judged
to be in the same parallel with the point now mentioned ; but
the conclusion for the longitude, is calculated only from a few
lunar eclipses, and by geoditical deductions from the meridian
of Hawk-Hill near Edinburgh.

Soil.——In a parish so extensive, there must be a considerable variety of soil. Little of it, however, is naturally rich,
The rising ground, in particular, which runs west from the
town towards Blackness, was originally thin and poor, with a
gravelly bottom, and the surface was covered, probably, for a
long time, with heath. About Blackness, the soil continues
equally thin, and the bottom is of till. But, to the north of
Blackness, particularly on the east end of the Hill of Balgay,
the soil is deeper, and consists of a rich black earth. Except
about the old castle of Dudhope, and on the low grounds behind
the town of Dundee, the soil of the Law is poor, with a bottom of till. The ground to the eastward of the Law, though
better, is not remarkably rich ; a good part of Craigie, which
consists of the best of it, was moor not 30 years ago, and the
bottom is generally till. To the eastward of Craigie, the soil,
in some farms of the Douglas estate, becomes better, and in-
clines to clay. The best land is in the bottom, where Dighty and Fiethy meet. It includes part of Baldovie and Drum-
gieth, and seems to be a deposit from these two *waters.* The
estate of Pitkerro, bounded on three sides by Fiethy, Dighty,
                                                         and

and the Burn of Murroes, confifts of a foil good and dry,
though rather thin, and the fouth bank of Duntroon is alfo
fertile. The worft land lies to the north of the hills of Balgay, Duntroon, and the Law But the neighbourhood of
this large town feems to place all thefe varieties of foil upon
a level. They are, in general, in a ftate of high cultivation,
and produce valuable crops. Inftead of large pieces of moor,
which, within the laft 30 years, were to be found every
where, there is hardly to be feen a fingle fpot. All is culture
or plantation, except a few acres of common, and very little
lies wafte through negleét.

Cultivation.—The number of people, who have farms, is
31 or 32. But of farmers, properly fo called, and who make
farming their only bufinefs, there are not more than 15. The
praétice of one of the moft induftrious and inteHigent, is as
follows. He rents 130 acres at 40 s. per acre : he keeps
conftantly 7 fervants, and 8 horfes ; he employs in fpring
3 ploughs, each wrought by 2 horfes, and in winter, 2
ploughs wrought by 4 ; and he ufes 4 caits, whofe dimenfions are 8 feet by 4. His land is laid out in 7 divifions cultivated in this rotation : 1 fallow, 2. wheat, 3. potatoes and
turnips horfe-hoed, 4. barley, 5. oats, with grafs feeds, 6. grafs,
chiefly fold green, and cut and carried off by the buyers, 7.
grafs cut for hay. In this rotation, the whole manure is
given to the wheat, and the fyftem feems to be approved of
by his neighbours, and generally adopted. He begins to fow
wheat in September, oats in March, barley in April, turnips
from the 10th to the middle of June ; and his crops of grain
are generally reaped in September. The reaping is wholly
performed by the fickle, and all the kinds of grain are bound
in fheaves, and, while on the field, fet up in fhocks. An acre
of good turnips fells from 7 l. to 10 l., according to the diftance
from

from the town. The buyer takes them up and carries them off the grounds, and none are fed off in the field. The potatoes are chiefly planted by Dundee manufacturers, who alſo clean them with hand hoes, and take them up, The farmer puts the ground in proper order for receiving them, and draws from 4 l. to 6 l. the acre. This practice is attended with the beſt effects, to the health and more eaſy ſubſiſtence of the manufacturer and his family; and to the farmer in clearing his land from weeds, which it does more effectually than any other method. An acre of good graſs, for green feeding, like the turnip, draws from 7 l. to 10 l. and even 12 l. The plough generally uſed is the improved Scotch one, though Small's plough begins alſo to be introduced. No threſhing machines have hitherto been employed, though there are many in various parts of the neighbouring country, and though one kind of them is ſpoken of with approbation. Probably the reaſon is, that we have no farms ſo large as to make them neceſſary, or to pay ſufficiently for the original expence. The corns, when brought off the field, are all ſtacked in the barn-yard, and generally raiſed about 3 feet above the ground, on wooden frames ſupported by ſtone pillars. Fanners have been, for a long time, the only inſtruments employed in winnowing. The principal manures, in addition to what every farm ſupplies, are dung from Dundee, and lime, chiefly from Sunderland. No ſervices are in this pariſh exacted from the farmers; and this oppreſſive cuſtom, though ſtill ſubſiſting in ſome other parts of Angus-ſhire, is here happily aboliſhed.

Cattle.—The greateſt part of the pariſh is incloſed with hedges and ſtone fences, but, except in ſome parts diſtant from the town, the incloſures are ſeldom uſed for paſture. The cattle of all kinds are good, but the pariſh is not remarkable for any peculiar breed. The farmers breed ſome horſes, but

by

by no means in number fufficient for the demands of the neighbourhood, or for their own labour. The market in Dundee,
for all kinds of butcher meat, is one of the beft in Scotland*.
No fheep are bred, or even fattened for fale, except a few by
Mr. Guthrie of Craigie. He has tried in his inclofures the
large fouth country breed, and endeavoured to introduce that
of Mr. Bakewell, with tolerable fuccefs. The birds aud quadrupeds, which are not domefticated, are the fame that frequent the other low country parifhes near the fea, and feem to
require no particular enumeration. No part of the parifh is
fubject to inundations, except the bottom where Fiethy and
Dighty join; but no confiderable damage is done, either to
the grounds, or to the crops upon them; and though the
equinoctial tides fometimes rife high, they have not, in any
perfon's memory, been hurtful.

Climate and Difeafes.—No part of the parifh can be called
unhealthy. The higher and weft part of the town of Dundee, and the whole ridge, on which the principal additions to
it have been built, is naturally as healthy a fituation, (from its
gravelly bottom, the conftant current of the tides, and its expofure to the S. W. winds,) as, perhaps, any in the world. E-
ven the fuburbs to the N. E. though on a bottom of till, are
healthy, for the declivity of the fituation prevents all ftagna-
tion of water. The low grounds behind the town are, indeed,

---

* The veal, in particular, has of late years become excellent, in confequence
of an improvement introduced, by a gentleman in the neighbourhood, in the
management of the calves. Inftead of confining them in low, dirty, and open
ftalls, they are placed in boxes raifed fome feet above the ground, by which
means they are more eafily kept clean, warm, and dry, and care is alfo taken
by giving a cover to every box, to exclude the light. In confequence of thefe
and fome other attentions, the veal equals, if not excells, the beft produced in
England.

deed, hitherto, but infufficiently drained, and the houfes to the fouth, which border on them, exhibit fome inconfiderable marks of dampnefs. But the principal caufes of unhealthinefs in Dundee, are the height of the houfes, the narrownefs of the tenements and of fome ftreets, by which the people were too much crowded upon one another. The bounds of the royalty were too confined for the increafing number of the inhabitants, and it was only within the laft 30 years, that they began to extend their buildings beyond its limits. But with all thefe defects, Dundee may be confidered as a very healthy place; the fmall-pox, indeed, is often epidemical and fatal, for inoculation is, hitherto, but imperfectly introduced; but fevers are feldom infectious, and agues almoft unknown. The crowded places of the town, indeed, are unfavourable to children, but probably not more fo than other crowded places; and as one evidence of its healthinefs, it may be mentioned, that in a diftrict containing 1800 inhabitants, only two perfons, in the fummer of 1789, were found confined to bed. Lefs rain falls here than at Perth, for, by the Carfe and Siedlaw hills to the north, and the Fife hills to the fouth, the clouds are attracted, and frequently carried away from this town and neighbourhood *. The village of the Ferry, in particular, at the eaft end of the parifh, near Broughty caftle, is uncommonly dry and wholefome, and, perhaps, better fitted for fea-bathing, than any other place on the eaft coaft of Scotland. The moft frequent endemial difeafes are confumptions and the fcrophula, by which laft, perhaps, the former are principally produced. The fcrophula feems chiefly to affect the families of linen-weavers, who fometimes feed poorly, and whofe manufacture is carried on in damp and low floors. We have no lake, or even pool of ftanding water

* No tradition or hiftory fpeaks of any damage done in Dundee by thunder, and probably the fituation and form of the Law is our fecurity, and enables it

to

water, except one, which is dry in fummer, and the declivity
of the ground in all places, fpeedily carries off the rain.

Foffils, Springs, &c.—Unlefs whin-ftone and porphyry
may be claffed among volcanic productions, nothing of this
kind has been difcovered. Thefe two, particularly the firft,
compofe the principal part of the hills and rifing grounds in
the parifh. The porphyry is chiefly on the lands of Balgay
and Blacknefs. There are, however, various quarries of
what we call free-ftone. This is much harder than the freeftone about Edinburgh, and is evidently ftratified. It is a
fand-ftone, and fometimes inclofes many pebbles, fuch as now
lie on all our fhores, and are rounded by the dafhing of the
waters. From the quarries of this kind in the neighbourhood,
and efpecially along the coaft, ftones for building in the town
are often taken. But the beft quarry, and what builders principally employ, is that of Kingoodie on the eftate of Mill-field,
in the parifh of Forgan ; and lighters bring the ftone immediately from the quarry. Though compofed of coarfer particles,

to act, in fome degree, as an electrical conductor. We have no water fpouts,
or whirlwinds, and, excepting the meteor, which, fome years ago, paffed along
the whole ifland no remarkable phænomena are remembered in the air. The
aurora borealis differs nothing from thofe in other places of Scotland, and, except during a fettled courfe of froft, it is generally followed by wind and rain
from the fouth. From a meteorological regifter, kept for fome years paft, by
Mr. Fairweather, a gentleman in the neighbourhood of the town, it appears, that
the annual average of rain, which fell from January 1783, to January 1792, is
22, 12 inches, or abftracting from the uncommonly rainy year of 1789, 21, 23,
that the average height of Faranheit's thermometer, for the months of June,
July, and Auguft, at two o'clock afternoon, was for the fame years 63, 85, and
for the months of December, January, and February, at 8 in the morning 34,
78. The houfe, where this regifter was kept, is fituated in the fouth expofure
of the bank below Blacknefs, and about 40 feet above the level of the Tay.

ticles, and incapable of being fo fmoothly polifhed as the
ftone from fome other quarries, particularly thofe of Craigie
and Invergourie, it is much more durable, and in many parts
of the great fteeple, built from it, in the 12th century, efpecially in the higher and more expofed parts, the marks of the
chiffel are ftill vifible. The colour is grey, inclining a little
to blue. Another fand-ftone of a redifh colour and fofter
texture, is found immediately weft from the town, and at high
water generally covered by the tide; but it is fo perifhable as
to be of little ufe. We have no figured ftones, no petrifac-
tions, no limeftone or marble, and no granite or other alpine
ftone, except a few loofe and detached pieces, which bear the
appearance of being rounded by water. A very fmall quantity of grey flate is found in the free-ftone quarries on the
lands of Craigie; but it is nothing different from the reft of
the quarry, except that it fplits into thinner ftrata. There
are no mines of any kind, nor any mineral fprings except
two, and thefe fo flightly tinged with iron, as hardly to deferve the name. Some excellent fprings break out near the
town, at the bottom of the Law, one efpecially called the *Lady Well*, whofe waters are conveyed in leaden pipes through
the different ftreets of the town, and fupply the greateft part
of it. The waters from moft of thefe, on boiling, leave a
ftony cruft on the veffels employed for that purpofe any confiderable time; but we have no fprings which, with propriety,
can be called petrifying.

Coaft Tides, &c.—The Tay is between 2 and 3 miles broad,
where it bounds the parifh, and it extends nearly along its utmoft length. The adjacent coaft is generally high and rocky.
At the weft end, along the lands of Balgay, it is perpendicular, and more than 40 feet high; along thofe of Blacknefs it
falls lower, till, in approaching the town, it becomes a precipice

pice of gravel, apt to be undermined by the sea, and encroached on by the wind. In all the tract of ground, west from the town, there are but one or two places where small vessels can come to land. The harbour of Dundee lies to the south of the rocks, on which the principal part of the town is situated; and here the ground slopes to the water more gently, and the harbour is capable of receiving vessels of 300 tons. Eastward from the flat ground, where the ancient part of the town was built, and along the estate of Craigie, the shore again becomes rocky, but in several places small vessels may come to land. Beyond this estate, the coast falls lower, excepting at one promontory called the *Hare Craigs*, and at the Ferry, near Broughty Castle, it becomes a flat *links*, with a fine gravelly beach, where larger vessels may safely approach. In the tides there is no peculiarity. As the current in the north sea flows south, we have high water about half an hour sooner than at Leith, and at the harbour the rise from low to high water is, in the highest streams, about 18 or 20 feet. Some rocks lie off the harbour, but, excepting 4, which have buoys, or beacons, they rise above the surface of the water. The current of the Tay, especially after land floods, is rapid. Many sand banks lie to the eastward between this harbour and Errol, and they are all on the north side of the river. The principal channel of the Tay is on the Fife shore, and it is only by this that vessels of any burden can go up to Perth or Newburgh. Continual incroachments are made by this river, on the low lands of the Carse of Gowrie, and the Inch of Mugdrum, opposite to Errol; and the soil which is washed away, comes down with the tide, and is deposited all along our shores, especially in the harbour. A bason, which they shut at high water, and open when the tide has left the harbour, was, for a long time, the only resource for clearing away the soil, which is thus deposited. The

same

fame method is ftill employed, but a more effectual one has lately been adopted, of opening arched paffages in fome of the piers. Through thefe the current moves rapidly, and prevents the foil from fettling ; and before this contrivance the harbour was in danger of being filled up. To the eaft of the harbour, all the way to Broughty Caftle, there is an excellent road for fhips of any burden, which can get within the bar, acrofs the mouth of the river. This is about 3 miles below Dundee, and as veffels can hardly attempt to crofs it, in a ftorm, many fhipwrecks happen on the coaft beyond it, when the ftorm is from the eaft, and the veffels are found too near the fhore. The principal fcene of thefe wrecks is St. Andrew's bay, and the coaft of Angus between Barry and Arbroath. Even within the bar, and till the veffels have paffed Broughty Caftle, the coafts on both fides are dangerous, confifting of flat fands.

River and Sea Productions.——The frefh water ftreams of Dighty, Fiethy, and the Burn of Muroes, have trouts in them, and Dighty has fome pikes, but no falmon ; except at the end of the fifhing feafon, when a few of what are called *foul fifh*, or *kelt*, are caught, and no fifh of almoft any other kind, except fome fea trout, after it leaves the parifh, to fall into the Tay at Menyfieth. Though the Tay abounds in falmon, there are but 4 or 5 fifhings on all our extent of coaft ; nor do almoft any white fifh, except a fpecies of flounders, called *frefh waters*, come within the bar. In the fands of the river we have a few fmall crabs ; one bank yields periwinkles ; fhrimps are caught on all of them, and fmelts in the channel, on the fhore of Fife, near Balmerino, where the water becomes lefs falt than at Dundee. In fome years, towards Auguft, large fhoals of porpoifes appear, and regularly go up and down with the tide, from the mouth of the river as far as Errol, in purfuit of falmon, but no method has hitherto been found of catching them. Seals are numerous, and alfo deftructive

to

to the falmon ; but various methods are practifed of catching
thefe ; and as they foon leave the places where they are once
difturbed, they are now feldom feen farther up than Monyfieth. The falmon, caught in the river, go principally to
the London market, frefh or pickled. To carry them frefh,
the method firft fuggefted by Mr. George Dempfter, of pack-
ing them in ice, has been found of the greateft confequence,
and is now conftantly adopted. The price of falmon here is
always regulated by that of the London market, and generally goes beyond it. Our falmon fifhings begin later than towards Perth, and confequently lefs is carried in a frefh ftate
to London. The rent of all the falmon fifhings in the river
probably exceeds 3000 l. annually ; but of this rent, thofe on
our fhores yield a very inconfiderable part. The currents of
the Tay being rapid, the channels of its waters are often
changed, and, confequently, in this part of the river the falmon often change their courfe, and the annual value of any
particular fifhing alters. A fifhing on the Fife fhore, oppofite to Broughty Caftle, was let in 1789, at no greater yearly
rent than 40 l. and in that year the tackfman is faid to have
cleared no lefs than 300 l. As the parifh is fituated a good way
within the bar of the river, we have no fea weed for manure.
Some kelp is made, but in fo fmall a quantity, that the fhores
yield no rent ; and any perfon who pleafes is allowed to burn
it. I know of no uncommon plants in the parifh, or any uncommon fhells upon its fhores ; neither fpunges nor corals
are to be found.

On the fea coaft, without the bar, great numbers of fea-
fifh are caught ; haddocks, whitings, cod, ling, plaice, dab,
flounders, foles, turbot, holibut, fkate, mackarel, and herrings.
Of thefe, the haddocks were the principal, and the moft readily bought up. They were fome years a goin fuch plenty, as
to be an important article of food for the common people ; but

for

for more than three years they have entirely left the coaft.
They were always in feafon, except from February to May.
The cod and ling are not plentiful, and they are inferior in
quality to thofe taken farther north. The mackarel and herrings come from beyond Fife Nefs, and are principally taken
in Autumn. All the towns of Angus afford excellent
markets for all thefe kinds of fifh, the town of Dundee efpecially ; but it is now poorly and irregularly fupplied. Between Monyfieth and Arbroath, confiderable quantities of
crabs and lobfters are found. The lobfters went chiefly to the
London market, till lately, that by overfifhing, none were to
be had of a proper fize, and, on this account they were for
fome time fpared, and more of them come to the market of
Dundee. Mufcles and cockles come from the mouth of the
Eden, near St. Andrews, and are fold by meafure. The defeét
of our fea fifhing is, that the fifhermen live too far up the river,
and, their boats being fmaller than in the times when fmuggling prevailed, they do not go out to deep enough water, and
cannot always venture to crofs the bar, We have no oyf-
ters, and all attempts to fettle them in the river, have hitherto been unfuccefsful.

Antiquities, Curiofities, &c.—On the top of the Law of Dundee, which is the moft remarkable hill in the parifh, there
are the remains of a fortification, the ditch of which is ftill
vifible. Though the whole inclofure, which is of a fquare
form, is not of the fame ftruéture with the towers, which
have been fuppofed to be cemented by the force of fire, one
fmall part of it has been thus compaéted. Probably on this
the fires for alarming the town were lighted ; and, by the frequent lighting, fome of the ftones have been put in fufion.
Along a good part of the fhore on the eftate of Craigie, feveral urns of unburnt clay, containing afhes, have been found,

and

and feveral ftone coffins with bones ; and, though the moft of
thefe are of the common form, fome, without any difference
in the fize of the bones, are only three feet fquare. On the
lands of Balgay, there is one of thofe fubterraneous dwellings,
or places of retreat, afcribed to the ancient Picts ; and,
although it has not been yet explored, it is certainly of uncommon extent.—The fkeleton of the firft elephant diffected
in Britain, was fome years ago to be feen ; the diffection was
made by Dr. Blair, an eminent phyfician of Dundee, and a
a memoir which he drew up concerning it, is to be found in
the London Philofophical Tranfactions.—From the council
minutes, which yet remain, it appears, that coal mines were
wrought in Scotland, at a much more early period than is
commonly believed ; for they fhew, that in the 16th century,
coals were the principal and common fuel. The fame minutes furnifh many evidences of the uncertain and changeable
value of money ; for, in 1589, the price of a boll of coals,
which probably confifted, as at prefent, of 800 lb. weight,
and which now fells at 6 s. coft, in 1610, 1 s. 6$\frac{2}{3}$ d. Mr.
David Lindfay the parfon, (who afterwards was bifhop of
Brechin, and probably tranflated thence to Edinburgh,) values
13 bolls of meal, 13 bolls of oats, and 10 bolls of wheat, paid
him out of the Abbey of Lindores, at no more than 8 l. 6 s.
8 d. yearly ; and in place of that quantity of victual, has that
annual fum fettled on him by the council : and, in the fame
year, Mr. James Gleg leaves the regency or profefforfhip of
St. Salvator's college, St. Andrews, in order to be chofen rector of the Dundee grammar fchool, with no greater yearly falary, than 16 l. 13 s. 4 d. and no higher quarterly payments
from his fcholars, than 6$\frac{2}{3}$ d. The plague alfo appears in ancient times to have been very frequent ; and, befides the
dreadful ravages it made in Dundee about the year 1566, and
for

for the laft time in 1607, the inhabitants feem to have never been perfectly free from alarms concerning it *.

Population.——As to the ftate of the population of the town and parifh, in remote times, it is impoffible to give any accounts; nor can thofe which we may attempt to give, even for the laft century, be deemed fully fatisfactory. The greateft part of the ancient records and documents, is faid to have been carried off or deftroyed, at the various fieges of the town, and efpecially when it was ftormed by Monk; and though fome council minutes remain, as far back at 1587, and a record of perfons inrolled as burghers, beginning in 1513, they afford very little affif-tance in this inveftigation. The regifter of baptifms and marriages, reaches no farther back than 1645, and contains no more than five complete years before the fatal affault in 1651. As, however, we have of late years, three actual enu-merations of the inhabitants, one in 1766, when their num-ber was found to be 12,426; one in 1781, when it turned out 15,700; and one in 1788, when it was 19,329, we are enabled, from a comparifon of the marriages near thefe pe-riods, with the marriages about 1651, to form fome probable conjectures about its former population. The annual ave-rage of the marriages for the 5 years, previous to 1651, is 85.
But

* Under the head of antiquities may alfo be ftated the various attacks and fieges of the town. It was twice taken by the Englifh in the days of King Ed-ward I. and as often retaken by the heroes Wallace and Bruce, and the caftle was demolifhed by the latter. It was again taken and reduced to afhes by Richard II. and a fourth time by the Englifh, who, in the reign of Edward VI. held Broughty Caftle. The Marquis of Montrofe took it by affault, and gave it up to pillage, which feems to have been prevented by the approach of an ar-my of the Covenanters; and to cover his retreat from them, the north and eaft parts of it were fet on fire. The laft and moft deftructive fiege, when it was again taken by affault, and completely pillaged, was in Cromwell's time by Ge-neral Monk.

But the annual average of the marriages, for the 5 years, immediately preceding 1766, is 140; and as 140 to 12,426, the actual number of inhabitants, in 1766, fo is 85 to 7544. The average number of marriages again for the 5 years preceding 1781, is 149, and as 149 to 15,700, fo is 85 to 8957; and, in like manner, as 215, the average number of the marriages for the 5 years preceding 1788, is to 19,329, fo is 85 to 7641. Thefe are the three refults for the number of the inhabitants in 1651; the medium of the three brings it out 8,047; and, it is probable, that this conjecture does not err widely from the truth. It is true, that a fimilar comparifon, inftituted between the averages of the baptifms, at thefe different periods, would bring out in 1651, a population not lefs than 12,597; but more refpect feems, on many accounts, to be due to the regifter of marriages, than to that of baptifms. All marriages, whether regular or not, have hitherto been carefully recorded; but, befides that many neglect, or find it inconvenient, to record their children's names, (and thefe omiffions are much more readily overlooked, in large places, than in fmall), it is to be obferved, that previous to 1651, there were few or no fectaries; whereas, fince the revolution in 1688, and efpecially, fince the rife of the Independents and Seceders, about 1732, many have thought regiftration in the records of the Eftablifhed Church, inconfiftent with their religious principles: confequently, the number of recorded baptifms, muft now bear a lefs proportion to the number of inhabitants than it did formerly; and, the refult, for the former population, which is drawn from them, muft come out too great.

The lofs of people in the fiege by Monk, and efpecially in the carnage at the ftorming of the town, appears, on many accounts, to have been great, and cannot be eftimated at much lefs than a fixth part of the whole inhabitants. Of 159 children, born within the eight months immediately following, no lefs than

than 25 are poſthumous; and as 159, to 8047, the whole number of inhabitants, ſo is 25 to 1265, the number that may be ſuppoſed to have been deſtroyed. It is true, that this diminution of inhabitants does not produce any immediate effect upon the marriages, or baptiſms, recorded in the regiſter; nay, that in the ſix ſucceeding years, the marriages are more numerous than before the ſiege. But among theſe, 66 are the marriages of Engliſh ſoldiers; and though the baptiſms, during this period, are not upon the whole increaſed, but in a ſmall degree diminiſhed, 255 of them are of ſoldiers' children. Beſides, the money ſpent by a ·numerous garriſon could not fail to attract people by the hopes of profit; and, the exact diſcipline of Cromwell's troops, and the regular diſtribution of juſtice, which took place during the whole time of his uſurpation, gave them full and unuſual ſecurity in their various occupations. But on the withdrawing of the garriſon, the deficiency of inhabitants, becomes immediately evident. Notwithſtanding the acceſſions which the garriſon has been ſuppoſed to attract, a calculation from the marriages brings out, after the reſtoration, a diminution of 875 in the population; and, towards the end of the reign of Chales II. and during the whole reign of James VII. a diminution of 1420.

This diminution of population cannot be aſcribed to the flight or removal of the inhabitants, on the foreſight of the ſiege; for many perſons, and ſome even of the higheſt rank, had repaired to Dundee, as a place of ſecurity, and ſtrength. Among theſe, I find the Earls of Buchan, Tweddale, Buccleugh and Roſeberry; the Viſcount of Newburgh; the lords Balcarras, Elibank, Yeſter and Ramſay; and the maſter of Burley; 15 perſons alſo bearing titles of knighthood; 11 other gentlemen of landed property; 9 of the Faculty of Advocates; 24 writers, merchants, and indwellers of Edinburgh; and 6 citizens of the Canongate, Leith and Muſſelburgh.

Some

Some even of the clergy from the fouth found it neceffary to take fhelter in Dundee particularly Meffrs. Oliver Colt ; at Muffelburgh, Stevenfon at Dunbar, and Reid of the Weft Kirk Edinburgh. All thefe are mentioned in the regifter, as parents or witneffes to the baptifms recorded in it. One of the children recorded is Anne, afterwards Dutchefs of Monmouth; and the houfe where fhe was born is ftill pointed out*. In this deftruction of fo many inhabitants, many ftrangers were involved, thofe efpecially who appeared as defenders of the town. The governor Lumifden, of the family of Invergelly in Fife, is faid, on the irruption of the Englifh, to have taken poffeffion of the great fteeple ; and, being foon after obliged to furrender at difcretion, he and all with him were maffacred in the church jrd. In the fame place alfo, the

two

---

* It may, perhaps, be an object of curiofity, at leaft, to an inhabitant of Dundee, to know the names of the perfons whofe pofthumous children are recorded, and, who probably fell in the fiege, or after it. They are John Duncan, Donald Dunbar, Robert Ritchiefon, James Guthrie, Andrew Kinneries, merchants; Robert Bultie, unmarried, of a refpectable mercantile family now extinct; Major Robert Lindfay, probably fon of one defigned late of Kinnettles; Thomas Annand, taylor; George Barrie, mealmaker; David Elder, weaver; Thomas Nicol and Alexander Hill, maltmen; William Glenny, feaman; John Nicol baxter; George Anderfon, hammerman; and of perfons whofe defignations are not given, James Angus, unmarried; James Thain, John Difton, John Johnfton, Thomas Smith, John Kennedy, John Lyon, Thomas Watfon, William Oughterlony, James Stibbles. As an object of fimilar curiofity, the following not inelegant epitaphs, on the tomb ftones of two other perfons, who feem to have been of confiderable note, are inferted.

" *Monumentum* ROBERTI DAVIDSON, *prætoris vigilantiſſimi, qui, dum fortiter &*
" *magnanimiter urbis oppugnatione dimicabat, lethaliter ab hoſtibus vulneratus, pro civi-*
" *tate et ſuis vitam reddidit. Cal. Septembris, Anno Salutis humanæ MDCLI.*

" *Monumentum* GEORGII BROWN, *prætoris meritiſſimi, qui, hoc præturæ munere*
" *per decennium feliciter defunctus, undiſque pugnando lethaliter ab hoſtibus vulneratus;*
" *quibus vulneribus per Martem languidus, mortem, naturæ debitum, pro civitate et pa-*
" *triæ reddidit.* 2do. *Nonas Octobris, Anno Dom.* 1651. *Ætatis ſexageſimo."*

two batallions of Lord Duffus's regiment are ſaid to have been ſlaughtered; and, another body ſuffered the like fate, in the ſquare called the fiſh-market. No unuſual provocation appears to have been given to this ſeverity. On the contrary, Mr. Gumble, general Monk's chaplain, and who writes his life, ſpeaks in high terms of the governor, for his gallant and brave defence. His head was, notwithſtanding, cut off and fixed upon a ſpike, in one of the abutments at the ſouth weſt corner of the ſteeple; and, till a few years ago, when the ſtone where the ſpike was inſerted, fell down, the remains of it were obſervable. The ſame indignity appears alſo to have been done to others. It is a tradition here, that the carnage did not ceaſe till the third day, when a child was ſeen in a lane, called the Thorter-Row, ſucking its murdered mother. Several perſons alſo, on this occaſion, were carried priſoners to London, probably along with the 300 officers ſurpriſed by Monk's Colonels, Alured and Morgan, at Alyth, when, collecting a body to raiſe the ſiege. Among the priſoners, were Mr. Andrew Affleck, the parſon, or firſt miniſter, and Mr. John Robertſon the Vicar. They were detained at London till ſpring 1653; and, after their return Mr. Robertſon was ſome time confined in the common priſon of Dundee. Mr. Affleck was anceſtor to the two brothers, Admiral and Captain Affleck in the royal navy. The date of this mercileſs aſſault, was the firſt of September 1651.

Though no probable account can be given of the population in remote times, the town of Dundee appears to have been long ago a place of conſiderable note. Edward I. thought it of ſufficient conſequence to be occupied by an Engliſh garriſon; and, the illuſtrious WALLACE, (with his companions John Blair, probably of the Balthayock family, and Sir N. Campbell of Lochow,) is ſaid, by tradition, to have received his education at the Dundee ſchool, and in this ſituation,

tion, to have begun his exploits, with the death of the son to the Englifh governor. Of the 4 boroughs, Edinburgh, Perth, Dundee and Aberdeen, which were of fuch confequence, in all the reigns, after that of Robert Bruce, as to give fecurity for the obfervation of national treaties, it was the third in rank : Its fhare, in the reign of James VI. of the whole public taxes, was a 25th part, and of thofe laid upon the boroughs, fometimes a tenth part, but more frequently a 5th ; and of the 1200 merks impofed upon the towns of Dundee, Forfar, Arbroath and Perth, for fitting out the yacht, *Mary-gallant*, to fetch home the king and queen from Denmark, the proportion paid by Dundee was 700. At the ftorm by Monk, Gumble fpeaks of it as a very rich and thriving place ; he tells us, in particular, of 60 fhips taken in the harbour, and fent away loaded with booty, confifting chiefly of plate and money ; and, difapproving of the rapacity of the plunderers, mentions, with apparent fatisfaction, the lofs of the whole fleet, in croffing the bar of the river.

A calamity, probably no lefs fatal to the town of Dundee, than the fiege and ftorm by Monk, was the fevere 7 years dearth in the end of the laft century. The annual average of marriages for 5 years, was at that time reduced to 54; and from the effects of this calamity, we never recovered till feveral years after the rebellion in 1745. Though the union of the kingdoms put an end to the arbitrary and tyrannical proceedings of the government in Scotland, it produced a new caufe of depreffion to this particular diftrict. Our ftaple manufacture was the fpinning and weaving the coarfe woollens, called *Plaiding.* Thefe were fent to the Dutch market, and there thickened and dyed, for clothing to the troops in various parts of Germany. This branch of trade, we have, by the lofs of our Dutch and French privileges, loft fo completely fince the Union, that now no remainder of it is to be found. The annual

average

average of the marriages, for the 5 years preceding 1746, does not exceed 56; this gives a population no greater than 5302; and from other reasons, it is probable, that this conclusion is not much below the truth. At the cross, in the principal street of the town, there were not in that year, above 4 or 5 houses completely built of stone, all the rest were partly of wood. No shop rented at more than 2 l., or at the utmost 3 l.; the retailers who rented them were generally poor, and three shops at the cross, which three years ago were sold for 450 l. each, were then entirely shut. At that time, also, there were only two churches, for public worship; and though there were no Seceding meeting-houses, and the Independent congregation was very inconsiderable, if one church was well filled on Sundays, the other was nearly empty.

We have no register of burials, that can be depended upon, except for the last 5 years; and this we owe entirely to the care and attention of Dr. Willison, one of our principal physicians. As the insertion of the whole would swell this account to too great bulk, the facts which follow, as seeming to be most important, are extracted from it. From February 1st. 1787 to ditto 1788, the number of burials was 552; from 1788 to 1789, in which period a very malignant kind of small pox raged, the number was 867; from 1789 to 1790, it was 609; from 1790 to 1791, when the small pox again raged, accompanied with the chincough, it was 840, and from 1791 to 1792, 890. The annual average of burials, therefore, for these 5 years, is 752; and the proportion of deaths, to the whole number of inhabitants, may, with probability, be reckoned nearly that of 1 to 31. The excess of the burials in 1791, above those of any year, wherein the small pox did not prevail, is principally to be ascribed to fresh accessions of inhabitants; for, though a putrid sore throat was at that time epidemical, I do not find, after the most minute inquiries,

that

that it was fatal to more than 50 people. The proportion of burials, of males to thofe of females, is nearly as 110 to 125 ; whereas the proportion of births, of males to thofe of females, taken from the record of baptifms, by a medium of averages for 5 years, at different periods, is nearly as 145 to 128. The average number of children, dying under 2, is 236 : from 2 to 5, 98; and of ftill-born children 50. The moft fatal period to people advanced in life, is from 60 to 70, where the annual average of deaths is 57 ; and to young people paft childhood, from 15 to 25, when the fame average is 47. The moft fatal months are January, March, and December, the averages of burials in thefe being refpectively 88, 73, 74. But, perhaps the moft important fact in the whole regifter, and which ought to excite attention from the perfons moft averfe to the practice of inoculation, is, that, while in 1787 and 1789, the average number of children dying under 5, was only 171, a fimilar average for the years 1788 and 1790, in which the fmall pox raged, arofe to the aftonifhing fum of 420. The whole number of people reported as dying above 90, in all the 5 years of the regifter, is 25; of whom one was in the 99th year; another above the 100th, another in the 102d, and another probably in the 107th year of their feveral lives. The name of the laft was James Peter, who died in 1790. A correfponding date of his father and mother's marriage, was certainly found in the parifh regifter of Dunnichen. Their marriage was faid to have fubfifted only 1 year, and he affirmed, that he was their only child.

Since the enumeration in 1788, the town continues to increafe with greater rapidity than before ; and the whole inhabitants of the town and parifh can hardly be eftimated at lefs than 24,000 ; they are certainly rated fufficiently low at 23,000. They refide chiefly in the town and fuburbs ; and, as the inhabitants, of what may be properly called the coun-

try

try parifh, do not exceed 1100, (and this is nearly double their number in 1759), the town and fuburbs of Dundee may be faid to contain from 22,000 to 22,500 fouls. The return to Dr. Webfter in 1755, for the town and diftrict, was only 12,477 fouls; fo that calculating the population now at the medium number of 23,500, the increafe is 11,123 fouls. On the borders of the parifh, there are two villages, the North Ferry near Broughty Caftle, part of which runs into the parifh of Monyfieth, and our proportion of people in it is 166 : the other is Loch-eye, chiefly in the parifh of Liff; and in this our proportion is hitherto but inconfiderable.

Manufactures. The principal and ftaple manufacture of Dundee is linen of various kinds; viz. 1. Ofnaburghs, and other fimilar coarfe fabrics of different names, for exportation, and which alone, till lately, were fubjected to the national ftamps. The quantity of thefe ftamped, between November 1788 and ditto 1789, amounted to 4,242,653 yards, valued at 108, 782 l. 14 s. 2 d.; and fubtracting from this a fourth part, fuppofed to be brought from fix neighbouring parifhes, to the Dundee ftamp offices, there will remain for the quantity made in this parifh, 3,181,990 yards, in value, 80,587 l. 0 s. 8 d. 2. All the different forts of canvas for fhipping. This fabric is entirely confined to the town, and the quantity annually made may be rated at 704,000 yards, and valued at 32,000 l. The cloth of this kind, made by fome of the principal manufacturers, is thought to be fuperior in quality to any other in Britain; and, by a regulation now introduced, and for which we are chiefly indebted to Mr. Graham of Fintry, of fubjecting it to the infpection of public ftamp-mafters, will probably retain its character. A procefs is alfo known, by which the buyer, at a fmall additional expence,

may

The quantity annually made, may amount to 16,000 yards, and may be valued at 800 l. 4. Bagging for cotton wool, in quantity 165,000 yards, and in value 5,500 l. 5. Some diaper by one company lately established. 6. The greatest part of all the linen necessary for household purposes; but the quantity and value of this cannot be exactly ascertained.

Besides all these kinds of linen, the manufacture of cotton has been lately introduced, and will probably soon become a very important branch of business. Seven companies are already engaged in it. They employ about 400 men, women and children, in spinning cotton into yarn for wool. They are supposed to spin annually 135,000 lbs. of yarn, valued at 20,250 l.; and, with warp, which they buy from distant cotton mills, most of these companies have begun to work up their yarn into callicoes, handkerchiefs, and coarse waistcoats. One company also spins yarn for muslin, to the annual value of 3000 l. An English company from Lambeth is also engaged in establishing an woollen manufacture, where every branch of the business, from the wool to the finished cloth, is proposed to be carried on. The looms employed in all the kinds of weaving, and in all parts of the parish, are from 1800 to 1900.

The manufacture of coloured thread has been established in Dundee for 50 or 60 years, and was for a considerable time peculiar to it. This business is in the hands of 7 different companies or masters, who use 66 twisting mills, and employ about 1340 spinners, and 370 servants, to make the yarn into thread. The quantity annually made is computed at 269,568 lb. and valued at 33,696 l. The spinners live in distant parts of Scotland, where labour is cheaper than in Dundee.

The value of leather, tanned annually in Dundee, is computed at 14,200 l. About 32 persons are employed in tanning, who use 5000 l. worth of oak bark; about 12 as curriers,

curriers, in dreffing part of what is tanned for upper leathers to fhoes; 95 in making boots and fhoes for exportation, and 200 in fupplying the confumption of the town. The value of boots and fhoes exported may be about 4385 l. As the demand for tanned leather has, for fome years, greatly increaf-fed, confiderable difficulty is found in procuring raw hides, and the price of oak bark is doubled. This bufinefs is upon the increafe. Two new enterprifing and active companies have of late engaged in it, fo that probably it will be more than doubled.

Two companies are engaged in manufacturing cordage of all kinds for fhipping, and ropes for all the various ufes of the country. They employ about 30 perfons, and they alfo carry on the whole bufinefs of fhip-chandlers. Soap was fome years ago manufactured to a confiderable amount; but this bufinefs now declines, and laft year only yielded of duty to government the fum of 1828 l. 19 s. $0\frac{1}{4}$. It is thought that this bufinefs will not only be abandoned here, but that it will foon be totally loft to Scotland. The fuppofed caufes are either regulations of excife, partial to England, or fu-perior rigour in carrying the common regulations into execu-tion. It is poffible, however, that the real caufe may be foolifh attempts to underfell their richer Englifh neighbours. It may here be mentioned, as an article of curiofity, that foap making was an art known in Dundee, as far back as the 16th century.

Within thefe 3 or 4 years, the manufacture of glafs has been introduced, and the company engaged in it have erected two glafs-houfes; one for bottles, and the other for the white kinds of window glafs. They employ in the bufinefs 100 perfons, and laft year it yielded to government a duty of 3046 l. Ma-ny perfons are alfo employed in manufacturing tobacco and fnuff; and one company is engaged in a fugar houfe, but of its

importance

importance to the community, no particular account has been obtained.

Befides thefe, and fome other branches of manufacture, omitted as being yet in their infancy, (for example, caft iron and falt,) or though long eftablifhed, fufficiently accounted for by the taxes they pay to Government, 2 banking companies are eftablifhed in Dundee ; and two diftant companies, one in Edinburgh, and one in Paifley, have opened bank offices. The quantity of paper money, in conftant circulation from all the four, is eftimated at 160,000 l. Infurances againft fire are alfo made by a company, confifting of 50 or 60 perfons, whofe property is fuppofed to amount to half a million ; and by whom, though formed into a company only a few years ago, infurances are already made to the value of 800,000 l.

Revenue paid to Government.—Some part of the revenue, arifing from Dundee to Government, may be accurately or nearly afcertained, but a much more confiderable part muft be left to conjecture.

Of the firft kind are the duties of excife for the year, ending with the 5th of July 1792, and communicated in the moft obliging manner, by Mr. Mitchell, fupervifor ; and they are accompanied with a comparative ftate of the excife duties in 1751.

	In 1751,						In 1791.		
	L.	s.	d.				L.	s.	d.
Malt, -	811	13	$1\frac{1}{4}$	-	-	-	1436	7	11
Ale and beer, -	1214	15	$3\frac{1}{2}$	-	-	-	1690	2	1
Candles, -	160	4	2	-	-	-	622	2	$10\frac{1}{2}$
Hides, -	283	11	$8\frac{1}{4}$	-	-	-	1017	1	2
Soap, -	none			-	-	-	1828	19	$0\frac{1}{4}$
Glafs, -	none			-	-	-	3406	0	$5\frac{1}{2}$
Bricks, -	none			-	-	-	14	17	6
Total,	L. 2470	4	3	Carried over, — L.			10,015	11	0

Cuftom-

Brought over, —	L. 10,015	11	0
Cuſtomhouſe duties for the year ending January 1. 1792, and communicated with like readineſs, by Mr. Hunter clerk of the cuſtoms, - -	6341	17	11
Land-tax, and other taxes in the country part of the pariſh, levied by the country collector, - -	341	8	1
Town-ceſs, and other taxes within the royalty, levied by the town's collectors - - - -	949	19	0
Exciſe licences of all the various kinds, about, -	512	2	0
Ale licences, about, - - - - -	280	18	6
Duties on 78,447 lb. of ſnuff and manufactured to-bacco, paid at the places of original importation,	4902	18	9
Produce of the poſt office in 1791, about, -	1600	0	0
Of the ſecond kind, are the duties on ſalt, allowing 4 buſhels yearly to 5 perſons,	690	0	0
Duties on 583½ tons of ſugar, of which 7 20ths are ſuppoſed to be unmanufactured, 8 20ths refined, and 5 20ths ground or powdered, and reckoned equiva-lent in taxation to 621 tons, - -	9315	0	0
Duties on 47743 lb. of tea, eſtimated at, - -	895	2	6
Duties on ſtamped paper not leſs than, - -	1000	0	0
Exciſe duties on wines and ſpirits imported immedi-ately from foreign parts, - - -	2030	16	6¼
Ditto on ditto, from other parts in the kingdom, ac-cording to a mean of three eſtimations. -	5970	0	0
Duties on innumerable other articles, manufactured ſoap, groceries, drugs, ſtarch, indigo, cambric, muſ-lin, ſilk, paper, newſpapers, perfumery, malt-liquor, hops, &c. &c. &c., imported - -	12,000	0	0
So that the revenue ariſing to government, from the trade and conſumption of Dundee, can-not be eſtimated at leſs than, - -	L. 56,845	14	3¼

In the laſt article the valuation is by no means too high, for
the duty on ſoap alone will make up the greateſt part of it; and
the quantity made in Dundee does not ſupply one fourth of the
demands of this ſingle pariſh; ſo that it is not improbable, that
a more juſt eſtimation would bring out a revenue greater than
60,000 l. Several of theſe ſums are not, indeed, directly paid in
Dundee, but they are equally real taxes upon its traders and inhabitant s

habitants. With refpect to thofe on ale and malt, it ought not to pafs unobferved, that they have for a long time gradually decreafed, and do not now yield a fum equal to its produce in 1745, when the parifh did not contain above 6000 people. In that year the town's grant, of two pennies on the pint of ale, is faid to have yielded 500 l. In 1757 it gave 423 l. 9 s. and its produce in 1791 was no more than 326 l. 6 s.; this difference is fuppofed to arife, in a great meafure, from the various taxes; by which the malt liquor here has been fo much debafed, that it ceafes to be the drink ufed in focial meetings, or for refrefhment from the fatigues of labour; and the people, deprived of their ancient, exhilerating, and wholefome beverage, have recourfe to intoxicating and enervating fpirituous liquors. The increafed ufe of thefe is certainly a moft alarming circumftance. They are fold in no lefs than 179 licenfed houfes; and the number of non-licenfed ones, where they may be procured, is believed to be very great; whereas formerly the town was fufficiently, and perhaps, too well fupplied by five or fix.

Shipping, Exports, Imports, &c.—On the 5th of January 1792, there were 116 veffels, belonging to the port, navigated by 698 men, and meafuring 8550¼ tons. Of thefe, 34 were employed in the foreign, and 78 in the coafting trade, and 4 in the whale fifhery. By Mr. Hunter, clerk of the cuftoms, the author of this account has been favoured with the following comparative ftate of fome of the principal articles of trade, in the years 1745 and 1791.

Total tonnage cleared outwards to foreign parts

	In 1745.		In 1791.
	500 tons.	-	1,279 tons.
Ditto cleared inwards from ditto,	1280 do.	-	10,520 do.
Inwards coaft-wife, -	no account,	-	40,923 do.
Outwards, ditto, - -	3000 do.	- -	20,055 do.

Goods

	In 1745.	In 1791.
Goods imported. Flax from Russia,	none	2348 tons
Ditto from Holland,	74 tons	72 do.
Hemp,	none	299 do.
Tow or codillio,	none	24 do.
Clover feed,	100 lb.	51½ do.
Lintfeed,	1406 hhds.	1036 hhds.
Fir timber,	98 loads	1706 loads.
Fir balks,	100	6300
Deals,	10,500	13,100
Swedish iron,	50 tons	45 tons
Goods brought coast-wise. Cotton wool,	none	35 do.
Tea from London,	none	47,743 lbs.
Porter,	none	1080 hhds.
Coals from the Forth,	no account	28,021 tons
Sugar, in 1745, no account but in 1756,	62 tons	583½ do.
Goods sent coast-wise. Linen, brown and white,	1,000,000 yards,	7,842,000 yards
Thread, white and coloured,	12,544 lbs.	130,752 lbs.
Sail-cloth,	none	280,000 yards
Cotton bagging,	none	65,000 yards
Barley or big,	3393 qurs.	23,917 yards
Wheat,	350 do.	3097 do.

To these evidences of the thriving state of Dundee, and indeed of the whole neighbouring country, a variety of others might be added. In 1772, no more than 5 or 6 houses were to be seen between the west end of the royalty and Blackness; now upwards of 100 acres have been feued out, in the same district for building on, and upwards of 4000 people settled in it. About 1770, the feu duty, even for the lands nearest the town, did not exceed 3 l. or 3 l. 10 s. the acre, and this was supposed to be an advantageous price; now lots of 10 or 12 acres, of a much greater distance, are feued by Mr Hunter of Blackness, at 10 l. and subfeued at 14 l. the acre. Among the latest feus near the town, may be mentioned about 4 acres of land, chiefly under the management of the Kirk-session.

feffion. Thefe, altogether, for many years paft, were rented at 3 l. Laft year they were feued at 40 l. the acre. In like manner in 1754, when there were only two churches on the eftablifhment for public worfhip, the feat rents of that portion of them, which was the Town's, properly amounted to no more than 21 l. 4 s. 7 d. Now, when there are 7 eftablifhed churches and chapels, the feat rents of the fame portion amount to 175 l.

Befides the general advantages derived from the conftitution of the Britifh government, and the liberty and fecurity its fubjects enjoy, in all their lawful occupations, the particular caufe of the increafe and profperity of Dundee is, undoubtedly, the bounty allowed by Parliament on all manufactured linens. By this the induftry of the inhabitants was firft fet in motion, and encouraged; and their confequent profperity, if it be not an evidence in favour of bounties in general, is, at leaft, a decifive one, that, in fome cafes, they are wife and judicious, and may be productive of the greateft benefit. Whether the linen manufacture could now be fupported without the bounty, or whether the fpirit of induftry, which is now awakened, could be eafily and profitably diverted into other channels, is a queftion on which it would be prefumptuous in any private perfon to pronounce, and, perhaps, any experiment on the fubject might be dangerous.

Prices of Provifions, Labour, &c.—The average prices of beef through the year, and without diftinction of particular prices, is 4 s. 6 d. the ftone, and this is alfo the general price of pork. Mutton, through the year, fells at from 4 d. to 5 d. the pound, and veal from 3 d. to 6 d. the weight is Dutch, confifting of 17 oz. 4 dr. per pound. Hens have rifen to 15 d. each; chickens to 4 d. and 6 d. each; ducks to 1 s.; geefe fell from 2 s. 6 d. to 3 s. each; turkies from 5 s. to 8 s.; pigeons at 4 d. the pair. The wages of a maid-fervant are

from

from 3 l. to 4 l. yearly, and of a labouring man-fervant from 7 l. to 10 l. Mafon's daily wages are from 1 s. 8 d. to 2 s.; thofe of houfe carpenters from 1 s. 3 d. to 1 s. 6 d. and of day labourers 1 s. at an average through the year.

Conſtitution, Privileges, &c.—The privileges of the town of Dundee, as a free and royal borough, are very ancient. A charter by King Robert Bruce, dated March 14th, in the 22d year of his reign, and proceeding upon a recognition of its privileges by a jury, mentions its being poffeffed of them in the time of his predeceffor, William, who began to reign in 1165 ; and that they were as ample as thofe enjoyed by the town of Berwick, or by any borough in Scotland. This charter, the recognition on which it proceeds, with the defignations of the jury, and the commiffion to Bernard, Abbot of Arbroath, and Mr. Alex. Frafer, Chancellor of Scotland, to prefide as King's Lieutenants at the trial, whether now in exiftence or not, were in the poffeffion of the Council not above 50 years ago ; and the writer of this article has had an opportunity to fee copies of them, with tranflations from the Latin, made by Mr. George Bruce, then rector of the grammar fchool. Thefe rights appear alfo to have been confirmed and enlarged by many fucceeding princes ; particularly, by David Bruce, James II. James IV. Queen Mary, James VI. and Charles I. So uncommon are fome of thefe, that by an edict of David Bruce, the villages of Coupar in Angus, Kettins, Kirriemuir, and Alyth, are prohibited from holding markets; and all perfons difcharged, under the higheft penalties, from attending them, *as being within the liberties of Dundee.* Befides a confirmation of rights, Queen Mary's charter conveys to the town all the poffeffions of the Dominican friars, Minorites, Francifcans, and Gray Sifters, St. Clement's church, and its chaplainries ; with all their revenues and lands, among which were a third part of the lands of Craigie ; and, in particular

3   ticular

ticular, the *place and yards* belonging to the Grey Cordelier friars, for this special reason, " that the former burying ground " in St. Clement's church-yard was in the *middyies* of the town, " and by burying in it *peft* and other contagious ficknefs might " be *ingenerit.* and made to *perfeveir.*" All thefe former grants are alfo mentioned at length, and confirmed with additions, by the charter of James VI. dated at Holyroodhoufe, January 16. 1731, and finally confirmed by Charles I. His charter is called *the great charter*, and bears, that all its articles were ratified in Parliament, Sept. 14. 1641.

Ample, however, as thefe privileges were, they appear to have been continually difputed by the Scrymfeours of Dud-hope, who, for fignal fervices done under the illuftrious WALLACE, had been by him created Conftables of the caftle, and continued to enjoy that hereditary dignity. The bounds between the powers of the Conftable, and the privileges of the citizens, feem never to have been accurately determined, and confequently have become the fubjects of frequent con-troverfy, and occafions of dangerous riot. The Conftable's powers efpecially appear to have excited the greateft jealou-fies, when, as often happened, they were united to any of the offices of the magiftracy. About the year 1604, Sir James Scrymfeour having made an attempt to render himfelf perpe-tual Provoft, to change the election of the council into a mere nomination, and to fubject all caufes, civil and criminal, to his own authority, the greateft commotions were excited, and the peace of the town was for many years difturbed. The citi-zens, however, under the direction chiefly of the Fletcher fa-mily, at laft prevailed ; and the Scrymfeours loft all their in-fluence in the council, and appear to have been expelled. Re-fentment for this affront feems to have increafed the ufual a-nimofity, and it arofe, at one time, to fuch extravagance, that the Conftable obtained a writ of *Law-burroes* againft the coun-

fellors,

fellors, and probably the whole community ; nor were they difcharged from its operation, till John Fothringham of Powrie became fecurity for them to the value of 20,000 merks. It was not till October 12. 1643, that thefe differences were fettled, by an agreement, under the direction of Sir George Halyburton of Fotherance, and Sir John Leflie of Newton, Lords of Seffion. Even after this agreement, many of the acknowledged powers of the Conftable were grievous and humiliating to the inhabitants ; and thefe powers were never finally abolifhed, till the general abolition of all hereditary jurifdictions.

The conftitution of government eftablifhed in Dundee, or what is called the *Set of the Borough*, though apparently republican, is a fpecies of oligarchy, not materially differing from thofe eftablifhed, in general, over all the towns in Scotland. The Town Council is compofed of 20 perfons, including the magiftrates, confifting of a provoft, and four bailies. The annual election of thefe magiftrates, and alfo of the dean of guild, and treafurer, is on the Thurfday immediately previous to Michaelmas. But the council for the enfuing year is chiefly chofen on the preceding Tuefday, and all the meafures fixed, which are generally decifive in the election of the officers juft now mentioned. The whole 20 counfellors affemble on that day, and choofe 8 new counfellors, of whom 5 muft be taken from the guildry, or body of free merchants, and 3 from any feparate three of the incorporated trades. No more new counfellors than 8 are neceffary, becaufe the 4 bailies muft be members of the new council *ex officio*. With the addition of thefe 8 new members, they proceed to make up *leets*, or lifts, for the offices of provoft, bailies, dean of guild, and treafurer. The leet for the provoft is limited to people, who, at any time formerly have been bailies; the leet for bailies to former counfellors; that for the dean of guild to prefent bailies; and the *leet* for the treafurer

furer is alone unlimited. When two perfons have thus been *leeted*, for every one of thefe feven offices, the powers of two particular old counfellors, as to any farther fhare in the election expire, and the number of old and new counfellors is reduced to 26. The *leets* are then tranfmitted to the convener of the 9 incorporated trades, to be by him laid before his deacons and their conftituents. On the Thurfday thefe 9 deacons affemble in the town-hall, along with the 26 old and new counfellors, and proceed to elect from the leets, by a majority of votes, the 5 magiftrates, the dean of guild, and the treafurer. Thus, including the three remaining bailies, who continue in the council without election, a body of 18 new counfellors is formed for the enfuing year, and all the former offices expire. On the Tuefday following, thefe 18 choofe the remaining two.

From this account, it muft be evident, that the formation of the new council is almoft entirely in the power of their predeceffors, and that a fociety, thus conftituted, is but in a very fmall degree dependant upon the community, whofe interefts are intrufted to their management. No appeal whatever is made to the guildry, or great body of merchants, who may be confidered as the *ariftocracy* of the place ; and the only controul the council can receive, in the election of their fucceffors, is from the deacons of the incorporated trades, who may be confidered as the reprefentatives of the *people*. Unlefs, however, a confiderable divifion, which feldom happens, fhould take place among the counfellors, and at the fame time the deacons remain united, this controul muft be of very little confequence. Without, therefore, a greater degree both of intelligence and public fpirit, than falls to the common lot of humanity, fuch a fociety muft be under ftrong inducements to confider itfelf as a fraternity diftinct from the community ; and having different interefts, it will certainly be fufpected of entertaining fuch perfuafions, and its conduct, efpecially specially when uncontroulable, as at present, by any superior tribunal, will always be viewed with jealousy, and is in danger of becoming, in some degree, arbitrary and interested.

It would, however, be unjust not to acknowledge, to the honour of the magistrates and council of Dundee, that, in many instances, they have exerted themselves with laudable zeal and success, in promoting the public good. The building and endowing new churches, the paving and lighting streets, the opening new ones, especially a new passage to the shore, the building new piers, and the general improvement of the harbour, are works which they have executed within these 10 or 12 years, and which are both of great importance, and entitle them to no small share of praise. Many equally important, no doubt, yet remain to be done, and some may have been neglected; but to these, it is to be hoped, according as their revenues may enable them, they will not fail to turn their attention.

The revenues of the town, not appropriated to particular purposes, may amount annually to 2200 l. If to these we add the revenues of the guildry, amounting to 80 l ; of the hospital, for decayed burghers, amounting to 300 l.; the fund arising from some lands, but chiefly from seat rents, for building and repairing the churches, computed at 588 l. ; the interest of money mortified for bursaries and similar purposes, amounting to 60 l. ; and if we also include 400 l. levied from poor's rates ; the members of council will be found to have under their management an annual sum not much short of 4000 l.

While there was a Parliament in Scotland, Dundee was represented in it by one member or commissioner. It is now only one of 5 boroughs, who, all together, send but one member to the British Parliament ; the other four are Perth, Forfar, St. Andrew's, and Coupar in Fife. Every one of the

councils

councils in their boroughs chooses a *delegate*, and the 5 delegates elect their representative.

Ecclefiaftical State, &c.—It is impossible to ascertain, with accuracy, the ecclefiaftical state of the parish, previous to the Reformation. The number of religious houses was certainly greater, than has appeared in any published accounts of ecclefiaftical antiquities; but the ancient writings being in general lost, and the buildings converted into private property, and varioufly demolished and rebuilt, they are now incapable of being traced. It is probable, that the church dedicated to St. Clement, converted into a *Tolbooth*, or town-house, at the Reformation, and situated where the present town-house stands, had been the parish church; and certainly, the area behind it, now used for a meal-market, and the lanes, by which it is surrounded, composed the common burying ground. But, since the Reformation, the great one built by David Earl of Huntingdon, (which, when entire, was one of the largest and most magnificent in the kingdom), has been the parish church. Its form was that of a crucifix, with a very noble square tower, or steeple, at the west end, through which was the great entry. The height of the tower, which is still entire, is 156 feet; its area, within the walls, 27 feet, and without 40. The length of the nave was 120 feet, its height 63, its breadth 40, and the breadth of each of its ailes 30. The length of the choir is 95 feet, its height 54, its breadth 29, and the breadth of each of its ailes 14¼. The length of the crofs part of the building, which had no ailes, is 174 feet, and its breadth 44. According to tradition, this church was destroyed by Edward I.; and probably the nave was never afterwards repaired. What had been repaired was also again destroyed in Edward VI's time, by the English, then in posfeffion of Broughty Castle; and the destruction, either at the first or second time, appears to have been accomplished by fire.

fire. The crofs part of the building lay uncovered till 1588, when it was again fitted up for ufe, by means of general taxations laid on the inhabitants, by the authority of the town council, and by voluntary contributions. One of the principal contributors was captain Henry Lyell of Blacknefs, who, in an infcription, (on which are his arms, the fame with thofe of Lovell), affumes the merit of the whole.

At the Reformation, only two minifters feem to have been eftablifhed in the parifh, one called *the Parfon*, and the other *the Vicar*. The Scrymfeours of Dudhope, conftables of the caftle, were patrons of the firft charge, and the patronage of the laft belonged to the community. As the care of the parifh was too laborious for two minifters, Mr. James Robertfon the vicar, on obtaining in 1608, a fixed ftipend of 800 merks, refigned to the patrons his vicarage; and, about 1609, they appointed in his room an additional minifter, Mr. William Wedderburn, who, in 1613, received alfo a fixed ftipend, equal to that of Mr. Robertfon, and gave up to the council the more cafual and infufficient produce of the vicarage. Though thefe tranfactions do not appear to have been authorifed, by any decree of the Lords of Erections, and no confent appears to have been either afked or obtained from the patron of the firft charge, the patronage of both the others was confidered as the undoubted property of the community. The parifh was thus fupplied with three minifters, one drawing his living from the parfonage teinds, and the other two from the various funds within the borough ; and they have always officiated as colleagues in the two places of worfhip, the choir and the fouth part of the crofs building in the ancient church. As the inhabitants were found too numerous for being accommodated in two churches, the magiftrates, in the year 1759, fitted up the north part of the crofs building as a chapel of eafe ; and the town continuing to increafe, they built, in 1789, a large and handfome new church, on the fituation of

the

the ancient nave ; and, by a decree of the Lords of Seffion, both were erected into churches on the eftablifhment, for two additional ftipendiary minifters, who officiate as colleagues in both by turns. As the town-council had, after the Revolution, acquired the patronage of the firft charge by purchafe, they are now confidered as undoubted patrons of all the five.

The ftipends of the two ftipendiary minifters, on the old eftablifhment, are each 140 l. The firft minifter's ftipend, including his glebe, and an old allowance for houfe rent, exceeds thofe of his colleagues a few pounds. No part of it affects the teinds of the parifh, except one chalder of meal, and another of barley, and 66 l. 13 s. 4 d. in money. With refpect to all the three, it is to be obferved, that 20 l. of each ftipend is an addition made by the council, only three years ago, upon account of the increafed expence of living, and continues no longer than the lives of each incumbent. The falaries of the two ftipendiary minifters, on the new eftablifhment, are no greater than 120 l. each.

Befides thefe 5 eftablifhed minifters, two others, ordained and in the communion of the Church of Scotland, officiate in two Chapels of Eafe. One of thefe chapels was built in 1772, by the joint exertions of the Kirk-Seffion, and the 9 incorporated and united trades, chiefly by means of donations and charitable contributions, and continues under the management of thefe focieties. It is as large almoft as any of the other churches, and its minifter receives a falary of 100 l. The other was built in 1789, by a feparate congregation of the *Relief* perfuafion, now, on their own application, received, along with their minifter, into the church. He receives a ftipend of 90 l. and the chapel may contain 800 or 900 people. A third chapel alfo, under the direction of the Church of Scotland, belongs to a congregation of Highlanders, who

have

have lately emigrated from their native country. Their clergyman officiates in the Gaelic language, is yet unordained, and they have not been able to afford him any higher salary than 30 l. All these churches and chapels are considered as in one and the same parish, and all their ministers and elders compose only one Kirk-Session.

The dissenting congregations, with the number of persons, belonging only to this parish, of which they are in part composed, including their children and all occasional attendants from the parish, according to the accounts by their own ministers or principal managers, are as follows. 1. One meeting, of the *Scottish Episcopal* form, consists of a clergyman, and 370 persons. The clergyman is titular *Bishop* of one of the districts into which the people of his persuasion are distributed. 2. One *Independent* meeting, of the sect denominated *Glassites*, from the late *Mr. Glas*, has several pastors or preachers, and 1160 persons. The preachers are distinguished in the congregation by the names of *Bishop* and *Elders*. 3. One meeting of the *English Episcopal* form, consists of one clergyman and 420 persons. 4. One meeting of *Seceders*, of the *Burgher* form, has one clergyman and 784 persons. 5. One of the *Antiburgher* sect has one clergyman, and 650 persons. Besides these, there are also other separate societies, of *Roman Catholics, Anabaptists, Bereans*, now said to be split into three sects, *Methodists, Unitarians*, and *Independents* of another form. The attendants of all these together, cannot exceed 400, so that the whole number of dissenters, including children, in this parish, amounts to 3784. The principal Independent congregation affords a decisive proof of the importance of early marriages to population. It was formed by Mr. Glas, about the year 1732, and at that time consisted of no more than 71 members, men and women. It has now collected 1160, and the increase is much more the effect of an

indispensible

indifpenfible law of the fociety, enjoining *early* marriages, than of any new acceffions of profelytes. Befides the importance of the law to population, it appears, from this experiment, that it is alfo of the utmoft confequence to prevent licentiouf-nefs, and to promote early induftry. The ufual objections of its tendency to produce a debilitated race, and to increafe the number of the poor, appear to be in a great meafure frivo-lous; for, in confequence of the regulations of the fociety, very few of their poor have hitherto been burdenfome to others, and their young people do not feem to be inferior in health or vigour, to the ordinary natives of the town.

Charitable Funds and Diftributions.—The funds, and annual diftributions of charity in Dundee, are very confiderable, and merit a more complete detail, than the writer of this article is enabled to give. Thofe committed to the management of the Kirk-Seffion are the principal funds; and, for the year **1791**, were as follows:

Intereft of money mortified, and rents of land acquired by
    fuch money, - - - - - L. 95 4 6¾
Dues allowed by law, or cuftom for marriages, - 55 13 0
Fines alfo allowed by law from delinquents, - - 1 15 0
Sale of the effects of penfioners after their deaths, - 35 8 3
Collections at the doors of the 4 churches, and the Chapel
    of Eafe in the Cowgate, - - - - L. 640 13 8¾

In all, - - - - - - L. 828 14 6½

From this fum, the diftributions and other expenditure were
    as follows:
To 243 ftated penfioners, of whom 196 were enrolled for
    life, - - - - - - L. 531 0 0
In occafional charities through the year, and to the fame pen-
    fioners on three extraordinary occafions, to wit, after the
    communions in the fpring and autumn, and at the begin-
    ning of the year, - - - - - 175 13 7

                              Carried over, L. 706 13 7

Brought over,	L. 706	13	7
For nurſing orphans, and children deſerted by worthleſs parents, chiefly natural children, - - -	25	8	0
For books and education to poor children, ſalaries to teachers of ſchools in the ſuburbs, and ſtipends due by law to the miniſters, from the kirk-ſeſſions lands, - -	33	1	6
To 7 church officers or beadles, - - -	L. 51	2	8
In all, - - - - - -	L. 816	5	9
So that in the year 1791, the ſurplus was, - -	12	8	9¼

In the year 1790, inſtead of a balance ſaved, a debt of 81 l. 5 s. 7¾ d., had been contracted, though the diſtributions were 85 l. 12 s. 6 d. leſs. But on the intimation of this to the congregations, their collections were immediately and cheerfully increaſed, ſo as to produce an annual riſe of 160 l. 17 s. 0¼ d. The conſtant weekly allowance to penſioners, as may appear from the above ſtatement, is no greater than 10 d. and a ſmall fraction, and may perhaps be thought too ſcanty. But it ought to be conſidered, that it is an average allowance; that the greateſt part of the penſioners are capable of earning ſomething by their work; that the principal uſe of ſtated charities is merely to ſupply the deficiencies of ſuch earning; and that, when they become ſo liberal as to render work unneceſſary, or when living by charity ceaſes to be diſhonourable, they are utterly deſtructive of prudence, foreſight, ſobriety and economy.

Other funds, principally or wholely under the management of the kirk-ſeſſion are,

Rents of lands, and ſums mortified by Mr. Gilbert Guthrie, for educating poor boys, - - - -	L. 140	0	0
Each boy receives yearly 3 l. 6 s. 8 d. for 3 years, and as much when they end.			
Similar rents by———for the ſame purpoſe, - -	61	0	0
Other rents for poor widows, and diſtributed among 21 of them, - - - - -	53	14	0
	L. 254	14	0

So

So that laft year the whole funds of charity, under the management of the Kirk-Seffion, amounted to 1083 l. 8 s. 6½ d.
Thefe funds, particularly Guthrie's mortification, will, in a
few years, be confiderably increafed. To this, the principal
part of the 4 acres of land, mentioned as feued at 40 l. the
acre, belongs. It is to be obferved, that the management and
difpofal of all the feffions funds cofts not a fingle farthing
of expence.

The annual diftributions, from funds under the management
of the Town-Council, or levied by their authority, are as follows :

From the hofpital for decayed burghers,	- -	L. 130 0 0
From the Guildry,	- - - -	46 0 0
Poors rates levied within the royalty,	- - -	400 0 0

This laft fum, after paying the expence of levying and
diftribution, was laft year divided among 120 penfioners.
It began to be levied only a few years ago, for the avowed
purpofe of fuppreffing beggars. It has not produced this effect, and, notwithftanding, has rifen from 100 l. to 400 l.
Though this tax compels the covetous, and thofe who rarely
attend public worfhip, to take fome part in the maintenance
of the poor, and on this account, has the appearance of juftice, it is liable to many objections. It tends to impair voluntary charity ; it falls as heavily on the moft charitable and
liberal, as on the covetous and licentious ; by being confined within the royalty, it takes no hold on the opulent perfons
in the country part of the parifh, the proprietors of the land efpecially, who profit more by the induftry of Dundee, than
any other fet of men ; at the pleafure of any magiftracy, it
may be extended beyond all juft and moderate limits ; and,
being like their other funds, under their uncontroulable difpofal, may be perverted into an engine of borough politics, and
be-

become in future, a grievous nuisance. At present, however, it has produced no real or perceptible evils ; particularly it has not, as in England, become extravagant and destructive to economy, nor rendered it in any degree more difficult for strangers to obtain a settlement.

Other distributions are,

From the fraternity of seamen, - - - -	L. 390 13	6
From the general fund of the 9 incorporated trades, -	56 14	0
From the particular funds of the same trades, -	167 19	0
From the united and pendicle trades, supposed, - -	70 0	0
From several public and private societies, supposed, -	30 0	0
From the Scottish Episcopal meeting, - -	12 0	0
———— English ditto, - - - -	16 0	0
———— Burgher Seceding ditto, supposed, -	25 0	0
———— Antiburgher ditto, ditto, - -	18 0	0
———— Independent meeting, who, from principle, neither give nor keep any account of their charities, supposed, - - - -	300 0	0
———— All the other religious societies, supposed, -	40 0	0
Besides the charities now enumerated, there are also bursaries at the university and grammar school, in the gift of the council, amounting to, - - -	60 0	0
Mr. Henderson's charity school for poor children, -	25 0	0
A dispensary, on which was expended last year, -	140 0	0
Mr. Stephen's mortification for boys at School and college, in the gift of the Provost, the minister of the Murraygate district, Mr. Dempster of Dunnichen, and Mr. Hunter of Balskelly, from which there is at present paid, -	79 0	0
Dr. Brown's mortification, now in the management of his immediate trustees, whom failing, it devolves on the Kirk-Session, - - - -	128 0	0
Miss Graham's mortification towards the education of an orphan girl, - - - - -	2 5	0
	L. 1560 11	6

So that altogether, the money bestowed last year, in various charities, amounted to. - - - - L. 2377 5 3

The

The Difpenfary was eftablifhed in 1782. It is entirely fupported by voluntary contributions, and has been of the greateft ufe. The prefident and principal benefactor is Lord Douglas. But the contributions of the remaining heritors, (a very
few excepted,) either to this or to any other charitable inftitutions of the place, notwithftanding all the advantages they derive from it, are hardly worth the mentioning. To the Difpenfary, it is alfo now propofed to add an Infirmary ; and the
liberal and numerous fubfcriptions already obtained, leave
little reafon to doubt, that the purpofe will foon be carried into execution.

General charaƈter.—The people of Dundee have been for
a long time entitled to the reputation of induftry, regularity
and economy ; and, notwithftanding the increafe of their
wealth and numbers, a juft claim to this reputation ftill continues. As their wealth has been almoft entirely the refult
of great attention and induftry, it is preferved by the fame
virtues, and they are ftill ftrangers to extravagant and ruinous luxuries. One inftance of economy and ancient fim-
plicity of manners, will, in fome parts of Britain, hardly meet
with credit ; that, though we have many burghers, worth
from 5000 l. to 40,000 l. there are not in the whole town,
more than 9 male houfehold fervants ; and of thefe, not one
belongs to any perfon, who can, with propriety, be faid to be
engaged in trade. This economy does by no means exclude
cheerful and frequent focial intercourfe, or abridge their real
comforts and recreations. It does not even banifh a liberal
hofpitality ; and inftead of leffening their humanity and compaffion for the miferable, the people of Dundee are inferior
to none in generous exertions and contributions, either for the
relief of particular diftreffes and misfortunes, or for the eftablifhment and maintenance of public beneficent inftitutions.

The

The riſe of the wages of labour, has not hitherto produced any conſiderable bad effects, even upon the common people ; but, on the contrary, has been generally employed to increaſe their lawful comforts, to feed and clothe them better, and to encourage them in the more early eſtabliſhment of families ; and the proportion they beſtow, in all charitable contributions, at leaſt equals, if not exceeds, that of their ſuperiors in opulence. Yet it would be inconſiſtent with truth, not to mention, that proſperity has introduced among ſome, a degree of licentiouſneſs unknown in former times ; and one alarming ſymptom of it ought not to be concealed, that, notwithſtanding the great acceſſions made, ſince the year 1788, to the number of inhabitants, the number of annual marriages has hardly received the ſmalleſt addition. The people of Dundee may be alſo characteriſed from their religious habits ; and no where in Scotland is public worſhip better, or perhaps ſo well attended. Their numerous ſects indicate their zeal and attachment to religious principles, and perhaps an exceſs of attention to religious controverſies ; but theſe give very little diſturbance to the general harmony, and inſtead of increaſing bigotry they ſeem to weaken it. Though ſome ſects, not only on their firſt riſe but even at preſent, cannot be acquitted of harſh and uncharitable opinions, concerning thoſe who do not adopt their ſentiments, mutual toleration evidently prevails ; and each begins to ſuſpect, that the dictates of their own party have no better claim to *infallibility*, than thoſe of others.

As to the general ſize of the inhabitants, it is certainly inferior to that of the people in the ſouth and weſt parts of Scotland, and even of their neighbours in various parts of Fife : and though the linen manufacture be the great ſource of their opulence and increaſe, its influence does not ſeem ſo favourable as might be wiſhed to health, or friendly to the production of a vigorous and hardy race.

Remarkable

Remarkable Perfons and Families.—Among remarkable and diftinguifhed perfons may be mentioned, 1. ALEXANDER SCRYMSEOUR, one of WALLACE's heroic companions, the perfon to whom, after he had recovered the town from the Englifh, he committed the reduction of the caftle, and whom he put in poffeffion of the hereditary dignity of conftable: 2. Sir JOHN SCRYMSEOUR one of his defcendants, who became Vifcount of Dudhope, and adhering to Charles I. loft his life in the battle of Marfton Muir: 3. His fon who followed the fortunes of Charles II, accompanied him with a regiment to the battle of Worcefter, and returning with him at the reftoration, was created Earl of Dundee. Befides their dignity of conftables, the chiefs of this family were hereditary ftandard-bearers of Scotland. They continue to be reprefented by the Scrymfeours of Birkhill, now Wedderburns of Wedderburn, who, on the death of the Earl of Dundee, without immediate heirs, were unjuftly fpoiled of their honours and inheritance. 4, ROBERT PITTILLOCK, commonly pronounced *Tillock*, and now fpelled *Patullo*. In the wars of Charles VII. of France, for the recovery of his kingdom from the Englifh, particularly in their final expulfion from Gafcony, he acquired the moft fignal honours ; and was the firft captain of the famous Scottifh guard, then formed, and to whofe fidelity the French kings for feveral centuries committed their perfonal protection. 5. JAMES HALYBURTON, defigned on his tomb-ftone, uncle to Halyburton of Pitcurr. To this perfon, his country is indebted, as one of the moft early and able promoters of the reformation. By his influence chiefly, Dundee became the firft town in Scotland, where the reformed religion was openly profeffed. He headed the Dundee troops, who went to the defence of Perth, againft the vengeance threatened by Mary the regent. By his able conduct in encamping and conducting the Proteftant forces, affembled at Coupar, the at-

tempt

tempt of the popifh troops, under the French general D' Oyfel, to reduce St. Andrews and feize the chief leaders of the reformation, was defeated ; and by him and his brother Alexander, at the head of their fellow citizens, one of the principal attacks againft the town of Perth was carried on, and the popifh garrifon diflodged. He was provoft of Dundee for 33 years. From gratitude and refpect to his memory, his funerals were defrayed at the public expence ; and, what was then reckoned a mark of peculiar honour, his grave was lined on the fides with mafon-work, and arched over, and a monument erected to his memory. Dundee has alfo produced fome perfons of confiderable eminence for fcience. It is believed, that JOHN MAR, the mutual friend of the great Baron Napier, inventor of Logarithms, and of Mr. Edward Briggs, and who brought about, and was prefent on their firft interview at Merchifton, was one of its native citizens. He appears to have been diftinguifhed by James VI. before his fucceffion to the Englifh crown, and to have gone up with him to England in the royal houfehold. To another citizen, JAMES MAR, probably grandfon of the former, we owe a chart and foundings of the whole north fea, fo accurate, that, though laid down about the beginning of the prefent century, it has hitherto received few improvements of importance. By him, in particular, the bank, which bears his name, was difcovered and delineated ; and his native town is peculiarly indebted to him for his accurate draught and foundings of the enterance into Tay, and the whole paffage up the river. The family of thefe eminent perfons ftill fubfifts. In other branches of literature, we count the well known HECTOR BOECE the hiftorian, who was Principal of the King's College in Aberdeen, and one of the chief reftorers of learning in his time ; and, in the *literæ humaniores*, Dr. KINLOCH, phyfician to James VI. Mr. GLEG, rector of the grammar fchool, and Mr. GOLDMAN, merchant.

Some

Some Latin poems of the three laſt are to be found in the collection of the *Poetæ Scotigenæ*, which, for taſte as poems, and
elegance as Latin compoſitions, are inferior to no modern productions.

One of the moſt eminent citizens of Dundee, in the end of
the laſt, and beginning of the preſent century, was its provoſt, GEORGE YEAMAN of Murie. This gentleman repreſented the town in the laſt Scottiſh or Union Parliament, and the
diſtrict of boroughs, to which the town now belongs, in
the firſt and ſecond Britiſh parliaments ; and to him his
native country, eſpecially this part of it, is more indebted, than to any repreſentative ever ſent from Scotland.
By his good ſenſe and addreſs principally, the projects, of tax-
ing hides *by tale*, and barley for malting *by meaſure*, (than
which none could have been more injurious to a country,
where the former are ſo diminutive in ſize, and the latter ſo
comparatively mean in quality,) werè defeated ; and, when the
Frith of Forth was exempted from the general duty laid on all
coals carried by ſea, (a duty which the poor, in countries deſtitute of coal, have ſeverely felt and bitterly complained of,)
he procured, that the Tay ſhould be included within the
bounds of the Forth, and that the legal limits of the mouth
of this river ſhould be the Red Head in Angus, and St. Abb's
Head in Berwickſhire. Dundee has alſo had the honour
of being repreſented in many parliaments, by GEORGE
DEMPSTER, Eſq. of Dunichen, another native citizen. Of
this gentleman's merits from his country, it would be improper in his life time to ſpeak, and they cannot be ſuppoſed
better known to the writer of the preſent memoir, than to all
his countrymen.

Among the FAMILIES, who have had their original in Dundee, may be mentioned the truly honourable one of the FLET-
CHERS of Salton, diſtinguiſhed for giving birth to the celebrated

ed and enlightened patriot, ANDREW FLETCHER. They were
ſettled in Dundee as merchants, in the 16th century, and poſſeſſed of the lands of Inverpeffer near Arbroath; diſtinguiſhing themſelves, during the courſe of the 17th century, as
magiſtrates of Dundee, and like their deſcendants, in vin-
dicating its liberties, againſt the arbitrary claims and encroachments of the family of Dudhope; and from theſe
anceſtors, it is probable, that he embibed ſome portion of
his patriotic ſpirit. He ſprung from a ſecond ſon of this
Dundee family, and his deſcendants are now its repreſen-
tatives, the elder branch having failed ſome years ago, by the
death of its laſt male, Major HENRY FLETCHER of the marines.
Another branch of it is the family of Balinſhoe, which produced the two brothers, Sir ROBERT and Colonel FLETCHER,
lately diſtinguiſhed in the Eaſt Indies.

The preſent Lord LOUGHBOROUGH, chief juſtice of the common pleas in England, is alſo deſcended of a family long reſpectable in Dundee. The chiefs of it were ſucceſſively town
clerks for near 200 years, and frequently the town's commiſſioners to the parliament. In this ſituation they acquired the lands of Kingennie and Blackneſs, and were honoured
with the title of baronets. This title is now carried by Sir
JOHN WEDDERBURN of Ballendean, a native of Dundee, and
male repreſentative of the family.

Advantages and Diſadvantages.—The principal advantages
of Dundee are,—the noble river on which it is ſituated, opening to the inhabitants, a ready communication, not only with
the London market, but with thoſe of the principal and moſt
opulent countries of Europe; and alſo giving them a conſiderable extent of inland navigation:—The fertile countries in its
neighbourhood, the Carſe of Gowrie eſpecially, full of thriving, rich, and intelligent farmers; whoſe induſtry, if it was
firſt ſet in motion by the opulence of towns, and their increaſ-

ing

ing demand for country produce, now amply returns the favour, by equal demands on the towns for their merchandife
and manufactures :—The induftry, fobriety, and frugality of
its inhabitants, which virtues, having been confirmed by long
habit, will probably continue to be reputable for a long period
to come. In addition to thefe, it muft draw the moft fignal
benefits from the excellent turnpike roads lately conftructed,
and continuing to be extended through all the principal diftricts of Angus, and the neighbouring parts of Perthfhire.
For thefe the town is entirely indebted to the exertions of a
few country gentlemen ; and though its inhabitants have had
no fhare, either in the trouble or the rifk of the undertaking,
they will be probably the principal fharers in the profits ; for
their markets inftead of being often fhut up, and becoming
inacceffible, will now be open at all feafons of the year, for the
heavieft goods ; and the people in diftant parts will no longer be
under the neceffity of repairing to the lefs abundant markets of
inferior towns. But if Dundee enjoys thefe advantages, it is
not without its difadvantages and defects. Among thefe the
following feem to be the moft remarkable :—The lanes, and
even feveral ftreets are uncommonly narrow, and the dwellings
of the inhabitants too clofe upon one another ;—the greateft
part of the families living by half dozens, as formerly in Edinburgh, under the fame roof, with common ftairs, without
back yards or courts, and many poffeffing only fingle rooms :—
The late additional fuburbs have been built without any general plan, and without the leaft regard to health, elegance or
cleanlinefs ; though no fituation perhaps in the world, prefented better opportunities to provide for all the three :—There is
an almoft total want of public walks and open places, to which
fedentary or delicate people may refort, and children be carried for air and exercife. Several have been, or are about to
be converted to private purpofes : one, which is the beft and
moft important, is generally inacceffible, through the badnefs

of

of the lane that leads to it ; and, the high roads being deftitute of foot paths, thofe who have the greateft need of air,
find themfelves, for a great part of the year, confined to their
houfes, at leaft they cannot get beyond the ftreets ; and thefe
circumftances are the more vexatious, that the inhabitants of
the royalty are taxed annually about 130 l. for *road-money*, but
find themfelves and their magiftrates totally excluded, in confequence of a late law, from any direction in the application
of it :—The principal burying place is too fmall, in proportion to the parifh. The expence of interment in it is confidered by the poorer people as too great. Two of the moft ancient burying grounds in the parifh are uninclofed, fo that
thofe, who, for cheapnefs, have recourfe to them, fuffer the
mortification of feeing the remains of their friends treated
with indignity ; and, from the ufe of one of thefe, the poor
have, of late years, been totally excluded.—But the greateft
of all the difadvantages of Dundee, is the almoft total want of
public inftitutions, even for the moft fimple and neceffary
parts of education ; nor, excepting a reputable grammar
fchool, is there an opportunity for parents to have their children inftructed in any branch of human literature ; and this
defect is not fupplied by any tolerable public library.

Other difadvantages, at leaft caufes of difcontent, arife from
the nature of feveral public laws and inftitutions. Complaints of this kind are expreffed by the trading people, who
have fuffered lofs in confequence of the law of *perpetual
entails*, or who are expofed to fuffer it. They think, that
property of every kind ought to be liable for the debts it has
given opportunity to contract ; that the contrary practice is
unjuft, and the laws which authorife it, nothing different from
licences to a fpecies of fwindling. Befides the aftonifhing
quantity of land in the neighbouring parts of the country,
brought, of late, under this kind of fettlement, it is believed,

that

that the proportion of this parish, subjected to it, is not much less than 3000 l. a-year.—Some complaints are also made on the subject of the late *corn law*, as tending to diminish the freedom of trade in this important article, and to render it more precarious. The merchant alleges, that, while his ship is at sea, he is not sure whether the port, to which, from confidence in the law, he ordered his corn, may not, by proclamation be shut up: and certainly it has been attended with some considerable inconveniencies; for, during the last spring, seed-corn, even from England, though often of the utmost importance to this country, and various articles of household provision, which the country does not yet supply, were, by its operation, laid under an absolute *prohibition*, or a duty which, with equal efficacy, prevented importation. The intercourse for corn was not at that time permitted, even with the county of Fife, from which we are separated only by the river; and at the present time, (November the 12th 1792,) though the harvest has been bad, and the price of grain considerably raised, two vessels with grain and meal, one of which lies in the harbour, and the other is daily expected, will not be permitted to unload their cargoes. Besides these complaints, though the people here are happily free from the *coal duty*, to which their more northern neighbours are subjected, it is only from the duty on Scottish coal; and the present sudden advance in the price of this article, from 4 s. to upwards of 6 s. for 800 weight, must, while they are not relieved by importations from England, be severely felt by all the poor.—With respect to the discontents, which prevail in Dundee, about the state and mode of the representation of the people in parliament, and that they are governed by a magistracy in a great measure independent on them, these are not peculiar to this place, but common to it with all the towns in Scotland.

One

One diſadvantage of Dundee ariſes from its ſituation, and hardly admits of a proper remedy. It is the diſtance at which it is placed from any large freſh water river, with falls ſufficient for moving the various machinery, now ſo important to manufactures. The neareſt falls of this deſcription are on Dighty, and in the pariſh of Monyfieth ; but they are too diſtant for deriving full advantage from the population of Dundee.

Miſcellaneous Obſervations.—In the year 1782, the corns were much damaged by exceſſive rains, the harveſt was not completed till towards the end of November, and a conſiderable dearth followed. The inhabitants, however, exerted, on this occaſion, their uſual generoſity ; and at one time, with a view of alleviating the diſtreſs of the poor, the ſum of 200 l. was raiſed in the ſpace of two days. But the intention of raiſing this ſum was much more laudable, than the application of it. It was employed, together with the produce of other funds, in keeping the market prices of grain below the common rates of the country, a benefit in which the rich, and they who had no need, were partakers equally with the poor ; and the conſequence was, that they who had grain to ſell, carried it to other markets, which were free from ſuch timid and impertinent regulations, and where they received their prices immediately from the buyers, without having the trouble of applying, for any part of them, to truſtees of public money. Accordingly, the ſupply of the Dundee market, as might have been eaſily foreſeen, was, through the whole ſeaſon, ſcanty and difficult ; and depended entirely on the influence the magiſtrates could exert with country gentlemen, and the more opulent claſs of farmers. Even the ſupply of many families, who were not under the neceſſity of going daily to market, became a buſineſs of conſtant and vexatious ſolicitation. The

people

people of Aberdeen, where the dearth was greater, are faid to have acted much more wifely, by raifing the market price of grain, and to have advertifed large premiums to every importer of it ; and we are told, the confequence was, that their market was filled as well as in the ordinary times of plenty ; and the prices, of neceffity, foon fell to their proper level. A fmall quantity of the provifion made by government, for the poor of the northern parts of this ifland, was alfo at this time allotted to Dundee ; and the Kirk-Seffion received fome unfolicited donations, amounting to 60 l. for the poor under their infpection. In thefe, the fhare which Lord Douglas, according to his ufual humanity, contributed, was no lefs than 50 l.

In the two former centuries, the prices of various neceffaries of life, as meal, malt, ale, leather, fhoes, &c. were regulated by the magiftrates and council ; and in making, altering, and executing their regulations, they created much vexation to the dealers, and much ufelefs trouble to themfelves. The price of no neceffary of life is now regulated in this manner, except of bread made from wheat flour ; and neither does the attention of the magiftrate to this article, feem to be of much greater ufe, than it was to the others, where it has long been laid afide ; nor, though it fhould be fuppofed of ufe, does the method of regulation adopted here feem to be advantageous. On the contrary, it is perhaps the very reverfe of what it ought to be ; for the price of bread, concerning which all are judges, remains fixed, and the weight, which few have opportunity to examine, or even fometimes to know, is variable. It is probable, that were this bufinefs freed from the influence of corporation laws, it might be as fafely as any other committed to the management of thofe engaged in it ; and, that by their feparate interefts and competition, it would be equally guarded from combination and abufe. Indeed, no corporation laws whatever feem to be entitled to much refpect ; all

of

of them tend, more or leſs, to create monopolies againſt the public ; nor do they always promote the good of the very ſocieties
they were meant to favour.   The prices of admiſſion to the exerciſe of any buſineſs in Dundee, though not ſo extravagant as
in other places, particularly in Aberdeen, are, notwithſtanding, taxes frequently found to be inconvenient.   A merchant
pays to the Guildry for freedom to himſelf and his poſterity,
8 l. 6 s. 8 d. and half this ſum for freedom to himſelf only ;
an apprentice to a merchant pays 1 l. ; a handycraftſman 8 l.
6 s. 8 d. for admiſſion into any of the 9 incorporated trades ;
and, except at the times appropriated to public markets, no
ſtranger can, without a conſiderable tax, expoſe his goods to ſale
for a ſingle day.——Of perſons belonging to Dundee, who have
been condemned, baniſhed their country for life, or executed,
upon account of felonies, the writer of this account cannot,
after much inquiry, find more than *three* during the whole
courſe of the preſent century.   Since *Bridewells*, or penitenti-
ary houſes, have been eſtabliſhed in Edinburgh and Glaſgow,
Dundee has been much more peſtered than formerly, with vagrants and perſons of doubtful character, and *ſwindling* and
petty thefts are more frequent.   This will probably produce
a *Bridewell* in Dundee.   An eſtabliſhment of this kind is
certainly neceſſary, and the common priſons, and preſent in-
flictions of juſtice, are by no means ſufficient to ſupply its
place.   With reſpect to our priſons, though among the beſt
in Scotland, they are deſtitute of any court or area where the
priſoners may enjoy the open air,   This, however, is at preſent, the leſs neceſſary, as the laws of the country are ſuppoſed inhumanely, to exclude debtors from the privilege of
breathing the ſame air with others ; and, it is but very ſeldom, that felons ſuffer long confinement, in the priſons of
places not viſited by the Circuit Courts of Juſticiary.

    In this town, there are ſeveral public buildings ; but, ex-
cepting

cepting the ancient church and steeple formerly described, the spire of the chapel in the Cowgate, and the town-house, none of them seems, as a piece of architecture, to be entitled to much attention. The last is certainly a building of uncommon taste and elegance. It was planned by the elder Adams, and does him honour.

Among the regulations unfavourable to the freedom of the market, and consequently to the interests of the inhabitants, those might have been mentioned which relate to the trade in coals. There are only 4 births, or places at which vessels loaded with them are permitted to deliver their cargoes; and, if these places are occupied, all other vessels, however great the demand may be, are excluded, and must continue shut up, unless the cargoe should be sold in wholesale to one person, or unless the master, if he means to retail, will consent to sell below the current price. The first occupiers, accordingly, must reduce their prices, or see their rivals carry off all their customers. The intention of this regulation was, no doubt, to prevent any unfair rise of prices from combinations among the masters. But its real effect is to increase the risk and expence of the trade, and to induce those who are engaged in it to have recourse to other ports, rather than sell at a diminished profit, or at a loss. Perhaps there is no branch of business, wherein those intermediate dealers, often branded in law by the names of *forestallers* and *regretters*, would be more necessary, or where the encouragement of such would tend more to the general benefit. When the importer must also turn retailer, the time in which he should be fetching a new cargo is lost, and he brings fewer coals in any given period to market; and he and all his ships company must be paid for their time, instead of one regretter.

In the foregoing account, there are, no doubt, many articles omitted; particularly the *brewing* and *ship-building* manufactures. In the firſt, a numerous company is now engaged, but the chief part of the buſineſs is in the hands of particular brewers, denominated by the legal term of victuallers. Of theſe, there are 66 maſters, who employ 63 journeymen and apprentices. They make their own malt, and brew it into that kind of drink called *Two-penny*, which, till debaſed in conſequence of multiplied taxes, was long the favourite liquor of all ranks of people in Dundee. It was a liquor neither much boiled nor fermented, and always uſed within two months after being made.——Shipbuilding is ſaid to be executed here with great advantage and ingenuity. In it two maſters are employed, with 31 journeymen and apprentices ; and 6 are employed by two boat-builders.

PARISH OF DUNNICHEN.

Situation, Extent, and Name.

THIS parish is situated in the county of Forfar. It is 15 miles to the north-east of Dundee, 9 north-west of Arbroath, and 3½ south-east from Forfar. It is bounded on the east by the parish of Forfar; on the north by Recobie; on the south by Carmislie; and on the south and east by the parishes of Kirkden and Recobie. It contains about 3200 Scots acres. It takes its name from the largest hill in the parish. *Dun*, a Gaelic word, is invariably applied in Scotland to hills on which some castle, or place of strength, has stood; *Ichen* is unknown, but probably a proper name. On the south side of the hill is an eminence, now called Cashells, or Castle-hill, with visible remains of the foundation of some antient building. The only other hill in this parish is called Dumbarrow, probably from having been the burial place of some person of eminence. A rock on its north side is still called Arthur's Seat. This hill is not so high as that of Dunnichen. The hill of Dunnichen was lately measured with great geometrical accuracy. The mill stream of Muirton fulling mill, at the base of the hill, is 200 feet above low water mark in the harbour of Arbroath; and the height from

that

that ſtream to the higheſt part of the road over the hill is
443$\frac{4}{10}$ feet, above which the higheſt ſummit of the hill may
riſe about 80 or 100 feet ; ſo that the height of the hill is
about 700, or 720 feet above the level of the ſea. The hill
of Dunnichen runs about 3 miles, in a ſouth-eaſt direction ;
its ſummit forming the northern boundary of the pariſh.
The pariſh extends, from eaſt to weſt, about 4 miles, and
from ſouth to north, in one place, about 3 miles, narrowing
a little to the eaſtward.

Diviſion of Property, and Deſcription of Soil and Surface.—
This pariſh conſiſts of three eſtates :

	Acres.
Dunnichen, containing . . .	1800
Dunbarrow	600
Tullows, conjectured	800
Total	3200

The ſoil, in general, is fertile, producing wheat, flax, oats,
and barley. The ſeaſons are late, on account of its elevation.
One field is now ſown with wheat near the ſummit of the hill
of Dunnichen, and at leaſt 500 feet above the level of the
ſea ; no ſmall proof of the poſſibility of extending agriculture
ſucceſsfully on the ſides of the high hills of Scotland. Dunnichen, containing about 50 acres, is in the center of the pariſh. The moſs of it was drained about 30 years ago, and
now affords a large ſupply of peats : In all probability it will
furniſh the neighbourhood with fuel for about 30 years longer, and may then be made a rich meadow. The reſt of the
fuel is coal, brought by land from the port of Arbroath ; and
a ſmall ſupply from extenſive fir plantations, about 30 years
old.

Rivers,

Rivers, &c.—This parish contains no river nor lake. It is watered by one small brook, called Vinny, some say Finny, or Attle, which takes its rise in a neighbouring moss. It runs from west to east, along the south base of the hill of Dunnichen, and in its course turns one flax mill, and one mill for washing yarn. It joins Lunan water about 4 miles below. The burn of Craichy, which forms one of its sources, turns a corn mill. It contains some trout, much diminished of late in their number, by flax being steeped in and near its stream. A small brook runs out of the moss of Dunnichen, and falls into Vinny at the eastern extremity of the parish.

Manufactures, Villages, and Fairs.—Many weavers, principally of course linen, inhabit this parish. An attempt is now making to introduce the manufacture of coarse cottons. Dunnichen is itself a very small village, consisting of the houses of the proprietor, the manse, a public house, and the houses of a few mechanics and labourers, not exceeding 14 in all. To the eastward is the village of Drimmitormont, a very old village, inhabited by weavers, each of whom occupy six or eight acres of land. In the year 1788, a farm of 66 acres, called Letham, has been laid out by the proprietor of Dunnichen for a village. Streets have been marked out on a regular plan, and lots of any extent are let upon perpetual leases, at the rate of L. 2 an acre. It contains already about 20 families, and new houses are rising on it daily, the situation being favourable for such a plan, by having Vinny water on the south, the perennial brook of Dunnichen moss running through it, plenty of freestones on the farm itself, and thriving woods and a moss in its neighbourhood. Here a fair or market has lately begun to be held, once a fortnight, on Thursdays, for the sale of cloth, yarn, and flax; and L. 400 or L. 500 are
some-

sometimes returned in one market-day. An old established fair is annually held at Dunnichen, on the 2d Wednesday of March, old style, called the fair of St Causnan. It is a toy fair, at which neither horses, corn, nor cattle, are sold.

Church and Stipend.—The church is small and old. It was dedicated to St Causnan. There are some doubts, even in the Popish-kalendar, of the existence of this saint, although a large well near the church also bears his name; and the falls of snow, which generally happen in March all over Great Britain, is in this neighbourhood called St Causnan's Flaw. The minister's stipend is about L. 70 a year, paid chiefly in oat-meal and barley, besides a glebe of 4 arable acres, and 2 acres of grass ground.

School.—There is a parish school here. The schoolmaster's salary is L. 8 : 6 : 0 yearly, with a house, school-house, and kitchen-garden. The present schoolmaster, by his assiduous application to the duties of his office, has raised a considerable school, having seldom fewer than 50 or 60 scholars, whom he teaches to read and write English, arithmetic, and Latin, when any of the children require that branch of education.

State of the Poor, Parochial Funds, and Records.—There may be about a dozen of poor and indigent persons belonging to this parish, principally reduced to poverty by old age or distempers. A sufficient fund for their maintenance arises from the voluntary contributions of the parishioners, collected on Sundays, and at the time of the sacrament. It amounts at present to about L. 20 Sterling a year, and is yearly increasing; and from it a reserve of L. 62 : 1 : 10 has been made as a provision for bad seasons. Of these poor people some

receive

receive a quarterly, and some a weekly allowance, according as their necessities require. The fund is managed by the clergyman and kirk-session, who being intimately acquainted with the circumstances of every poor person in the parish, are enabled thereby to proportion the supply to their wants and exigencies.

This parish affords one, among perhaps many instances in Scotland, how safely the maintenance of the poor may be left to the humane and charitable disposition of the people, and how unnecessary it is to call in positive laws to their assistance; for, if such laws provide funds for maintaining the poor, they also provide poor for consuming the funds.

Population.—This parish has much increased in its population since the returns made to Dr Webster about 40 years ago, and it still continues on the increase. At the above mentioned period, it contained only 612 inhabitants; whereas it appears, from a survey made last year, that their number amounts to 872, whereof 75 belong to the anti-burgher meetings of Forfar and Dumbarrow. An abstract of the marriages, baptisms, and burials, for the last ten years, is subjoined.

Years.	Baptisms.	Marriages.	Burials.
1781	19	10	14
1782	19	15	20
1783	29	9	12
1784	22	5	13
1785	25	12	30
1786	24	7	45
1787	29	10	14

Years.	Baptifms.	Marriages.	Burials.
1788 .	22 .	4 .	18
1789 .	33 .	14 .	10
1790 .	25 .	3 .	14
	237	89	190
Yearly average	24	9	19

As the difproportion between the deaths of males and females appears fomewhat extraordinary, it is inferted from the grave-digger's Report.

	Men.	Women.
1781 .	11 .	3
1782 .	18 .	2
1783 .	9 .	3
1784 .	11 .	2
1785 .	27 .	3
1786 .	40 .	5
1787 .	12 .	2
1788 .	18 .	0
1789 .	7 .	3
	153	23

Difproportion nearly $6\frac{5}{8}$ to one.

Mode of Cultivation and Produce.—This parifh, like the reft of the country, has of late received confidèrable improvements in agriculture. About 30 years ago, the old fyftem began to be altered. Leafes, which formerly were few, and feldom granted for a longer term than 9 years, have lately been

been granted for 19 years, and the life of the tenant, and some for longer and more indefinite terms. On the principal estate in the parish called Dunnichen all servitudes were abolished, viz. thirlage to the mill and blacksmith's shops, carriages, and bonnage, a word of Gothic extraction, which means shearing corn. Money-rent was substituted in the place of oat-meal, barley, kane-fowls *, yarn, and mill-swine. The farms were inclosed with fences of free-stone. Better houses and offices were built. The breed of cattle and horses was improved. Turnip, potatoes, kale, and clover and rye-grass, were planted and sown for winter provision. The distinction of out and infield was laid aside, and all the fields were cropt and cultivated in due rotation. But these improvements were much facilitated by means of a valuable manure which began to be used about that time in this and the neighbouring parishes, viz. shell marl, to which the late considerable increase of the value of the lands may in a great measure be ascribed. This valuable manure being found in greater plenty in this neighbourhood than any where else in the kingdom, or even perhaps in the known world, it may not be thought impertinent to describe it more particularly. About two miles north from Dunnichen, there are a chain of lochs which abound with marl, viz. the lochs of Forfar, Restineth, Recobie, and Balgavies. In these lochs, it lay long an inaccessible treasure, till, about forty-five years ago, Captain Strachan, proprietor of the loch of Balgavies, began to drag it, much in the same manner that ballast is dragged from the bed of the river Thames. This he performed with so much success, as not only amply to supply his own farms, but to have a surplus for his neighbours. His example was
soon

* Part of the rent was formerly paid in fowls, which were called kane.

foon followed on the other lochs; and, about 30 years ago, the late Earl of Strathmore, by means of a drain, lowered the furface of the water of the loch of Forfar, thereby opening a ftill more extenfive fupply of marl; and, in the year 1790, Mr Dempfter of Dunnichen drained the loch and mofs of Reftineth, by which an inexhauftible mafs of fhell-marl has been made acceffible. Marl is fold at 8 d. a boll, containing 8 folid feet; fixty bolls are commonly ufed for the firft dreffing of an acre of land. Its qualities are precifely the fame with thofe of lime Which of thefe manures is preferable, has been long a fubject of frequent difpute among the farmers; but the chemical analyfis of marl fhews clearly that marl is in every refpect the fame with lime, and poffeffes the additional advantage of being found in a pulverifed ftate, and requiring no calcination previous to laying it on the land. The fimilarity of the two has been ftill farther evinced by Mr Dempfter having conftructed a kiln on a plan fuggefted by Dr Black • for calcining marl, which, after calcination,

makes

* The conftruction of the kiln, and method of calcining the marl, will appear from the following extract from a letter of Dr Black's to George Dempfter, Efq; dated 28th November 1789.

" There is no doubt but that fuch marl as you defcribe may be burned to very good lime, if the proper degree of heat can be applied to it. In a country where the only fuel is peat, I have no hopes of fuccefs with the Reverberatory. With fuch fuel, in fuch a furnace, it would be expenfive beyond meafure, and perhaps impracticable, to produce the neceffary degree of heat. Neither is the experiment likely to fucceed in a drawkiln, in which fo much duft and rubbifh muft be produced by the defcent of the lime, and attrition of the maffes againft one another, that the paffages for the air would be too much obftructed. But, in a kiln in which the maffes of marl would be little difturbed, the operation might fucceed very well. I would therefore prepare the marl as the harder kinds of peat are prepared in fome places, by laying it, while foft, on a plot of

grafs,

makes a very strong cement. The calcination of marl will, it is hoped, prove an useful discovery in this neighbourhood, to which other lime must be fetched from the distance of 14 or 16 miles.

The improvements made in this parish have been principally confined to the estates of Dunnichen and Dumbarrow. Dunnichen paid, about 30 years ago, nearly L. 300 of yearly rent,

grass, and forming it into a bed some inches thick ; this bed, while drying, may be a little compacted, by beating it with the flat of the spade or shovel, and, before it be quite dry, it may be cut into pieces of the size of peats. The best kiln for burning it should have nearly the shape of a draw-kiln, or should have a much deeper cylindrical cavity than the vulgar kilns in which lime is burnt ; it may be from 20 to 30 feet deep, and from 8 to 9 feet in diameter ; the top of it should be covered with a dome or arch, having an opening at top, 3 feet diameter, to let out the smoke, &c. and a door in the side of this dome for introducing the materials ; at the bottom, where the kiln is a little contracted, should be a grate 5 feet square, the bars of which being loose, might be drawn out occasionally. In charging this kiln, lay first 18 inches depth of peats over the whole grate, then throw in prepared marl and peats intermixed until the kiln is filled to the top, and at the top of all there should be some peats without any marl ; then shut up the door at the top of the kiln with stones and mud, and throw in the kindling at the vent of the dome. The fire will be slowly communicated from the top to the bottom, so as to charr the whole peats, and to expel the remains of humidity from the masses of marl ; and this will be accompanied with very little consumption of the inflammable matter ; but, when the whole is charred, it will begin to burn with abundance of heat, first at the bottom, and gradually upwards, until all the peats are completely consumed. Then, by drawing the bars of the grate, the kiln may be drawn. I cannot say what proportion the peats should bear to the marl, but am of opinion that a very moderate proportion may be sufficient in the middle and upper parts of the kiln. To know whether the marl is thoroughly burnt, slake the lime with water when fresh drawn from the kiln, and try if the slaked lime will dissolve in aquafortis, or spirit of salt, without effervescence."

rent, in corn, money, and other articles, in kind. The farm-buildings were ruinous hovels; the ground was over-run with broom, and furz or whins, and many parts of the arable land were wet and boggy, and all without trees. It has, since that time, been drained and inclosed. Most of the muirs, which make a fifth part of the estate, have been planted with thriving timber. The fences of many of the fields are surrounded with hedge-row trees. The land has been marled. The present rents may be fully treble the former. The arable ground now lets, when out of lease, from L. 1 to L. 1 : 10 : 0 per acre. The meanest cottager is now better lodged than the former principal tenants. Wheat grows well on several of the farms. There is no where better flax, turnips, potatoes, and artificial grasses. There are several different systems of cropping the ground. The rotation of the best land is oats, flax or fallow for wheat with dung, barley, and sown down with grass seeds, grass for the three or four following years. A second rotation is, two crops of oats, a crop of barley, a green crop, a crop of oats or barley, with dung, and sown down with grass-seeds, hay cut one year, and the grass pastured three or four. Ten bolls of wheat are raised on an acre, and sixteen stone of scutched flax *. The inclosed fields are let for 40 or 50 s. an acre for pasture, and for L. 5 an acre for flax. Compost dunghills are in general use, with a certain proportion of marl, about 8 or 10 bolls to an acre, which is found to answer well; and it is generally now understood that, if fields are not over-cropt, they cannot be over-marled. It is difficult to ascertain accurately the increased produce of an acre, in consequence of the improved agriculture. But it is universally allowed that the farmers were poorer when the rent

of

* A stone of flax is worth 12 s.

of their land was from 4 to 5 s. an acre, than now when they pay three or four times that sum.

Minerals.—Little search has been made for minerals in this parish. The most valuable is free or grit stone ; it is easily quarried, and is found in every part of the hill of Dunnichen, and other par s of the parish, and is very fit for building houses and stone-fences. A few strata of whin-stones appear in some places, and a coarse iron-bar in the hill. No symptom of coal has as yet discovered itself any where in this county.

Air and Climate.—The air of this parish is supposed to be remarkably healthy, from the many old people in it ; and the climate is nearly the same with that of all the eastern coast of the island. In the spring, and beginning of summer, easterly winds generally prevail after mid-day, attended with chilliness, and sometimes fogs, though in a less degree than nearer the coast of the German Ocean. The heaviest rains come in autumn and winter, from the south-east, attended by violent winds, which last sometimes two or three days, and occur twice or thrice in the year.

Antiquities.—There are only a few antient tumuli or barrows in the parish, which, when opened, are found to contain human bones, in rough stone coffins. Pots of a coarse earthen ware are also sometimes found in them. Neither coins nor arms have as yet been discovered in or near them, to assist our conjectures as to their date. In the moss of Dunnichen have been found very large roots of oak trees, and some horns of the red-deer, and also a stratum of coarse marl below the moss, and six feet under sand.

High

High Roads.—The late act obtained two years ago, for e-
recting turnpikes on the great roads, and for commuting into
money the ſtatute labour for improving the parochial roads,
promiſes ſoon to effect a thorough reformation on the
roads of this country. The commutation has nearly quadru-
pled the effective labour applicable to the roads, and this
muſt be employed within the pariſh where it is levied The
proprietor of Dunnichen intruſts the application of the fund
to the principal farmers in the pariſh, who are far from
grudging to pay a tax from which they reap ſo much benefit. Many of the roads have, in the firſt year of the tax,
been formed, and the dangerous parts amended. The ſum
levied in this pariſh is about L. 27 Sterling yearly, and that
of the whole county exceeds L. 2000 a year. Turnpike
roads, between Cupar of Angus, Forfar, Arbroath, Dundee,
Cupar of Angus, and Meigle, and from Dundee to Montroſe,
are in great forwardneſs, and will probably be fully completed in the courſe of this and the next ſummer, in ſpite of
ſome antient prejudices, by which their progreſs has been
conſiderably retarded.

Miſcellaneous Obſervations.—The ſmall-pox frequently proving fatal to the children of the pariſh, Dr John Adam of
Forfar has attended ſome days this ſpring for inoculating
all the children of the pariſh *gratis*. But, although this meaſure was publicly recommended in church by the miniſter,
and privately by the whole kirk-ſeſſion, yet, ſo ſtrongly do
the antient prejudices prevail againſt this mode of communicating the diſtemper, that only nine or ten children have
been inoculated. They have all recovered ; and it is hoped
that inoculation will ſoon become general in the pariſh, from
the ſucceſs with which this firſt experiment has been attended.

Ai-

Although the granting of leafes for nineteen years, at leaft, is now become univerfal, yet there prevails a confiderable diverfity of opinion among proprietors of land as to the expediency of including the life of the farmers in their leafes. Some advantages, however, feem to give a decided preference to this laft fort of leafe. The tenant knows he is fettled for life, and is therefore afraid to over-crop his land, left he fhould thereby injure himfelf. Many law-fuits are thereby avoided on this fubject. The tenant is alfo fuppofed to be more attentive to the repairs of his buildings and fences ; and he certainly requires a much lefs vigilant infpection on the part of the proprietor, or his factor.

In order to protect the newly planted trees round the farmer's inclofed fields, the proprietor of Dunnichen has given the heirs of the tenants a right to one third part of them, at the expiration of the leafe ; and he engages not to profecute the tenants for any accidental dammage the trees may fuffer from cattle, or otherwife. The tenants on this eftate confider the trees as a part of their own property, and are at pains to protect them from injury, and to have other trees planted in the room of fuch as have fuffered. A fenfible warmth is derived to the fields from fuch of thefe fence-rows as have been planted fifteen or twenty years ago.

It is apprehended, until farms are tranfmitted from father to fon, like an inheritance, as is much the cafe in England, agriculture will not attain all the perfection of which it is capable. *Veteres migrate coloni*, is an odious mandate, marking bad times for the country. When leafes are granted for the tenant's life, he has a chance of getting his fon's life added to his own, by paying a moderate fine to the proprietor.

When

When the estate was begun to be improved, many of the tenants were unable and averse to the modern system. These were generally left in possession of their houses, with a small portion of land, on a lease for their own life and that of their wives. The remainder of the ground was laid out into new farms, and let to more enterprizing tenants.

It may not be improper to explain the meaning of some words used in this account, which, though well understood at present, will require to be explained to after generations, full as much as the most barbarous customs of our ruder ancestors require to be explained to us.

Thirlage *.—When the proprietor of a barony or estate builds a corn-mill on it, he obliges all his tenants to employ that mill, and no other, and to pay sometimes nearly double what the corn might be ground for at another mill. As this servitude tends to make millers careless and saucy, it will without doubt soon be universally abolished.

Smiddy or Smith's Shop.—Formerly one blacksmith, who was also a farrier, was only allowed to exercise his business on a barony or estate. He had the exclusive privilege of doing all the blacksmith and farrier work. For this he paid a small rent to the proprietor, and every tenant paid him a certain quantity of corn. About thirty years ago, a person of this description had this sole right on the barony of Dunnichen, for which he paid L. 1 yearly.

Services.—These are of various kinds. On some estates, the

---

* Some of these customs have been briefly explained in different notes in various parts of this volume.

the tenants are bound to dig, to dry, and to fetch home and build up, as much peat as is neceſſary for the proprietor's fuel through the year. In this manner the tenants are employed during moſt part of the ſummer. It prevents them from fallowing and cleaning their grounds, fetching manures from a diſtance, ſowing turnip, &c. On other eſtates, it is the duty of the tenants to carry out and ſpread the dung for manuring the proprietor's land in the ſeed time, which frequently interferes with his own work of the ſame kind. It is alſo the duty of the tenants to fetch from the neighbouring ſea-ports all the coal wanted for the proprietor's uſe. The tenants are alſo bound to go a certain number of errands, ſometimes with their carts and horſes, and ſometimes a-foot, a certain number of long errands, and a certain number of ſhort ones, are required to be performed. A long errand is what requires more than one day. This is called *carriage*. Tenants are alſo expected to work at any of the proprietor's work a certain number of days in the year. In ſome places, this obligation, it is ſaid, extends to 52 days, or a day in the week.

Bonnage—is an obligation, on the part of the tenant, to cut down the proprietor's corn. This duty he muſt perform when called on. It ſometimes happens, that, by cutting down the proprietor's crop, he loſes the opportunity of cutting down his own.

This whole catalogue of cuſtoms is ſo adverſe to agriculture, and to the true intereſts of the proprietor, that, in a ſhort time, their very names will probably be obſolete, and the nature of them forgotten.

The following plan of a navigable canal, not indeed within the

the bounds of the parifh, yet, being connected with it, ought to be mentioned. In the year 1788, Mr Whitworth the engineer was employed to take a furvey of the country, for the purpofe of bringing a navigable canal from the port of Arbroath to Forfar. That gentleman made out an accurate plan of this canal, which he reported to be highly practicable. It required 25 locks to conduct it from Muirton Fulling Mill to Arbroath ; the diftance 13 miles 1 firlong and 2 chains ; the perpendicular height above low water-mark 196 feet. The expence he computed at L. 17,788 : 17 : 8. As there is no reafon to believe the trade on this canal would at prefent defray this expence, the plan is laid afide, and the furveyor's Report is depofited in the town-clerk's offices in Forfar and Arbroath. This ufeful work will probably be refumed again when the country fhall have attained more wealth, and further improvements. It would ferve to convey coal, lime, and wood, into the center of a very populous country deftitute of thefe articles.

PARISH OF EDZELL.

(Presbytery of Brechin.—Synod of Angus and Mearns.
—County of Forfar.)

By the Reverend Mr ANDREW HUTTON.

Surface and Extent.

EDZELL is situated on the N. E. corner of the county of Forfar. The body of the parish is a kind of peninsula, formed by the two radical branches of the North Esk, called the East and West Waters, which here unite, and form what is properly stiled the North Esk, a considerable river, separating the counties of Forfar and Kincardine, and containing many lucrative salmon fishings. This peninsula is about $2\frac{1}{4}$ miles in length, by $1\frac{1}{4}$ in mean breadth, and is considerably distinguished from the rest of the parish in soil and fertility. The soil here is generally light black earth, or sharp gravel, with a tinge of clay; and the bottom is gravel or yellow sand. Beyond this is another district, betwixt the hills and a projection from them, about $2\frac{1}{4}$ miles in length, from E. to W. and 1 mile in breadth, the soil of which is more mixed with clay, upon a bottom generally of cold wet clay. This quarter will sometimes yield good crops of oats and bear, but is not so grateful to the farmer as that of the former district. Beyond this, the parish stretches 6 or 7 miles up the East Water, with a breadth of about $\frac{1}{4}$ of a mile. Here the soil is

still

ſtill inferior, being ſtony or ſandy, with a bottom of gravel, mixed with large ſtones or rock.

Proprietors, Rent, &c.—The firſt of theſe three diſtricts, about one half of the ſecond, and the whole of the third, belong to the Honourable W. Maule of Panmuir. The remaining part belongs to Sir Alexander Ramſay Irvine, Bart. The firſt diſtrict, whoſe ſurface is almoſt a dead flat, never fails, with good management, to produce, in ordinary years, good crops of oats, bear, (rough bear or Cheſter), peaſe, turnips, flax, and potatoes. The land, though leſs ſtrong and rich than in many other places, is dry and early. It has happened for a courſe of years, that when the crops have greatly failed in other places of the country, the farmers in this quarter have enjoyed crops much above the rate of their neighbourhood. Artificial graſs, eſpecially white clover, proſpers well; but that rich and permanent ſward of graſs which is found in more powerful ſoils, is wanting here. Rent, in this quarter, does not exceed 9 s. *per* acre, which is eaſy to pay, from the induſtry and improvements of the preſent leſſees. About 60 acres of village lands, occupied by about a dozen of families, give 15 s. or thereby. The tenants in this quarter ſtand chiefly by grain and black cattle. The two other diſtricts have not the ſame advantages, as labour upon them is liable to be kept back in ſeed-time; and the crop, from the wetneſs of the bottom, is ſubject to be caſt too late in harveſt. One half of the middle diſtrict, whereof the ſoil is inferior, rents ſtill lower than the former diviſion. The other half yields about 10 s. In this quarter, the tenants have the advantage of ſheep, in addition to their grain and black cattle. The rent of the third diſtrict, which is far from means of improvement, and which is ſtill more expoſed to bad ſeaſons, cannot be well aſcertained. The pro-

fits

fits of the farmer arise more from sheep and cattle than from grain.

Climate.—The air is generally sharp and piercing, as the surface of the parish is for the most part bare of shelter, and is opposite to two glens, which generate a current of air. No unwholesome vapour can arise, on account of the quick circulation of water, as there is every where a ready communication with the rivers, whose channels are deep and rapid.

Natural

Diseases.—There are no very remarkable instances of longevity. One man, who had been born, and lived most of his life in this parish, died a few years ago, near to the age of 100. Another gave an account of himself, which must have made him to be above that age ; but it appears from the records, that his claim was not well founded. One woman now lives in the village above the age of 90, and is still able to move about : another is 86. Several have reached above 80. The most prevailing complaints are, asthma amongst the men, and hysterical disorders amongst the women, rheumatism in both sexes. These may, in part, be caused, or not a little heightened, by poor diet, hard labour, and sorry lodging. Consumptions are also fatal to persons in this parish. No peculiar epidemical disorder prevails. Several years ago, many were cut off by an infectious putrid fever, which was, however, more fatal in some neighbouring parishes. The people are fast surmounting their prejudices against inoculation. Some observe, that the ague was frequent in their youth ; but the complaint is now hardly known.

Antiquities.—The castle of Edzell is one of the most magnificent ruins any where to be met with. It long belonged to the family of Lindsay, and now belongs to Mr Maule of Panmuir. It consists of two stately towers evidently in different stiles, and built at different periods. These are connected by an extensive wall ; and large wings went backwards from the towers. Tradition says, that the square tower, the most ancient, was built and possessed by the family of Stirling, from whom it descended to Lindsay of Glenesk. Of the former family, no traces now remain in these parts. The Lindsays of Glenesk, afterwards of Edzell, make a distinguished figure in Scottish history. Buchanan mentions several remarkable actions in which these chieftains

(reguli

Natural Productions.—The water of the North Esk has obviously a petrifying quality; because the rocks through which it runs are of all degrees of consistence, from sand in the very first stage of concretion, to stones of sufficient hardness for all the purposes of ruble building. There is also a lime-quarry, to which all the tenants of the proprietor have right. It has been of some service for a long course of years; but the difficulty of procuring fuel to burn the lime-stones, is a bar in the way of its being very extensively useful. There are still many spots of natural birch. But there is not a doubt this parish once abounded with fine oak and beech, as stately trees are often found in the mosses. There is a tradition,

(*reguli de Glenesk*) were engaged. After coming to the possession of Edzell, their power surpassed that of any other family in the county One of this family, about the beginning of last century, built a small castle, called *Auchmull*, in this parish, and another, called *Innermosk*, in Lochlie, as lurking holes, while he was forced to skulk several years for the murder of Lord Spynie. One of them succeeded his cousin, Earl Crawfurd, who had disinherited his own son; but the honours and estate afterwards reverted to the natural heir. The last of this family left the country about 1714, having greatly degenerated from the martial character of his progenitors, and afterwards died in the north of Scotland, or in Orkney, in poverty and wretchedness. This family, like other powerful chieftains, possessed the power of life and death upon their estate. The place of execution still retains its name.

In two different parts, appear those monuments of antiquity commonly named *Druidical temples*. Two of these are found at Culindie, considerably up the glen, within a few yards of one another. They consist of tall upright stones, inclosing elliptical spaces; the largest about 45 feet by 36, the smallest somewhat less. There is in one the appearance of a small portico or entrance. They must be of very great antiquity; because the stones of which they are formed, though exceedingly hard in consistence, are yet hollowed and wasted away by the weather. Several miles further south, at Dalbogg, is a third, but not so entire as the two former. The ground on which they stand is considerably elevated.

tion, that the elevated grounds, dividing the upper and lower quarter of the parish, were formerly clothed with wood; now they bear only heath. Previous to 1714, there were some avenues to the castle of most stately beech, of which hardly a vestige now remains. The late Earl of Panmure, about 20 years ago, made two plantations, chiefly of Scotch fir; one of them about 4 miles in circumference, the other of less extent. Both are thriving admirably, and promise advantage to the proprietor, and much benefit to the country.

Birds and animals are much the same as in other parts of the country. Birds of passage are, the cuckoo, swallows of different species, sea-gulls occasionally, from a loch in the neighbourhood. Birds of song are, linnets, thrush, blackbird, red-breast. Wild animals are, fox, hare, otter, polecat, weasel. No deer are inhabitants of the parish, although a severe storm sometimes occasions a visit from them. There is a considerable salmon fishing. The fish are mostly disposed of by contract with merchants in Montrose concerned in the London trade. The sheep may amount to about 2000. The horses and cattle are not distinguished by any remarkable circumstance. Till lately, the horses were in general rather of middling strength, but the breed is gradually improving. It is believed that the parish supplies itself with that article, but it does not much more. The farmers here have not hitherto attended much to search out the best breed of either horses or cattle. The better sort may average about 18 l.; the inferior much lower. Best oxen, from 3 to 4 years old, about 6 l. Best cows about 5 l.; inferior, 3 l.

State of Agriculture.—Under this head, the circumstances of the parish, compared with what they were 30 years ago, offer a very pleasing subject of contemplation. At that period, the greater part of it had been recently held of tacksmen

under

under the York Buildings Company, by a precarious and cruel tenure of one, two, or three years. The tenants had no encouragement to induſtry, and they were not induſtrious. Almoſt their only mean of ſubſiſtence aroſe from their ſheep. The land hardly repaid labour ; 40 or 50 threaves (4 ſtooks) have been often talked of as then inſufficient to yield a boll of grain. In tearing the miſerable ſoil, they uſed often 6 horſes, ſuch as they were, never leſs than 4, often 4 horſes and 6 cattle. Lime, as a manure, was almoſt unknown. *Now*, they enjoy the ſecurity of leaſes, judiciouſly granted, to encourage the erecting of good ſteadings, and improving the ground. Lime has been employed with great ſucceſs. An inſtance lately occurred, of about 16 bolls of oats, and another of 20 bolls of bear, after one. The uſual average may be about 6 returns of the ſeed. The ground is almoſt never let out of cropping, without being laid down with graſs ſeeds. The ordinary ſpace of ſo lying is 4 years, of which the firſt, and ſometimes the ſecond, is hay ; the remainder paſture. From two fifths to one half is generally in graſs. The land is cropped 4 years, of which one or two are green crops. Turnips ſuit well, but are not yet cultivated to the height which they will probably ſoon reach, as it is not as yet very common to raiſe them for the purpoſe of feeding. Every one has them in greater or leſs quantity, as winter food for milch cows and young cattle. Flax ſuits this ſoil. The average quantity raiſed may be about 16 acres. Cabbage, as a field crop, has been tried in ſeveral caſes with good ſucceſs. The quantity of potatoes raiſed is very conſiderable, as almoſt every family is connected with land, and ſupply themſelves with that moſt uſeful root. The grain is ſuch as may be expected. It is neither ſo weighty nor valuable as that produced from carſe or richer inland ſoils ; but it is, in general, at leaſt equal to that of the ſurrounding country.

try. No wheat, and but little barley, is raiſed. The bear is not remarkably large·in the grain, but is thin in the rind, weighs well, and recommends itſelf to the maltſter and meal-maker. Oats, in ordinary years, give 16 pecks of meal, of 8 ſtone, after 16 pecks of grain. Until within a few years ago, the old Scotch plough was univerſally uſed, even on the moſt clear and eaſy ſoils ; and the harneſs was ſuch as the ordinary farm ſervants could make. Now, Small's plough, with the ſhort iron head, and caſt metal mould-boards, is getting into uſe. Harneſs, of the moſt complete kind, is every day coming into faſhion. Two horſes, with one man to work them, are now pretty general, and will ſoon be wholly eſtabliſhed, as the price of labour is high ; and more attention will be paid, of courſe, to the rearing and keeping of horſes. It appears that agriculture, at ſome diſtant period, was purſued to conſiderable extent ; becauſe the preſent race of tenants, notwithſtanding their great progreſs in improving waſte lands, have not yet gone ſo far as their forefathers reached. Many tracks of land are found, with the marks of cultivation, pretty far up the hills, and in many other ſpots now covered with heath, which the farmers of the preſent day have not yet been able to overtake.

Rent.—There are two farms above 50 l. ; 10 from 20 l. to 50 l. ; upwards of 30 below 20 l. ; ſome ſo low as 3 l. inde-pendent of the village lands, which are occupied by 13 per-ſons at about 48 l. Total rental at this time 950 l.

Population.—There is ground to believe, that population, in the laſt century, was at leaſt equal to what it now is. From the entry of baptiſms in the old records, it appears that the village (Slateford) was then more populous than now. There are intimations of other villages, of which there is now little

more

more than a veſtige. Many farms are named which do not
now exiſt; and the adjoining farms have not received a proportional increaſe. The foundations of buildings are frequently found where there is not now a houſe. Indeed it
would not be ſurpriſing that population ſhould flouriſh in the
immediate vicinity of a powerful family, ſo able, in turbulent
times, to protect its retainers, and diſpoſed to encourage ſet-
tlers, by the appointment of village fairs, markets, and otherwiſe. The pariſh would ſeem to have loſt, in point of population, from the Revolution till within the ſpace of 20 or 30
years ago, when the numbers have probably increaſed.

Population Table.

Number of ſouls in 1755	862	In the village - 117
————————— in 179½	963	In the country - 846
Males - -	470	Married perſons - 294
Females - -	493	Children of each mar-
Under 10 - -	228	riage at an average 4$\frac{1}{11}$
Males - -	111	Widowers - - 14
Females - -	117	Widows - - 24
Between 10 and 20 -	212	Bachelors above 50 - 10
Males - -	114	Unmarried houſeholders
Females - -	98	under 50 - 10
Between 20 and 50 -	371	Unmarried women above
Males - -	163	45 - - - 8
Females - -	208	Epiſcopalians - 40
Between 50 and 70 -	114	Bereans - - 10
Males - - -	63	Seceders - - 2
Females - -	51	Roman Catholic - 1
Between 70 and 100 -	38	Perſons not connected
Males - - -	19	with any denomina-
Females - -	19	tion - - 2

Perſons

Persons who cannot read, strangers - -	3	Alehouse-keepers -	4
Proprietors (non resident) - -	2	Smiths - - -	5
		Taylors - -	9
Clergyman - -	1	Waulkmiller - -	1
Schoolmasters (1 parish, 1 Society, 1 private)	3	Masons - -	2
		Drystone dykers -	3
Average scholars taught English, writing, arithmetic - -	45	Wheelwrights and turners - - -	2
		Wrights - -	5
Merchant - -	1	Shoemakers - -	5
Shopkeepers - -	3	Flaxdressers - -	4
Maltman - -	1	Weavers - -	13
Carter - -	1	Lint-miller - -	1
Male farm servants -	66	Houses inhabited -	205
Female ditto - -	50	—— built within 4 years - -	24
Day labourers - -	17	—— turned to other purposes, ditto -	6
Cottarmen, servants to their landlords -	16		

Manufactures, Exports, &c.—No manufactures are carried on. The only shadow of them is, that the weavers generally make pieces of coarse cloth for country use, which they sell at the different markets in the neighbourhood. The exports are, oats, bear, meal, black cattle, sheep, yarn, butter, cheese, fowls, eggs, and coarse cloth. The imports are, wood, iron, leather, house and farming utensils, salt, tea, sugar, spirits, fine cloth, many of the necessaries, and almost all the luxuries of life. These, however, are not yet consumed in an extraordinary quantity; and the exports do certainly far overbalance the imports [*].

Circumstances

* *Prices of Provisions.*

	40 *years ago.*					*At present.*
Meal *per* boll -	8 s.	-	-	-	-	15 s.

Bear

Circumstances and Character.—The people are nearly of one class and condition. Their way of living arises, either wholly or in great part, from the culture of the ground. Their manners are suitable to their condition. Most of the farmers are now in easy circumstances, the consequence of the hard labour, frugality, and attention of the present generation. They have not laid aside those good habits. With few exceptions, they are distinguished for integrity, sobriety, and diligence. Acting from a sense of their relation to their Maker, they are, of course, punctual and serious in performing the duties of religion. Their devotion, too, is of a rational, tolerant nature, not breaking out into heats against those who entertain different opinions, but manifesting itself in

	40 years ago.	*At present.*
Bear *per* ditto -	8 s. - -	15 s.
Eggs *per* dozen -	1½ d. 2 d. -	5 d. 6 d. 6½ d.
A fowl - -	4 d. - -	9 d. 10 d.
Butter *per* lib. of 24 oz.	4 d. - -	8 d. 10 d. 11 d.
Butcher meat *per* stone	2 s. 6 d. - -	4 s. 4 s. 8 d. 5 s.

Prices of Labour.—A sufficient ploughman's fee from 7 l. to 8 l. subsistence about 4 l. - Total L. 11 or L. 12 The cottager's encouragement, being in ground and servitudes, may be rather better for himself; but, all things weighed, cheaper to his master. This useful class of men, who are going fast out of fashion, form in their families the best nurseries of male and female servants.

Young men from 14 to 19, fee 4 l. 10 s. or 5 l. subsistence 4 l. - - - - Total L. 9 0 0
Herds for cattle from 11 to 14 years of age, fee 1 l. 10 s. subsistence 3 l. - - - Total L. 4 10 0
Female servants, average fee about - - 4 0 0
Men shearers for whole harvest, with subsistence 1 10 0
Women ditto, ditto - 1 2 0
Men shearers, and mowers of hay, about the village, *per* day, with subsistence - - - 0 1 0
Women ditto - - - - - 0 0 9
Day labourers in summer, with meat, 6 d. and 8 d. without, 10 s. and 1 s.

in an equal and charitable fpirit. The diffenters from the
eftablifhed Church attend occafionally upon it, and live with
the minifter and people as if there was no difference in their
views. Splendid acts of beneficence do not fall within their
lot. But the poor in the feveral quarters of the parifh, in
fuch fevere feafons as this, in point of fuel, find themfelves
cared for by their neighbours, when even the good aliment
from the feffion funds could not command the carriage of
that effential article. In the year 1783, fo diftrefsful to
Scotland, the farmers in the body of this parifh had a better
crop, and more fafely got in, than in almoft any part of the
country. Several of them manifefted their good difpofitions,
by fending meal to be difpofed of by a proper perfon in a
centrical fpot, to fuch houfeholders as were recommended by
the kirk-feffion, confiderably below the market price. The
people here are, in general, extremely contented with their
condition; and they have no fmall caufe to be fo, as even
the pooreft of them, both men and women, who enjoy
health, have abundance of work, and good encouragement.
Even the cottars, fubtenants, tradefmen, and labourers, who
have families, have their children fought after almoft as foon
as they are able to do any thing; and the education of the
young folks is often helped forward by thofe with whom
they refide, in order to attach them more ftrongly as fervants. The people here have no propenfity to emigration
and adventure. Not above one or two are in the army, and
none in the navy. A confiderable number of the prefent
inhabitants were born in other parifhes, but all are natives of
Scotland. To this contented, quiet fpirit, it is probably owing that flagrant crimes do not occur. It is beyond a doubt,
that the people are much improved fince laft century, both in
morals and in manners. In the old records, there are inftances of perfons fubjected to difcipline for dragging nets on
the

the Sabbath; and farmers, with their wives and servants, convened in parties for drinking, fighting, and scolding, on the Lord's day during divine worship. Such irregularities would now cause horror.

Disadvantages.—One disadvantage under which this parish formerly laboured, was the want of opportunities of giving their children education, from the inconvenient form and circumstances of the place. That is now remedied, to a certain extent, by a school appointed under the Society for propagating Christian Knowledge, (whose institutions are producing admirable effects), above two years ago in one quarter, and by a private school established since, by the aid of one of the proprietors, in another. The encouragement of the parish schoolmaster is pitiful, and, from the alteration of circumstances, in no respect what it was originally intended to be. Another disadvantage, which probably never can be remedied, so far as to render this corner the seat of any extensive manufacture, is scarcity of fuel. The mosses are generally steep, and far distant; and the labour of preparing and carrying home peat, &c. is excessive; and even these are nearly exhausted. Montrose, the sea-port town, is distant about 12 miles, which greatly enhances the price of coals. The proposal, however, to remove the coasting duty, is a most gracious and seasonable motion, and, we may hope, will contribute, with other circumstances likely to happen, to allow that useful article at a reasonable rate. Other fuel is turf, cut from the muirs, and broom, which is of service, while the improvements in agriculture allow any to remain.

Poor.—The number of poor, upon an average of the last 6 years, is 12. The average of the sum distributed to them for the same period, 18 l. The session funds arise, in part,

from

from the intereſt of a ſum of money, in part from the voluntary collections in the church, which average 14 l. Theſe
two maintain the poor in ſuch a way as not only to be free
of complaint, but to give full ſatisfaction to themſelves, and
to thoſe who live around them. If any happen to be wholly helpleſs, board is allowed for them to their neareſt relations; or, if they have none ſuch, perſons are paid for undertaking the care of them. There are two ſtated meetings,
at Whitſunday and Martinmas, for the purpoſe of fixing the
rates of the following half year, and for purchaſing clothes.
There is no great danger of impoſition, as the poor muſt have
reſided 3 years, at leaſt, before any aid can be given. The
elders in each quarter, by converſing with neighbours, and
by their own obſervation, are able to form a pretty juſt
judgment of their neceſſity.

Eccleſiaſtical State.—The church is a very old, ſtrong building, incommodious in itſelf, and inconveniently ſituated for
the whole pariſh. The date of the building is not known ;
but it muſt have been erected long before the year 1641, as
I find that the kirk-ſeſſion in that year paid the " Sclaitter
" for poynting the kirk, 5 l. 13 s. 4 d. Scots. It. Mair of
" drink ſiller to his boy, 6 pennies." The manſe was built
71 years ago, indifferently executed at firſt, in a low ſituation,
has been often repaired at a conſiderable expence, and now
is in bad condition. The ſtipend is about 61 l. with a glebe
worth about 7 l.: but a proceſs of augmentation is now
depending. The Crown is patron.

UNITED PARISHES

OF

ESSIE AND NEVAY,

(COUNTY AND SYNOD OF FORFAR, PRESBYTERY OF
MEIGLE.)

By the Rev. Dr PLAYFAIR.

Situation and Extent.

THE pariſhes of Eſſie and Nevay, 3—4 miles from
weſt to eaſt, and 2—3 from north to ſouth, are bounded on the eaſt and ſouth by the pariſh of Glammis, on the
ſouth-weſt by Newtyle, on the weſt and north by Meigle
and Airly ; lying in the preſbytery of Meigle, commiſ-
ſariot of St Andrew's, ſynod and county of Forfar ; in
extent amounting to 8 ſquare miles, that is, about 5120
Engliſh or 4096 Scotch acres ; whereof about 2500 are
cultivated, 530 in paſture, 220 covered with wood, and the
remainder heathy and barren.

Surface

Surface and Soil.—The northern declivity of the Sidla hills compofes one half of both parifhes. The foil of this divifion is a thin black mould, on a bottom of mortar ; but, its expofure notwithftanding, it is more fertile, and yields earlier crops, than any part of that ridge which fronts the fouth. Towards the fummit of the hills the foil degenerates, and is fit for planting or pafture only. The higheft part of the fouthern boundary does not exceed 950 feet above the level of the adjacent plain.

The foil of the lower part of the parifh is various. In Nevay, a level and marfhy tract, containing fome mofs on a ftratum of fand, is a continuation of the extenfive mofs of Meigle. No marl has been found in the former, though there be abundance in the latter. That tract ftretches eaftward to the church of Effie, and north to the Dean. Some plots of it are cultivated ; the reft affords indifferent pafture. A low and flat territory, north of Effie, confifts of a ftrong and rich clay, ill cultivated, and liable to be partially inundated by the river, which, in time of heavy rains, overflows its low banks. To the eaftward of the church the foil is thinner, but friendly to vegetation.

Climate.—A greater quantity of rain falls in this diftrict than in the low country fouth of Sidla. Laft fpring (1793) the fields in this neighbourhood were refrefhed by copious fhowers, while the Carfe of Gowrie, and territory to the eaftward, remained dry and parched. The reafon of this difference feems to be, that all clouds and vapours from the fouth-weft are divided near the mouth of the river Earn, and attracted partly by the Sidla Hills, and partly by an elevated ridge ftretching along the north coaft of Fife ; fo that little rain from that quarter falls upon the interval between thofe mountains. But, favoured as Strathmore is in this refpect, the weather in general is extremely variable.

able. The ſpring is late; the autumn frequently cold and rainy; and during winter the piercing north-eaſt wind prevails. The mildeſt month in the year is July. Seed-time begins about the end of March, and is concluded in two months; the hay-harveſt is in July, and corn-harveſt from the beginning of September to the end of October.

Rivers, &c.—The Dean, which flows from the loch of Forfar, forms the northern boundary of Eſſie, and runs weſtward to the Iſla, into which it falls near Meigle. As this deep and ſluggiſh river paſſes through a very level country, there are few falls ſufficient for the purpoſe of machinery. Between its ſource and termination, the difference of elevation does not exceed 40 feet in the ſpace of ten miles. At Cookſtown, however, a mile W. N. W. of the church of Eſſie, there is a corn and a lint mill, both on the north bank of the river, and a communication to the ſouthward is opened by a bridge lately conſtructed. This river is noted for the large ſize and delicious taſte of its trouts. It contains alſo pike and perch, but no ſalmon, except a few *black fiſh* or *kelt* in autumn.

A rivulet, which riſes in the hill of Nevay, and is augmented by a ſmall ſtream from a drain in the marſh already mentioned, forms the weſtern limit of the pariſh of Eſſie, and county of Forfar. In its progreſs northward it turns a mill, below which it loſes itſelf in the Dean.

Another rivulet, called the burn of Eſſie, deſcends from a hill in the Sidla ridge, bathes the wall of the church-yard, and falls into the Dean. On this rivulet there is a lint-mill about a quarter of a mile S. E. of the church, on the turnpike-road to Glammis. There is no lake nor ſtagnate water in either pariſh.

Eſtates.

Eftates.—Towards the conclusion of laft century, the names of the proprietors of both parifhes were, the Earl of Strathmore, the heirs of Lord Couper, Nevay of that Ilk, Blair of Balthayock, and Lamy of Dunkennie. Three of thefe families have difappeared, two remain. The parifh of Nevay now belongs to the Right Honourable James Stuart Mackenzie, Lord Privy Seal of Scotland; and that of Effie is divided among five proprietors, none of whom has a feat in the parifh. The lands are under the management of frugal, induftrious and fubftantial farmers. The proprietor of Nevay lately granted new leafes to his tenants on this and his other eftates in Strathmore. His moderation and generofity on that occafion will not be foon forgotten. Every occupier of a farm was fecured in the poffeffion of it, upon condition of paying a very fmall rife of rent. Had the ufual methods of fcrewing and racking tenants been adopted, the landlord might have greatly increafed his revenue; but he preferred the pleafure of making feveral hundreds of people comfortable and happy.

Farms.—The extent of farms is from 50 to 500 acres. The number of the moft confiderable is thirteen. They are in general larger than thofe in the fame diftrict 40 years ago. The enlargement of farms is attended with fome difadvantages. When cottages are demolifhed, their inhabitants are conftrained to retire to towns in queft of lodging and fubfiftence. When thefe nurferies of population fail, a fufficient number of working people cannot be eafily procured, and the fcarcity of a commodity proportionally enhances its value. The want of labourers is moft fenfibly felt in time of harveft. Some farmers find it neceffary to employ bands of fhearers from the north country, who cut down the corn at the rate of 6 s. or 7 s. *per* acre, and as foon as this work is finifhed, retire to the mountains.

In

In a rainy feafon the hufbandman cannot always collect day-labourers fufficient to manage and bring home the crop, fo that part of it is fometimes loft. This inconvenience is never known where cottagers are one of the productions of the foil.

The beft arable land is let below 20 s. the acre. No rent is paid *per* advance. No fervices are required, except the carriage of fome coals from Dundee. A few of the tenants have power to fubfet; but this privilege is not generally granted. The valued rent of both parifhes is about L. 1200 Scots; the real rent is L. 1270 Sterling.

An acre of good land well cultivated produces, in fucceffion, 10 bolls oats, peafe 5 or 6, wheat 8, turnip valued at L. 5 Sterling, barley 10 bolls, fown grafs 180—240 ftones of hay, befides another crop for green feeding the fame feafon. The prices of grain and hay are regulated by the market at Dundee. The expence of labour, provifions and implements of hufbandry is the fame as in the neighbouring parifh of Meigle, (fee Vol. I. p. 515.)

Inclofures.—Inclofing and fubdividing, partly by ftonewalls, and partly by a ditch and bank fet with quick, were introduced about 30 years ago by the proprietor of Nevay. A great proportion of the whole diftrict is now inclofed with fences of the latter kind, which fhelter the fields from inclement blafts more effectually than ftone walls, but in a calm and moift feafon prevent a free circulation of air, and thereby prove hurtful to the crop. The ditches, however, being fufficient drains, render the fields in all feafons fit for cultivation. The practice of pruning hedges, fo as to make the top flat and the fides perpendicular, prevails. A better plan has been adopted in fome neighbouring diftricts, *viz.* to flope both fides gradually till they meet in a fharp ridge at top. By this mode of dreffing a hedge, every part

of

of the plant being expofed, receives its proper nourifhment. In Nevay, rows of trees are planted in the hedges, which embellifh the country, but eventually muft be prejudicial to the thorns, and the adjoining part of the fields.

Manures.——Befide the dung of the farm-yards, and compoft, confifting of weeds, ditch-fcourings, ruins of mud-walls, &c. confiderable quantities of marl are ufed. This excellent manure, whofe qualities and operation are now well underftood, is fetched from the moffes of Baikie and Meigle. The original price is 8 d. *per* boll, containing 8 folid feet. Sixty bolls are allowed to an acre ; but, by many experiments formerly made in the parifh of Bendochy, it appears that a larger proportion will not injure the foil, if it be not overcropped. Marl incorporated with compoft anfwers better than when mixed with farm-yard dung. It is ufually fpread on the furface of fallow, or on grafs, fome time before a field is broken up.

Live Stock.——Little attention is paid to the different breeds of animals. 141 horfes are ufed for the purpofes of hufbandry ; but moft of thefe are purchafed from diftant counties. No black cattle are employed, though a few are reared. Sheep are entirely banifhed.

Mines, &c.——Near Caftletown there is one mineral fpring, and another on Sidla, a mile fouthward of Effie ; but their qualities and virtues are unknown. A fmall vein of filver ore, too inconfiderable to be wrought, was difcovered feveral years ago in the fouth-eaft corner of the parifh. An excellent freeftone quarry, in the parifh of Nevay, at the foot of Sidla, has been lately neglected. The ftone is of a light grey colour, and admits of a fine polifh.

Fuel.

Fuel.—Peats are found in the moſs of Cookſtown. The appriſed value of every cart-load, together with the expence of digging, winning, and carrying it two or three miles, may amount to 2 s. 6 d. Three cart-loads for domeſtic uſe are ſcarcely equal to one boll coals of 56 ſtones avoirdupois weight, the price of which, including carriage 12 miles, is 9 s. The ſcarcity and dearneſs of fuel have induced many of the inferior claſs to leave this part of the country.

Plantations.—There are few trees in this diſtrict, hedge-rows excepted. On the eſtate of Dunkennie, a mile eaſt-ward of the church of Eſſie, a ſmall thriving plantation of Scotch fir diverſifies the ſcene; and part of Sidla Hills was planted by the late Earl of Strathmore. A plantation of foreſt-trees on a barren tract to the weſtward, would be equally ornamental and uſeful.

Houſes.—There is no town nor village in Eſſie or Nevay; for the cottages near the church of the latter do not merit either of theſe appellations. The farm-houſes and offices, with a few exceptions, are neatly built of ſub-ſtantial maſon-work. The dwelling-houſe confiſts of two ſtories covered with ſlate. The huts of ſubtenants and mechanics have ſtill a mean appearance, though more comfortable than at a preceding period. The farmer's mode of living is as much improved as his habitation. His attire is decent, his houſehold-furniture not inelegant, and his table plentifully ſtored. In affluence he rivals the middling order of proprietors, and in hofpitality excels them.

Antiquities.—About a mile weſt of the church of Eſſie, on the north ſide of the turnpike-road through the Strath, there is an ancient fortification, ſurrounded on the weſt, ſouth, and eaſt ſides, by a very deep and broad itch, and on on the north by a rivulet, whence the ditch was filled with water. Within a vast earthen mound or rampart is an area 120 yards in length, and 60 in breadth. Some antiquaries have ascribed this work to the Romans; but their route lies 2 miles northward, on the opposite side of the river Dean. Some coins of Edward I. having been found in the area, it is probable this fort, or castle, as it is vulgarly called, was constructed by the army of that invader. Vestiges of a large encampment may be traced at no great distance on the farm of Inglestown, a name which seems to favour my conjecture. At the church of Essie there is a stone 6 or 8 feet long and 2 broad, with several hieroglyphical characters engraven upon it, representing a hunting match. The purpose for which this monument was erected is unknown. At present it lies in a rivulet, and must soon be defaced.

Population.—The population of this district has remained nearly the same for a century past. A. D. 1727, it contained 640 inhabitants. According to the report made to Dr Webster, the number of examinable persons was 500; and there are now (A. D 1793) 630 souls. Householders 132, servants of both sexes 102, weavers 29, tailors 4, shoemakers 5, wrights 5, masons 4, blacksmiths 3. Average of marriages 10, of births 20, of deaths 12.

Manufactures.—No manufacture has been ever established in these parishes, owing to their local situation, and distance from any considerable market-town.

Roads.—A turnpike-road from Perth to Aberdeen traverses the parish of Essie; and near the manse a toll-bar was erected several years ago; but the road westward to the limit of this parish is still unfinished, and thence to

Meigle

Meigle it is almost impaſſable during winter. There is no direct road from either pariſh to Dundee; but one from Glammis, and another from Newtyle, to that ſea-port, were lately completed; and the diſtance between one or other of theſe places and the moſt remote point in the diſtrict does not exceed four miles.

Church, &c.—There is a ſmall church in each pariſh, where divine ſervice is performed alternately. The church of Eſſie is ſituated on an eminence, 2 miles weſt of Glammis, and 5 from Meigle; that of Nevay ſtands on a riſing ground, formerly ſurrounded by a marſh 2½ miles S.W. of Eſſie. Both are mean fabrics. The date of the union of theſe pariſhes was prior to the middle of laſt century. The manſe, near the church of Eſſie, has a commanding proſpect to the weſt and north-weſt. It is well built, and the offices are in good condition.

By an old decreet of locality, the ſtipend was aſcertained to be L. 433 : 6 : 8 Scots money, and 4 chalders victual; and the glebe conſiſted of 4 acres of land adjoining to the manſe, 1½ acre at the church of Nevay, and an acre of graſs. An augmentation having been granted not many years ago, the living is now worth L. 90 a-year. The names of the miniſters ſince the reformation are, Mr David Brown, Mr Crichton, Mr Silveſter Lamy, Mr Adam Davidſon, Mr Alexander Finlayſon, Mr Maxwell of Strathmartine, and Mr Ogilvy, the incumbent.

School, &c.—The parochial ſchool and ſchoolmaſter's houſe are ſituated near the centre of the diſtrict, about 1½ miles S.W. of Eſſie church, in a barren ſpot at the foot of Sidla. The ſalary, with other emoluments annexed to that office, may amount to L. 12 Sterling. The number of ſcholars for ſome years paſt has been inconſiderable.

Character.

Character.—The inhabitants of this territory are ſober and induſtrious, ſtrangers alike to intemperance and diſſipation of every kind. The vice of dram-drinking, which if we may rely on Statiſtical information, ſo much prevails in many pariſhes of Scotland, is here unknown. There is not a tavern or alehouſe in either pariſh. Theſe people, however, are open, generous and hoſpitable. That ſervile ſpirit, which diffuſed itſelf among the lower claſs during the rigour of the feudal ſyſtem, no longer exiſts; and paſſions then predominant have ſubſided. They are neither proud nor paraſitical. Mild and peaceable, they are neither ready to reſent an injury, nor to harbour revenge. Attached to the national church, and the preſent form of government, they are not inclined to ſchiſm, nor prone to ſedition, nor liable to change. Not a few of them enjoy the benefits and comforts of ſociety, and all are contented with their condition.

PARISH OF FERN.

(*County of Angus.*)

By the Rev. Mr JOHN GILLANDERS.

Name, Situation, and Extent.

THIS parish is suppofed to take its name from a Gaelic word which fignifies *farm ;* probably in allufion to the quality of the foil, which is, in general, very good, and which might then be fuperior in fertility to the neighbouring diftricts. Others derive it from a word in the fame language, fignifying *the den ;* and if it was meant to apply to that part where the church ftands, it is very characteriftic, as it is fituated in a low place, of an elliptical form. The extent of this parifh is about 2 miles from eaft to weft, and 5 from fouth to north. It is fituated 6 miles from Brechin, (the feat of the prefbytery), and lies in the county of Angus or Forfar.

Soil, Climate, &c.—The greater part of the furface is a light loam, and has a good expofure ; the reft, which may comprehend a farm or two, has a clay bottom. In the hilly parts there are 5 fheep farms. The fheep walks are wholefome, few dying of the rot, or by any hurtful herbs. The climate, for this northern latitude, is mild and temperate, particularly towards the fouth ; in the hilly parts, fomewhat

more

more sharp, and cold ; yet the whole is accounted salubrious, there being no standing lakes or marshes, which are often so fatal to health. Of course, diseases arising from colds and damps are not frequent, and the people, in general, live to a good old age.

Rivers, Hills, and Trees.—There are two burns or rivulets in the parish, the *Cruick* and the *Noram.* The former has its source in it, and both abound with black trouts. The hills abound with the ordinary game of the Grampians. A-bout 25 years ago, it had a very naked appearance : There was no timber of any sort, but a few planes and ashes, in the old taste, round the garden dykes ; but now there are several hundred acres laid out in plantations of Scottish fir, and hard timber, all in a thriving state.

Cattle.—There are about 120 or 130 horses employed in husbandry, from 2 to 4 in a plough. On the sheep farms above 800 sheep are kept, of different breeds; and their wool sells, one year with another, from 14 s. to 20 s. *per* stone.

Fuel and Fossils.—The tenants have peat and furze from the hills, and drive some coals from the nearest sea-port towns, Montrose and Arbroath. Within these few years, there has been discovered, in the grounds, of the principal proprietor, a slate quarry, of a light blue colour, and pretty hard. A few cart loads have been taken out of it, but no farther trial has been as yet made.

Population.—For these 30 years past the population has been on the decrease. Many petty farms being con-verted into one, numbers of families have been driven into the towns ; and farms that formerly supported 5 or 6 fami-lies,

lies, are poffeffed only by one. The whole number of fouls, young and old included, is about 490. The return to Dr Webfter, in 1755, was 500, but the amount was probably more confiderable. The marriages laft year amounted to 4, the births to 9, and the deaths to 7. There are 3 fhoemakers in the parifh, 4 taylors, and 4 weavers.

Heritors and Rent.—There are only 4 heritors; two occupy their own lands, a third has only one farm, all the reft of the parifh is the property of one gentleman. The lands let at from 5 s to 25 s *per* acre. The valued rent is 23 : 4 l. 3 s. 4 d. Scots, or 192 l. 16 s. 11⅓ d. Sterling. The real rent, as now paid, has not been afcertained.

Agriculture.—The crops chiefly raifed are oats, peale, barley, lint, and graffes; for the moft part clover and rye-grafs. The feed time commences the 1ft of March, and the harveft commonly in Auguft. The principal proprietor has bound his tenants to a certain rotation of crops, and to inclofe about two thirds of their farms with ftone dykes, the value, of which is to be paid for, at the end of their leafes, by the landlord. They are alfo *thirled* to the mill for what corn they confume in their families.

Church and Poor.—The ftipend is 1000 merks Scots paid in victual, befides an allowance for communion elements in money. The manfe has been lately repaired, and the offices rebuilt. The poor are fupported by the weekly collections, the intereft of their funds, and fome grain from a mortification.

Wages.

Wages.—A taylor's wages is from 4 d. to 6 d. *per* day, with victuals. Farm servants get from 6 l. to 8 l. a year; household servants, nearly as much. Cottagers, who work daily to their masters, have, for wages, some land laid down with grass for a cow or mare, or permission to feed with the farmer's own cattle; their fuel led, with a house and yard free.

PARISH OF FERNELL.

(*County of Angus.*)

By the Rev. Mr DAVID FERGUSSON.

Name, Situation, &c.

THE antient, and true orthography of the pariſh, is *Fernell;* but it is uſually written *Fernwell*, or *Farnwell*. Fernell is ſaid to be of Gaelic origin; *fern* ſignifying, in that language, a *den*, and *nell*, a *ſwan;* ſo that it ſhould ſeem to have derived its name from an adjoining den, which, at that time, had been the abode of ſwans. On the north ſide of this den ſtands an old caſtle, once the reſidence of the anceſtors of the preſent family of Airly. The pariſh church is about three Engliſh miles ſouth of Brechin. The pariſh lies in the ſhire of Angus, preſbytery of Brechin, and ſynod of Angus and Mearns. It is about three Engliſh miles long, and two broad.

The pariſh of Kinnaird, which lies between the pariſhes of Fernell and Brechin, was diſjoined from that of Fernell, and formed into a ſeparate pariſh, about the year 1633. In the year 1771, at the inſtance of the heritors of the pariſhes of Brechin, Fernell, and Kinnaird, the Court of Seſſion annexed almoſt the whole of the pariſh of Kinnaird to Fernell,

and

and the reſt of it to Brechin ; which annexation took place in the year 1787.

Soil.—The ſoil is fertile, and generally low land, being ſituated in the middle of a ſtrath, which extends to Montroſe, about five miles diſtant to the eaſt. This part of the pariſh conſiſts of a very fine clay and loamy ſoil, perhaps as good as any in Scotland, and very much reſembles the ſoil of the Carſe of Gowrie, betwixt Dundee and Perth. The ſouth and weſt part of this pariſh is higher ground ; the ſoil alſo is of a different nature, and inferior quality, conſiſting chiefly of black earth. Some of the fields, in the eaſt part of the pariſh, are ſubject to inundations, from a ſmall river, which, taking its riſe in the muirs, and being increaſed by a number of ſmall ſtreams, ſometimes in autumn ſwells to an amazing ſize, overflows its banks, and breaks down the adjoining fences.

Rivers.—The only large river in the pariſh is the South Eſk, which riſes among the Grampian mountains, runs cloſe by the ſouth ſide of the town of Brechin, and after meandering beautifully through the ſtrath, diſcharges itſelf into the baſon, formed by the reflux of the ſea, on the weſt ſide of Montroſe. A conſiderable part of this river forms the boundary of the pariſh of Fernell, on the north. It abounds in ſalmon and ſalmon-trout ; and the fiſhing upon that part of it, which now belongs to the pariſh of Fernell, the property of Sir David Carnegie, in extent about two miles and a half, pays about L. 90 Sterling of yearly rent.

Population.—In May 1791, there were living in the pariſh 620 perſons, of whom there were,

Under

Under 10 years of age, - -	126
Unmarried, - - - -	297
Married, - - - -	172
Widowers and widows, - -	25
	620

Eight of thefe 620 were between 80 and 90 years old. Within thefe few years the number of inhabitants has decreafed confiderably by the enlarging of farms, and of courfe removing feveral families of farmers, cottagers, and fubtenants. In Dr Webfter's report, however, the number is only 509.

Table of births, marriages, and burials, before the annexation.

	Births.	Marriages.	Burials.
1784,	13	5	11
1785,	10	3	5
1786,	13	1	9
1787,	10	10	5
At a medium,	11	5	7

Since the annexation,

	Births.	Marriages.	Burials.
1788,	15	7	19
1789,	22	5	11
1790,	15	6	13
At a medium,	17	6	14

No regifter of burials was kept here before the year 1784.
The

The number of the principal farmers is 11 or 12, moſt of whom are married and have families. Several of them pay L. 100, ſome from L. 100 to L. 150 of rent; and one pays L. 250. There are ſeveral other ſmall farms, which let at different prices; as, 5, 8, 10, 20, or L. 30. There are only three or four families of diſſenters; of whom one or two are Epiſcopalians, and the reſt Non-jurors. There are no Seceders, nor Roman Catholics.

Productions.—There are about 2200 arable acres in the pariſh, of which 8 or 900 acres are of a rich clay ſoil. The greater part of the pariſh is incloſed; the haughs or low grounds, where the ſoil is richeſt, with thorn hedges; and the others with fences of earth and whins, or with ſtone dykes; which laſt is acknowledged to be the beſt of any. Several improvements in this way have been carried on of late years, and the farmers ſeem to be convinced of the benefit of incloſures. All the uncloſed ground is therefore to be incloſed by the heritors with ſtone dykes, the tenants paying the intereſt. The farm houſes are in general very good; they, as well as the offices, being built of ſtone, and covered with ſlate. The principal crops in the pariſh are wheat, oats, barley, and peaſe. The quantity of wheat ſown here, has, for ſome time, greatly increaſed, and the clay ſoil is peculiarly adapted for it. This year there are about 150 acres of wheat ſown. Of late, there has been almoſt no Cheſter bear ſown, barley being preferred, on account of its giving a greater return, and a higher price. A conſiderable quantity of peaſe, ſome beans, and a great deal of clover and rye-graſs, are ſown in the pariſh; and uſually about 30 acres of flax. Turnips and potatoes are a general crop all over the country. Yams are alſo ſucceſsfully cultivated for feeding cattle, and are ſaid to anſwer better with
milk

milk cows than turnips, as the milk of cows fed upon them
is not affected with the diſagreeable taſte, which the turnips
never fail to give it.   Oats, peaſe, and flax, are ſown from
the beginning of March to the end of April; barley, from
the middle of April to the middle of May; and turnips,
from the middle till the end of June, and are generally
ſown in drills.   September and October are the months for
ſowing wheat.   The harveſt generally begins about the end
of Auguſt, and, in ordinary years, the crop is got into the
barn-yards before the middle of October.   The loamy ground
is cultivated four years in tillage, and four years in graſs.
The clay lands are cultivated in ſix parts, viz. fallow, wheat,
peaſe, barley, clover, and oats.   A greater quantity of every
ſpecies of grain, than is neceſſary for the maintenance of
the inhabitants, is raiſed within the pariſh.   The unarable
ground conſiſts of paſture, waſte ground, and planting.   The
extent of the natural paſture cannot be exactly aſcertained ;
neither can the meaſurement of the land, denominated waſte
ground, be given; but it is neither extenſive nor uſeleſs, as it
ſerves to ſupply the inhabitants with broom or whins for fuel.
Of planting, there may be between 3 and 400 acres, the
greater part of which is Scots fir ; but in the pleaſure
grounds at Kinnaird, there is a great quantity of fine thriving wood of all kinds.

Church and School.—The ſtipend of Fernell, now, in conſequence of the annexation from the pariſh of Kinnaird, is,
103 bolls, 9 pecks meal; 32 bolls oats; 67 bolls and a firlot Cheſter bear, and L. 24 : 13 : 3 Sterling, communion elements included ; beſides a manſe, garden, and glebe of about
7 acres.   The late Earls of Southeſk were patrons of this
pariſh ; but, in conſequence of the forfeiture of their eſtate,
in the year 1715, the right of patronage is now in the poſſeſſion of the Crown.   Sir David Carnegie, Bart. of Southeſk,

eik, is the representative of the family, has his seat at Kinnaird, and is proprietor of all the parish, except Little Fithie, a small estate of about 100 acres, the property of William Gibson, Esq; who resides upon it. The manse and church were repaired in the year 1752; and the school-house was built in the year 1747. The schoolmaster's salary is about L. 10 Sterling *per annum*; and he has, at an average, twenty-four scholars, who are taught English, writing, and arithmetic.

Poor.—The number of poor in the parish is, at an average, 12. There is a mortification, by Dean Carnegie, of 800 merks Scotch; the annual interest of which, together with the interest of some former accumulated collections at the church door, amount yearly to about L. 19 Sterling, which is distributed among the poor. The funds have rather increased than diminished for some years past. No poor in the parish are allowed to go about begging; but this, as well as other parishes in the neighbourhood, is much oppressed by vagrants and sturdy beggars; an evil generally complained of, but never attempted to be remedied.

Wages.—About 40 years ago, the annual wages of the best labouring man servant was about 40 s. *per annum*; at present, they cannot be hired under L. 7 Sterling. About 40 years ago, maid servants wages were about 20 s. *per annum;* now they are L. 3, or something more yearly, besides some perquisites.

Fuel.—The fuel in general used among the lower ranks of the people, for a long time past, was turf, brought from Monthrithmont Muir; but that muir was, some years ago, divided among the gentlemen of property in the neighbourhood,

hood, and no turf was afterwards allowed to be carried out of it. In consequence of which, fuel is a scarce commodity here ; and that now used by the lower ranks is the branches of firs, which are pruned from the woods, or such broom and whins as the uncultivated grounds afford. Coals are also brought from Arbroath, about eight miles distance, where they are bought for 6 s. or 6 s. 6 d. *per* boll, (72 stone) free of any duty to government ; so that they are 1 s. 6 d. cheaper than at Montrose, where the duty is levied. No peats can be had within 12 or 14 miles.

Miscellaneous Observations.—In this parish there are 60 carts and 40 ploughs, 20 of which are ploughs constructed for four horses, and 20 for two horses ; so that the number of labouring horses is 120. The number of black cattle is supposed, at an average, to be about 600. There are no sheep kept in the parish, as there are no hills or waste ground to supply them with pasture. The roads were formerly kept in repair by the tenants, who had their labour appointed according to the extent and value of their farms. Last year the statute act took place, which converts the labour into money, at the rate of 1 l. 4 s. Sterling for every L. 100 Scots of valued rent. There was collected last year in this parish, including the tax on saddle and work horses, L. 31 Sterling, which is in future to be collected every year, for the purpose of repairing the roads. There are no manufactures carried on here, all the people being employed in farming, except a few who follow handy-craft employments, such as taylors, wrights, shoemakers, weavers, &c. They are a sober and industrious set of people, enjoying, in a reasonable degree, the conveniencies and comforts of society, and seemingly contented with their situation and circumstances. There are no ale-houses, nor is the want of them considered by the people as an hardship.

PARISH OF FORFAR.

(COUNTY AND PRESBYTERY OF FORFAR, SYNOD OF ANGUS AND MEARNS.)

By the Rev. MR. JOHN BRUCE.

———————

Name and Extent.

THIS parish, in all writings concerning the patronage, tithes, &c. is designed the parish of Forfar-Restenet; though the latter part of the name is seldom mentioned in conversation or in common writing. Restenet was perhaps the name given to the Priory, expressive of the purpose for which it was built, namely, a safe repository for the charters, &c. of the monastery of Jedburgh; but some take its derivation from a Gaelic word, *Risk*, signifying, as they say, a bog or swamp, which indeed answers to the situation.

Forfar is conjectured to be the same with the antient Or, and the Roman Orrea, signifying a town situated on a lake, to which description it exactly answers; and the lake to which it stands, has for many ages been known by the name of Forfar.

The parish is divided into burgh and landward; whether Forfar and Restenet have some time or other been two different parishes, parifhes, and afterwards united, is not certain; but the burgh and landward parts of the parifh have long had, and continue to have, diftinct interefts in fo far as relates to the fupplying of the poor, and they make feparate collections for them at the church door.

The form of the parifh is irregular, its greateft extent from N. to S. being about 6 Englifh miles, and from E. to W about 5; though in fome places, it does not exceed 3 Englifh miles in breadth and 4 in length. The town in which the church and manfe are built is fituated near the N. W. corner of the parifh. The loch of Forfar, the property of the Earl of Strathmore, and a part of the parifh of Glammis, formerly wafhed the border of the minifter's glebe in that part which lies contiguous to the manfe: and the eaftmoft houfe in the parifh of Forfar in within a gun-fhot of the kirk of Refcobie.

Town of Forfar.—Forfar is a royal burgh of confiderable antiquity, and the capital of the county of Angus or Forfar; the fheriff whereof has held his court for upwards of two hundred years in this town, which is pretty centrically fituated for the adminiftration of juftice. It is alfo the feat of the prefbytery of Forfar; confifting in all of eleven parifhes, the churches of which lie around it, at, or within the diftance of four computed miles, except that of Cortachie which is rather more than five.

The ground on which it ftands, with that for a confiderable way around, is uncommonly uneven, and covered, as it were, with hillocks of various fizes, as if nature had here, at fome period, fuffered a convulfion. Though low with refpect to the circumjacent ground on every fide excepting the Weft, it is high in comparifon to the general level of the country. The lakes and fprings, a mile to the eaft of it, run eaftward and empty themfelves into the German ocean at Lunan Bay. Its own fprings, and thofe on the weft fide of it, run directly

weft

weſt through the fertile valley of Strathmore, till they join the Tay near Perth; and ſuch is level of the country, that it has been thought practicable, and by ſome an object worthy of commercial attention, to open a communication by a canal between Forfar and the ſea in either of theſe directions *.

Forfar commands a fine view of the Seedlaw hills and the valley of Strathmore, terminated by the Grampians on the weſt, the moſt conſiderable of which is about 50 miles diſtant. In that direction is the famous Schihallion.

Forfar is perhaps a ſingular inſtance in Scotland, of a town of any note, built at a diſtance from running water; but the vicinity of the lake with its numerous ſprings, and the protection of the caſtle, a place in former times of conſiderable ſtrength, muſt have firſt invited the inhabitants of the country to ſettle and form a village, which afterwards becoming the occaſional reſidence of Majeſty, was diſtinguiſhed by conſiderable numbers of royal favours, the memory of which is preſerved in the names of places and fields within the royalty, ſuch as the King's muir, the Queen's well, the Queen's manor, the palace-dykes, the guard-breads, &c. †

The

* A few years ago, a young gentleman belonging to the navy conducted, for a wager, a ſmall boat all the way from the loch of Forfar by Perth to Dundee, and was obliged to leave the boat only in one or two places, where a ſudden fall of the water made ſailing dangerous.

† In the caſtle of Forfar Malcolm Canmore held his parliament in the year 1057, immediately after the recovery of his kingdom from the uſurpation of Macbeth,——A figure of the caſtle, cut in ſtone, remains upon the manſe and the market croſs, and forms the device of the common ſeal of the burgh; though nothing but ſome rubbiſh remains on the ſpot where it ſtood. It is probable, the moſt uſeful ſtones have been from time to time abſtracted for building houſes; and it appears that the weſt entry to the old church, and a great part of the materials of the preſent ſteeple, had been taken from it. From the extent of its territory, and the names of places, it would ſeem

The burgh is governed by a provost, two bailies, and twelve common counsellors, who are elected annually by themselves with the assistance of four deacons of crafts, who are also members of council, (but chosen by the members of the respective corporations,) and fifteen other burgesses nominated for the occasion, by the retiring provost and bailies.— The annual council, thus consisting of nineteen members, have the privilege of electing a delegate, to vote for the election of one representative in Parliament for the burghs of Perth, Dundee, St. Andrews, Forfar, and Cupar in Fife.—The revenue of the burgh, arising from lands, customs, &c. is supposed, *communibus annis*, to be little below L. 400 sterling clear, and it is yearly increasing.

The incorporation of shoemakers, which is still the richest in the town, was, previous to the year 1745, the most numerous; and the wealth of the place arose chiefly from their industry

seem, that the community had been enriched by repeated marks of royal bounty; nor do the inhabitants seem to have been insensible to the kindness shewn them by their sovereigns. A parliamentary ratification, dated 1669, of the Royal writ of *Novodamus*, dated 1665, proceeds upon the abstraction of the original charters and rights of the burgh, and the plundering of the inhabitants in 1651 for their attachment to the Royal Family, and particularly on " the faithful testimony and dissent " given be Alexander Strang, late Provost of Forfar, and commissioner for the " said burgh, against passing of the unjust act of the pretendit parliament, the " 16 of January 1647, entitled, Declaration of the Kingdom of Scotland " concerning his Majesties Person." This act, which bears such honourable testimony to the humanity and public virtue of the chief magistrate of Forfar, besides confirming all the ancient rights and privileges of the burgh, ratifies its right to the patronage and tythes of the parish, disponed by James and Sir George Fletchers of Restenet, and of any feus or rents payable out of the burgh acres to the priory of Restenet, the abbey of Coupar, and Lord Torphichen. In the year 1684, as appears from the date upon it, the market cross was erected, it is said, at the expence of the crown, and it stands to this day, a monument of the loyalty of Forfar, though in the eye of the police it is perhaps a nuisance as an incumbrance on the street.

duſtry in manufacturing a peculiar fabric of ſhoes, which they ſtill carry on to a great extent, it being well adapted to the uſes of the country people, particularly in the braes of Angus. —About the year 1745 or 1746 the manufactory of Oſnaburgh was introduced here, which from very ſmall beginnings has grown into a great trade, and has become the ſtaple of the place ; and the happy influence of which, particularly of late years, is viſible in the amazing increaſe of population and wealth, and the conſequent improvement of every thing.—This branch of manufacture was brought to Forfar by a gentleman ſtill living there, who has acquired by it a comfortable independence.—His brother, a weaver in or near Arbroath, (about the year 1738 or 1739) having got a ſmall quantity of flax unfit for the kind of cloth then uſually brought to market, made it into a web, and offered it to his merchant as a piece on which he thought he ſhould, and was willing to, loſe. The merchant, who had been in Germany, immediately remarked the ſimilarity between this piece of cloth and the fabric of Oſnaburgh, and urged the weaver to attempt other pieces of the ſame kind, which he reluctantly undertook. The experiment however ſucceeded to a wiſh.—Many hands were ſoon employed in the neighbourhood of Arbroath, where a Company was eſtabliſhed to promote the buſineſs, and from whence the diſcovery was brought to Forfar at the period above mentioned.—Before that time the flax was dreſſed by women ; there was no cloth made at Forfar, but a few yard-wides, called Scrims ; the number of incorporated weavers did not exceed 40, nor were there above 60 looms employed in the town. But in conſequence of the act for encouraging weavers, the trade increaſed ſo rapidly, that, before the year 1750, there were upwards of 140 looms going in Forfar, and at preſent there are between 400 and 500.

The knowledge of this art is ſo eaſily acquired, the call for
hands

hands fo great, that almoft every young man here betakes himfelf to it. He receives a part of the profit of his work from
the very day his apprenticefhip begins; in a year or two he is
qualified to carry on bufinefs for himfelf, and able to fupport a
family, and fo he marries and multiplies; and this facility of
acquiring a living at an early period of life is one great caufe of
the rapid increafe of population. To this alfo it is owing, perhaps, that other profeffions, lefs profitable and more difficult
to acquire, are feldomer purfued by the young men of this place;
and it is a fact worthy of notice, that there has not been above
one or two apprentice taylors in Forfar thefe feven years paft.

The Ofnaburgh trade is indeed a fluctuating one, and when
the demand for that fabric flackens at any time, it brings many of the young and unprovident into difficulties, and oftentimes adds to the number of the poor. But when the trade is
good (and it has been for fometimes paft more ftable and more
flourifhing than ever it was known before), the profits of it,
with the government bounty, are fufficient to fupport the fober
and induftrious weaver againft the influence of a falling market.—Manufacturers are juft now giving from 15s. to 20s. for
working the piece of ten dozen of yards, which a man of good
execution will accomplifh in nearly as many days; and a man
working his own web, has been known to produce 18 fuch pieces
by his own hands in the fpace of 19 weeks.—This however is
allowed by all to be extraordinary, though it fhews what fobriety and diligence may do.

The trade and wealth of Forfar having increafed fo rapidly
fince the year 1745, muft naturally be fuppofed to have produced great alterations in the appearance of the place and the
manners of its inhabitants. Accordingly their buildings, their
expence of living, and their drefs are almoft totally changed
fince that period. And there is a remarkable difference, even
within

within these 10 years, not only in all these respects, but also in their amusements.

About and before the year 1745 there were few private houses covered with slate, and the masonry of almost all of them was of a very inferior kind; since that time almost every new house has been covered with slates of a coarse kind, of which there are plenty in quarries within the royalty, and several of the principal ones with Easdale. A thatched house is scarcely to be seen, and the masonry of such houses as have been built of late years is neat and substantial; the inhabitants appearing to have caught a new taste in building from the pattern set them in the new Town-house and new Church, which are of neat modern architecture.

Like most towns in Scotland, Forfar had been built without any regular design, as every man's fancy dictated the situation of his house; now more attention is bestowed in regulating the streets in the extended parts of the town, as well as in removing irregularities in rebuilding houses in the old-street.—There are no uninhabited houses, new ones are extending the town in almost every direction, and house rents are rather on the rise. Most of the houses built for trades-people consist of two stories, having four apartments of about 16 feet square each, one of which, with a portion of the garret, is sufficient to accommodate a weaver with his loom, his furniture and his fuel, and he pays for it, and a few feet of garden ground, from 20s. to 45s. *per annum*, according to its distance from the market-place or its other advantages or disadvantages. The weaver generally prefers the low flat for his operations, and an open exposure, if possible, to the heart of the town *.

About

* About 50 or 60 years ago there were not above 7 tea-kettles, as many hand-bellows, and as many watches in Forfar: now tea-kettles and hand-bellows are the necessary furniture of the poorest house in the parish, and almost the meanest menial servant must have his watch.

About

About 1745 the common rent of an acre of burgh land was L. 10 Scotch, including 40d. for minifters ftipend. An acre of the fame land is now often let at from 50s to L. 3 *per annum*: Several of them near the town bring more than twice as much, and the whole of them have been lately found by a decreet arbitral

About the fame period, a leg of good beef weighing 4 ftone might have been purchafed for 5s.; a leg of tolerable veal for 5d. the higheft for 1s. and fome fo low as 2d¼.; mutton from 8d. to 1s. per leg; a fmaller fort from the Grampians, but of excellent flavour, from 4d. to 5d. per leg. Previous to 1745 there was no meat fold in Forfar by weight, and very feldom was an ox killed till the greater part of the carcafe had been befpoken.——A little before that two work oxen, weighing about 30 ftone each, were fold in one of the Forfar fairs for 50 merks Scots the head; and both the fize of the cattle and the price of them were thought a wonder.

An ox, worth at that time about 40s. fupplied the flefh-market of Forfar eight days or a fortnight, except on extraordinary occafions, from Chriftmafs to Lammas. Between Hallowmafs and Chriftmafs, when the people laid in their winter provifions, about 24 beeves were killed in a week; the beft not exceeding 16 or 20 ftone. A man who had bought a fhillings worth of beef or an ounce of tea, would have concealed it from his neighbours like murder. Eggs were bought for 1d. per dozen, butter from 3d. to 4d. per lb. and a good hen was thought high at a groat.

The gradual advancement of population, trade, and agricultural improvement, has produced the gradual rife in the price and confumption of all thefe articles, which within thefe laft twenty years are fome of them doubled, and many of them trebled; oat meal too has rifen, but not in the fame proportion with moft other articles. And there are few artificers who cannot well afford to treat themfelves and their families frequently with meat and wheaten bread, confiderable quantities of both being confumed by them. At an average, there is not lefs than L. 50. worth of meat fold in the flefh market of Forfar every week throughout the year.——Good meat brings from 3d. to 4d. and fometimes 5d. per lb. and can feldom be purchafed in quantities, even at the cheapeft periods, for lefs than 4s. per ftone. Eggs which ten years ago fold at 2d. per dozen are now rifen to 4d. and fometimes 6d. Hens are from 10d to 1s. Butter from 8d. to 10d. ½ per pound of 24 ounces Englifh——and other articles in proportion. Though this bears hard upon annuitants, yet it is univerfally allowed that labouring people purchafe more of thefe articles now, and are better able to do it, than when provifions were cheaper.

arbitral to be worth 25s. per acre, if let *in cumulo* for a leafe of 19 years.

Clover grafs-feed was firft fown in one of the burgh acres about 60 years ago, and the people around run to fee it as a curiofity; nor did it become general in this neighbourhood for upwards of 20 years after.

The foil of the burgh acres is of a light nature, and of no confiderable depth, having in general a gravel bottom, and it has been faid a thoufand times, that it and the ground a confiderable way round, would take a fhower every day in the year without prejudice; yet, being flanked by the range of Seed-law-hills on the fouth, of the Grampians on the north, the teeming clouds coming from the weft with the prevailing fummer-winds, often pafs over and fhed their fertilizing influence on the hills on either fide of this tract, while every thing in the intermediate fpace was burning up. The foil produces excellent barley, but the oat crops in general are light and punny. The difcovery of marle and the increafed quantity of hot manure from the town, has improved it very much of late, and the multiplied confumption of the produce has fo much excited the induftry and attention of the inhabitants, that moft of the old fields are in a ftate of high cultivation, while feveral extenfive ones improved from barren muir produce plentiful crops. It fhould be obferved, however, that the tackfmen of thefe acres are not in general able to pay the high rent which many of them do, from the produce of the ground, but one muft have a cow for his family, and another a horfe to carry him to a diftant market or bring goods from a fea-port, and he takes a piece of ground near him and pays a premium for his convenience *.

General

* The effects of this increafe of number, trade, and wealth, appear vifibly alfo in the drefs of all ranks, and even in the amufements of the more wealthy citizens. Twelve or twenty years ago, it was no uncommon thing to fee

the

General Character of the Inhabitants.—The general character of the inhabitants is that of industry and enterprise. As in other large assemblages of men, instances of dissipation are not wanting, and failures among trading people now and then happen; effects, which a sudden influx of wealth, and inexperience in the paths of extended commerce, seldom fail to produce and multiply; but it has been observed, to the honour of the merchants of Forfar, by the people from a distance who have had long and extensive dealings in this country, that there is no town in Angus, where they find fewer bankruptcies and more punctual payments.

Articles of commerce are greatly more numerous within these few years. Wine of various sorts, which was formerly brought from Dundee in dozens, and seldom used but as a medicine, is

the wife of a wealthy burgess going to church arrayed in a rich silk gown covered by a homely plaid; now silk mantles and bonnets, and fashionable head-dresses are no rarities; and even the servant maids begin in this respect to ape the dress of their superiors. Formerly a ball or social dance was not thought of above once or twice in a year, and the ladies in general appeared at it dressed in close caps like their grandmothers; for several years past there has been, during the winter season, a monthly concert of Italian and Scotch music, performed by the gentlemen of the place, and followed by a dance, well attended, and presenting a company of ladies and gentlemen dressed in the modern fashion. Entertainments of the same kind are sometimes given in summer; one in particular on the 19th of June, kept as an anniversary in honour of St Margaret, Malcolm Canmore's Queen, to whose munificence perhaps Forfar was much indebted. Buchannan styles her, "*Lectissima et singulari pietate Fœmina;*" and ascribes many of the best acts of her husband's reign to the influence of her piety and prudence, particularly the abrogation of Evenus' law of infamous memory. Tradition celebrates her attention to the good instruction of the young women in Forfar, and it is said it was the law of her table, that none should drink after dinner who did not wait the giving of thanks, and hence the phrase through Scotland of the grace drink. These festive scenes are in general enjoyed at little expence, and have contributed not a little to cultivate the manners, and to promote the harmony of this society.

is now imported in pipes, and is a very common drink at private as well as at public entertainments. Porter, which, about 20 years ago was scarcely known, is now brought from London in great quantities and is becoming a common beverage with the lowest of the people. Table-beer is seldom made by private families, but by the brewers in the town, who are a flourishing class of men; from 1600 to 2000 bolls of malt are consumed annually, but the consumpt of this article is lessened since the introduction of porter.

Superfine cloths, and all kinds of cotton, cloth and many other articles formerly got from Dundee, are now to be had in plenty in many shops in Forfar.

Dundee is the nearest sea-port town, and with which Forfar has most frequent intercouse, but it also carries on a trade with Arbroath and Montrose.—The communication with all these places will be greatly facilitated when the turnpike roads leading to them are finished. The turnpike act for this county commenced in June 1789, and the roads to Dundee and Arbroath are now nearly completed. Though the popular prejudice was at first against them, every one begins to see his interest in them now, since as much can be drawn by one horse as could formerly have been done with two, and the toll exigible for a one horse cart per day from Forfar to Arbroath or Dundee, is no more than 4d$\frac{1}{2}$. on either road. The turnpike road from Forfar to Perth is likewise in great forwardness, and will soon be compleated, to the general improvement of the estates through which it passes and the towns to and from which it leads.

One great drawback on the property of Forfar is the scarcity of fuel. Peats have indeed for several years past been obtained from the lands gained by draining the loch of Forfar; these are now nearly exhausted, and a new moss has been opened by the draining Loch-Restenet, which, in its turn, a

few

few years will fee to an end: at any rate the peats got from thence, though a convenient, are by no means a cheap article of fuel; for the poor man, could he afford the money all at once, would be much cheaper, and if cheaper he muft be more comfortable, with coal. A confiderable quantity of thriving firs are rifing on the town's property, and on fome of the eftates in the neighbourhood; but their number feems by no means adequate to the probable demand for firing, when the moffes fhall be exhaufted; fo that the community's fole dependence for this article, at fome future period, will be on coal, which at prefent is obtained from Arbroath and Dundee, at a very great expence, not lefs than from 9s. to 10s. 6d. per boll of 70 ftone Dutch. In fome places of the flate quarries in this neighbourhood, ftrata of culm-ftone have been found, fuch as indicate the vicinity of coal, and they excited no little expectation fome years that this ufeful foffil might be difcovered here. Some feeble attempts towards a difcovery were made by the proprietor of one of thefe quarries, and a few a-cres around it; but his finances were unequal to the expence, and he met with no fupport from the public.

There are few places within the royalty, in which a quarry of fome kind may not eafily be found, fo that both ftone and flate are comparatively cheap; but the expence of lime and wood, neither of which can be had but from the fea port towns or an equal diftance, will probably continue, with the high price of fuel, to obftruct in fome meafure the growing profperity of this burgh, till wealth and the fpirit of enterprize fhall open a communication by water between it and the fea.

In fpite of thefe difadvantages, however, Forfar is, and is likely to continue, a thriving place; fituated in the centre of a well cultivated county, the feat of the court of juftice, the members of which at a moderate computation bring L. 1500

a

a year to the town; the place of refort for the free-holders, not only for tranfacting the bufinefs of the country, but for the enjoyment of fociety in clubs, affemblies, &c. laying on a great road through the kingdom, and open by the turnpikes to a ready intercourfe with all her neighbours, poffeffed alfo of feveral fubftantial manufactures, conducted by men of fpirit and induftry, who daily ftretching out new paths of art and commerce, fhe muft rife, in the nature of things, to greater eminence than fhe has yet attained.

Many things doubtlefs are neceffary to the accomplifhment of this defirable end. A well regulated police, and the fup-preffion of a multiplicity of ale houfes, fo dangerous to the morals of the people, are particularly requifite. The clearing and lighting of the ftreets, and the introduction of water in pipes, are alfo objects worthy of attention, to which, it is hop-ed, in time, the people in power well apply their care.——It is alfo univerfally allowed, that nothing can contribute more to the civil and religious interefts of any fociety, than a facred attention to the education of youth. And where the funds of a parifh admit of it, as well as thofe of this diftrict can, there ought to be at leaft three eftablifhed fchools, one for La-tin-grammar, and the other learned or foreign tongues, one for Englifh folely, and one for writing and arithmetic. There are at prefent two eftablifhed fchools in Forfar, with tolerable ap-pointments, in each of which the mafter is permitted to teach all the branches of education promifcuoufly, a method calcu-lated to perplex himfelf and obftruct the improvement of his pupils. The fchools about the middle of this century were in confiderable reputation; but the town for many years paft has been rather unfortunate in the appointments made to thefe important offices. The magiftrates and council have, how-ever, of late taken fuch meafures as it is hoped fhall in future

ture fecure the good inftitution of youth, and raife the fchools to fome degree of celebrity *.

The church, fituated near the centre of the town, has been rebuilt within thefe few years, on a plan calculated to contain 2000 hearers. The fabric is elegant and commodious, but difgraced by the contiguity of the old-fteeple and fpire, the battlement of which it over-tops by 12 feet at leaft.

The town houfe has alfo been lately rebuilt; the front in the market place has an agreeable effect, but the apartments for prifoners are dark, damp, and difmal, almoft excluded from the fun, and the free circulation of common air; and the general utility of the whole fabric feems to have been fa-crificed to the attainment of one large upper room for public bufinefs and amufement. The cupola, alfo intended for an or-nament, conveys a mean idea of the genius of the architect. It is evident, alas! for the unhappy prifoner too evident, the genius of Howard fat not at his elbow, when he meditated this wretched defign.

The flaughter houfe, lately in the very centre of the town, has been very properly removed to the north fide of it; which, befides ridding the place of a noifome and dangerous incum-brance, muft contribute to the health of the inhabitants.

The air of Forfar may be faid in general to be falubrious; occafional fogs arife from the lakes and low grounds in the neighbourhood, but have nothing particularly noxious in them. Epidemical diftempers fometimes appear, but they are not more fatal than in other neighbouring communities, and

---

* Within thefe few years the manfe has been repaired at a confiderable expence at two thirds of the money which would have built a commodious one from the foundation; and yet it is a manfe ftill ftanding in need of re-pair; a proof among many of the inattention of heritors to their own inte-reft. Were fuch public works finifhed fubftantially at once, they would coft them lefs trouble and lefs expence.

and in general leſs ſo. On one occaſion the ſmall-pox carried off a great number of children, a circumſtance which may be expected ſome times to happen in places where the prejudice againſt inoculation has not ſubſided : this prejudice indeed, as well as other popular errors, daily loſſes ground; and it is to be hoped that the ſucceſs attending the practice of this important diſcovery will make univerſal converts of the riſing generation. In the caſe alluded to, the inoculated ſmall pox was introduced late in the ſpring, and children who had not been inoculated received the infection at the commencement of the ſummer months, which, happening to be warmer than uſual, aſſiſted in ſpreading the contagion. There are many active lively men in Forfar between 70 and 80 years old, ſeveral upwards of 80 years with all their faculties entire. One between 90 and 100, who is beginning to feel the infirmities of age ; and there was one buried in July 1781 who had attained the age of 100 *.

Poor.—The number of poor in the town is very conſiderable ; they are ſupported by money ariſing from lands purchaſed with the donations of Meſſrs Robert and William Strangs mentioned in the preceding note, about the year 1654, amounting to about L 96 yearly ; and the money collected weekly at the

* Of the antiquities of Forfar little can be ſaid, as its charters have been, for upwards of a century, conſigned to oblivion by the hand of rebellion and anarchy. A few trials of thoſe unhappy women called witches, together with the bridle with which they were led to execution, are ſtill preſerved as monuments of the ſuperſtition of our fathers; and the field in which they ſuffered is pointed out to ſtrangers as a curioſity.

Among the memorials of the good, is juſtly reckoned a very large bell, ſent by Robert Strang merchant in Stockholm as a tribute of reſpect to his native place; and a table of donations to the poor, to which the ſaid Robert Strang and his brother William contributed the principal ſhare.

the church door, which with the interests of certain savings in former times of plenty, amounts to about L. 100 yearly. Out of these sums, besides a monthly distribution of about L. 6 or L. 7 and occasional supplies in cases of urgent necessity, the poor are furnished with shoes, clothing, and house rent——Since the scarcity in the year 1783, when oat-meal was 20s. per boll, through the increase of the number of poor and the rise of provisions, the funds which before were accummulating have been scarcely adequate to the expenditure; and new methods are now trying to render the supply of the industrious poor more effectual, without increasing the burden of the community. The fact seems to be, that over-grown charity funds, are enemies to industry, as they encourage the idle and improvident, to depend upon them as a security against want in the evening of life. And so they will neither work nor save. For many years preceding the year 1788, provisions were more easily obtained by the poor, than now, by the great quantities of fresh fish with which the market of Forfar was supplied at very reasonable prices, by carriers who gained a livelyhood by bringing them almost daily from the sea-port towns. A supply which had its influence also on the price of meat. But since the year 1788 fish have been very scarce; the haddocks particularly have left our coasts entirely, and one great article for the subsistance of the poor, as well as a luxury for the rich, is withdrawn.

There is a weekly market held in Forfar every Saturday; it is well attended, and a great deal of country business is transacted there. A branch of the Dundee Banking Company, and one of the commercial Bank Company of Aberdeen, have been established here for these two or three years, and both have considerable employ *.

There

* It is a singular circumstance in the history of this burgh that it obtained
an

There are several well frequented fairs kept on the muir adjoining to the town; the custom of one of them was purchased some time ago from the Earl of Strathmore, and all make a considerable addition to the revenue of the burgh. From Martinmas to Candlemass there is a weekly market on Wednesday, free of custom, held on the street for the sale of fat cattle; and during the feed-time there is one weekly on the same day for the sale of work horses, all of which are well frequented, and occasion the spending a great deal of money in the town, by the country people who attend them *.

Surface, Soil, &c.—The Landward Parish presents a level prospect to the eye, intercepted only by the hill of Balnashinar directly to the south of the town, part of which is within the royalty, and from the top almost the whole parish, as well as a great extent of country beyond it, may be seen at one view. The west end of this hill is the place of execution of public justice, and it is said that it derives its name in the Gaelic, from the complaint of a Highland boy, following his grandfather, who had forfeited his life to the justice of his country.— The soil is various. To the north and south it is in general light and thin, with a gravel bottom, as in the burgh land; about the middle, from the east to west, spouty clay land.

Rivers

an act of the Scotch Parliament, in the reign of King James VI. changing its weekly market day from Sunday to Friday, At what time is was changed from Friday to Saturday, the incumbent has not been able to learn, but the reason of the change has evidently been, that Friday interfered with the great weekly market in Dundee, and that the other days in the week were kept as fair days by the other towns in the shire.

* It is perhaps proper to take notice of the inconvenience which arises to trading people, from the want of a proper and uniform standard of weights and measures. A pound of butter in Forfar is 24 English ounces; in Kirrimuir 3 miles distant it is 27 ounces, the same difference obtains in cheese, and a similar one in other articles.

Rivers and Lakes.—There are no rivers in the parish, and scarce any stream that deserves the name of a burn. Two trouting-rivers Lunan and Venny, indeed take their rise in this parish but are both inconsiderable rills in so far as connected with it. Such is the scarcity of water, that of 8 mills in the parish, six are driven by water collected from small springs which in summer do little execution, one is driven by wind, and another by a horse.

There were before the draining, three lakes in the parish, Forfar, Restenet, and Fithie; all abounding in pike, perch and eel; and since a communication has been opened by a drain between the Loch of Forfar and the river Dean, trout of a considerable size are sometimes taken; but none of these fish have been brought to market except eels, which some time ago were exposed in great numbers, taken in an ark at the outlet of Loch-Restenet.

The loch of Forfar, upwards of 20 years ago, was drained of about 16 feet perpendicular depth of water. About a mile in length and a quarter of a mile in breadth, of various depth, (from 2 to 22 feet in summer), still remains. No arable land has been gained by this draining, but a very considerable quantity of moss and marle. A cubic yard and an half of solid moss is supposed to produce a cart load of peats, valued, as they lie upon the bank, from 8d. to 1s. To this the expence of digging, drying, and leading must be added to make the full price, and that will be little short of the prime cost. Those who dig and dry them for sale, usually charge the people in Forfar half a crown for a small cart load of dried peats laid down at the door. The boll of marle, consisting of 8 cubic feet, brings 8d. to the proprietor, out of which he pays 1d. for digging or 1½d. for dragging; for they not only dig for the marle at the recovered land, but heave it from the bottom of the lake by a machine, such as is used for clearing the channel of of the Thames; and this operation requires the labour of three men, each of whom in good weather will make from 2od. to 2s. per day. The marle is an excellent manure for the improvement of waſte lands, and anſwers well in compoſt for moſt of the ground in this country; the rapid improvement of which is to be dated from its diſcovery. It is of two kinds, both produced from ſhells and both equally good, but differing very materially in their cónſiſtency. Both of them form, in a ſhort time, a dry and apparently ſolid maſs, and one ſpecies continues ſo, though carried to a diſtance, like ſlacked lime; the other by agitation of the carriage becomes in a manner liquid, and cannot without a very cloſe cart be conveyed to any conſiderable diſtance.

The draining of the lake coſt Lord Strathmore about L. 3000, and it has yielded him from L. 500 to L. 700 *per annum*, but both the moſs and the marle are now nearly exhauſted; and ſome years hence, perhaps, the drain being neglected, the loch may again riſe to its antient boundaries *.

Loch-

* Before this loch was drained, and near the north ſide of it, there was an artificial iſland compoſed of large piles of oak and looſe ſtones, with a ſtratum of earth above, on which are planted ſome aſpin and ſloe trees, ſuppoſed to have been a place of religious retirement for Queen Margaret. This now forms a very curious peninſula. The veſtiges of a building, probably a place of worſhip, are ſtill to be ſeen. And it is likely there might be ſome accommodation too for the occaſional reſidence of the prieſt of the place, as the remains of an oven were diſcernible not many years ago, and alſo ſomething of the furniture of a pleaſure garden. It appears that the loch has at ſome period ſurrounded the riſing ground called the manor, and the adjacent hill on which the caſtle of Forfar ſtood; which hill is not, as the authors of the Encyclopedia Britannica ſuppoſe, artificial, but a congeſtum of ſand and fat clay, evidently diſpoſed in various irregular ſtrata by the hand of nature. Beſides the fiſh above mentioned, the loch is frequented by water fowl of various kinds and in the months of July and Anguſt. About ſun ſet it is infeſted, or rather fiſhers upon it are plagued, by flies of the gnat kind, which faſten in great numbers on every part of their clothes, and leaving their ſkins, fly off ſportive as

from

Loch Reftenet, the property of George Dempfter Efq. of Dunnichen, has been lately drained. The extent of ground recovered does not exceed 200 acres, yet the value of the mofs and marle has been computed at above L. 50,000. Indeed the marle is fuppofed to be inexhauftible. Upon the S. W. fide of this lake, and almoft furrounded by it, ftood the priory and the parifh church, the ruins of which ftill remain. There is alfo ftanding in a pretty entire ftate, a very neat fteeple and fpire built of ftone and run-lime with a fort of fineering of polifhed afher. This is faid to have been a dependency of the monaftery of Jedburgh, where their valuable papers and effects were kept, as a place of fafety from the depredations of the Englifh borderers *.

Loch-Fithie, a little to the S. of Loch-Reftenet, a beautiful little fheet of water is alfo the property of George Dempfter Efq.—It has little, if any, either of mofs or marle in it, but abounds in pike and perch. It is about a mile in circumference, of various breadths, and furrounded by a beautiful rifing bank, which conceals the profpect of the lake till one comes juft upon it, and heightens the delight of the wanderer with unexpected pleafure. The banks are adorned with common firs, larch and fpruce trees, in fome places agreeably intermixed and well ftocked with finging birds. Every thing in this fpot confpires

from a prifon. The incumbent has often returned home, covered with their *fpolia opima*, after receiving no little entertainment from obferving their method of difengaging themfelves, which overbalanced the annoyance received from their buzzing.

* In this neighbourhood, and probably in the adjoining muir, in which there are the veftiges of a camp by fome fuppofed to be Roman, Buchanan relates, that a bloody but indecifive battle was fought, about the year 830, between Feredith the Pictifh Ufurper, and Alpin King of the Scotch. Several large ftones, fuch as are ufually found in Scotland commemorative of fimilar events, are ftill ftanding, though without any infcription, not far from the fuppofed field of battle.

pires to form a pleaſing retreat for the contemplative or the
gay. Its worthy owner has lately erected a handſome cottage after an Eaſt-Indian model, for the enjoyment of a ſum-
mer-day with his friends.

Woods, Rent, &c.—On ſeveral eſtates in the pariſh, as well
as on the property of the burgh, are thriving plantations of fir
from 20 to 30 years old, and it is generally ſuppoſed that an
acre of thriving fir trees 30 years old, would bring its proprietor at leaſt 20s. for every year of its growth, after paying all
expences. This is certainly turning waſte lands (and ſuch in
general are the lands on which fir thrive beſt here) to very
good account ; beſides that by the annual ſhedding of the leaves
the ſoil is enriched, and rendered fitter for the purpoſes of a-
griculture when the woods are cut down.—There are 10 heritors in the pariſh, of whom 4 reſide ; and there is beſides a
ſmall eſtate belonging to the poor of the burgh. The valued
rent of the whole pariſh is L. 2587 : 19 Scotch, and the real
rent is probably about as much ſterling *.

There are 3 large farms which bring about L. 200 of rent
and upwards, three that give about L. 100, 11 or 12 from
L. 40 to L. 100 and the reſt are ſmall poſſeſſions occupied in
general by weavers and other artiſts ; for weavers in the country part of the pariſh, as well as in the town, form the moſt
conſiderable body of labourers. A weaver in the country, in
general, has as much land as will maintain a cow or two, and
ſometimes a horſe, throughout the year ; and on moſt eſtates
in the pariſh, are little villages peopled chiefly by tenants
of this deſcription, who join their horſes together to form a
plough.

---

* There is a conſiderable part of the landward pariſh actually within the
royalty, the property of the community or of individuals who have feued
from it, and conſequently not comprehended in the above ſtatement and valuation of the county lands.

plough. The number of weavers in the country in 1791 was 155.

The mode of cultivation after ley is, in general, 1ft, a crop of oats; 2dly, lint or oats; 3dly, barley with dung; 4thly, turnips or fome other green crop; and 5thly, barley with grafs feeds, which remain four or five years under hay and pafture. This practice differs, however, with foil and feafon and other circumftances, and can hardly be obferved by the tackfmen of fmall pendicles, though every one of them has a part of his fmall poffeffion in grafs, turnips and potatoes, which laft is much cultivated throughout all the parifh, and forms an excellent fuccedaneum for meal and a ftanding difh on the tables of the rich and the poor.

The lands in general will yield from the fifth to the feventh return. Harveft is feldom reaped within three months after fowing, and in fome years, particularly in the fouth part of the parifh, which is very wet, it is much later. Agriculture, however, in its improvements, is keeping pace in this part of the country with manufactures. The fields are regularly laid out, inclofures are multiplying, and rents are double and treble what they were twenty or thirty years ago. One farm in particular, which let for a leafe of 30 years at about L. 50, has lately been let at between L. 300 and L. 400, and is ftill thought a good bargain *.

Population

* On fome of the eftates in the parifh, the exaction of bondage-fervice is ftill in ufe; and befides the ftipulated rent in money or grain, fome tenants pay poultry and pigs, and muft leave their own work at the landlord's call, to affift in ploughing, harrowing, cutting the corn, cafting peats, driving coal and other errands and carriages, in hay time and harveft, and at any other time of the year. This is indeed agreeable to bargain, and the number of thefe fervices is ufually fpecified and valued in the leafes; but they are generally as unpopular as impolitic, and accordingly begin to be omitted in new contracts of leafe. Mill thirlage alfo exifts in this parifh and is confidered as a grievance.

About 60 years ago, a principal farm fervant might have been had for 35s.

or

Population Table.

Number of fouls in 1755,	2450	Total in the country		1174
———— in 1781,	3800	Families do.	-	269
———— in 1790,	4625	Males 8 years old and up-		
———— in 1791,	4712	wards	- -	473
———— in 1792,	4756	Females, do	- -	463
Examinable perfons in the		In 1792, within the roy-		
burgh in 1790	2667	alty *	- -	3800
Under 8 years age, do.	785	Of thefe, examinable		2925
Total in the burgh	3452	———— under 8 years of		
Families, do. -	983	age	- -	875
Males 8 years old and up-		In the landward, in 1792		956
wards - -	1252	Of thefe, examinable		765
Females do. -	1415	———— under 8 years		
Examinable perfons in the		of age	- -	191
country part, in 1790,	936	Examinable perfons in		
Under 8 years of age, do.	238	communion with the		
		eftablifhed		

or 40s. the half year, and a woman for 40d. befides her harveft fee. Now many men fervants receive L. 12 fterling *per annum*, and few or none lefs than L. 7 ; and women fervants have from L. 3 to L. 4 a year with a lippie of lint ground, or fome equivalent called *bounties*. A man for the harveft demanded formerly half a guinea, now he afks from 30s. to 40s, and is fometimes in-treated to take more. A female fhearer formerly received from 8s. to 10s. now 20s. and upwards. Male fervants in agriculture, befides their wages, get victuals, or two pecks of meal a week in lieu thereof, with milk which they call fap. Cottars generally receive from L. 3 to L. 7 a year, with a houfe and garden, and maintenance of a cow throughout the year. On this fcanty provifion they live comfortably, and raife numerous families without burdening the public. A family of nine children has been reared by a labour-er of this defcription without any public aid. The cottar eats at his mafter's table, or has meal in lieu of this advantage. From 20 to 30s a year are given to a boy, from 10 to 14 years of age, to tend the cattle or to drive the plough.

* A confiderable part of what is called the country parifh is actually within the royalty; and there are fome houfes fuppofed to be in town, which are built on county lands.

eftablifhed church, at Whitfunday 1790, about - - 3213	Examinable perfons of the Epifcopal perfuafion about - - 240	
Annual number of communicants about 1800	Do. of the Seceffion about 150	

	Baptifed.	Married.	Buried.
In 1660,	41	26	—
In 1755,	68	—	51
In 1782,	141	43	81
In 1789,	143	45	51
In 1790,	147	34	107*

From the preceding ftatement of the population, it would appear that Forfar ought to be a collegiate charge.

Mifcellaneous Obfervations.—The poor in the country parifh are few, only about 8 or 10 very old or difeafed individuals claim the aid of the funds, and they are well fupplied at their houfes out of the weekly collections at the church, and the intereft of accumulated collections in former years of plenty.—They have alfo a few acres of land, purchafed by fuch contributions, as a referve againft years of fcarcity. All the above amount to more than L. 40 fterling. There is not a beggar in the country parifh, and only about five or fix belonging to the town, who are furnifhed by the kirk treafurer with a permiffion-ticket, to diftinguifh them from ftrangers and vagrants.

About half a century ago the population of the town and country parifh feems to have been nearly equal, the difproportion between them now will appear from the foregoing table. —There has been little alteration in the number of landward parifhioners fince the year 1781, though during that period there

* The great increafe of burials in 1790, was occafioned by the ravages of the fmall-pox.

there is an addition of near 1000 inhabitants to the town. The chief causes of this increase have been already pointed out.

The inhabitants of both town and country share alike the praise of industry, economy, and hospitality. If fewer instances of intemperance, impurity, and prodigality appear in the country than in the town in proportion to the number in each, it is perhaps chiefly, because simplicity of manners is less liable to corruption in the former than in the latter, from a multiplicity of low ale-houses, these seminaries of impiety and dissipation.—The farmers and manufacturers in the former, however, have experienced a change in their dress and expenditure as perceptible as what has taken place among the inhabitants of the burgh.

The parishioners are in general attached to the religious establishment of the kingdom. A small society of Episcopalians and another of Seceders form the sum of the sectaries.—A spirit of enquiry and a taste for reading is springing up, and popular superstitions begin to hide their heads. The subscriptions to the Encyclopedia Britannica, the Bee, and several periodical and other publications, scientific, religious, moral and political, are more numerous of late than could well have been expected; and they already shed an evident lustre on the conversation of many.

The presbytery of Forfar was disjoined from Dundee by an act of the provincial synod of Angus and Mearns, dated Arbroath, 17th April 1717, and the members held their first meeting by appointment at Forfar on 1st May following.

The stipend, as augmented in 1785, is L. 84 : 15 : 9d$\frac{5}{11}$ in money, and 31 bolls 2 pecks of meal, making, at the ordinary conversion, L. 100 neat, L. 5 for communion element money, with a house and garden, and a glebe consisting of about 7 acres.—The new church was opened for public worship on the 9th day of January 1791.——The oldest date upon the manse is 1619.

PARISH OF GLAMMISS.

(*County of Angus.*)

By the Rev. Mr JAMES LYON.

Name, Extent, and Surface.

THE modern name of this parish is *Glammiss*, but its etymology is unknown. It lies in the presbytery of Forfar, and synod of Angus and Mearns. It is about 12 miles in length, and the greatest breadth is 5 miles; but in some places it is hardly one. The greatest part of this parish is flat country, and lies in the heart of Strathmore, which is an extensive plain, situated at the foot of the Grampian mountains, and remarkable for its fertility. Large plantations of trees, together with the fields regularly divided and fenced by hedge rows, make the country round exceedingly beautiful. Part of this parish is rocky and mountainous, and the Sidlie hills run along the south side of it. They are covered with heath, and are not remarkably high.

Soil.—The soil is in general good. It has been well cultivated, and produces plentiful crops. About 60 years ago, the people were sunk in sloth and indolence; but a variety of causes have concurred to call forth their vigour, and to

roufe

rouſe them into action. Improvements have been, and ſtill are, carried on with ardour and ſucceſs. The diſcovery of marle has wonderfully contributed to the improvements in agriculture.

Fuel.—Amidſt the many advantages which the people here enjoy, the want of fuel is a great inconvenience. They generally uſe peats, of which there are plenty in different moſſes ; but they are dug at a conſiderable expence, and will ſoon be exhauſted. Some tranſport coals from Dundee, the neareſt ſea-port town, which is twelve miles diſtant from Glammiſs. This defect, however, will in a ſhort time be ſupplied by the extenſive woods planted by the late Earl of Strathmore, which are in a very thriving condition, and are a great ornament to the country.

Diſeaſes.—The air is rather moiſt, and neither very healthy, nor very unhealthy. Agues and melancholy habits are not much known here. Fevers and conſumptions are the moſt prevalent diſtempers, owing, it is ſuppoſed, to the moiſture occaſioned by the hills to the ſouth, and the great quantity of planting. We have no mineral ſprings of any conſequence.

Rivers and Fiſhes.—The river Dean, a deep running water, is ſupplied from the lake of Forfar. The Kerbet, and the burn of Glammiſs, run through the pariſh, and abound with plenty of fine red trout. There is a very conſiderable lake in the eaſt end of the pariſh, near Forfar, called the *Loch of Forfar.* It originally contained 140 acres ; but 60 of theſe have been drained, and a great quantity of marle and peat have been dug out, which has proved very advantageous to the Earl of Strathmore, the proprietor. When the lake

was

was drained, a number of curious antiquities were found, and are to be ſeen in the caſtle of Glammiſs.

Antiquities.——Within a few yards of the manſe of Glammiſs, there is an obeliſk, of rude deſign, erected, as is generally ſuppoſed, in memory of the murder of Malcolm II. King of Scotland. On one ſide of the monument, there are figures of two men, who, by their attitudes, ſeem to be forming the bloody conſpiracy. A lion and a centaur, on the upper part, repreſent the ſhocking barbarity of the crime. On the reverſe, ſeveral ſorts of fiſhes are engraven, as a ſymbolical repreſentation of the lake, in which, by miſſing their way, the aſſaſſins were drowned. In a neighbouring field, there is a ſtone on which are delineated a variety of ſymbolical characters ſimilar to thoſe already mentioned, and intended, as is ſuppoſed, to expreſs the ſame facts. At the diſtance of one mile from Glammiſs, near a place called Coſſans, there is an obeliſk, not leſs curious than either of the two preceding monuments. It is vulgarly called *St Orland's Stone*. No probable conjecture has been formed relating to the facts deſigned to have been perpetuated by it. On one ſide is a croſs rudely flowered and chequered; on the other, four men on horſeback appear to be making the utmoſt deſpatch. One of the horſes is trampling under foot a wild boar; and, on the lower part of the ſtone, there is the figure of an animal ſomewhat like a dragon. It has been thought that theſe ſymbols repreſent officers of juſtice in purſuit of Malcolm's murderers. There is a fortification on the ſummit of a hill, two miles ſouth-weſt from Glammiſs, known by the name of *Denoon Caſtle*. It probably was deſigned for a place of retreat in times of danger. It is encompaſſed by a wall, ſuppoſed to have been 27 feet high, and 30 broad. There are two entries, one to the ſouth-eaſt, and another to the north-weſt.

weſt. The whole circumference is about 340 Engliſh yards; but, although this wall be much defaced, and almoſt covered with graſs, yet there are evident traces of buildings in the intermediate ſpace. The only other work of antiquity in the pariſh, is the Caſtle of Glammiſs. This venerable ſtructure, the property of the Earl of Strathmore, and his chief ſeat in Scotland, is of very antient date. For ſome time it remained in the hands of the crown; and, in the year 1372, it was granted by Robert II. to J. Lyon, his ſpecial favourite, who not long after received his daughter in marriage. Since its original conſtruction, it has been greatly enlarged.

Quarries.—Beſides other quarries of inferior note in the pariſh, there is near the village of Glammiſs a freeſtone quarry, the ſtones of which are very durable, and are excellent for building and for millſtones. There are abundance of fine gray ſlate quarries, in different places, belonging to the Earl of Strathmore and Lord Douglas. About twenty years ago, an attempt was made to find out a lead mine near the village of Glammiſs. It was wrought a conſiderable time, and ſome ore was found; but the ſcheme was not perſiſted in.

Cattle.—A conſiderable number of fine cattle are fed in this pariſh. One dealer in this article is often poſſeſſed of ten thouſand pounds worth of cattle at a time, moſt of which he carries to the Engliſh market.

Population.—In the year 1783, the number of ſouls in the pariſh amounted to about 2040. In Dr Webſter's Report, the number is 1780. From the Regiſter, it appears that, in the year 1718, there were 63 baptiſms, in the year 1740, 60, and in 1750, 60. In the year 1784, there were

51 baptifms, 36 burials, and 14 marriages. In 1786, 47 baptifms, 38 burials, 17 marriages. From the 1ft of October 1789, to the 1ft of October 1790, there were 42 baptifms, 37 burials, and 16 marriages. There are a number of villages in this parish. The village of Glammifs contains about 500 fouls; the Newtown of Glammifs about 140; Arnefont 80; Cotterton of Hayfton 48; Nether-Handeck 39; Milltown of Glen-Ogilvie 67; and Cottertown of Drumglye 120. The number of farmers in the parish is about 80; fome of their farms are extenfive, and others but fmall. The number of weavers and manufacturers is about 70.

Heritors, &c.—The parish is divided among four heritors, the Earl of Strathmore, Lord Douglas, William Douglas of Brigtown, and Mr Henderfon of Rochilhill. Lord Strathmore's eftate contains about 6000 acres. The greateft part of the unarable ground confifts of thriving plantations, to the extent of about 1000 acres. The yearly rent may be from L. 2500 to L. 3000 Sterling. The value of land, on this eftate, has rifen confiderably within thefe fifteen years. One farm, in particular, which was rented at L. 52 twelve years ago, now gives L. 300. The rental of the eftate of Lord Douglas in this parish is about L. 500, an advanced rent from L. 200 fince the year 1770. The whole of this eftate contains about 3000 acres. The eftate of Mr Douglas of Brigtown in this parish contains about 70 acres, and the prefent rental is about L. 50. The eftate of Rochilhill contains above 200 acres, and brings about L. 70 yearly rent. The parish fupplies itfelf with provifions, and generally fends a confiderable quantity of meal and barley to different parts of the country.

Church.—The Earl of Strathmore is patron of the parish. The

The ſtipend is, of money, L. 52 : 15 : 6, with 40 bolls of meal, and 16 bolls of barley. The glebe contains rather more than ſix acres and a half, and is worth 40 s. an acre.

Wages.—The expence of a labouring ſervant is generally about L. 8 or L. 9 a year, with ſix bolls and a half of meal. Maid-ſervants wages are about L. 3, beſides maintenance.

Poor.—The number of poor ſupplied from the funds of the pariſh are about twenty, beſides others who receive charity occaſionally. The kirk ſeſſion have a number of ſeats in the church at their diſpoſal, for which they draw about L. 7 annually. The average of weekly collections is 10 s. 6 d. The ſeſſion have alſo about L. 200 at intereſt.

GLAMMISS

School.—There is a very flourishing school in Glammiss. The present schoolmaster is eminent in his profession. His salary and perquisites amount to about 50 l. Sterling, with a good house, which, besides his own family, accommodates some boarders. The number of his scholars is about 50, at an average.

Cattle.—There are about 1190 cattle in the parish; 272 horses, and between 700 and 800 sheep.

Miscellaneous Observations.—There is one good inn in the village of Glammiss, and 3 alehouses; besides two or three more of the last description, in different parts of the parish. The number of these alehouses is much reduced of late, which is not to be regretted, as they have always been found to have a very bad effect on the morals of the people.—A few farmers in the parish still employ cottagers in agriculture; but the generality find, that they get their work best done by hired servants. The tenants are bound to no services, except driving some coals, if required, and furnishing a proportion of carriages towards the building of their master's houses. They also furnish carriages for the building or repairing of the church and manse. The services formerly required of the tenants, made them little better than slaves.—The nearest post town is Kirriemuir, which is about 4 miles distant.

PARISH OF GLENISLA.

(PRESBYTERY OF MEIGLE, SYNOD OF ANGUS AND MEARNS, COUNTY OF FORFAR.)

By the Rev. MR. JAMES DONALD.

Name, Extent, &c.

GLENISLA derives its name from its local fituation, be-ing placed in a glen through which the river Ifla runs. —— From the head of this parifh to the foot, taking a ftraight line, it meafures about 18 Englifh miles, but if all the windings of the river are taken in, it meafures precifely 25 miles and one fur-long. Its breadth, at an average, will not exceed 2 miles.

The Ifla, which takes its rife from Caan-Lochan, formerly a deer foreft of the family of Airly, runs through the middle of the parifh. This river abounds with trout of a tolerable fize ; there are alfo falmon to be found in it, though they are prevented from getting far up by a fall of water below the mill of Craig, mea-furing betwixt 70 and 80 feet perpendicular, called Reeky-Linn, from the fmoke which conftantly afcends from the wa-

ter

ter. This fall makes a very grand appearance at all times, but more particularly when the river overflows its banks.

Soil, Climate, &c.—The soil is in general of a light nature, and full of stones. In the lower part of the parish, however, where improvements are carried on, it appears to be deep strong loam, producing good crops of corn and grass. In the upper part, lime stone is to be got in great abundance from three different quarries. But the expence of quarrying and burning prevents the inhabitants from reaping great benefit from it. Some of the more opulent of the tenants drive marle from the Loch of Kinnordy, about 9 miles distant, which manure turns out to very good account.

The air is very pure, and the people in general very healthy. The healthiness of the people, however, may be ascribed to their manner of living. They are not pent up in houses, nor employed in sedentary occupations like many others, but roam at large in the open air, tending flocks of sheep and cattle. Several instances of longevity are to be found in the parish; particularly one man in his 94th year, still vigorous and retaining all his faculties, another 82, and a third 76. During the summer months, it is very sultry, but frosts generally set in by the end of August, and the winters are commonly very severe.

The people, especially in the upper part of the parish, are late in beginning to sow, owing principally to the frosts which keep the ground long, particularly after a severe winter. It is often the latter end of March or beginning of April, before the seed-time is begun. This, of course, prevents the grain from ripening soon; so that it is frequently the middle, and often the end of November, before the crop is all got in.

The frost mists do much hurt here, particularly on the river side. They seem to manifest their noxious quality first on the potatoe stems. Some fields of barley have been rendered

almost

almoft ufelefs by them. The barley takes a deadly whitenefs after this happens, and the kernels when unhufked, immediately after the froft, are foft and watery, and in a fhort time grow fhrivilled and dry. Oats, when frofted, acquire in a few days a bluifh caft. Thefe frofts prevail here moftly in the month of Auguft.

Population.—On the 12th of July 1791, there were living in the parifh 1018 fouls; of whom 224 were under 10 years of age, 456 between 10 and 20, and 338 widowers and married —The return to Dr. Webfter in 1755 was 1852 fouls; fo that the population has decreafed confiderably fince that period.

No exact regifter of baptifms and marriages has been kept here for many years paft; fo that from what records belong to the parifh, little material can be learned. From thefe records it appears that for 9 years preceding 1792, there were 236 baptifed, and 93 couples married.

The greater part of the inhabitants have fmall farms, with a confiderable extent of pafturage annexed to them. About 54 of them are fmall proprietors or portioners, and a great part of thefe occupy their lands themfelves. There are juft now in the parifh 3 blackfmiths, 8 weavers, 7 taylors, and 4 wrights. What is remarkable, there is not a fhoemaker in the parifh. All the inhabitants are of the eftablifhed church excepting 8 Non-jurors, 5 Catholics, and 1 Burgher Seceder.

The general character of the people is, that they are humane, and when they form an attachment to a perfon, will exert their utmoft efforts to ferve him. They are not indeed fo induftrious as could be wifhed. The fummer months are moftly fpent in providing fuel and tending the flocks; while the winter months are moftly confumed in burning this fuel. With refpect to their morals, they are punctual in attending on public worfhip, worſhip, and as decent in their behaviour in other reſpects, as their neighbours around them.

Church and Poor.—The value of the living is L. 55 : 11 : 1$\frac{4}{12}$ ſterling. The glebe and garden may be worth about L. 3 ſterling. The king is patron of this living. The manſe and church are very old.

The number of poor who receive alms from the kirk-ſeſſion is about nine. The yearly ſum expended for their relief will not exceed L. 12 ſterling. This ſum is raiſed from the Sunday collections. What further ſupport they ſtand in need of is ſupplied by charitable and well diſpoſed perſons.—The funds belonging to the poor do not exceed L. 40 ſterling.—By ſome old records it appears, that in the year 1704, the Sunday collections did not exceed 3d. a week, now at an average they amount to 3s. 6d.——There are no travelling beggars belonging to the pariſh ; but in the time of ſheep ſhearing it is much infeſted with vagrants from adjacent parts of the country *.

Rent

---

* The price of barley and oats is generally regulated by the Dundee market. Indeed the grain produced in this diſtrict is not ſufficient for the conſumption of the inhabitants. Oat meal generally ſells at 15s. and barley meal at 10s, and 10s. 6d. per boll of 8 ſtones of 16 lb.—Beef, mutton, and pork, is no leſs than 3d. per lb. of 16 oz.—The price of a pig is 2s. 6d.—of a hen 8d.—of a duck 6d. and of a chicken 3d. Butter is ſold at 6d. in ſummer, and when ſalted, at 8d. per lb. of 22 ounces.—The ſtone of cheeſe is generally 5s. but the price varies according to its richneſs and age. Ewe milk cheeſe is ſometimes ſold at 7s. per ſtone.

The wages of men-labourers are generally 1s. per day, from March to September, with maintenance. The women ſeldom hire by the day, except in the time of ſpinning wool, when they receive 3d. per day with maintenance.

The day-wages of a maſon are 1s. 1d.—of a wright 1s.—and of a taylor 6d. with maintenance.

Farm-ſervants generally draw from L. 7 to L. 8 ſterling *per annum*, with maintenance.—Women ſervants receive L. 3 ſterling a year, along with ſome

bounties,

Rent and Produce.—There is but a very ſmall part of the pariſh incloſed. Indeed one of the heritors, ſufficiently aware of the advantage and propriety of improving ground covered with heath, has incloſed a good many acres of muir ground, adjacent to his houſe, with fir and birch trees, which preſently appear to be in a very thriving ſtate. Would his neighbours follow his example, the country would not wear the bleak aſpect it preſently does.—The beſt arable land lets at about 20s. per acre, but to this is annexed the privilege of hill paſturage. The rent of the pariſh may be between L. 600 and 700 ſterling. This, however, is varying every year. The heritors, as has been mentioned, are 54 in number, of whom about 32 reſide in the pariſh. It is impoſſible to aſcertain the number of acres contained in it, the arable ground bears but an inſignificant proportion to that which is covered with heath. The plough moſtly uſed in the upper part of the pariſh is the old Scotch plough, generally drawn by 4, ſometimes by 6 horſes, yoked a breaſt of one another;—what is peculiar, the driver always travels backwards. This mode, no doubt, has been adopted, on account of the weakneſs and ſmall ſize of the horſes, which are moſtly of the Highland breed.—In the lower part, the Engliſh plough is for the moſt part uſed, and is drawn by 2 horſes. One man holds and drives.

The vegetable produce is bear and oats, no wheat is ſown; turnips, and potatoes are raiſed in the lower part of the pariſh; in the higher part of it turnips are but now introduced, and indeed it is impoſſible this crop can turn out to advantage, while the inhabitants allow their ſheep to feed promiſcuouſly

after

bounties, which in value may amount to 6s. or 7s. ſterling. About 40 years ago, the wages of a man-ſervant did not exceed L. 1 : 6 : 8 ſterling a year with maintenance.

after the corns are put into the barn-yards. With refpect to animal productions, the country abounds in black cattle; thefe are generally of a fmall fize, but very durable; the largeft will not exceed the weight of 18 or 20 ftones of 16 lb. The number in the parifh at prefent amounts to about 1696. The fheep, which are generally kept in the hilly part, are but of a fmall fize; fome of the inhabitants, however, go yearly to the fouth of Scotland, where they purchafe numbers of black faced fheep, which turn out with them to good advantage. The precife number of fheep cannot be afcertained. The country abounds with muir fowl, and feveral gentlemen keep fhooting quarters, which they regularly attend during the feafon. Here are hares and foxes in abundance. Ptarmigans are alfo to be found at a place called Caanefs, towards the head of the parifh.

Mifcellaneous Obfervations. ——The roads are in very bad repair, and muft continue in the fame ftate till proper over-feers are appointed to infpect them, and the road money of the parifh appropriated to their repair. The bridges are only two in number (though the extent of water, from the head to the foot of the parifh, is about 25 Englifh miles.) Were a bridge built centrically between thefe two, which are 9 miles afunder, it would be a confiderable advantage to the country at large, and free many individuals from inconveniencies they prefently labour under. Indeed there are fome funds for a bridge already, and fubfcriptions might be expected to complete the fcheme, were there any public fpirited perfon to fet the work on foot.

Befide the parochial fchool, the falary of which is 100 merks, there is a fchool erected by the Society

for

for propagating Chriſtian Knowledge at Folda. The teacher draws yearly from the Society L. 10 ſterling. Both ſchools juſt now are in bad repair, and truly it is difficult to get theſe matters properly adjuſted among ſuch a number of heritors *.

* There are the remains of two caſtles, viz. the caſtle of Forter and the caſtle of Newtown. A great part of the walls of the former remain almoſt entire, but only the veſtiges of the foundation of the latter are to be ſeen. Both belonged to the Ogilvies of Airly, and in 1641 were demoliſhed by the Marquis of Argyle; an injury the family of Airly did not fail to reſent.

PARISH OF GUTHRIE.

(*County of Angus.*—*Prefbytery of Arbroath.*—*Synod of Angus and Mearns.*)

By the Rev. Mr. WILLIAM MILLIGAN, *Minifter of* KIRKDEN *.

Situation, Surface, Soil, and Extent.

THE parifh of Guthrie is divided into two parts, one of which is 6 miles diftant from the other, and lies directly fouth from it. The inhabitants of the fouthern part, in going to their own parifh church, pafs through the parifhes of Dunnichen, Kirkden, and Refcobie. This part is called *Kirkbuddo*, where it is faid there was once a chapel for religious worfhip. The moor of Montrithmont, nearly a plain, confifting of about 5000 acres, which was a common, probably ever fince it was covered by the fea, has been divided among the

* This account was drawn up by Mr. Milligan, at the defire of Mr. THOMAS CRAIG, minifter of Guthrie, who has been fettled in that diftrict for 39 years; but, being prevented by indifpofition, from drawing up the account himfelf, requefted Mr. Milligan to take the trouble of doing it.

the proprietors of the ſurrounding pariſhes of Kirkden, Kinnell, Fernel, &c. who are encloſing and planting their ſeveral
proportions. About 370 acres of this moor have fallen to
the ſhare of the pariſh of Guthrie. Almoſt the whole northern part of the pariſh ſinks gently to the ſouth and eaſt,
from the top, near to the north weſt end of it, called the
Hill of Guthrie, the higheſt part of which is probably not
much more than 500 feet above the level of the ſea. There
is no hill in the ſouthern part of the pariſh, but the loweſt
ground in it is probably near 700 feet higher than the ſea.
Moſt of the pariſh, eſpecially the ſouthern part, is too wet.
The annexed table ſtates accurately, the extent and kinds of
land in the ſouthern part of the pariſh, being the contents of
a map from a late menſuration. The northern part is
taken from the proportions of oats, barley, peaſe, &c. ſown
by the different farmers according to their own reports, and
cannot be ſuppoſed ſo accurate. The extent of it is, probably,
rather more, than is ſtated in the table.

Extent of the Pariſh.

Number of Acres, &c.	North part.			South part.			Total.		
	A.	R.	F.	A.	R	F.	A.	R.	F.
In paſture, - -	51	0	0	100	2	26	151	2	26
Arable, - -	1138	0	0	682	1	7	1820	1	7
In moor, - -	370	0	0	186	3	11	556	3	11
Under moſs, - -	-		-	85	2	39	85	2	39
———— water, -	-		-	2	0	36	2	0	36
———— wood, - -	15	0	1	49	1	1	64	1	2
Groſs contents, -	1574	0	1	1107	0	0	2681	0	1

Crops in 1791.

Number of acres under barley. - - - -	244
——————————— oats, - - - -	334
——————————— peaſe, - - - -	60
——————————— flax, - - - -	19
——————————— turnips, - - - -	31
Carried over,	688

Brought

				Brought over, 688
Number of acres under potatoes,	-	-	-	12
——————— Grafs,	-	-	-	372
——————— fallow,	-	-	-	66
				Total, 1138

Agriculture and Cattle, &c.—There is a regular rotation of crops, in the fouthern, as well as in the northern part of the parifh, and probably about the fame proportion of oats, barley, peafe, &c. ; but it is divided into fuch fmall parts, that it was impoffible to ftate them accurately. There are fix farms in the fouthern part, viz. one of 169 acres ; one of 65 ; one of 45 ; one of 47 ; one of 39; and one of 33 acres, all arable : and the reft of the eftate of Kirkbuddo is divided into no lefs than 25 fmall farms. The number of cattle and horfes are in proportion to the grafs, and the lands in cultivation. There are not above 3 or 4 faddle horfes, and fcarcely any fheep or hogs.

Rent and Proprietors.—The average price of land, lately let in the northern part, is about 15 s. and in the fouthern part, 10 s the acre. The valued rent of the parifh is 1500 l. Scotch, and the real rent above 1000 l. Sterling. The parifh is divided among 3 proprietors, only one of whom, (Guthrie of that ilk,) refides in it about 7 months of the year.

Church, School and Poor.—The kirk and fchool are fituated in the northern part of the parifh. The manfe is old and ruinous. The ftipend, including 2 chalders of meal, at the ordinary converfion, is below 50 l. Sterling. The glebe is a legal one. The church is an elegant building for fuch a country parifh. The walls, or at leaft a part of them, are faid to be about 300 years old, and they may ftand for 1000

years

years to come. Mr. Guthrie of Guthrie is patron *. The
fchool-mafter is well qualified for his office. The falary, including kirk dues, may be between 11 l. and 12 l. Sterling.
The fchool fees are the fame as thofe of Kirkden. The fcholars are numerous, but the fouthern part of the parifh can
reap no advantage from the fchool. The weekly collections,
and the intereft of a fmall fum of money, are found fufficient
for the maintenance of the poor, of which there are at prefent
only two fupported by the public funds, and two or three who
receive fmall fums occafionally.

Population.—The people, almoft without exception, are
fober, induftrious and contented ; and a few excepted, all
belong to the Eftablifhed Church. The return to Dr. Webfter,
in 1755, was 584 fouls. By a particular enumeration, taken
in 1792, the number, ages and profeffions of the inhabitants,
appeared to be as follows :

Number

* The parifh was erected into a provoftry by one of his predeceffors, as appears by the following citation from an old author, who had written an account
of the different diocefes of Scotland.

" Guthrie, in the fhire of Angus or Forfar, was a collegìate church, founded
" by Sir David Guthrie of that ilk, who was Lord High Treafurer in the reign
" of King James the III. for a provoft and three prebendaries, the number of
" which was afterwards increafed by Sir Alexander Guthrie of that ilk, his fon
" and heir, who was flain at the battle of Floudon, in the year 1513." Henry Guthrie, bifhop of Dunkeld, was defcended of a younger fon of this ancient
family. Families, like individuals, often rife to ftrength and notice, and decline again into weaknefs and obfcurity, fometimes fuddenly and fometimes
more flowly. This old family feems not yet the worfe of age. John Guthrie,
Efp; of that ilk, poffeffes a fine eftate in the fhire of Angus, though his predeceffors were advanced to the higheft honours, as far back as the reign of James
the III.

Number of perfons	In the northern part.		In the fouthern.		Total.
	Males.	Females.	Males.	Females.	
Under 10 years of age,	42	43	35	28	148
Between 10 & 20 —	50	36	25	30	141
———— 20 & 50 —	73	71	31	39	214
———— 50 & 70 —	20	12	15	12	59
———— 70 & 92 —	3	4	2		9
	188	166	108	109	
	108			166	

Total of males, 296 - - and femaIes, 275   571

Hence there is a decreafe within thefe 40 years of   -   13

Number of Families,	ʉ	76	Number of Merchants,	-	2
———— Farmers,	-	14	———— Brewers,	-	1
———— Weavers,	-	17	———— Retailers of liquors,		2
———— Taylors,	-	5	———— Male fervants,	-	50
———— Shoemakers,	-	2	———— Female fervants,	-	33
———— Smiths,	-	1	———— Tradefmen's fervants,		11
———— Coopers,	-	1	———— Apprentices,	-	2
———— Wrights,	-	2			

Lift of Births, &c. for the laft 10 years.

			Baptifms.	Marriages.	Burials.
In the year	1782	there were	17	3	6
	1783		12	3	9
	1784		15	2	10
	1785		14	2	11
	1786		9	1	10
	1787		16	3	8
	1788		17	2	10
	1789		14	6	4
	1790		13	4	9
	1791		12	6	20
Total in 10 years,			139	32	97
Average,			13 9-10	3 3-10	9 7-10

Fuel.—The northern part of the parifh is fupplied with coals from Arbroath, and the fouthern part with peats from

a

a moſs, part of which is in the pariſh. Coals are uſually from 6 s. to 6 s. 8 d.; but this year they have been 7 s. at the loweſt, and for 4 or 5 months paſt 8 s. the cart load, of 70 ſtone Amſterdam weight.

Antiquities.——In the ſouthern part of the pariſh of Guthrie, there are upwards of 15 acres of moor, which are part of a Roman camp. The reſt of it is in the pariſh of Inverarity. The *vallum* and *foſſa* are yet very diſtinct, and of a conſiderable height and depth. The caſtle of Guthrie, ſuppoſed to have been built by Sir Alexander Guthrie, who was ſlain at Floudon, is a ſtrong building, and is ſtill entire. The walls are about 60 feet high, and 10 feet thick. It has a prodigious maſſive iron door. This caſtle and its door are at once a monument of the ancient grandeur of the family of Guthrie, and of the rudeneſs and barbarity of thoſe times, when men could not live ſecure, but in ſuch ſtrong towers. The garden of Guthrie is a mixture of ancient and modern taſte; it has ſeveral beautiful box hedges cut in various figures, and in perfect preſervation, though very ancient. Some ſuppoſe the garden to be nearly as old as the caſtle.

PARISH of INVERARITY.

(COUNTY OF FORFAR.)

By the Rev. Mr JOHN WEBSTER.

Situation and Extent.

INVERARITY is in the prefbytery of Forfar, and Synod of Angus and Mearns. It is bounded by the parifh of Kinnettles on the W.; Murrays on the S.; Carmyllie on the E.; and by Forfar on the N. The parifh is about 3 miles fquare.

Agriculture, Rent, Wages, &c.—Here and in the neighbourhood, there is a growing fpirit for agriculture. Marl is the chief manure. It is brought from the diftance of 5 miles; and from 40 to 50 bolls are put upon an acre. Its effects are moft fenfible and beneficial upon light dry land; and if laid on in a greater quantity, it will operate powerfully, even on a foil that has a tendency to be moift. For the firft feafon it does little good; but afterwards its effects will continue for 6 or 7 years. At the end of that time, the marling operation may be renewed, but it is pretended, the quantity of marl ought to be diminifhed in proportion to the number of times that the field has been marled. The

moft

most approved method, is to mix it with earth and dung, about 1 part marl, 1 earth, and 2 dung. This compost, by spreading it equally, prevents dangerous effects; and also causes it to *work* sooner than when marl is laid on by itself. What in some measure may have retarded the progress of agriculture here, is the old system of bondage and cottagers, which still prevails. This practice has continued, on account of very long leases having been formerly given. Of cottagers, there are to the number of 60 families, and the bondage in which they are held by the great farmer, has evidently an effect in rendering them less industrious; not having the command of their own time, they are brought not to know its value, and from being idlers when paying bondage abroad, they learn to be lazy at home; besides, as they hold their cottages from year to year, every little improvement they should make, would render them only more dependent on their master. As the old leases of the great farms expire, these cottagers are getting leases from the proprietor. From this, and the abolishing of personal services, it is not doubted but their situation will be improved, and the most powerful motive be given to excite their industry.

There are but few inclosures in this parish in proportion to the extent of arable ground. Corn therefore is principally cultivated. Where a field has been under cultivation and inclosed, it may let from 18 s. to 21 s. the acre; where it is otherwise, it will not give above 15 s. The valued rent is L. 2987 : 6 : 8 Scots; the real rent about L. 2000 Sterling.

Labourers get a shilling a-day without their victuals; farm servants have from L. 8 to L. 10 the year, and maid-servants from L. 3 to L. 4; and the wages of all of them are still gradually rising, which shews that both manufactures and agriculture are in a thriving condition.

Plantations.

Plantations.—The want of incloſures has had the ſame effect here, as in other places, of retarding the plantation of
trees : A circumſtance to be regretted, as woods and hedge-
rows add to the beauty, and improve the climate of a country. It gives pleaſure to mention, that the principal proprietor is buſy in planting the whole of his waſte lands,
which muſt eventually turn to good account. An acre of
land will contain 1500 trees at 6 feet diſtance. In 20 years,
each of theſe may ſell for 2 d.; and this amounting to
L. 12. 10 s. yields a rent of 10 s. yearly. In planting waſte
lands, eſpecially on the declivity of a hill, it would be a
good practice to lay two furrows together with the plough;
which would give the trees planted between them a greater
depth of ſoil ; and what is of ſtill greater advantage, the
ground would be kept dry, and the trees, on that account,
thrive much better.

Birds of Paſſage, &c.—Dotterels, rails and woodcocks,
viſit this pariſh. At their firſt appearance dotterels are very tame ; but after having been ſhot at they become remarkably wild. They have become much rarer, ſince the
country was improved. Woodcocks come here in the end
of September, and remain till April; one of them built a
neſt in this neighbourhood ; but the neſt and eggs were deſtroyed. We have a few grouſe; and which are conſiderably larger in ſize than upon the Grampians.

Population.

Population.—The return to Dr Webſter, about 40 or 50 years ago, was 996. According to the pariſh regiſter, there were at an average——

A. D.	Marriages.	Baptiſms.	Burials.	Souls.
1716	14	37		962
1720	9	38		988
1730	18	41	23	947
1740	9	33	26	897
1750	13	31	25	853
1760	11	37	25	931
1770	9	34	23	852
1780	8			860
1789	16			900

There are 169 families, $5\frac{1}{2}$ to each family. Thoſe of 10 years and under, are to thoſe above that age as 2 to 9. There are 1 Roman Catholic; 7 Epiſcopalians; 33 Seceders. The population from 1716 to 1770 is calculated from baptiſms, and burials being multiplied by 26 and 36, and the half of the whole product being taken for the number of ſouls required, that of 1780 and 1789 is aſcertained by actual enumeration. It ſhould thus appear, that the population of the pariſh during the preſent century has been very much the ſame : Many cauſes may have contributed to this ; the number of large farms, of ſmall poſſeſſions, and of cottages continued nearly equal ; and, though our increaſed wealth ſhould have produced more children, yet having no trading village to keep them at home, thoſe who were not needed for the uſual domeſtic purpoſes, may have gone in ſearch of employment to the many manufacturing towns, with which we are ſurrounded. From the cottagers being in more eaſy circumſtances than formerly, it is probable there may now be a greater proportion of ſouls under 12

years

years of age; but the higher wages of labouring servants having led the farmer to do more work with fewer hands, the one circumstance may counterbalance the other, and therefore may have kept the population of the parish almost stationary.

Poor, &c.—Families who occasionally need relief from the poors fund, have been gradually diminishing, and beggars have become exceedingly less numerous; at present we have not one belonging to the parish; but in 1741 the kirk-session gave 32 of them a badge and a licence to beg. Later than that period the heritors were obliged to assess themselves for supporting the poor; now our weekly collections are more than adequate for that purpose. At the interval of every 20 years there was, at an average, collected each Sunday,——

A. D.	s.	d.
1710	0	4
1730	1	3
1750	2	7
1770	5	3
1790	7	0

Were we therefore to judge of the wealth of the parish by this standard, we would conclude, that it had increased in the proportion of 1 to 21: This estimate would, however, be too high; because as there was formerly a much greater number of parochial beggars, those who had to give more charity in private, might give less in public: Yet allowing for this, and comparing what was given at different periods for the relief of families, who may be supposed to have been in similar circumstances, the wealth of the parish must be 8 or 10 times greater than it was in the beginning of the present century. Our former poverty, and indeed the poverty of the country in general, is strongly

ly

ly marked by the defcription given of thofe who folicited charity as beggars :—Stranger gentlemen,—poor gentlemen,—diftreffed gentlemen,—are the appellations very frequently given them ; and what muft have been the poverty! what the fpirit of the times! when, as the record informs us, a gentleman accepted a fourpence, and a young gentleman, recommended by a nobleman, was relieved by a fixpence !

Antiquities.—The only antiquity worth mentioning is a Roman camp called Taerfauds, in the moor of Lower. It is nearly a rectangular parallelogram, about 300 by 700 yards. There is another camp, Battledykes, about 8 miles to the north of this, in the parifh of Oathlaw, and, from the traces of a *via militaris* extending between them, it is probable that thefe two encampments were connected together. Neither hiftory nor tradition give any diftinct account of either of them. Some antiquaries fuppofe them to have been built by Agricola in his 6th campaign, when he obtained his victory over the Caledonians, under Galgacus their chief.

Character of the People.—They are, in general, induftrious and fober ; pleafed with their fituation, but not without ambition to improve it ; remarkable for their attendance at church ; and improved both in their moral and religious character.

PARISH OF INVERKEILOR.

(*County of Forfar.*)

By the Rev. Mr JOHN CARNEGIE.

Name.

THE antient name of this parish was *Conghoillis*, as appears from a charter describing the lands of Boisack. Its present name is *Inverkeilor*, from the Gaelic word *inver*, implying the mouth of a stream, there being a rivulet named *Keilor*, which empties itself into the sea, about a mile from the village.

Situation, General Appearances, &c.—The parish is situated in the county of Forfar, or Angus, presbytery of Aberbrothock, and synod of Angus and Mearns. It is of an oblong form, and extends from the sea westward, about six Scots miles in length; and its breadth at a medium is about $2\frac{1}{2}$ miles. The general appearance of the country is pretty level, except on the north side, where the ground rises from the river Lunan, and forms a beautiful bank, mostly of good arable land, sloping to the south.

Soil, Air, Diseases.—The soil of the parish varies, but is in general dry and fertile; the air is pure and healthy, but in the months of April and May, thick fogs frequently rise

from

from the fea. The ague was formerly the moft prevalent diftemper ; but of late the rheumatifm has become more general.

Rivers and Mills.—The river Lunan runs eaftward through this parifh, and takes its rife, about four miles from the weft end of it, near Forfar. This river has its fource from a well, called *Lunan Well*, a little above a chain of lochs, viz. Reftenet, Refcobie, and Balgaves, through which it paffes, and in its courfe is fed by feveral burns. It flows with a clear current, and after a variety of beautiful windings, falls into the fea at Redcaftle. It formerly abounded with fine trouts, and fome pike, but of late the fifh have fuffered much from watering lint in the river, or in burns that run into it ; and from fifhing with nets. In the courfe of this river, through the parifh, there are 15 mills, four of which are corn, four barley, five lint, one flour, and one oil mill.

Sea-coaft.—The extent of fea-coaft is about five miles, of which, that along the bay of Lunan, (which affords a fafe anchorage for fhips, except in a ftorm from the eaft), is flat and fandy, and overgrown with bent ; but the coaft on the fouth is high and rocky, where there is a remarkable promontory, the Red-head, on the eftate of the Earl of North-efk, whofe feat, Ethie-houfe, lies near it. It was built by Cardinal Beaton, and was one of his country feats. This cape is 45 fathoms in height ; it is feen at a great diftance from fea, and abounds with a variety of fea-fowls. At the Red head there is an inexhauftible quarry of fine free ftone. And below the rocks, pebbles, known by the name of *Scots pebbles*, are numerous ; among which there are fome of the colour and denfity of an amethyft.

Fifh.

Fish.—On this part of the coast there is a small fishing town, called *Ethie-haven*, inhabited by ten industrious fishermen, who employ two boats. The fish caught are haddocks, skate, cod, ling, holybut, and sometimes turbot. Salted cod, (about nine inches in length), were sent to the London market, and sold at 5 s. *per* hundred. In the year 1755, a lobster fishing commenced, which considerably hurt the fishing of skate, killing, ling, and holybut; but the small fish were not found to be scarcer. In London the demand for salted cod ceased, but lobsters found there a good market. In the year 1760, a salmon fishing was begun on Redcastle and Lunan sands. It was pretty successful that season, but not since; perhaps, in some measure, owing to steeping lint in the river Lunan, which communicates with the bay. The white fishing continued much the same, till the year 1786, from which period, both the great and the small fish, have been very scarce, particularly the haddocks.

Fuel—The fuel commonly used is coal, brought from the Frith of Forth, and sold at the harbour of Aberbrothock, at 6 s. 6 d. a cart load, being 72 stone. But on all that pass the Red-head, northward, there is a tax of $18\frac{1}{2}$ d. *per* boll. There are indeed still some whin and broom in the country, but the supply from these is become, by the improvements in agriculture, exceedingly scarce.

Population.—There are no records of this parish, farther back than the year 1739; since which time the population has increased. The number of souls at present in the parish, is 1747. In Dr Webster's report, the number is 1286. The births at an average of seven years, amount to 45 *per annum*, the marriages to 14, the burials to 24. But it must be observed, that the number of burials cannot be exactly ascertained, afcertained, as many of the parifhioners bury elfewhere, and fome from other parifhes bury here; and it is only when the mort-cloth is given, that the deaths are recorded.

There are fix heritors in the parifh, of whom four are refident. The number of tenants is 48, of ploughs 98, and thefe, except a few, are drawn by two horfes. There are 353 houfes in the parifh. The average number of fouls in each family, is about 5. The following tradefmen are all houfeholders: weavers 46, who are chiefly employed in making coarfe green linen cloth, or Ofnaburghs, which they fell to the greater manufacturers in towns, intended for the Weft-Indian and American markets, and exported from London and Glafgow; carpenters 9,—taylors 8,—fhoemakers 5,—blackfmiths 5,—flax-dreffers 6,—mafons 3,—coopers 2, —bakers 2,—brewers 3,—retailers of ale 5. The inhabitants are all of the eftablifhed church, except four families of Epifcopalians, and one family of Seceders.

Rent and Crops.—The valued rent of the parifh is 6354 l, 6 s. 8 d. Scots. The real rent is 3179 l. 13 s. 6 d. Sterling. The rate at which land is let, is various: fome farmers pay from 7 s. 6 d. to 20 s. *per* acre. There is no map of the parifh, but the number of acres is reckoned to be about 7083. Of thefe one half is annually employed in raifing wheat, barley, oats, peafe, &c.; and betwixt 70 and 80 acres at an average, in raifing flax. The other half in hay, pafture, fummer-fallow, and potatoes, which afford a very general fubfiftence; and in turnips, on which cattle are fed after the foggage. The tenants find their advantage in breeding cattle, a confiderable number of which, both fat and lean, go to England yearly. The produce of the parifh is more than fufficient to fupply its inhabitants.

Poor.

Poor.—The average number of poor on the roll, is about 20, who receive according to their circumstances, from 2 s. to 7 s. *per* month. The annual amount of the sum, expended for their relief, and for occasional charities, is about L. 54 Sterling, which arises chiefly from the weekly collections, and from the interest of a small mortified sum.

Church —The stipend is, meal 68 bolls at 7 stone *per* boll, bear 48 bolls, wheat 12 bolls, money L. 17 : 2 : 2$\frac{2}{7}$, including L. 5 for communion elements; a glebe four acres arable, and L. 20 Scots for grafs. Both kirk and manse are old, and need frequent repairs.

School.—The number of scholars is various ; there have been from 30 to 70. The schoolmaster's salary is 100 merks from heritors, and eight bolls of oats in seed-time from the tenants. The school fees *per* quarter are, for reading 1 s. reading and writing 1 s. 6 d. arithmetic 2 s. and Latin 2 s. He has likewise some emoluments, arising from the offices of session-clerk and precentor, together with a house and garden.

Roads.—About two miles of the post-road, leading from Aberbrothock to Montrose, run through this parish. It has been hitherto kept tolerably well in repair by the statute labour. Two tolls have been lately erected on it, with a view to the alteration of its course. The turnpike road betwixt Aberbrothock and Forfar, passes, for about two miles, through the west part of the parish.

Antiquities.—At the mouth of the river Lunan, on an eminence, stands an old venerable ruin, named *Redcastle ;* it is said to have been built by William the Lyon, and used as a

royal

royal hunting feat, which is probable from the names of fome farms, belonging to the Earl of Northefk lying very near it, but in the parifh of Lunan, as *Hawkehill, Courthill* and *Cothill;* likewife in reference to a royal hunting-feat, *Kinbleth-mont,* in this parifh, the feat of Mr Lindfay-Carnegie of Spynie and Boifack, implies the *King's-blythe-mount.* About a mile from Ethie-houfe, eaftward, nigh the fea, ftand the remains of a religious houfe, called *St Murdoch's Chapel,* where divine fervice was performed by the monks from the abbey of Aberbrothock. At a place called *Chapeltown,* there are the remains of the chapelry of Quytefield, now annexed by charter to the eftate of Mr Lindfay-Carnegie; and which is the family burying ground. There are veftiges of Danifh camps, both in the lands of the Earl of Northefk, and of Mr Lindfay-Carnegie. Thofe on the ground of the latter are near a farm-houfe, called *Denmark.* Although, owing to the cultivation of the country, the veftiges are not now remaining fo very diftinct, ftill the tradition is ftrong, and the name of *Denmark* feems to warrant it.

Improvements.—Since the fettlement of the prefent incumbent, agriculture has been amazingly improved. There was then little wheat fown, no barley, (the firft boll of which the prefent incumbent imported from Eaft-Lothian); no grafs-feeds, nor fummer-fallow, few inclofures, and thofe of earth. At prefent, agriculture, in every branch, is in a ftate of cultivation, little inferior to the Lothians. Of late, the knowledge of improvements, and the value of farms, have increafed with a rapid progrefs. And within thefe 10 or 12 years, a fpirit of improvement has been particularly obfervable. Farmers are fo fenfible of the advantages of inclofures, that all the fences now going on are of ftone. Their houfes of late, efpecially of thofe who have any encouragement, from the length of their leafes, are neat, commodious, and fubftantial, with a complete fteading or fet of offices. The houfes of cottagers and tradefmen, are generally now of ftone, and fome of them flated. It muft be obferved, that in building here, there is a local convenience, as on every eftate in the parifh, there is plenty of free ftone. This fpirit of improvement has not produced, in the parifh at large, the depopulating effects that have marked its progrefs in other parts of Scotland. A junction of farms has taken place in but a few inftances ; and in thefe, owing to fome local inducements, viz. ground lately feued, and the adjacency of a river, the lofs to population is fully compenfated, by many new houfes built for tradefmen.

PARISH OF KETTINS.

(County of Forfar—Synod of Angus and Mearns.
—Presbytery of Meigle.)

By Mr John Ritchie, *Student in Divinity at Markinch.*

Extent, Situation, and Roads.

THE length of the parish of Kettins, from E. to W. is 4 miles; the breadth, from S. to N. is 3. The village of Kettins is distant from Perth about 12 miles E. by N. and about 14 N. W. from Dundee. The church is 1 mile S. E. of Coupar. The turnpike road, from the latter to Dundee, passes through the parish. It is not yet finished. A road extends to Perth along the foot of the Sidla hills, but is not frequented.

Gentlemens Seats, Surface, &c.—*Lintrose,* the seat of Mungo Murray, Esq; was formerly called *Todderance,* and belonged to ———— Haliburton, Esq; whose grand-father, Lord Todderance, was a Senator of the College of Justice, and a nephew of the house of Pitcur. Lintrose is a mile westward of the church, and is environed by fertile fields and thriving plantations. *Haliburton House,* a modern mansion, upwards of half a mile S. E. of Kettins, formerly the ordinary residence of the family of that name, is now the property

property of Lord Aboyne *. It ſtands in a plain, and is ſurrounded by ſtately plantations. A detached part of the pariſh, called *Bandirran*, lies about 6 miles S. W. and contains a gentleman's ſeat. The greateſt part of the pariſh is level, and incloſed with hedges of thorn, or fenced with ſtone dykes. The ſouth part gradually riſes to the ſummit of the Sidla hills, and is partly covered with heath and paſture.

Villages, Rivulets, and Mills.—Kettins has 7 villages belonging to it, and is itſelf the largeſt. The village of that name, where the church ſtands, is pleaſantly ſituated on a rivulet, which deſcends from the Sidla hills, and paſſing through Coupar, loſes itſelf in the Iſla, near 5 miles W. of the latter town, after having turned 5 mills in its courſe. The number of rivulets within the pariſh is 2, and they ſerve 10 mills.

Soil.—The ſoil is various. A great part of the low pariſh, the higher grounds chiefly, and the hill ground, have a light thin ſoil, and are partly covered with heath and paſture. In many places a ſtrong red clay or mortar prevails, and in ſome it is wet and ſpungy. The greater part of the pariſh, however, is tolerably fertile. Much of this diſtrict is let to ſmall tenants, who, beſides farming, follow ſome trades, chiefly that of weaving coarſe linen.

Agriculture, Produce, Cattle, &c.—The ſame manner of cropping

* The family of HALIBURTON were very active in bringing about the Reformation of the Church of Scotland, and in the laſt century had an extenſive property in this country. The Caſtle of PITCUR, a mile ſouth of the church, and now in ruins, gave title to the ancient and honourable family of HALIBURTON, the chief of that name.

cropping and improvements, that is followed in Coupar and the neighbouring parishes, is practised here, and the produce is much in the same proportion. Here, too, the same disadvantages, scarcity of firing, and the distance from lime and coal, operate as a check on the industry and improvement of the farmer.—There are a few dealers in cattle in the parish, who keep grass parks, and drive their fed cattle to Falkirk, or to England.—There are now no sheep in the parish. A few were kept to pasture on the hill of Peatie till lately.

Rent and Proprietors.—The valued rent of the parish is 5129 l. 16 s. 8 d. Scotch. The present rent is unknown. The land, at a medium, lets at 17 s. Sterling per acre.—The number of heritors is 8, whereof 7 are resident. Lord ABOYNE is chief heritor.

Ecclesiastical State.—The Crown is patron. The stipend was formerly 8 chalders 9 bolls 7 pecks of victual, but has been lately augmented. The church was built in 1768 *, and repaired in 1791. The manse was built from the foundation in 1792. The name of the present incumbent is JOHN HALIBURTON.

Poor and School.—The poors money, collected at the church doors, together with a rent arising from a mortification on land, amounts to 50 l. yearly. The number of poor at present on the roll is 14. The school house was repaired in 1782. The salary was augmented in 1790, by a decreet of the

---

* The church of KETTINS anciently had six chapels depending on it, viz. one at a village called *Peatie*, another at *South Coston*, a third at *Pitcur*, a fourth at *Muiryfaulds*, a fifth at *Denhead*, and a sixth on the south side of the village of Kettins. Most of these were within small inclosures used as burying places.

the Commiffioners of Supply. It was formerly 100 l. Scotch. The prefent fchoolmafter has taught with reputation a good number of years, and has, with his fmall emoluments, brought up a numerous family.

Population.—The population of Kettins has varied at different periods, as will appear from the following table:

STATISTICAL TABLE OF THE PARISH OF KETTINS.

In 1726, the number of examinable perfons above 12 years of age, was * - - - - 1100
To which may be added, for thofe under that age, at leaft - - - - - 300
_____
1400
In 1755, the return to Dr Webfter was - - 1475
_____
Increafe in 30 years 75
In 1793, the total number of inhabitants was only 1100
_____
Decreafe in 38 years 375
_____
Total number of baptifms, from 1722 to 1726, inclufive - - - - - 450
Annual average of ditto during that period - 90
Ditto of ditto, from 1751 to 1755, inclufive - 45
Ditto of burials, during that period - - 40
Ditto of ditto, from 1787 to 1791, inclufive †. 33
Families

* The regifter of births and marriages has not been regularly kept for fome years paft. There are no feffion records prior to the 9th of Auguft 1650.—A record of that date mentions two kirk-feffion regifters before that period.

† There is nothing remarkable in the proportion of males and females, nor in the prices of labour, or of the neceffaries of life, in this diftrict, different from thofe of Coupar.

Families in the parish	218	Teachers	-	3
Families in Kettins	40	Brewers	-	2
Roman Catholic ditto	1	Smiths	-	6
Widowers -	5	Wrights -	-	13
Widows -	8	Sieve-makers	-	3
Bachelors -	5	Day-labourers	-	27
Unmarried women	4	Masons	-	2
Weavers -	62	Cooper	-	1
Looms -	100	Flax-dressers	-	3
Farmers -	41	Gardeners	-	2
Drovers -	3	Bleachers	-	3
Shoemakers -	7	Public houses	-	5

Bleachfields, Longevity, &c.—There are 3 bleachfields in the parish, *Borland, Baldinnie*, and *Kirk-steps*. The two first whiten annually 100,000 yards, the last about 30,000 yards. —Few very remarkable instances of longevity have occurred within the recollection of the inhabitants, though to hear of people dying at the advanced age of 90 and upwards is not uncommon. There was a man alive last autumn (1793) at the age of 106. There are no epidemic diseases peculiar to this parish. Inoculation for the small-pox is by no means general, especially among the lower classes.

Antiquities.—There are no Roman ways, nor Druidical circles in the parish *. At *Camp-muir*, a village belonging to

Kettins,

---

* Some tumuli have lately been found in this parish, when digging materials for the turnpike road: One at Pitcur contained at least 1000 load of stones. In the center of this cairn, a few flat unwrought stones, and without date or characters, contained some human bones. A cairn of a very small size was found a mile farther south on the new line of road, and scarce distinguishable from the pasture around. In the center, an urn was found full of bones.

Kettins, and upwards of a mile N. W. of the church, there are ſtill viſible the outlines of a camp, ſuppoſed to be Roman, as noticed in the account of Coupar. At Baldowrie there is an erect Daniſh monument, 6 feet high. It contains ſome figures, but they are almoſt entirely defaced.—The Caſtle of *Dores* ſtood on the ſummit of the hill *, ſouth from Pitcur. Tradition reports it to have been ſome time the reſidence of MACBETH. The following names are doubtleſs of Celtic derivation : *Baldowrie*, *Baldinnie*, *Balunie*, *Balgove*, and *Airdlair*.

* On this hill, great quantities of aſhes are ſaid to have been diſcovered. From this circumſtance, it is concluded to have been one of thoſe hills, where fires uſed to be kindled in antient times, to alarm the country on the approach of an enemy. On the eaſt quarter of this hill, and cloſely by the ſide of the new road, the workmen quarrying ſtones came upon an excavation in the ſolid rock, in which they found ſome half conſumed bones of a ſoft conſiſtence. The hole was about 3 feet wide either way, and ſeemed to direct its courſe towards the ſouth. There was no entrance from above obſerved, for at leaſt half a mile in any direction from this place.

PARISH of KINGOLDRUM,

(COUNTY OF FORFAR, SYNOD OF ANGUS AND MEARNS, PRESBYTERY OF MEIGLE.)

By the Rev. MR JAMES BADENACH.

Name, Extent, Surface, Climate, &c.

THE origin of the name feems to be uncertain. It is faid to be derived from the Gaelic, and to fignify, " The Town between the Drums." This fignification is, at leaft, expreffive of the local fituation of the kirk and kirktown, which ftand between two drums or eminences, with the burn of Cromby running between them. The parifh is about 7 miles from N. to S. and $2\frac{1}{4}$ from E. to W. It is properly a hilly or mountainous diftrict, with fmall rivulets between the hills, in which there is good angling for trout. In the north part of the parifh the mountains rife to a confiderable height, efpecially Catlaw, whofe elevation above the level of the fea, has been found, by barometrical menfuration, to be 2264 feet, and at the bafe of which, on the N. E. there is a chalybeate fpring, ufeful in

weakneffes,

weakneſſes. On Catlaw, and the adjoining mountains, partly green, and partly heath, there is excellent paſture for ſheep; and Catlaw mutton is remarkable for its ſuperior delicacy and flavour. There is but little flat land; almoſt the whole of it ſloping gently with a north or ſouth expoſure. The climate is nearly the ſame throughout the whole pariſh, and any variation is owing to expoſure and local ſituation. Along the braes of Balfour and Baldovie, lying to the ſouth, and ſheltered with a riſing ground on the north, the air is rather milder and more temperate than in any other part of the pariſh; and both ſpring and harveſt ſomewhat earlier. The air, however, in general is cold and ſharp, yet extremely healthy; and to the ſalubrity of the air and the water, it may probably be owing that agues never make their appearance. The prevalent diſeaſes are fevers, colds, ſore throats, and conſumptions.

Soil, Produce, and Rent.—The ſoil is various: In ſome places it is a kind of clay, cold and wet; in others a light ſand; but in general is a rich black mould. The principal crops are barley and oats. Of late years wheat has been raiſed in particular places, eſpecially in the braes of Kenny and Baldovie, with great ſucceſs. Turnip and potatoes, clover and rye graſs, are common in every part of this pariſh. A ſmall quantity of peaſe is ſown chiefly for fodder, and on every farm more or leſs flax-ſeed, for domeſtic uſes. More grain is raiſed than is conſumed by the inhabitants; a part of their barley is bought by a diſtiller in the pariſh, and the remainder, with the oats, wheat, and meal, are carried to the Dundee and the Kirrimuir markets. Both ſpring and harveſt are later than in the vale of Strathmore, to the ſouth, owing to more frequent ſhowers among the hills, and to a keener air in the narrow openings between

I them,

them, than in a wide extended vale. The foil is in moſt places of excellent quality, and climate only is wanting to render it extremely productive. The valued rent of the pariſh is L. 2555 Scots; the real rent about L. 1600 Sterling. Moſt of the leaſes were granted ſeveral years ago, and many of them are ſaid to be extremely reaſonable. The arable acre is from 5s. to 18s. and the number of arable acres is between 3000 and 4000. There is no map of the pariſh, nor can the waſte land and rough paſture be aſcertained with any degree of preciſion. There are 8 heritors, 1 of whom reſides conſtantly, and another occaſionally.

Improvements.—Within the laſt 20 years conſiderable improvements have been made. The ſituation is favourable for manure, from being in the immediate vicinity of an inexhauſtible fund of ſhell marl, a part of which lies in the pariſh, and belongs to the proprietor of Balfour, from which his own tenants have privilege, by their leaſes, to any quantity which their improvements require. Beſides laying out the fields in a regular manner, fallowing, and marling, ſeveral farms have been incloſed with ſubſtantial ſtone fences, an improvement which greatly enhances their value. Planting likewiſe is going on in different places, and in particular upon the eſtate of Captain Wedderburn of Pearſie, where, beſides a conſiderable portion of the arable land being incloſed, there are plantations to a great extent. A good deal of attention has alſo been paid to the breeding of horſes and cattle, as well for ſale as for private uſe, and the breed of both has of late years been much improved. Upon the eſtate of Pearſie, cattle, bred out of ſmall highland cows, have ariſen, from the richneſs of the paſture to ſuch a ſize, as to bring L. 10, L. 12, and ſometimes

times L. 15 a head, for turnip-feeding, or heavy carriages.

Antiquities.—On a hill called the *Schurroch*, to the westward of the church, there are in three different places, equally diftant from each other, feveral large ftones, erected in a circular form, called here Druds altars, which is evidently a corruption of Druids altars, and fhows them to have been places of Pagan worfhip. Upon the top of another hill, called Catlaw, already mentioned, which bounds this parifh on the north, there is a very large cairn of ftones, in a circular form alfo; but whether ufed as a place of worfhip, or of obfervation, from whence fignals were given to the country, on the approach of an enemy, is uncertain. The caftle of Balfour, formerly the principal refidence of Ogilvy of Balfour, an ancient family, and a defcendent of the family of Airly, has fome claim to antiquity. As there is no date to be feen upon any part of the walls, which are ftill ftanding, it is not generally known in what year it was built. The ftructure is evidently in the Gothic ftyle ; and, from facts connected with it, about which there is no uncertainty, muft be upwards of 200 years old, and might probably have been erected about the middle of the 16th century. The family of Balfour is funk into the family of Fotheringham, and Colonel Fotheringham of Pourie, by the female line, is proprietor of the eftate of Balfour, the moft extenfive, and the beft land of any in the parifh.

Population, &c.—According to Dr Webfter's report, the number of fouls was then 780. The population is diminifhing. The prefent number is about 600. Of whom are 18 or 20, who are Epifcopalians; and 2 men and 1 woman, who are Seceders. The number of families is 129. The

The births, marriages, and deaths, as inserted in the parish-register for the last 10 years, are as under :

Years.	Births.	Marriages.	Deaths.
1781	18	6	14
1782	15	0	9
1783	18	7	16
1784	13	5	10
1785	18	5	10
1786	9	8	12
1787	15	5	8
1788	17	3	14
1789	16	8	9
1790	16	7	12
1791	15	10	11

No manufactures are carried on in the parish. There are but few tradesmen of any description, and these few are employed for parochial purposes ; almost all the rest of the inhabitants being engaged in the operations of husbandry. The decrease of population, as above stated, is owing partly to the union of farms, and partly to tradesmen and smaller tenants removing to villages and sea-port towns, from interest or convenience. In consequence of this decrease, together with the flourishing state of manufactures in Angus, the wages of labouring servants have arisen in a *quadruple ratio*, within the last 40 years *.

Stipend,

* For example, the best ploughman in this parish, and perhaps in the Braes of Angus, could have been hired about 40 years ago, for L. 2, or L. 2, 5 s. in the year ; whereas good ploughmen are receiving at present, from L. 8 to L. 9. The rise in the wages of women servants, day labourers, and harvest reapers, is in the same proportion ; and, for the last ten years, has been more rapid than in any period of the same extent, within the 40. The farmer is however enabled to meet this advance of the price

of

Stipend, Poor, &c.—The ſtipend is 82½ bolls victual, and L. 22 : 8 : 3 $\frac{6}{12}$ money, beſides a manſe and glebe of a-bout 4 acres. The church was originally a parſonage, belonging to the Abbey of Arbroath; and the greater part of the preſent ſtipend is payable from abbey-lands in that neighbourhood. Towards the end of the 12th, or in the beginning of the 13th century, a donation of the pariſh was made to the abbey by Sir Allan Durward of Lentrathen, and this donation is ſaid to have been confirmed by a charter from the Hoſtiary of Scotland, of date 1253. From the time of the donation by Sir Allan Durward, until ſome years after the middle of the 16th century, the lands of Kingoldrum continued in the poſſeſſion of the Abbey, and about the year 1565, the greater part of them is ſaid to have been feued *cum decimis incluſis.* The burden of the ſtipend continued ſtill to fall upon the Abbey, and after the erection of the Abbey into a temporal lordſhip, it devolved upon the titular of the tithes. The conſequence of which was, that, by the decreet of proviſion, dated in the year 1635, more than one half of the preſent ſtipend was allocated upon abbey-lands in the neighbourhood of Arbroath, from which it continues to be payable to the miniſter of Kingoldrum till this day.—In a pariſh in which there is no village, and ſcarce any houſeholders who have not ſome employment adequate to their ſuſtenance, there cannot be many who ſtand in need of alms. The number at preſent upon the poors roll amounts only to 5; all of whom

of labour, upon theſe grounds, that fewer ſervants are neceſſary, and more work is performed by the ſame number of ſervants than in any former period; becauſe a third, or certainly leſs than a half of the ſame farm yields better grain, and a greater quantity of it, than the whole did 30 or 40 years ago; and becauſe his grain, his horſes, and his cattle, his poultry, his butter, and his cheeſe, are brought to a better, and for the moſt part to a ready-money market.

whom are heads of families, and receive a weekly allowance. Befides collections in the church on the Sundays, there is a confiderable fund belonging to the poor, the intereft of which, together with the weekly collections, is fufficient for every purpofe of parochial charity. In the year 1782, the year in which the prefent incumbent was ordained, it does not appear that the number of poor increafed, and the only difference between that and other years, feems to have been a more liberal difburfement to fuch as were already upon the roll.

Manners, &c.—Plainnefs of manners and honefty in their dealings, characterize the inhabitants of this diftrict. In their feveral occupations they are induftrious, and at the fame time carry on their bufinefs without noife and without feuds. Many of them are in eafy circumftances, and all live within their income. Their ftature is about the middle fize; their food plain, and they poffefs all the fpirit and activity of Highlanders. In profeffion they are Prefbyterians, and well attached to the family on the throne. If their zeal is temperate, it is not the lefs real; want of enthufiafm being no proof of indifference, but, on the contrary, of foundnefs in principle. Whether the parifh has produced any eminent men, either in fcience or in arms, is uncertain; it is faid, however, to have given birth to a famous actrefs on the Englifh ftage.

PARISH OF KINNELL.

(COUNTY OF ANGUS.)

By the Rev. Mr. Chaplin.

———————

Name, Situation, &c.

IT is said, that Kinnell fignifies the *head of the pool*, the church and manfe being placed near a deep pool in the water of Lunan. It is fituated in the county of Forfar, prefbytery of Aberbrothock, and fynod of Angus and Mearns.——The foil is of two kinds. One is clay, and naturally wet ; the other light, producing good crops in a moift feafon, but much parched when it is dry. The air is healthy. No ficknefs prevails to any extent. Sometimes in the month of February there are fevers, but chiefly among the poor, in confequence of their low diet, damp houfes ,&c.————There are no mineral fprings, lakes, or woods in the parifh. The water of Lunan runs through a part of it, in which, are excellent burn trouts, which are in perfection in the 'months of June and July.

Population, &c.——The antient ftate of its population cannot now be known. The return to Dr Webfter, in 1755, was 761 fouls ; but, this is fuppofed to be a miftake, as, till

withia

within these 25 years, they never exceeded 600. They now a-mount to 830. The increase is owing to the tenants having use for more hands, being busied inclosing their farms, and improving them with lime and marle. There are likewise a number of small possessions, which give great encouragement to population. There are no villages, nor any uninhabited houses in the parish. At an average for the last 10 years, there have been 6 marriages, 20 baptisms, and 12 deaths yearly.————There are only 3 heritors, none of whom reside.

Rent, Tenants, &c.————The valued rent is L. 2,700 Scots, the real rent about L. 1,700 sterling. There are 18 greater, and 50 smaller tenants. Some of the greater pay from L. 50, to L. 150 *per annum*. The smaller, who are generally trades-men, pay from L. 5 to L. 15 yearly.————There are 2,000 arable acres, and from 4 to 500 of muir. The acre is let from 10s to 15s.————There are 160 horses, and about 600 black-cattle : No sheep.————The principal crops are oats and barley ; some pease and beans ; a great deal of clover and rye-grass. A considerable quantity of flax, and some wheat, are also raised. Turnips and potatoes are now a general crop all over the country. There is much more grain raised, than is necessary for the support of the inhabitants. There was no-thing remarkable in the state of the parish, in the years 1782, and 1783 ; meal was dear, but there was no real scarcity.

Church, &c.————The church was built in 1766, and the manse in 1726. All the inhabitants of the parish very regu-larly attend the established church, except one Seceder, and three of the Episcopal persuasion. The king is patron. The living consists of 60 bolls meal, 32 bolls bear, and L. 27 : 14 : 6 in money, besides a garden and a glebe of six acres.

School.

School.—The legal falary is 200 merks Scots. Perquifites are, for a marriage, 2s 6d. for the baptifm of a child whofe parents are above the rank of cottagers, 1s. from cottagers, half a merk Scots; and for certificates, 4d. For teaching Englifh, 1s, per quarter; for writing and arithmetic, 1s 6d; and for Latin, 2s. In the fummer, there are from 30 to 40 fcholars, and, in the winter 50 and upwards.

Poor.—There are, at prefent, 8 perfons on charity, at 4s. each per month; befides feveral others, who get cloaths, fhoes, and coals, once a year. The fum fpent yearly for their fupport, is about L. 26 fterling, arifing from weekly collections, feat rents in the church, and the intereft of fome money belonging to them. The Seffion is very attentive to their neceffities, allows none of them to beg, and pays the fchoolmafter for teaching their children. But a great many beggars, from diftant places, infeft the parifh continually.————It has been faid, that all the parifhes in Scotland, except two or three in the Highlands, can maintain their own poor at home:—Why, then, are they allowed to wander about, oppreffing the country at large?

Antiquities.—There was a mound of earth lately opened in the parifh, and feveral human bones found in it of a large fize. There was alfo an urn, containing burnt human bones. The outfide of it was ornamented clay, and the infide charcoal. It is probable, that the burning of the dead was confined to the chief ranks, as being both troublefome and expenfive. When burnt, they were put into earthen urns, as among the Greeks and Romans, and a barrow of earth thrown up in proportion to their rank.——Buchanan fpeaks of a battle, in the reign of James II. between the Lindfays and Ogilvies, about the year 1443. Tradition adds, that the battle was fought near this

this place, and that a man, of the name of Irons, was slain in the pursuit. On account of his extraordinary size, his boot and spur were taken off, and hung up in an aisle adjoining to this church, belonging to the family of Airly. The boot in a course of years, would fall down and perish ; but the spur still remains on the wall, covered with rust. It measures 8 inches in length, and $4\frac{1}{2}$ in breadth, and the rowel is as large as a crown piece.

In 1790, a boy, going from school, found, under a bit of slate, a considerable number of silver pennies ; some of them were in good preservation, considering how long they have been under ground, and have the following inscription, *Ed. R. Angl. Dns. Hyb.* The reverse is, on some of them, *Civitas London.* on others, *Civitas Cantor. Civitas Dublinensis.*

Miscellaneous Observations.——The roads are tolerable.—— The statute-labour is sometimes exacted in kind, and sometimes commuted. There are no stone bridges in the parish, no turnpikes, no services of any consequence ; no post-office. The nearest is Aberbrothock, about 4 miles distant.——No peat, some bad turf ; but plenty of coal, from Aberbrothock, for 6s the boll, which is 70 stones weight.

General Character.——The people are sober, regular, and industrious. No emigrations, no banishments, no murders, no suicides in the memory of the oldest. There are two ale houses in the parish, which have no bad effects on their morals. There is a considerable alteration to the better, within these 20 years, in dress, manner of living, houses, &c.

PARISH of KINNETTLES,

(County of Forfar, Synod of Angus and Mearns,
Presbytery of Forfar.)

By the Rev. Mr David Ferney.

Name, Extent, Surface, Soil, Air, &c.

THE name is of Gaelic derivation, and fignifies " out
" from the bogg." This name applies with peculiar
propriety to the old manfion-houfe of the eftate of Kinnettles, which was built clofe to a piece of marfhy ground,
ftill called the Bogg *. The church being built within the
boundaries of this eftate, that circumftance probably gave
the name of Kinnettles to the parifh. The form of the
parifh is nearly a fquare, having about 2 Englifh miles
for the length of each of its 4 fides. The fouth line or
boundary feems, however, to be rather fhorter than any
of the other three. The parifh is divided by a hill, one
part of which is called Brigton, the other Kinnettles.
The hill is arable, except a few acres of rocky land on
that

* The manfion-houfe is now removed about a furlong farther from the
marfh.

that divifion of it which belongs to Kinnettles, which are planted. There are a few acres of woodland on the Brigton fide. The hill continues to defcend to the S. within a fmall diftance from a rivulet which runs through the fouthern diftrict of the parifh. The weftern defcent contains 4 inclofures, and then dies away into flat land. The northern continues the length of 3 inclofures; afterward the land is rather level, comprehending 3 inclofures alfo. There is a like number on the eaftern defcent, which is divided into two parts. South of the rivulet a range of floping banks declines to the N. as far as the rivulet. The plantations and pleafure grounds of Brigton extend on both fides of the little river with a fweep about an Englifh mile in length. The houfes of Brigton, Kinnettles, Inverighty, with the pleafure ground, have a good effect.—Our foil is various, confifting fome of it of brown clay, fome of loam, of loam with a mixture of clay, of loam with a mixture of fand; fome of it is in quality almoft mere fand. Of this laft kind there is but a fmall proportion. Our clay and black foil are deep and fertile; fome of the ftrong land yields from 8 to 12 bolls an acre, particularly in oats after ley, when it is well laid down. Even the light foil has produced good crops with marl and kindly treatment.—The air is not fo much infefted with fogs as in fome other diftricts in Scotland, being rather dry and healthful. We have no difeafes that can be faid to be local. Agues are fcarcely known; fevers not epidemical; melancholy habits are equally rare here as in moft other diftricts. The moft epidemical fever in my remembrance, was about the beginning of fpring 1789, after an uncommonly wet winter, in a village low and wet. Our air is fharp in winter, and frofty in proportion as the Grampians are covered with fnow. We have feveral freeftone quarries,

ries, which are made use of for building houses and fences; some of them yield stones well adapted for the purpose of hewing.

Animals.—Cattle and horses are in considerable numbers, 607 of the former, 130 of the latter. No sheep, but a few (about 40) kept principally for the use of gentlemens families *. The farmers in the parish rarely follow the plan of rearing cattle on their best farms; they rather buy in and fatten. Were they, however, to adopt the plan of rearing, they have the means of so doing up to 36 and 80 stone weight, when the cattle have attained the age of 4 or 5 years; and such cattle would bring, if fat, from 5 s. to 7 s. the stone, according to the demand and the pitch to which they may happen to be fed.

Population, &c.—According to the return made to Dr Webster in 1755, the number of souls was then 616. The state of population cannot be traced far back with any degree of exactness. The taste for enlarging farms, and razing cottages, has contributed not a little to diminish the number of inhabitants in this and most country parishes in Angus. This diminution, however, is not so great as might be expected from the number of houses demolished. Farmers and others, keep more female servants than are necessary, solely for the business of husbandry, and the service of their families. When not engaged in domestic and farming business, they can find employment for them in spinning yarn for the green linen manufacturers. But the

---

* We have no migratory birds, except green plovers, swallows, and the cuckoo, which appear in the month of April; and the woodcock, in the beginning of winter. The swallow disappears about the month of September, the cuckoo about the month of July.

the number gained in this manner is not equal to the number loft by the razing of houfes. The amount of the prefent
population is 621, comprehending all ages ; males 325 ;
females 296. There is no town in the parifh, only 1 village, containing 78. The number of births for 10 years
preceding April 1790, was 165, making 16¼ yearly. There
is no regifter of deaths kept here. Since 1783, on account
of the tax, there has been a regifter of burials, which contains all that have been buried here, whether parifhioners
or ftrangers. This would have given certain information
of the deaths in the parifh, had it not been cuftomary here
not to confine the burying of their dead to the church-
yard of the parifh. From October 1783 to October 1790,
there have been 28 marriages. But this article may readily occafion a miftake, and a return of many more marriages may poffibly be given than have actually taken place
in it. When the bridegroom refides in one parifh, and the
bride in another, there may be a report of the fame marriage from both thefe parifhes.

Males.		Females.	
Under 10,	68	Under 10,	49
From 10 to 20,	91	From 10 to 20,	81
—— 20 to 50,	116	—— 20 to 50,	118
—— 50 to 70,	42	—— 50 to 70,	43
—— 70 to 100,	8	—— 70 to 100,	5

The oldeft inhabitant at prefent is a woman in her 90th
year, and 2 men going 85. I recollect no tradition of remarkable old age here. Exclufive of pendicle tackfmen,
who depend not on farming alone for their fubfiftence, we
have 16 farmers, befides 2 gentlemen who farm part of
their own eftates. Their families in all contain 167 perfons. There are 3 farms, on which the poffeffors do not
refide;

3

reside ; and 1 of these yields the highest rent. The circumstance of non residence on these farms diminishes considerably the number of this class. The number of heritors is
5, and 2 of them reside. The number of manufacturers
is 58 ; of handicraftsmen, 20 ; apprentices, 6. Household
servants are 5 male, 16 female. There are 76 labouring
servants, 51 male, 25 female ; here I have marked only
hired servants. With most of our farmers, the sons and
daughters of the family supply, in a considerable degree,
the place of servants. There is 1 artist employed in conducting a flax-yarn mill. Labouring servants often go
from one parish to another. We have 2 residing heritors,
Mr Douglas of Brigton, and Mr Bower of Kinnettles, or
of Kincaldrum. Their families consist of 25 persons, exclusive of domestic servants. Lord Strathmore is one of the
heritors, but has no mansion-house here ; also Mr Simson
of Inverighty, who has a mansion-house here, but resides
in Edinburgh. There is 1 clergyman, 26 Episcopalians, 5
Roman Catholics, 1 Seceder, 589 of the Established Church,
93 married men, 45 bachelors at the age of 21, widowers,
12 ; marriages, upon an average, may produce $5\frac{14}{15}$. There
is no account of any having died of want. No recollection of murders or suicides, except one suicide committed
by a woman about 20 years since *. Very few have emigrated.

* We have bands of sturdy beggars, male and female, or, as they are
usually called, tinkers; whose insolence, idleness, and dishonesty, are an
affront to the police of our country. These persons are ready for prey of
all kinds. Every thing that can supply them with provisions, or bring
them money, is their spoil, if it can be obtained with any appearance of
safety. They file off in small parties, and have their places of rendezvous,
where they choose to billet themselves at least for one day ; nor do they
fail generally to make good their quarters, as the farmer is afraid to refuse to answer their demands, or to complain of the oppression under
which he labours.

grated. None have been banished, or obliged to leave
the parish for want of employment. No uninhabited
houses. The number of the inhabited is 126; the propor-
tion of houses to the number of inhabitants is as 1 : 4$\frac{117}{126}$.
On account of the increased size of farms, and the practice
of inclosing, population does not seem to be so great now
as it was 25 years ago. Farmers were then accustomed to
have 1 or 2 houses on their farms, with a small quantity of
land, which were intended for the accommodation of one
or two married servants. Since the inclosing and labouring of ground with attention have taken place, that accommodation for married servants is withdrawn, and o-
ther servants are thereby discouraged from marrying. The
servant finds, too, that when married, he cannot so easily
find a place with a farmer, whom, perhaps, he would be
most willing to serve; nor are masters, in general, fond of
retaining married servants. In fact, there is no class a-
mong whom marriages are so infrequent, as farmers servants.

Productions, Agriculture, &c.—Almost all the vegetables,
plants and trees in Scotland are to be found here, and thrive
in our soil and climate; and we have such animals as are
common to the low countries of Scotland. Rent of best a-
rable land is from 18 s. to L. 1, 5s. the acre. Size of farms
is from 42 to 200 acres, and upwards. Farms, at an average, about L. 88 yearly. There is at least 4-5ths of the
parish inclosed. The number of acres under the different
crops, at present, is nearly as follows:—583 in oats, 335 in
barley, 26 in wheat, 33 in pease, 28 in lint, 84 in turnips,
22 in potatoes, 174 in cutting grass, and 777 in pasture; a-
mounting in all to nearly 2065$\frac{1}{4}$ acres. There are 31 ploughs,
drawn by 3 or 4 horses; 56 carts; 1 coach; 1 two-wheel-
ed chaise. Exclusive of what some heritors retain in their
own

own hands, the land-rent of the parish may be about L. 1600 Sterling. The parish supplies itself with provisions. Besides what is sufficient for that purpose, a considerable quantity of oat-meal is sent to the neighbouring towns; and perhaps $\frac{2}{10}$ of our barley is conveyed partly to the towns in the county, and partly to others at a greater distance, to be manufactured there. The attention of our farmers has never been turned to the raising of hemp. We know not what it is in this country to turn land into grass, without sowing it with grass-seeds. All our hay-grass, and pasture on land fit for tillage, are artificial grasses. We have some pasture (about 120 acres) on mire and moss ground, which is natural grass; such lands having not, as yet, been brought under culture. There are about 20 acres of moor, and 12 or 16 of plantations. The grass-seeds sown here are red and white clover, about 19 or 20 lb. to the acre, 2-3ds red, and 1-3d white. We add 6 or 8 pecks of rye-grass seed, which has frequently a mixture of rib-grass or plantane. Commonly this artificial grass is cut the two first years for hay, and house-feeding for cows and horses in summer. I attempted once to introduce the tall yellow clover, and commissioned a quantity of the seed of that grass, as being of a less dangerous quality than the red clover. I was disappointed, having got only a dwarf, grovelling, unprofitable kind, instead of that which I commissioned. I never attempted to introduce it again, nor has it as yet found its way into the parish *.

Stipend,

---

* Our wheat, in general, is sown from the end of September to the 20th of October. We sow oats as soon as the ground is sufficiently dry for receiving it. Sometimes land is fit for seed in February, as in 1779; at other times, not till the middle of April. The desirable time for our soil, in general, is to begin about the 10th or 15th of March. On dry land, in good condition, with a good season, there will be a luxuriant crop,

though

Stipend, School, Poor, &c.—The ftipend, in money, is L. 44 : 3 : 3$\frac{10}{12}$ Sterling; in victual, 2 chalders of meal, and 1 chalder of barley, each kind valued at 13 s. 4 d. which, with the old glebe, about 6 acres, and 2$\frac{1}{2}$ acres of moor, obtained in lieu of a fervitude, at L. 1, 10 s. the acre, the whole may be rated at L. 88 : 18 : 3. In point of benefit, I am much at a lofs how to eftimate a glebe. A minifter labouring it at the expenfe of L. 14 for a man-fervant's wages

though fown fo early. In wettifh land and not into fuch order, there will be little ftraw, and altogether a deficient crop, if it be not fown confiderably later. Englifh barley, which demands our beft foil, and in the higheft condition, requires to be fown from the 20th of April to the 5th of May, in order to produce good and fufficiently early grain ; Scotch barley, from the beginning to the 15th of May ; common Scotch bear, from the 10th to the 25th of May. Our peafe are of the haftings kind, and do not require to be fown before the middle or 20th of April. Lint-feed, from the 20th to the end of April. It was earlier with fome laft feafon, by 14 or 20 days ; but where this was the cafe, the feed lay uncommonly long in the ground without fhooting ; fome of it was fickly during a good part of fummer ; nor could it be faid to be fooner ready for pulling, than that which had been fown about the ufual time. Smart nights and mornings are frequent about the end of April, rendering the lint crop very uncertain, if it get above ground before the 1ft of May. They plant potatoes from the 20th of April to the beginning of May ; and fow turnips from the 10th to the 20th or 22d of June. The reaping time muft vary according to the nature of the fummer. Hay, which is not intended for feed, is cut from the 1ft to the 10th of July ; what is intended for ryegrafs feed, 8 or 10 days later. Lint harveft is from the 12th to the 25th of Auguft, fometimes a few days later. The earlieft and lateft commencement of barley harveft, which I remember, was the 15th of Auguft, and the laft day of September. In the years 1775, 1779, and 1783, the barley harveft began from the 15th to the 18th of Auguft ; in the year 1782, it began the laft day of September. The barley harveft ufually begins about the 1ft or 5th of September. Wheat is cut down about the fame time with barley. Our barley, for the moft part, begins to be cut down about 10 or 14 days before the beginning of oat harveft. In 1779, the corns on dry farms were all got in by the 10th or 12th of September. In 1782, they were not got in with fome till the 22d of November : with others, fome days later.

wages and board, with two horfes kept for the purpofe, muft be a confiderable lofer. It was an unlucky circumftance, in affigning land to minifters, that the Legiflature did not think of allotting more. 20 or 25 acres might have been managed with very little additional expenfe. The Crown is patron. The manfe was built in 1737, and was repaired in 1785. The time at which the church was built is not known; it got a repair a good many years ago.—The fchoolmafter's falary is L. 5. Number of fcholars, from 20 to 30, at 1 s. 3 d. the quarter, for 3 quarters of the year. The fees are L. 4 : 13 : 9; fees for regiftration of baptifms and marriages, and falary as feffion-clerk, L. 2 : 8 : 4. The amount of the whole is L. 12 : 2 : 1; a fum lefs by L. 2 Sterling than the income of a common labourer.—The number of poor is 7. The annual contributions are about L. 13, 16 s. There are fome feats in the church belonging to the poor, which yield L. 2, 12 s. yearly. Intereft of money, about L. 2, 8 s. In all, L. 18, 16 s. *.

Mifcellaneous

* The price of meat, 40 years ago, may be rated at 1 d. the pound. Now all kinds of butcher meat, of the beft quality, fetch from $3\frac{1}{2}$ d. to 4 d. the pound. Hens were then 4 d. and now about 1 s. and other poultry in the fame proportion. Butter, 40 years ago, was 4 d. the pound ; now it fetches from $7\frac{1}{2}$ d. to 10 d. Cheefe, I prefume, was not fold by weight at the diftance of 40 years, but was then proportionably low ; now it fells from 5 s. to 6 s. the ftone, the ftone confifting of 24 Englifh pounds. Wheat is now from 18 s. to L. 1, 7 s. ; bear, from 10 s. to L. 1. Thefe higheft prices of wheat and barley have not been paid for many years, except in 1782. The ufual price of barley and oat-meal is from 12 s. to 16 s. Forty years ago, grain was in general from 3 s. to 5 s. cheaper.—Wages, without board, for a day-labourer, are 1 s. or 1 s. 1 d.; a carpenter, 1 s. 4 d. ; tailor, 1 s. 1 d. ; bricklayer and mafon, 1 s. 6 d. or 1 s. 8 d.—The fuel generally made ufe of is peat. Gentlemen ufe coal in their families ; it is alfo part of the fuel in fome farm-houfes. Many burn nothing but peat, broom, and furze. We are under the neceffity of reforting for peat to a neighbouring parifh, at the diftance of about 2 Englifh miles from a great part of this diftrict. Any mofs we have in
the

Miscellaneous Observations.—We labour under no difadvantages, but fuch as are common to us with almoft all
the county of Angus ; the want of falt, lime and coal.
We have all the advantages which are enjoyed by other
inland diftricts ; and are fupplied with marl from pits near
the boundaries of the parifh. Houfes unconnected with
land, dont yield, I think, L. 12 Sterling. Farm houfes are
in *cumulo* with the farms. Such houfes being now an article of confiderable expenfe, the landlords begin to fpe-
cify a rent, according to a certain rate of intereft on the
money laid out in building, *viz.* about 7 *per cent.*—The
writer

the parifh, is not dug. Our coals are from the Forth, by fea-carriage to
Dundee. Mofs-dues to the proprietor, are 9 d. in one mofs, 6 d. in another, the cart-load. The ufual price of coal is 4 s. the boll, the boll
weighing 56 ftone.—The rate of common labourers wages is the fame as
that of farmers fervants.

Hufbands wages, - - -	L. 8	0 0
Meal. in place of maintenance, 2 pecks a-week, with milk,	5	17 0
Induftry of the wife, befides the care of the family, -	2	12 0
Amount of their funds for one year, , -	L. 16	9 0

This a-week is 6 s. 3¾ d. I make no doubt but it may fuffice for the
plain diet and clothing which fuch families ufe. Let us fuppofe the family to be numerous, I allow only the hufband and wife, and 5 children, to
depend on this weekly allowance, viz. one child of 8 years, one of 6, one
of 4, one of 2, and an infant. When the youngeft of thefe 5 is born, a
boy or girl of the family, who had reached the age of 10 years, goes to
fervice, and the burden of that child is taken away. A boy or girl at 8
years of age becomes ufeful in the family, and enables the mother to ufe
her induftry for increafing their funds. When a few of the children get
above 10 years, they increafe the living of the family very confiderably.
If the labourer be a farmer's fervant, the farmer generally allows him a
day for digging peats, and fome draughts of carts for bringing home his
fuel.—The wages of male fervants, in hufbandry, are in general about L. 8
Sterling, with maintenance in the family, or 6½ bolls of oat-meal yearly,
with a fufficient quantity of milk. A maid-fervant has L. 3 Sterling, with
maintenance.

writer of the Roman department of the Univerſal Hiſtory, is ſaid to have been a native of this pariſh.—The people in general are of an equal degree of ſtrength, compared with the inhabitants of other counties in Scotland. We have ſome who may be accounted ſtrong. One man, in particular, might ſtand high in the liſt of ſtrong men in any county of Britain. The talleſt man, within our bounds, wants, I think, about half an inch of 6 feet high. They are of different ſizes, from about 6 feet down to 5 feet 4 or 5 inches, perhaps a very few below that height. The ordinary ſtature is about 5 feet 7 inches. Women, in general, are about 5 feet high. Excluſive of ſhoes, we have ladies, whoſe height is from 5 feet 4 to 5 feet 7 inches. The complexions of the people, are ſome ruddy, ſome pale. They have all, however, a healthy appearance; and are pretty remarkable for an acuteneſs of genius, which enables them to attain to dexterity in the different occupations in which they employ their talents.— The people are very much diſpoſed to induſtry. The only manufacture is green linen, or oſnaburgh. There are 58 hands employed in that branch of weaving. We have a ſpinning mill for flax yarn. It is on a ſmall ſcale, intended to contain 120 pirns. A corn mill is converted to that purpoſe. It is in contemplation of the Company to extend their plan, if the experiment now making ſhall anſwer their expectations. In the mean time, they are buſy adjuſting their apparatus, of which they have made trial; and the yarn which it throws, looks well, and is thought to be of a very good quality. This work is carrying on by virtue of a leaſe of patent privilege from a Company in England.—We have but very few inſtances of fondneſs for a ſeafaring life. Nor are the people much addicted to a military one : the army not having, at any period, in the memory of man, obtained any conſiderable ſupply here.

here. The inhabitants in general are œconomical, and
augment, rather than diminiſh their ſtock. They are well
clothed and fed. Superior induſtry affords them a plentiful ſupply of the neceſſaries and comforts of life. Among
one claſs, however, œconomy does not ſeem to have been
much regarded.——The whole landed property has been
transferred by ſale ſince the year 1743. Prices of land
have been, I preſume, about 25 years purchaſe, or perhaps
a little more.——We have few calls for extraordinary exertions of humanity : in clamant caſes of diſtreſs, I can eaſily believe our people capable of extraordinary beneficence.
They enjoy, in a conſiderable degree, the advantages and
comforts of ſociety : contented with their accommodation,
few remove to diſtant parts of the country, or emigrate to
foreign countries.——The circumſtances moſt extenſively
diſtreſſing, are thoſe which affect the manufacturers of
green linen. They depend on two countries, Ruſſia for
their raw materials, and the Weſt Indies and part of A-
merica for the ſale of their manufacture. A bad crop of
flax in Ruſſia, or the jobbing ſpirit of the merchants there,
or extraordinary profits to the importers of the flax, often
reduce the profits of theſe manufacturers to a mere trifle.
This evil, I think, might be removed, if flax raiſing could
be brought to a ſyſtem, which would render a flax crop
equally certain with any other crop. Our ſoil is pretty
much adapted to the raiſing of flax, and the plan of farming here is ſuch, that the farmer could eaſily employ a
few acres in cultivating it. In this caſe, there would be
only the chance of the ſale market againſt the manufacturers. But although grievances were redreſſed as much as
poſſible, it is ſtill a queſtion, whether that is not the moſt
deſirable manufacture which is ſupplied with materials
from the country itſelf, and has the benefit of a home
market, founded on the natural demand of the inhabitants
                                                        for

for the manufactured articles *.—As to the manners of
the people, they are diftinguifhed from thofe of a period
30 or 40 years ago, as there is more induftry, attention, enterprife and fobriety. Their cuftoms are much the fame

as

* The public road from Perth, through Strathmore, which paffes thro'
this parifh, is repairing on a new plan, and will foon be finifhed within
our bounds, unlefs it fhall be deemed neceffary to widen it. It was begun to be repaired in autumn 1789. Owing to the fpirited plan of fubfcriptions from the gentlemen in the county, the road from Forfar to Dundee, part of which paffes through this parifh, is proceeding on the fame
plan. All the county roads in Angus are to be repaired from the fub-
fcription-fund. We are much indebted to the exertions of Mr Douglas
of Brigton, who tranfacts and fuperintends the bufinefs of the road from
Forfar to Dundee, and for feveral miles on the Strathmore road. To render the road convenient, fteep banks are avoided, and on Mr Douglas's
ground in this parifh, the road takes a new direction for 1½ miles through
inclofures of land of very excellent quality. The rule is not to admit, if
poffible, above 1 foot of rife in 20. Thefe roads have turnpikes, and all
the county roads either have or are to have them. Our farmers are much
reconciled to turnpikes, and imagine that the accommodation obtained in
this way, is cheap. Statute-labour is not exacted in kind. Since the plan
by fubfcription took place, the commutation-money is to be applied to the
repairing of the private roads. We have two bridges in the parifh; one
on the road from Forfar to Glammis, was built by fubfcription, at leaft in
part, about 21 years fince, and is in good condition; the other, on the
road from Forfar to Dundee, is intended to be taken down, and another
built at fome fmall diftance.—In the year 1782, our drieft lands were not
fit for receiving feed till the 16th or 17th of April. There was not a blade
of oats to be feen till about the 12th of May, in this neighbourhood,
which is rather an early diftrict. The barley-feed time was very backward. About the 29th of May, we had rain for 50 hours, without in-
termiffion. The fummer was cold and wet; and on the 16th of Auguft,
we had an uncommon flood, which chilled the ground fo as to deprive it
of the warmth neceffary for filling and ripening the corns. On the morning of the 12th of September, we had hoarfroft as thick as at Chriftmas.
About 7 o'clock that morning, the fun was bright, and had influence fufficient to melt the froft; and, in a few minutes, peafe and potatoes had the
look of having been dipped in boiling water. The effect of this froft
made the farmer imagine that harveft was nigh. The corns affumed a
whitifh appearance, and the firft rain threw it in appearance feveral ftages
back.

as at that period. Their drefs is more gay, and expenfive ; their living more plentiful. Though it is not the cafe in this parifh, to any confiderable degree, in fhow, expenfe, manner of living, and drefs, there is an imitation of fuperiors creeping into the country. Perhaps 30 years ago, the boundaries between the ranks were more diftinctly marked, and more attentively obferved. Inferior ranks begin not to fcruple to invade the boundaries of thofe above them. The genius of the people leads them to induftry and enterprife ; befides, they are very communicative. This difpofition fuffers no experiment to lie concealed, either as to the manner

back. The corns were changed from green to whitifh, and from whitifh to green, according as froft or rain happened to prevail. Our lower, ableft, and beft lands, which will produce 8, 10, or 12 bolls of oats an acre in good years, yielding from 15 to 16, or perhaps 17 pecks of meal the boll, that year yielded 4 or 5 bolls an acre, and thefe yielding not above 8, 10, or 11 pecks of meal the boll. I heard of fome oats in the county, which yielded only mill duft, inftead of meal. Barley of that crop, which was much ufed for meal, fell greatly fhort, both of its ufual quantity and quality. The higher grounds, raifed above the region of the noxious hoarfrofts, had a more equal progrefs towards ripening. And thefe high, weak, light grounds, not reaped till the month of November, produced oats, yielding about 15 pecks of meal the boll. Thefe grounds were lefs hurt by the froft and rain. Of that crop, farmers paying confiderable rents, could fcarcely procure as much oat-meal from their farms, as was fufficient for their own fami ies, and oats for fowing their ground. People, both in towns and the country, traverfed the country. and particularly this parifh, where we had feveral mills, and thought themfelves lucky if they could obtain a peck or two of meal, to fupply the immediate and urgent demands of their families. They would gladly have given more than the high current price, to have been affured of finding it at any particular place. The fcarcity continued through fummer 1783 ; and had it not been for a fupply of Englifh oats from Leith, I doubt not but fome muft have perifhed for want. Some farmers, forefeeing the diftreffed condition of the country, fowed fome barley early. Great quantities of potatoes were planted, and the harveft of 1783 was early. By thefe means, the country obtained a fpeedy and pretty plentiful fupply. Amidft the fcarcity of provifions, there was one comforting circumftance. The people, in general, were not diftreffed for want of money.

ner of conducting it, or as to its fuccefs. Their fpirit of
enterprife makes them eafily adopt a new plan, when fairly recommended by its fuccefs ; and their induftry fecures
their doing juftice to any plan which they may adopt.
Free from the fetters of prejudice, they follow, let the
leader be whom he will, if they are warranted by fair,
well tried, fuccefsful experiments. That fpirit has brought
this country to be able to fupport double or triple the
number of inhabitants, which it could have done 30 or 40
years ago. A great deal of wafte ground has been brought
under culture ; and lands which then would have yielded
3 or 4 bolls an acre, now produce 8 or 10, and fometimes
more. This is the cafe, more or lefs, with the country of
Strathmore, and in the county of Angus : I know no part
of the country where farming is carried on to greater perfection than in this very parifh.—Befides a great increafe
in the quantity of corn, there is a confiderable addition of
profit by the rearing and fattening of cattle. Inftead of
the ftinted and famifhed breed, of which the farmer's ftore
confifted 40 years ago, cattle can now be reared to a confiderable fize, and fetch a decent price, to compenfate the
trouble and expenfe ; fatted cattle generally fell well. Our
farmers fatten through the winter, fome 10, fome 16, fome
20, fome 30 cattle. Some of thefe are partly fed with turnips, ftraw and hay ; fome with turnips and hay. Such
as are fed wholly on turnips and hay, can be brought to
a degree of fatnefs, not exceeded in any part of Scotland.
The greateft part of our pafture and hay foggage is employed for the purpofe of fattening. Turnip crops keep
the land clean, and the great proportion of pafture gives
them vigour to produce good corn crops when broken up.
—There is a grievance, which, though in one view, it affects
but a fingle individual in a parifh, yet is very extenfive in

its

its influence; I mean the pitiful living of schoolmasters. In fact, there is no occupation among us, or in the country in general, from which greater profits may not be obtained. What extent of learning and qualifications is to be demanded or expected from a person, whose office yields him hardly the bare necessaries of life? I think we are just on the verge of having schools remaining vacant; the office being stripped of every thing that can induce a man of any capacity to accept of it.—Allow me to make another observation. In respect to the poor, matters seem to be very improperly conducted. We are importuned by people from almost every county in Scotland; whose stories may be true or false; and whose circumstances may therefore entitle them to charity, or may not. Much good would accrue to the public, if such vagrants were confined to their respective parishes. Their circumstances might then be exactly known; temptations to falsehood would be taken away; idleness would be prevented; persons able to contribute in any respect to their subsistence, would be obliged to exert their industry, or would suffer the reward due to their neglect. Here, however, an objection occurs, namely, That some parishes, from the scantiness of their funds, and the great number of their poor, are unable to supply, in any comfortable manner, all the poor within their bounds. Where collections, dedicated to the support of the poor, are not sufficient for necessary supplies, let there be assessments. This would oblige landed gentlemen, and others, on whom such assessments might be chiefly laid, to exert themselves, by introducing manufactures, or other means of subsistence. The number of poor would thereby be diminished; those who might still need parochial supply, would be less indigent, and others become able to bear a part of the burden of the unavoidably poor.

poor. So long as mankind are supported by strolling, the industry and ingenuity of thousands must be lost to the community, and vice cherished to a considerable degree. —The decrease of population in country parishes, and the great resort of people to towns, is an evil much to be regretted. Though this mode should continue, it is not improbable that there may be still a gradual increase of inhabitants over Scotland. But the question is, by which of these two plans may population be supposed to increase most; whether, by a well peopled state of country parishes, or by extending and crowding the towns. In all infectious distempers, such as fevers, small-pox, measles, hooping cough, the danger to children is greatest in towns. As to inoculated small-pox, the distemper may be introduced in towns at a favourable season, and, when introduced, it takes its range of infection, and before its course is finished, the hot unfavourable season arrives, and the distemper generally becomes malignant and fatal. In the country, infection from this distemper may be more easily avoided, and I hope to see whole parishes taking such rational views of inoculation, as to agree to have all their children, who have not had the distemper, put under inoculation, at the same time, during the favourable season; a victory over prejudice, not to be expected universally in large towns. But dropping this consideration, the sickly looks of many children, in large, crowded, ill situated, or ill constructed towns, show that the country is the preferable place for children. Inhabitants of large towns are sensible of this, who rejoice in the opportunity of having them settled in the country, especially after they have been ailing, as the only means of restoring their health and vigour. But how is the prevailing resort to towns to be prevented, when the present taste is, to raze or suffer almost every house

houfe to go to decay, which is not conducive to the benefit of a farm ? Might not the building one or two neat
villages in every country parifh, be the means of prevent-
ing this great concourfe of inhabitants to the towns. They
might be erected in a dry fituation, and calculated for convenience as well as health. Suppofing thefe villages to be
inhabited by mechanics, manufacturers, day-labourers,
farmers fervants and widows, there might be one or two
fmall farmers connected with the village, who might have
leifure, and be induced to perform carriages to the villa-
gers for hire *.

* Perfonal fervices are ftill performed here. They are fpecified and
limited. Occupiers of a houfe and garden, or of a houfe, garden, and one
or two acres of land, perform fome days work occafionally, as the proprietor may happen to require them in the courfe of the year. Such tenants as poffefs ground fufficient to enable them to keep a horfe, befides
the above fervices, are bound to perform two horfeback carriages in the
courfe of the year, as far as Dundee, which is about 12 miles, or to a fimilar diftance. Greater tenants are bound to bring a certain number of
bolls of coals from Dundee to the proprietors houfe, which require 2 or 3
days work of their carts Befides, they muft give a day's work of all their
reapers, for cutting down the proprietors corns. Thefe go by the general name of fervices, in place of the old arrhage and carriage, which were
very comprehenfive. *Arrhage*, I take to be from the Latin, *aro*, to till;
and implied the driving out of the manure for the proprietor's farm,
ploughing and harrowing his ground reaping in harveft, and bringing
home his hay and corns. The old fervice of carriage was very unlimited,
and very tyrannically exacted.—From 16 to 30 years back, from the prefent time, about 37 cottages were razed. or became ruinous. From 10 to
17 years back, 10 or 11 new cottages have been erected; an increafe of
fmall houfes has begun to take place; a mill, for fpinning flax-yarn, is
building; and a village is begun, for accommodating the hands to be employed, which will require a confiderable number of houfes. The employing of cottagers in agriculture, increafes population. A houfe for accommodating a family, is a confiderable inducement for a fervant to marry; and, from having a houfe and an acre or two of land, a fervant is
more inclined to remain in his mafter's fervice. Hired fervants are apt to
be touchy and petulant, by being lefs dependent, as having it more eafily
in

in their power to remove from one place to another. A hired fervant, however, has the chance of obtaining more extenfive knowledge, by fome-times changing his place.——There is no poft-town nearer than Forfar, a-bout 3 miles diftant from the centre of this parifh. We have one ale-houfe; no inn. Ale-houfes are not fo much reforted to, as 30 or 40 years ago.

PARISH OF KIRKDEN.

(COUNTY OF ANGUS.)

By the Rev. MR. MILLIGAN.

Name, Situation, Extent, &c.

THE parifh has two names, *Kirkden,* alias *Idvie.* The firft only is in common ufe ; and is evidently derived from the fituation of the kirk and manfe, which are built in a den. It derives its other name from the barony of Idvie.— It is about 5 Englifh miles in length, and the broadeft part of it does not exceed 2. About the middle, for near a mile, it is very narrow.—Kirkden lies in the prefbytery of Arbroath, in the fynod of Angus and Mearns, and in the county of Angus or Forfar. The foil is various. About 1200 acres are dry kindly land, mixed with fmall ftones, called by the farmers, a beachy foil. This part is, in general, fooneft fit for the feed in the fpring ; and the crop upon it is fooneft ripe in autumn. About 900 acres are deep dry land, and the bed is till. The remainder is a cold clay bed, and is naturally wet and fpungy, but has been greatly improved by draining.

Air,

Air, Climate, Diſeaſes.——The air is commonly clear and
ſalubrious, excepting ſometimes in the evening, about the end
of April, or the beginning of May, when the wind is weſter-
ly. In the pleaſanteſt days, and ſometimes for ſeveral days
together, we ſee the fog riſing on the German Ocean, about
3 or 4 o'clock in the afternoon ; and, even when we enjoy the
moſt delightful ſunſhine, we know, that, in an hour or two,
we ſhall be involved in *darkneſs*, that may almoſt be *felt*. So
flowly does the *damp* approach, that it is often ſome hours before it reach us, after we ſee it a-coming. In general, however, the inhabitants are remarkably healthy. About 25 or
30 years ago, the ague, eſpecially in the ſpring, was ſo general, that many farmers found it difficult to ſow and harrow
their lands, in the proper ſeaſon, owing to their ſervants being ſo
much afflicted with it. At preſent, this diſeaſe is little known
in this pariſh, or in the neighbourhood. This is perhaps
owing to the draining of the grounds, the great change
that has taken place in the mode of living, dreſs, &c. Every
year, ſeveral children die of the ſmall pox, the prejudices a-
gainſt inoculation being ſtill very great. In vain, the patriotic Mr Dempſter provided, laſt ſeaſon, an able phyſician and
proper medicines : Though inoculation, by theſe means,
might have been got *gratis*, hardly one accepted the generous
offer.

Rivers and Fiſh.——The Finny and Lunan, both of which
riſe in the pariſh of Forfar, either paſs along, or partly inter-
ſect the pariſh of Kirkden. There is excellent burn-trout in
both, which are, however, every year, much deſtroyed with
the watering of flax, either in the rivulets themſelves, or in
places from whence the deadly ſtreams run into them. Eels
are alſo caught in the ſeaſon ; and ſea fiſh are brought from
the coaſt in conſiderable quantities.

Manufactures.

Manufactures.——There is hardly a houfe in the parifh, where one or more women are not employed in fpinning yarn, for the Ofnaburgh weavers. Many millions of yards of Ofnaburgh cloth, are, every year made in this county, of which this parifh manufactures its proportion. The women all fpin with both hands; and a good fpinner can earn 3s, or 3s 6d, *per* week. Girls of 13, or 14 years of age, earn 2s, and many of them 2s 6d a week; and they reckon their board only about 1s 6d. For this reafon, many, inftead of going to fervice, continue with their parents and friends, merely for the purpofe of fpinning, as being a more profitable employment, and, in which they enjoy more liberty. But there are many, who do not like to be fo clofely confined to fpinning, and therefore go to fervice, where only a ·part of their time is fpent at the wheel. Weavers are interfperfed, at fmall diftances, all over the country; and moft of them give out flax, and pay the current price for fpinning it. Much of the flax grows at home; but great quantities are alfo brought from abroad. Till lately, the manufacturers of this neighbourhood went to Forfar or Arbroath, for the ftamping and fale of their webs; but now there is a market, every fortnight, for thefe purpofes, at the neighbouring village of Letham.

Population.——On the laft day of October 1790, the number of perfons living in the parifh of Kirkden, properly parifhioners, were 727; of whom there were 359 males, and 368 females.

Below

	Males.		Females.
Below 10 years of age -	80	- -	91
Between 10 and 20 -	98	- -	69
———— 20 and 50 -	124	- -	154
———— 50 and 70 -	43	- -	47
Above 70 - -	11	- - -	6
———— 80 - -	3	- -	1
	359		368

Thomas Lyal, Efq. of Gardyn, the oldeſt man now living in the parifh, was 85 years old, the 9th of October, 1790, and is yet a healthy man. A labouring man of this parifh died laſt year, aged 92 years, and a few days. The return to Dr Webſter of the population of Kirkden, in 1755, was 563. The inhabitants have therefore encreaſed 160. The caufe feems to be the flourifhing ſtate of manufactures.

The parifh regiſters being very inaccurately kept, no certain conclufions can be drawn from them. From 1780, to 1787, incluſive, the number of marriages were about 71, and of burials, 66.

Divifion of the Inhabitants.——In this parifh there are 133 families; 17 of which, confiſt, but of two perfons each; and 2 or 3 folitary individuals. Of the above there are 4 refiding heritors, 33 farmers, (perfons who have no other occupation) 26 weavers, 5 wrights, 4 taylors, 2 mafons, 2 cadgers, (fifh-carriers,) 4 blackfmiths, 3 fhoemakers, 6 millers, 2 creamers, (perfons who go through the parifh, and neighbourhood, and buy butter, hens, eggs, &c. moſtly for the Dundee market,) and 19 labourers. The above are all heads of families. There are about 60 labouring fervants, male and female; but almoſt all the females are chiefly employed in fpinning; and there are 9 or 10 houfehold fervants in the heritors

ritors families. Many families have no occafion to hire fervants, having a fufficient number of children to perform their work. And the faucinefs of fingle fervants makes others engage cottagers, whofe family ties make them more dependant and humble. Thus evil produces good, and pride prevents depopulation. Each of thefe married labourers has a houfe and yard; a cow maintained fummer and winter; 52 ftones of meal; the carriage of their coals and other fuel; and commonly, fome ground allowed them for lint: and fome of them have L. 5, fome L. 6, and fome of them L. 7 in money. Befides thefe fervants, reapers are engaged for harveft; a good female fhearer at about L. 1, and a male at about L. 1 : 6. All the inhabitants are of the eftablifhed religion, except the refiding heritors, and 1 or 2 in their families, in all about a dozen, who belong to the church of England; and about 21 Antiburgher Seceders, including children.

General Character. ———The inhabitants of this parifh, with very few exceptions, are an induftrious, civilized, and contented people. No perfon has been banifhed from it, nor been guilty of murder, fuicide, or any atrocious crime, within the prefent century; if we except thofe, who, from miftaken loyalty, followed the Pretender, in 1745.

Chriftmas is held as a great feftival in this neighbourhood. On that day " the fervant is free from his mafter," and goes about vifiting his friends and acquaintance. The pooreft muft have beef or mutton on the table, and what they call a dinner with their friends. Many amufe themfelves with various diverfions, particularly with fhooting for prizes, called here *wad-fhooting.* And many do but little bufinefs all the Chriftmas week; the evening of almoft every day being fpent in amufement. All the lower claffes of the people ftill obferve the old ftile.

Church.

Church.———The church was built in the year 1749; and the manſe was repaired, and the office houſes rebuilt in 1783. The living conſiſts of 16 bolls of meal, 6 bolls of bear, and 850 merks Scots, (L. 47 : 4 : 5$\frac{4}{12}$), in money, and 6 acres of land; in all about L. 66 ſterling a year.———The Crown is patron.

School.———The ſchoolmaſter's ſalary is 100 merks Scots, (L. 5 : 11 : 1$\frac{4}{12}$), with ſome perquiſites which do not exceed L. 3 *per annum.* There are few ſcholars.

Poor.——The number of poor at preſent, who receive occaſional alms, is 10; but all of them have property, and earn moſt of their ſubſiſtence, except 3 old perſons. They live in houſes near their children, who are in a thriving condition. They receive out of the poors funds, the price of a boll of meal, one after another, as they require it, on applying to the elders, any Sunday after ſermon, and alſo money to buy fuel in the ſeaſon. Orphan children are boarded at the rate of L. 4 ſterling *per annum.* No perſon, properly belonging to this pariſh, is in the habit of ſtrolling about as a mendicant. Indeed, in this manufacturing country, ſuch as are able to go about and beg, are generally fit, unleſs they have infant children, to earn their bread at home, the women by ſpinning, and the men by filling pirns, (rolling up yarn upon lake reeds, cut in ſmall pieces for the ſhuttle). By experience, we have found it to be a great ſaving of our poors funds, to aid thoſe who are ſinking into poverty, before they fall too low. To ſupport the, poor we have the weekly collections and ſeat-rents of a loft, in the church, erected out of the poors money, in all about L. 15 or L. 16 *per annum*; and L. 156 lent out upon intereſt, at the rate of 4$\frac{1}{2}$ *per cent.* This fund, for theſe 16 years paſt, has been fully adequate to the demands of the poor,

without

without any application to the landholders; who, about 20
years ago, were in the ufe of contributing annually a certain
fum for their relief. The poor are not only well provided
for, but very well fatisfied with the attention that is paid them.

Divifion and Rent of Lands.——The whole extent of the parifh is nearly 3500 acres; about 3000 of which are arable, and
the remainder planted, or moor, not yet improved. It is divided among 6 proprietors, 4 of whom refide in it. Only a-
bout a half of the parifh is yet inclofed; but the inclofing proceeds apace; the better fort of farmers being very fenfible of
the great advantage which may be derived from it.

There are about a dozen of perfons, including 3 proprietors, who farm from about 30 to 150 acres each. The
reft of the parifh is divided into fmaller portions, from 36
down to 6 acres; for there are very few families in the parifh,
who have not one, or more cows, not excepting thofe who
live partly on charity.——The rent of moft farms, lately
let in leafe, taking the good and bad land of the farm, at an a-
verage, is 15s. One large inclofed farm, however, lately let
at L. 1 the acre.——The late leafes are, in general, for 19
years. For a crop of lint land, fome pay L. 5, and fome (this
year) L. 6 : 3, the acre. Thofe who let the land, plough and
harrow it, and carry the flax to and from the watering.——
Perfonal fervices, thofe badges of antient flavery, are ftill partly continued, though lighter than formerly, and now limited.
Several of the tenants, however, are altogether freed from
them. It is a pretty common thing, to pay a certain number
of kain fowls. Some of the tenants are obliged to give a
draught of one, or more horfes, for a fpecified number of
miles, if required; or to fend one or more carts for coals to
the proprietor, and to give, perhaps, a day of all their reapers,
in

in harveſt, upon receiving notice the evening before. The e-vil conſequences, which muſt reſult from this, are obvious.

Mode of Cultivation——There are 44 ploughs in the pariſh all drawn by horſes; but many of them hardly deſerve the name of ploughs; for ſeveral of thoſe, who rent about 12 or 15 acres of land, keep only one horſe, and, joining with another in the ſame ſtate, with theſe two, commonly but indifferent, horſes, they cultivate both farms. A tenant with two ploughs, and 8 ſtrong horſes, is ſuppoſed able to manage a farm of 200 acres to great perfection. It is true, there are often but two horſes in the plough; and he ſtirs his barley ground ſometimes, with one horſe only, while the other horſes are doing other parts of the farm work.——The mode of farming is various, according as the tenants, who have old leaſes, are ſkilled in huſbandry, or otherwiſe, or according to the taſte, and knowledge of the proprietor, by whom, in the late leaſes, they are often tied down to a certain rotation of crops. In general, however, about half of the land is in grain of various kinds, and the other half ſown with graſs ſeeds. Whatever number of crops, in grain, are taken, the land lies as long in graſs. The following is a common rotation: After graſs, 1ſt, oats, 2dly, turnips, peaſe, potatoes, or lint; 3dly, barley and graſs ſeeds, keeping it in graſs three years.

Stock and Produce.—The ſtock in this pariſh principally conſiſts of black cattle and horſes: there are almoſt no hogs, and not above 150 ſheep. In regard to produce, after ſupplying the pariſh itſelf, large quantities of meal are annually ſold in the neighbouring towns; and about 1200 bolls of barley, (31,600 ſtone), are annually exported. Through the whole ſummer, butter and cheeſe are weekly carried to the different markets around us.

Fuel

Fuel.--This parish, and the neighbourhood, bring most of their fuel from Arbroath. The cart load of coals, (72 stones), costs generally 6s 8d. besides carriage; yet this is our cheapest, as well as best fuel, for there is little peat in this neighbourhood, and none in this parish.

Roads and Bridges——The roads have, till last year, been made by the statute labour, which was, long ago, found altogether insufficient, for making and keeping them in good repair. The labour of one parish was often carried out of it, to make a road in another, while the roads, within the parish itself, were exceedingly bad.

In 1790, an act of parliament was obtained, to raise money by turnpikes, for making certain county roads, therein laid down. In this act, the statute labour is converted into money, at the rate of L 1 : 4, sterling, on the L. 100 Scots of valued rent, to be raised yearly, till the parish roads are made. By this act, no money can be levied in one parish, to make the roads of another.

The turnpike act met with considerable opposition, before it was carried in the county; as most improvements do in their infancy; and there are still grumblers: But the gentlemen now seem all agreed; and the most respectable farmers acknowledge, that turnpikes must be a great advantage in this county, where roads were formerly, at no time good, and, in winter, were so deep, as to be almost entirely unpassable.

Antiquities.—A plain in the parish of Kirkden, between the Finny and the Lunan, seems, in days of yore, to have been often a field of blood. There is an obelisk in it; and many Roman urns, with bones in them, have, at different times, been dug up. The obelisk is niched into a large stone. There are on it, some imperfect figures of horses, &c. It is supposed by
some

some, to have been erected, upon the defeat of the Danes by Malcolm II. about the same time with the cross at Camiston, in the parish of Monikie, mentioned by Buchanan. Near this obelisk, there was a green hillock, consisting of sand and gravel, which was cut away 16 years ago, in straighting the road; in which some graves were found. The bones in them were by no means of a larger size, than those belonging to persons in modern times.

In this parish there are two artificial conical mounts, called Laws : the law of the barony of Idvie, and that of Gardyne. The last is now covered with fir trees. The gallows stood upon the top of the Law. Thomas Lyal, Esq. was told by David Philip, sometime ago, a tenant in the parish, that he (David Philip) saw two Highlandmen taken in this parish, with stolen cattle, and immediately judged, condemned, and hanged, on the Law of Gardyne. The Law of Idvie has also an aperture on the top, where probably the gallows stood, or was occasionally erected, in feudal times

The castle of Gardyne was built in 1568. It is firm and entire. An addition, to make it a more commodious dwelling, has been added in later times. The castle is romantically situated, on the brink of a precipice, at the bottom of which, there is a beautiful plantation of thriving trees, through which there runs, a purling stream, of the purest water.

Miscellaneous Observations.—There is a mineral well in the parish, which has cured swellings and sores of the feet and legs, merely by washing, after the applications of several physicians had proved ineffectual.————Potatoes are beginning to be more used in the towns ; but, in this parish, they are seldom eat by the labourers, even by those on public charity, excepting in the months of October, November, and December.————None, belonging to this parish, stroll about begging; yet many Randies (sturdy vagrants) infest this country, from the neighbouring towns, and the Highlands; who, from an undiscerning humanity, and sometimes, perhaps, from timidity, are but too much encouraged.———— A very great change in the appearance of the people has taken place within these few years. About 15 years ago, all the men servants wore coarse home-manufactured cloth and bonnets. There were then seldom three men's hats seen at church on a Sunday. Now most of the men servants wear, on Sunday, good English cloth, (at least what goes by that name); and there is hardly a bonnet to be seen in church. ————Many of the lower classes of females still continue to cover their heads with the plaid in church: But several of them wear cloaks and silk hats, and begin to dress after the manner of those in the more southern counties of Scotland. ————Within the last 10 years, about 9 or 10 cottages have become ruinous; but a greater number, and houses of a better sort, have, in that time, been built.

PARISH of KIRRIEMUIR.

(COUNTY OF FORFAR, SYNOD OF ANGUS AND MEARNS, PRES-
BYTERY OF FORFAR.)

By the Rev. MR. THOMAS OGILVY.

Name, Extent, Surface, and Soil.

KIRRIEMUIR, commonly pronounced Kellamuir, is a
Gaelic word, and fignifies Mary Kirk. The form of
the parifh is irregular. Its greateft length from S. E. to N.
W., is 7 or 8 miles, its leaft 4. The greateft breadth from
S. W. to N. E., is about 7 miles; the leaft 6. The northern
part, called Glenprofen, from the river Profen which runs
the whole length of it, is bounded on the S. by Kingoldrum;
on the E. and N. by a ridge of mountains which feparates it
from Cortachy and Clova; and on the W. by another ridge
of mountains which feparates it from Glenifla and Lintrathen.
This glen is about 12 miles long; and, with the tract of
country which lies along the burn of Lednathie, Glenuig,
Glenlogie, and fome fmaller glens which are comprehended
under

under the general name Glenprosen, may contain 24 or 30 square miles. The face of the country is various. For about a mile to the N. of the parishes of Glammis and Forfar, it is almost flat. Then it rises gently about 2 miles more, forming almost one continued sloping bank, till within a few hundred yards of the town, which stands nearly in the centre of the southern part of the parish, and is separated by a narrow valley or den, about 100 feet deep, from the above bank. To the E. and W. of the town, it is almost level. The rest of the parish is beautifully diversified with hills, and dales, rivers, woods, and plains. The hills, however, those in Glenprosen excepted, are of no great elevation, and are either cultivated, or planted, or afford tolerable pasture. Glenprosen is altogether hilly and mountainous. A few of the hills are covered with grass, except on their summits; and a few of them are rocky; but they are, in general, covered with heath, interspersed, however, with innumerable patches of grass, probably produced by the many rills which tumble down their sides. Some of these hills are interfected by rivulets which have their source in the glens formerly mentioned; and in the glens are several hundred acres of flat mossy ground, partly covered with bent and rough grass, which afford good pasture for young cattle during the summer months, as the hills do for sheep. In Glenprosen, the soil is partly thin and light, partly mossy, and, in general, wet. In the southern part of the parish, are all kinds of soil; but a black mould, on a bottom of mortar, predominates. This, when dry, produces heavy crops of all kinds of grain; but being in many places wet and spongy, the harvest is often late, and the grain of rather an inferior quality.

Rivers, and Woods.—The river Esk, which has it source in Clova, forms the N. E. boundary of this parish for about
2 miles

2 miles. The Profen takes its rife in the N. W. extremity of it; runs the whole length of the glen to which it gives name; afterward feparates the parifhes of Cortachy and Kingoldrum for about 2 miles; then Kirriemuir and Cortachy for about 2 miles more; and falls into the Efk near Invercarity. The Carity has its fource in the parifh of Lintrathen; traverfes that and the parifh of Kingoldrum; and, after a meandering courfe of about 4 miles in this parifh, is loft in the Efk at Invercarity, to which it gives name. Thefe rivers fwarm with fmall trout, which afford excellent fport for the angler; and, in the fummer months, a great number of fea-trout refort to the Efk and Profen. This trout is red, of an excellent flavour, and by many people preferred to falmon. Some years ago, falmon were likewife plenty in the Efk; but now, owing to the dam-dikes towards the mouth of the river, their numbers here are inconfiderable. The Gairie has it fource about 2 miles to the W. of the town in the meadow, formerly the Lake of Kinnordy. After paffing the meadow, it glides along a channel cut for it out of folid rock, till within 300 or 400 yards of the town. Then, changing its courfe to the S. E., it defcends into a narrow valley; and, in its fall, turns a corn and malt mill, a flax, and 2 fulling mills. Directing again its courfe to the E., it meanders along the den, which is of a ferpentine form, about 200 yards to the S. of the town, and 60 feet below the level of the loweft part of it. At the eaftern extremity of the den, which is about a mile long, it takes a fouthern direction, and after beautifying and enriching the parks of Logie, again turns to the S. E., and, after a courfe of about 10 miles, which, in a direct line, would not exceed 5, falls into the Dean a little to the E. of Glammis Caftle. Before the Lake of Kinnordy was drained, in 1740, this was a confiderable ftream; but now, in a dry fummer, it is fcarcely fufficient to turn a mill.

This

This parish, to the E. of the town, was once a continued forest, called Platane. At present there are no woods of great extent; though a considerable quantity both of hard and soft timber, of all kinds and ages, is interspersed up and down the parish, especially on the estate of Kinnordy, the proprietor of which is giving his seat every embellishment which wood can bestow, as well as ornamenting the country, by planting every piece of waste ground on his estate. Mr. Ogilvy of Clova, has likewise planted, within these few years, 300 acres of Scotch and Larix firs, besides hard wood; and continues to plant a certain number of acres every year. There is, besides, in Glenprosen, a considerable quantity of natural wood, mostly birch; and, were it not for the sheep, it would soon become a forest, as the upper part of it, which is still called the Forest of Glenprosen, has evidently been.

Climate, &c.—The climate varies considerably. The lower part of the parish is far more mild and temperate than Glenprosen, except in the middle of summer, when, owing to the reflexion of the sun's beams from the hills, the latter is perhaps warmer than the former. And, about the boundaries of the parishes of Glammis and Forfar, the air is milder than about the town, and to the northward of it. Scrofula and consumptions are the most common disorders; and we are sometimes, though rarely, visited with putrid fevers. The air is clear and salubrious; the people rather above the common size, well made, strong, active, and healthy. The ague, which is common in the lower parts of Strathmore, is unknown here; and, often, whilst Forfar, Glammis, and Meigle, are enclosed in mist, there is none at Kirriemuir. There are no instances of a remarkable longevity; but many arrive at 80; and 2 or 3 died lately who were above 90.

Cultivation,

Cultivation, &c.—Part of this parish was enclosed many years ago, and is in a state of high cultivation; and, in every part of it, improvements are carrying on. Such, at present, seems to be the spirit for improvements in agriculture, both among the proprietors and tenants, that if they go on for a few years longer, as they have done for 15 years past, there will be little waste ground in the parish. What is wet, they are draining; what is uncultivated and arable, they are bringing into tillage; what is not arable, they are planting. Much has been done in all these ways; and a great deal still remains to be done. And here the means of improvement are to be had in great abundance. The Lake of Kinnordy, which is completely drained, and the meadows of Logie, which are not drained, contain an inexhaustible supply of fine marl. Nor is encouragement wanting to engage the tenants to use it. For the proprietor of Kinnordy sells it considerably cheaper than any other marl in the county; though, in quality, it is, by many, reckoned inferior to none. Accordingly, it is carried not less than 14 miles. The town likewise affords a great deal of manure, which, within these 3 years, has risen from 8 d. and 9 d. the cart load, to 16 d. and 18 d. This is a clear proof of the spirit for improvement; and, as another, it may not be improper to mention, that a small estate about 2 miles to the N. of the town, sold last year at 60 years purchase, though one half of it is under lease for a life, and the other for 9 or 10 years. Few, if any, leases are now let, in which the tenant is not bound to a regular rotation of cropping; and those who have old leases, and are not bound, begin to find it their interest to follow one. The rotations most common are, 1st, oats or flax, after ley; 2d, turnip or potatoes; 3d, oats; 4th, barley with grass-seeds; 5th, hay; 6th, 7th, and 8th, pasture; then oats or flax, &c. as before. Instead of 3 years, some pasture 5; and, in place of making

hay

hay the firſt year of the graſs, ſome are beginning to paſture that year, and to cut for hay the ſecond. This, they think, gives them hay of a ſuperior quality, and rye-graſs ſeed in the greateſt perfection. A few never make any hay for ſale ; but paſture all the years. Inſtead of taking only 1 crop of corn after the ley, ſome take 2. The whole dung of the farm is laid on with the turnip or potatoes ; and when it is not ſuf-ficient for all the ground allotted for green crop, they fallow, and ſometimes dung and ſow wheat in October. At pre-ſent, however, wheat is not a common crop here ; the far-mers finding that barley is, in general, more profitable, eſ-pecially when the value of the turnip is confidered. Ano-ther rotation much approved of, when dung can be command-ed, is, 1ſt, oats after ley ; 2d, turnip or potatoes ; 3d, bar-ley with graſs-ſeeds ; 4th, hay, or the graſs cut green ; 5th, paſture ; 6th, oats, or flax, &c. as before. Here likewiſe the dung is laid on with the turnip, &c, which are always horſe-hoed. Another mode of culture practiſed here, deſerves to be mentioned. Mr. Kinloch of Kilrie, having the command of the river Gairie, begins, in the month of November, to flood his encloſures at Logie, and continues to do ſo at inter-vals, till the middle of April. Theſe encloſures have been in graſs ſince the year 1770 ; and, in conſequence of the above practice, are now the earlieſt aud beſt graſs fields in the coun-ty ; and there is not, perhaps in Scotland, any ſuperior to them. Before the above period, they let at from 10s. to 12s. an acre. Laſt ſeaſon, 1792, from 3 l. to 4 l. 10 s. Sterling the acre†.

Neither oats nor barley are raiſed in ſufficient quantities to ſupply the conſumption of the pariſh ; but black cattle, lean

and

† Small's plough, with a metal mould-board, is getting into general uſe ; and few farmers are without a roller.

and fatted; sheep for the butcher, poultry, butter, cheese, honey, wool, and tallow, to a considerable amount, are annually
exported. The farmers have lately turned their attention to
the breeding of horses. By consequence the breed has been
much improved, and a large sum of money saved the parish,
which used to be sent out of it for that useful animal. The
most intelligent of the breeders of sheep have likewise changed their system; and, instead of buying the greatest part of
their stock, when a year old, at the Linton market, as was the
practice some years ago, they are begun to rear nearly as many
lambs as serve them. The sheep reared here are altogether
white. They are not so heavy as the Linton sheep: but their
wool is finer, and their mutton of a higher flavour.

Town, Manufactures, &c.—Kirriemuir, a burgh of barony,
is of considerable antiquity; but the date of its erection is
here unknown *.

Situated near the foot of the braes of Angus, in a fertile,
extensive, and populous district, Kirriemuir is the mart to
which the inhabitants of the neighbouring parishes chiefly resort. Hence no town in the county has a better weekly market; in none of its size is more trade carried on. Nine carriers go regularly to Dundee twice, and often thrice a-week,
loaded

---

* It is, however, certain, that the jurisdiction of its bailie was very great;
and, it is said, extended even over the hill of Dundee. It stands in a very healthy
and pleasant situation, partly on a flat, and partly on an inclined plane, on the
S. W. side of a hill of the same name, along the northern brow of a beautiful
den, through which runs the small river Gairie. In form, it very much resembles an anchor; that part of it which lies along the den, in the level situation,
forming the arms; and that which stands on an inclined plane, the shank of the
anchor. The prospect of the lower part of the town is bounded by the southern
brow of the den; but from the higher part is seen almost the whole of Strathmore.

loaded with the produce, or manufactures of the diſtrict, and bring from thence flax, ſugar, tea, porter, rum, and all kinds of merchant goods ; and two come twice a-week from Montroſe. And it is to be obſerved, that theſe carriers ſeldom bring coals. The town is ſupplied with that article by Dundee carriers, or the farmers in the neighbourhood *. Two annual fairs are held here, in July and October, for ſheep, horſes, and black cattle ; and for flax, wool, labouring utenſils, and houſehold neceſſaries. It contains 492 houſes, 471 families, 10 brewers, who are likewiſe innkeepers, 12 retailers of foreign ſpirits, 3 of wine, about 20 of ale and whiſky, 27 merchants, 228 weavers, and 1584 ſouls.

Two tan-yards have been eſtabliſhed here for ſome time, and a third is erecting. A diſtillery was begun ſome months ago, in a ſituation than which none could be better adapted for the purpoſe ; and in building the houſes neceſſary for it, the proprietor had in view the eſtabliſhment of a brewery at the ſame place, ſhould a proper perſon be found to undertake it. About 1200 pair of ſhoes are made annually for exportation ; and the manufacture of coarſe linen is carried on to a very great extent. Oſnaburgh, ſcrim, and birdy, to the amount of about 38,000 l. Sterling, were manufactured from September 1791 to September 1792. This is more than was ever before manufactured in one year, and muſt have been owing to the flouriſhing ſtate of the trade, which was never better than it is at preſent, December 1792 †.

Population.

---

* It is 16 miles from Dundee, 20 from Arbroath, 15 from Brechin, 5 3-4ths from Forfar, and 5 from Glammis.

† A journeyman weaver can, with eaſe, gain 16 d. a-day, and a woman 8 d. at ſpinning. And to ſuch perfection have ſome of the people here arrived in this buſineſs, that many women, when they exert themſelves, can gain 12 d. and even 15 d. a-day ; and a weaver lately wrought, on a wager, in 18 hours and 20 minutes,

Population.—According to Dr. Webster's report, the number of souls then, was 3409. At present they amount to between 4000 and 5000. Males born in 1792, 68, females 70, marriages 43.

Ecclesiastical State, Stipend, Schools, Poor, &c—It appears that there were once 4 religious houses in the parish, besides the one presently used as a parish church, and the chapel in Glenprosen, where the minister still officiates 2 or 3 times a-year *.

An

20 minutes, a web of birdy, consisting of 91 yards, for working which 8 s. was then paid. This has greatly raised the price of all kinds of labour. In 1786, the wages of a labouring man servant were from 5 l. to 7 l.; of a woman from 2 l. 10 s. to 3 l.; of a mason from 15 d. to 18 d. a-day; of a joiner from 12 d. to 15 d. At present, 1792, they are as follows : of a man servant, from 7 l. to 10 l. of a woman, from 3 l. to 4 l. 4 s.; of a mason, from 20 d. to 24 d. a-day; of a joiner, from 15 d. to 18 d. All kinds of provisions have likewise risen in proportion; if we abstract from the quality, which has been much improved since the above period. Beef, mutton, and lamb, sell at from 3 d. to 4½ d. the pound; veal at 2½ d. to 4 d.; honey at 6 d. to 12 d. the pound, Dutch weight; fowls at 9 d. to 14 d.; eggs at 3 d. to 4 d. a dozen; butter at 9 d. to 11 d. the pound of 27 oz.; cheese at 6 s. to 8 s. the stone, of 27 English pounds. The price of victual is very much regulated by the market at Dundee. Oatmeal and barley are, at a medium, about 14 s. the boll.

* One at a place called Chapeltown, about 3 miles to the N. of the town; one at Killhill, about 3 miles to the E. of it; one near Balinshoe; and one in Kirriemuir. It is probable that the one near Balinshoe was built by the proprietor, for the use of his own family; as the site of it is still enclosed with a good wall, and used as the burying place of the Fletchers of Balinshoe. Whether the others belonged to private families, or the parish in general, and when any of them were used as places of public worship, is uncertain. But the proprietor of the site of the one in Kirriemuir is, to this day, called Sainty, and not thirled to a mill in the neighbourhood, which is the case with every other proprietor in the town; and a piece of ground adjoining, now used as a garden, is in old writs called the Kirk-yard.

An elegant church was built here in 1787, to which Charles
Lyell, Efq. of Kinnordy, the principal heritor and fuperior
of the town, added a handfome fpire, which is feen through
the whole of Strathmore. The manfe was built in 1774;
but fo ill executed, that it was found neceffary to repair it
in 1787. It is now a fubftantial and commodious houfe.
The ftipend is 112 bolls of victual, $\frac{2}{3}$ meal, and $\frac{1}{3}$ bear, and
470 l. Scotch, including 50 l. for communion elements, and
20 l. for grafs-money, with a glebe of 4 acres. Lord Douglas is patron.—The fchoolmafter's falary is 200 merks, with
a commodious houfe and a fmall garden, befides 1 l. 12 s.
Sterling, mortified to him, many years ago, by a Mr. Ogilvy
a clergyman in London, for teaching 4 boys of his own
name *.

The number of fcholars varies from 60 to 100. There are
2 private fchools in the town, at one of which the numbers
are much the fame as at the parochial fchool. At the other,
are taught from 20 to 40 fcholars. In the country part of
the parifh; there are 4 fchools, at which from 100 to 150
children are taught to read Englifh.

The number of poor families which conftantly receive alms,

is

---

* Mr. Hendry of the parifh of Kenfington, London, a native of this parifh,
by his will, bequeathed to the minifter and elders 1400 l. Sterling, in truft, the
intereft of 1200 l. to be laid out in educating, and furnifhing with books, pens,
ink, and paper, 12 boys, or, as many more as it will educate; and the intereft
of the remaining 200 l. to be paid to the fchoolmafter for keeping the accounts.
Some difficulties arofe about fome parts of Mr. Hendry's property, and the ex-
clufion of the truft in his will; fo that his executors did not think themfelves
fafe to pay the money without an amicable fuit in Chancery. This was begun
in 1784; and in 1786, the Chancellor found the money due, with 1½ years intereft; but, inftead of ordering it to be paid, he directed it to be laid out in
the funds, and a plan to be given in how it was to be expended. This was done
foon after; but the legacy has not yet been paid. It is, however, expected that
payment will be ordered in the courfe of next term.

is at prefent 19. The only fund for their fupport arifes from
the intereft of a fmall fum faved by the feffion in former
years, to anfwer any emergence, collections in the church,
dues for lending mortcloths, fines from delinquents, and the
fale of the effects of penfioners after their death. Thefe, for
the year 1792, amounted to 99 l. 9 s. 8¼ d. The diftributions to the above penfioners, and fome other occafional charities, with 4 l. 6 s. paid to the feffion-clerk and beadle, a-
mounted to 86 l. 16 s. 2 d.; fo that in 1792, there was a faving of 12 l. 18 s. 6¼ d., although the allowance to each pen-
fioner was never more liberal, being from 3 s. to 7 s. a-month,
befides the rent of their houfe, and from 5 s. to 10 s. to affift
them in buying fuel *.

Mifcellaneous Obfervations.—A little to the W. of the town
is a globular hillock, and contiguous to it, a circular pond
evidently excavated to form the hillock. In a difpofition to
the eftate of Kinnordy by one of the Douglas family, this
hillock, which is called the Court Hillock, and a road to it,
is referved. The pond is commonly called the Witch Pool,
and was lately converted into a refervoir for the mills on the
Gairie; a much better ufe than, if we may judge from the
name,

* In 1762, the collections made in the church were, each Sunday, at a medium, including what was collected at the difpenfation of the Lord's Supper
9 s. 9¼ d. In 1772, the church was vacant; but in 1770, they were 14 s. 2 d.;
and in 1790, 1 l. 8 s. 10 d.: A clear proof this of the growing opulence of the
parifh, as well as of their charitable difpofition. But in order to have the a-
mount of their charity, we muft add a confiderable fum given to be diftributed
among poor families, not penfioners, by two of the heritors who are Epifcopalians, and, therefore, feldom or never attend the church; and a very large fum
given by the people to ftrolling beggars, moft of whom, inftead of being objects of charity, are very fit objects for a houfe of correction. Such, however,
is the difpofition of the people, that their purfe is open to every vagabond who
can tell a plaufible tale of woe; and as much fquandered in this way as would
make all the poor in the parifh live comfortably.

name, the superstition of our ancestors led them to apply it.
At Invercarity there is a Gothic building of cut stone in
good repair. When it was erected, is uncertain; but it must
have been before the 15th century. It consists of 4 stories,
and each storey, except the uppermost, which is divided into
2, of only one apartment. The walls are about 9 feet thick,
project considerably near the top, and terminate in a parapet
not more than a foot thick. Between the parapet and roof,
there is a space for 2 or 3 men to walk abreast, and immediately above the gate 3 square apertures, through the projection of the wall, so placed, that a stone dropped through
them must fall upon a person standing at the gate. To the
E. of the gate which fronts the S., are some vestiges of a
wing, demolished, it is said, by the Earl of Crawford, in
1445, in some family feud between the Lindsays and Ogilvies,
one of whom was then proprietor of Invercarity *

---

* This town was in great distress in 1782, not so much from a scarcity of victual, for some of the farmers never had a better crop, as from a resolution entered into by the people not to give above a certain price. Consequently the
farmers carried their victual to the best market; and this place was threatened
with a famine. To prevent this in future, a society was established in 1785,
called the Weaver Society. Each member, at his admission, pays a certain
sum, and so much a quarter afterward; and, in case of sickness, or inability to
work, he is entitled to a certain allowance a-week; and in the event of his
having a widow, she receives a small annuity. The funds, which are now considerable, are employed in purchasing meal, which is sold to the members at
prime cost, and to others, at a trifling profit. This society has been of great
use to the parish. Another, on much the same plan, called the Society of Shoemakers, was established some months ago. There are 3 mosses in the parish,
and several others on the boundaries of it. From these, the common people
are supplied with fuel; but the mosses being much exhausted, it is now procured with difficulty; and after a wet season, the poor are almost starved.
This is the chief disadvantage under which the parish labours; and is likely to
be, in some measure, remedied by the great quantity of thriving timber lately
planted here, and in the neighbourhood; and by the turnpike road making to
Dundee, the nearest sea port.

7

APPENDIX.

STATISTICAL TABLE *of the Parish of* KIRRIEMUIR, *for* 1792.

Length in English miles, about	20	Average of births for 10 years	
Breadth,—from - -	2 to 7	preceding 1792, - -	$125\frac{1}{10}$
Population in 1748, -	3407	* Marriages in 1792, - -	42
—————— in 1792, -	4358	Births, - - -	139
Inhabitants in the town in 1748,	670	Number of families, -	1047
—————————— in 1792,	1584	—— houses inhabited, -	923
Inhabitants in the country in 1748,	2737	—— houses built within these	
—————————— in 1792,	2774	10 years, - -	121
Number of males, -	2190	—— ditto pulled down, -	45
—— Females, - -	2168	—— married persons, -	748
—— Persons under 10 years of		—— children, at an average,	
age, - -	1022	from each marriage, -	6
—— under 20, - -	2079	—— twins born in the parish for	
—— under 50, - -	3719	the last 10 years, -	40
—— under 70, - -	4247	—— bachelors above 50, -	13
—— under 80, - -	4352	—— unmarried women above 45,	37
—— under 90, - -	4358	—— widowers, - -	78
			Number

* *No regular register either of marriages, or deaths, has been kept. But in* 1784, 109 *deaths are recorded. In some subsequent years, only* 48, 56, &c. *are recorded. Nor can the register of baptisms be depended on ; for, since the duty on registration was laid on, many, rather than pay it, neglect to register.*

Number of widows,	-	140	Female servants occasionally, -	251
Members of the Established			Flaxdressers, - -	18
Church, - - -		4069	Carriers, - - -	9
Seceders, about - -		180	Day-labourers, - -	47
Roman Catholics, -		2	Poor,—from - - 15 to 30	
Episcopalians, - -		107	Capital of their funds about - 70 l.	
Proprietors residing *, - -		3	Annual income,—from 70 l. to 100 l.	
———— non-residing, - -		7	Young persons taught english,	
Clergymen †, - - -		2	writing, and arithmetick, 300 to 400	
Merchants and shopkeepers, -		30	Latin,—from - - 8 to 24	
Surgeons, - - -		2	At the University, - -	2
Schoolmasters, - - -		7	Persons serving in the army dur-	
Farmer above 500 l. a-year, -		1	ing the last war, supposed, -	36
Farmers above 100 l. - -		4	Ditto in the navy, supposed -	16
Ditto above 50 l. - -		15	Number of acres in Scotch mea-	
Ditto under 50 l. and above 10 l. ‡,		58	sure, supposed, from the best	
Innkeepers, - - -		14	information, to be as follows,	
Smiths, - - -		12	exclusive of the hills and glens:	
Masons, - - -		28	Arable, - - -	6650
Carpenters, - - -		50	Meadow, or natural grass, -	1170
Weavers, - - -		516	Woods and plantations, -	1560
Shoemakers, - - -		56	Wheel-carriages, at present -	2
Tailors, - - -		39	Carts, - - -	253
Butchers, - - -		4	Ploughs, - - -	127
Millers, - -		25	Valued rent, in Scotch	
Bakers, - - -		7	money, - L. 8104 10 0	
Gardeners, - -		9	§ Real rent, 1792, in Ster-	
Male domestick servants, - -		4	ling, about - 6700 0 0	
Female domestick servants, -		96	Rents spent in the parish,	
Male farm servants, - -		290	about - - 4200 0 0	
				VALUE

* Besides the above, there are from 40 to 50 small proprietors here, called feuars, most of whom reside.

† There is in Kirriemuir, a Scotch Episcopal Chapel; but the clergyman resides at present in the parish of Kingoldrum.

‡ A part of the parish is divided into small portions, from 2 to 10 acres, which, in general, are occupied by weavers, who pay from 2 l. to 10 l. of rent. As farming is their employment only occasionally, they are numbered among those of the trade which they follow.

§ In the above sum, the rent of the town, which is between 1100 l. and 1200 l., is included.

VALUE of STOCK.

Number of draught horfes; about 507, valued at * 8 l. each. Total, L. 4056 0 0
——— faddle and carriage horfes, 13, ——— 30 l.   -   -   390 0 0
——— cattle, about   -   † 1945, ——— 6 l.   -   11,670 0 0
——— fheep, about   -   - 3200, ——— 10 s. 6 d.   -   1680 0 0

                    Total value of ftock,   -   L. 17,796 0 0

* *The value of the horfes ufed in the parifh, is from* 10 l. *to* 30 l., *when at their prime ; but, becaufe many of them may be aged, they are valued as above.*

† *In the above number, are not included the cattle grazed and fed in the grafs enclofures, which may amount to* 600. *Many of the cattle reared here have been fold at* 10 l., 15 l., *and fome even at* 18 l. ; *but, becaufe the greateft number are of an inferior quality,* 6 l. *has been judged to be the medium.*

STATISTICAL ACCOUNT

OF

SCOTLAND.

PARISH OF LETHNOT.

(COUNTY OF FORFAR.)

By the Rev. Mr JOHN TAYLOR.

Annexation and Situation.

THE parishes of Navar and Lethnot, prior to the year 1723, were two separate charges : Before their union, the parish of Lochlee and Lethnot were one charge. The minister resided at Lethnot, and preached two sabbaths at Lethnot, and the third at Lochlee. But, as Lochlee is distant from Lethnot ten computed miles, and as the road was found always inconvenient, and often dangerous, especially in winter, it was judged proper by all concerned about the year 1723, to disjoin Lochlee from Lethnot, to make the former

former a ſeparate charge, and to annex Navar to the latter. Navar and Lethnot, thus united, lie in the county of Forfar, the preſbytery of Brechin, and the ſynod of Angus and Mearns. They are ſurrounded by the Grampian hills on all ſides, except towards the eaſt, where there is a ſmall opening, through which the Weſt-water iſſues, and the plain of the Mearns is ſeen. The only part of the Grampians, that lies to the ſouth of them, is the hill of Caterthun remarkable for having on its top the remains of a very ancient fortification. Oppoſite to Caterthun, which is the higheſt top of a long ridge, running nearly from eaſt by north to weſt by ſouth, are the Grampians on the north, nearly in a parallel direction to the long ridge of Caterthun, but much higher. Along the bottom of theſe, Navar and Lethnot are ſituated, the breadth of the arable land from the bottom of Caterthun on the ſouth to the uncultivated parts of the higher Grampians on the north, being nearly 3-4ths of a mile all along, and the length about 5 miles. Lethnot, which lies eaſtward, is bounded on that quarter by the pariſh of Edzel, and part of the pariſh of Stricathrow, on the ſoutheaſt and ſouth by the eaſtern part of the ridge of Caterthun, which ſeparates it from the pariſh of Menmuir; on the weſt by the Weſt-water, which ſeparates it from Navar; and on the north, by that part of the Grampians, called the *hill of Wirran,* or *the hill of ſprings,* (as the word Wirran is ſaid to ſignify,) which ſeparates it from the pariſh of Lochlee. Navar is bounded on the ſouth and ſouth weſt by the weſtern part of the ridge of Caterthun, which divides it from Menmuir; on the weſt it is ſeparated from the Glens of Fern, Tannadice, Cortachy and Clova, by a great extent of the Grampian mountains; and towards the north, others of theſe mountains divide it from the pariſh of Lochlee. But beſides that part of the pariſhes, which is ſituated as above deſcribed, there is a conſiderable number of ſmall

farms,

farms, which lie fcattered on the Weft-water and other fmall rivulets, extending a good way among the hills in a north-weft direction from the church of Lethnot, the moft diftant being upwards of five miles from it.

Soil, Marl, &c.—The foil in both parifhes is various, fome of it is of a clay nature, fome a rich loam with a till bottom, and there is fome haugh ground adjacent to the Weftwater with a fandy bottom. The ancient name of the Weft-water was Dy; it has its fource among the hills about twelve miles north-weft from the church of Lethnot, and it receives in its progrefs a great number of rapid rivulets. There are appearances of unfhapely rocks here and there on its banks, and at one place there is found limeftone of a reddifh fandy nature, mixed with veins of freeftone. The farmers quarry the limeftone, and find it to anfwer well with their lands. But there is no freeftone quarry within the parifhes, and though fome of the rocks, which feem in general to be compofed of what is commonly called *fcurdy ftone*, might anfwer for building, yet there is no quarry of them opened for that purpofe. There is in the hill of Wirran, a fpecies of rock of a bluifh colour, and of a very fine texture, very like to that of the fmall blue flates, from which the farmers quarry lintels for doors and windows. They can have thefe pieces almoft of any length and breadth they pleafe; but as the rock is at fome diftance, it is feldom wrought. What is of greater confequence to fome of the farms of the parifhes is a vein of clay or rock marl, which runs from the eaft end of Lethnot to the weft of Navar, in a line nearly eaft by north to weft by fouth. This vein extends beyond the boundaries of the parifhes. It is found on the lands of Balfour at the diftance of five miles eaft, and it is found a little north of the Houfe of Fafque, the feat of Sir Alexander Ramfay, at the diftance of feven miles from
this

this place. A great quantity, no lefs than 300 of our cart-
loads are neceffary to manure an acre. But when it is put
on in fufficient quantity, it is far preferable to lime, its virtue remaining for many years. It is of different colours,
fome bluifh, and fome purplifh mixed with veins of a cream
colour. It effervefces, like limeftone, with aqua fortis, and
anfwers beft with thin dry land. However it can be of ufe to
the adjoining farms only, becaufe with refpeët to thofe at
the diftance of a mile or two from the pit, the expence and
labour would exceed the profit. It is found at fix, eight,
and in fome places ten feet below the furface. It is laid on
ley and fpread in fummer, and continues to incorporate
with the furface during the winter-rains and froft, and the
field is broken up in fpring for oats.

Mineral fprings.—There is a great number of mineral
fprings within the parifhes, all of a chalybeate nature ; fome
of them are ftrong, and prove beneficial in complaints of the
ftomach and gravel. People of the neighbourhood frequently vifit them ; but there is no refort to them by perfons at
a diftance, though it is believed they would prove as falu-
tary in fome complaints as the wells of Pananach, which
are in high repute.

Fifh.—In moft of the fmall rivulets, which fall into the
Weft-water, there is trout of the common kind ; and in the
Weft-water itfelf, there are three fpecies of frefh water
trout ; 1_ft_, Thofe of the common kind about eight or nine
inches long; 2_dly_, The yellowifh trout confiderably larger ;
and 3_dly_, A fpecies of trout called _Par_, about the fize of a
common burn trout, with a fmall head, and fides beautifully clouded. Befides the above kinds, there are alfo fea-
trouts, which come up from the fea in May, from one to
two pounds weight. There is likewife plenty of fmouts,

(as

(as they are commonly called) or smelts, which are a slender clear-skinned species of trout about eight or nine inches long : They are supposed by some to be young sea-trout, but their flesh is white, whereas that of the sea-trout is reddish like salmon.

Distempers.——On account of our being surrounded by high hills, we are exposed to frequent and strong gusts of wind, by which the atmosphere is kept pure and healthy. The distempers most prevalent are inflammatory and pleurify fevers, owing to the frequent and sudden changes of the weather, and to the peoples being exposed to hard exercise, wet clothes, and a sudden stopping of the perspiration. There is a distemper, called by the country-people the *leaping ague*, and by physicians, *St Vitus's dance*, which has prevailed occasionally for upwards of 60 years in these parishes, and some of the neighbouring ones. The patient first complains of a pain in the head, and in the lower part of the back ; to this succeed convulsive fits, or fits of dancing at certain periods. This disease appears to be hereditary in some families. When the fit of dancing, leaping or running seizes the patient, nothing tends more to abate the violence of the disease, than the allowing him free scope to exercise himself in this manner till nature be exhausted. Another distemper, with which the constitution of some families here is tainted, is the scrofula or king's evil, owing very probably to cold, and to a poor aliment. But in general the climate seems favourable to longevity. Within these last 16 years, four persons have died, who were above 90 ; one of them was 106.

Population.——Dr Webster's state of the population about 40 years ago was 635 souls. The number of people has decreased considerably within these last 20 years. In 1777 and 1778, the
number

number was 555, of whom 268 were males, 287 were females, 65 were under ſix years of age, 99 were under 10 years,
50 were Nonjurors, and 2 were Bereans. But in 1790,
the number was only 505, of which 256 were males, 249
were females, 62 were under ſix, and 98 under ten. There
are at preſent ſix tailors, ſeven weavers, two ſmiths, and
two wrights, within the pariſhes. In 1790, the number of
Nonjurors, or more properly now, Epiſcopalians, was 56. The
cauſe of the diminution of the number of people is, that in
no leſs than ſix caſes, two farms have, within theſe fourteen years, been joined into one. Beſides the number of
ſubtenants is alſo conſiderably diminiſhed. There were ſixteen houſes, then inhabited by ſubtenants, which are now
ruinous. In ſome caſes, the poſſeſſors, being old people,
died out; and in others, the farmers choſe to have their
poſſeſſion of land in their own hand, becauſe they could
turn it to more advantage; beſides they wiſhed to leſſen
the number of their ſubtenants, becauſe they found it inconvenient to lead fuel to them, and to perform other ſtipulated ſervices. The diminiſhing of the number of ſubtenants and the uniting of farms, it is preſumed, is an evil
not peculiar to this corner. The conſequence is, that there
is, and has been for ſome time, a great difficulty in procuring ſervants.

Births, Marriages and Burials for the last ten Years.

	Male Births.	Fem. Births.	Mar.	Bur.
In the year 1781	9	5	5	11
1782	10	5	6	9
1783	9	6	10	7
1784	9	4	4	9
1785	9	6	2	6
1786	6	9	7	12
1787	5	4	7	7
1788	11	6	3	8
1789	3	5	5	7
1790	8	6	8	12
Sums	79	56	57	88
Yearly average	$7\frac{9}{10}$	$5\frac{6}{10}$	$5\frac{7}{10}$	$8\frac{8}{10}$

In the year 1778, there were 119 inhabited houses; but in 1790, the number was only 103. The number of married persons or couples in 1778, was 85; in 1790, the number was 74. There were 15 bachelors, widowers included, keeping houses by themselves, and for the most part old men, in the year 1778. The number of persons of the same description in the year 1790 was 13. As to the number of children produced by marriages, there are many instances here, when young people marry, and are in easy circumstances, of their having eight children; many where there are ten children, and some where there are thirteen. But when people advanced in life marry, the number of children is two or three, and sometimes none. Many of our young people remove from the parishes, but not for want of employment. They get higher wages to the southward, and some remove for the sake of learning, a particular trade

or

or art, as their genius leads them. None have perished
from want, since the end of the last century, when there
were seven years of general scarcity, and when some persons were found dead with cabbage, kail-roots, &c. in their
mouths.

Sheep.—The number of sheep is about 6770, of lambs
1256. But as a great number of lambs perish through the
weakness of the ewes, owing to severe winters and springs,
there are brought annually from the southern counties about
678, part of them lambs, but for the most part year-olds,
because these last stand the winter better. Hence the annual increase arising from lambs produced at home, and
from those brought from the south, is about 1934. But of
these generally one third is destroyed, before they come to
full maturity, some by foxes, some by severe winters and
springs, some are amissing, and many are cut off by a dif-
ease, which is here called *the Braxes.* Hence it happens,
that the sale of old sheep annually amounts only to 2-3ds of
1934, that is 1289. The south country, or what is here
called the *Yarrow brood*, are of a larger size than the native kind, and bring a higher price from the butcher; but
their wool is much coarser. There is now such a mixture
of the two breeds, that hardly any of the native kind are
to be found pure. The wool of the native kind, several
years ago, used to sell at 1 s. 3 d. *per* lb., and at present it
easily brings that price, when pure; while that of the Yarrow breed brings only 10 d. or 11 d. The pound consists of 24 ounces English. Many of our farmers begin to
think that they would have acted more wisely, had they encouraged their own native breed: for they find, in the *first*
place, that the Yarrow breed requires much more pasture;
2dly, That they do not stand the winter so well; and, *3dly*,
That their wool is of a much coarser quality. A wedder
of

of the native breed when full grown, fells at 10 s. 6 d. or 11 s. and the Yarrow kind brings 14 or 15 s. It is obferved here, that the nature of the fheep's pafture greatly affects the wool. A farm where there is much wet marfhy ground, and that rough kind of grafs which grows on fuch ground, always produces coarfe wool.

The fineft wool is produced, where the fheep have young tender heath, and fhort fweet grafs to feed upon.

The difeafe formerly mentioned under the name of *Braxes,* in this place, proves fatal to many of the young fheep. It feizes them towards the end of harveft, when they are in beft condition, and the moft thriving are cut off by it. When their bodies are opened, the blood is found extravafated in their bowels, and in a putrid ftate. It appears to be infectious; for when the difeafe begins, numbers perifh, and they are cut off by a fhort illnefs. No method is found fo effectual for ftopping the progrefs of the malady, as removing the fheep to a pafture at fome diftance. When the young fheep are carried to a diftant pafture, it is fome time before they become acquainted with it, fo that for a few days at leaft, they muft be but half-fed. This confideration induced an ingenious man in a neighbouring parifh, to confine his young fheep a good part of every day within their pens, at the time when the Braxes began to make its appearance, that they might be prevented from filling their ftomachs, when attacked by it, and this precaution had the defired effect in faving their lives. There are others who fay, that they have tried this precaution without fuccefs.

Horfes and black cattle.——The number of horfes within the parifhes is 147: many of them are of a fmall fize, only a little larger than the Shetland breed. The number of black cattle is 601. The number of calves reared annually
is

is about 130; but befides thefe, there are between two and three dozen fed for the butcher.

Heritors, farms, &c.—The heritors of Navar and Lethnot, are three in number, none of whom refide. The valued rent is L. 1031 : 13 : 9 Scots : The real rent is about L. 410 Sterling. The proprietor of the greateft eftate gave leafes (a little after 1760) to all the tenants in the lower part of the parifhes for two nineteen years and a life; and for one nineteen and a life, to thofe in the upper or more hilly part of the eftate, obliging the tenants to carry on certain pieces of improvement fpecified in their leafes. They became obliged to build fubftantial houfes on their refpective farms, to inclofe a certain portion of the farm, to bring in and improve baulks, and fuch pieces of wafte ground as were fit for improvement, and to plant an acre, or half an acre, according to the fize of the farm, of young trees in fome convenient place, and to keep a fufficient fence around them till grown up. Some of the tenants have completely fulfilled thefe ftipulations. All the farms are fet upon moderate terms, fome at 7 s. *per* acre, fome at 5 s. and fome as low as 2 s. 4 d. Their fize is very various; fome confift of 30 acres, fome of 50, fome of 80; there is one of 100 acres, and another of 160. The rent of thofe farms which lie in the lower part of the parifhes, is made to rife at the end of every nineteen years of the leafe. Thus the farm of 160 acres, which paid L. 33, for the firft nineteen, pays now yearly during the currency of the fecond nineteen L. 39, and is bound to pay for the firft nineteen of the life L. 45.

All the tenants have already increafed the value of their farms very confiderably by improvements, and by bringing wafte ground into cultivation : But there is ftill a good deal of wafte ground on moft of the farms, which will require the induftry of many years fully to improve. Moft of the larger farms confift of what was formerly two farms.

Agriculture.

Agriculture.—The number of acres arable, may be estimated at 1200. Of these about 400 are allotted to oats, 200 for Chester bear, 30 for pease, about an equal number for turnips, potatoes and cabbage ; all the rest lie in grass, about 144 acres being sown with red clover, white clover, and rye-grass. The number of ploughs is 28 ; but about 30 or 40 years ago, the number was upwards of 40. The cause of the decrease is, that in many instances, two farms have been joined into one since that period, and besides, in the hilly part of the parishes, several farms which were formerly in cultivation, are at present lying in grass, and meant to be kept in that state, as pasture for cattle and sheep. Twenty-eight ploughs, indeed, are more than sufficient for all the labour ; tho' on the larger farms there is work enough for the ploughs employed. On a small farm of 18 or 20 acres, one plough of four small horses is more than enough ; so that the uniting of small farms, which lie contiguous, may be sometimes considered as a wise plan, and as tending to the advantage of the country, at least in respect of the landlord.

Within these last 30 years, the art of farming is greatly improved in this place. It is only about 20 years ago, that the farmers began to clean their land by sowing turnip, and to sow grass seeds. Since that period there has been a great spirit of industry and improvement. As lime answers well with their land, they have been in the practice for several years of bringing it from a great distance. Some of them bring it at least 12 statute miles. Hence the quantity of grain produced at present is far greater than what was produced 30 years ago. At present the parishes can spare annually, at an average, about 500 bolls, part in oats and oatmeal ; but the greatest part, bear in grain, which is carried to Brechin and Montrose. The beginning of our seed-time here is very various, owing to the spring snow lying long near the bottom of the hills. Generally we begin to sow oats
before

before the middle of March, and bear about the middle of
April. In the years 1782, 1785, 1788, and 1789, April
was begun, and the firſt eight days of it near gone, before
there was any ſowing here. But in 1787, 1790, and 1791,
ſome of our farmers began to ſow peaſe and oats in February, and all of them in the firſt and ſecond week of March.

The beginning of harveſt here is alſo various. Generally
it begins about the firſt or ſecond week of September, and
is finiſhed before the firſt of November, and all the corns
got in. But in the year 1782, there was no reaping till
the 3d of October, and it was the 20th of November before
all the corns were got in. Crop 1782 in this place, as in
the greateſt part of the kingdom, turned out very unproductive. The ſnow and froſt came on before the corns
were ripened. However, with what the people had reſerved of the former crop, and with the ſcanty ſupply which
crop 1782 afforded, they were able to ſubſiſt till crop 1783
came in aid, without ſeeking any aſſiſtance from abroad ; or
at leaſt, if a ſmall portion of meal was brought from Montroſe, and ſome bolls of ſeed-oats bought, there was more
ſold out of the pariſhes, to people who came from Dee ſide,
and other places. It is the practice of many in theſe pariſhes
to have their girnals or meal-cheſts always pretty full, that
they may be prepared againſt a bad crop. Experience has
taught them this precaution, becauſe the harveſts here are
often precarious, and the corns ſuffer either by wind, or by
the winter coming on before they are fully ripened. There
is but little flax raiſed here. It does not generally ripen ſufficiently, to tempt a farmer to riſk many acres on its cultivation. Yet moſt of the farmers in the lower part of the
pariſhes ſow a peck or two for the uſe of their own families,
and they reckon it a tolerable crop, if they have between
two and three ſtone after the peck of lintſeed. The ſtone
conſiſts

confifts of 24 lb. Englifh, or 22 lb. Amfterdam. There is no *common* pafture except the hills.

Difadvantages.—Among the difadvantages to which this place is expofed, may be reckoned a long continuance of fnow in the fpring, by which the operations of hufbandry are interrupted, and the feed-time retarded; and on this account, our corns are but feldom fo well ripened as thofe in the low country. While good oats in the low country yield fixteen pecks of meal *per* boll, we reckon them good here, if they yield fifteen. The winters here are always more fevere than in the low country, and our farmers are often interrupted in their operations by ftorms, while thofe to the fouthward of the hills can plow and cart. Befides they frequently fuffer very confiderably in fevere winters and fprings by the lofs of fheep and lambs. Our diftance from Brechin, which is the neareft market-town being five computed miles, and the road acrofs the fteep hill of Caterthun, often rendered impaffable for horfes by the fnow, may be reckoned another difadvantage under which this country labours.

Stipend, &c.—The ftipend is L. 51, 19 s. Sterling, and 16 bolls oatmeal. The glebe may be eftimated now at five guineas yearly. The church is probably two or three hundred years old. It was covered with lead until the year 1742, and then flated. A minifter of the parifh, fo many years ago, that neither his name nor the period of his incumbency is remembered, lived and died a bachelor, and having money, he bequeathed it to cover the church with lead. It is faid, that his body lies interred in a ftone coffin in the eaft end of the church. As to the manfe, it is but a modern edifice. It was built about the 1723. The King is patron of the parifh.

School.

School.—There are two ſchools within the pariſhes; the eſtabliſhed ſchool, and another founded on private donation. The pariſh ſchoolmaſter's living conſiſts of 100 merks Scots, paid by the heritors and tenants, fees for baptiſms, marriages, and ſchool-fees, and may be eſtimated at L. 11 or L. 12. For a few months in winter, the number of ſcholars is ſometimes above 40, but through the ſpring and ſummer, only about a dozen attend the ſchool. Reading, writing, and arithmetic, are the only branches taught. The other ſchool, which is fixed on the Weſt-water about four computed miles from the former, is kept only during the winter half-year. This ſchool was firſt erected about 1750, and a fund of 500 merks Scots, appointed for ſupporting a teacher, which fund, about two years ago, received an addition of L. 20 Sterling.

Poor.—Our number of poor at preſent is eight. They are ſupplied by our Sabbath-collections, and the intereſt of a fund of L. 460, a proviſion abundantly ſufficient to anſwer all reaſonable demands. Our weekly collections have been continuing to riſe gradually for ſome years. Our funds being ſo conſiderable, we judged it improper to apply for any of the Government's bounty in 1783. About 50 years ago, it was common for upwards of 20 young people belonging to the pariſhes to go a-begging in the winterſeaſon for want of employment and ſupport; whereas at preſent the farmers find it very difficult to procure either at home, or from a diſtance, a ſufficiency of young people to ſerve them. There is not a perſon belonging to theſe pariſhes permitted at preſent to go a-begging.

Prices.—The price of an ox, 40 or 50 years ago, was L. 2, 10; ſuch an ox would now ſell at L. 6, 15. An old ewe ſold formerly at 1s. 1d.; ſuch an ewe would now
ſell

fell at 4 s. 6 d. or 5 s. A good wedder fold formerly at
3 s. 6 d. or 4 s. ; fuch a wedder would now give 11 s. Mutton and beef fold formerly at 1 d. *per* lb.; it now fells at
4 d. Sheep were formerly cotted or lodged in a houfe fummer and winter, a mode of treatment much againft their
profperity. Cattle were formerly fed on bear-chaff and
bear-fhag, by which is meant the refufe of the bear which
did not ftand the wind ; at prefent they are fed on turnips,
hay and fheaves of fhort oats. A good hen fold formerly
at 4 d.; fuch a hen would at prefent bring 10 d. Butter
fold formerly at 4 d. *per* lb.; it now brings 9 d. The
pound here is 22 oz. Amfterdam, or 24 oz. Englifh. A
ftone of cheefe weighing 22 lb. Amfterdam, or 24 lb.
Englifh, fold formerly at 3 s.; it now brings 5 s. and 5 s. 6 d.
A boll of oats with fodder fold formerly at 11 s. $1\frac{1}{3}$ d.;
it now fells at 15 s. A boll of bear in grain fold formerly
at 7 s.; it now fells at 13 s. A boll of oat meal fold formerly at 8 s. 4 d. ; (during the years of fcarcity indeed, in
the end of the laft century, meal fold at 20 d. *per* peck ;)
a boll of oat meal fells now at 13 s. 4 d. Our boll is
8 ftone Amfterdam.

Wages, &c.—A labouring man's wages *per* day about
40 years ago, were 2 d. and his meat ; his wages at prefent
are 6 d. and his meat. The wages of a hireman, that is,
a man-fervant hired for the half year, capable to hold the
plough, and work with horfes, were formerly 16 s. 8 d. ;
fuch a man's wages now are L. 3, or L. 3, 10 s. A maid-
fervant's wages formerly were, for the fummer half year,
10 s. with bounties, by which is meant, an ell of linen, an
apron and a fhirt : Her wages for the winter half year
were 5 s. with fame bounties ; the reafon why her wages
were higher in fummer, was, becaufe fhe reaped in harveft ;
a maid-fervant's wages at prefent, for the fummer half year,

are

are L. 1, 5 s. with bounties of an ell of linen, apron and ſhirt, beſides, ſhe alſo ſtipulates for a week to herſelf, during which ſhe goes to her parents houſe and works for herſelf, and is allowed a peck of meal for maintenance during that week. Her wages for the winter half year are L. 1, with ſame bounties, week and meal. A tailor's wages formerly were 2 d. and meat; they are now 6 d. and meat. A weaver formerly charged at the rate of 1 d. *per* ell, for weaving cloth of a certain ſpecies; he now charges 3 d. *per* ell for ſimilar cloth. A pair of coarſe ſhoes formerly coſt 1 s.; ſuch kind of ſhoes now ſell at 3 s.

In this place, the common labourers, when married, have a ſmall ſettlement from a farmer, of about one and an half, or two acres, ſufficient to maintain two cows and 24 ſheep; the farmer does all neceſſary work for the land, in way of tilling, harrowing, leading home the corns, and bringing a certain quantity of fuel from the hills. The ſubtenant is always bound to ſerve the farmer in harveſt, and in the winter half year. The encouragement given him, upon the whole, is ſuch as may enable him to bring up a family without aſſiſtance from the poors funds. Though he have a riſing family of ſix children, the eldeſt under twelve, it would be thought ſtrange here, while he, his wife and children were well, if he ſhould deſire any ſupply. When the ſcheme of the ſituation of the labouring poor in England is conſidered, there occurs only one caſe in which a ſupply would be judged neceſſary here. The caſe is where the woman is deſerted by her huſband, and left with ſix children, four of them being too young to earn any thing: It is to be obſerved that children in this place become uſeful at eight or nine years of age: During ſummer they are employed as herds by ſubtenants. Thus their parents are freed from the charge of their maintenance; beſides they get a ſmall fee of about 5 s. It is to be obſerved alſo, that a

woman's

woman's work in this country turns to more account than it appears to do in England, and our mode of living is lefs expenfive. Such a woman as is mentioned in the above cafe, could gain, in this country, in the way of fpinning, about 18 d. a-week, and manage her family-concerns. The young girls in this country, by the time they are 13 or 14 years old, can fpin 5 or 6 hafps of yarn in the week: A woman that has nothing to interrupt her, fpins about 12 hafps; the price for fpinning a hafp is 3 d. Poor people here, inftead of tea, fugar and butter, live commonly on pottage and milk. It is only old, infirm or difeafed people, who are unable to work, and the ordinary poor, who receive fupport from the poors funds. As for tradefmen and artifans, they have fmall fettlements from the farmers, of about 2 acres each: They are generally bound to reap in harveft, and for fome days work in the bufieft time of fummer. Upon the whole, by the accommodation of their fmall fettlements, and the profits of their occupations, they are enabled to live comfortably, and to bring up families. The lower clafs of people here, as well as thofe above them, are, in general, fober, induftrious and frugal; and but few of them fail in early life to make provifion for the infirmities of old age.

Antiquities, &c.—The remains of what is fuppofed to have been a Druidical temple, ftill appear near the bottom of the hill of Wirran in Lethnot, and it is faid that there were formerly to be feen, the remains of other two in Navar. Though at prefent there is but very little wood in the parifhes, it is plain that there muft have been a good deal long ago, becaufe in many places where peats are

are found, large trunks of black oak are also difcovered.

Eminent Perfons.—Among thofe worthy of being mentioned, James Black deferves a place. This man, born in
1677, though his ftation was originally mean, raifed himfelf by his prudence and induftry, and did more fervice
to his country than many of high rank and opulent
fortunes. During his life he procured the building of
the Gannachy bridge on the North Efk, and contributed
almoft all the money that was neceffary for that purpofe;
a bridge which at this day could not be built for lefs than
L. 160; and at his death he left 50 merks Scots as a fund
for its fupport, befides 1000 merks, for other ufeful and
pious purpofes, *viz.* 300 merks towards building a bridge
at Balrownie, on the road that leads from this place to Brechin; as alfo 200 merks for the poor in the parifh of Fettercairn, and 500 merks for fupporting a fchool in the
Weft-water, which has been already mentioned. On his
tomb-ftone the following infcription is engraved.

No bridge on earth can be a pafs to heaven,
To generous deeds let yet due praife be given.

Fuel.—The general fuel of the parifhes is turf, peat and
heath. The providing of fuel here, is a work of
great expence and labour, on account of the fteepnefs
of the hills, and the diftance of the moffy ground. Many of the farmers, and many alfo of the fubtenants find
it expedient to bring yearly a few coals from the port of
Montrofe, diftant 10 computed miles, which may be reckoned equal to 15 ftatute miles. The boll there, weighing

ing 70 ftone Amfterdam, cofts about 8s. On account of
the high cuftom-houfe duty at Montrofe, our people go
fometimes to Arbroath, which is at leaft 4 ftatute miles
farther diftant, where the coals are fold from 18d. to 2s.
cheaper the boil. It is furely partial, and therefore impolitic, to make the duty on coals higher at Montrofe
than at Arbroath.

Roads and Bridges.—The roads within the parifhes, though
greatly improved within thefe laft 20 years, are ftill but
indifferent. The people are very fenfible of the advantage
of good roads; this indeed may be always expected to be
the cafe, where a fpirit of induftry and improvement prevails. The ftatute-labour is exacted and allotted to roads
within the parifhes, and fometimes to that great road without the parifhes, which leads to Brechin. There are no
turnpike roads within the parifhes. There are no lefs than
7 bridges within the parifhes, 2 of them of about 50 feet
fpan each. There does not feem any occafion for more.

Mifcellaneous Obfervations.—Within thefe laft 50 years,
a great alteration has taken place in the manners, drefs, and
way of living of the people in this place. About 50 or 60
years ago, there was neither a fpinning wheel nor a reel
within the parifhes. The rock and the fpindle were then
ufed, by which aw oman could fpin at an average only $3\frac{1}{2}$
hiers in the day. They ufed then alfo, what was called
the hand-reel, a machine equally flow for work. A woman
can with as much eafe at this day, fpin 12 hiers, as a woman
could have fpun $3\frac{1}{2}$ hiers then. A hier is 240 threads, or
rounds of the reel, each of them 91 inches long. About
50 years ago, neither buckles were ufed for fhoes, nor metal
buttons for clothes. There were then very few carts with-

in

in the pariſhes. Loads were then carried on horſeback. Prior to the 1745, there was not a tea-kettle within the pariſhes, except the miniſter's; now there is not a farm-houſe without one, and ſeveral of the ſubtenants uſe the ſame piece of furniture. Formerly there was little beef or mutton uſed. Even a farmer's family thought themſelves ſufficiently provided in fleſh-meat with one old ewe killed about Chriſtmas. For ſuch a family at pre-ſent 16 ſtone of beef, and 2 good ſheep are conſidered as a moderate proviſion. About 20 years ago, neither barn nor mill fanners for cleaning victual were to be ſeen; at preſent each of the three mills has a ſet of fan-ners, and there are but very few farmers, whoſe barns are not furniſhed with the ſame uſeful machine. There has alſo been within theſe 4 or 5 years, a barley-mill erec-ted, much to the convenience of the neighbourhood. For-merly the people, eſpecially ſuch as were wealthy, lived frequently in fear leſt their houſes ſhould be broken, and their property plundered; at preſent they live ſo ſecure in ſome places, that, as is ſaid, they are ſeldom at the pains to bolt the door under night.

UNITED PARISHES of LIFF and BERVIE,

(COUNTY OF FORFAR, SYNOD OF ANGUS AND MEARNS, PRESBYTERY OF DUNDEE.)

By the Rev. Mr THOMAS CONSTABLE.

Union, Extent, Surface.

THE union of the parishes of Liff and Bervie took place in Nov. 1758. Liff comprehended the old parishes of Logie and Invergowrie; both of which, as appears from the records of the kirk-session, were united to it before the middle of the last century. But Logie, *quoad sacra*, has from the same remote period, belonged to the parish of Dundee, and a considerable proportion of the stipend payable out of it, been allowed to the minister who has the charge of the country parish there *. On the W. and S. E. owing to the

---

* The motives to this transaction cannot now be discovered; but most probably originated from the relative circumstances and connexion of both parishes, a part of Logie, as it is said, having been formerly encroached,

the interfections of the neighbouring parifhes, the form of Liff and Bervie is very irregular. It may be reckoned, on an average, 3 miles in length, and the fame nearly in breadth. The appearance of the furface is in general high-ly pleafing. The ground rifes with an eafy afcent for the fpace of 3 miles from the river Tay, except towards the S. E. where the end of the hill of Balgay, which is very moderate in height, and either wholly planted or cultiva-ted, and a low narrow dale, extending from thence weft-ward through the village of Bervie, intervene. Along this agreeable expofure, are interfperfed houfes, trees, and fields in culture. The higher grounds form, as it were, a ridge, ftretching fomewhat obliquely from W. to E. Be-hind thefe, is a bleak, extenfive tract of moor, where are fome thriving plantations of fir, but hardly any mark of improvement or cultivation. This moor falls northward in gradual declivity, and forms, with the oppofite grounds, part of that Strath or valley, which beginning in the parifh of Lundie, and extending eaftward a few miles, is called Strathmartin, an appellation given to one of the parifhes adjoining this diftrict. In the middle of this ftrath, runs a fmall and rapid ftream from the loch of Lundie, which meets an additional fupply, collected here from the hills above Auchterhoufe, and is then called the water of Digh-ty. This brook is the northern boundary of thefe united parifhes, dividing them from Auchterhoufe, and is nearly parallel to the courfe of the Tay, the principal boundary

on

croached upon by one of the principal ftreets of Dundee, Logie there-fore, comprehending the lands of Logie, Blacknefs, and Balgay, as being part of another fpiritual charge, falls not properly to be confidered in this account of the united parifhes of Liff, including Invergowrie and Bervie.

on the fouth. In this diftrict, there are two other ftreams; one from the E. through Locheye, and another from the W. which meet about half a mile from Invergowrie, before they fall into the Tay. After junction, they are called the burn of Invergowrie; and here, in the months of March and April, fea-trout are fometimes found of 4 lbs. weight.

Climate, Chalybeate Spring.—There are no endemial diftempers. The air is pure and wholefome, owing in a great meafure to the ebbing and flowing of the Tay on one fide, and the ground rifing from it to a confiderable height on the other. In one low and confined fpot, occupied chiefly by manufacturers, few or no difeafes appear, that are not common in the moft healthy fituations. Among the oldeft inhabitants, is a married couple, whofe joint ages make 175, and who have lived together 59 years. There are many of both fexes in this diftrict, whofe lives are prolonged to upwards of 80 years. Confumption and rheumatifm, diforders the moft fatal to fociety, efpecially in the country, owing principally to the want of good and comfortable accommodation among the poorer clafs of people, are not more prevalent in this than in other quarters, where the fame proportion of the people lead fedentary lives. Nay, many perfons from Dundee, of delicate and fickly conftitutions, have found their health greatly improved by a few months refidence here in fummer; and there can be no doubt, that the chill wind and damp vapours from the eaft, which prove fo unfriendly to the reftoration of health, are lefs fenfibly felt here, than in places more immediately adjoining the mouth of the river. In all cafes, therefore, where fea-bathing is not required, this quarter perhaps ought to be preferred.—There is a chalybeate

spring

ſpring at the village of Bervie, which was formerly reſorted to with advantage, by valetudinary perſons in the
neighbourhood, but which is now in no great repute.
From the taſte of the water, and the colour of it, when
mixed with ſpirits, it would appear to be ſtrongly impregnated with iron.

Population.——According to Dr Webſter's report, the number of ſouls at that time was 1311. The number of inhabitants at preſent in the weſt part of this diſtrict, compared
with the amount of the whole, bears no ſort of proportion
to what it did at the beginning of this century, nor even
within a much ſhorter period. Two oppoſite cauſes have
united to produce this remarkable difference : 1ſt, The alienation of the lands belonging to the feuars of Liff; and,
2dly, The late introduction, and rapid increaſe of manufactures, to be afterwards explained, particularly in the eaſt
quarter of this diſtrict. The lands of Liff were part of an
endowment to the monaſtery of Scoon, and appear to have
been feued out by the commendator of that monaſtery into
eight parts, about the time of the Reformation. This laid
the foundation of a village, formerly denominated the
Kirkton of Liff, which from ſundry particulars in the ſeſ-
ſion-record, but more eſpecially from comparing the number of elders in it, with thoſe in the other diviſions of the
pariſh united, appears to have contained in 1650, one third
at leaſt of the whole inhabitants, who, it is obſervable, according to a report made by the miniſter about that time
to the preſbytery of Dundee, amounted to 400 and upwards. This village continued to increaſe, and was in a
flouriſhing ſtate until ſome time after the beginning of the
preſent century, when almoſt the whole of theſe lands
in feu, came into the poſſeſſion of a principal heritor, and
in

in confequence of the improvements made by his extended
pleafure-ground, and the excambion of glebe and other lands,
little now remains of the former appearance and condition
of this fpot. The village of Bervie, diftant about a mile from
that of Liff, has alfo in former times been more confiderable.
At prefent, it feems to labour under peculiar difadvantages, and muft in a fhort time be entirely deferted, unlefs
thefe fhall be removed. But though population may have
declined in the weft, it has of late years increafed beyond the ordinary proportion in other quarters of this diftrict, particularly in the eaft, at Locheye and Milehoufe.
This will appear from comparing the number of examinable perfons in the years 1753 and 1792. By a furvey
of the inhabitants in January 1792, the number of examinable perfons, or of thofe above 10 years old, amounted
to   -   -   -   -   1451

By decreet of annexation for Liff and
    Bervie, dated Auguft 1753,
The examinable perfons in Liff were re-
    ported to be   -   -   -   -   650
The examinable perfons in Bervie,   150
                                              ———   800

Increafe of examinable perfons from 1753 to 1792,
    a fpace of 39 years,   -   -   651

This unufual increafe has arifen chiefly from fome confiderable feus granted out of the eftate here, belonging to the
family of Lundie, between the years 1735 and 1740,
which proving convenient for manufactures, has been fub-
feued fince that time, and is now remarkably filled with
inhabitants. New houfes are erecting on it every year;
but no fort of attention is paid to form or method in pla-
                                                        cing

cing them. From the annexation, the inhabitants of the parifh of Bervie have rather diminifhed than increafed, fo that the whole addition made to the number of people for almoft 40 years in both parifhes, has been entirely on the fide of Liff *. It is further to be remarked, that at that period the population of both Liff and Bervie, was probably much lefs than it had been for many years before, at leaft during the interval between the improvements above mentioned, and the eftablifhment and growth of manufactures, and hence that the amount of examinable perfons at the annexation of the parifhes, is not, ftrictly fpeaking, to be confidered as conveying a proper idea of the ancient ftate of population in this diftrict. The prefent number of the inhabitants amounts to 1790 : Of this number, there are 339 reckoned under the age of ten, which falls fomewhat fhort of the ufual proportion, owing to the late irregular acceffion of fettlers, the frequent change of fervants, and the various fuccefs of manufactures. The native inhabitants are few in comparifon with the ftrangers who have fettled lately. There are many of the former who are able to trace their anceftors back for feveral generations ; and, in particular, there is one family, who without any change of circumftances, unlefs what has necefarily been produced by the gradual and flow operation of time, now inherit the fame fpot cultivated by their forefathers, prior to the æra of the Reformation.

The

* Thofe who are curious about inveftigations of this fort, may from the above account, and the different enumerations given of the inhabitants of Liff, inform themfelves pretty accurately of the ftate of its population from 1650 to 1753, and from thence down to 1792, including a period of no lefs than 142 years.

The householders amount to - - - 348
Of these, the number of weavers, exclusive
   of servants, is - - - 172
Brewers, who at same time retail their own
   ale, - - - - 2
Retailers of ale and spirits, - 7
Tailors, - - - - 13
Shoemakers, - - - 5
Smiths, - - - 4
Masons, about 4 of whom live in the houses
   of their parents, - - 15
Wrights, - - - 12
Flaxdressers, - - 5
Day-labourers, - - 35
Carters, - - - 10
                             —— 280

Two residing heritors, farmers, feuars, small tenants, and a few females, householders, make
   up the remainder, amounting to about - 68

Marriages, on an average of 6 years, ending January
1792, according to the record of the kirk-session, amounted to 15; baptisms to 58; and burials to 29. In cases
of marriage here, it often happens, that the man is far
less advanced in life than the woman he marries. The former depends much on the experience of the latter, and
generally too on the savings of her industry, to enable him
to begin with some comfort a married life: This disparity
of years happening on the side of the woman, must needs
be a hinderance to population *.

Soil,

* The register of baptisms especially in so populous a district as this,
is not to be considered as giving an accurate account of the births in it.
                                               Children

Soil, Agriculture, &c.—The soil varies in different places, but in general that of the higher grounds is light,
mixed with sand, and has sometimes rock for its bottom, and
sometimes mortar. The lower grounds are either of a black
soil, inclining to loam, or of clay. At present upwards of
2000 acres are divided into 12 farms, none of them containing less than 100 acres, and one 400 nearly. The remaining
grounds in the district, allowing for about 400 acres plantation, and perhaps even more for roads and moor or
waste, particularly towards the extreme boundary on the
north, are for the most part occupied by smaller tenants, or
by feuars. Some of the more considerable farms have
rented of late at two guineas an acre ; but one half of these
being either liferent tenures, or held upon old leases, the
medium rent of the whole cannot be estimated higher than
from L. 1, 5 s. to L. 1, 10 s. Smaller holdings rise in value, in proportion to their vicinity to Dundee, those especially

Children that are still-born, or die unbaptized, are never mentioned in
the public register ; besides, there are parents, who sometimes from neglect, and sometimes from parsimony, do not insert in it their childrens
names, and by Dissenters this duty is often omitted entirely. Some allowance may likewise be necessary respecting the deaths here. Many persons
from other quarters having settled of late years in this district, some of
these after death are conveyed to the parishes whence they came, and
others are interred privately in the neighbouring church-yard of Logie,
which appertains to these united parishes, but has become more the burial place of people from Dundee. And in all cases, unless the mortcloth
here be called for, (which is sometimes prevented, in the instance of burials at Logie, by private mortcloths being hired cheaper in Dundee,)
no mention is made in the record of the persons deceased. The burying-
ground in each of these united parishes is still kept sacred for the reception of the dead ; but the church-yard of Liff, and next to it, that of
Logie, are most frequently used. Very few in comparison are buried in
Bervie, and in Invergourie not above two burials on an average will happen in the year.

cially that are calculated for a residence to an industrious
and poor family, and which consist only of a house, and
one or more acres of land. Accordingly, while the village
acres about Liff and Bervie, upwards of 4 miles from market, pay a rent of L. 2 a-year, those of far inferior quality in Locheye and Milehouse, (so called to mark the distance from Dundee), originally feued between 1735 and
1740 at 10 s. an acre, yielded some years ago L. 3 feu-duty;
and in one place adjoining the late turnpike-road, they now
give L. 5 or L. 6. As the same line of road passes through
the less inhabited quarter of this district on the north, a
considerable tract of ground in the strath or valley mentioned there, which, for the most part, is now rated only at a-
bout 10 s. the acre, may be expected in time to rise in
value. The situation is precisely similar to that of Locheye, but farther removed from market, and the land in
general seems more susceptible of improvement and cultivation.

The method of cropping must needs be supposed to vary according to the difference of soil and exposure; but
even where these are the same, one fixed and uniform rotation is not yet adopted. On one or two farms, where a
regular mode of cultivation is going forward, the succession
of crops is as follows: 1*st*, Oats; 2*d*, Fallow; 3*d*, Wheat;
4*th*, Turnip and potatoes; 5*th*, Barley, with grass-seeds;
and, *lastly*, two years grass, cut the first year and pastured
the next. Lint and pease make sometimes a part of the
green crop, but, in general, not much of either is sown. In
the lighter soil, whereof a large proportion of this district
is composed, both fallow and wheat are often laid down.
Marl is sometimes employed as a manure from the neighbouring parish of Foulis, especially in the higher grounds
                                                   towards

towards the north and weft, and in the back moor of Liff, but lime is generally preferred, and is brought fometimes from England, and fometimes acrofs the Tay from the oppofite county of Fife, and landed at Invergourie. Befides the dung made on their farms, the farmers are often obliged to get an additional fupply from Dundee; and every lading of a cart and pair of horfes from thence, cofts them no lefs than 1 s. 6 d. exclufive of tolls and carriage. The beft improved land here rarely yields above 10 bolls of wheat or any other grain the acre. Inftances have indeed occurred of much higher returns than this, but they are too rare to be confidered as a ftandard by which to eftimate the produce in general. A confiderable part of the diftrict is enclofed with ftone fences, but few of the enclofures, however, remain long in grafs for pafture or grazing; thofe that are let for this purpofe are rouped annually, and bring from L. 2, 10 s. to L. 3 Sterling the acre.

The Scotch plough, with amendments, is in common ufe: At the fame time, from the late general fpeculation and improvements on this ufeful machine, it has become more than ever an object of attention both here and in the neighbourhood, and many farmers are at great pains to have their ploughs fafhioned after the moft approved models. It is the practice to employ two horfes in each plough, unlefs the occafion renders the addition of one or more neceffary. Two threfhing machines have been erected for fome time; they go by means of horfes, and are looked upon as ufeful both in refpect to profit and convenience. There are 5 corn-mills, a flour-mill, a fnuff-mill, and three mills for cleaning yarn. Thirlage and kain are ftill continued upon fome lands, but thefe feem the only
exactions

exactions of which the farmers and smaller tenants have to complain.

The number of draught-horses about 180, and of these not above a dozen or fifteen may be said to be kept for convenience, or for any purpose but that of husbandry. Very few horses are bred here or in the country around, and accordingly their price has advanced beyond all former expectation. Forty pounds Sterling is now considered as a very moderate price for a pair of ordinary cart-horses, and they are seldom to be had for less than fifty. Milch cows are very numerous, every family almost, whether with or without land in their possession, having one or more of them. No attention is paid, especially by the poorer sort of people, to their breed, and in general they are of a diminutive size. Their number may amount to 382. In Locheye and Milehouse alone there are about 117 for the use of the families in that quarter. But neither there, nor in one or two places more of this district, are the cows and horses maintained by the produce of the land in possession of their respective owners. A very considerable share of the provision necessary for them is purchased from the neighbouring farmers, who find it their interest often to answer demands of this sort, by exposing to sale in different lots, one or more fields of standing corn, grass, or turnip, as they can best spare of each. In this way it happens, that in some years a considerable quantity of oats and barley is brought from neighbouring parishes into this district, but this is nothing equivalent to the different kinds of grain, and of barley especially sold out of it. The yearly amount of what is thus disposed of, cannot be accurately ascertained ; it is, however, certain that, unless in years of extraordinary scarcity, this district will do far more than support itself. Besides, there are several portions of land now lying waste and neglected, which, if properly improved,

ved,

ved, would fully indemnify both the expenſe and trouble. There are a good number of calves reared, and ſome cattle alſo are fed for the market; but this practice is by no means univerſal. The market-town is Dundee, where there is a ready ſale for grain of every ſort, hay, milk, butter, cheeſe, poultry, &c. And to thoſe who have not the means of ſubſiſtence within themſelves, every article except potatoes is as high as in Dundee, where the expenſe of living has increaſed of late, with the induſtry and wealth of the inha-bitants. It is a pleaſure to ſay, that the principal farmers are in general accommodated with good houſes, but the dwellings of the ſmaller tenants, and indeed of the great bulk of the inhabitants, are as yet ill adapted either for health or comfort *.

Manufactures.—This diſtrict, from ſeveral portions of it being let in crofts or ſmall poſſeſſions, is highly favourable to the eſtabliſhment and growth of manufactures. Hence, in every hamlet within its bounds, as Liff, Bervie, Den-head, &c. the weaving of linen cloth has become the principal employment. But the quarter which is both the moſt populous, and contains the greateſt number of manu-facturers, is that ſtrip of land, which having on the ſouth the hill of Balgay, and forming with it a narrow valley, is com-prehended under the names of Locheye and Milehouſe. The peculiar

---

* They are kept however neat and clean, and this taſte may ſoon lead to ſubſtantial improvements. The common wages of a ploughman, from L. 8 to L. 10 a-year, either with his victuals in his maſter's houſe, or 2 pecks of oat-meal a-week, and a proportional quantity of milk for ſubſiſ-tence by himſelf. The wages of women-ſervants, L. 3, including *boun-ties* or preſents, which however are ſtipulated for. The hire of a day-labourer from 9 d. to 1 s. with his victuals; but for two years paſt, it has riſen beyond this, owing chiefly to the contract work done upon the new roads leading from Perthſhire through this county.

peculiar attractions of this fpot to manufacturers, befides its
being in the country, and at a convenient diftance, either for
carrying what they can fpare to market in Dundee, or for
bringing neceffaries from thence, are thefe : 1*ft*, The promife of a fixed refidence, almoft the whole land having
been fubdivided into fmaller feus and poffeffions, a family, according as they are able, may either purchafe or rent,
what will ferve for a commodious habitation. 2*d*, Every
web of cloth, as foon as it comes from the loom, may here
be difpofed of, without the trouble and expenfe of conveying it for fale to a diftance. The firft merchant weavers
were, a family of the name of Coock, who continue ftill in
the fame line, with much credit and advantage to themfelves, and to whofe induftry and example this diftrict is
principally indebted for its prefent flourifhing condition.
But 3*d*, What above every other advantage has tended to
enhance the value of this fpot to manufacturers, and without
which it might have remained ftill in its original unim-
proved ftate, is a fmall brook or ftream, that paffes from
Milehoufe weftward, through Locheye, and furnifhes a fupply of water for boiling and bleaching, as much as is neceffary of the cloth manufactured in the diftrict. Thefe
caufes combined, point out Locheye and Milehoufe as a
highly convenient ftation for manufacturers. The houfehold linen made in this diftrict is not worth mentioning,
and the number of Ofnaburghs is comparatively fmall.
The ftaple manufacture is coarfe linens, which are carried
to London, fome of them for confumpt in Britain, others
for exportation. They are named from their breadth,
as yard wides, 3 quarter wides, and wide thin linens, and
the price of each fort is regulated by the quality of yarn
of which it is made, according to the market. A very
fmall proportion of the yarn made ufe of, is fpun in this diftrict, though feveral women apply themfelves to it ; every

weaver

weaver being for the moſt part ſupplied with that article from Dundee. Some of the cloth manufactured is ſold by individuals at firſt hand, at Dundee and Inchture; but the quantity thus ſold does not amount to more than is pur-chaſed by the merchant weavers in this diſtrict, from neigh-bouring pariſhes, who, therefore, may be ſaid to deal to the extent of the whole cloth manufactured here. The mer-chant weavers are 5 in number, and are themſelves included in the liſt of operative manufacturers. All of them, one excepted, who buys to the greateſt extent, diſpoſe of their whole ſtock either in Dundee or Perth, or Cupar of An-gus, preferring a ſmaller gain at home, to the riſk of a greater in the hands of correſpondents at London. Almoſt half of their cloth is bleached before it is ſold, and of late they have adopted the method, of what is termed here *dry-bleaching*, which is nothing more than after boiling the cloth in water, mixed with a due quantity of pot-aſhes, to waſh the lees from it, and leave it to whiten on the ground by the action of the ſun and weather, without, as former-ly, ſprinkling water upon it. The cloth by this means is equally well bleached, and much labour as well as expenſe is ſaved. The following is a pretty accurate ſtatement of the webs manufactured in one year, and the prices at which they are commonly ſold by the manufacturers.

Webs.		Price.
3800 yard wides, and 3 quarters wides, at L. 2, 10 s. the web,		L. 9500
550 yard wides,	at L. 2, 12 s. -	1430
150 3 quarter wides,	at L. 3, - -	450
60 ditto,	at L. 4, - -	240
300 Oſnaburghs,	at L. 3, - -	900
4860		L. 12,520.

Of

Of the above webs, 2830 were bleached, and in that ftate being fit for fhirting and many important ufes, the profit at fecond hand is more confiderable than that on the *green* or *unbleached*. Confidering the number of weavers who are houfeholders, and that feveral among them keep 1 or 2 fervants, or more properly apprentices, it may perhaps be expected, that a third more cloth at leaft fhould be manu-factured in the year within this diftrict. In reply, this much may be obferved, that fome of thefe houfeholders are at an advanced period of life, that the greater part have more or lefs to do of rural labour on their fmall poffeffions, and that many quit their own employment entirely, and en-gage with the neighbouring farmers, in the time of harveft. It would tend greatly to promote and encourage manufac-tures here, were a ftamp-office eftablifhed as at Inchture and Meigle *.

Antiquities.—Under this head may be mentioned a tem-ple, called Druidicial, meafuring in circumference about 43 yards. A Roman camp, as defcribed by Maitland in his hiftory of Scotland, which, from its vicinity to the frith of Tay, he confiders as having been one of thofe which, ac-cording to Tacitus, *In vita Agric.* contained occafionally both the land and fea forces. There were obvious traces of this camp remaining a very few years ago, which the plough has fince entirely effaced. The fpot, however, is ftill diftinguifhed, being known by the name of *Catter Milley*, evidently a corruption of the words *quatuor mille*, meaning thereby to exprefs either the number of troops affembled in this fortrefs, or the diftance of the encampment

---

* The number of looms employed in this diftrict, amounts to 276; ap-prentices and fervants to 104.

ment from some other station.   Within the confines of this
district on the east, is a place named Pitalpie or Pit of Alpin, from its being the scene of that memorable engagement in the 9th century, between the Picts and Scots, in
which the latter were routed, and Alpin their king, with
many nobles, slain *.   Near to the present church, and immediately within Lord Gray's inclosures, are some remains
of the foundation of a castle, long known in the country by
the name of Hurly Haukin.   It is now impossible to judge
with any certainty of its original dimensions, but it has evidently been of considerable size and strength, and surrounded on all sides, except the north, by a pretty deep natural
fosse.   In digging about the remains, burnt ashes were found
and an iron spur, of the kind long ago worn.   It was built
by Alexander I. King of Scotland, and the history of it
tends to throw light on the ancient state of this district †.

                                                    Invergourie,

* The King's head, after the battle, being fastened to a pole, was
carried by the enemy to Abernethy, at that time the most considerable
Pictish town, to be exposed there to public view; but his body, according
to tradition, was buried at Pitalpie.   On the top of a little hill east of
Pitalpie, is still to be seen a large stone, called The King's Cross, having
a hole in the middle about a foot deep; as the Scots were encamped, it
is said, at no great distance from the Tay, the King may have fixed his
standard in this stone.   Not very remote from this is another little hill,
in which were discovered eight or ten graves, having the bottom, sides,
and top of flag-stones.   The head of each grave was due west.   The
bones mouldered away on being touched.

† Alexander, according to the custom in those days, having a donation made him at his baptism, by the Earl of Gourie, his godfather, of
the lands of Liff and Invergourie, no sooner succeeded to the throne, than
he began to erect this palace, as Fordoun calls it.   He was not however
long permitted to remain in it without being disturbed.   Some of his fol-
lowers or attendants from Mearns and Murrayshire, having joined in a
conspiracy to seize on his person, the plot was discovered, in the moment
                                                              they

Invergourie, as a place of Chriſtian worſhip, is of remote antiquity, and perhaps the moſt ancient on this ſide the Tay. The firſt church was built by Boniface *, a legate or miſſionary, on his landing there with ſome attendants from Rome, during the 7th century. The ſame perſon pro- ceeding into the interior parts of Angus, founded other churches. The walls of the church of Invergourie, uſed in later times, are ſtill very entire ; but they indicate no ſupe- rior antiquity or workmanſhip, and are probably thoſe of a fabric leſs ancient than the firſt. The church-yard is on an eminence of a ſingular ſhape, which, on one ſide, is often waſhed by the Tay ; and ſome people, from the variety of mould dug up, have conjectured, that the whole or greater part of this eminence may have been compoſed of forced earth. We ſhall finiſh this article, with an ac- count of a ſubterraneous building diſcovered a few years ago near Lundie Houſe, which, it is believed, will be ac- ceptable

they were endeavouring to force the doors of the palace in the night, and the King, aſſiſted by his chamberlain Alexander Carron, the ſon of that Carron whom Malcolm III. had diſtinguiſhed by the ſurname of Serim- geour, and preferred to the office of carrying the royal ſtandard, happily effected his eſcape. Embarking then at Invergourie, he directed his courſe to the ſouthern parts of the kingdom, where he raiſed a great force in order to repel and puniſh this inſurrection. But before proceeding in his expedition, he founded, as a tribute of gratitude to God for the late deliverance and protection he had experienced, the church of the monaſtery of Scoon, and made over to that church *in dotem et glebam*, the Lands of Liff and Invergourie formerly aſſigned to him as a preſent by the Earl of Gourie. Vide Fordoun's Sco. Chron. alſo Buchan. Hiſt.

* Vide Boeth. Hiſt. alſo Archbiſhop Spottiſwood, and Forbes on Tithes. The two latter agree in one account, which is evidently copied from Boece, but with very great inaccuracy. They make Boniface to have landed at the mouth of a ſmall river, dividing Angus from Mearns, A. D 697. ; whereas Boece points clearly at Invergourie as the landing place, and mentions the fact as having happened about A. D. 620.

ceptable to many readers. This building was difcovered
in a field that had long been under culture, and often had
refifted the plough, in paffing along the fpot under which
it refted. In digging this fpot, to remove the ftones which
occafioned fuch interruption, they were found in general
to be of a furprifing breadth ; but at the fame time, either
violently rent afunder, or difturbed in their pofition by
the frequent intercourfe and collifion of the plough. And
it appeared on their removal, that thefe ftones had been in-
duftrioufly brought hither, and ferved to cover certain artificial receffes or buildings, which now difcovered themfelves. Among thefe different buildings, which are to be
confidered as compartments of one and the fame fabric, lay
one of them at a fmall diftance from the others, but connected with each by a paffage or communication about two
or two and a half feet wide ; and it was diftinguifhed alfo
by its fuperior fize and dimenfions. This principal com-
partment was about 6 feet in breadth, 12 in length, and 5
in height ; the walls and floor were of ftone. It extended
in the direction nearly from eaft to weft, and befides the
paffages already mentioned, leading from it to the other
compartments of the building, was furnifhed with one towards the fouth, peculiar to itfelf, and fuppofed to have
been the main entrance. The whole of this ftructure was
extremely rude. Many of the ftones that compofed it, inftead of being laid flat, or in fuch a way as accords with
fkill in the art of building, were placed endwife in the
walls. There were no arches, though the feveral compartments required them ; the upper courfe on the walls on
each fide was of large ftones, with their ends projected in-
wardly, and the opening or vacuity between covered all
the way, with others of a correfponding breadth. At the
fame time, confidering that no mark of any tool or inftrument was to be feen, and that no mortar of any kind had

been

been ufed, the walls were certainly put together with much
unity and compactnefs. The building ftood on the fhel-
ving fide of a rock, but the different compartments were
placed fo irregularly with refpect to one another, and with
fo little appearance of regard to order or method, unlefs in
fo far as that each fhould communicate with the larger
and principal one, that nothing could be inferred from
their relative fituation to one another. On the compartments being firft opened, all of them were filled with a
rich black mould, which, whether it had been purpofely
depofited there, or in the courfe of generations paft, had
infinuated itfelf from the furface above, through the cover-
ftones not being entire, and having been difturbed by the
plough, cannot with certainty be determined. But upon
removing this earth, were obferved the remains of fome
burnt matter, and feveral fragments of bones, fo fmall as
rendered it impoffible to afcertain whether they belonged
to the human body or not; likewife were found fome
querns or hand-mills, about 14 inches diameter, which, as
they appeared to be much worn, had no doubt been ufed
for grinding corn of fome kind, although they had been
made with fo little dexterity, that it is not eafy to conceive
how they could have anfwered that purpofe. In the centre of fome of thefe querns was faftened a fmall bit of iron *
fhowing the handle to have been of that metal. Before this
building was clofed up, it was minutely furveyed by the
late Sir David Dalrymple, Lord Hailes †.

Ecclefiaftical

---

* Cæfar Comment. lib. 5. c. 12. Utuntur (Britanni) aut ære, aut ta-
leis, ferreis ad certum pondus examinatis, pro nummo. Nafcitur ibi
plumbum album in Mediterraneis regionibus, in maritimis ferrum.

† Subterraneous buildings of the fame kind are reported to have been
accidentally fallen upon in this neighbourhood, in particular, in the parifhes of Aughterhoufe, Foulis, and Tealing. And it is the vulgar opinion, and by no means improbable, that there are others beneath a particu-

Ecclefiaftical State.—During the long and intricate procefs about the right of patronage to Bervie, previous to
the admiffion of the incumbent May 1785, a propofal was
fet on foot to build a Seceding meeting-houfe in this diftrict.
And after incredible pains beftowed in gaining profelytes,
and raifing contributions, this propofal was at length carried into execution. A place of worfhip and dwelling-
houfe were erected, and foon a paftor was called. But not
long after his fettlement, fome proceedings of his own clergy againft him not meeting the general fatisfaction and
opinion of the people, they fplit into two parties, the one for
fupporting the clergy's fentence, the other the right of the
minifter. Some points in queftion by the latter, were
long and zealoufly contended for at law, and the conteft fubfifted with no fmall prejudice to the peace and morals of
many concerned, till lately, that a compromife took place,
on the minifter refolving to withdraw from his charge. A
fucceffor to him is not appointed; and in this fituation of
things, the number of that communion in the diftrict cannot prefently be afcertained. According to the beft advice,
they never exceeded 120, and of thefe a few families have
been always Seceders. They now fall fhort of this a-
mount, as fome of them, in confequence of the late difference, have returned to the Church. There are three or
four families of the clafs of Independents, and but a few
individuals of any other fect or perfuafion. The inhabitants at Milehoufe frequent divine worfhip, efpecially in
the winter feafon, at Dundee, but all attend their own
church at the miniftration of the Sacrament.

Church,

lar fpot in this diftrict which yet remain to be explored. When time or
accident fhall lay thefe open, it is to be hoped, that more light will be
afforded the antiquary, for afcertaining the origin and caufe of thefe fingular and hitherto neglected monuments of human workmanfhip and
defign.

Church, Manſe, Stipend, School, Poor, &c.— The preſent church-fabric, except the aiſle, which in every view ought either to have been raiſed higher or rebuilt, was erected in 1774, to accommodate the inhabitants, and reſts nearly on the foundation of the former building. Either the foundations muſt have given way, or the maſon-work been ſlightly executed, as ſome rents already appear in the walls. When the bulk of the inhabitants reſided in the weſt part of the diſtrict, the ſituation of the church was then more convenient. The manſe, which is placed a little way from the church, is alſo modern, and was built about the time when theſe pariſhes were united in 1759–1760. It is a handſome building, but the roof is much decayed, and the inſide work very ſuperſicial, and by no means correſponding with the outſide appearance. It ſtands about 297 feet above the high water mark at Invergourie, and commands a varied and delightful proſpect, comprehending the Tay in its courſe for ſeveral miles, with a well clothed, fertile tract of country on the one ſide of it, and the ſteepy boundary of Fife on the other. The ſtipend is 7 chalders victual, and money about L. 53 Sterling, including L. 8, 14 s. which is no part of the teinds of this diſtrict, but of a grant conjointly to two other miniſters and the miniſter of Bervie. The glebe and garden contain about 10 acres. Heritors, comprehending thoſe of Logie pariſh, 9. The whole valued rent L. 6680 Scots. —The average number of ſcholars at the parochial ſchool does not exceed 35. The ſituation is centrical enough with reſpect to the whole diſtrict, but yet not very commodious for one or two places, which contain by far, comparatively, the greater number of the inhabitants. Beſides, the acceſs to ſchool from the weſt, is in a great meaſure ſhut up, and in winter the roads in every other direction are to children almoſt impaſſable. To theſe cauſes, the

the firſt of which it were difficult to remedy, are chiefly to
be aſcribed the low ſtate of the parochial ſchool, and the
introduction of 5 private ones, for the moſt part indifferently taught. At the former, the quarterly payments are,
for Engliſh, 1 s. 6 d.; for writing, 2 s.; for arithmetic, 2 s.
6 d. The ſalary allowed the ſchoolmaſter is L. 7 : 1 : 10
money, and 2 bolls 14 pecks oat-meal; as ſeſſion-clerk,
he receives L. 1 : 15 : 6, and about L. 3 : 1 : 6 more
for baptiſms and marriages. The whole emoluments are
too inconſiderable for a teacher of any merit and capacity.
—With reſpect to the poor, there has never been any aſ-
ſeſſment for their maintenance. The funds for their relief
ariſe from the dues of mortcloths, proclamation of marriages, rents of a few ſeats in the church, money at intereſt, but
chiefly from the collections at the church door. Beſides the
number now on the roll, amounting to 12, there are ſeveral
families and individuals which require occaſional ſupply.

Miſcellaneous Obſervations.—The principal plantations are
on the eſtates of Lord Gray and Colonel Duncan of Lundie. Thoſe ſurrounding the houſe of Gray, are reckoned
highly beautiful, and certainly do honour to the taſte of
that accompliſhed nobleman, John Lord Gray, by whom
they were laid out. The diſtrict abounds with what is
here called freeſtone, but in ſtrata ; the prevailing colour
is grey, inclining to blue. Some grey ſlate has been
found, but very little whinſtone. A proper pier at Invergourie would be of ſingular advantage for the importation
of lime, and coal which is the principal fuel in this quarter.

PARISH of GLENTRATHEN, or LINTRATHEN,

(County of Forfar, Synod of Angus and Mearns, Presbytery of Meigle.)

By a Friend *to* Statistical Inquiries.

Extent, Surface, Soil, &c.

MANY diſtricts in Scotland afford little information or entertainment to a Statiſtical inquirer. Among theſe may be ranked the pariſh of Glentrathen, or Lintrathen. It is 8 miles from N. to S. and 4 from W. to E. Elevated on the ſkirts of the Grampian mountains, from 500 to 1000 feet above Strathmore, this diſtrict has a bleak and barren aſpect. The ſurface is uneven, conſiſting of hills, vallies, and mountains. Near the ſouthern boundary there is a bank of tolerably fertile land, about a mile in length and half a mile in breadth, fronting the S. and gently ſloping to the rivers Melgam and Ila. A mile northward of the church, in a deep valley, there are ſome well cultivated and fruitful fields. But the greater part of what is called arable land, is a thin and mooriſh ſoil; which

yields

yields corn of a very inferior quality. Several vallies, fit only for pasturage, extend northward among the hills, which are covered with short heath, and buried in snow during winter. There are few trees of any age or growth in this part of the country.

Rivers.—The Melgam, a confiderable stream, has its rise beyond the N. W. boundary of the parish, runs S. E. along the base of a mountain, forms a small cataract in the village of Glentrathen, and after a circuitous course, in a rocky channel, falls into the Ila below the walls of Airly Castle. The Carrity, less than the preceding, defcends from the northern part of the parish, and bathes the foot of Catlaw in its progress eastward to the South Efk.

State of the People, &c.—In this fequestered district, there is no town, no village of note, no feat, no mines, nor minerals, no natural curiosities, few manufactures, and little trade; no innkeeper, no baker, no writer, no furgeon, no butcher, no apothecary, and one Seceder only. Hamlets, coarsely built of stone and earth, and covered with thatch, thinly fcattered in the vallies, or on the fouthern declivities of the hills; and a mean village compofed of defpicable huts, crowded together on the rocky bank of the Melgam, almost oppofite to the church, indicate the poverty of the inhabitants, who feem to be in a rude state of fociety.

Antiquities, Lakes, &c.—About ¼ mile N. N. E. of the church, there is an artificial eminence, whofe fummit commands an extensive profpect. On this fpot a gibbet was erected for those unfortunate perfons, whom the fervile court of a defpotick baron had condemned to death. Vestiges of the hangman's habitation appear at the foot of the tumulus, and the name of a neighbouring plot of land per-

petuates

petuates the memory of this infamous practice. To the weſtward of the village, about a quarter of a mile, lies a circular lake, upwards of one mile in diameter, and in ſome places of conſiderable depth. It is fed by rills from the ſurrounding heights, and ſends forth a ſmall ſtream to augment the Melgam. Pike, perch, and trout are found there in abundance. The border of this lake is not garniſhed with a ſingle tree, ſhrub, or bulruſh. Half a mile N. W. on an elevated heathy tract, are many tumuli, or cairns. There, perhaps, a battle was fought by ſome contending chiefs, but tradition is ſilent. Near the W. end of the lake, there are remains of an extenſive encloſure, ſaid to have been a deer park belonging to Sir Allan Dorret of that ilk. The ruins of this gentleman's reſidence may be traced on the S. W. declivity of the hill of Formal, near the bank of the Ila *.

Population, Agriculture, &c.—A territory ſo unpropitious cannot be well inhabited. The population of this pariſh has not been recently aſcertained. The report to Dr Webſter, 50 years ago, was 1165 ſouls. From the regiſter of baptiſms and burials, the number of inhabitants
at

* Some time before the Reformation, he was proprietor of the greater part of the pariſhes of Glentrathen and Kingoldrum. The latter he bequeathed to the Abbey of Aberbrothick; and the former he gave to his daughter, who married to one of the family of Airly. The patronage and teinds of the chapel which he built or repaired in Glentrathen, were transferred to the prior and convent of Inchmahomo. This priory, and others, were granted by James VI. to John then Earl of Mar, and erected into a temporal Lordſhip, called the Lordſhip and Barony of Cardroſs, in favour of the ſaid Earl and his aſſignees. That family becoming bankrupt, it was judicially ſold by the Court of Seſſion, A. D. 1746, and purchaſed by Mr John Erſkine of Carnock, Profeſſor of Law. The teinds and patronage of this pariſh were purchaſed from Mr Erſkine by the family of Airly, A. D. 1770.

at prefent may be computed at nearly 900. Of thefe about 50 are denominated farmers, who occupy certain proportions of land, out of which they tear a fcanty fubfiftence. Few improvements have been made there in agriculture. The old fyftem prevails. Some plots of turnip, flax, and fown grafs appear; but oats and barley are the principal productions of the ill cultivated foil. Of thefe a fufficient quantity is raifed to fupply the neceffities of the natives; but there is no proper encouragement to induftry. However facred the promife of a feudal lord may be held, little exertion will be made, or can be expected, where no leafes are granted, and where heavy fervitudes are impofed; while a tenant fubfifts at the pleafure of the proprietor, and is bound to perform twelve carriages to the diftance of 20 miles, even in feed-time or harveft, he will not difplay that vigour and enterprize, by which his brethren in other parts of the country have arrived at eafe and opulence. This is a difgraceful remain of a fyftem humiliating to man, and hoftile to all improvement; a fyftem which, about 50 years ago, prevailed in all its rigour throughout the northern part of Scotland, but which every enlightened landlord, defirous of the profperity of his country, and of his own intereft, has now abandoned. There are no enclofures nor plantations of trees, and fcarcely one fifth of the parifh is arable. The whole, perhaps, ought to be converted into grafs farms, the coldnefs of the climate, and poverty of the foil, being inimical to cultivation. No marl has been found in this parifh; and fuel for the purpofe of burning lime cannot be obtained. With difficulty the inhabitants procure peats, turf, and heath for domeftick ufe. Thefe are dug out of Newton mofs, or torn from the furface of the mountains; and the preparing and carrying home of that fuel confumes a great part of fummer.—There is no trade nor manufacture in this corner, but fuch as is neceffary to the accommodation of the natives, and their wants are few.

few. Deſtitute of the elegancies, and moſt of the conveniencies of life, their deſires are limited. They enjoy little,
and with that little are contented. Attached to their naked
ſoil, they are temperate and ſober.

Heritors.—The number of heritors is five, none of whom
reſides in the pariſh. The valued rent of the moſt conſiderable proprietor is L. 1074 Scots ; of the real rent I have
not been informed.

Church, Stipend, School, Poor.—The church is an old,
dark, diſproportioned fabrick, built at two different periods.
The manſe is a wretched hovel, covered with thatch. The
abject ſtate of this habitation is not owing to any reluctance
in the heritors to grant repairs, but to another cauſe, which
has now ceaſed to operate. The ſtipend is L. 400 Scots,
and 40 bolls victual. The late incumbent, far advanced in
life when promoted to this charge, officiated 20, and his
two immediate predeceſſors 107 years. Walter Ogilvy,
Eſq; of Clova, is patron.—The parochial ſchoolmaſter has a
ſalary of ſix or ſeven bolls oats, collected from the tenants,
and ſome trifling fees. On this miſerable allowance he has
contrived to ſupport a family upwards of ſixty years. The
hut in which he reſides is hardly fit to accommodate the
meaneſt beggar.—The number of poor on the ſeſſion-roll is
from 5 to 7. The funds allotted to their relief are the rent
of a gallery in the church, the intereſt of a ſmall capital,
the mortcloth money, and a weekly collection of 10 d. or
1 s. The prices of labour and proviſions are the ſame as
in the neighbouring pariſhes of Kingoldrum and Gleniſla.

Language.—The names of the pariſh, and many places
in it, ſeem to be partly Gaelic and partly Anglo-Saxon ;
but the language ſpoken by the inhabitants is Engliſh, or a
dialect of it peculiar to North Britain.

STATISTICAL ACCOUNT OF LENTHRATHEN.

By the Rev. Alex. Thomson, Minister.

THE late minister, though a man of sense and learning, yet labouring under the infirmities of old age, when statistical inquiries were set on foot, did not undertake writing the account of this parish. An anonymous account, however, was soon published; but not being so complete as could be wished; which indeed could not be expected from a person, who was probably a stranger to the district; it therefore occurred to the present incumbent, after receiving Sir John Sinclair's last letter, requesting some additional information on the same subject, that this might be a proper opportunity of writing a brief Statistical Account of the parish, comprehending as much of the information desired as can be obtained, or as circumstances will admit.

Extent,

Extent, Surface, Soil, &c.

The parish extends from north to south, about ten miles; and from east to west, between five and six; not exceeding the distance of four miles from the most fertile and improved part of Strathmore. It may be divided into two districts, the northern and the southern. The northern, or the upper part, consisting chiefly of hills and vallies; the former, of no considerable height, produces, in its present state, better crops of grass than corn, on account chiefly of the distance from manure. But that the land is by no means of an inferior quality clearly appears from the exertions of some individuals, and particularly of one tenant, who, happening to be in better circumstances than ordinary, by which he has been enabled to do justice to his ground, has had, for some years past, such returns, as may vie with the productions of some of the most fertile, and best improved soil in Strathmore. In the lower district, extending from the southern extremity, about three miles north, the ground is, in general, very fertile, and produces excellent crops of oats, barley and turnip, being advantageously situated within four miles of marle, a very useful manure in this country. This part of the parish has a fine exposure, lies in the form of an oblong, gently declining to the south.

Rivers.—The river Isla bounds the parish on the west. This beautiful stream, after running through Glenisla, the neighbouring parish to the north, falls, upon touching this parish, into a deep rocky channel; and after five miles of a circular course, it leaves the parish at the castle of Airly, a romantic seat of the Earl of Airly, and runs nearly in a south direction, down to the fertile fields of Strathmore. It
may

may not be improper to mention a beautiful cafcade, called the Reeky-Lin, about two miles weft from Airly Caftle, where the Ifla falls, with impetuofity and noife, from a rock apparently fixty feet high, into a whirl-pool ; the appearance of which, efpecially when the water is in flood, is fo grand, that many lovers of natural curiofities have come from a confiderable diftance to behold it. A little farther down is what is called the Slug of Achranny, where the banks on each fide are remarkably high and fteep, and the water confined between two rocks very near each other, tumbles down a precipice, exhibiting a tremendous appearance. The other river, Melgum, is much lefs than the former, though it is a very pretty ftream, abounding with excellent trout of a large fize, that can be eafily catched with the fly in the angling feafon. The river runs nearly through the middle of the parifh and joins the Ifla at the Caftle of Airly. About two miles up from this junction, it tumbles over four rocky precipices from fifteen to thirty feet high, called the Loups of Kenny, the banks on each fide being uncommonly fteep. In high water efpecially, the fpectator is entertained with an appearance peculiarly grand and majeftic. About half a mile farther down, the river moves for a fhort way (till it falls into the Ifla) in a moft pleafant ferpentine den covered on each fide with natural wood, which delights the eye of every perfon who can relifh the beauties of nature. And this leads me to obferve, that as this parifh in general is fertile and improveable, and wafhed with the two above mentioned rivers, it wants only wood to make it one of the moft pleafant and beautiful places in this or any other northern county. Some clumps, however, of afhes of confiderable fize appear about moft of the farm fteadings, which afford fome fhelter and embellifhment. One farm particularly, called Kinnaird, fcarcely half a mile eaftward from the

church

church and a farm of very good foil, is adorned with one
hundred afh trees, fome of confiderable age;——and about
half a mile farther eaft there is another farm named Shan-
nally, originally the feat of a gentleman formerly one of the
heritors of the parifh, where there is ftill to be feen a good
number of very fine old trees, of different kinds, that are
very confpicuous at a diftance, and attract the particular
notice of any perfon who comes to take a view of the
country.

State of the People, Buildings, &c.——The inhabitants are,
in general, difcreet, honeft and inoffenfive ; and fome of the
farmers are well refpected. Their drefs is plain ; and on
Sundays they are always clean and neat ; and the writer of
this account has the fatisfaction to declare, that they are
very regular in their attendance on public worfhip; and
have every appearance of unaffected devotion. Here, no
religious difputes or controverfies prevail, as the people are
all, with the exception of two or three, of the eftablifhed
church ; and as they are fo fenfible to believe, that religion
confifts not fo much in entertaining this or that opinion, as
in decency and propriety of conduct. It is furely fome
proof of their good behaviour, that there has been no criminal trial from the parifh, nor any feditious mob in it from
time immemorial. In this and in the neighbouring parifhes, inoculation has been adopted, efpecially among fome
of the moft refpectable families. It is however a pity, that
a confiderable number of the country people are ftill pre-
judiced, through ignorance and miftaken ideas, againft this
noble invention, though it is to be hoped their prejudices
will be gradually removed. With regard to building, the
houfes are generally one ftory of mafon work covered with
thatch. Of late fome have been built of two ftories and
flated

flated. The farmers are, upon the whole, very comfortably lodged, having, even in houfes of the fmalleft fize, one fnug neat apartment with a bofom chimney, always kept clean and decent, in which they entertain their neighbours who occafionally vifit them. If they are ftrangers to the luxuries and refinements of fome other people in the fame line, and which to a fuperficial obferver may indicate greater profperity, it may be confidently affirmed that they are ftrangers to many of their vices, and that they enjoy a greater degree of comfort and happinefs.

Population, Trades People, Agriculture, and Stock.——The number of fouls may be computed at nine hundred and twenty. Any decreafe fince Dr Webfter's report may be owing to fome alterations of farms which have taken place within thefe forty years, and to the diminution of cottagers, and their not being employed by the farmers fo much as formerly.

Abstract of baptisms and marriages for the last ten years.

Years.	Baptifms.	Marriages.	Years.	Baptifms.	Marriages.
1788	21	5	1793	26	7
1789	29	4	1794	22	9
1790	24	5	1795	22	6
1791	23	8	1796	24	10
1792	28	10	1797	18	8

No regifter of burials has been kept for fix years paft.—— In this parifh refide at prefent five fquare wrights, three blackfmiths, one wheelwright, one fhoemaker, three tailors, twenty weavers, one brewer, and one mafon. With regard to Agriculture, I find in the northern divifion, where the tenants have a great dependence on the fale of cattle and fheep, the poffeffions are fmall, renting from four to

twelve

twelve pounds fterling. Here, from the diftance of manure, &c. improvements are but in their infancy. In the
fouth and more improved part, there are two tenants, each
of which poffeffes upward of 150 acres arable, befides pafture to a very confiderable extent. About twelve rent from
50 to 100 acres arable. On fome of the fmall farms, the
tenants are rather backward in adopting the new fyftem :
but others even of that defcription are very attentive and
induftrious, there being no lefs than 600 acres in the parifh
in proper culture, with fufficient quantity of fown grafs,
fallow and turnip, and the rotation of crops is not altogether regular ; there may be nearly about one half in corn
crop, and the other half in fown grafs and fallow. Very
few farms here being meafured, the number of arable acres
is not known.

There are five heritors in the parifh, the Earl of Airly,
Charles Lyell, Efq. of Kinnordy, John Smyth, Efq. of Bal-
harry, James Ogilvy, Efq. of Iflabank, and John Milne,
farmer of Blackdykes. Of thefe, Lord Airly is by far the
moft confiderable proprietor, having more than two-thirds
of the parifh. It has been particularly remarked, that this
Nobleman has granted but very few leafes to his tenants,
and this fcheme has been confidered as hoftile to improvement. It does not become a clergyman to enter into con-
troverfy, but it is an undoubted fact that the tenants of the
noble family of Airly, both here and in other parifhes, have
always been remarkable for eafe and opulence. Few of the
old refidenters or their defcendents have ever been removed,
a confidence between the landlords and tenants having prevailed time immemorial. The farmers all declare their fatisfaction to continue at the prefent rent, fome of their poffeffions being very low rated, and none above the value ;
and if the proprietor and tenant have agreed upon a certain

number

number of carriages to be paid as part of the rent, it does not appear to be confiderable. I have been certainly informed, that there was a time, when the whole carriages on the eftate of Airly were offered to be commuted at a moderate converfion, but to this the tenants would not agree. A-mong the few leafes granted to tenants in the parifh, fome are very low rented, and without any carriages. But thofe who have no regular leafes, have been in ufe to poffefs on agreement for a period of between fourteen and nineteen years; and as thefe agreements are never broke through, the tenants confider themfelves as in perfect fecurity, and they live fatisfied and happy. May this amity long con-tinue. On this head, I think it rather the bufinefs of a clergyman to preach the gofpel of peace to his hearers, than to make any attempts to raife difcord between his parifhion-ers and their mafter where none prevailed before. But, if the mode of letting farms that has, for fome time, been adopted in this parifh, fhould be confidered as in any de-gree difcouraging, I am certainly informed, that leafes are to be granted to fuch tenants as have no title of poffeffion, and who may chufe to have them. It is undoubtedly no fmall mark of encouragement and fatisfaction, as well as of induftry, that fome of the greater farmers have inclofed very confiderable parcels of ground; and within thefe few years, have cultivated from wafte land covered with heath and whins, forty, fixty or more acres, which they have dif-covered to be by no means of inferior quality, and which have produced very good crops of corn and barley.

With regard to the amount of live ftock and their value, I am informed, there are about 200 horfes, worth, at an average, from eight to twelve pounds fterling, nine hundred cattle, worth at an average, when about three years old, from five to feven pounds fterling; and near to 200 fheep,

worth

worth from ten to eighteen shilllings. How much animal food may be consumed in the parish I am uncertain; but not less than one thousand pounds worth of live stock are sold out of it annually. In this parish there are four corn mills, one waulk mill, and a lint mill. In the latter, not less than five hundred stone of lint are dressed yearly, which is raised mostly in the parish. Formerly there was a sufficient quantity of moss, and though it is now a good deal exhausted, yet the most of the parishioners are well enough served with fuel; and they are certainly not in a worse situation in this respect, than many neighbouring parishes. I cannot ascertain the real rent exactly: but it is computed at an average, from nine to ten shillings per acre, though some of the ground is let at twenty shillings.

Church, Stipend, School, Poor.——The church is old and rather small for the parish: but it is proposed to enlarge it or to build a new one. There was a new manse built about three years ago, consisting of six rooms, a kitchen, milkhouse and cellar, with other conveniences; so that the clergyman is as decently and comfortably lodged as any in his station can reasonably expect. The stipend was, since the year 1720, not more than 400l. Scots, with two chalders and a half of victual; but an augmentation was obtained in 1796, and it is now three hundred and thirty-six pounds Scots, and thirteen bolls of victual; so that at an average, the living will amount to upwards of one hundred pounds sterling, with a glebe of more than the legal size, of excellent soil, and about three acres more for which the Minister, for time immemorial, has paid no more than twenty-two shillings sterling, little more than seven shillings per acre. By the goodness of the family of Airly the present incumbent pays no more. He has been nearly five years settled. The Hon.
Walter

Walter Ogilvy of Clova, is patron. There is a very sufficient school-house built of mason work and slated, but not
yet quite finished within. Both master and scholars will be
perfectly well accomodated. The number of scholars may
be reckoned from 16 to 20 in summer, and from 40 to 60
in winter. As to the school salary, which is only eight bolls
of corn; it may be mentioned, that there was lately a school
master, who resided in that capacity about sixty years in the
parish; and that no augmentation to the salary took place,
might be owing to his not demanding it; and that the
tenants from long acquaintance, and from a regard for the
man, gave him yearly, perhaps, double the quantity of oats
to which he was legally entitled. The number of poor on
the session roll is from five to seven. The funds are about
120l. sterling; the interest of which, with the rent of a gallery in the church, and from four to five shillings of weekly collection, with the mort-cloth money, is sufficient to support the few that are really indigent.

Lakes, Antiquities.——About a quarter of a mile west from
the parish, there is a lake, commonly called the Loch of
Lintrathen, surrounded by rising grounds, excepting on the
east. There are several lakes in this county of Angus; but
this is universally allowed to be incomparably the finest. It
is nearly circular, about one mile from east to west, and
three in circumference. It is believed to be fed mostly from
springs, as the few very small rills from the surrounding
heights, would be insufficient for that purpose. The water
is transparent. In some places the depth is immense——but
where it could be done, attempts have been made to discover marle, which, however, have not yet been found successful. Could this manure be found in the loch, to drain it
might be practicable. It abounds in pike, perch, trout and

eel,

eel, all of exquisite quality. The trout, of a large size, taste very much like those of Loch Leven. It is very remarkable, that, in this lake, the trout have not been known to take the fly, except in a very few instances. About half a mile north west from the Manse are to be seen several cairns, perhaps memorials of some engagement, but there is no tradition ; and on a rising ground, not far from this, there is a stone of about fourteen feet high, and four in diameter. It stands perpendicular : and near it are other two of about the same size lying on the ground. But as there is no inscription upon any of them ; and as tradition is silent, I can say nothing about them. Near the west end of the lake there was an extensive inclosure, and there are still some remains of it, which, tradition says, was a deer park belonging to Sir Allan Durward of that ilk. On the south-west declivity of the hill of Formal, near the river Isla, may be seen the ruins of this gentleman's house.

PARISH of LOCHLEE,

(COUNTY OF ANGUS.)

By the Rev. Mr JOHN PIRIE.

Name, Situation, and Extent.

LOCHLEE is evidently derived from a loch situated in a deep bottom, almost surrounded with steep and high hills; at the east end of which, the parish church stands.—The parish is situated in the north corner of Forfarshire, in the presbytery of Brechin, and Synod of Angus and Mearns. It is surrounded with high hills, part of the Grampians, a narrow opening at the east end excepted, through which the river North Esk passes to the low country; and it is nearly intersected in two or three places by hills. It is about 12 miles long from E. to W. and 6 miles broad from N. to S. if regard is had to its pasture grounds; and there are about 8 miles betwixt the most distant dwelling houses from E. to W. and 4 from N. to S.; it is nearly of the same breadth from end to end.

Surface

Surface and Soil.—The hills are for the moſt part ſteep, rocky on the ſides, and covered with heath. There is nothing in the pariſh deſerving the name of meadow ground, even the valleys being covered with heath, the grounds under tillage excepted, and a few ſpots of inconſiderable extent, producing buſhes, ſpratt and bent, intermixed with other coarſe graſs. The ſoil under culture, is thin and light, generally on a bottom of gravel, and in many places full of ſtones. The extent of the arable land is very inconſiderable, when compared with that of the whole pariſh, there being only a few ſmall ſtripes under tillage, along the different branches of the river ; and it does not appear practicable much to increaſe the quantity.

Productions.—The amount of grain produced, is very inconſiderable, and, at an average, does not ſupport the inhabitants. This, in a great meaſure, is occaſioned by an unfavourable climate. The ground being locked up with froſt, or covered with ſnow, during the winter and great part of the ſpring ſeaſon, it is commonly the 1ſt or 2d of April, before the tillage for the enſuing crop commences, a few farms in the eaſt end of the pariſh excepted. The ſeed time being late, and generally very cold, the crop is oftentimes checked in the following September, by froſt and unſeaſonable weather, before it has had time to come to maturity. The bear, if it eſcapes the September froſt, is for the moſt part well filled ; but the corn is often very unproductive, it being frequently as late as the middle of November before the harveſt is concluded. In 1789, a great part of the grain remained in the fields, till the ſecond week of December. Potatoes and turnips have lately been introduced, and if the climate would permit, theſe uſeful roots would thrive well.

Climate

Climate and Difeafes.——The climate varies in different parts of the parifh. Although much colder than in the low country, yet, in the eaft end of the parifh, it is more temperate and warmer than in the weft end, where the winter fnow frequently lies upon the hills, until the end of May, and fometimes the middle of June. The air is reckoned healthy ; the inhabitants are not fubjeƈt to fevers of any kind, nor is there any other difeafe peculiar to the place. The ague never makes its appearance in any form, within the bounds of the parifh, although that difeafe is common, in the adjoining parifhes of Fettercairn and Edzell. In May 1782, after an exceeding cold and wet fpring, the wind blowing generally from N. E. a fever made its appearance in the parifh, which, in the fpace of 6 weeks, cut off 35 perfons. It was attended with fymptoms fimilar to what accompanies an inflammation of the Pleura : The perfons affeƈted had their fpittle mixed with blood, within a few hours after the fever feized them ; they felt a pain at or below their left pap ; and died upon the 5th or 6th day. The pain, however, did not affeƈt their breathing fo much ; nor did it feel fo acute as is commonly the cafe in a pleuritic fever. The greater part of thofe who died, were 30 years of age and upwards ; they were all above 18. Two only recovered of all that were feized. It is not remembered that a fever, fimilar to the above, has happened in the parifh.

Population.——From an account taken in 1723, when Lochlee was disjoined from Lethnot, there appears then to have been, 400 examinable perfons in the parifh ; in 1766, the number of fouls in it amounted to 600 ; at prefent (1792) there are 178 men, 237 women, and 193 children below 12 years of age, making in all 608 fouls. Although, from the above ftatement, it might be concluded, that

that the population has varied little or nothing ſince **1723**; yet it appears, in faɕ, to have been a little on the increaſe, at leaſt ſince **1766**. The natives had formerly a ſtrong attachment to the place, and ſeldom left the pariſh. Although the ſame attachment ſtill continues, yet the price of labour in the low country has advanced ſo conſiderably, within the laſt 20 years, as to induce ſeveral of the young men to leave the pariſh ; a circumſtance, which will account for the great difference, betwixt the number of men and women at preſent reſiding in it. The return to Dr Webſter, in **1755**, was 686 ſouls.

Births, Marriages and Deaths in the Pariſh ſince October **1**. **1783**.

Years.	*Births.*	*Marriages.*	*Deaths.*
Oɕt. 1. 1784	17	7	13
1785	17	6	12
1786	13	8	13
1787	14	6	11
1788	15	1	13
1789	20	6	9
1790	13	5	3
1791	12	2	8
1792	10	4	13

Poor.——The number of poor upon the pariſh roll, does not often amount to 12. The intereſt of a ſmall fund, together with the weekly collecɕtions, amounting together to about L. 6 Sterling yearly, is divided among them ; and if at any time, one or more are bed-rid, it is cuſtomary to hang up a bag in the mill for them, into which the tenants put a handful of meal, when they grind their corn. There are no travelling beggars, belonging to the pariſh, and very few paſs through it at any time, except in the months
of

of June and July. At that feafon 120 and upwards, traverfe yearly, begging wool; of whom, many feem to be
real objects of charity, but numbers of them appear to be
of a different defcription. They come from Dundee, Arbroath, Montrofe, Brechin, Stonehaven and Aberdeen, for
the above purpofe.

Rent, Proprietor, &c.—The yearly rent of the parifh in
1714, amounted to L. 218; 39 wedders, at 3 s. 4 d. a-head;
31 ftone and 10 lb. of butter, at 4 d. the lb; and 46 dozen
and 2 poultry, at 3 s. 4 d. the dozen; the tenants paying,
every fifth year, the double of the money rent: By ad-
ding a fifth of the money rent, and taking the value of
the wedders, butter and poultry, in cafh, the yearly rent
of the parifh in 1714, amounted to L. 284 : 4 : 6$\frac{2}{7}$ Sterling.
The prefent rent (1792) is L. 385, 12 s. Sterling. From
time immemorial, the whole parifh belonged to one heritor. For fome centuries before 1714, the proprietor's family name was Lindfay. His manfion-houfe, called Invermark, a place about half a mile from the church, continued to be the ordinary place of his refidence, until he married the heirefs of Edzell, which happened at leaft 200
years ago, when he removed to the caftle of Edzell. The
walls of Invermark are ftill entire. In 1714, David Lindfay, the laft proprietor of that name, fold both Lochlee and
Edzell, to the Earl of Panmure. The Honourable William Maule of Panmure, is the prefent proprietor of the
parifh.

Tradefmen.—There are 4 wrights, 4 tailors, 3 weavers,
2 fmiths, and one fhoemaker in the parifh. The wrights
and fmiths are but occafionally employed, and therefore
have time to attend to fmall crofts of land, a few black cattle and fheep. There is nothing but coarfe woollen cloth
and

and some sheeting manufactured; but these articles afford constant work for the weavers. The inhabitants have been long in the practice of wearing shoes made of coarse leather, which go by the name of Forfar brogues, or black leather shoes; the shoemaker, therefore, is able to accomplish all the demands made upon him in his line, as these black leather shoes are to be had in Brechin and Forfar, and in most of the markets in the neighbourhood. A day-labourer receives 6 d. Sterling, and his meat *per* day, or 9 d. without victuals. In 1772, a day-labourer received 4 d. and his meat; a wright receives 8 d. and his meat; and a tailor 6 d. and his meat *per* day. In 1772, a man servant's wages for the half year was from L. 1, 5 s. to L. 1, 10 s. Sterling, with pasture for a score of sheep; his fee for the half year is now from L. 2, 10 s. to L. 3 Sterling.

Rivers, Loch, and Fish.—The principal branches of the river North Esk, which falls into the sea about 2 miles N. E. from Montrose, take their rise in the parish; these are the waters of Lee, of Mark, and of Tarf. The water of Lee passes through the loch, from whence the parish takes the designation of Lochlee.—Lochlee abounds with trouts, eels, and char. The trouts are generally of a large size, but very poor, not only in the loch, but also in the water of Lee, while it runs separately from the water of Mark; the trouts in Mark and Tarf are clear and fat, but not so big as in Lee. The loch is a mile long, and about the fifth part of a mile broad.

Sheep, &c.—There are 9200 sheep. lambs included, 130 goats, 192 horses, and about 600 black cattle in the parish. The horses and black cattle are small. About 6000 of the sheep are of the black faced kind; above 2000 are of a crossed breed, obtained by keeping black faced rams with ewes

of

of the white breed; the remainder are reckoned white sheep. It is believed, however, that, by not attending to the rams in the proper season, the true breed of white sheep is entirely gone. The first of the black faced sheep were brought into the parish about 30 years ago. Before that period, three glens in the west end of the parish, viz. Unich, Mark, and Lee, extending to several square miles, were set apart for the pasture of black cattle during the summer. Unich is still employed for that purpose, and had in it, during the months of June, July and August last, upwards of 300 black cattle, for which the glen-keeper received about 1 s. 6 d. Sterling *per* head. The other two glens are now chiefly employed in the pasture of sheep. There are about 1000 black faced lambs reared in the parish yearly. The remainder are bought, either in lambs, from L. 5, to L. 5, 10 s. the score, or in hogs, from L. 9, to L. 10 the score, but chiefly in hogs, in regard many of the bought lambs die in the autumn, of the sickness. The wool of the black faced sheep is very coarse, and is sold at different prices, according to the manner in which it is treated; a considerable quantity of it is sold unwashed, for about 8 s. the stone, part of it is washed, but very indifferently, viz. by driving the sheep three or four times through a pool of water, and sells at about 10 s. the stone; what is cleansed by hand washing sells at about 12 s. the stone. The tenants are unanimously of opinion, that the pasture has an influence upon the quality of the wool. Perhaps, it might be proper also to take the climate into the account. The west end of the parish, where the greater part of the black faced sheep pasture, is very cold, and in the winter much exposed to storm. The crossed breed and white sheep, are all brought up in the parish, the wool of the latter sells at 16 s. the stone; and, in a few farms in the east end, where great attention is paid to the sheep, it sells from 1 s. 2 d. to 1 s. 3 d. the pound. Some of the

the old people remember the time, when wool from this pa-riſh, was ſold in Aberdeen, at 30 s. Sterling the ſtone. Smearing with tar and butter, is not much practiſed, except when the ſcab is ſuſpected; many of the lambs, are, in the autumn, ſmeared with tobacco juice, mixed with black ſoap, and a little ſtale urine, allowing about four pounds of ſoap to twenty pints of tobacco juice. The tobacco juice effectually kills the vermin.

Wild Animals.—There are many foxes in the pariſh; they commit great depredations among the young ſheep. Although the pariſh is at a conſiderable expence yearly, in paying a fox-hunter, there are ſo many rocks and large cairns, where the foxes find ſhelter, that it appears ſcarcely practicable to extir-pate theſe animals by hunting. A few of them are poiſoned in the winter ſeaſon, by dragging a piece of ſalted fiſh well ſpiced with powdered *nux vomica*, along a hill ſide, and leaving it near water. If the fox comes upon the tract, he ſoon finds the bait, eats it, drinks and expires inſtantly. The only dif-ficulty lies in finding open water in time of a ſevere ſtorm, and without this, the *nux vomica* does not kill. If he does not drink immediately after eating, he commonly eſcapes by throwing it up. Arſenic would, no doubt, prove an ef-fectual poiſon with or without water; but as the inhabitants are very inattentive, it might be dangerous to uſe it. There are many wild cats alſo in the rocks and cairns, but they do little or no hurt among the ſheep. There are plenty of white hares in the hills, and ſeveral deers, and a few roe-bucks traverſe the glens. The rocks abound with eagles and hawks, and the hills with moor fowl. There are but few partridges in the pariſh.

Roads and Bridges.—Until 1764, there were no roads within the pariſh fit for wheel-carriages, ſince that time the inhabitants have, by ſtatute labour, made a tolerable cart
road

road from the eaft end of the parifh to the weftmoft dwelling houfe in it. The only place of accefs for wheel carriages is at the eaft end; and, it is probable, this will always continue to be the cafe, the furrounding and fteep hills, in every other quarter, rendering it difficult to make a cart road to Glenmuick, Glentamir, Navar or Clova; and the little intercourfe with thefe places rendering it unneceffary. Many of the tenants have alfo made private cart roads for their own conveniency, fo that carts are now much ufed. Before 1764, there were no carts in the parifh. There are 3 ftone bridges, one upon Tarf, another over Mark, and the third about a mile below the junction of Lee and Mark. The above bridges were all built fince 1749.

Fuel.—Hitherto the inhabitants have been well fupplied with peats; but as the moffes, in feveral places upon the low ground, are nearly worn out, their fuel will be obtained with greater difficulty and labour, in a few years hence; in regard that the hills, although in many places covered with inexhauftible mofs, are, at prefent, inacceffible; and it would require very confiderable fums of money to make even tolerable roads of communication.

Ecclefiaftical State, &c.—From the time of the Reformation to 1723, Lochlee and Lethnot made but one charge; the minifter refided at Lethnot, where he had a manfe and glebe. It appears by a decreet paffed in 1717, that the ftipend amounted to 1000 merks Scotch, with L. 50 Scotch for communion elements. During the above period, the minifter preached two days at Lethnot for one day at Lochlee, and in tempeftuous feafons of the year, the inhabitants of Lochlee remained without public worfhip altogether. As a remedy for this difadvantage, John Lindfay of Edzell, at that time alfo proprietor of Lochlee, by a deed of mortification, dated

dated at Edzell, " the twentie twa day of Auguſt, ane
" thouſand ſix hundereth fyftie nyn years," ſet apart two
crofts of land, adjoining to the church of Lochlee, 100 merks
Scotch, 6 bolls of oat-meal, with paſture for one horſe, one
cow and 20 ſheep, for the maintenance of a catechiſing
reader at Lochlee, whoſe office was to convene the pariſhioners in the miniſter's abſence, to read a portion of
ſcripture, and to pray with them. In 1723, Lochlee was
made a ſeparate charge. Lethnot and Navar being joined
together, and the manſe and glebe of Navar with nine hundred merks Scotch of ſtipend, and L. 50 Scotch for communion elements, were decerned to belong to the miniſter of
Lochlee. In 1726, the heritor agreed to build a manſe at
Lochlee, and to the deſignation of a new glebe there, in excambion for the glebe and manſe of Navar ; in the execution
of which, it was found, that the glebe of Navar was equal in
value to four ſeventh parts of a farm, near the church of
Lochlee, called the Kirk-town. The miniſter of Lochlee,
therefore, now enjoys as a glebe, four ſeventh parts of the
arable land, graſs and hill paſture, that formerly belonged
to that farm, and L. 54 : 3 : 4 Sterling of ſtipend and communion element money. The manſe was built in 1750,
and is at preſent in tolerable repair. The walls of the
church, although apparently very old, are ſtill in good repair ; the roof was thatched with heath till 1784, when it
was covered with ſlates. Since the year 1723, the mortification above mentioned has been enjoyed by the parochial ſchoolmaſter, he having no other ſalary. The Honourable Society for propagating Chriſtian knowledge, have,
for many years appointed a ſchoolmaſter, to teach in corners
of the pariſh moſt diſtant from the pariſh ſchool, a meaſure
that has tended very much to diſſeminate knowledge in it.
The church and parochial ſchool are near the centre of the
pariſh, if regard is had to the boundary of the hill paſture;

but

but they are far otherwife in refpect of the inhabited part, there being only three families refiding weft from the church. The King is patron of the parifh. The church of Lochlee is fituated about 8 miles from the church of Glenmuick, 10 from the church of Edzell, 9 from the church of Lethnot, 8 from the church of Clova, and 20 miles from Brechin, the nearest poft town. The only road for wheel carriages from Brechin to Lochlee, lies in a direction north from Brechin for about 7 miles, till it crofs the Gannachy bridge, in the parifh of Edzell; when, for feveral miles along the north fide of the river North Efk, it takes a north wefterly direction. It enters Lochlee at the eaft end, and from thence to the church. There are 6 miles in the direction of weft, or rather W. S. W.

Mifcellaneous Obfervations.—The farmers are fubjected to no fervices by the heritor, with the following exception, that each tenant is to furnifh a man and horfe for two days in the year, to attend the proprietor, if defired; and in proportion to their rents, to carry materials for building and repairing the church, manfe, fchool, and public buildings in the parifh. The rents are paid *forehand*, that is to fay, the rent for crop 1793, is paid, the firft half, at Whitfunday 1792, and the laft half at Martinmas 1792.—The rocks abound with limeftone, but fo full of fand as to require no additional mixture when ufed as mortar *. It makes, however, a ftronger cement, when ufed in building, and ftands the froft better than the lime brought from the low country.—There is a vein of lead ore that runs through the parifh, in a direction nearly eaft and weft. About the year 1728, a company
of

---

* This fort of lime, which has naturally enough of fand mixed with it, is by far the beft calculated for plaiftering the outfide of houfes, &c. but is not fo good a manure.

of miners were employed for ſome time in making a trial of it. They gave it as their opinion, that it was well worth the working; but as they had no overſeer, and their employers reſided at a great diſtance, the trial came to nothing, and was given up.

Character.—The inhabitants are, for the moſt part, regular in their lives, none of them, ſince the commencement of this century, having been ſubjected to any criminal proſecution, except one accuſed of murder, who was fugitated in 1776. Dram drinking, indeed, has, of late, become more frequent among them, and may be productive of other bad practices. The character of the people, however is, on the whole, reſpectable; and if they want ſomewhat of that poliſh, which prevails in more fertile and more populous diſtricts, they are alſo free from many of thoſe faſhionable vices, by which the others are diſtinguiſhed.

UNITED PARISHES OF LOGIE AND PERT,

(COUNTY OF FORFAR, SYNOD OF ANGUS AND MEARNS, PRESBYTERY OF BRECHIN.)

By the Rev. Mr ALEXANDER PETER.

Name, Situation, Soil, Air, &c.

IT seems probable, that the parish of Logie, or Logie-Montrose, as it was formerly called, was annexed to the parish of Pert perhaps about the year 1610 or 1615. *Logie*, which is a very common name through Scotland, is said to be of Gaelic extraction, and to signify a ' flat or ' low situation,' which particularly corresponds to that of the Old Church of Logie, which is situated in a hollow or low ground, by the side of the Northesk river. *Pert* is of uncertain origin. The Old Church of Pert is likewise situated on the banks of the Northesk, very near the Old North Water Bridge, and about 3 miles up the river

from

from Logie. The United Parish is something of an oblong, or rather elliptical form, though by no means regular ; its greatest length from E. to W. is more than 4 English miles, and its greatest breadth from S. to N. about 3 miles. The lower part of it lies along the banks of the river North-esk, which, by a beautiful curve, divides it towards the north and east, from the parishes of Marykirk and St Cyrus. The upper part is pretty high, generally bending with a gentle declivity to the river, though good part of it likewise has a southern exposure.—The soil, chiefly in the lower parts, is a deep clay, yielding, even in an uncultivated state, plenty of natural grass. That, in the higher grounds is partly a light loam, and partly of a black moorish cast, with a clay bottom, spontaneously producing in its natural state, or when left uncultivated, a short heath, intermixed with furze and broom.—The air is in general sharp and salubrious, though now and then rains and fogs from the sea, perhaps, in some measure, contribute to render it unwholesome. The most prevalent distempers are fevers, which sometimes prove highly infectious and epidemical. This was particularly the case in 1787-8, when, in little more than the space of a twelvemonth, about 30 individuals died of a malignant fever, which generally produced a delirium about the 4th or 5th day, and cut them off in less than a week after. Perhaps an officious, though ill-judged attention, shown by the people in visiting their sick neighbours, tended to spread the contagion, which might be aggravated by the want of a due regard to cleanliness, and to the admission of fresh air. It was remarked, that though several young persons who were seized with that fever recovered, no one advanced in life, or even above the age of 30, experienced a recovery. The other diseases most common are, gravel, rheumatism, and consumptions. The small-pox also at times make considerable ravages, and, no doubt,

doubt, prove the more fatal, as the common people still show a very general averſion to inoculation. The plague raged here in 1648.

Springs, Rivers, &c.—There are ſeveral ſprings, though not of very great celebrity; one of them is a ſtrong mineral, which is ſaid to be ſerviceable in ſtomach diſorders. There is a ſpring well in the old church-yard of Logie, which was formerly much reſorted to by people who had ſores There is a very copious ſpring in Martin's Den, that would fill a bore of 4 inches diameter, nouriſhing great abundance of water, with creſſes in its ſtream. And there is in a field, near the ſpot where the old manſe of Pert ſtood, a plentiful ſpring of excellent water, likewiſe feeding a great quantity of water-creſſes. Both this, and the ſpring in Martin's Den, are ſuppoſed to be anti-ſcorbutic. There is no lake, nor any river, except the Northeſk already mentioned, commonly called the North Water, dividing the counties of Angus and Mearns. This river furniſhes a title to the noble family of Northeſk, who formerly poſſeſſed a large track of land in the pariſh of Pert, and neighbourhood, on both ſides of the river, now in the poſſeſſion of the Earl of Kintore and others. Roſe Hill, which gives title to the eldeſt ſon of the Earl of Northeſk, is an eminence on the road ſide, near the gate of Ingliſmaldie, (a ſeat belonging to Lord Halkerton, now Earl of Kintore,) and a little to the northward of the North Water Bridge; whereas the Southeſk, which runs paſt the town of Brechin, gave title to the Earl of Southeſk, who was attainted in 1715.

The North Water produces excellent trout and ſalmon; the latter, ſome years in conſiderable quantities. In that part of it which bounds the pariſh of Logie Pert are caught, ſome years from Candlemas to Michaelmas, (the legal term

of

of fishing here,) upwards of 120 stone, though some seasons often not half that quantity. The salmon-fishing in this part of the river has for some time past, been much hurt by a dam-dike belonging to a proprietor of the fishing below, the height of which prevents the salmon from getting up the stream. To remedy this evil, recourse has lately been had to a process at law. The salmon here are chiefly caught with the net, though angling both for trout and salmon is likewise frequently practised. The salmon are reckoned in greatest perfection during the months of February, March, and April. They are commonly sent for sale to the Boil-house at Montrose, where, at an average, they bring about 5 s. the stone ; from thence they are exported to the London market. When sold on the spot, towards the beginning of spring, they frequently fetch 6 d. a pound.

Minerals, &c.—There are here several freestone quarries, the rock rather soft, and at no great depth from the surface. What stones they have hitherto produced, have been used by the proprietors for their own private purpofes. But what particularly deserves notice, is the limework, which for some years has been carrying on, and is still carrying on to greater and greater extent in the district of Pert. Limestone was first discovered here about the year 1780. For some time it was wrought in the usual way, but of late an attempt has been made by the principal proprietor, and with no inconsiderable success, to work it by mining, in the same manner as coal is wrought in the southern parts of Scotland ; and a subterraneous drain, intended to be about 15 fathoms deep, and 400 yards in length, is now begun to be cut for clearing off the water from the quarries. The main stratum, or vein of limestone, extends from the Northesk nearly in a S. W. direction, through the whole parish

parish of Pert, and enters the parish of Strickathrow, where it is likewise wrought to some extent. There are several veins, under one another, at different depths from the surface. One principal vein is at the depth of about 6 feet, and nearly 12 feet thick. To use the style of the workmen, it is covered with a strong scourdy stone, mixed with lime, and the pavement or bed is a thick body of reddish freestone, in which are several thin seams of limestone. The vein now mining, which is supposed to be rather of superior quality to the rest, is at the depth of more than 40 feet. The several quarries are said to have produced this year, upwards of 16,000 bolls of shells ; each boll of shells yielding about 3 bolls of lime of exceeding fine powder. The lime is reckoned remarkably good, and is very fit either for building or manure. It is sold by wheat measure at 1 s. 9 d. *per* boll ready money, and 1 s. 10 d. credit. There are a good many hands employed in this work, especially in spring and summer, perhaps from 20 to 30 or upwards. Good hands are allowed 1 s. 2 d. a-day, and when engaged by the quantity, at the rate of 6 d. the boll. About L. 2 being allowed for powder for 1600 or 1700 bolls. The limestone is burned with what is called Coom Coals, (the same the blacksmiths use,) brought from Inverkeithing and other parts of the frith of Forth to the port of Montrose, and from thence carried in carts to the lime-work. This coal is generally purchased on the spot, at 3 s. 6 d. the boll, the freight to Montrose, exclusive of custom dues, is about 1 s. 5 d ; the cartage from Montrose to the quarries, (about 7 miles distance,) 2 s. the boll or 72 stone. In consequence of the above advantage of lime, improvements are fast advancing in this neighbourhood, and the value of land is every year rising. One proprietor is said to have let some of his farms at quadruple rent, after having fallowed, limed, drained, and inclosed the ground.

The

The duty on coal, for burning lime into manure, falls very heavy, and the taking it off, would not only operate a an encouragement to the farmer, but might tend much to the improvement of the country in general.

Animals, Birds, &c.—The animals of the wild kind are chiefly hares, foxes, weasels, and polecats. The birds are, crows of different kinds, especially the rook, the raven, and the carion crow ; partridges, blackbirds, herons, thrushes, sky and wood-larks ; magpies, robins, wrens, linnets, goldfinches, bulfinches, wood-pigeons, hawks of different species. Gulls are found to flock hither before a storm from the sea, and we have prodigious flocks of sparrows, which are peculiarly destructive to early grain. There is likewise found here in gardens, about the fruit season, a bird called by some the oosal, said to be but a recent visitor in this part of the country, pretty much resembling the blackbird, only of a lighter dun colour. It devours small fruit very voraciously. We have three species of the swallow. Our migratory birds are the cuckoo and swallow, which last makes its appearance in May, and disappears about the end of October. The moor of Pert furnishes the lapwing, appearing in March, and disappearing about the end of harvest. In that moor also are plovers, wild ducks of different species, snipes, and wild geese, which, though they do not nest here, lodge in the moor, sometimes in hundreds during the night. The parish also breeds a considerable number of black cattle of a middling size.

Population.—According to the return made to Dr Webster, the numbers were then 696. There can be no document found for ascertaining with precision the state of the population here at a very early period. It appears from the

session

seffion register, that between the years 1720 and 1730, the number of births each year, at an average, was from 20 to 24, the number of marriages from 4 to 7, and the number of deaths from 12 to 16; from which it should seem, that the population then was nearly as great as at present. There are two circumstances which have tended much to diminish the population here, as well as in several places of this neighbourhood, the monopoly of farms, and the different mode of farming which has of late years been adopted. There are in this parish sundry instances of two or more farms having been joined into one, which must occasion a diminution of tenants; and as several of the farmers now make use of hired servants in place of cottagers, and plough with one man and two horses, in place of two men and four horses formerly used; this, likewise, though no doubt a more œconomical scheme, is less favourable to population, and tends to the decrease of numbers. Owing to these causes, the number of individuals would be reduced below what it formerly was, were it not for two other causes, proving more than an overbalance, the limeworks already mentioned, and some bleachfields, &c. in the district of Logie, which afford employment to a confiderable number of hands. The amount of the population in the month of February this year (1791) was about 999 individuals, of whom 469 were males, 530 females. None reside in towns, one family excepted, who generally reside for some months during the winter season in Montrose. There is likewise a lady with her maid-servant, not included in the above amount, who reside during the summer in the old manse of Logie. There are only two places in the parish, which, with any sort of propriety, can be called villages, *viz.* North Water Bridge, and Mains of Craigo, the one containing only about 70 individuals, and the other about 60. The annual average of births for 7 years last past,

has

has been nearly 24 ; of deaths between 11 and 12 ; of
marriages more than 5. Of the 999, there were under

the age of 10,	-	-	-	230
From 10 to 20,	-	-	-	202
From 20 to 50,	-	-	-	377
From 50 to 70,	-	-	-	163
From 70 to 100,	-	-	-	27

Of thefe about 6 or 7 are 80 and upwards, none of them,
however, have arrived at 90.—The number of farmers having families, and who earn a livelihood by farming, is a-
bout 36. Of thefe about 5 or 6 pay from L. 100 to L. 200
Sterling of yearly rent ; the fecond clafs from L. 20 to L. 50
or more ; and the third clafs from L. 5 or L. 6 to L. 20.
Befides thefe, there are feveral who occupy fmall tacks,
which they hold chiefly of landed proprietors ; but which,
being infufficient for their fubfiftence, they have recourfe
at times to hiring for manual labour, or exercife fome trade,
fuch as weaving, &c. In this parifh, befides the bleachers
and millers afterwards to be mentioned, and thofe employed under them, there are 5 fmiths, 2 coopers, 9 wrights, 4
mafons, 10 weavers, 7 tailors, 4 fhoemakers, 1 butcher, 1
dyer, 4 merchants or fhopkeepers, 2 flax-dreffers, and about
20 apprentices and journeymen in whole under thefe. A few
hands are occafionally employed in falmon fifhing, one fer-
ryman at the boat of Craigo, feveral miners employed at the
limeworks, a few houfehold fervants, above 80 labouring fervants, male and female, and 2 ftudents. More than one third
is fuppofed to have been born in other parifhes or diftricts of
Scotland. There is no nobility refident in the parifh ; of gentlemen heritors 2 refide, 3 are non-refident. There is one
furgeon, who was in the navy.—All our people are of the
Eftablifhed Church, except 2 or 3 Seceders, 8 or 10 Epifcopalians, and about half a dozen of perfons, who call themfelves Bereans ; no Roman Catholics.—The annual births
are

3

are to the whole population, nearly in the proportion of 1 to
42. Suppoſing both parties pariſhioners, the proportion between the annual marriages and the whole population would
be nearly as 1 to 99 ; but as it frequently happens, that ſome
one of the parties married belongs to a different pariſh,
this muſt vary the proportion accordingly, and make it
conſiderably leſs. The annual deaths to the whole population, may be, on an average, as 1 to 86 or 90. The number of married men having houſes is about 160 ; the number of bachelors having ditto, 14, and widowers having
ditto, 10. Each marriage, at an average, produces between
4 and 5 children. None were ever known here to have died
for want. The people in general being ſober and induſtrious, ſuch crimes as murder and robbery are unknown.
One or two ſome years ago emigrated to America, though
from no neceſſity, or want of good employment at home.
None have been baniſhed from the pariſh as far back as can
be remembered. A few cottages have been ſuffered to fall,
but others in general have been built in lieu of them.
The number of inhabited houſes is about 224, and the
number of perſons at an average to each inhabited houſe,
is between 4 and 5.

Manufactures, &c.—The following are the principal :
Two maſter bleachers reſiding with their families, one at
the bleachfield of Logie, the other at the bleachfield of
Craigo. At Logie bleachfield, belonging to a company in
Montroſe, who have the field in tack from the proprietor
of Craigo, there is a complete apparatus for bleaching of
thread, and the quantity bleached here annually is from
60,000 to 70,000 ſpindles, which is almoſt wholly diſpoſed
of at the London market. This work, which was ſet a-going about 30 years ſince, but which has of late been on the
increaſe, affords employment each ſeaſon to about 40 hands,

men,

men, women, and boys. Finding their own victuals, they receive of wages from 3 s. to 5 s. a-week, according to their age and expertness at the business.—Craigo bleachfield, which is likewise rented from the proprietor of Craigo by a gentleman in Montrose, is at present subset to a bleacher. It was formerly used for bleaching of thread, but is now chiefly employed for whitening cloth. It affords work during the proper season to 6 or 7 hands, at about 8 d. a-day. Both fields lie on the banks of the Northesk, within half a mile of one another. The rent is extremely moderate, only a good deal has been laid out on proper houses, machinery, &c. At the mill of Craigo, besides the mill for grinding meal, there is a mill for cleaning yarn for the duck manufacture, and brown sheeting; it likewise contains an apparatus for beating coarse thread, and furnishes pretty constant work for 3 hands, each of whom may earn at the rate of 10 d. a day Here also is a flax mill, employed in breaking and scutching flax, after a much improved method, at the rate of at least 1500 stones avoirdupoise yearly. This mill gives constant employment to about 8 hands, each earning from 7 s. 6 d. to 9 s. a-week. The flax wrought here is all for home consumption. Near the above is a waukmill and dyehouse. At the mill of Logie, besides a meal and barley mill, there is hard by the river side a snuff mill, held in feu from Craigo by a merchant in Montrose. Between 30 and 40 years ago, when this mill was first erected, and when importation of tobacco was allowed at the port of Montrose, there were annually manufactured here, and sold at about 1 s. the lb. for exportation, near 40,000 lb. snuff. Since the importation of tobacco at Montrose was prohibited, this manufacture has considerably declined. Tobacco for this mill is now conveyed coastwise by the Canal from Glasgow. There is now only one person employed here, and about 5000 lb. of snuff annual-

ly

ly manufactured and fold for home confumption, at the rate of 2 s. 4 d. the pound. There is likewife here a mill, with 10 beaters for beating thread. In the united parifh are 3 meal mills, employing a miller, befides affiftants. The whole parifh of Pert is under thirlage to the mill of Pert, fome paying $\frac{1}{5}$, and others $\frac{1}{21}$ multure, befides knavefhip, &c. The whole land of Craigo is under thirlage to the mill of Craigo at $\frac{1}{21}$, befides knavefhip, &c. There is no thirlage at the mill of Logie. This thirlage, which is a fort of old feudal tenure, by which tenants and others are bound at a certain fixed rate, to have their corns ground at certain mills, is generally confidered as a grievance, and is at fome mills a prelude to very indifferent ufage.

Agriculture, &c.—Some woodlands on the eftate of Craigo are found to produce a confiderable variety of mofs, no fewer than 14 or 15 different fpecies, fome of which have been tranfmitted for the infpection of the Royal Society at London. Some of the old woods are Scots fir, others a mixture of hard wood, fuch as afh, elm, oak, birch, &c. The young plantations on the different eftates in the parifh confift partly of Scots fir, and partly of larix, fpruce, plane, elm, beech, afh, birch, in fhort, an intermixture of all kinds, commonly raifed in nurferies.—About 450 acres have been planted here within thefe 10 or 15 years paft; and of thefe about 270 acres were inclofed, and nearly planted out the 2 laft years.—According to the beft computation, there are from 180 to 190 horfes in the parifh, young and old; about 740 black cattle, exclufive of calves, about 200 of whicn are annually brought up. There was formerly a great number of fheep in this parifh; but fince the inclofing of fields and fowing of artificial grafs took place, the breeding of fheep has in a great meafure meaſure been given up ; ſo that there is ſcarcely **now** 100 ſheep in the whole pariſh, and theſe are chiefly kept for the uſe of the table. The pariſh can afford itſelf a very tolerable ſupply of various kinds of proviſions. It does not export any conſiderable quantity; but finds in general a ready market for grain of different kinds at Brechin and Montroſe, where it is bought partly for the uſe of the inhabitants, and partly by commiſſion for exportation to other places. Both at Brechin and Montroſe, but eſpecially the latter, a good deal of bear and barley is ſold for malting. Till of late years very little ground was ſown in artificial graſſes. It is ſaid the firſt ever known in the pariſh was about the year 1746 or 1747; when a perſon in the pariſh of Pert having ſown a ridge with clover, got a public proclamation made for people to keep off their ſheep and cattle from it, which brought many to ſee it as a matter of curioſity. Oats are generally ſown about the end of March, and begin to be reaped about the 1ſt of September, and ſometimes later. Barley is ſown about the middle of April, bear later ; and both are commonly reaped rather earlier than oats. Peaſe are ſown and reaped much about the ſame time with oats. Wheat is ſown here in September and October, and reaped about the ſame time with barley. The ripening of the different corn crops is rather retarded by the liming now ſo much in uſe. Flax is ſown about the end of March, and reaped the 1ſt of Auguſt. Turnips are ſown about the middle of June ; graſs feeds according to the different crops with which they are ſown out; and hay is uſually cut in July. The groſs amount of the pariſh in Scots acres, with the different ways in which theſe at an average are employed, are as follow :

Groſs

Grofs amount, exclufive of farm-fteadings, (that is, farm-houfes and their offices), roads, gardens, &c. 3860 acres.

	Acres.
Annually employed in oats, - -	740
—————————— in barley and common bear, -	420
—————————— in peafe, - -	144
—————————— in wheat, - -	70
—————————— in flax, - -	46
—————————— in fallow, turnips and potatoes,	160
—————————— in hay for cutting, -	270
—————————— in pafture, including waftes, -	890
—————————— in moor uncultivated, -	350
—————————— in woodlands, - -	770
	——
	3860

The valued rent is L. 3816 : 9 : 4 Scots. The real rent, including the value of what the feveral proprietors hold in their own poffeffion, furplus rents, rents of mills, bleach-fields, &c. lime works not included, may be from L. 1800 to L. 1900 Sterling. The number of ploughs is about 55 ; of carts 64. Several of the ploughs are of the old Scotch kind, others of a lighter conftruction. The beft arable land in the parifh lets at about a guinea an acre ; that of an inferior quality at about 10 s. or 15 s. The number of farms is rather diminifhing, owing to junction or monopoly. Moft of the parifh of Pert, and a good part of Logie, is inclofed, partly with hawthorn, and partly with furze hedges on funk fences. No doubt hedges are a great benefit in point of fhelter, as well as ornament. They are only found inconvenient in a wet harveft and low fituation. The hawthorn likewife harbours prodigious flocks of fparrows, which devour confiderable quantities of grain. Perhaps ftone fences, built pretty high, might in fome refpects

be

be preferable, as sheep could be more commodiously kept within these ; and surely it is a circumstance much to be wished, that the breed of sheep were more encouraged here than it now is. Many of the people in the parish have still an unreasonable aversion to inclosing, notwithstanding its many obvious advantages.

Advantages and Disadvantages.—It is an advantage, that the centre of the united parishes, lying at nearly an equal distance from the market towns of Montrose and Brechin, about 4 or 5 measured miles from either, there is found a ready sale for grain. poultry, butter, cheese, eggs, &c. But then there is a disadvantage resulting to those of the parish who have such articles to buy ; because on acccunt of the demand at these towns, enhanced of late by a number of monied men, who have settled in these places and neighbourhood, there is no article of provision can be purchased within the parish, but at a very dear rate, and even higher than in the above market towns. There is likewise a temporary disadvantage, which those especially of the poorer class are beginning to feel : The coal has here, for a considerable time, been the principal article of fuel, yet the common people have in a good measure likewise depended partly on furze and broom, and partly on turf and peat. The furze and broom begin to fail, as most of the wastes, from whence these were procured, are either inclosing or converting into corn ground. The article of turf becomes still scarcer, as the moors from which that was got, are now for the most part inclosed and planted, and the low country mosses which furnished peat, become every day more and more exhausted, so that in a few years a total failure of them may be apprehended ; and as to peats from the hills, the distance from hence, which is 10 or 12 miles, part of it very steep and disagreeable road, renders it extremely difficult,

cult, as well as expenfive, to procure them; fo that the parifhioners here, in a fhort time, will be chiefly confined to
two articles, wood and coals. Burn-wood at prefent is
by no means plentiful; and though there be a good many
rifing plantations in the parifh, yet thefe moftly confift of
hard wood; and, at any rate, feveral years muft elapfe before they can prove ferviceable in the way of fuel. On this
account, there will be at leaft a temporary neceffity of u-
fing a greater quantity of coal, which will fall very heavy
on the poorer fort, by reafon of the additional tax on that
article, all to the north of the Red Head, a promontory
near Arbroath. It is hoped the Legiflature will be induced to abolifh this very partial and unreafonable tax.
Under this article, it may be proper to remark, that the
bleachfields, lime quarries, &c. in the parifh are a very confiderable local advantage, as they furnifh employment, efpecially during the fpring and fummer feafons, to near 80 individuals; befides, the fmaller tenants, and others who have
horfes, earn no inconfiderable profit, by carting coals to
the lime-works from Montrofe.

Stipend, School, Poor.——The value of the living, including
the glebe, is one year with another about L. 80 Sterling.
The patrons are the Crown, and the New College of St
Andrew's *per vices.* The fchoolmafter's falary, including
fchool fees, and other perquifites, is better than L. 20 Sterling a year, befides a free houfe and garden. He has in
the winter feafon from 40 to 50 fcholars, and in fummer
from 30 to 40. His terms for Latin and arithmetic are
2 s. 6 d. the quarter; writing 2 s.; reading Englifh 1 s. 6 d.
The number of poor in the parifh at prefent receiving alms,
is about 25. The annual amount for their relief, may be,
one year with another, about L. 40 Sterling.

Prices of Provifions, Labour, &c.——All kinds of butcher
meat fell nearly at 4 d. the lb. except pork, which is about
$3\frac{1}{2}$ d.

3½ d. ; eggs, 4 d. the dozen ; fowls, from 1 s. 8 d. to 2 s. the pair, according to the ſeaſon ; chickens, 7 d. the pair ; ducks, 1 s. 4 d. ditto ; butter, at an average through the year, may be reckoned at 8½ d. the lb. ; whereas, about 30 or 40 years ago, beef or mutton could have been bought here at 1¼ d. the lb. ; a pair of good chickens, at 2 d. a dozen ; eggs, at 1 d. ; butter, at 4 d. the lb. and other articles in proportion.—The wages of an ordinary labourer are about 8 d. a day in winter, and 10 d. in ſummer, finding his own proviſions ; of a maſon, about 1 s. 8 d. ; of a wright, about 1 s. 4 d. ; of a tailor, 1 s. if he finds his own victuals, and 6 d. if victuals are afforded him. The maſons and wrights moſt frequently work by the piece.—Coal, Scotch and Engliſh, is the chief article of fuel here, though peat, turf, furze, broom, and wood, are likewiſe occaſionally uſed. The Scotch coal is at preſent about 8 s. the boll at the port of Montroſe, the boll weighing 70 ſtone, cartage from thence about 1 s. 6 d. or 2 s. the boll, according to the diſtance. The Engliſh coal, which is likewiſe much uſed, is about 1 s. 6 d. the barrel, ſix barrels being ſuppoſed rather better than a boll of Scotch. Peat from the moſſes in Fettercairn pariſh, about 6 miles diſtant, is bought on the ſpot out of ſtacks at 1 s. the foot, the cartage about 1 s. 6 d. the cart load. The cart load of broom or furze, coſts from 1 s. to 1 s. 6 d. ; turf can ſcarcely be got at any price ; dead wood is ſold here at about half value. With regard to the expence of a common labourer when married, if he have a family conſiſting of three or four children, it cannot be leſs than L. 12 or L. 13 Sterling a-year ; yet if he and his wife be frugal and induſtrious, they may make a ſhift to earn a tolerable livelihood, eſpecially, if they have a kail yard, and maintenance for a cow, as is pretty generally the caſe here. The man may gain at the rate of 8 d. or 9 d. a day, the wife, by ſpinning, may earn 8 d. or 1 s. a-week,

even

even when occasionally engaged in nursing; and the children, when 7 or 8 years of age, begin to be hired out as herds. Though the food of the labourer be but coarse, yet he has plenty of meal, potatoes, and milk, and his bed is generally good. Pottage, brose, and flummery, are the peasants three ordinary meals. The wages of men servants in husbandry throughout this parish and neighbourhood, are from L 6 to L. 7 Sterling a-year, and they are commonly engaged half yearly. The wages of women servants, who are likewise engaged by the half year, are about L. 3 a-year, together with what is called bounties, consisting usually of an apron and a yard of coarse linen, value in all about 3 s. The harvest wages of men reapers are, now for good hands about L. 1, 5 s. and women ditto about 16 s. 8 d. besides victuals. When engaged by the day, men get about 1 s. women, 8 d. and their victuals.

Stature, Manners, Dress, &c.—The people are ordinarily of a middling stature, the men being from 5 feet 5 inches high, to 5 feet 10, and the women from 5 feet 2 or 3 inches, to 5 feet 7, though there are several of the men 6 feet, and of the women 5 feet 9 or 10. There are instances of some individuals having reached the height of 6 feet 3 or 4 inches.—The people in general are disposed to industry, and seem fond of agriculture. There are no manufactures carried on in the parish, excepting the limeworks, bleaching, &c. already mentioned, only the women find excellent employment in spinning factory yarn, given out by the shopkeepers in the parish, for which at present they get at the rate of 1 s. and even 15 d. the spindle. The people do not seem to possess any fondness either for a seafaring or military life; the former, however, they look upon to be rather more reputable than the latter, which, on account of its supposed connexion with profligacy and
irreligion,

irreligion, they regard in a degrading point of light, and when the ſon of ſober and diſcreet parents inliſts to be a ſoldier, they give him up in a manner for loſt. Though the pariſhioners here in general cannot be charged with want of œconomy, or with being more expenſive or luxurious than their neighbours, yet it muſt be acknowledged, that their mode of living now is widely different from what it was 30 or 40 years ago. About that time, excepting in the houſes of perſons of property or in a genteel ſtation, tea was unknown ; but now there is ſcarcely a houſe in the pariſh, excepting thoſe in indigent circumſtances, in which tea is not uſed at leaſt once a-week, and by many of the farmers twice a-day. Formerly butcher meat was ſeldom or never uſed by the lower or middling ranks, except about Chriſtmas, but now it is no unfrequent article at any ſeaſon of the year. Next to oat and bear meal, potatoes, which begin to be much cultivated, conſtitute the principal food of the poorer claſs.—The mode of dreſs likewiſe, within theſe 20 or 30 years paſt, has undergone a very conſiderable alteration. Formerly the women of inferior ſtations appeared at church on Sundays in bed blankets, or tartan plaids; but now they wear ſcarlet plaids, or duffle cloaks and bonnets ; and maid-ſervants are ſometimes as well dreſſed as their miſtreſſes. Formerly farmers and reſpectable tradeſmen were contented with the blue bonnet, and with ſay for their beſt clothes, while hiremen and apprentices wore coarſe grey, or white woollen cloth, home made ; but now, not only farmers and maſter tradeſmen, but farmers ſervants, apprentices, and cottagers, frequently appear at kirk and market in hats and Engliſh broad cloth. Formerly clocks and watches were not uſed in the pariſh, excepting, perhaps, by the laird or miniſter ; but now, in general, every farmer has his eight-day clock, and almoſt every ſervant has his watch.—With regard to the ſtyle in which

which the gentry in this parish live, it can scarcely be reckoned more splendid and sumptuous than it was 20 or 30 years ago, though, generally speaking, there is an increase both of splendour and luxury in many places of the neighbourhood, occasioned chiefly by the influx of wealth from the East and West Indies.

Antiquities.—There are in the parish or district of Logie, at nearly a mile to the west of the mansion-house of Craigo, and a little to the right of the public road, leading from the Old North Water Bridge to Montrose, three remarkable tumuli, called the three Laws of Logie, and not far from thence, on the border of the parish of Montrose, a fourth tumulus, called Leighton's Law. Of the three Laws of Logie, two have been opened, in digging sand or gravel for the roads. In one of these, some years ago, was found a stone coffin ; not any ways cut or wrought, but consisting of separate pieces in a natural state, something resembling grey slate stones. Within it was a human skeleton, having the bones of an extraordinary size, mostly entire and of a deep yellow colour, but when touched, exceedingly brittle. The second Law was found to contain four human skeletons, deposited only at about a foot depth from the surface, likewise consisting of exceedingly large bones ; and at a very little distance from these was found a beautiful ring, supposed to be of ebony, as black as jet, of a fine polish, and in perfect preservation. This ring, which the minister of the parish has in his custody, is of a circular form, flat in the inside, and rounded without ; its circumference is about 12 inches, and diameter 4. The thickness of its rim in the middle is more than half an inch, and its greatest breadth about an inch and a half, which diminishes in a gradual proportion till it is only about ¾ of an inch. It lets in an ordinary hand, would fit a pretty
large

large wriſt or arm, and perhaps may have been worn as a bracelet by ſome perſon of diſtinction. In the ſame tumulus, at about 4 feet from the ſurface, was found an urn full of aſhes, ſomething in the ſhape of a common bottle without a bottom, lying horizontally, with the neck end cloſe, and of a ſubſtance reſembling a crucible. There were likewiſe diſcovered in the ſame place ſeveral cavities, near 6 feet from the ſurface. The third and largeſt of the three Laws, which has not yet been broken up, contains a ſpace equal to the $\frac{1}{8}$ of an acre, nearly circular, with a ſort of foſſe round it, filled up with round ſtones, intermingled with pieces of glaſs. There is reaſon to believe, that theſe Laws, if duly examined, would be found to contain many more bones, urns, &c. : but there is no tradition concerning them, by which it can be aſcertained whether they have been raiſed by the Danes or Romans, or ancient Caledonians. Mention is made by Buchanan in his hiſtory of Scotland, to which Gordon alludes in his Itenerarium Septentrionale, that about 1000 years ago, a little before the celebrated battle of Luncarty, in the reign of Swino, a party of Danes landed at the mouth of the Eſk, and fought in that neighbourhood ſeveral ſkirmiſhes with the Scots ; and it is not improbable but theſe Laws or mounds might have then been raiſed, in burning or burying the ſlain. Or, as Law is a word of Saxon origin, perhaps theſe tumuli might have been begun by the Saxons, who, at a very early period, are ſaid to have made incurſions all along the coaſt of this iſland. The three Laws, with the adjacent ground, have been lately incloſed and planted by the proprietor of Craigo.—Eaſt from the above Laws, in a ſtraight line, and within a plantation of Craigo's, are three large ſtones ſet up on end, with two others very near them, in a ſimilar poſition ; and to the eaſt of all are the remains of a circular ſort of building, about 16 yards in diameter. The ground

was

was lately trenched, but no mark of human bones difcovered. This is conjectured to have been a drudical temple.

Roads, Bridges, &c.——There are two, or rather three public roads, leading through the united parifh. Befides thefe,
are fundry private or by-roads. Till a year or two
ago, the roads in the parifh were made and kept in repair
by ftatute labour; but by a late act of Parliament, the ftatute labour in this county was converted into money. By
the act, the occupiers of lands, whether proprietors or tenants, are liable to pay yearly, an affeffment in money, for
the lands occupied by them refpectively, according as the
faid lands ftand valued in the tax roll of the county, at a
rate not exceeding the fum of L. 1, 4 s. Sterling for each
L. 100 Scots of valued rent. Accordingly in this parifh,
now, the landed proprietors being affeffed in proportion to
their valued rents, levy the affeffment from their tenants
according to the real rents they pay, and they again from
their fubtenants; the proprietors, at the fame time, being
accountable for what they themfelves occupy. This mode
is deemed rather more favourable to the poorer clafs of inhabitants, than the exaction of the ftatute labour in kind,
but is thought more burdenfome on the farmer. Turnpikes are confidered as by no means neceffary here; and
the erecting of them at prefent would be rather an unpopular meafure.——With regard to bridges, 2 have been built
this fummer in the parifh of Logie, chiefly by fubfcription,
on the road leading from Marykirk to Montrofe. On the
weft public road are 2 fmall bridges, built fome years ago.
As to being kept in repair, they are now upon the fame
footing with the public roads. The principal bridge in the
parifh, and which connects it with the Mearns, is the
North Water Bridge, confifting of 3 arches, of exceeding

strong

ftrong work. This is now commonly called the Old Bridge, with a reference to the new one, which fome years ago was built acrofs the North Water, near the mouth of it, on the great coaft road. The old North Water Bridge was built by John Erfkine of Dun, fuperintendant of Angus and Mearns, upwards of 200 years ago. Concerning the builder of this North Water Bridge, popular tradition fays, " That having had a dream or vifion, that unlefs he fhould build a bridge over Stormy Grain, where 3 waters run in one, he would be miferable after death. Accordingly go-ing out one day in a penfive mood, and walking along the banks of the North Efk, he met an old woman near the fpot where the bridge now ftands, and afking the name of the place, received for anfwer, that it was called Stor-my Grain, where 3 waters run in one. Hence, recog-nifing this to be the fpot to which his dream alluded, he immediately fet about building a bridge there; but the bridge being founded, and the work going on, a fpeat in the river fwept it away, upon which he ordered the bridge to be begun anew. But after it was confiderably advanced, it tumbled down a fecond time. Mr Erfkine was now fo much difcouraged, that he fell into a deep melancholy, and kept his bed. One day, however, obferving a fpider attempting to weave a web, he faw it fall down; making a fecond attempt, it was equally unfuccefsful; but trying a third time, it fucceeded. Accordingly encouraged by this, he caufed it be begun a third time, and had the good for-tune to fucceed." Whether there be any real ground for this traditionary ftory or not, it is by no means abhorrent from the caft of mind that characterifed thofe times.

Mifcellaneous Obfervations.—In 1782, the crop was not all got in till confiderably after Martinmas. Ten bolls of bear were then purchafed at the feffion's expence, for the ufe

of the poor at the rate of 24 s. the boll, and were either fold
at a reduced price, or given gratis; befides a prefent of 10
bolls, confifting of a mixture of oats, barley, rye, &c. received then from Government, was diftributed among the poor.
Oat-meal here at that time fold at 2c s. the boll.—There
are two principal alehoufes, in a manner neceffary, as being on public roads, with one or two more, perhaps, lefs
requifite. The bad effects of thefe on the morals of the
people are not very perceptible, though the increafe of public houfes both in town and country is always to be regretted. The heavy Excife laws, and the enormous duty
on malt, make beer lefs brewed. in private families than
formerly, though perhaps, whifky is more ufed. Within
thefe ten years paft, near 30 new houfes or cottages have
been built in the parifh where there were none before;
perhaps, about half a dozen during that fpace have been
pulled down, or fuffered to fall into ruins. Employing cottagers in agriculture, is thought by fome of the farmers
here to be lefs frugal than keeping hired fervants in the
houfe, though it no doubt, is more favourable to population.—The meadows and lower grounds on the Northefk
are very fubject to inundations, which have fometimes done
confiderable damage, efpecially in the time of harveft. In
1774, when the river rofe to an almoft unprecedented
height, it fwept away a great deal of cut corn, and laid flat
fundry fields that were uncut, fpoiling them with fand;
and laft autumn, an uncommon flood fwept away from a
farm in this neighbourhood, on the oppofite banks of the
river, more than half an acre of ground, with about 60 bolls
of lime lying upon fallow; at any time fix hours of wind
and rain from the S. or S. E. will make it rife, fo as to o-
verflow all its banks.—In the year 1784, a very remarkable meteor was feen here, as it was through the moft part of
the kingdom, as well as in fome foreign parts. It made

its

its appearance about 7 o'clock in the evening, moving in a rapid and majestic manner, something in a direction from N. W. to S. E. having its visible magnitude equal to that of the full moon, and a light much superior ; at length it disappeared as it were in the ocean. This meteor must have been of prodigious bigness, its velocity immense, and its altitude many miles.—The common people here make use of the ordinary Scottish dialect, with less tone than they speak in Fife, though not near so short as they do in Aberdeenshire. With regard to the names of places in the parish, many of them seem to be of Gaelic or Celtic extraction.—Property in land here is very often changing ; of this there have been no less than four material instances in the united parish of Logie and Pert, within 8 or 10 years past ; and during that period, or little more, near the banks of the Northesk, and within the extent of 5 or 6 miles, no fewer than 8 estates have been in the market, and changed their proprietors. This rapid alienation of property, may in one instance or two be accounted for on political considerations, but is chiefly imputable to the two following causes :—Some of the old proprietors having been men of pleasure, and not sufficiently attentive to their worldly interest, were obliged to sell their land from the impulse of necessity, or pecuniary embarrassment ; others of them, again, who had several children, having, in contradiction to the old feudal spirit, made liberal provision in their settlements for the younger branches of their families ; this rendered the sale of their estates unavoidable on their demise. Land sells here at 25 or 30 years purchase, and seems to be on the increase.—The people are by no means ungenerous or uncharitable, according to their circumstances ; if at any time they see virtue or industry in distress, their chearful and ready support is not wanting ; but when vice is plunged into wretchedness, perhaps their pity is too much withheld,

from

from not making a proper difcrimination between the perfon and the crime, the vice and the mifery it involves.
The people enjoy the comforts and advantages of fociety
in a very tolerable degree, though the increafe of taxation,
and of the price of provifions, efpecially with regard to
the poorer clafs, operates as a confiderable abatement. Several of the tenants enjoying long leafes at the old rent,
which is nearly one half lefs than what their farms would
let for at prefent, have in their hands the means of a comfortable fubfiftence, and by induftry and frugality may become rich. But the new leafes in general being pretty far
ftretched, and the wages of fervants every year growing
higher, thofe, it is to be prefumed, who hold fuch leafes,
if they are not extremely active and induftrious indeed,
muft find confiderable difficulties. Were the wages of fervants rendered in fome meafure ftationary, and greater
moderation obferved in the raifing of rents, not only might
tenants and their fervants be on a more eligible footing,
but landed proprietors would enjoy greater and more permanent fecurity, befides the generous fatisfaction of not entirely
engroffing the fruits of honeft induftry. Were there premiums allotted by monied men for the improvement of
barren ground, and the melioration of ground already in
fome meafure cultivated, (the improvement or melioration
to be eftimated by an impartial jury,) many beneficial con-
fequences might enfue.

PARISH OF LUNAN.

By the Rev. Mr GOWANS.

Name, Situation, Extent, &c.

LUNAN, antiently Lounan, or Inverlounan, is so called from a river of that name, near the mouth of which the church stands. The source of the river is a quagmire, at a small village called Lunan-head, in the neighbourhood of Forfar; the Gaelic word *Labnon* signifying boggy or marshy ground. Lunan is situated in the county of Forfar, presbytery of Aberbrothock, and synod of Angus and Mearns. It is nearly a rectangle, about 2 miles long, and 1 broad, being one of the smallest parishes in the county. It is bounded on the north by Marytown and Craig; on the west by Kinnell; on the south by Lunan water, which divides it from Inverkeillor; and on the east by the German Ocean. The extent of sea-coast is about a mile, being a portion of Lunan Bay, famous as a place of safety for ships in all hard gales, except those from the east. The shore is sandy, and bounded with hillocks overgrown with bent; but the adjoining land is for the most part steep and high. The ground rises so rapidly from the river towards the north, that, when viewed from the south, the parish has the appearance of being situated on the side of a hill; but, at the top, it becomes again flat, and con-

tinues

tinues fo to the diftance of feveral miles beyond the parifh.
The fituation is at once pleafant, and advantageous for agriculture. The higher ground commands an extenfive view of
the country around, and of the German Ocean; and the
floping ground anfwers well for draining, which in many
places is much wanted; for the land abounds with boggs and
fprings, or what hufbandmen call *fpouts*. The greateft part
of the parifh ftands on rock of moor-ftone, commonly called
fcurdy: It is of a dark blue colour, and of fo clofe a texture
that water cannot penetrate it; and the furface of the ground,
efpecially during the winter months, is confequently very
loofe and wet. This rock is the only ftone found in the parifh fit for building. It is quarried by blafting with gunpowder, by which it is broke into fuch irregular pieces, that,
unlefs the mafons be at uncommon pains, walls built of it are
not water tight.

Soil, Produce, Rent, &c.—The foil of the higher part of
the parifh is frequently fhallow; but of the lower, deep and
rich, except a little on the fea-fhore, which is fandy. The
land is on the whole fertile, and produces grain of the beft
quality. The rent of the arable land is at prefent from 9 s.
to 15 s. Sterling an acre, but will probably be raifed at the
expiration of the prefent leafes, fome of which are not long.
No value is put on wafte or pafture ground. The valued
rent of the parifh is L. 1550 Scots; the real rent about
L. 525 Sterling.

There are eight farms in the parifh, very different in fize
and rent; and this number has been the fame beyond the
memory of man. Six of thefe farms, called the Barony of
Lunan, meafuring 790 acres, including 196 acres of moor,
common to them all, belong to the Earl of Northefk. Arlukie,

lukie, meafuring 400 acres, including 180 acres of moor, or coarfe pafture, belongs to Robert Stephen, Efq; of Letham. Lunan, meafuring 215 acres, including 62 acres of moor and wafte ground, belongs to Alexander Taylor Imray of Lunan. The whole parifh, accordingly, when the glebe is taken into the account, confifts of 973 acres arable, and 438 wafte land. Of thefe, 40 acres annually bear wheat, 187 barley, 270 oats, 45 turnip or cabbage, 10 potatoes or yams, 16 flax, 40 peafe, 324 fown grafs, and 40 lie fallow. Some tenants have made attempts to inclofe part of their farms with fences of earth topped with furze; but few of them are fo complete as to anfwer the purpofes of a fence. The farmers appear fully fenfible of the advantages of inclofures; and moft of them in the neighbourhood have begun to inclofe with ftone-walls; a practice which would be generally adopted, were it not for the difficulty in fome places of getting ftones, and the fhortnefs of many leafes. The parifh does much more than fupply itfelf with provifions; more than one half of the produce being annually carried to market, to which there is eafy accefs by the high road. This road, and the bridges on it, were chiefly made, and have been hitherto wholly kept in repair, by the ftatute labour, which was fometimes exacted in kind, and fometimes commuted; but, by an act of parliament paffed 1790, it was made turnpike, which farmers at prefent confider as a very great grievance. The feafon for fowing wheat is October; oats from the middle of March to the middle of April; barley in May; and turnip in June. Hay and harveft time generally continue from July to September. There are in the parifh 250 black cattle, 62 horfes, 21 carts, and 16 ploughs, drawn ufually by 4 horfes or 4 oxen, except in the feed time, when 2 horfes only are ufed; and then the number of ploughs are about a third more.

Prices

Price of Proviſions, Labour, Servants Wages, &c.—Proviſions have riſen in price ſince the commencement of the preſent century at leaſt two-thirds, and in ſome inſtances more. Butcher meat is at preſent from 3 d. to 4 d. a pound; chickens 3 d. a piece; hens and ducks 1 s.; butter 9 d. and cheeſe 3 d. a pound. The wages of a maſon are 1 s. 8 d. a day; of a carpenter 1 s. 4 d.; of a taylor 1 s.; or 6 d. with victuals; of a day labourer in huſbandry 1 s. The wages for harveſt-work of a man are from L. 1 : 5 : 0 to L. 1 : 10 : 0; of a woman from 18 s. to 20 s. The yearly wages of a male ſervant are from L. 6 to L. 8; of a female ſervant L. 3. Servants wages are nearly trippled within theſe laſt 50 years. Farmers prefer men ſervants who are unmarried to cottagers, chiefly becauſe they are always at hand, while the cottagers go to their own houſes after the ſtated hours of labour. Cottagers, however, are preferred for harveſt-work, as they do not require lodging, which it would be difficult to find for ſo many as are wanted at that ſeaſon. When a cottager is employed through the whole year, which is done in a few inſtances, he is allowed a houſe and yard, with about L. 6 of wages. Some eat in the farmer's houſe; and others are allowed, in name of maintenance, 6¼ bolls, or 52 ſtones of oatmeal, with paſture for a cow; but, in the latter caſe, the wages ſeldom exceed L 5, or L. 5 : 10 : 0 at moſt. By the wages he receives, with the produce of his wife's induſtry, ariſing chiefly from ſpinning, he is enabled to live pretty comfortably, to bring up three or four children, and to give them an education ſuitable to their ſtation. It is evident, indeed, that doing this with an income of about L. 10 muſt require good economy; but, unleſs it be wanting, there are no cottagers in ſtraitened circumſtances. Their ordinary food conſiſts of meal, partly of oats, partly of barley, potatoes, and milk. A family of few perſons, viz. a wife and four

children,

children, the hufband eating at his mafter's table, will confume 6 bolls of oat-meal, value L. 4 ; 4 bolls of barley-meal,
value L. 1 : 16 : 0 ; and 3 bolls of potatoes, value 10 s. 6 d.
There remains about L. 3 : 15 : 0, which is generally found
adequate to all the other neceffaries of fuch a family.

Population.—From comparing the prefent number of inhabited houfes and of baptifms, with thofe of any particular
period of the prefent century, it does not appear that the parifh has fuffered any material alteration in population. If
there be any difference at all, it feems rather to have increafed in a fmall degree. The prefent amount of its population
is 291 ; of thefe 136 are females, and 155 males ; among
whom are 46 married or widowers, and 26 marriageable
batchelors. There are 46 fouls under 10 years of age, 74
from 10 to 20, 114 from 20 to 50, 51 from 50 to 70 ; and
6 from 70 to 100. The annual average of births, for 50
years backwards, is about 9, being in proportion to the whole
population as 1 to 32, of marriages 3, and of deaths 4. A
farmer's family, at an average, confifts of 10 perfons. There
are in the parifh 13 weavers, 1 carpenter, 1 blackfmith, 1
fhoemaker, and 4 apprentices. The number of fervants in
the parifh is 68 ; of people born in other parifhes there are
176 ; and it is remarkable that there is but 1 farmer, and a
very few other houfeholders, who were born and now refide
in the parifh. The number of children for each marriage is,
at an average, about 4. All the inhabitants, except one female fervant, who has only a temporary refidence in the parifh, are of the eftablifhed church.

Church.—The value of the minifter's living, including the
glebe, at a moderate converfion of what is paid in victual, is
about 88 guineas. The patronage of the parifh belonged to
the

the Earl of Panmure, and fell to the crown by forfeiture in 1715; but the reprefentative of that family is ftill titular of the teinds. From that period, to 1781, the right of prefenting to the church lay dormant, government being either ig-norant of the forfeiture, or not careful enough to claim the patronage. The prefent incumbent, who is married, was ad-mitted minifter of Lunan in April 1790. Mr Walter Mill, or, as he is called by fome hiftorians, Sir Walter Mill, a Po-pifh prieft, held the office of paftor of Lunan 20 years; but, afterwards embracing the doctrines of the Reformed, he was forced to abandon his charge. He was apprehended in the town of Dyfart by order of Cardinal Beaton, carried to St Andrew's, tried, condemned, and burnt, at the age of 82, in April 1558. One of the minifters, Mr Alexander Pedie, who died in 1713, bequeathed fome plate for the Lord's Supper in the church of Lunan, on this fingular condition, that any Epifcopal congregation within feven miles of Lunan requiring them fhould have the ufe of them for that purpofe. There is a marble monument erected in the church to his memory, for upholding which his widow bequeathed an an-nuity of L. 4 Scotch, payable to the kirk-feffion. The church is an old edifice, repaired in 1773. The manfe and offices were built in 1783, and ftand nearly a mile north of the church.

Poor.—The poor in the parifh of Lunan have been always well fupplied. They have never been numerous, which has occafioned the funds to be uncommonly large. Befides the weekly collections, there is a capital of L. 500, for the main-tenance of the poor, and other purpofes to which parifh funds are ufually applied. The number on the poor's roll has been generally from four to fix; but, from 1783 to 1790, there were eight; and confequently, during that period, the

dif-

disbursements of the session were much about equal to the whole income. The dearth, at the commencement of that period, was certainly the cause of the additional number; for they are again reduced to six, who receive from 3 s. to 4 s. 6 d. a month, with a small sum annually for purchasing fuel. As no heritor, nor any person of superior rank, resides in the parish, and the congregation is small, the weekly collections, which are only from one to two shillings, would not be nearly adequate to the wants of the poor, were it not for the annual rent arising from the accumulated stock. The origin of this capital appears to have been legacies left long ago for the behoof of the poor.

School.—David Jameson, formerly a farmer in the parish, left 2000 merks Scots, half of the interest of which was for the poor, and the other half was made payable to the schoolmaster for teaching six poor scholars. Till lately, this was all the schoolmaster enjoyed; but, by decreet of the commissioners of supply, the heritors are now burdened with the payment of 200 merks Scots of yearly salary. This, with the salary, and usual emoluments belonging to the offices of session-clerk and precentor, and fees for teaching from 30 to 40 scholars, makes a living of about L. 25 Sterling.

Miscellaneous Observations.—The English, or that dialect of it peculiar to North Britain, is the only language used or known by the inhabitants of Lunan. Many places in the parish, it is probable, owe their names to their being situated in the neighbourhood of Redcastle, now a ruin, in the parish of Inverkeillor, and formerly a royal residence. Hence Courthill, where the courts of justice had been held; Hawkhill, where the King's faulconer had resided; and Cothill, where the shepherd, it is likely, had his habitation and cots
for

for his flock. The names of some places are evidently derived from the Gaelic, as the name of the parish, and Dunbart-
net (called also Drumbartnet) from Dun a hill, which is so named from being situated on an eminence. There is a salmon
fishery at the mouth of the river, but it has been very unproductive for several years past, yielding nothing but trout,
with which the river formerly abounded. They are now
much destroyed by the steeping of flax, large quantities of
which have of late years been raised in the district. It is not
improbable but this operates also as a cause of the salmon
having deserted the bay, where they were sometimes caught
in great plenty. The fishery is annexed to the farm of Lunan, and no particular rent specified for it. Besides the stated rent, tenants, in some instances, are bound to give their
landlords, in the summer, one draught of their carts; their
servants a day in the hay-harvest; and their reapers a day in
autumn. The difficulty of getting people to hire at a time
when all are busy, is the reason assigned for continuing to
exact the two last. Tenants require like services of their
subtenants; but they are always limited to a certain number
of days, and seldom exceed three or four yearly. Tenants in
general complain more of being obliged to grind their corn
at some particular mill, and pay high stipulated multures, a
custom which prevails almost universally in North Britain,
than of these trivial services, which are seldom exacted so ri-
gorously as to make them distressing. The fuel commonly
used in summer is turf, or broom, valued from 1 s. to 2 s. a
cart load, of which there is plenty in the parish; and, in
winter, coals, 70 stone of which, called a boll, cost 6 s. at
Arbroath, where no duty is exacted.

Rev. John Gowans.

The following miftakes occurred in the account of Lunan.

Page 463. l. 9. After the word Forfar, add, 'from which 'circumftance the name is fuppofed to be derived;' and *for* Laonon *read* Lônon.

P. 465. l. 1. *for* Arlukie *read* Arbikie.

466. laft line, *for* few *read* five.

467. laft line, *for* 88 *read* 80.

470 l. 4 from the foot, *for* turf *read* furze *or* whins.

UNITED PARISHES OF LUNDIE AND FOULIS.

(Counties of Angus and Perth.—Presbytery of Dundee. —Synod of Angus and Mearns.)

By the Reverend Mr ANDREW HALLY.

Erection and Constitution.

THESE parishes, originally distinct, were united in 1618, by decreet of the High Commission, and have ever since been under the charge of one minister, who dispenses ordinances alternately at each church; but, as they lie in different shires, (Lundie in Forfar, and Foulis in Perth), each parish continues to have its own kirk-session, poor's box, and session register. It will therefore be proper to describe each of them separately. And, first, of

LUNDIE.

Name, Extent, Surface, Soil, &c.—LUNDIE, the name of the largest lake in the parish, as well as of the parish itself, is of Gaelic origin, being derived from *Linn-Dé*, which signifies the *water or pool of God*, probably on account of its great extent; as high hills, of old, were called *the hills of God*, and deep waters, *the waters of God*. It is of a circular form, and contains 3258 acres, of which 2000 are arable, about

110 in lakes, 119 in meadow ground, and the remainder hill
and pasture. It is surrounded by Siddley-hills on the north
and west. The south slope is green, and affords good pasture. The north or back part is heathy. The middle of
the parish is pretty flat, and the soil is sufficiently productive, except in rainy or late seasons, when the crop is seldom
got in without damage. The air is not unhealthy *, though
it must necessarily be moist, from the number of lakes and
fens in the parish.

Lakes and Echo.—There are 4 lakes, all of which are supposed to be full of marl, from the specimens that have been dug
from their sides; but none of them have as yet been drained.
Lundie loch, which is about a gun-shot from the church,
covers 72½ acres, and is 60 feet deep in some places. All
of them abound in pikes, perches, and eels; but there are no
trouts, or any other kind of fish in them. These lakes are
the fountains of Dighty Water, which is so beneficial to the
country in general, particularly to Dundee; and which
empties itself into the sea at Monyfeith, about 10 or 12
miles from this.—At a small hill, about 60 feet above the
lake of Pitlail, there is a remarkable echo. When a person
stands upon this hill, the surrounding mountains of Siddley
forming a kind of amphitheatre, he will find a loud cry distinctly repeated three times at least, if not four †.

Heritors

* There are no local distempers prevalent in either of these
parishes. The most frequent disease is the rheumatism. Instances of extraordinary longevity sometimes occur. One man
died here, about 20 years ago, aged 106; and many have exceeded 80.

† The following anecdote strongly marks the simplicity of country people:—One summer evening, a young fellow sat down on
this hill to divert himself and some friends, by playing on the
shepherd's

Heritors and Rent.—There are 3 heritors, but none of them reside in the parish. About 30 years ago, the land rent of Lundie was superior to that of Foulis; but the case is now reversed, which may be owing to the long leases or diferent tacks granted, by which the principal heritor of the former parish has not had it in his power to inclose and improve the ground, whereby the greater part of it is still in its natural state. The difference between the rent of Lundie and that of Foulis cannot be stated with precision; the former is reckoned not much under 1000 l; and some idea of the advance of rent may be formed from one farm, which, in 1642, was let at 50 merks Scotch, but is now esteemed a good bargain at 100 l. Sterling.

Agriculture, Produce, and Cattle.—The chief productions are barley, oats, potatoes, and flax. There is more of this last article raised here than at Foulis, but not so much artificial grass. Several farmers have tried the culture of wheat, but have all given it up, except one. The seed time for oats is from the 1st of March; for barley, about the 20th of May; and for wheat, from the middle of September to the end of October. Considerable quantities of oats, barley, and oat-meal, are exported, besides supplying the inhabitants. The crop is somewhat later than at Foulis.—There are 140 horses, and 364 cattle; 28 ploughs, chiefly of the construction recommended by Mr James Small, in his Treatise on

Ploughs,

shepherd's pipe, an instrument upon which he was reckoned a good performer. But he had hardly played a single tune, when, hearing his music distinctly repeated three times over, he got up in great terror, averring that the Devil was certainly in the place; that he had never before engaged with *Satan*, and he was determined he never would again; whereupon he broke his pipe in pieces, and could never afterwards be prevailed upon to play any more.

Ploughs, &c. ; and about 37 carts, with hay tops for leading corn. Where the ground is level, and the ridges ſtraight, theſe ploughs are managed by two horſes only ; and one man both holds and drives, which occaſions a conſiderable ſaving of time and labour *.

Population.—For theſe 30 years paſt, the population has varied little ; though, from the regiſter of baptiſms and burials, there appears to be a great increaſe ; the number of the former, within that period, being 343, and that of the latter only 145. The number of inhabitants, at preſent, is 334, all of whom attend the eſtabliſhed Church, except two or three Seceders. Of theſe, there are 16 farmers, who keep two ploughs each ; 2 ſmaller ones, who have a horſe and ſome cows ; 14 weavers and 2 wrights, who have a cow and an acre of ground apiece ; 2 taylors, 2 ale-ſellers, and 1 ſmith. There is alſo a ſmall bleachfield, with a waſhing-mill, beetles, &c. and a thread mill, which give work to 14 or 15 people.

F O U L I S.

Extent, Surface, and Soil.—This pariſh is of a triangular form, lying nearly eaſt and weſt. The greateſt length is four

meaſured

* The average annual wages of a plowman, in both pariſhes, are 8 l. though ſome have 10 l. ; thoſe of a maid-ſervant 3 l. including bounties ; ſuch as 2 yards of linen and an apron, with ground for 2 lippies of lintſeed. About 40 years ago, the wages of the former were only 2 l. and of the latter 20 s. with the bounties. A day's wages of a man employed in agriculture are 1 s. or 8 d. with his victuals ; thoſe of a wright 10 d. a maſon 1 s. and a taylor 8 d. with their maintenance. Theſe wages are found ſufficient for the ſupport of themſelves and families while in health ; and, when in diſtreſs, they are aided from the funds.

meafured miles, and the medium breadth fomewhat more than one. It contains 1200 acres of arable land, and 744 of hill, wood, and pafture ground —The foil is, in general, rich, well cultivated, and moftly inclofed. The ground has an eafy flope towards the fouth, which renders the fituation very agreeable. There is only one hill, called the *Black Law*, which, though noted for good pafturage formerly, is now become of little value, by the total removal of fheep from it. There are neither rivers nor rivulets in either of the parifhes, but feveral lakes. One, which was called the *Piper Dam*, and which covered 55 acres, was drained about 15 years ago. A confiderable quantity of marl, as well as of peats, has been dug from it. It not only fupplies the parifh, but part of the neighbourhood, with that fpecies of manure, and yields a confiderable fum yearly to the proprietor.

Heritor, Tenants, and Rent.—The whole parifh is the property of Sir William Murray of Auchtertyre, Baronet, who does not refide in it.—More than one half is occupied by one farmer and his fon ; another farms 180 acres, a third 150, and the reft is divided into about 20 fmall farms. The rent is above 1000 l. Sterling. The farms let at from 10 s. to 20 s. an acre.

Agriculture, Produce, and Cattle —About one third of the arable land in this parifh, amounting to nearly 400 acres, is laid out in green crops, grafs, turnips, potatoes, and flax. The reft produces wheat, oats, and barley. Foulis was the firft parifh in this country where a regular rotation of crops was attempted. It is about 20 years fince the proprietors introduced it, and the fuccefs encourages the continuance. The feed time is the fame as at Lundie; and the crop is generally all cut down and gathered in by the 1ft of October.

The

The parish, besides supplying itself with provisions *, exports considerable quantities of grain. There are about 90 horses, and 300 head of cattle. The number of ploughs and carts is much the same as at Lundie.

Population.—Owing to the enlarging of farms, and throwing several possessions into one, the population has decreased to the number of about 100. The number of baptisms, during the first ten years of the present century, was 163; and, during the last ten years preceding 1790, only 91. Yet, during the last 30 years, the number of baptisms exceeds that of the burials by nearly one third, there having been 300 baptised, and only 208 buried in the parish within that period. The number of inhabitants, at present, is 314, all members of the established Church, except 8 or 9 Seceders; among whom there are 10 weavers, 2 wrights, 2 taylors, 1 smith, 1 shoemaker, 1 distiller, and 20 small farmers, each of whom has a plough, some with 4 horses, and others 1 or 2, besides the 4 great farmers above mentioned. But the present state of both parishes will best appear from the following

Statistical Table of the united Parishes of Lundie and Foulis.

Length in English miles,	7½	Number of births for 30	
Breadth, - -	1½	years preceding 1790,	643
Population in 1790, -	648	Ditto of deaths, -	353
———— anno 1755,	586	Members of the Establish-	
		ed Church, -	636
Increase,	62	Seceders - -	12
		Proprietors,	

* The prices of provisions have risen greatly of late in both parishes; beef, mutton, veal, &c. from 2 d. to 4 d. *per* lib.; hens from 6 d. to 1 s.; butter from 4 d. to 9 d.; wheat from 14 s. to 21 s. *per* boll; barley from 10 s. to 15 s.; and meal in proportion.

Proprietors,	-	-	4	Perfons employed about the	
Clergyman,	-	-	1	bleachfield, - -	15
Schoolmafters,	-	-	2	Diftiller, - - -	1
Farmers above 50 l. *per an-*				Poor, - - -	10
num,	-	-	4	Horfes, - - -	230
Ditto under 50 l.	-		38	Cattle, - - -	664
Keepers of ale-houfes,	-		2	Carts, - - -	74
Smiths,	-	-	2	Ploughs, - - -	56
Wrights,	-	-	4	Total extent in acres,	5257
Weavers,	-		24	Ditto of arable ground,	3200
Shoemaker,	-	-	1	Rent in Sterling money a-	
Taylors,	-	-	4	bout - -	L. 2000

Ecclefiaftical State of both Parifhes.—The manfe, and a glebe of fix acres, are fituated at Lundie. The ftipend confifts of 4 chalders of victual, one half meal, the other barley, and 30 l. in money, including communion elements. It may be eftimated at 70 l. *per annum.* Colonel Alexander Duncan of Lundie is fuppofed to be patron of both parifhes, though Sir William Murray claims the patronage of Foulis. The church of Lundie lies exactly 3 miles and 120 feet diftant from Foulis, in a north-weft direction. When it was built cannot be afcertained; nor is there any thing very remarkable about it, except an elegant monument lately erected at the eaft end of it, by Lady M. Duncan of London, in memory of her hufband, the late Sir William Duncan, phyfician to his Majefty, who lies interred there. But the church of Foulis merits particular notice, as a remarkable piece of ancient architecture. It is 88 feet 10 inches in length, and 27 feet 9 in breadth, and is built all of hewn ftone. It is perfectly entire, without the leaft fymptom of decay, although it was built in the year 1142, during the time of the Crufades, as appears by an infcription on a large oak beam that fupported the organ loft, having been erected in confequence

of

of a vow made by the wife of one of the lords of this place, that, " in cafe her hufband fhould return in fafety from the holy wars, fhe would build and endow a church *." It was made collegiate by Andrew the firft Lord Gray, who placed therein a provoft and feveral prebends, with fuitable endowments, in the reign of James II. On the top of the eaft gavel of the church there is a crofs ; in the church-yard there is another, 8 foot high ; and, about 10 or 12 years ago, there was a third crofs, 14 or 15 feet high, with fteps all round, about a quarter of a mile north from the church. A new roof was put on the church about four years ago.

Schools and Poor.——There are two fchools, one in each parifh, but both are poorly provided, the legal falary of each being only 40 l. Scotch. The average number of fcholars attending each is 30 ; and, though aided by voluntary fubfcriptions, the encouragement is fo trifling, that the parifhes are often expofed to changes, and as often but indifferently fupplied. The average number of poor in each parifh is 5. The collections at church, with the dues of the mort-cloth, and the intereft of a fmall fum lent, has hitherto been found fufficient for their fupport ; and none are allowed to beg.

Mifcellaneous

* Part of this infcription is ftill legible, viz. *Hoc Templum ftructum fuit Anno Millefimo centefimo Quadragefimo fecundo ab A. Gray.*——There are feveral other remains of antiquity to be feen here, particularly a number of paintings upon a wainfcot partition, (which feparates Lord Gray's burial-place from the church, and is fuppofed to be equally ancient), reprefenting our Saviour in various attitudes, the Apoftles, with the infignia of their martyrdom, the Roman Centurion, &c. At the weft end of the church, there are the remains of a large font, befides another without, and a third within the door. About 20 years ago, there ftood in the eaft end of the church a large black oak table, which went by the name of *the altar.* It was placed before a prefs in the wall, with an iron door. Upon thefe are reprefentations of priefts in their facerdotal robes, &c.

Miscellaneous Observations.—The roads were formerly made by statute labour, which is now commuted. Turnpikes are beginning to be erected ; the people, in general, approve of them ; but some of the inferior ranks are not yet reconciled to them.—The fuel generally used here is coals, at the rate of 3 l. *per* chalder. Some peats are also used.—The principal advantages of Lundie and Foulis are their vicinity to the Tay, by which lime and coals are easily procured, and the extra produce of the parishes exported.—The names of several of the villages are derived from the Gaelic ; *e. g. Balshando*, the old black town on the back of the hill ; *Lincrieff*, a town on the side of a hill, with trees, and the like : Others from their situation ; as *Smistown*, because mists lie long upon it, &c.— The people, in general, are sober, regular, and industrious. They enjoy, in a reasonable degree, the comforts of life, and seem to be contented with their condition.

PARISH of MAINS of FINTRY,

(COUNTY OF FORFAR.)

Communicated by the Rev. Mr CHARLES PEEBLES.

Name, Situation, Soil and Climate, &c.

THE ancient name of this parish was *Strathdighty*, being part of that pleasant strath, through which Dighty directs its course to the frith of Tay. The present name is Mains of Fintry, from the old family seat of Fintry, which is near the church. It belongs to the presbytery of Dundee, and synod of Angus and Mearns. It is 4 miles long, and 3 broad about the middle; but becomes considerably narrower toward the extremities. The water of Dighty, which runs from west to east, intersects the parish into nearly two equal parts; and from the banks of this beautiful stream, the ground rises gently to the north and south. The face of the country has a sweet and delightful appearance, being all inclosed with thorn hedges, which are in a very flourishing state. They shelter and beautify the fields; but at the same time attract great flocks of birds,

which

which deftroy much of the grain. There is alfo a good number of large oak and afh trees, and fome thriving plantations in the parifh. The foil in the haughs is a deep loam, and produces excellent crops. The reft of the parifh, with fome little exception, is a pretty deep mould upon till, and is very fertile. The air is dry and falubrious, there being no ftagnated water in the parifh. Hence there are no epidemical or topical difeafes, and the people in general enjoy very good health ; only they are now and then vifited by confumptions and fevers.

Population.—From the regifter of baptifms, this parifh appears to have been much more populous 80 years ago than at prefent. At that period, the number of fouls was above 1200. In the year 1768, it contained only 660. This decreafe was occafioned by ejecting the fubtenants, and enlarging the farms ; and from the people removing into the neighbouring town of Dundee, where employment was more eafily procured. It is now increafing very rapidly, from the encouragement given to labourers, and from the amazing number of hands employed in bleaching, and other manufactures carried on upon the water of Dighty. Hence, in the year 1790, the number of fouls was found to be 878, which is confiderably greater than it was 40 years ago.

STATISTICAL

STATISTICAL TABLE of the PARISH of MAINS of FINTRY.

LENGTH in English miles,	-	4	Number of Seceders, - -	40
Breadth, - -		3	——— Proprietors residing,	2
Population in 1790,	-	878	——— —— non-residing,	5
Ditto, in 1755, -	-	709	——— Clergymen, -	1
			——— Tradesmen, -	42
——Increase, -	-	169	——— Apprentices, -	10
Annual Average of Births,	-	28	——— Schoolmasters, -	1
——— —— Deaths,	-	10	——— Farmers, -	25
——— —— Marriages,		9	——— Souls in their fami-	
Number of Males,	- -	600	lies, - -	225
——— Females, -	-	278	——— Male servants, -	70
——— Persons under 10			——— Female ditto, -	40
years of age,		210	——— Poor, - -	8
——— —— from 10 to 20,		250	Annual average of their sup-	
——— —— 20 to 50,		250	port, - - -	L. 10
——— —— 50 to 70,		150	Number of Ploughs, -	43
——— —— 70 to 100,		18	——— Four-wheeled Car-	
——— Families, (about 6 in			riages, - -	1
each), - -		154	——— Carts, -	84
——— Members of the			——— Horses, - -	1500
Established Church,		838	——— Black Cattle, -	300

Valued rent, in Scotch money, L. 1933   6   8
Real rent in Sterling ditto,   2500   0   0

Number of Acres under Oats,	200	Number of Acres under Flax,	20
——— ——— Barley,	300	——— ——— Turnips,	50
——— ——— Wheat,	100	——— —— in Pasture, -	300
——— ——— Potatoes,	30	——— — Sown Grass, -	700

Church,

Church, School, Poor, &c.—The King is patron of the living of Mains. The stipend is worth about L. 90. The church seems originally to have been a Roman Catholic chapel, as the fount is yet to be seen, and a small press in the wall, with an iron door, in which perhaps were deposited some of their sacred relics. It is very ancient, and, though it lately received some repairs, is still in a ruinous condition. The manse * was built in 1760, and, though not a large house, is very sufficient and commodious. The poor are all maintained in their own houses; their funds arise from the collections on Sabbath, which may be about L. 10 *per annum*, from the produce of

---

* There is an old castle near the manse of great antiquity. It was built in the year 1311, but by whom is uncertain. It was for a great series of years, the property and residence of the Grahams of Fintry. The buildings are in the form of a square, with a strong tower in the front. There is only one principal gate, which is towards the west. It has a good deal of out-works, and seems to have been a place of considerable strength. Tradition relates, that during the feudal system, its proprietors maintained almost a constant war with the family of Powrie, another strong hold in the neighbouring parish. Above the principal gate there is a passage, which seems to have been designed for the inhabitants to pour down boiling water, or stones, or any other offensive materials, upon their assailants when they attempted to force it. This old castle stands upon a pretty steep bank of a small rivulet, which separates it from the minister's garden. It is surrounded with very high trees, which, when covered with foliage, almost conceal it; and the chimney heads appearing over their tops, with here and there a peep of the old ruins, have a very picturesque appearance from the windows of the manse. The foundations of the old castle, one of the proprietors of which (viz. Claverhouse) distinguished himself in persecuting the Presbyterians, under Charles II. were lately dug up by a farmer. There appeared to have been a Popish chapel belonging to the house, as the fount, altar piece, &c. were discovered. There are in the church yard two stone coffins, of about two and a half feet deep, which consist of four large stones, secured at the corners with bars of iron. Tradition relates, that the plague once raged in this parish, and that the bodies of some of the unhappy sufferers were there inclosed.

of the mortcloth, and a two-wheeled machine for carrying the dead, which is fometimes let for hire ; and from the interest of a fmall mortification. The fchoolmafter's falary is 100 merks Scotch ; the fchool wages are very fmall, and oft ill paid. His whole living does not amount to above L. 14 a-year. Upon this he could not poffibly fubfift, were it not for the encouragement he has for boarding. It is furely a pity, that fuch a ufeful clafs of men, who lay the foundation of all morality and religion, cultivating the tender mind, and " teaching the young idea how to fhoot," fhould be fo fhamefully neglected. While the Legiflature is meliorating the fituation of the clergy, furely the poor fchoolmafters ought not to be neglected.

Agriculture and Produce.—Land here is rifing in its value, and is generally fold at 28 or 30 years purchafe. The ufual rent* is 30 s. *per* acre at an average. They begin to fow about the latter end of March, and reap in the months of September and October. The rotation of crops is 3 of grafs, 1 of oats, and 1 of barley ; then a green crop, followed by a crop of oats, or barley fown with grafs feeds. Sometimes, inftead of the green crop, the land is fummer fallowed, and fown with wheat ; after which the ground is manured, and a crop of oats or barley taken. The farmers find the artificial graffes to be very profitable, as they fell very high, either on the ground or when turned into hay. It is very common to receive L. 5 the acre for rye-grafs and clover uncut, and 8 d. the ftone when cut and dried. The cultivation of turnips, too, amply recompences
the

* The rent of cottages is from 20 s. to 30 s. yearly. A labouring man earns in fummer 1 s. *per* day, and in winter 8 d. ; tailors have 8 d. *per* day and their victuals ; wrights 1 s. 2 d. ; mafons 2 s. ; good labouring men fervants have L. 10 *per annum*, and maids L. 4. The average price of meal is 1 s. the peck ; of potatoes 7 d.

the hufbandman, whether he fells them on the ground, or feeds cattle with them; and he fcarcely ever fails to have a good crop of barley after this valuable root. Some of the farmers alfo raife a few yams, which are good feeding for horfes, given raw, for they are not fit for boiling. The potatoes alfo thrive here pretty well, but they are generally planted too thick in the drills, which are too near each other. The drills fhould be always fo far feparate, as to allow the plough to get up amongft them, to lay to or take away the earth, as may feem neceffary. The farmers feem averfe to fowing of flax, as they think their ground not proper for it; it would furely be a very valuable crop if it could be raifed, as there are fo many linen manufactures carried on here. But of this the farmers, who underftand their bufinefs very well, are the beft judges. The horfes are almoft all employed in hufbandry. They are generally ftout, well made, and of a good fize. The black cattle are of a middle fize, about that of the Galloway breed. There are a few cows, however, approximating to the large Englifh kind. Many more calves are produced than can be reared. Hence they are fattened and fold to the butchers in Dundee; but it would, perhaps, be a more profitable plan, if the farmers could afford to keep them, till they were 3 or 4 years old, and then fell them to the graziers. There is little or no cheefe made in the parifh. Much more emolument arifes from felling the milk in Dundee.

Minerals, Fuel, &c.—There are freeftone and flate quarries in the parifh. Some years ago there was a mineral fpring, which was reckoned medicinal, and frequented by many people, who received much benefit from it; but its fource being covered by the building of a bridge, it has difappeared for fome time paft. The only fuel now made ufe of here is coals, brought by water from different parts of Fife.

They

They coſt at the ſhore 6 ½ d. *per* cwt. Here they are free of duty, but this is a burden ſeverely felt by many other parts of the country. It is much againſt the increaſe and proſperity of manufactures, and ſhould be removed by the Legiſlature.

Advantages, &c.—This pariſh being ſituated near Dundee, finds a ready market for every article the inhabitants have to ſell; who can, with equal eaſe, procure any thing they want from that town. The farmers have plenty of manure from it, and being ſo near the ſhore, the lime is pretty reaſonable; which, with dung, anſwers all the purpoſes of manure. This pariſh alſo poſſeſſes advantages over ſeveral places of the country in point of climate. None of it lying very high, (being moſtly dry and ſheltered with hedges) they have their harveſt more early, and do not run ſuch a riſk of loſing the crop by ſhaking winds or early froſts. And in an exigence, plenty of hands can always be got from Dundee to cut down the crops ſpeedily. Many of the people look upon it as a great inconvenience, to pay toll, when they ſcarcely touch upon the turnpike, and while their own bye-roads are almoſt impaſſable; but it is to be hoped this diſadvantage will ſoon be removed.

Manufactures.—Dighty, the only river in the pariſh, drives more machinery for its ſize than, perhaps, any water in Britain; every fall upon it turns a mill; ſo that within this pariſh, though not above 4 miles in length, there are no fewer than 33 mills erected for different purpoſes. There are ſeveral corn mills, barley mills, and mills for waſhing and cleaning yarn. There is one erecting at preſent for ſpinning flax, upon a capital of L. 4000, which, it is ſuppoſed, will give bread to a great number of both young and old people, and bring conſiderable emoluments to the proprietors; one frame is already up, by which

which they have had a fpecimen of the work. They fpin
with amazing quicknefs, and make very good yarn, only
as it is drawn out dry, it appears rough. This might,
perhaps, be obviated, if they could fall upon any method
of wetting the flax while it is fpinning, which would render the cloth more fmooth, and give it a finer appearance.
There are nine bleachfields in the parifh, three of which
are carried on upon a very large fcale. They bleach a
great quantity of coarfe cloths, which they call Soldier's
farking and Ofnaburgs, moft of which they export. This
demand for yarn and cloth, affords a profitable employment
to the women in this place, who, as they fpin with both
hands, can eafily make 8 d. a-day. There are alfo upon
the water of Dighty, a wauk mill and a fnuff mill. In
fhort, a perfon has only to come to this water to fee the
happy effects of induftry and manufactures, and to what a
height they may be carried. While the manufacturer enriches himfelf, he does a real benefit to fociety, by employing
thofe hands, who muft have either become burdens upon the
public by afking charity, or nuifances by worfe practices.

Character.——The inhabitants of this parifh are of an ordinary fize, and generally ftout and well proportioned.
They are humane, induftrious, well difpofed, and, in general, regular in their attendance upon the ordinances of religion. They enjoy the comforts of life to a confiderable degree, and, though they are by no means niggardly, are pru-
dently economical, and contented with their circumftances.
The young men do not feem much inclined either to the army
or the navy. A few of them, however, have made choice
of a feafaring life. Though there are 3 petty public houfes
in the parifh, that fell ale and whifky, yet they have no
bad effect upon the morals of the people. There have been

no

no inftances of fuicide, nor of any executed or banifhed for capital crimes, in the remembrance of any now living.

As it may doubtlefs prove entertaining to many readers, to obferve the progrefs of manners in the fpace of 30 years, the following comparifon is added, between the ftate of this parifh in 1760 and in 1790, in fundry particulars.

COMPARATIVE STATEMENT *of the parifh in* 1760 *and* 1790.

In 1760, Land was rented at 6 s. an acre, on an average only 2 fmall farms were inclofed.

In 1790, Land is rented at 30 s. an acre, all inclofed with ftone dikes and thorn hedges.

In 1760, No wheat was fown in the parifh, except one half acre by the minifter, no grafs nor turnip feed was fown, and no kail nor potatoes planted in the open fields.

In 1790, Above 100 acres are fown with wheat; about three fifths of the ground are under grafs, turnips, kail, and potatoes.

In 1760, Land was plowed with oxen : only a few horfes were kept to draw the harrow in feed time, and bring in the common harveft. L. 7 was thought a great price for a horfe.

In 1790, Oxen are not employed in agriculture. Farmers have their faddle horfes, worth from L. 24 to L. 30, and work horfes from L. 20 to L. 25 each.

In 1760, The wages of men fervants, that followed the plough, were L. 3 a-year: of maid fervants, L. 1, 10 s.

In 1790, Men fervant's wages are L. 8, fome L. 10 : maid fervant's ditto L. 4.

In 1760, Day labourers were got at 6 d. a-day; tailors at 3 d. wrights at 6 d.; and mafons at 10 d. a-day.

In 1790, Day-labourers receive 1 s.; tailors 8 d. wrights 1 s. 2 d. and mafons 2 s. a-day.

In 1760, No Englifh cloth was worn but by the minifter and a quaker.

In 1790, There are few who do not wear Englifh cloth : Several the beft fuperfine ; cotton vefts are common.

In

In 1760, Men's stockings in general were what was called plaiding hose, made of white woollen cloth; the women wore coarse plaids: not a cloak, nor bonnet, was worn by any woman in the whole parish.

In 1760, There were only two hats in the parish; the men wore cloth bonnets.

In 1760, There was only one eight day clock in the parish, six watches, and one tea kettle.

In 1760, The people in this parish never visited each other, but at Christmas. The entertainment was broth and beef; the visitors sent to an alehouse for five or six pints of ale, and were merry over it without any ceremony.

In 1760, Beef and mutton were 2 d. *per* lb.; butter 5 d. *per* lb.; cheese 2 s. 6 d. *per* stone, and eggs at 1 d. halfpenny *per* dozen.

In 1760, In this parish there were four meal mills, one washing mill for cleaning yarn, one wauk mill, and one snuff mill.

In 1760, There was one bleachfield in the parish, which employed 10 persons.

In 1760, Children at school had a piece of pease bread in their pockets for dinner.

In 1790, Cotton and thread stockings are worn by both sexes, masters and servants; some have silk ones: the women who wear plaids have them fine, and faced with silk; silk plaid cloaks and bonnets are very numerous.

In 1790, Few bonnets are worn; the bonnet-maker trade in the next parish is given up.

In 1790, There are 30 clocks, above 100 watches, and at least 160 tea-kettles, there being scarce a family but hath one, and many that have two.

In 1790, People visit each other often; a few neighbours are invited to one house to dinner; six or seven dishes are set on the table, elegantly dressed; after dinner a large bowl of rum punch is drunk; then tea; again another bowl; after that supper, and what they call the grace drink.

In 1790, Beef and mutton are 4 d. *per* lb.; butter 10 d.; cheese 5 s. 4 d. *per* stone, and eggs 6 d. *per* dozen.

In 1790, There are 3 meal mills, 17 washing mills, 5 mills for beating thread and cloth, one wauk mill, one snuff mill, and 5 barley mills.

In 1790, There are 9 bleachfields which employ above 100 persons.

In 1790, Children at school have wheaten bread, sweet milk, butter, cheese, eggs, and sometimes roast meat.

In

In 1760, Every perſon in the pariſh, if in health, attended divine worſhip on Sunday, which
was regularly and religiouſly
obſerved. There were only 4
Seceders in the pariſh.

In 1760, Few were guilty of any
breach of the 3d command-
ment. The name of God was
reverenced and held ſacred.

In 1790, Much lukewarmneſs
prevails, with regard to religious inſtruction ; and a conſequent inattention and indifference, as to worſhip and crdi-
nances. Sunday is far from
being ſo ſtrictly obſerved, and
the number of Seceders has increaſed tenfold.

In 1790, The 3d commandment
ſeems to be almoſt forgotten,
and profane ſwearing abounds
greatly.

PARISH of MARYTON,

(County of Forfar, Synod of Angus and Mearns, Presbytery of Brechin.)

By the Rev. Mr James Wilson.

Boundaries, Eſtates, Extent, Air, &c.

THIS pariſh is bounded on the N. by the river of Southeſk and the baſon or back ſands of Montroſe; on the S. by the ſea and the pariſh of Lunan. There are only now two eſtates here, Old Montroſe and Dyſart. Old Montroſe was the property of the great family of Montroſe, till the reign of Charles II. We then find it in the poſſeſſion of the famous Earl of Middleton. Since that time it has paſſed through the hands of a great many, and is now the property of Sir David Carnegie, Baronet, of Southeſk. From its name, one might be apt to imagine, that there had been a town here before the preſent town of Montroſe was built; but of this there remains no tradition. Bonnyton, which is now joined to Old Montroſe, was the ſeat of the family of Wood. It is only within theſe

few

few years paſt that the remains of the old caſtle fell down.
It had been regularly fortified, with a complete ditch a-
round it, which ſtill remains entire. Dyſart belongs to
Thomas Carnegie, Eſq; of Craigo, and was purchaſed not
many years ago by his family. None of the heritors reſide.—This pariſh contains altogether from 2500 to 3000
acres of land. The valued rent is L. 3000 Scots, and the
real rent about L. 1700 or L. 1800 Sterling. The lands
in general are not high rented. In the greateſt part of this
pariſh the lands lie very low, almoſt on a level with the
ſea; this, together with the fogs that riſe from the baſon of
Montroſe, makes the air damp. This pariſh often, eſpecially in the ſpring months, when the eaſterly winds prevail is involved in a cloud, when it is bright ſun-ſhine a
mile or two to the weſtward. Agues were very common
here before the low grounds were drained; out ſince that
event took place, the people are in general healthy, and
many of them live to a good old age. It were to be wiſhed that the lower claſſes could be prevailed upon to inoculate their children for the ſmall-pox; but no arguments
will perſuade them to lay aſide their abſurd prejudices. If
this mode were adopted, the lives of many children might
be ſaved to the community.

Population, &c.—According to Dr Webſter's report, the
number of ſouls was then 633. This pariſh is not very
populous, their being no villages in it, nor manufactures of
any kind. The whole pariſh is divided into large farms;
and theſe requiring only a ſtated number of people for their
cultivation, any increaſe that may ariſe muſt go to other
places for employment. Being ſo near the port of Montroſe, a great many of the young men go to ſea. There
are no records of the number of inhabitants before the preſent incumbent was ſettled in 1778. In 1779, the number
of

of people above 15 years of age was 369; in 1786, a period of 7 years, there were 367 people above 15 years of age, and 142 under 15, in all 529. In January 1793, another period of 7 years, the state of the population is as follows :

Under 10 years of age,	-	139
Between 10 and 20,	- -	92
———— 20 and 30,	- -	81
———— 30 and 40,	- -	71
———— 40 and 50,	- -	70
———— 50 and 60,	- -	28
———— 60 and 70,	- -	30
———— 70 and 80,	- -	15
———— 80 and 90,	- -	3
Total,		529

The increase since 1786 is 20; and the cause of it is, some of the principal tenants having subset part of their lands. The average of the number of baptisms, as nearly as can be ascertained for 14 years past, is annually 18; marriages 5; and burials 12; but it is to be observed, that the register of baptisms, burials and marriages, is not so regularly kept as formerly, owing to the tax upon the registration, trifling as it is. The common people, not being compelled to pay it, rather choose to save 3 d. than to have either a baptism, burial or marriage, inserted in the register.

Soil, Agriculture, &c.—The soil in this parish is various, according to the situation. Upon the low grounds of Old Montrose it is a strong deep clay, commonly called in Scotland Carse land, admirably adapted for wheat. There is a small ridge of hills that runs through the parish from E.

E. to W. and divides Old Montroſe from Dyſart. The ſoil upon theſe riſing grounds is in general a very fine loam, which bears excellent crops of barley, turnips and graſs. Upon the lands of Dyſart, as they lie higher, the ſoil is of a lighter quality than Old Montroſe.—This pariſh is in a pretty high ſtate of cultivation, and would have been much more ſo, were it not for the pernicious effects of long leaſes and low rents, leaſes let many years ago, and many years of them ſtill to run. Improvement of land on a large ſcale, and to extent, did not take place in this part of the country till of late years, when the old leaſes were at an end, and the rents were raiſed. Farmers, like men of other profeſſions, muſt be ſpurred on to induſtry by neceſſity. Thoſe who poſſeſſed the old leaſes found that they could live as their fathers had done before them, and were ſatisfied with the day of ſmall things. If they got a livelihood with eaſe, they were not anxious for wealth, when accompanied with exertion. It would be injuſtice, however, not to acknowledge, that ſome of the tenants who poſſeſs the old leaſes are now beginning to go on with ſpirit and induſtry : but that was not the caſe, till they were ſhown a good example ; and perhaps, but from neceſſity, that example would never have been ſhown them. There is much fine land in this pariſh let at 10 s. the acre, and even under that ; and yet the tenants are not more wealthy than their neighbours, who pay 30 s. the acre for land of no better quality. What can be the reaſon of this, but that the former are not ſo induſtrious as the latter, owing to long leaſes and low rents. Great as the improvements are, which have been made in this part of Scotland, within theſe few years paſt, yet the land is by no means arrived at that value to which it is capable of being raiſed. —There are two modes followed in cropping the ſtrong clay land in this pariſh. The one is firſt a fallow, with 50

bolls of lime fhells to the acre, and well dunged ; the land
is then fown with wheat. The next crop is peafe or
beans ; after that barley and grafs feeds, generally red clover ; 1 year in grafs, which is cut and given to the horfes
in the houfe. After the grafs, oats ; then a fallow again,
and fo on. The other mode is firft a fallow, then wheat ;
peafe or beans after the wheat ; then barley ; then oats.
After the oats, a fallow, and fo on. There are likewife
two modes followed in cropping the lighter foils. One is,
the land is made free of weeds, and the foil reduced ; it
is then limed and dunged, and fown with turnips in the
drill ; after the turnips, barley and grafs-feeds ; two years
in grafs, the firft cut for hay, the fecond for pafture ; then
a crop of oats ; after this turnips, &c. according to the a-
bove rotation. The other mode is, the land having been
4 or 5 years in grafs is limed, and broken up for oats ; after
the oats barley, then a green crop ; after that barley and
grafs-feeds, when it is laid down for pafture, and remains
in that ftate 4 or 5 years. The average returns of an acre
are, wheat 10 bolls, barley 8 bolls, oats 8, beans from 8 to
14, peafe from 4 to 10. The grain in general is of a very
fine quality. An acre of turnips is worth from L. 4 to
L. 5 Sterling. A good deal of flax was formerly raifed in
this parifh, but that practice is now much given up, it having been found by experience not to be profitable. The
hufbandry is almoft all carried on by horfes, there not being
above one oxen plough in the parifh. Ploughs, with 2
ftrong horfes in each, are univerfally ufed. The tenants
breed a good many of their horfes themfelves. The farmers, upon the lighter foils, likewife rear a number of black
cattle ; but the ftrong land not being well adapted for pafture, the tenants keep but few cattle through the fummer.
In order to confume the ftraw, and make dung for the
farm, they either purchafe cattle in the autumn and fet
                                                              them

them off in the spring, or take into their straw yards cattle from the graziers, who pay so much a-head for them, according to their size *.

Advantages.—This parish derives much advantage from its vicinity to the town of Montrose, where the farmer has always a ready market for every thing that he can raise, and where in return he can purchase whatever he wants for the use of his farm or his family. Another very great advantage is the open navigation from Montrose to Old Montrose, where coals are landed for fuel to the inhabitants, and likewise great quantities of lime both from Sunderland and Lord Elgin's lime-works, for manure. Vessels of 50 or 60 tons burden can, at stream tides, land with ease at the harbour of Old Montrose. A canal has been projected, and perhaps one day will be carried from thence to Brechin. This would complete the navigation between Brechin and Montrose, and would of course not only

* *Price of Labour.*—The price of labour is very high. The wages of a common ploughman are from L. 8 to L. 10 Sterling a-year; a servant maid from L. 2, 10 s. to L. 3. A stout man will get from L. 1, 10 s. to L. 2 for the harvest; a woman from L. 1 to L. 1, 5 s. The wages of a common labourer are 1 s. a-day. Yet notwithstanding the high price of labour, the common people are not richer than formerly: Although their revenue be greater, they add nothing to their capital, seldom think of saving any thing to support them in their old age. All is spent upon the back and the belly; they eat and drink better, and are better cloathed. The ploughman now despises the home-made suit of blue or grey, and all of the same piece: He comes to church on Sunday dressed in a coat of English cloath, a fancy vest, corduroy breeches, white thread stockings, plated buckles, &c. All of them wear hats; not a Scotch bonnet is to be seen. The dress of the women is as much changed as that of the men. The country lass makes her appearance at church, or a wedding, dressed in the manufactures of Manchester, Glasgow, and Paisley. Thus the improvement of the land is the enrichment of the kingdom, and the fail could not be spread without the assistance of the plough.

I

only be of singular advantage to both these towns, but like-wise to all the adjacent country *.

Maryton-Law.—Maryton-Law is a small eminence si-tuated upon a rock upon the top of one of the hills for-merly mentioned. It is evidently artificial, and probably in former times has been either an alarm post, as it com-mands a great extent of country, or a place where the great family of Montrose distributed justice to their vassals. From the top of it is one of the most beautiful prospects in Scotland. To the north, (close under the eye), is the rich and fertile country extending from Brechin to Montrose, on both sides of the river Southesk, where are interspersed a num-ber of elegant gentlemens seats; a fine view of both towns, with the bason and harbour of Montrose, and in the back ground are the Grampian hills. To the east is the well cul-tivated parish of Craig, with a great expanse of the Ger-man

* *Fisheries.*—In the river Southesk, which is the northern boundary of this parish, there is great plenty of fish, salmon, grilse, sea-trout, finnocks, and a variety of river-trout. In the month of May. a prodigious quantity of beautiful clear small trouts, called smouts, make their appearance. They are evidently the salmon-fry that were spawned in the autumn be-fore, and are then going down the river to the sea, where they arrive at maturity, A vast variety of aquatic birds frequent the bason, or, as it is commonly called, the back sands of Montrose, especially in the winter season; such as wild geese, ducks of various sorts, and in amazing num-bers; a variety of gulls, cormorants, sea-magpies, golden-eyes, curlieus, he-rons, &c. &c. The wild geese arrive in great flocks about the end of October, and generally remain till March. They frequent the fields in the low grounds through the day, where they feed upon the wheat-stub-ble in autumn, and the green wheat in winter: They always return to the bason at night. The ducks, on the contrary, remain in the bason through the day; but when the night falls, they go to the land, and feed upon the barley-stubble fields. Both the geese and ducks are very fine birds for eating. In severe storms, of long continuance, there are likewise some swans in the bason; but they do not remain long. There are great plenty of partridges in this parish, and some quails, but they are rare: Hares are scarce, there being little cover.

man ocean. To the ſouth is Lunan bay, the red head of Arbroath, and the proſpect is terminated by the frith of Forth, and the coaſt of Lothian.

Stipend, School, Poor, &c.—The manſe was built 4 years ago, and is one of the beſt finiſhed in the county. The ſtipend is 76 bolls of meal, 45 bolls of barley, and L. 19 Sterling in money. The glebe conſiſts of about 6 acres of very good land. The King is patron.—The ſchoolmaſter's ſalary is about L. 5 Sterling a year; and as the pariſh is ſmall, his perquiſites are not conſiderable. A new church was built laſt year, which is both elegant and commodious, and to the praiſe of the heritors be it ſpoken, not a farthing demanded for ſeat-rents; a practiſe by no means common in Scotland, but highly worthy of imitation.—The poor are maintained from the intereſt of a fund of about L. 500 Sterl. and the weekly collections, which are very trifling, owing to the greatneſs of the poors funds, the people not being very apt to give, when they know that there is little occaſion for their charity. Theſe great funds are a loſs to any pariſh. They are the cauſe of a number of poor coming into it, when they know that they will be maintained. They tend to make the lower claſſes greedy and lazy, and to live beyond their incomes, and very careleſs about ſaving any thing to provide for a family, or to ſupport them in old age. They likewiſe put a ſtop to that charity among the common people, which is the bond of affection between man and man, and which tends more than any thing elſe to humanize the mind.

Manners.—The people of this pariſh, except 5 or 6 individuals, are all of the Eſtabliſhed religion, and very regular in their attendance on public worſhip. They are quiet and inoffenſive, and mind their own buſineſs; and as there is but one alehouſe in the pariſh, they are in general ſober, not being much led into temptation.

PARISH of MENMUIR.

(COUNTY OF FORFAR.)

By the Rev. Mr JOHN WAUGH.

Origin of the Name:

IF *Men* or *Mun* in the Celtic, as has been faid, means a mofs or bog, then Menmore will fignify the great mofs, which etymology receives confiderable credit from the face of the parifh to the fouth, and the remains of marfhy grounds in that quarter.

The name was anciently *Menmure* and *Menmore,* the laft fyllable of which is well known to be a common termination to names of places in this kingdom, fuch as *Strathmore,* the great valley, *Kenmore,* the great head, and *Benmore,* the great hill. It fhould feem, not only from legendary report, but from a fine fpring which ftill goes by his name, that in the times of Popery, the church here had been dedicated to St Aidan, which appellation was alfo given fometimes to the parifh itfelf. This holy man was Britifh; his name appears in fome of our kalendars; he flourifhed in the 7th century, and is faid to have been Bifhop of Lindisfarne before that fee was transferred to Durham. Under the aufpices of Ofwald, king of Northumberland, he converted his fubjects to the Chriftian faith. That he was in deferved efteem in that country, along with Bede and St Cuthbert, there is no doubt.

Situation,

Situation, Extent, Surface and Soil.—This parish is situated in the shire of Forfar, in the presbytery of Brechin, and Synod of Angus and Mearns. It is rather more than 5 English miles in length, and about 2, at a medium, in breadth. The general appearance of the country is flat, especially to the south and east, except the northern division of the parish, which is hilly and covered with heath. The rest of the grounds, particularly on the slopes, are very fertile : The soil seems to be a sandy clay, not very deep, and towards the water side sharper, with less loam and more gravel intermixed.

Climate and Distempers.—The air may be called healthy, though, from the vicinity of the hills, it is cold, and very often in the summer evenings after sun-set, there is a chilly breeze from that quarter. In the low lands it is rather marshy, and the air is moister, which, with the nature of the food, may encourage the scurvy and King's evil. This latter complaint, with the slow inflammatory fever, are the prevailing distempers. The disease called *Sibbins*, and described some years ago by Dr Gilchrist, has made its appearance once or twice in this parish ; and this distemper, called, in the account of a neighbouring parish, the *louping gout*, was first noticed here.

Mineral Spring.—On a farm called Bathall there was a mineral well, which was in considerable repute some years ago; but is now very little resorted to. It is of the chalybeate kind, and good for stomachic complaints. But the poor people in those diseases, for which Spa waters are recommended, commonly prefer that of Panana or Arbroath.

Population.—The number of people in this parish, according to Dr Webster's statement, amounts to 743. By a very correct list taken last spring, (1791,) there were 900 souls, fouls, viz. 432 males and 468 females, which makes an increase of 157; although, from examining the register of baptisms for a considerable time back, it appears, that the population is rather on the decline. The births are, at an annual average, nearly 27, deaths 22, marriages 8. Of the two latter no exact records are kept, and consequently the calculations may not be so perfectly correct. The number of farmers is 36; of manufacturers, the weavers, who are the only people of that description that are here, 12. The different sectaries or dissenters, are about 60, viz. 2 Roman Catholics, who do not properly belong to the parish, but come from the north; 10 Seceders, who attend a meeting in Brechin; and 48 Episcopalians.

Farming and Produce, &c.—There are 55 ploughs in the parish and 100 carts. The old Scots plough is commonly used. On 2 farms they still use oxen. In some places the small plough is introduced. The parish supplies itself with provisions, excepting butcher meat and small groceries, which people in a country situation need from market towns; but in return for these they send in fat cattle, and export pretty large quantities of grain, especially oats and rough or Chester bear. On some of the larger farms, where they have a greater proportion of pasture, a good deal of cheese and butter is made and sold at Brechin or Kirrymuir. The soil, in several places, seems peculiarly favourable for raising flax. Four or five persons have lately obtained premiums for this article; and this summer, with the assistance of the Board of Trustees, a mill for dressing lint has been erected on the water Cruick, which, it is to be hoped, will meet with encouragement. Peas and oats are sown here as soon after Candlemas as the weather will permit, though, in some late seasons, they are hardly finished by the middle or even the end of April. Flax is sown about the beginning of that month, and through the whole of it. When it is a dry

spring,

spring, the farmers wiſh to get their bear earlier ſown, than in more ſouthern or in leſs expoſed ſituations, as the cold nights and froſty air of October have frequently injured this grain of late years. Barley is little cultivated, though rather coming in; both it and the Cheſter bear will ſometimes anſwer very well, when the ſummer is warm, though not ſown till near Whitſunday. Turnips begin to be ſown after that is over, which thrive very well here, ſeldom miſgive, on account of the fly and ſlugg, as they do in England, and are univerſally ſown with the hand or a machine in drills, and afterwards cleaned repeatedly with the common plough. A good many potatoes, red cabbage, boricole, and ſome yams for horſes, are cultivated with ſucceſs in the ſame way : Theſe are reckoned a profitable crop, beſides preparing the ground for oats. By this intermediate produce, and the ſucceeding one, with the help of manure, being very plentiful, the farmers reckon themſelves greater gainers than thoſe who raiſe wheat at the expence of exhauſting their land, and loſing a crop by fallow.

Diſadvantages.—The improvements in agriculture, and the pariſh in general, lie under certain diſadvantages, which deſerve to be mentioned. There is neither lime nor marl in the pariſh, and it is a great labour, and occupies a good deal of the ſummer's work to bring them from pits or hills at 4, 6, and even at 12 miles diſtance. Another hindrance to improvement, and a great diſadvantage to the pariſh, is the kind of fuel and the manner of obtaining it. There are few peats; turf is the principal firing. Theſe are none of the beſt, tedious in caſting, winning and leading, in wet ſeaſons very difficult to dry; and by the cultivation of waſte lands, the whins, divot and room, are almoſt worn out. Thus, the poor houſeholder, after all his fatigue, has ſometimes nothing but his labour for his pains, and is obliged to
buy

buy coals from the ports of Arbroath and Montrose, the first 15, the other 10 miles from Menmuir. These coals, to such as have them to purchase, will come to 12 s. and 13 s. the cart-load. If they go to Arbroath, the distance is very great; if to Montrose, they are 1 s. 6 d. or 2 s. the boll dearer, from the heavy duty that is exacted whenever sea coal passes a little promontory called Redhead. So heavy is this burden, that it is found to be more frugal to burn small coal from Newcastle, than what comes from the Frith of Forth. This grievance, which hurts the poor, and checks very much all spirit of enterprise and manufacture, might be removed by a new tax on some less needful commodity, or by an equalization of the duty; perhaps an additional halfpenny levied in general on Fife and Lothian coal might answer the end.

Heritors and Rent.—There are 6 heritors, only two of whom reside in the parish. The valued rent is L. 283 : 3 : 11 Sterling. The real rent is L. 1599 a-year. The average rent of farms may be L. 50. The general rent of the best arable land is about 12 s. the acre. The farmers are convinced of the advantages of inclosures, although they are as yet but rare. In several new tacks the tenants have bound themselves to inclose with dry stone-dikes, for which they are to receive 10 s. a rood at the expiration of their lease. The victual raised annually amounts to 5704 bolls. There are 218 horses; 1030 black cattle, and 1447 sheep.

Wages.—A stout day-labourer may be hired for 8 d. with victuals. In winter wages are less. In harvest a man's wages are 1 s. a-day, and a woman's 10 d. Day-labourers, when industrious, can bring up their families without difficulty. The wages of domestic servants, at a medium, are L. 6 for a man, and L. 3 for a woman. The wa-

ges

ges of artisans vary much : Some carpenters will be got for 8 d. a-day, others can hardly be hired for 1 s. 6 d. The case is similar with regard to tailors. Some of them only demand 4 d. and others 8 d. a-day, just as they happen to be dextrous at their trade, or much employed.

Poor.—There are 10 at present on the funds. The annual amount of contributions for their support is, at an average, L. 14; besides which, L. 6, 10 s. arises from funds lying in the heritors hands, at the interest of 5 and 4¼ *per cent.*

Church.—The church was built in 1767. The stipend varies with the price of victual. It consists of 6 chalders, viz. 32 bolls of bear and 64 of oats, with L. 25 Sterling, in which it is chiefly paid. Including the glebe, which is scarcely 6 acres, but very good ground, the ecclesiastical benefice is, *communibus annis*, rather above L. 90 a-year. The patron is John Erskine, Esq; of Dun.

School.—There is but one school in this parish, and that but ill attended. There are hardly 10 scholars in summer, and in winter the greatest number never exceed 30. The encouragement given to the master is extremely poor. A paltry house, about 100 merks of salary, and the emoluments not above L. 2.

Antiquities.—On the top of a hill called *Caterthun*, there are the remains of a very remarkable fortress. It consists of an immense quantity of loose stones, ranged round the summit of the mountain in an elliptic form. Whether these are the ruins of a stupenduous wall, or whether they were at first only heaped together, does not certainly appear; though, from their present state, one should imagine the latter was the case. It is supposed by anti-

quarians,

quarians, that this was a Danifh or a Pictifh camp; and what puts this hypothefis beyond doubt, is, *firft*, plain indications of a foffe or ravin all around; and, *2dly*, on the next hill, a fortification of the fame figure, but of lefs note, being compofed of earth; whereas, in Caterthun, the great curiofity is the vaft number of ftones. Whether we confider the fize of fome of thefe, the whole mafs *in cumulo*, the height to which they have been conveyed, the diftance from which 'tis likely they were brought, there being no quarry or rock in the adjacent moors; or, in fine, whether the curious reft on one, or on all thefe circumftances, this ftructure, rude as it is, may well excite wonder, and affords much fubject for refearch. Some travellers, who have narrowly examined thefe ftones, tell us, that on fome of them they difcovered coarfe outlines of birds, beafts, &c. Within the ring or oval circumference, the earth is covered with foft grafs and bent; whereas, without the ing, the heath and mofs is very luxuriant over the hill. The fpace inclofed by the ftones may be near two acres. Among thefe ftones fome herbs appear, but the Digitalis or foxglove is moft confpicuous. There are up and down flight eminences, or fmall tufty hillocks, underneath fome of which, 'tis not improbable, lie concealed arms, bones, urns, or fome *notitiæ* of the original formation of thefe remarkable ramparts. But there is another object vifible at firft glance, which muft be mentioned. It cannot be better defcribed than by borrowing fome of the words of a writer, who obferves, when fpeaking of the appearances on the top of Craigphadrick, ' Within this inner fpace, there are other marks of artificial ' operation, viz. a portion of ground, feparated from the reft, ' near the weft fide. This is in the fhape of a *parallellogram*, ' the dike and ditch of the inclofure eafily to be difcerned. ' But what has been the intention of this piece fet apart, 'tis ' difficult to determine. It might perhaps have marked ' the refidence of thofe of high rank, or been a place appro-
' priated

' priated to religious use.' As *Caterthun*, at a little distance, appears to be of a conic shape, and has a range
of stones about its summit like a crater, some travellers
imagine it to have been formerly a volcano. This may be
the case with some other hills in the north of Scotland ; but
the structure in question is plainly a work of art, and not of
nature. There is nothing like lava which might point out
the operation of internal fire ; nothing like the vitrification
of these Highland castles formed by artificial fusion, neither
is there any mark of masonry ; so that it must rank with
Duneval and *Dunjardel* in Inverness and Nairnshire, and o-
ther fortifications of dry stone. With regard to the main object, the time when, and the people by whom this strong
hold was first erected, history is silent, and consequently recourse must be had to the most probable conjecture. Little
need be said on this head after the suppositions of Messrs
Pinkerton and Pennant, whose writings with those of others
may easily be consulted. The last of these authors has given, in one of his first tours in Scotland, a view of Caterthun, with its dimensions. Some people in this country
would trace the origin of Caterthun no higher than what
in the Celtic its name implies, ' the Thieves-hill ;' but this
seems to fix it to an æra much too recent. That the
northern freebooters, or *Catterin*, as they are vulgarly called, availed themselves in their expeditions southward, of
this and other places of strength, there is no doubt. On this
account also it might receive its present name ; but it has
been clearly a strong camp before the period of their incursions, probably in the Danish or Caledonian wars. Some
suppose Tacitus speaks of this place in his history, and 'tis
also said, that in later days the celebrated Marquis of Montrose and his army signed the Solemn League and Covenant

on

on the top of this mountain *. There is a cluster of burrows, about a mile to the north of the church, which were believed, by the common people, to be graves of Picts or Danes killed in battle; but as, upon one of them being opened, bones were found very entire, one should imagine they belonged to a later transaction. A little rivulet hard by has two passes, called the Scotch and Englishman's ford, which seems to confirm this opinion, and to fix their date about the reigns of Charles I. or II. when there were frequent skirmishes in this country between the Presbyterian and Royal forces. There is one burrow detached from the rest, which is called *Beattie's Cairn*, and the place ' the ' *Mansworn Rigg*,' i. e. the perjured land. There is a tradition which agrees with this appellation, and affords a striking picture of the spirit of ancient times. Two lairds quarrelled about their marches, and witnesses were brought to swear to the old boundaries. One of these chieftains, provoked to hear his opponent's servant declare on oath, that he then stood on his master's ground, pulled a pistol from his belt, and shot him dead on the spot. It was found, that to save his conscience, he had earth in his shoes brought from his laird's land. The person who punished such prevarication, in so summary a manner, was proprietor of Balhall. Before the Carnegies bought the principal estate here, these lands were possessed by a family named *Collace* or *Coleffy*. Their funeral vault is in the church yard. One of them distinguished himself as follows

* Some travellers pretend to have found on its summit several figured stones with hieroglyphic characters, and likewise a piece of a broken statue. One, in particular, † makes mention of certain gold coins with inscriptions, in the possession of some gentleman in Angus, which were got on Caterthun. If the gentleman, in whose custody these curious pieces are, would lay them before the Antiquarian Society, it might tend to remove the obscurity in which the history of this mountain is involved.

‡ Vide *Ruddiman's Magazine*, August 31. 1775.

lows in the battle of Brechin. When the Earl of Crawford fought in this engagement, to revenge Lord Douglas's murder by James II. there was in his army one
Collace of Balnamoon. This man being affronted at not receiving a promise of the lands of Fern from Crawford, on
their eventual victory, left him, while the combat was yet
doubtful, and brought over to Huntly and the loyalists
the best part of his commander's forces, consisting of battle-ax,
long spear, and broad sword men. This turned the for-
tune of the day, and forms a very important fact in the
history of that time, as several writers acknowledge it was
a most critical event to James, and established the Crown,
which, till that decisive engagement, had only tottered on
his head.

Miscellaneous Observations.—The inhabitants of this parish are disposed to industry and economy. The women,
in particular, spin a great deal of lint into coarse yarn for
the duck or sail-cloth factory. They spin with both
hands, a practice little known in the south of Scotland,
which enables them to earn 3 s. a-week. This makes it
sometimes difficult to get domestic servants, seeing they
can make their bread easily at home. There are three
persons in this place who take in the flax undressed; one of
these keeps constantly two hecklers employed, to prepare
the lint for spinning; which, on being returned in yarn, is
carried to Montrose, as the few manufacturers who reside
here are principally employed in making coarse plaidings
and linen of a finer quality for home consumption. The
roads are improving. They are still made and repaired by
the statute labour, which is not commuted. There are no
tolls, and the general idea is that they would be oppressive.
There are 2 bridges over the water called Cruick, on the
great road to Brechin. One of these was built 3 years ago,

for which purpofe L. 30 was obtained from the county, and L. 40 raifed by fubfcription. There are 5 corn mills on Cruick water, and a fulling mill on a fmall rivulet to the north. At one of thefe mills about 400 bolls of pot-barley are annually made for the London market. There is only 1 licenfed ale-houfe in the parifh, and it is rather a convenience than a nuifance. Cottagers are here almoft u-niverfally employed in labour. Several farmers think that they are both cheaper and more fteady labourers than hired fervants. Many of the cottagers live very comfortably.

PARISH of MONIFIETH,

(COUNTY OF FORFAR, SYNOD OF ANGUS AND MEARNS, PRESBYTERY OF DUNDEE.)

By Mr JAMES ROGER, *Preacher of the Gospel.*

Situation and Extent.

THIS parish is pleasantly situated on the S. border of the county of Angus. The S. E. point of the parish is about a mile west from the light-house, built in the year 1753, which stands beside the narrow, variable, and difficult entrance into the æstuary of the Tay, formed by a sand-bank, seen at low water, stretching from the coast of Fife in a N. E. direction, and lies about 9½ miles S. W. from Arbroath, about 7 miles N. E. from St Andrew's, about 7½ miles east from Dundee, 56° 27′ N. lat. and 2° 55′. W. long. from Greenwich. From the S. E. point of the parish, along the æstuary, about the distance of 3½ miles, is its S. W. boundary. From the æstuary, it stretches N. W. to the distance of about 6 miles, decreasing irregularly to a point, in form of a wedge, inserted

between

between the parishes of Dundee and Murroes, on the S. W. and W.; that of Barry on the S. E. and of Monikie on the E. N. E. N. and N. W. No actual survey has been made of the parish; but he who supposes it to contain 3710 Scotch acres, will not be far from the truth. The parish seems anciently to have been of less extent than at present. Its proportion of the links which skirt the coast, may be safely supposed above 400 acres, and seem all once to have been covered with water. Adjoining to these links in this parish, tradition relates that some part belonged to the parish of Ferry-Port-on-Craig on the opposite side of the æstuary; but what that part was, or when the separation was made, it might be vain, at this distance of time, to enquire.

Surface, Rivulets, &c.—From the N. W. point of the parish, out of a well at the foot of the hill of Dodd, in that low range, reaching thence to the Knockhills near Arbroath, and about 4 miles E. from the hill of Lorn, in that high ridge of hills called Sidla, which extend from Perth to Redhead, and are the southern boundary of Strathmore, there issues a rivulet which waters for about a mile the S. W. border of the parish, crosses it in an eastern direction, and after meandring through the parish of Monikie, returns, and dividing this parish for about $\frac{1}{4}$ mile from that of Barrie, and receiving the name of the Buddon Burn, loses itself in the æstuary. About $1\frac{1}{8}$ mile S. W. from the Buddon Burn, and about $\frac{1}{8}$ mile in the same direction from the village of Monifieth, the river Dighty falls into the æstuary, after a S. E. course of about 11 miles from its rise in the lake of Lundie, and about $1\frac{1}{2}$ mile from its entrance into this parish. Where the Dighty enters the parish, it is joined by the Burn of Murroes, which, rising in the western part of the parish of that

name,

name, runs eaftward, and at laft wafhes for a mile, the S.
W. boundary of this parifh. From the N. W. point of
the parifh, about the diftance of 2 miles, the road from
Dundee to Brechin croffes the rivulet, which, near its ef-
flux into the æftuary is called Buddon, in a northern direction. About 4 miles from the N. W. point of the parifh, the old road from Dundee to Arbroath croffes the
Burn of Murroes, in an eaftern direction. About 5 miles
from the N. W. point of the parifh, the new turnpike-
road from Dundee to Arbroath croffes the Dighty in a
N. E. direction.

Beach.—Within water-mark, on the bounds of this parifh, a very few rocks only are feen ; the far greater part
is fandy and level. The links which fkirt the coaft, and
ftretch from the village of the Eaft Ferry, fo called, in
contradiftinction to that of the Weft Ferry, in the parifh
of Dundee, to which it joins, rife in a few places into
fmall knolls, but oftener approach to a plain.

Soil.—From the links on the W. of the Dighty, the
ground fuddenly rifes, and then gently declines towards
that river ; and the foil is generally an excellent loamy
black. From the links on the E. of the Dighty, there
fpreads for more than a mile almoft a level plain ; and the
foil is at firft light and fandy, but extremely fertile, and
then affumes a rich blacknefs of colour. Black and excellent, the ground now gradually fwells towards certain
hills of inconfiderable height, which at large intermediate
fpaces traverfe the parifh from N. to S. from the village
of Drumfturday-moor, built on the fides of the old road
from Dundee to Arbroath, to the vicinity of the village
of the Eaft Ferry, near Broughty caftle. From thefe hills
the ground again defcends towards the Burn, near its termination

mination, called Buddon, and in its descent, by degrees, loses its excellence. It again rises somewhat towards the N. W. point of the parish, and shews to the eye of the traveller spots yet moorish and waste.

Hills.—Of these some may deserve notice. The highest and most remarkable, is the most southern of that collection of hills called *Laws*, in the vicinity of the village of Drumsturdy-moor. Its height has not been ascertained by measurement; but is supposed not much to exceed 530 feet above the level of the sea. It lies from E. to W. is of an oval figure, and is covered with a pleasant verdure; its summit is 133 yards in length, 66 yards in breadth, and 316 yards in circumference. From this hill westward, may be seen the coast of Fife, the level and pleasant country, which stretches to the rich and populous city Dundee, part of the fertile carse of Gowrie, and almost all the æstuary, as it beautifully winds to Perth, and the distant prospect is bounded by the mountains in the shire of Argyle. South and eastward may be seen the bay of St Andrew's, the hills of Lothian, the agreeably varied country to Arbroath, and the German Ocean to the utmost extent of the horizon. Around the summit of this hill, are to be seen the broad foundations of an ancient fortress; and on the E. end of it, several large vitrifications, or masses of sandy and whin-stones firmly united, by means of the fusion of certain parts of the whin-stones *.

From

---

* These vitrifications have plainly been caused, by the application of external fire; as small pieces of burnt wood are found in the heart of the masses when they are broken. But the question occurs, how was this fire applied, so as to vitrify these masses ?—One ingenious gentleman has conjectured, that before the use of lime, as a cement, was introduced by the Romans into the island, whoever wished to strengthen their forts,

made

From this hill of Laws, at a little distance S. W. is the Gallow-hill of Ethiebeaton, on which, it is said, the Barons who were the proprietors of the adjoining farms of Ethiebeaton, Laws and Ornochie, were wont to sit in judgment on their vassals, and to hang such as were convicted of theft. Farther to the S. is the hill of Balgillo, which will be included in the account of Broughty castle, in its immediate neighbourhood.

Broughty castle.—Broughty castle * is situated on the most southern point of this parish, whence to the coast of Fife,

is

made a wooden frame, of the same dimensions they wished their defence to be, filled it with sandy, and whin or plum-pudding stones, set fire to the frame, and by the entenseness of the heat, vitrified the inclosed mass, and produced a strong munition. (See William's treatise on vitrified forts.) A second agrees to the conjecture of the first in every thing but this, that fire was applied to the frame, not by friends who wished to strengthen the fort, but by enemies who wished to demolish it. (See Essay on Vitrified Forts in Phil. Tranf. Ed. Vol. II.) But by whatever process the vitrifications on other hills have been effected, it appears probable, that the vitrifications on this hill have been effected, neither at the construction nor demolition of its fortress, but at a different period. When that period was, it is not easy with precision to tell; but surely a supposition which occupies little time, where supposition only is to be had, can do no harm. In A. D. 838, the Picts had been finally expelled by Kenneth II. whose father King Alpin, in a battle fought on a plain N. W. from Dundee, they had taken prisoner, and with barbarous cruelty slain. Most of the Picts at their expulsion sought for shelter in Denmark, whence, it is said, their ancestors sprung. Incited by them, the Danes rose for revenge, and frequently invaded the eastern coast of Scotland. From these wasting invaders, the fortress on this hill might afford a temporary refuge. On the E. end of it, which is most conspicuous, fires might be kindled to alarm the more distant parts of the country, when these incursions happened in the night; and the frequent fires might at last vitrify the stones which they touched.

* The following note, the substance of which has been extracted from the Kirk-session records, will afford a proof that there is no reason to question,

is not above a mile diftant. It might thus, it is not unlikely, be originally fpelled *Borghtay*, from Borgh, a fecurity,
and Tay ; or, the fecurity of the Tay. When it was built
will not, perhaps, be eafily afcertained. It cannot be one
of the caftella, or forts, which Tacitus, in his life of Agricola, fays that general erected, in the third year of his expedition, when he came to the æftuary of the Tay ; for
thefe forts, we are informed by Boece, in the fourth book
of his Hiftory, were erected not on the north, but on the
fouth fide of the æftuary ; not in the county of Angus, but
in the county of Fife. Dr Macpherfon feems to be right,
who fuppofes that the fquare towers, like Broughty, were
built at a much later period. The earlieft mention of it
with which I have met, is in the year 1492, when, according
to the credulous Boece, in the Delineation of the Scottifh
Kingdom, prefixed to his Hiftory, it witneffed a foolifh pro-
digy.

---

ftion, as fome do, whether Broughty belongs to this parifh. Towards the
end of laft century, a man committed a trefpafs within the bounds of
Broughty, for which he was fummoned to appear at the tribunal of the
Kirk-feffion. He refufed obedience, under pretence that Broughty belonged not to this parifh, but to that of Caputh, in the neighbourhood of
Dunkeld, about 26 miles N. W. To afcertain the true fituation of
Broughty, the minifter wrote to a Mr Webfter, then its proprietor ; who
replied, that it lay neither in the parifh of Monifieth nor of Caputh, but
in that of Kirriemuir, about 16 miles N. On this the minifter applied to
the prefbytery, who by their deed annexed Broughty and its pertinents
for ever, *quoad facra*, to the parifh of Monifieth. Had the Kirk-feffion
records been fully confulted, it would have been found that Broughty
was already annexed, not only *quoad facra*, but *quoad temporalia*, to this
parifh ; for there it is exprefsly faid, that on December 12, 1658, Broughty
among others paid for the reparation of the church. It follows not indeed always, that a place belongs to that parifh for the reparation of
whofe church it pays. It feems, however, an acknowledgment of Broughty's belonging to Monifieth parifh, that it paid for the reparation of the
church there. For had there been any evidence that Broughty belonged
not to this parifh, Mr Webfter, its proprietor, when called on, would
furely have been able to produce it, and not have founded his opinion
wholly on tradition.

digy. From the year 1547 to 1550, it was the scene of deeds not unworthy to mention, and which are connected with events that form a striking æra in history.

On the death of James V. of Scotland, Henry VIII. of England, to save that blood and treasure which were expended in defence of either nation, sought to unite the two neighbouring kingdoms, by the marriage of his young son Edward, to Mary, the infant Queen of Scots. To this measure all that nation had sworn agreement: But, incited by Cardinal Beaton and the Queen Dowager, who dreaded the downfal of the Popish religion, by an union with a heretical nation, they were prevailed on basely to break their oath. To enforce acquiescence, Henry arose in his might, and at his death the cause was espoused by Edward Seymour, Duke of Somerset, who was elected Protector of the kingdom during the minority of Edward his nephew. Moving along the eastern coast of Scotland with a numerous army, which was seconded by a powerful fleet, on Saturday, September 10. 1547, he met the 30,000 Scots under the conduct of the Earl of Arran, Regent of the kingdom, on the west of the river Esk, near Musselburgh, and discomfited them with great slaughter; but was soon after, by reason of the advanced season of the year, and intelligence he received of designs forming against him in England, forced to return thither, without completely prosecuting his victory. Immediately on this his fleet, besides the fortresses on the isles in the æstuary of the Forth, seized this of Broughty, and filled it with an English force *.

Ancient

* As the Duke of Somerset departed with his army by the east of Scotland, the Earl of Lennox, who had received a disgust in the court of that kingdom, and had been honoured with the alliance of Henry VIII. entered by the west. His presence spread terror and dismay, and none met

but

Ancient state of rivulets, roads and hills, &c.—From time immemorial the rivulets and river above mentioned have run in their present channels; but of late the roads in this parish have undergone confiderable alteration. Within the laft twelve years, the road from Dundee to Brechin has been made wider and ftraighter. Within twice that number of years, the old road from Dundee to Arbroath was formed; and the new turnpike road is yet fcarcely finifhed. Within the laft 50 years, no trees fhaded any hill in the

but to do him homage. The heart of Arran, the regent, which was never intrepid, now fhrunk within him. To conceal his fear, however, he collected the fcattered remains of his enfeebled hoft, and, from the weftern parts of Scotland, where he had taken refuge after the unfortunate action at Muffelburgh, marched by Perth and Dundee to blockade the caftle of Broughty. After having lain before it from the 1ft of October 1547 to the 1ft of January 1548, he departed from the fiege with the lofs of one of his beft generals, and with that of all his ordnance, lamenting his doom to perpetual misfortune. Infpirited with this fuccefs, the Englifh fortified the hill of Balgillo, about half a mile northward, and, notwithftanding the active exertions of James Haliburton, provoft of Dundee, with a hundred horfe, and of Sir Robert Maule, in his caftle of Panmure, about fix miles northeaftward, and about half a mile eaft from the prefent beautiful feat of that family, in the parifh of Panbride, laid wafte Dundee, and moft of the county of Angus. With rage the Earl of Argyll heard the report. He collected his valiant clans, and, indignant, marched to Broughty; but felt the mortification of repulfe. Not long after, a fimilar fate awaited three regiments of French, commanded by D'Effe, and as many regiments of Germans, commanded by one of their own princes. At laft diffentions at home, and war with the French abroad, engaged the whole attention of the Englifh. Provifions, arms, and ammunition, ceafed to be regularly fent to their garrifons in Broughty, and the fort of Balgillo; and thus, on February 20, 1550, they fell an eafy prey into the hands of the allied army of Scots, Germans, and French, commanded by Des Thermes, the fucceffor of D'Effe. Both fortreffes were then difmantled; and though they have been more than once repaired and fortified, yet hiftory defcribes them as the fcene of no action which merits record. At prefent, there are only a few veftiges of fortification to be feen on the hill of Balgillo; and Broughty caftle is faft wafting down to ruin.

the parish, as at present they shade several ; and within the same period, the extensive and beautiful plantations
around the two seats Fintry and Grange were reared. The
house of Fintry stands where the Dighty enters the parish,
and is a modern elegant mansion. Nearly where the Dighty
falls into the æstuary, stands the house of Grange, which
displays marks of ancient magnificence.

Population.—According to Dr Webster's report, the
number of souls in 1755 was 1421. In this parish there
are at present 1218 persons of all ages. Of these 620 are
males, and 598 females. There are 246 families, of which
233 belong to persons who have been married, and 13 to
persons who were never married. Below the age of five,
there are 136; between 5 and 10, 183; between 10 and
20, 223; between 20 and 30, 251; between 30 and 40,
132; between 40 and 50, 136; between 50 and 60, 86;
between 60 and 70, 53; between 70 and 80, 15; between
80 and 90, 3. The three villages of the parish are thus
peopled : In the village of Drumsturdy-moor, there are
132, *viz.* 70 males and 62 females; in that of Monifieth,
175, *viz.* 84 males and 91 females; and in that of the East
Ferry, 230, *viz.* 114 males and 116 females. Of late years
there have been annually married 12, been born 39, and
died 18. The great inequality of deaths to births, seems
to arise from this : Many inhabitants of this parish early in
life settle in Dundee ; many go aboard merchantmen, may
perish by the dangers of the sea, or be impressed into ships
of war, and perish by the hands of the enemy *.

Agriculture.

* The parish appears at no former period to have been much more populous than at present. About the year 1660, the annual average of marriages was 5 of births 26 : and of deaths 14 : So that whether a calculation
be made from the marriages, births, or deaths, the increase in population

Agriculture.—The ſubſiſtence of the people is chiefly by agriculture. Of the 3710 acres of which the pariſh may conſiſt, 140 may be ſuppoſed in plantation, 400 in links, and 170 otherwiſe unarable. Of the remaining 3000 acres, the one half may be ſuppoſed in fallow, paſture, and green crops. Of the other half, nearly 100 may be ſuppoſed in wheat, and the reſt equally divided into oats and barley. Here the farms are generally extenſive. There are ten farms that rent between L. 99 and L. 200; two between L. 200 and L. 300; one between L. 300 and L. 400; one between L. 400 and L. 500; and one between L. 600 and L. 700. Below L. 99 of rent, there is no ground poſſeſſed by any farmer, properly ſo called. The other poſſeſſors of land are the 46 pendiclers, who are generally tradeſmen, and hold a few acres of a proprietor; and the forty-two cottagers, who have each a houſe and an acre or two from a tenant. Here the means of improving land are embraced, and their good effects are viſible. Sea-weed cannot be found in ſufficient quantity on that part of the coaſt which belongs to this pariſh, to be of uſe as a manure. Marl alſo lies at too great a diſtance, as well as the dung of Dundee, much to profit the farmer. There is, however, abundance of lime brought from the ſouth of Fife, and from north and ſouth Sunderland, in England, which is landed

3   at

tion muſt have been conſiderable. If a calculation be made from the births, the pariſh will be found to have increaſed in number 406, which is preciſely one-third of its preſent inhabitants. From the period now mentioned to the preſent time, the increaſe in population has been gradual. About the year 1750, indeed, the annual average of births was 44; but that of marriages was only 9; and of deaths 15. Some years before 1750, a malignant fever had raged, which ſent many to their graves. The extraordinary number of births in the years which immediately followed, only filled up the breaches the fever had made. About the year 1760, the annual average of births was only 35, and that of deaths was 18. The marriages are omitted in the record.

at the villages of Monifieth and the Eaſt Ferry; and of which about 6000 bolls of Wincheſter meaſure may be annually uſed in this pariſh as a manure. The crops in the lower part of the pariſh are very liberal; but thoſe in the upper part are leſs productive. The time of ſowing and reaping in the lower part, is much the ſame as in the eaſt of the Carſe of Gowrie, or the centre of Strathmore; but in the upper part is latter. Though a conſiderable quantity of grain be yearly exported from the villages of Monifieth and the Eaſt Ferry, yet its price is regulated by the market at Dundee.

Cattle.——Beſides a conſiderable number of cattle fed on common paſture, there are between 300 and 400 fattened every ſummer in graſs encloſures, and about a fifth part of that number fattened by turnips in winter. A few ſheep paſture part of the links.

Within the laſt 50 years, the agriculture of the pariſh has been much improved. It ought not to be omitted, that this was entirely owing to Mr Hunter, then proprietor of Grange, a gentleman whoſe name deſerves to be recorded. Some years before 1750, he, firſt of this pariſh, began to encloſe land, and between the years 1750 and 1752, to uſe lime as a manure. In the year 1753, he introduced the culture of turnips, and in the year following, that of potatoes. By fallow, dung and lime he prepared his grounds for the crop, and he ſowed them at the proper ſeaſon with graſs-ſeeds. Now had his fields begun to aſſume a fairer ſurface and a ſofter mould; but ſtill their upleaſing form remained. The ridges were wide at one end, narrow at the other, and bent in various curvatures. They were ſoon rendered regular and ſtraight. His fields lay beſide the road to the pariſh-church, and the pariſhioners, as they paſſed, beheld their beauty and fertility with wonder.

What

What they beheld they imitated, and many foon faw with fatisfaction their own fields covered with a fimilar beauty and fertility. The old Scottifh ploughs were difmiffed apace ; and at prefent there is not one in the parifh. The old Scottifh plough improved, however, continues in general ufe. A few of Small's newly invented make, have been introduced, but are found to fucceed only in lands that are level and free from incumbrance. There is but one thrafhing machine in the parifh, ufed on the largeft farm. The other farmers employ men to thrafh out their grain, called lot-men, who generally refide in the neighbourhood, and receive as wages the twenty-fifth boll of grain they thrafh out, with breakfaft, and a fmall allowance for dinner.

None can ever hope to fee the agriculture of this parifh increafed, but by a very fmall part of the links. They muft either be allowed to remain, as at prefent, in pafture ; or be planted with trees. If they were planted, the roots of the trees would harden the foil, and prevent the encroachment of the fea. An extenfive clump of firs planted in the links of the neighbouring parifh of Barrie has thriven well. If fome plan of this fort be not adopted, the period perhaps, is not diftant, when they will all be again completely inundated. From the links between the light-houfe and the village of Monifieth, (a fpace of about 2 miles,) within the laft 40 years, the fea has plundered upwards of 50 acres.

Fifheries.——The fifheries of this parifh are inconfiderable. The falmon fifhings pay a yearly rent of no more than L. 130. Fifteen years ago, before any were fent from this parifh to London, they were fold in the adjacent villages, and in Dundee at $1\frac{1}{2}$ d. the lb. Since that period, a pound of falmon has not been fold under 4 d. At firft fight, it

would be thought beneficial to the falmon fifhing, if a method could be invented, by which the porpoifes, or *Gair
fifh* as they are called, which devour fo many falmon,
might be deftroyed. But it is to be confidered, that the
fear of the porpoifes forces the falmon nearer to land than
they would otherwife be willing to come. If the porpoifes were deftroyed, the falmon would be fafer; but the
fifher would catch lefs in his net.

About 10 years ago, the white fifhing on this coaft began to decline. Soon after, the haddocks, which were
caught in the greateft abundance, totally left the coaft.
While they remained, they chiefly had given conftant employment to 3 large boats belonging to this parifh, which
earned annually, at an average, L. 100 each. The 3 boats
are ftill retained, and frequent their old fifhing grounds;
but as they feldom catch any other kinds of fifh than fome
cod and ling, or when any other kinds chance to be
caught, as it is in fmall quantity, they afford a very fcanty
and precarious fubfiftence. Whether the haddocks were
banifhed by lack of proper food, or purfued by fome vo-
racious enemy, it is the lefs important to inquire; as they
have now begun, in fmall quantities, to revifit our coafts.
A few fmall fhell fifh might be found within the bounds
of this parifh, if one were at pains to gather them. Lobfters and crabs are caught in their greateft perfection on
this coaft, in the parifhes of Panbride and St Vigeans.

Manufactures.——There is little in this parifh which deferves the name of manufacture. There are only 38 weavers, who, as they at one time weave ofnaburghs, and at
another time houfehold cloth, and are fcattered over the
parifh, the quantity of cloth which they weave cannot eafily be afcertained. But it muft be very inconfiderable,
as feveral of them occupy a few acres of land, which requires

quires a portion of their time. There is an oil mill on the Dighty, which annually extracts oil from 800 bolls of lint-ſeed. A ſmall quantity of oil only is uſed in the neigh-bourhood, and is ſold at 1 s. 3 d. a Scotch pint. The reſt is ſent to London. A ſmall quantity of oil duſt alſo is ſold in the neighbourhood between 6 d. and 8 d. a ſtone A-voirdupois, and is uſed in ſpring, before the riſing of the graſs, to increaſe the milk of cows, and to aſſiſt in foſter-ing calves. The reſt made up in cakes about 18 inches long, 5 broad, and 1½ inch thick, are put into caſks and ſent to England, up the river Humber in Yorkſhire, to fatten cattle. But though there be little in this pariſh which deſerves the name of manufacture, yet it is well ſtored with thoſe who furniſh the neceſſaries and conveni-encies of life. Beſides the 38 weavers and 2 oil-millers, there are 3 corn and 7 flax-millers, 1 fuller, 3 flax-dreſſers, 4 gardeners, 10 tailors, 20 ſhoemakers, 9 blackſmiths, 8 maſons, 13 wrights, 2 bakers, 3 brewers of ale, 9 ſellers of drink, and 5 ſellers of ſmall wares. Beſide the oil mill, there is on the Dighty a corn and fulling mill, together with a thread mill belonging to a manufactory in Dundee. The Dighty, in its progreſs through this pariſh, affords many fine falls of water, on which machinery might be erected, and by which manufactures might be greatly improved.

Rent, &c.—The preſent rent of the pariſh may be eſti-mated at L. 3832 : 2 : 9. In the year 1656, during the uſurpation of Cromwell, when the lands of the different counties in Scotland were valued for the purpoſe of taxa-tion, the rent of this pariſh was preciſely L. 457 : 13 : 9¹¹⁄₁₂; which is leſs than an eighth part of the preſent rent *.

Poor.

* The prices of proviſions, of the implements of huſbandry, and of la-bour are high. The price of 1 lib. butter, 10 d. ; 1 lib. cheeſe, 3 d. ;
1 lib.

Poor —The charity which this parish gives to the poor, is a branch of expenditure which does it honour. There is collected in the church every Sabbath throughout the year at an average 7 s. 3 d. exclusive of the larger sums collected at the time of the celebration of the sacrament. These collections, and a considerable sum arising from money at interest, with the lending of a hearse and mortcloths, and the letting some seats in the church, more than amply supply the necessities of the 12 poor of late years commonly on the list, and of the two which the general dearth of last year has added *. Before the year 1678, several sums had been

---

1 lib. salmon, 6 d. ; a hen, 1 s. 3 d. ; dozen eggs, 7 d. The price of a pair of horses is L. 52, 10 s. ; harness, L. 3. 3 s. ; a cart, L. 10, 10 s ; a plough, L. 2, 2 s. ; a pair of harrows, L. 1, 1 s. The wages of a male servant a-year, are L. 10 ; a female servant a-year, L. 4 ; a male reaper, L. 1, 4 s. ; a female reaper, L. 1 ; a labourer a-day without board, 1 s. 3 d. The prices of provisions, implements of husbandry, and labour, have much increased within the last 40 years. At the commencement of that period, the price of 1 lib. butter was 4½ d. 1 lib. cheese, 1½ d. ; 1 lib. salmon, 1½ d. ; a hen, 4 d. ; a dozen eggs, 1 d. The price of a pair of horses was L. 10 ; harness, 5 s. ; cart, 10 s. ; a plough, 9 s. ; a pair of harrows, 2 s. The wages of a male servant a-year, were L. 2, 2 s ; a female-servant a-year, L. 1, 6 s. ; a male reaper 11 s. 8 d. ; a female reaper, 10 s. ; a labourer a-day without board, 6 d.

---

* In the year 1578, the usual collection on Sabbaths was $\frac{8}{12}$ d. ; and on June 29. the same year, the fund of the poor amounted to no more than 6 $\frac{2}{x}$ d. These days afforded small provision for the present exigence of the poor, and laid up little in store against the season of uncommon need. The cottagers gave to the masters of whom they held their little hovels, all the children they needed as servants. The rest found it often vain to apply to a trade, for almost every man was his own tradesman. Away, therefore, they were sent by the cravings of hunger, to beg that bread which they could not earn, and the poor preyed on the poor. Before 1651, the times seem to have grown better ; for the usual collection on Sabbaths that year was 4 $\frac{2}{12}$ d. ; and on Sabbath November 23, the parishioners were able to collect L. 2, 5 s. for the support of their brethren in the

been bequeathed to the kirk-ſeſſion for the benefit of the poor ; and the uſual collections on the Sabbaths had riſen to 8 d. an increaſe of preciſely 12 times in the ſpace of a century ; from that to the preſent year 1793, the weekly collection has increaſed nearly 11 times. The charity which the pariſh thus gives to the poor, is no doubt owing in a great meaſure to its increaſed opulence. It will not be ſuppoſed, however repugnant to their liberality, that in common with many other pariſhes, they enjoy that uſeful inſtruction which a church and two ſchools may be expected to communicate.

Church, Stipend, Heritors, &c.—The church, which is ſituated at the village of Monifieth, is an ancient building ; but the period of its conſtruction is unknown. It muſt have been built before the æra of the Reformation, as on the E. end of it is a quire, in which maſs, in the days of Popery, was wont to be celebrated *. The church-living, including

56

the priſon of Dundee, who had been taken captive by the Engliſh army under General Monk, as they paſſed through this pariſh to the ſiege of that city, and which ſum Mr John Barclay, the miniſter, and another gentleman, were commiſſioned to carry.

* Tradition relates, that there were once at the ſame time four chapels in the pariſh ; one at the Eaſt Ferry, where there is ſtill a burying-place ; a ſecond on the banks of the Dighty, at the Miln of Balmoſſie, the foundation-ſtones of which were dug up by the preſent farmer ; a third on that ſpot in the land Ethiebealin, which is ſtill called Chapel Dokie ; and the fourth at Monifieth. The chapel at Monifieth, it is ſaid, being found likely to endure the longeſt, was made, as it continues at preſent, the pariſh church, and the reſt were ſhut, and ſuffered to decay ; but when this happened, tradition is altogether ſilent. Before the Reformation, Monifieth was annexed to the dioceſe of St Andrew's. In 1560, when Preſbyterianiſm was firſt eſtabliſhed in Scotland, its ſuperintendant was appointed to reſide in Brechin. After 1606. it belonged to the Preſbytery of Dundee, and Synod of Angus and Mearns.

56 bolls of meal, 56 bolls of barley, 8 bolls of wheat, L. 45 : 6 : 8, a manfe, garden, and offices, 4 acres of glebe, and a right of pafturage, may be eftimated at L. 147 a-year. The Hon. Mr Maule of Panmure is patron. Sir Alexander Ramfay of Balmain, Baronet, is the principal heritor. Befides thefe two gentlemen, there are feven others who are heritors None of the heritors are refident.

Schools.—Of the two fchools, one is parochial. Its falary of L. 11 : 2 : 2,$\frac{8}{12}$, the fchool-houfe and garden, the emoluments arifing from proclamations and baptifms, L. 2 for the office of clerk to the kirk-feffion, and the fees, for teaching 50 fcholars, may yearly amount to L. 40. Here was Mr William Craighead, for feveral years fchoolmafter, a man whofe treatife on arithmetic is not wholly unknown to the lovers of that fcience, and who died in 1763. The other fchool was founded by the generofity of Sir Alexander Ramfay in 1782, for the benefit of the upper part of the parifh. He has endowed it with 2 acres of land, and a garden rent free, befides an annuity of 2 bolls of meal ; 20 s. are given by the kirk-feffion to the teacher, and thefe emoluments, with the fees for 20 fcholars, may be worth L. 15 a-year.

Character of the People, &c.—As their fituation is fo falubrious, that multitudes refort every fummer to the villages of the Eaft and Weft Ferry for the benefit of fea-bathing ; as the employments of few are fedentary ; as the ground is no where marfhy ; as the accefs to coals is eafy ; they are generally healthy. But it is of more importance to characterize the minds than the bodies of a people ; it is of more importance to be told, that within the laft 80 or 90 years, this parifh has increafed as much in religion and morals,

morals, as in the arts of life. The kirk-feffion regifter informs us, that from 1676 to 1710, a period of 34 years, during the miniftry of Mr John Dempfter, the laft Epifcopal clergyman at Monifieth, and from whom the prefent Mr Dempfter of Dunnichen, fo well known for his patriotifm is defcended, the ftricteft church difcipline was obferved. From among the numerous proprietors, who then fhared the lands of the parifh, but whofe race have all long fince left the poffeffions of their fathers, and are gone, he felected feven elders to watch over the morals of the people, and the fame number of deacons from among the tenantry, to watch over the ftate of the poor. Great was then the need for infpecting parochial conduct. Little regard was paid to the Sabbaths. On thefe days fome were occafionally convicted of having fifhed with the rod or the net. Scarcely was there a Sabbath on which fome delinquent was not juftly and publicly reproved; and it was feen neceffary, after public worfhip was finifhed, to fend a committee of the kirk-feffion to perluftrate the inns of the parifh. By degrees decency and devotion began to reign. The pious exhortations and worthy example of Mr Dempfter and his kirk-feffion were long remembered and imitated, after death had ftilled their voices, and withdrawn their prefence. At this day the parifhioners attend the church with the utmoft regularity and gravenefs of deportment; and they are extremely fteady in their religious principles. About two years ago, the fects called Burgher and Antiburgher built each a conventicle in this vicinity; but they are thinly attended, and have not been able to gain over from this parifh more profelytes than 20, of whom 15 are Burghers, and 5 Antiburghers. There are only two other fectaries in the parifh, the one an Independent, and the other a Methodift. But the inhabitants of this parifh are not only regular and decent

in

in their attendance on church, fteady in their religious principles, but diftinguifhed for their induftry and fobriety. Suc-
cefsful diligence has given to feveral the bleffings of moderate wealth ; and laborious exertion has been able to banifh
from the dwellings of all, fave the 14 poor on the fund, the
wretchednefs of abject poverty. Since the beginning of
the prefent century, none in this parifh has deprived himfelf of life, been deprived of it by the law, or been doomed
to exile.

PARISH of MONIKIE,

(COUNTY OF FORFAR).

By the Rev. Mr WILLIAM MAULE.

Situation, Soil, &c.

THIS parish is 6 English miles in length, and 4 in breadth. Its form is almost triangular, one of the angles terminating in the sandy desart situated at the mouth of the Tay. On the S. W. and W. it is bounded by the parishes of Monifieth and Murroes; on the S. E. by Barrie; on the E. by Panbride; on the N. by Carmylie, and on the N. W. by Inverarity and Tealing.— The face of the country is diversified by several large hills. The soil and air are very various. The S. part of the parish is distinguished for fertility. In the N. and N. W. the soil is more moist, the air colder, and vegetation more slow; insomuch, that the inhabitants of the former have frequently their harvest gathered in a month or 5 weeks before those of the latter. The interposition of a large hill, or ridge of hills, called Camustoun, or Dunie, makes a considerable alteration in point of climate.

Agriculture.

Agriculture.—The rent of the beſt land is from 5 s. to 15 s. the acre, but that of ſome of the worſt has been recently 16 s. 8 d. Of the beſt land, the leaſes are old, having been let about 23 years ago, moſt of them for twice 19 years, and a lifetime, the rent riſing 1 s. the acre at the 20th year. At that period, little or nothing had been done in the way of improving land, and the tenants were in general poor; moſt of them are now in eaſy, ſome of them in opulent circumſtances; they are in general frugal and induſtrious. Of thoſe farms, one which happened to be let for only 19 years at L. 52 Sterling, and which conſiſts of about 170 acres, was let again within theſe laſt 4 years at L. 120; and the preſent tenant being a ſkilful and induſtrious farmer, is likely to make more money than the former, who laboured in the old way. Were the leaſes of the other farms expired, they could all be let for more than twice the preſent rent. In the ſouthern part of this pariſh, the farms are for the moſt part incloſed. Every farmer finding his account in breeding and fattening cattle, raiſes annually ſeveral acres of turnip. Wheat has long been cultivated in the ſouthern, and which is the moſt fertile part. For the laſt 6 or 7 years, the farmers diſcontinued the ſowing of this grain, ſeveral of them having met with conſiderable loſſes by blaſting. But they are now beginning to try it again, and have this year been ſuccefsful. Good artificial grafs is alſo produced. By an article in their tacks, moſt of the tenants are bound to have a third of their farms always in grafs. Much attention has of late years been paid to the raiſing of flax. About 25 years ago, when a great proportion of the ground conſiſted of natural paſture, every farmer had a large flock of ſheep. At preſent, there are not in this pariſh above 2 or 3 who have ſheep at all. In the N. and N. W. parts

of

of the parish, there are large tracks of moor, formerly
waste and uncultivated, covered wholly with heath, infomuch that a person might have travelled a confiderable
way without feeing any other vegetable. At prefent
thofe tracks contain plantations of thriving young wood.
In a track of moor which forms the northern extremity of
this parifh, there are fettled 15 or 16 families, who, by
their induftry, have rendered arable, and in fome degree
fertile, confiderable fpots of land formerly wafte and barren. The valued rent of the parifh is L. 4608 : 6 : 8
Scotch. There are about 23 confiderable farms, fome of
which confift of more than 200 acres.

Population.—This parifh contains 2 large villages, one
of which having about 30, and the other 25 families, and
2 or 3 villages lefs populous. According to Dr Webfter's
returns, the numbers were 1345. The number in 1772
was 1033; at prefent it is 1278. There is reafon to believe, that about the beginning and middle of this century,
the parifh was more populous. The diminution of the
number of people is owing to the union of farms; the
farmers alfo employ fewer hands than formerly. Many of
the cottagers are exterminated. Since commerce began to
flourifh, feveral manufacturers, who fubfifted partly by a-
griculture, have gone to large towns. The annual average
of births for the laft 10 years is 32. The annual average
during a period of 10 years fubfequent to 1718, and during 10 years fubfequent to 1742, appears from a well
kept regifter, to have been 41. For fome years paft, the
annual average of deaths has been about 19. The number
of marriages annually for 7 years paft has not exceeded
13.

Church.

Church, Stipend, School and Poor.—The church seems to have been built or renewed in 1678. The manse and offices are at present somewhat ruinous. The value of the living depending chiefly on victual is in different years different. During the 7 years of the incumbent's ministry, the stipend, at an average, has been L. 115 Sterling a-year. The manse and glebe cannot be estimated, both together, at more than L. 10 or L. 12 Sterling.—The schoolmaster's income as schoolmaster, session-clerk and precentor, is a-bout L. 35 Sterling a-year. The number of scholars is from 40 to 50.—The poor are in general well provided for. None of them are reduced to the necessity of begging. The number at present on the roll is 15. The annual average of collections is about L. 23 or L. 24 Sterling. There are of seat-rents belonging to the poor about L. 12 Sterling; and there is lying at interest at $4\frac{1}{2}$ *per cent.* 200 Sterling.

Miscellaneous Observations.—The roads in this parish at present are not in the best condition. That from Dundee to Arbroath, which intersects the lower part of the parish, is in bad weather almost impassable. There is a turnpike-road begun to be made, which, though a mile farther south than the old road, yet being quite straight, will shorten the distance between these 2 towns. About 7 years ago, a road was formed leading from Brechin to Dundee, and passing through the northern part of this parish. Upon this road there was built about 5 years ago, a strong massy bridge, 55 feet high, with a single arch, over a precipice at Denfiend, or the Fiend's Den, a place deep and winding. —Near the 8th mile-stone, E. from Dundee, there is a ridge of small hills, called the Cur-hills, where within these 14

years

years feveral ftone coffins have been found. In the vicinity of the fame place, were found upwards of 6 feet below the furface of the earth, feveral trees, oak, fir and birch. There were alfo found urns, covered with broad ftones, below which were afhes, fuppofed to have been human bodies reduced to that ftate by burning. To the fouth of the Cur-hills were found feveral heads of deer, and horns of a very large fize, among marl, about 9 feet below the furface.

Within thefe 3 or 4 years, there have been 5 or 6 large neat new houfes, and feveral fmaller ones built. Every farmer almoft has within thefe 10 years made fome addition or improvement to his dwelling houfe, or to his offices.—T ere are 2 confiderable inns in this parifh, and feveral petty ale-houfes. The confumption of fpiritous liquors has within a few years greatly increafed, the quality of the ale brewed in this part of the country being worfe than formerly; yet the morals of the people feem to have fuffered little by the change. No bufinefs of any confequence can be tranfacted by the common people but in the ale-houfe. But the vice of drunkennefs, and the crime of theft, are in this and other parts of the country more rare than about 30 years ago, when the lower clafs of people having fewer objects to excite their induftry, were more idle, and confequently more profligate.—About 35 years ago, the wages of a ploughman were in this neighbourhood L. 2, 10 s. Sterling; of a carter L. 2; of a female fervant from L. 1, 5 s. to L. 1, 10 s. At prefent, a ploughman is thought good for nothing, who does not receive L. 7 or L. 8. The ufual wages of female fervants are from L. 3 to L. 4. About 30 or 40 years ago, a farm which is now worked by 3 ploughs, having each 4, fometimes on-

ly

ly 2 horſes, employed 5 cattle ploughs, having each 10 oxen. Farms where 2 ploughs drawn by 4 horſes are now found ſufficient, were formerly wrought by 3 ploughs drawn by 10 oxen.

TOWN AND PARISH OF MONTROSE.

(COUNTY OF ANGUS.)

By the Rev. Mr ALEXANDER MOLLESON.

Origin of the Name.

THE ancient name of Montrose seems to have been **Ce-lurca** *. Many derivations have been assigned for its modern appellation. The most probable is from the Gaelic, in which language *Moinrofs* signifies " the fenny pro-" montory," and it is called by the vulgar, Monrofs to this day †. Buchanan and others, have given it a derivation more flattering than just, when they assert, that it proper-ly means the *Mount of Rofes* (Mons Rosarum). Yet, in allusion to this fanciful derivation, the seal of the town is impressed

---

* See Boethius. To this name alfo Johnston alludes in the following lines :

" Aureolis urbs picta rofis ; mons, molliter urbi
    " Imminet ; hinc urbi nomina facta canunt :
" Et veteres perhibent quondam dixiffe Celurcam ;
    " Nomine fic prifco et nobilitata novo eft.

† See Irvine's Nomenclat. Scot. 158. Baxter. (Glofs. Ant. Brit. 170.) de-rives it from *Mant-e-rofe*, " the mouth of the ftream." Others from *Mon-trois*, from the three hills in its neighbourhood, the Forthill, the Horloge-hill, and the Windmill hill. On the whole, *Moin-rofs* is the moft probable.

impressed with roses; and the motto is, " *Mare ditat, rosa*
" *decorat*," (the sea enriches, and the rose adorns).

Situation.—This parish is situated in the presbytery of
Brechin, in the synod of Angus and Mearns, and in the
county of Angus or Forfar. It may be considered under
two heads, the town and the country district. We shall begin with giving a concise account of the country part of
the parish. The town will require a more minute and particular description.

1. *Country district.*

Extent, &c.—The length of the parish, from north to
south, is about 3 English miles. Its breadth from east to
west, is about 2½. The general appearance of the district is
flat; but towards its northern extremity it rises gradually,
and terminates in a hill of no very considerable height, called,
the hill of Montrose. The country in the neighbourhood, being
fertile and well cultivated, affords a delightful prospect in
almost every part of this parish. A beautiful and extensive
expanse of Ocean; ships frequently sailing in all directions;
the town and bason of Montrose; the arches and ornaments
of the bridge of Dun; the windings of the river Southesk,
with the rich fields upon its banks; the charming valley of
Strathmore; a number of gentlemen's seats, and the plantations around them; the venerable steeples of the ancient
city of Brechin, and the celebrated Grampian hills stretching from the German Ocean, farther to the west, than the eye
can penetrate, must charm every traveller of taste. They afford also a permanent entertainment, to every inhabitant
of Montrose, who takes a pleasure in contemplating the sub-
lime and variegated works of nature.

Rivers,

Rivers.—To this parish belong two very considerable rivers. The one, the Northesk, separates the shire of Angus from that of Kincardine or the Mearns, and runs through the northern extremity of the parish, into the German Ocean. The post-road from Montrose to Aberdeen, crossing this river near its mouth, and the ford, often varying, it frequently proved fatal to travellers; the inhabitants of Montrose, excited by the activity of Alexander Christie, Esq; provost at that time, and aided by a generous public, together with a liberal donation from the annexed estates, built, in 1775, a handsome bridge, consisting of seven arches, across this ford. This bridge is of great advantage to the neighbouring country, and opens, upon the eastern coast, an easy communication with the northern part of this kingdom. The river sometimes swells to a great height; and, as its banks are low, the adjacent fields in this parish, suffer, on such occasions, considerable damage. The proprietors, however, cannot complain, for it fertilizes their lands, and the salmon fishing on both sides renders their estates much more valuable, than they would otherwise be. The Southesk separates this parish from that of Craig. After many beautiful meanders, gliding through the bason, and passing by the harbour of Montrose, this river falls into the German Ocean, about a mile from the town.

Over this river it is proposed to make a bridge, first from the Fort hill to the island of Inchbrayock, and then a small one, from Inchbrayock to the lands of Craig. Estimates have already been given in, of one bridge with the piers of stone, and the rest of wood, of another entirely of wood, and of a third intirely of stone. Subscriptions, to a considerable amount, have been obtained, and an act of parliament having also passed last session for that purpose, this great work will probably soon be accomplished. It is certainly a great undertaking

undertaking for ſuch a place; but it will doubtleſs contribute much to the advantage of Montroſe, will add to the value of lands in that neighbourhood, and, if the roads are once put in proper order, will be an additional inducement, to bring the mail-coach, along this coaſt, to the north of Scotland, the benefit of which will be very great.

Baſon.——The baſon of Montroſe is a beautiful piece of water, nearly circular, and about three miles in diameter. At low water, it is moſtly dry, but at high water, it has a charming effeęt from the weſt ſide of the town, waſhes the garden-walls, and tends much to the cleanlineſs of the place. Veſſels, of 50 or 60 tons burden, come to the eaſt and weſt ſide of the baſon, without any riſk. This is of great advantage to the ſurrounding heritors, as they can bring lime and coals, by water, very near their different eſtates.

In the laſt century, an attempt was made to cut off a conſiderable part of the baſon, and convert it into arable land, by running a dike from near the Fort hill, along the bank of the river Southeſk, towards the eſtate of Dun. The ſcheme was nearly carried into execution; and, as the ſoil is a ſtrong clay, it would have been very advantageous to the proprietors. But the perſons who had the management of this undertaking, quarrelling among themſelves, the work went on but ſlowly; and when the dike was nearly completed, a ſtorm aroſe, and levelled the whole with the ground. The foundation of this dike is ſtill viſible, and the ſcheme appears rational; but all thoughts of carrying it into execution, even on a ſmaller ſcale, ſeem, at preſent, to be abandoned. Some houſes in the town, are known to have been built of ſtones, which compoſed a part of this dike. It is ſtill called the *Drainers* dike.

State of Property, &c.—The country part of the parish, besides many small feus, is divided into eight larger properties;
of these, the estate of Kinnabar, which once belonged to the
family of Montrose, one of whose titles, to this day, is Baron
of Kinnabar, is the most considerable.   It is rendered more
valuable by the fishing, and the improvement of some waste
ground.   The present mansion-house is undergoing considerable repairs, and lies in a romantic elevated situation,
surrounded by trees. The soil of Kinnabar, and of the estates of
Charleton, Newmanswalls, Borrowfield, and Hedderwick,
is, in general, very good, and cultivated with spirit, according to the best schemes of modern improvers.   Even where
the low lands have a light soil, as they have long received
town manure, they are very productive of all kinds of
grain and turnips, especially, when, before breaking up, they
are clayed upon the grass.   The upper grounds, are, in
general, of a thin and muirish soil, but much improved
of late, by the above manure, and lime from the adjoining
parish.

The valued rent amounts to L. 2200 Scotch, or L. 183,
6 s. 8 d. Sterling. There are in the parish about 3080 acres
occupied as follows :

	Acres.		*Acres.*
In wheat,	60	Carried over,	1000
— Oats,	400	Sown or artificial grasses,	1000
— Barley,	350	Pasture,	400
— Pease,	100	Waste and heath,	400
— Turnips,	70	Wood,	250
— Potatoes,	20	Marshes,	30
Total in grain,	1000	Total,	3080

The medium rent of land in the parish is L. 1, 10 s. a-
year in the country district.   Some lets at L. 2, 10 s. and
some

ſome borough lands at L. 4 the acre, which is the higheſt. The price of the latter, ſometimes riſes ſo high, as L. 100 the acre.

In the country part of the pariſh there are, at an average,

Horſes, - - - -	130
Cattle, - - - - - -	500
Sheep, - - - -	100
Carts, - - - - - -	56
Horſe ploughs, - - -	37
Cattle, ditto, - - - - - -	3
Four-wheeled carriages, - -	5

No earths uſeful in manufactures have as yet been diſcovered, except clay for bricks, which is very good for that purpoſe. The trees are moſtly young, and principally conſiſt of planes, elms, birch and larix.

Mineral Springs.—There are ſeveral ſprings in this pariſh, of the chalybeate kind, but none of them ſtrong. There is one nigh the town, of a different ſort, which is certainly worthy of a chymical analyſis. About 50 years ago, Dr Thomſon, phyſician in Montroſe, made a variety of experiments on the water of this well, by which it appears, that it bears a conſiderable reſemblance to that of Scarborough, and has nearly the ſame qualities; notwithſtanding which, it has not been of late much frequented by ſtrangers, nor even by the people of Montroſe. Other wells are more reſorted to, not, perhaps, becauſe they are more efficacious, but becauſe they are at a greater diſtance, and in greater vogue with people of faſhion.

Sea Coaſt.—As far as this pariſh extends, the ſhore is ſandy and very level. There are no rocks or currents, from the mouth of the one river to that of the other. The

tide

tide of flood runs S. W. along the shore. The two nearest head lands are the Red-head on the south, and the Tod-head on the north. At the former, with off-shore winds, the anchorage is very good.—In the beginning of this century, however, a fleet of merchant ships, sailing to a Dutch settlement, with stores of all kinds, were wrecked upon this northern coast, and one or two were lost in the mouth of the Northesk.

2. *Town of Montrose.*

Situation, &c.—The latitude of the town of Montrose is 56° 34′ north; and its longitude from London is 2° 10′ west. It is pleasantly situated on a gentle eminence in a peninsula, formed by the bason, the river Southesk and the German Ocean. The neck, which connects with the main-land on the N. E., formerly, must have been much narrower than at present; as, from the appearance of the links, it is evident, that the sea has retired from its former limits, almost a mile. This is the voice of tradition, to which every spectator must assent.

Air, Diseases, &c.—From the situation of Montrose, it may naturally be imagined, that the atmosphere is replete with aqueous particles, and very piercing in cold weather, and when the wind is from the east. But, as the town is built, on a sandy dry soil, and there are hardly any stagnant waters or lakes in the neighbourhood, it is not subject to those march miasmata, which occasion agues and fevers. The most prevalent diseases of Montrose, are, of the chronic sort, such as, rheumatism, toothach, sore-throat, scurvy, scrophula, &c. Phthisis pulmonalis, frequently proceeding from scrophula interna, is not uncommon in this place. The hypochondriac, or hysteric disease, prevails

much

much among all ranks, eſpecially the vulgar. When fevers occur, they are almoſt conſtantly of the nervous tribe. Every malady proceeding from a relaxed ſtate of the fibres prevails here. This relaxation is occaſioned, by our atmoſphere being replete with marine vapours, and a copious mephitic exhalation, emitted from the baſon, when the water retires. From this account, putrid diſeaſes might be ſuppoſed to be among our endemics, but they are not. The true putrid ſore-throat is a rare diſtemper here; and our nervous fevers, unleſs neglected, or improperly treated, rarely aſſume the putrid diatheſis. The humidity of our atmoſphere is probably corrected by a conſiderable mixture of ſaline particles.—The water is excellent, and to be had in abundance. It is conveyed about 3 miles in pipes of lead, and iſſues from wells in different parts of the town.

Antiquities.—Among the few antiquities, which Montroſe can boaſt of, the Fort hill, which takes its name from the caſtle, built on its ſummit, deſerves to be particularly mentioned. From its poſition, it was well adapted to command the town, the harbour, and the ſhipping in the river. The main current of the river probably flowed, in former times, on the other ſide of the iſland of Inchbrayock, and it has evidently made very conſiderable encroachments on this hill. A well was diſcovered a few years ago on the brink, and, when the water is clear and ſmooth, another has been ſeen a good way into the river. Both of them, in all probability, have been once within the fort. The inhabitants remember, that the river at the Fort hill was not near ſo deep, nor ſo broad, as at preſent. Tradition ſays, that in ancient times, perſons on the oppoſite banks could almoſt ſhake hands. Another memorable and valuable piece of antiquity

antiquity belonging to Montrofe is an hofpital, or *maifon de Dieu*, which has been allowed to go to ruin ; but the revenues are preferved, and are under the management of the Town-council, and a mafter of the hofpital of their appointment. One of the moft ancient houfes in the town, (now belonging to, and poffeffed by Mr Scott of Logie), is famous for being the houfe, where the celebrated Marquis of Montrofe was born ; and in which the pretender flept on 13th February 1716, the night before his efcape. Next morning he went on board a frigate, which lay in the road, and conveyed him fafe to France.

Population.—The following ftatements will pretty clearly prove a progreffive increafe of population.

	For 10 years, ending 1770.	Ditto, ending 1790.
Annual average of Marriages,	35	52
——————————— Baptifms,	73	96
——— ——————— Burials,	118	160

The lifts of marriages and burials may be depended on. The lift of baptifms is as exact as could be procured. But the inattention of parents, and the backwardnefs of many to pay the fchoolmafter his dues, is a matter of very general complaint throughout Scotland, and contributes to render fuch lifts lefs accurate, than might be wifhed. If we multiply 127, which was the number of burials from 1ft January 1685, to ditto 1686, by 36, the parifh, at that time, would contain about 4572 inhabitants. According to this method of computation, the number of fouls, from 1740 to 1750, were, at an average, only 4248 but, from 1780 to 1790, they increafed confiderably.

The following lifts were extracted from the minifter's parifh rolls, which are made up with all poffible accuracy :

In

	In Town.	In the Country.	Total.
Number of ſouls in 1776,	4465	909	5374
Ditto in 1784, —	4866	950	5816
Ditto in 1790, —	5194	1000	6194

When it is conſidered, that the manufacture of canvas, ſince the peace of 1783, has been, in a great meaſure, given up, and, that trade, ſince that time, has not been very briſk in Montroſe, it will be acknowledged, that the population in this town, has, of late, increaſed, more than might have been expected. Gloomy ſpeculatiſts predicted, at the concluſion of the American war, that many would emigrate from this corner. A very few did emigrate, and theſe few have given no encouragement to others to follow their example.

Public Buildings.—The public buildings in Montroſe moſt worthy of notice, are, 1. The old town-houſe, which is ſituated in the middle of the principal ſtreet. A part was fitted up for the grammar-ſchool, and a part for the public priſon. As the rooms and cells in the priſon were too few, and ill-contrived, this houſe is repairing, in ſuch a manner, that men and women, debtors and criminals, may have ſeparate apartments, correſponding with their ſtation and their crimes.

2. The new town-houſe, built in 1763, towards the ſouth end of Murray-ſtreet, with its front directed to the Port. It is conſtructed according to the modern taſte, with rooms, where the magiſtrates aſſemble, &c.

3. The Pariſh Church.—The old church of Montroſe was a Gothic ſtructure, rendered very gloomy and irregular, by large additions to the galleries and to the building itſelf. It was originally, however, venerable and well proportioned.

portioned. Having fallen into decay, the heritors, town-council, kirk-feſſion, trades, and proprietors of ſeats, agreed unanimouſly to build another in its ſtead; the dimenſions of which, are 98 by 65 feet over walls. The plan has been formed with deliberation;— it has been compared with modern churches;—it has been ſubmitted to the in-ſpection of ſome ſkilful architects;—and, it is to be hoped, will be executed in ſuch a manner as to merit public appro-bation *.

4. The Epiſcopal chapel.—This chapel was founded in 1722. It is an ornament to the town, and was even praiſed by the author of the Rambler, in his Tour through Scot-land, as a neat and cleanly place of public worſhip.

5. Public Schools.—In this town there are a great num-ber of private ſchools, in which all ordinary branches of male and female education are taught; but the public ſchools, patroniſed by the town-council and kirk-feſſion, are three. The grammar-ſchool, in which Latin alone is taught. The writing-ſchool, in which, beſides writing, are

* It is but juſtice to the inhabitants of Montroſe, to take this opportu-nity of ſtating the very liberal and Chriſtian-like manner, in which the dif-ferent ſects have uniformly conducted themſelves to each other. The town-council and ſeſſion, lately petitioned the managers of the Epiſcopal and Anti-burgher churches, that the members of the eſtabliſhed church might have the liberty of enjoying divine ſervice in their meeting-houſes, till the pariſh-church was rebuilt. They, and their congregations, not only granted this petition, but declared, in the handſomeſt manner, their willingneſs to ſubmit to conſiderable inconveniencies, in order to accommo-date their fellow Chriſtians to their wiſhes. It is not long ſince the Anti-burgher congregation applied for liberty, to have their miniſter ordained in the eſtabliſhed church, as their own was repairing at that time, and liberty was readily granted. Thus they have ſoon found an opportunity to expreſs their gratitude in kind, and given occaſion to remark, that a generous action may meet with a return in a way little expected.

are alſo taught arithmetic and book-keeping. The Engliſh ſchool, in which are taught the reading of Engliſh, according to the new method, and the principles of Engliſh grammar. Some of the maſters of the public ſchools, teach, in private, other branches, ſuch as French, mathematics, geography and muſic. The public ſchools were formerly in different rooms in the middle of the town ; but, two years ago, very handſome and ſpacious ſchools were built, in an open area in the links, where the boys and girls enjoy ſalubrious air, and have ample ſcope for amuſement, without endangering either their health or their morals.

6. The Public Library.—Some literary gentlemen, eager to read a variety of publications, not to be had in the place, and which they could not conveniently purchaſe, reſolved to enter into a ſociety, for the purpoſe of forming a public library. It was begun in 1785, and is, at this time, in as flouriſhing a condition as could well be expected. Such inſtitutions, evidently tend to increaſe knowledge, and to diffuſe a taſte for learning, and therefore ought, as much as poſſible, to be encouraged *.

7. The Lunatic Hoſpital.—This is one of the moſt uſeful and patriotic inſtitutions belonging to this or any other town. Before it was built, the magiſtrates were frequently under the neceſſity of confining lunatics in the common priſon, ſituated in the middle of the town, where they were liable to have their diſorders increaſed, by the publicity of the place of their confinement, and often exhibited the moſt ſhocking ſcenes of blaſphemy and deſperation. At
length,

* The public teachers of youth and ſtudents at the univerſities, have the benefit of the library *gratis*. Convinced of its great utility, ſeveral gentlemen have already preſented to the library valuable books, and ſome have preſented works of their own compoſition.

length, in 1779, Mrs Carnegie of Pittarrow, juſtly celebrated for her public ſpirit, ſuggeſted the plan of a lunatic hoſpital, to be erected in the links near Montroſe. By her influence, a petition, ſigned by ſome perſons of diſtinction in the town and neighbourhood, was preſented to the magiſtrates, requeſting their aid for erecting ſuch an hoſpital; and ſoon after, a ſubſcription was opened for that purpoſe, which ſucceeded beyond expectation. Sixty nine lunatics have already been admitted into the houſe, ſome from places ſo diſtant as Perth, Aberdeen and Edinburgh, of whom 14 have been cured, 6 removed greatly better, 21 died, and 28 remain in the hoſpital *.

Conſtitution

* It is propoſed, as ſoon as the funds will permit, to fit up a ſick ward; in the mean time, 57 patients, labouring under dangerous diſeaſes, have been taken into the hoſpital, manyǀof whom required chirurgical operations. Twenty ſix have been cured, 10 relieved, 8 removed incurable, 10 died, and 6 are under cure; 1324 out-patients have received advice and medicine *gratis*, 410 of whom have been cured, 389 relieved, and 2 died. Such was the ſtate of the hoſpital at the beginning of 1790. As it was erected by ſubſcription, it has been hitherto ſupported by funds annually granted by the magiſtrates of Montroſe, by collections at the church and Epiſcopal chapel, by a collection through the Synod of Angus and Mearns, and the voluntary donations and contributions of the humane and liberal. Several lunatics from the pariſh of Montroſe have been admitted, *gratis*, and, from other pariſhes, whence liberal contributions have been received, at ſo low a rate as L. 8, L. 7, L. 6, and even L. 5 a-year. But, without further liberal donations, and the continuance of annual ſubſcriptions, the funds muſt be inadequate to ſupport the inſtitution, in ſuch a manner as its friends would wiſh. The medical gentlemen of Montroſe, give both advice and attendance *gratis*; and the treaſurer is equally diſintereſted. The humanity and frugality of the maſter and miſtreſs, and the order and cleanlineſs of the houſe, merit the higheſt commendation. Several pieces of coarſe ſheeting have been made, from the yarn ſpun by the lunatics in their lucid intervals. At ſuch times, they are alſo occaſionally employed in painting, reading, gardening, knitting ſtockings, ſpinning, and working with the needle. A piece of painting, in the miſtreſs's room, done by one of the lunatics, is, as ſuch, a conſiderable curioſity.

Conſtitution and Income of the Borough.—Montroſe is a royal borough, united with thoſe of Aberdeen, Bervie, Brechin, and Arbroath, in chuſing a member of Parliament. The corporation has continued in nearly the ſame ſtate, for about 450 years. It is compoſed of 19 members, *viz.* the provoſt, 3 bailies, dean of guild, treaſurer, hoſpital maſter, 10 merchant councillors, and 2 councillors from the trades. The old council elect the new, and they may continue themſelves, in office, as long as they pleaſe to hold together. The conſtitution requires no change of merchant councillors yearly; but the 2 trades councillors muſt be changed every two years. They may, however, be ſucceeded by their predeceſſors. The revenues of the town are not very ample, and have been conſiderably burdened by building an addition to the pier, making a new market for butchers meat, erecting lamps, improving public walks, ſubſcribing to public works, building new ſchools, and augmenting the number of teachers and their ſalaries, &c.; but they are managed with care; and if nothing unforeſeen happens, will receive an addition not many years hence. The provoſt has L. 40 yearly, allowed him to defray the expences of making burgeſſes, and entertainments on the King's birthday, or at the election of magiſtrates, &c. That appears to be a very economical meaſure, as probably, more than double that ſum would be inſufficient to defray theſe expences, without ſuch a regulation.

Commerce and Manufactures.—As the harbour of Montroſe is the moſt commodious of any, between the river Tay and the bay of Cromarty, the trade of this town, has, for a long time, been conſiderable. In the beginning of this century, and till about the year 1744, Montroſe was diſtinguiſhed by its ſhipping. It was alſo famous for a

market

market for linen yarn, which was brought from all parts
of the counties of Angus and Mearns, and fold here, whence
it was fent to London and Manchefter. A great market, called Rood fair, was held here in the beginning of May, which
was formerly much reforted to, but is now much on the decline. About 50 years ago fmuggling was much practifed here,
and indeed almoft every where on the coaft of Scotland,
and fcarcely any fort of manufacture was carried on.

The firft manufacture, of any confequence, that of
canvas, was erected here by a company in 1745. It was
carried on, for many years, to a great extent, and anfwered
well. Soon after, it was followed by another company on
a large fcale, and afterwards by many fmaller ones, particularly during the laft war. As the fame thing happened
in other places in the kingdom, this article was fo much
overdone, at the peace of 1783, that all the great companies
here, and moft of the fmaller ones, gave up, turned their
working-houfes into dwelling-houfes, and fold off their
machinery and utenfils, &c. Little, therefore, is now attempted in that line, compared with what was done before.

During this period, two different companies fet up a large
manufacture of coloured and white thread, and were followed by others on a fmaller fcale. One of the larger companies has given up; but the other continues, and has found it,
as yet, a very profitable branch of bufinefs. It is at prefent
the moft confiderable article of manufacture in the town.
Some brown fheetings and Ofnaburghs are alfo made here,
and a pretty confiderable trade is carried on, in the commiffion line, in Ofnaburghs and yarn fent to Glafgow. The
cotton manufactures have been lately attempted, and various
fmaller articles, as ftockings, &c. are manufactured. There
is a good tannery, and rope-works belonging to different
companies.

This

This town has been long distinguished for making and exporting excellent malt, and for making good malt liquor of all kinds. A public brewery, especially for small beer, has been lately set up. But private families, in general, brew for their own use. The strong ale made here, is esteemed, by good judges, equal to the Burton ale.

To Montrose, there belong, commonly, about 16 or 18 fishermen, but many of them are old, and for some years past they have had very indifferent success. Haddocks are just now remarkably rare, and consequently extremely dear. The mussels belonging to this place are excellent, both for bait and eating, and they are never dangerous. They are to be found in great plenty, all over the river and at the harbour. Oysters have been laid in a deep part of the river, to try if they will succeed there, but a sufficient time, for a full trial of the experiment, has not as yet elapsed. Incredible numbers of lobsters were, some years ago, taken on this coast. Pennant, in his tour (1772,) p. 2, mentions, that 60,000 or 70,000 were, at that time, sent annually to London; but that branch of commerce is now laid aside, as not sufficiently advantageous. Quantities of white fish, as cod, turbot, &c. might be taken on the great sand banks off this coast. The Long forties extend parallel thereto; and beyond that, lie, Montrose pits, (see Hammond's chart of the North Sea), a great bank with six pits in it. If we reckon from the surface of the water, they are from 40 to 100 fathoms deep. Those banks swarm with fish, but are nevertheless much neglected. Attempts have, indeed, been made for some years past, but unsuccessfully, owing to the misconduct of the persons employed.

There are at present 3 ships, belonging to Montrose, concerned in the whale-fishing business. They generally go to Davis Straits. The trade is very precarious, but they have, upon the whole, been more successful than many others.

At

At the harbour of Montrofe, there is a good wet dock, where fhips are built and repaired, not only for this, but for other ports.

In 1783, a plan was adopted, and patronifed by feveral gentlemen and merchants of Montrofe, for infuring fhips and goods at fea. It has been carried on ever fince. As there is alfo in this place a branch of the office at Dundee, for infuring houfes and furniture againft fire, moft of the property, belonging to the inhabitants, may be infured in the town itfelf.

The port of Montrofe, which comprehends within its bounds, all the coaft, from the Tod-head on the north, to the lights of Tay on the fouth, had, in 1789, the following number of fhips, and quantity of tonnage belonging to it.

	Number of Ships.	Tonnage.
Montrofe and Ferryden,	53	3543
Arbroath, - -	29	1539
Johnfhaven, - -	12	457
Gourdon, - - -	6	192
Eaft and Weft Havens,	3	118
Total Ships,	103	Total Tonnage, 5849 *

Duty

---

* The principal articles imported from foreign parts, in the year 1789, into the port of Montrofe, including Arbroath, were nearly as follows :

Afhes pearl, -	14 tons.	Iron, -	166 Tons.
Afhes wood, -	27 ditto.	Clover feed, -	17 ditto.
Flax,	578 ditto.	Whale blubber,	299 ditto.
Hemp, -	69 ditto,	Whale fins *alias*	
		Whale-bone,	14 ditto.
		Fir timber,	1479 ditto.
			Battes,

Duty on Coals.—The duty on Scotch and Engliſh coal, paid in Scotland, amounts to about L. 11,000 a-year. Of this ſum, the diſtricts belonging to the cuſtom-houſes of Aberdeen and Montroſe, pay the principal part. In the year 1788, Montroſe paid L. 2285, and Aberdeen L. 4735. The heavy duty impoſed on Scotch coal, carried coaſtwiſe by ſea, begins at the Red-head, between this and Arbroath. Montroſe is, of conſequence, the firſt town to the northward of the Frith of Forth, where it is paid. It is a duty undoubtedly impolitic, partial and oppreſſive. It is impolitic, as it diſcourages population and induſtry in the north of Scotland. It is partial and oppreſſive, as the richeſt and moſt populous parts

Battens,	-	-	25 hundred.	Spruce beer, 76 barrels.
Deals,	-	-	172 ditto.	Tar, 21 laſts.
Lintſeed,	-	-	298 quarters.	

Beſides ſundry other inferior ſpecies of wood, and miſcellaneous articles of ſmaller value. The principal articles exported in 1789, from this port, including Arbroath and Johnſhaven, of which no ſeparate account is kept, are nearly as follow:

Barley and beer,	-	-	-	-	-	6971 quarters.
Malt,	-	-	-			8287 ditto.
Sail-cloth,	-	-	-			5561 ells.

Beſides ſmall quantities of oats, oat-meal, beer-meal, wheat, flour, tow, &c.

Salmon ſhipped at Montroſe.

In 1788,	-	-	-	-	-	-	1200 kitts.
—— 89	-	-	-	-	-	2000 ditto.
—— 90	-	-	-	-	2500 ditto.

The quantity of freſh and kippered ſalmon, ſold here, cannot be eaſily aſcertained.

In the year 1789, beſides other goods, too various and numerous to admit of ſpecification, there were brought coaſtwiſe, into this port and its creeks, from England and the Frith of Forth,

Great coals,	-	-	-	17,446 tons.
Small coals,	-	-	-	-	2,490 London chalders.
Culm,	-	-	-	-	-	3,577 ditto.
Cinders,	-	-	-	-	375 ditto.

parts of Scotland pay no part of it, and the most remote and poorest parts of the kingdom pay the whole. A grievance of this kind, merits the attention of Parliament, and ought to be redressed, by abolishing the tax altogether, or substituting an equivalent in its stead on some other article, to be levied throughout all Scotland. Such a tax would be the meerest trifle to the kingdom at large, could be grudged by none, who had any regard to substantial justice, and would deliver this part of the country from a grievous burden, without the removal of which, neither its commerce nor its agriculture can prosper.

Poor.—The number of paupers in this place is very great. This is owing in part to the many charitable institutions in Montrose;—to the character its inhabitants have long maintained of kindness to strangers, and liberality to the poor;—and partly, indeed, to the different manufactures, to which men advanced in life, and reduced in circumstances, repair for bread to themselves and numerous families, and who, within a few years, become a burden on the public.

Of the funds allotted for the use of the poor, those belonging to the church-sessions are the largest, and managed, in general, with the greatest impartiality; without any respect to persons, station, employment, or principle, religious or political. The monthly pensioners amount at present to about 168. Besides these, occasional supplies are ordered for others at the monthly meetings. Such persons as, in the interval, are reduced to temporary distress, apply to the elder or church-warden, belonging to the division of the town or country parish, where they reside, who recommends them to the moderator of the session. Upon this, the moderator issues out an order to the treasurer, called a *precept*, to give them

them a fupply, feldom exceeding half a crown. The paffing traveller, who is well recommended, as an object deferving the compaffion of the public, receives alfo occafional fupply, upon producing to the treafurer the moderator's precept. Thefe occafional fupplies, during the interval of the meetings of the feffion, amount to from L. 30 to L. 40 a-year.

A tolerable idea of the nature and extent of thefe funds, now and formerly, may be deduced from a brief detail of the income and expenditure, towards the conclufion of the laft century, and at the prefent time.

Income, from 1ft February 1685, to ditto 1686.

Collected at the church-doors, -	L. 73	5	4¼
Received from William Durrow, -	19	5	7¼
———— for the mortcloth and bells, -	18	6	6
One fixteenth part of the loadening of the fhip Elizabeth, belonging to the feffion, -	15	15	11¼
Free-will offerings, by merchants and mafters of veffels, - -	12	2	8
Intereft of money for one year, at 6 *per cent.*	11	13	4
Collected, at difpenfing the Lord's Supper, -	10	12	5½
———— for the relief of James Ogilvie, prifoner with the Turks, - -	6	13	4
Collections at fea, - -	8	7	2
Received from James Gentleman, -	2	3	10
Fornication penalties, - - -	2	1	8
For Roffie's daughter's interment in the church,	1	13	4
For the clerk's wife's interment in ditto, -	1	13	4
Trifling articles, - - -	2	7	6
Total income, - - -	L. 186	2	1

Expenditure,

Expenditure, from 1ſt February 1685, to ditto 1686.

	L.		
Monthly penſioners, to the number of about 62,	77	5	8¼
Orphan's board, ceſs, church officers dues, &c. &c. &c. Miniſters ſtipend from the ſeſſion's lands, ſeſſion-clerk's fees, &c. -	21	19	5¼
Given to ſundry poor, by the ſeſſion's orders, at different times, - -	19	8	2½
The miniſter's precepts to the treaſurer, -	17	18	7½
Given for the relief of James Ogilvie, the money collected for that end, - -	6	13	4
For repairing the one ſixteenth part of the ſhip Elizabeth, - -	3	14	4
For repairing the church, -	1	8	4
For a pair of joggs, lead, and putting them in,	0	4	1¼

	L.		
Total expenditure, -	148	12	1½
Total income, -	186	2	1
Balance in treaſurer's hands,	37	9	11½

Income from 1ſt January 1789, to 1ſt January 1790.

Collected at the church door, - -	94	6	3¼
Received for land rents, - -	73	0	0
Collected, at diſpenſing the Lord's Supper, in May and November, -	39	9	9
Received for burials, and liberty to erect monuments, - -	26	10	2½
Houſe-rents, - -	23	13	2
Seat-rents in the ſeſſion's loft, and the body of the church, - -	6	5	0
Received, out of the effects of ſuch as died, when ſupported by the ſeſſion, -	1	0	0½

	L.		
Total income, -	264	4	5¼

Expenditure,

Expenditure, from 1st January 1789, to 1st January 1790.

	L.	s.	d.
Monthly pensioners, to the number of about 168,	L. 89	6	6
The minister's precepts to the treasurer,	32	6	9
Orphans board, and clothing to ditto,	30	4	$7\frac{1}{2}$
Schoolmaster's salaries, and church-officer's fees,	18	8	$4\frac{1}{2}$
To the lunatic hospital,	14	0	0
Distributed to the poor at November sacrament,	11	0	0
Incident charges,	10	6	3
Interest of money borrowed,	6	14	8
Paid for waiting on people in distress,	6	7	0
To poor children restrained from begging,	6	6	0
Church-servants fees, and expences at both sacraments,	4	17	6
Minister's stipend and cess,	5	13	10
Repairing the church,	4	2	$5\frac{1}{2}$
Coffins given to poor persons by the session,	3	11	6
Treasurer's fees,	3	0	0
Communion elements, at the November sacrament,	2	13	0

	L.	s.	d.
Total expenditure,	L. 248	18	$3\frac{1}{2}$
Total income,	264	4	$5\frac{1}{2}$

Balance in the treasurer's hands, L. 15   6   0

The hospital funds, which are under the direction of the town-council, have been so much improved, that they amount, at present, to about L. 108 Sterling a-year. They are restricted, entirely, to the relief of decayed burghers. Mortified money, to the amount of about L. 1600 Sterling, was left by John Milne, Esq; of Old Montrose, Baillie Aughterlonie, Mrs Grahame, Provost Thomas Christie, &c. under the direction of the magistrates and ministers, &c. The interest tereft is diftributed, at particular feafons of the year, among the poor at large, belonging to this parifh. The family of Hedderwick, mortified a fmall fum to the poor at large, both in the town and country parifh, and another to pur-chafe for the poor in the country parifh, Bibles and New Teftaments.

The failor's box is not rich, as many of the mariners fcruple to pay the dues. It affords, however, to the widows, &c. of fuch as are connected with it, occafional fupplies to pay houfe-rent, buy coals, &c. Shipwrecked failors, tra-velling to their own homes, if their ftory is judged to be genuine, may alfo expect fome charity from this fund.

The trades funds were formerly confiderable; but fome years ago, they were more than exhaufted by a ruinous law-fuit. By perfevering economy, and fome donations, they are at prefent emerging out of debt.

As, notwithftanding all thefe funds, and the generofity of many individuals, there are fome poor perfons, belonging to Montrofe, who could not fubfift without applying to the public at large; the magiftrates, and church-feffion, meet at a particular time of the year, and give out badges to fuch as they know to be under the neceffity of begging. Thefe licenfed beggars go through the town the firft day of every month, but are not allowed to beg at any other time, nor to go beyond the bounds of the parifh. They are fup-plied fo liberally, that they receive nothing from any of the public funds, except when lying on a fick-bed. Their number, at prefent, is about 40.

At the fame time, as idlenefs is very pernicious to mo-rals, efpecially to the morals of the youth, the council and church-feffion give a monthly penfion to fome orphans, and other poor children, to reftrain them from begging, to which they would otherwife be obliged to have recourfe.

Convinced,

Convinced, also, of the importance of an early Christian education, the church-session send a number of poor children to school, and pay for their education, till they are able, at least, to read the scriptures. There are, at present, about 50 such on the roll. They are at different schools, which are visited annually, that their progress in learning may be ascertained.

Ecclesiastical State.—There are few people in Montrose, who do not, occasionally, at least, attend some place of public worship. The great body of the people are presbyterians. Hitherto, there has been only one church belonging to the establishment; but it is large, and much crowded. The charge is collegiate· The stipend of the senior clergyman, is in money L. 48 : 14 : 7$\frac{11}{12}$, with 48 bolls 3 firlots 2$\frac{1}{4}$ pecks of bear, 55 bolls 2 firlots 2$\frac{1}{4}$ pecks meal, and 3 bolls 2 firlots of wheat, but without a manse or glebe. The stipend of the second minister arises from an annuity, laid on houses within the royalty, by act of Parliament, at the rate of 5 *per cent.* of yearly rent. It amounts, at present, to upwards of L. 100; and if levied with strictness, would considerably exceed the stipend of the first charge.

The following, is as accurate an account, of the numbers belonging to the religious sects, in this place, as could well be obtained.

	Souls.
Persons, young and old, belonging to the Established Church, - - -	4774
Ditto, belonging the Church of England,	720
Ditto, belonging to the Secession, including Antiburghers and Burghers - -	376
Ditto, belonging to the Episcopal Church of Scotland, - - - -	134
Carried forward,	6004

Brought forward, 6004

Perfons belonging to two fects of Independents,   92

Anabaptifts,   -   -   -   -   40

Bereans of different kinds,   -   -   20

Unitarians,   -   -   -   -   10

Quakers,   -   -   -   -   -   4

Perfons unconnected with any particular religious Society,   -   -   -   -   24

In all, 6194

Though the religious fects in Montrose are thus numerous, and perfons belonging to three or four different kinds,
are fometimes to be found in the fame family, they live, in
general, in great harmony.   About the beginning, and towards the middle of the prefent century, religious zeal, carried to an extreme, produced very bad effects ; and, if the
clergy were not difpofed, to go as great a length as their
hearers, they were perfecuted much by anonymous letters,
threatenings of profecution, and evil fpeaking ; but, in this
refpect, the times are happily changed.   Some bigots may
be found every where, but here they are much reduced in
number, and are daily diminifhing.   The clergy belonging
to the different fects, are on a friendly footing ; the people,
in general, attend public worfhip very regularly, and
behave with becoming decency in the houfe of God. There
are few places, where, upon the whole, the Sunday is better
kept ; though it muft be confeffed, there is, in this refpect,
a falling off here, as well as elfewhere.

Amufements.—The people in Montrose have amufements
of various kinds, both in fummer and winter. Social vifits
take place at all feafons, and fuch recreations as commonly
attend

attend them. The gentlemen hold a monthly club, which is well attended by perfons of diftinction, both in the town and neighbourhood. During fummer, many go to the wells, or retire to the country to enjoy rural felicity. Such as remain at home are frequently entertained with exhibitions calculated to gratify curiofity, or to increafe knowledge. Playing at the golf is a favourite and wholefome amufement. There is excellent ground for this purpofe, and alfo for walking; as a large part of the links is level, and dry at all feafons. Playing at bowls and billiards is alfo frequently practifed. Cards, fometimes, engrofs too much time. In the proper feafon, fome retire to the hills for fhooting, and their friends at home judge of their fuccefs, by the prefents they receive. During the winter feafon, there is an affembly every three weeks. It is conducted with the greateft decorum, and none but proper company are admitted. Actors occafionally perform here, and undoubtedly meet with too much encouragement, though their mode of living is fuch, that they generally depart in poverty, and leave debts behind them. At Chriftmas, and the new year, the opulent burghers begin to feaft with their friends, and go a round of vifits, which takes up the fpace of many weeks. Upon fuch occafions, the graveft is expected to be merry, and to join in a chearful fong. Inftrumental mufic has been, for many years paft, much neglected. Public or private concerts are rare. This is the more to be regretted, as mufic is a very innocent, chearful, and rational amufement, and if more cultivated, might divert the attention from other objects, which injure the health, or deftroy the morals of the people.

Conclufion.—Montrofe is juftly accounted one of the firft provincial towns for its fize in Scotland, or perhaps in Great Britain. It receives, on account of its neat and
cleanly

cleanly appearance, many encomiums from ftrangers. The houfes, if not elegant, are, on the whole, well built and regular; but, like thofe of Flanders, their gabel ends are often turned towards the ftreet. With one or two exceptions, they are now all of ftone, and many of them covered with blue flates. In the principal part of the town, each family poffeffes a feparate houfe. But beyond the port, and at the fhore, the cafe is otherwife. Hence it is more populous, than a ftranger would be apt to imagine. As it is a town more diftinguifhed by the refidence of perfons of opulence and fafhion, than of commerce and induftry, and often, but efpecially in time of war, full of foldiers and failors, the vices, which predominate in thefe diffipated times, are not uncommon. But, on the whole, the character of the people is refpectable, poffeffing a degree of public fpirit, of hofpitality to ftrangers, and of charity to the poor, rarely to be equalled.

PARISH of MUIRHOUSE, or MURROES,

(COUNTY OF FORFAR, SYNOD OF ANGUS AND MEARNS, PRESBYTERY OF DUNDEE.)

By the Rev. Mr ALEXANDER IMLACH.

Name, Extent, Climate, &c.

THERE are many places in Scotland of this name, though this is the only parish so called, perhaps from its original state; no other etymology can be ascertained. The church and manse are situated in the S. E. corner of the parish, 5 miles from Dundee. The parish is of small extent, a considerable part is very good arable land, some moor-ground; a moss, the property of Colonel Fotheringham of Powrie, and a valuable marl-pit, belonging to Mr Guthrie of Guthrie. The air is dry, and very healthy in the southern part of the parish. Agues did prevail about 30 years ago; but the marshes being drained, they no more appear. In the northern part of the parish the air is not so dry, mists frequently arising. There fevers distress the inhabitants, and the harvest is 10 or 12 days later than in the

southern

ſouthern parts. A turnpike-road goes through the pariſh, in a line from Dundee to Brechin, lately made, which will be of great benefit to the inhabitants.

Proprietors.—1. The Honourable William Ramſay-Maule of Panmure, heritor of Ballumbie ; where there are the remains of an old fortified caſtle. This eſtate was formerly the property of a family, of the name of Lovell. To one Alexander of that family, the celebrated Catherine Douglas (whoſe arm was fractured when attempting to ſtop the aſſaſſins who murdered James I. King of Scotland, in the town of Perth) was married, and lived in this caſtle. 2. John Guthrie, Eſq; of Guthrie, proprietor of Weſter and Eaſter Gaigies, as alſo Muirhouſe. Weſter Gaigie has been long the property of that family, where ſometimes a ſon reſided. Their principal ſeat is at Guthrie, where there is an old caſtle, and a collegiate church, endowed by Sir Alexander Guthrie ; he, or one of his ſucceſſors of that name, was killed with James IV. at the battle of Flowden. 3. Colonel Alexander Fotheringham, Eſq; proprietor of Weſter Powrie, Myretown, Whitehouſe, Middle Brighty, and Mill of Brighty. Weſter Powrie had been a conſiderable time the reſidence of that ancient family. They live now at an elegant ſeat, named Fotheringham, in the pariſh of Inverarity. 4. Alexander Wedderburn Eſq; of Wedderburn, formerly named Eaſter Powrie ; his ſurname was originally Scrymſeure, the repreſentative of the noble family of Scrymſeure's of Dudhope and Dundee. He aſſumed the name of Wedderburn, when called to the ſucceſſion of the Wedderburns of Eaſter Powrie, where there are the remains of an old caſtle, the reſidence of Gilchriſt, Thane of Angus, from whom all the Ogilvys in Scotland are ſaid to be deſcended. 5. Mr James Ogilvy, miniſter of the goſpel

at

at Effie, where formerly a family of the name of Guthrie, the progenitors of Mrs Ogilvy in the maternal line, refided. The valued rent of the parifh is L. 2304 Scots, of which Colonel Fotheringham poffeffes L. 714: 3: 4; Guthrie, L. 561: 2: 8¼; Wedderburn, L. 533: 6: 8½; Ballumbie, L. 350; Wefthall, L. 145: 7: 4¼. The real rent is 3 times, and more, than what it was 30 years ago. There being no towns or villages of any extent, manufactures do not exift; a few weavers here and there excepted.

Population.—According to Dr Webfter's report, the number of fouls then was 623. The number of inhabitants is greatly diminifhed, owing to the monopoly of farms, the mode of labouring, and the farmers fome time ago difcharging feveral of their fubtenants and cottagers. In former times, they laboured the ground with ploughs, drawn by oxen, each of thefe ploughs required 2 fervants; whereas, they now ufe ploughs drawn by 2 horfes, and 1 fervant. Upon 1 farm, it is known that the farmer who occupied it, at a former period, employed 13 men-fervants, whereas the prefent tenant employs no more than 5. Then 3 ploughs drawn by oxen were employed, and 6 horfes kept; now fix horfes perform the whole labour; fo in proportion over all the parifh. And if the proprietors of Wefter and Eafter Gaigies, and Muirhoufe, had not let a great part of their lands in pendicles or fmall farms, our numbers would not have been worthy of mentioning. The depopulation of the parifh is afcertained, by comparing the prefent with former regifters of baptifms. In the years 1734, 1735, 1736, 1737, and 1738, the average was 24.6 baptifms yearly. In the years 1761, 1762, 1763, 1764, and 1765, the average was 20.8. In the years 1787, 1788, 1789, 1790, 1791, and 1792, the average is 15.5. In that part of Eafter Gaigie, which is fituated in this parifh, (a great part of it lying

in

in the parish of Monifieth), there are 32 men and women, and 12 children under 10 years of age ; of these men 7 are weavers. In Wester Gaigie, there are 72 men and women, and 20 children ; of these are 2 wrights, 5 weavers, and 1 heckler. On the land of Muirhouse, there are 58 men and women, and 11 children ; of these 8 are weavers, 2 tailors, 1 mason, 2 smiths, 1 gardener, 2 shoemakers, and 2 millers. In the lands of Wester Powrie, the most extensive estate in the parish, and of the greatest valued rent, there are 97 men and women, and 38 children ; of these 1 miller, 2 smiths, and 5 weavers. On the lands of Wedderburn, or Easter Powrie, 40 men and women, and 26 children ; of these 1 smith. On Ballumbie, 26 men and women, and 15 children, 1 weaver. On Westhall, 9 men and women, and 6 children. Sum, 344 men and women, and 128 children ; in all 462.

Agriculture.—About 30 years ago, improvements began to take place, and the mode of labouring underwent a great change ; then lime began to be used as a manure, and the land, when let out, was sown with grass-seeds. Formerly, after ley, two crops of oats ; then giving what dung they had, a crop of barley ; then oats, and let out again : Few pease were used. Since lime was introduced, the mode of labouring is as follows : 1st year, fallow ; 2d year, barley ; sometimes, but seldom, wheat ; 3d year, oats ; 4th, green crop ; 5th year, barley and grass-seeds along with the barley, cut for hay one, sometimes 2 years ; then pastured 2 or 3 years. The farmers, from experience, find it more profitable to take fewer crops, both of corn and grass, *viz.* two years in grass, and 3 years in corn. Before they began to improve, every farmer had a flock of sheep ; now they have none. The land being mostly open,

open, the sheep they found destroyed their grass in the winter time *. Though the farmers labour with horses, they bring up a good many cattle; some rear 8; others 10; and some 12 yearly. They do not bring these to market, till they are 3, sometimes 4 years old; and then they will receive for each L. 7 or L. 8 Sterling. Some farmers sow a few turnip, and feed some cattle; but this practice does not generally prevail.

Character of the People, &c.—They are a sober, regular, and industrious people, and mostly employed in farming, (the few tradesmen already mentioned excepted). In the parish there is neither brewer nor baker. Within these 30 years, their situation is greatly altered to the better, and I can, with safety, say, that more money has been acquired by farming in this parish, and the vicinity, these 30 years past, than for 200 years before that period; though, at the same time, their mode of living is greatly improved, their houses more comfortable, and better furnished; they even use some of the luxuries of life. I shall make one observation, (which is hardly worthy of notice): When the present incumbent settled here, which was in the year 1761, there were only 2 tea-kettles in the parish, though

* Though the number of servants are greatly diminished, their wages are very much increased. About 30 years ago, a principal man-servant would have hired himself for a year, at the rate of L. 2, or L. 2, 10 s. now they receive L. 10 for the same space of time. Then, a day-labourer would have hired for 3 d. a-day, and his victuals; now they receive 1 s. and their diet, for the same space of time. Then a reaper in harvest would have been hired for the harvest for 12 s. Sterling; now they will receive L. 1, 10 s. for the same space.

though now there is ſcarcely a houſeholder who does not uſe that luxury.

Poor.—In this pariſh, properly ſpeaking, there are no begging poor; they are ſupported in their houſes by the weekly collections, the intereſts of a ſmall capital, and the rents of two galleries in the church; the heritors and their tenants being never aſſeſſed for their maintenance. In the 1782, when victual was ſcarce and high priced, and Government contributed for the relief of the poor in the north of Scotland, this pariſh declined receiving any part of the contribution, judging that other pariſhes might ſtand more in need of relief.

Stipend, &c.—The Crown is patron.—The ſtipend, communion-elements, and money for graſs, (the glebe not being of legal extent), do not exceed L. 90 Sterling, eſtimating the victual at 10 guineas the chalder. In the year 1647, one Mr James Gardner, who was clergyman here, died. During his miniſtry, ſeveral changes happened in the government, diſcipline and worſhip of the Church of Scotland, of which a ſhort account is ſubjoined, and brought down to the reſtoration of Charles II. in the year 1660 *.

---

* The General Aſſembly met at Glaſgow the 8th June 1610, authorized the Epiſcopal government, and put a period to the firſt eſtabliſhment of the Preſbyterian form in Scotland. The act of Aſſembly 1610 was afterward ratified by Parliament 1612. This revolution was brought about by James VI. at firſt by fair means, and under ſpecious pretences; but at laſt the non-conformiſts were ſeverely perſecuted. King James had been very active to prepare the General Aſſembly for his purpoſe. He had prevailed with the Aſſembly at Montroſe in the year 1600, to authorize 14 miniſters to vote in Parliament, not as biſhops, but as commiſſioners from the Kirk, and on theſe he had ſettled the revenues of the 14 biſhops

fhops of Scotland ; but by act of Affembly they were to be as much fubject to their prefbyteries as ever. He had prevailed with the Affembly at
Linlithgow, *anno* 1606, to appoint conftant moderators, and each moderator was to have L. 100 penfion from the King. The 14 commiffioners
for the Kirk were to prefide in the Synods. After thefe and other fteps,
having got the Affembly at Glafgow prepared and packed for his purpofe,
he prevailed with them to diveft themfelves, and all the inferior judica-
tures, of that ecclefiaftical power which, in former times, had been vefted
in them by the laws of the land ; and thus this firft Epifcopacy was introduced in a church-way, which was an event much defired by the King,
and which he had almoft defpaired to obtain. It may be obferved, however, that this was but a mixed kind of Epifcopacy : For, by the Affembly at Glafgow, it is exprefsly provided, That the bifhops, in all
things concerning their life, converfation, office, and benefice, fhould be
fubject to the cenfure of the General Affembly.

As this alteration was made in the government, fo a fimilar one took
place in the difcipline of the Church. For, in the fame year 1710, the
King fet up the High Commiffion Court, and committed the rod of difcipline to them. The members of this court were all the bifhops, all the
commiffaries in Scotland, with many of the nobility and gentry, and feveral minifters. They had power to judge in all caufes that concerned religion or a moral life, either in clergy or laity. They had no law, however, for their authority, but an act of Privy Council. They had power
to fufpend, deprive, depofe, imprifon, banifh, fine, &c. It was a moft
arbitrary court, and could ufe the perfons and properties of the fubject as
it pleafed, without form or procefs of law. Churchmen had the power
of the civil, and laymen that of the fpiritual fword. As by this court,
the power of the bifhops, fo was the King's fupremacy, exalted to a great
height.

An alteration was alfo made in the worfhip fome years after this. In the
Affembly met at Perth in the year 1681, the famous five articles, called the
Perth articles, were enjoined. Thefe were, private communion to fick
people, private baptifm, kneeling at the facrament of the Supper, confirmation by the bifhops, and keeping fome holydays. Thefe articles were
ratified by act of Parliament 1621 ; but met with greater oppofition, both
in the Parliament and Affembly, than the eftablifhment of Epifcopacy.
They were very difagreeable to both laity and clergy, as appears from the
numbers who fuffered from the High Commiffion Court, during 20 years,
for non-conformity to Epifcopacy and the Perth articles ; till at laft,
gaining the nobility to their party, Epifcopacy was rooted out with all
its dependencies in 1638. Prior to 1610, the ftandard of worfhip was the
order of Geneva, otherwife called Knox's Liturgy, fuited to the infant
ftate

 state of the Church, newly emerged from the darkness of Popery. In the year 1637, the bishops made an attempt to impose on the Church, a liturgy, or service-book, by the authority of an act of Council, without a church-law. The opposition to which, kindled the flame which destroyed the church and monarchy, and had almost consumed the three kingdoms.

Anno 1638. The National Covenant, otherwise called the King's Confession, being prepared, was renewed and subscribed with great joy in the Grayfriars Church by a great number of all ranks, convened at Edinburgh for that end. The bulk of the nation having acceded to the Covenant, they obliged the King to grant them a free General Assembly and Parliament. The General Assembly met at Glasgow, November 21. the same year. They approved the National Covenant, and declared it to be the same in substance with that signed by King James VI. and his household, *anno* 1581. In this Assembly, all the General Assemblies after the year 1605 were declared null, the High Commission Court, the Book of Canons, their Liturgy, the five articles of Perth, were declared unlawful; the 14 bishops were all either deposed or excommunicated, except three who accepted of single charges. They restored the Presbyterian government and discipline as at first.

Next year, the General Assembly met at Edinburgh, Aug. 17. and with the consent of the King's Commissioner, condemned Episcopacy as unlawful. They appointed the Covenant to be subscribed and sworn to by all his Majesty's subjects in this kingdom, of whatever rank and quality. All these acts were ratified and confirmed by Parliament in the King's presence, *anno* 1641.

Upon renewing the National Covenant, the civil war began between the King's party and the covenanters. The first blow was struck at the bridge of Dee, and a victory gained by the Earl of Montrose, at the head of the men of Angus and Mearns, for the covenanters.

Anno 1643. The form of the Solemn League and Covenant between the two kingdoms of Scotland and England, having been prepared by the committees of the General Assembly, the Convention of Estates, and the Commissioners sent from England for that effect, was unanimously approved by the General Assembly at Edinburgh, August 17. that year. It was also approved by the Convention of Estates of Scotland, as also by the Assembly of divines at Westminster, and both Houses of Parliament, and on the 30th of October, sworn to and subscribed in the High Church of Edinburgh, by the commission of the Church, the Committee of Estates, and the English commissioners, who had staid at Edinburgh till the Covenant was sent up to London and returned again. The imperemptory orders were then dispatched to all presbyteries to cause the Covenant to

be

be fworn to and fubfcribed to by all the profeffors of the Reformed religion, and by all his Majefty's good fubjects.

In the Solemn League, the government of the Church of Scotland is fecured, their loyalty to the King declared, but limited with their religion
and liberties, and they are bound to extirpate Popery and Prelacy in
both kingdoms; yet they are not bound exprefsly to introduce Prefbyteries into England. In this particular, the fectarians outwitted the Prefbyterians. For, though the Epifcopal government was totally abolifhed
in England, yet the Prefbyterian never was thoroughly fettled in that
kingdom. In a word, the defign of the Prefbyterians in the Solemn
League was to introduce an uniformity between the two kingdoms in doctrine, worfhip, and church-government, and they made confiderable advances in that work, but the Independents and Sectarians had no fuch
defign.

In 1643, the Affembly of divines fat down at Weftminfter. They
continued their feffions four or five years, and correfponded with our
Affemblies and their commiffions. Our Affemblies fent Commiffioners to
the Weftminfter Affembly. In the firft year of their meeting, they a-
greed on propofitions as to church-government, and the ordination of minifters, which were approved by our General Affembly. But as to the
directory for worfhip, the Weftminfter Affembly, as appears by their letter
to our Affembly, did not advife it to be fo ftrictly impofed, as to make
it unlawful to recede from it in any thing.

The Weftminfter Affembly agreed on a Confeffion of Faith, in 1647,
which was approved by our Affembly met at Edinburgh, Auguft 3.
that year. They agreed alfo on the Larger and Shorter Catechifms,
which was approved by our Affembly in 1748. Thus thefe two Affemblies carried on the work of Reformation and Uniformity, in fo far as
both churches agreed in their principles concerning doctrine, worfhip,
and government. But after the year 1648, no more progrefs was made in
this intended uniformity. Our divifions in Scotland, and the prevailing
power of the fectaries in England, put a final ftop to all thefe defigns of
uniformity and reformation in both kingdoms.

King Charles I. being at this time prifoner in the Ifle of Wight, the
Parliament of Scotland demanded, that the King fhould be liberated, and
brought to London in fafety and honour, and that religion fhould be eftablifhed in England according to their covenant and treaties, and for this end
appointed an army to be raifed of 30,000 foot and 6000 horfe. The General Affembly infifted, that he fhould be obliged to fettle religion in his
dominions according to the covenants. Both parties were loyal, and for the
King's liberation, but differed on the terms. The Affembly made an act,
commanding all minifters to preach againft engaging in war with England,

land, as a breach of the Solemn League. The Parliament made an act to the contrary. The ministers were very much embarrassed, but such as obeyed the Assembly were safest.

The Parliament sent their army into England, under the command of the Duke of Hamilton. They were defeated at Preston, Aug. 17. by Cromwell. This was called the unlawful engagement, and all who did engage in this war were obliged, by act of Assembly next year, to make public satisfaction for their offence. These offenders performed their penance without repentance; so that, by this piece of discipline, neither the interest of religion nor of the church was much advanced.

Anno 1649, Jan. 30. King Charles was basely murdered by Cromwell and the sectarian party. This execrable fact was detested and abhorred by all the Presbyterian party, who by no means acceded to it, though it be falsely and maliciously imputed to them by some. They lost a fine army, fighting for the King when a prisoner; and before he was brought to his trial, they, by their Commissioners at London, gave in their protestations against his trial; and, upon the melancholy event of his death, called home his son, and set the crown on his head. The General Assembly, in their letter to King Charles II. dated Aug. 6. 1649, have these words : " We do from our hearts abominate and detest that horrid fact of the " Sectaries against the life of your Royal father, our late Sovereign, so it " is the unfeigned and earnest desire of our souls, that the ancient monar- " chical government of these kingdoms may be established and flourish in " your Majesty's person all the days of your life, and may be continued " in your Royal family." Cromwell defeated our army at Dunbar and Hamilton, and in the year 1653 raised the General Assembly, and suppressed that court during his administration, but allowed Presbyteries and Synods to meet. The Church's loyalty to the King and Royal Family was very shocking to the Usurper. They had brought home the King and crowned him at Scoon, Jan. 1. 1651, having settled with him their claim of right, or the terms of his government. But the Usurper prevailed, and drove the King out of the island, and forced the whole kingdom into a subjection to his most arbitrary government. The Church stood firm and unshaken in their loyalty to their exiled King and the monarchy, praying for him by name in the face of the English soldiers, and exerted themselves to the utmost for his restoration, and when the oath of the Tender was urged, abjuring the King and Royal Family, all of them, as is said, Mr Sharpe excepted, refused it.

PARISH OF NEWTYLE.

(*County of Forfar.*)

By the Rev. Mr ALEXANDER SMALL.

Name, Situation, and Extent.

THIS parifh was formerly written *Newtyld*, but is now fpelt Newtyle. It is fituated in the county of Forfar, in the prefbytery of Meigle, and fynod of Angus and Mearns. Its extent is about $1\frac{3}{x}$ miles in length, from eaft to weft, along the Sidlie Hills, on the eaft of the Glack of Newtyle, (an opening in the Sidlie Hills, affording a paffage from Strathmore to Dundee); it is $1\frac{3}{4}$ miles from fouth to north, over the Sidlie hills, and one mile broad; the remaining $\frac{3}{4}$ of a mile, along the hill, being pretty nigh fquare.

Soil, Climate, and Difeafes.—The country is hilly on the fouth, and flat on the north. The foil is a mixture of black earth and clay; and, in fome places, of fand and gravel. In general it is fertile and well cultivated. Horfes and cattle, of a good fize and value, are raifed here. There is but one flock of fheep. The air is dry and healthy, excepting in fome marfhy places toward the north. Slow fevers are frequent here, and fcrophulous complaints not rare; which laft are very fevere in the fpring.

Population

Population Table for the Parish of Newtyle.

Number of inhabitants, in 1755,	913
Population in 1791,	594
Decrease,	319
Number of males,	306
—— females,	288
Inhabitants of the village, chiefly weavers,	230
—————— in the country,	364
Annual average of births,	15
——————— of deaths,	12
——————— of marriages,	5
Number of persons under 10 years of age,	104
——————————— from 10 to 20,	131
——————————— from 20 to 50,	257
——————————— from 50 to 70,	84
——————————— from 70 to 100,	18
Number of merchants,	3
——— notaries public,	1
——— farmers,	21
——— persons in their families, about	112
——————— their servants, about	80
——— manufacturers, about	230
——— taylors,	3
——— shoemakers,	3
——— wrights,	3
——— lintdressers,	5
——— persons born in other parishes,	300
——— inhabited houses (4 in each at an average)	149

There is only one family of Seceders, and no other sectaries. The proportion between the annual births, and the whole population, is nearly as 1 to 39. The proportion between the annual marriages and the whole population, is nearly as 1 to 118. The proportion between the annual deaths, and the whole population, is nearly as 1 to 49.

Rent, Agriculture, &c.—There are about 1600 acres of arable land in the parifh. Thefe are divided into 15 large farms, which are let at from 80 l. to near 200 l.; and 6 fmall, which draw from 6 l. to 12 l. a year. The average rent of the beft arable land is from 17 s. 6 d. to 20 s.; and of inferior land, 10 s. or 12 s. *per* acre. Some of the farms might draw 3 l. or 4 l. *per* acre, if they were near a town. What is efteemed the beft plan of farming here, is to have a farm divided into four parts, and to lay down one fourth in clover and rye-grafs, another in oats, another in turnips, potatoes, and peafe; and another in barley, and grafs fown with it; and fo in rotation. Very little wheat, and fcarcely any hemp, are raifed. There are 59 ploughs, many of which labour but fmall portions; and there are 106 carts. The parifh fupplies itfelf with provifions, and exports a confiderable quantity of grain, particularly barley. Wheat is fown in September and October, oats in March and April, and barley generally in May. Harveft, for the moft part, is in September and October. There are more than 800 acres of hills, moraffes, &c. all divided among the tenants. Some good marl is found in the parifh. No land has been fold in it for a confiderable number of years paft.

Language.—Englifh is fpoken here in the Scotch dialect. Names of places are chiefly derived from the Englifh; but there are alfo inftances of derivation from the Gaelic. Auchtertyre, the name of a farm here, feems to be Gaelic; *Uachdair Tir*, i. e. *the head* or *the upper part of the good land;* its fituation being at the foot of the Sidlie hills. Kinpurney,
(another

(another farm), is Gaelic; *Ceann Buerne,* is the *head of the ſmall ſtreams,* the land being ſpouty, and many ſtreams iſſuing from it. *Balmaiv,* in Gaelic, ſignifies *a good town.*

Eccleſiaſtical State.—The living, including the glebe, is from 80 l. to 100 l. at an average. The ſtipend is chiefly paid in victual, viz. two thirds meal, and one third barley. The Right Hon. James Stewart M'Kenzie, Lord Privy Seal for Scotland, (proprietor of the whole pariſh, excepting three farms), is patron. The manſe and offices were built in 1771, and the church in 1767.

State of the Poor.—There are 5 penſioners, who receive alms monthly; beſides 2 or 3 who get occaſional charity. The annual contributions amount to 13 l. or 14 l. which would not anſwer the exigencies of the poor, if there were not ſome ſtock laid out upon intereſt.

Price of Proviſions and Labour.—Beef, mutton, veal, pork, &c. are ſold at 3 d. 3½ d. and 4 d. *per* pound. Geeſe are ſold at from 1 s. 8 d. to 2 s. 6 d.; chickens at 4 d.; hens, 1 s. and 1 s. 4 d. which is triple the price they coſt formerly. Butter is ſold at 8 d. or 9 d. *per* pound; cheeſe at 4 s. 6 d. *per* ſtone; eggs at 4 d. *per* dozen, which uſed to be ſold at 1½ d. about 20 years ago, &c. Wheat is ſold from 1 l. to 1 l. 4 s. *per* boll; oats, from 12 s. to 14 s.; and barley, 8 l. Scotch, at an average. The wages of day labourers are 6 d. in winter, and 8 d. in ſummer, beſides their victuals. Wrights or carpenters get 8 d. in winter, and 1 s. in ſummer, with their maintainance. Maſons, who commonly board themſelves, get 1 s. 8 d. in ſummer. Day labourers, at public works, ſuch as roads, &c. have 1 s. 3 d. *per* day, when they board themſelves. The annual wages of a married ſervant, including

including his houfe, croft of land, meal, &c. may be worth
15 l. a fum rather fmall for the fupport of a family. Thofe
of male fervants, are from 7 l. to 10 l. *per annum,* and of female fervants about 3 l. which is near 4 times the value of
what they were about 30 years ago; and yet the fervants fave
no more money now than formerly, owing chiefly to their
extravagance in drefs.

Antiquities.—Near the Kirktown of Newtyle are the ruins
of the Caftle of Hatten, built by Laurence Lord Oliphant,
in 1575. Near the Caftle of Hatten, fome traces are dif-
cernible of what is called the Caftle of Balcraig, (*Baille
Craig,* i. e. *the town of a rock, fituated at the foot of a hill.*)
There are fome traces of a camp at Auchtertyre, about a
quarter of a mile from the Kirktown of Newtyle, where
Montrofe's army is faid to have taken their ftation for fome
nights, while the Marquis himfelf lodged at a neighbouring
caftle, after burning the houfe of Newton of Blairgowrie,
then the property of the father of the late Provoft Drum-
mond of Edinburgh. There is a tower built by the Lord Privy
Seal, on the top of Kinfurney's hill, (a part of the Sidlie
Hills), which ferves as a land mark. From this tower St.
Abbe's head is feen, and fome parts of 10 or 11 adjacent
counties. This hill appears to have been anciently made
ufe of as a proper place for kindling fires, to warn this and
the neighbouring counties of the approach of enemies.

Defcription of the People —The general fize of the people,
in this parifh, is about 5 feet 6 inches: A few individuals
have attained the height of 6 feet. They are very induftrious, in general, and more than one half of the houfeholders are weavers, and poffefs a fmall portion of land.
They are not fond of a military life, and few inlift in any
corps.

corps. They are in general ſober and economical ; enjoy, in a reaſonable degree, the comforts and advantages of ſociety, and, on the whole, ſeem pretty well ſatisfied with their condition. Their ſituation, however, might be meliorated, by greater exertions of induſtry, and by ſuperior knowledge of agriculture, and the other arts of civil life.

Miſcellaneous Obſervations.—Coals are the fuel uſed here. They coſt from 4 s. 6 d. to 5 s. *per* boll at Dundee. There are ſome peats, of a bad quality, and dearer than coal, uſed for kindling fires. Roads were kept in tolerable repair by the ſtatute labour, till laſt ſummer, when it was commuted. Now there are turnpikes, of whoſe utility many are not yet ſatisfied, though it is hoped they will be ſo, when the roads are completed. The general ſcarcity, in 1782-3, was felt here. The kirk ſeſſion bought meal for the poor, and ſold it at a reduced price. Oat meal ſold, in ſummer 1783, at 1 s. 3 d. ; peaſe and bear meal, at 11 d. the peck. The poor, in ſome of the hilly countries, bought coarſe flour, and mixed it with bran, of which they made bread. Hence the miſerable ſtate of the country may eaſily be conceived.

PARISH OF OATHLAW.

By the Rev. Mr THOMAS RAIKER.

Situation, Extent, &c.

THE antient name of this parish seems to have been Finhaven. It is situated in the county of Angus, presbytery of Forfar, and synod of Angus and Mearns. It is 5 miles long, and about 2 broad. It is bounded by the parish of Tannadie on the north; Aberlemno and Refcobie on the south; Carraldstone on the east; and Kirriemuir on the west. The general appearance of the country is flat. The air is moist.

Hills.—The hill of Finhaven lies on the south side of the parish, in a direction from east to west, for the space of 10 miles. On the top of this hill are the remains of an old castle : The foundation of the whole of it is yet visible. Its dimensions are 137 yards in length, and 37 in breadth, nearly in the form of a parallelogram. The foundation seems to have been built without mortar. The ruins discover something like vitriable stones, and plainly appear to have undergone the action of fire. It is said that the family of Finhaven were wont to retire to this castle in times of danger. There are evident marks of a well on the west end of it. The height of the

hill

hill is about 500 yards from the level of the country. At the foot of it, immediately ſouth of the caſtle, there is an appearance of a crater of a volcano, and all around ſomething that reſembles lava.

Rivers.——The river Eſk runs through the pariſh; and, it is thought, might eaſily be made navigable from the Kirktown of Tannadice to Montroſe, about 12 miles diſtant. In its preſent ſtate, it runs in a ſerpentine direction through a very fertile country. Formerly it abounded with ſalmon; but, on account of the number of crubs, there are now few or none. The rivulet called Lemno has lately been turned into a canal, which runs the whole length of the pariſh, from eaſt to weſt, and biſects it. It might eaſily be made navigable for ſmall boats. It joins the river Eſk below the old caſtle of Finhaven.

Population.——The number of inhabitants in this pariſh is believed to have been nearly the ſame for ſeveral years paſt.

Souls	430
Males	217
Females	213
Annual average of births	10
————— of deaths	4
————— of marriages	3
Perſons under 10 years of age	110
Between 10 and 20	97
Between 20 and 50	160
Between 50 and 70	50
Above 70	13
Heritors (none of them reſide)	6
Farmers	34
	Families

Families confisting of	1 person			1
	2			1
	3			4
	4			3
	5			3
	6			3
	7			1
	8			6
	9			1
	10			1
	11			2
	13			3
	15			1
	17			2
	18			1
	19			1
	21			1
	23			1
	28			1
	33			1
	44			1

Land rent of the parifh about L. 1178 Sterling.

Ploughs 34
Carts about 70

Poor.—The number of the poor of this parifh is, at an average, two. The annual amount of the contributions for their
relief is about L. 15 : 16 : 8 Sterling. The number relieved
at prefent is from two to four. The elders of the kirk-
feffion, in the different parts of the parifh, give information
concerning the ftate of the poor. In 1782, the kirk-feffion
purchafed a fmall quantity of corn, made it into meal, and
divided it among poor families.

Price

Price of Labour and Provisions.— he increase of labourers wages in husbandry, since the year 1740, has been very great. For 20 years after that period, their wages were from L. 2 to L. 3 a year; at present they are from L. 5 to L. 10 a year, and maintained, as formerly, in the family. Women servants wages, during the period already mentioned, were L. 1 : 10 : 0; they are now from L. 3 to L. 4. Day labourers, at the same period, got 2½ d.; at present they get from 8 d. to 10 d. exclusive of victuals. Harvest wages for the season are from L. 1 to L. 1 : 10 : 0; by the day 1 s. and victuals. Oatmeal is the principal food of the labouring people. The price of it, from 1740 to 1760, was about 8 s. and 10 s. 6 d. a boll; at present, and for some years past, it has been from 12 s. to 14 s. The general mode of living was much the same at both periods. Butter is from 6 d. to 9 d. a pound. Cheese from 5 s. to 6 s. a stone.

*Stipend.—*The money stipend is L. 500 Scots; and there are 2 chalders of victual. The manse, offices, and garden, are estimated at L. 6 Sterling, and the glebe at L. 4. The patron of the parish is Lord Aboyne.

*Antiquities.—*There is a vestige of a camp, supposed to be Roman. Its dimensions are 1200 yards in length, and 600 in breadth. There are 2 tumuli in it, which have never been opened. According to tradition, it was part of a great forest, called the Forest of Claton, which extended from Finhaven to Kirriemuir, about the distance of 6 miles. The site of the camp is now a well cultivated farm, called Battle-dykes. The names given to the other farm houses on the forest are descriptive of its former situation, such as Birkenbush, Drakemire, Forrester-Seat, King's-Seat, Wolf-Law, &c.

Rev. Tho. Barker.

To fatisfy you concerning the number of our paupers – that we have no more than two receiving charity, is a certain fact, both old women, and widows; and what is ftill more, one of them does not properly belong to us, but to a neighbouring parifh, and came to refide with a daughter married to a labouring man here. A few years ago, I hinted to Mr. Howlett a reafon why we have fo few paupers here, viz. We have neither brewers, nor beggars, nor baftards, nor bankrupts; but a fober, frugal and laborious people; no idlers nor drunkards; every family brew their own beer; no fectaries. We have indeed a family or two with a number of young children that we occafionally relieve with fmall fums; and it is fometimes with difficulty that they will be prevailed upon to accept of them, but no longer than they can do for themfelves, which is often at a very early age.

PARISH OF PANBRIDE.

By the Rev. Mr ROBERT TRAIL.

Name, Situation, Extent, and Surface.

THERE is reaſon to believe that this pariſh was called Panbridge about 200 years ago, and that it was an abreviation of Panbridget; the church here, which is very old, being built by St Bridget, or at leaſt in honour of her. An inſcription has been ſeen on an old grave ſtone, mentioning that it was erected in memory of ſuch a perſon of the pariſh of Panbridge. *Pan* is probably a corruption of the Latin word *fanum;* if ſo, Panbride ſignifies Bridget's church. This pariſh is ſituated in the county of Forfar, in the ſynod of Angus and Mearns, and in the preſbytery of Aberbrothock. It is more than 5 miles long, and about 2 broad. It is bounded by the ſea on the ſouth; by the pariſhes of Barrie and Monikie on the weſt; by Carmylie on the north; by Arbirlote on the north-eaſt; and a detached part of St Vigians on the ſouth-eaſt. The general appearance of the country here is rather flat than hilly; but there is a conſiderable declivity for ſome miles from the north to the ſouth end of this pariſh. The ſhore is flat, and very rocky.

Population.

Population.—Dr Webſter's ſtate . . 1259
In 1765, the number of inhabitants was exactly 1183
In 1790 1460
Annual average of baptiſms from 1762 till 1790 . 39
———— ———— of burials from 1767 till 1790 . 27
———— ———— of marriages . . . 10
Seceders 20
Epiſcopalians 4
Independants 2
Heritors 1

The number of baptiſms in 1790 was 55, which is 4 more than was ever known here before.

Poor.—The number of poor varies from 8 to 10: They are all maintained in their own houſes; and there is not a beggar in the pariſh. But, beſides the ordinary poor, there is a conſiderable number of houſeholders in indigent circum-ſtances, each of whom get a boll of coals from the ſeſſion yearly. The funds bearing intereſt do not much exceed L. 100; but a conſiderable ſum ariſes from the mortcloth and hearſe fees. The weekly collections in church are from 5 s. to 7 s. or 8 s.

Stipend.—The ſtipend is ½ chalder of wheat, 3 chalders of oatmeal, 2 chalders of barley, and L. 30 : 5 : 6 Sterling; in which ſum is included L. 5 for communion elements. The glebe conſiſts of 4 acres, 1 rood, and ſome falls, of very good land. The King is patron.

Miſcellaneous Obſervations.—There is one mineral ſpring of the chalybeate kind, but it is not much frequented. There is plenty of ſea-weed along the coaſt for manuring land; but it has rarely been made into kelp. Haddocks, cod, &c. were
wont

wont to be caught here; but for some years past scarcely any haddocks have been seen. Every crew pays 5 merks for the privilege of fishing. The price of provisions and labour is greatly increased. About 27 years ago, beef was 2 d. a pound; it is now $3\frac{1}{2}$ d. and 4 d. A fowl, which could then have been bought for 5 d. is now 9 d. or 10 d. The parish exports articles of provision. A taylor's wages is 6 d. a day and his meat; a carpenter's 8 d. and his meat. Some labourers get 6 d. and others 8 d. and their meat. The English is the only language spoken here. Exclusive of the large inclosures of Panmure, the yearly rent of the parish exceeds L. 1000. Hector Boece's ancestors, for several generations, were lairds of Panbride. A short history of the county of Angus, written in elegant Latin by a Mr Edward, minister of Murroes, in the presbytery of Dundee, containing both a geographical description of it, and an account of every family of note, was published in 1678.

Errata   PARISH OF RESCOBIE (pages 587–597)

The publisher apologises for the confusion in pages 587–592 of this volume, caused by the fact that two printed versions of the original are in existence. The correct version of these pages is included at the end of the book, together with details of the resultant amendments to the index.

PARISH OF RESCOBIE.

(COUNTY AND PRESBYTERY OF FORFAR, SYNOD OF ANGUS AND MEARNS.)

By the Rev. Mr. THOMAS WRIGHT.

Name, Extent, Lakes, Climate, &c.

THE name is of uncertain origin, and its etymology so doubtful, that the writer has not been able to learn, and therefore cannot say whether it be Latin, Gaelic, Celtic, &c.; but it is applied to denote a certain district

trict of country called a Parifh ; and, like moft local names, has probably been framed at firft from fome real or fuppofed affinity to the fituation.——The figure of the parifh is irregular, but the contents may be about 16 or 18 fquare miles, moftly in cultivation, with fome thriving fir plantations, and very little wafte ground. It has no river nor confiderable ftream, but yet is fufficiently water-ed for domeftick and agricultural purpofes; and particu-larly, it is interfected by the loch of Refcobie, which is a mile long, wafhed by the loch of Balgavies, in the pa-rifh of Aberlemno, on the N. and E., and was fo on the S. and W. by the loch of Reftennet, in the parifh of Forfar; but lately this laft mentioned loch was taken off by a drain, a project which at firft was by many thought rather problematical; but the fuccefs has afford-ed ample juftification, by affording fpeedy indemnifica-tion, together with the permanent fource of a very hand-fome revenue to the owner, a gentleman of celebrity in the political world, and long and well known by the honourable appellation of a *friend to his country*. Still, however, the fprings and rills, which formerly fed this drained lake, continue to difcharge themfelves by the drain into the loch of Refcobie, from whence, through the loch of Balgavies, iffues the chief branch of Lu-nan water, which gives name to a bay on the German Ocean, into which it falls about 12 miles E. from this kirk.

All thefe lakes abound in marl; a manure of approved and extenfive ufe in hufbandry, eagerly fought after by the induftrious farmer; and where it is fkilfully applied, producing very great effects, being nearly fimilar to lime

in

vanced age, as is ſaid, of 104, and we have living inſtances upwards of 80 and 90 ; our people are not liable
to frequent ſickneſs, nor have we any local or peculiar
maladies.

Soil and Agriculture.—The ſoil is various ; part of it rich
and fertile, part of it poor and barren ; but Nature has
furniſhed the thrifty farmer with a ready and effectual
remedy for the poverty of the ſoil, and the worſt may be,
and is made productive by the due application of marl.
In conſequence, the value of land is much increaſed ; the
new farmer does not boggle at promiſing double or triple
the former rent, and it is the laird's buſineſs to look to the
payment. And though, from want both of means and
ſkill in adventurers, failures may ſometimes happen, this
does not diſcourage others from ſtepping forward even on
higher terms ; ſo that, in general, farming is a profitable
employment, and the people are ſubſtantial and in eaſy
circumſtances, the effect as well as the reward of diligence
and induſtry, in an improved ſyſtem of management, a-
greeably to the old obſervation, " The hand of the diligent maketh rich." And indeed the genius of the country
at large, encouraged by an increaſed product and ready
markets, " bleſſed both in their baſket and ſtore," is ſtrongly bent to agricultural improvement, on which, it is to be
hoped, the New Board of Agriculture will ſoon ſhed its
friendly influence. This is one of the happieſt directions
which the genius of a country or people can take : it occupies their talents, and time uſefully and laudably, and,
affording ample ſcope for their ſchemes and fancies, prevents them from running wild, and takes them off from
thoſe jars and controverſies, whether of politicks or reli-

gion,

even on higher terms; so that, in general, farming is a profitable employment, and the people are substantial and in easy circumstances, the effect as well as the reward of diligence and industry, in an improved system of management, agreeably to the old observation, " The hand of the diligent maketh rich." And indeed the genius of the country at large, encouraged by an increased product and ready markets, " blessed both in their basket and store," is strongly bent to agricultural improvement, on which, it is to be hoped, the New Board of Agriculture will soon shed its friendly influence. This is one of the happiest directions which the genius of a country or people can take : it occupies their talents and time usefully and laudably, and, affording ample scope for their schemes and fancies, prevents them from running wild, and takes them off from those jars and controversies, whether of politicks or religion, which always have been, and ever must be, more pernicious than serviceable to society.

The kinds of grain in use, are oats and bear, mostly barley, some pease, and a little wheat here and there, with a large proportion in sown grass : Hence corn and cattle are the staple articles of our product, there being a very few sheep. The cultivation of lint is also in practice, and generally succeeds well. On the article of culture, I have to add with pleasure, that

Intellectual improvement proceeds apace : About 16 years ago, in the course of visiting the parish, there were found 3 people who could not read, and were become too old to learn; at present, it is not known if there

be

ceed 30 : There being no regiſter of deaths, their number is not exactly known.

Dreſs, Manners, &c.—Our people are uſually decent in their dreſs, ſometimes ſhowy ; and in a holiday ſuit, e-mulous of their betters. In their converſation, ſenſible ; in their manners, diſcreet and humane ; in their various employments, diligent and induſtrious (the ſpirit of in-duſtry not being confined to farming) ; and to their praiſe, it ſhould be known, that in theſe times of alarm and danger, their conduct is quiet, peaceable, and loyal : in religion, ſerious, ſober, moderate, charitable, ſympathiſing, obſer-vant of religious ordinances ; and chiefly of the Preſbyte-rian perſuaſion. The pariſh church is the only place of worſhip in our bounds ; but we have ſome Epiſcopalians, and a few Seceders. As to the Epiſcopalians, they are ſo pre-valent and powerful be-ſouth the Tweed, it would hardly be ſafe, even at this diſtance, to ſay that they can err ; and as to the Seceders, poor folk ! they are ſo few and ſmall be-north the Tay, it might be reckoned an illiberal attack on weakneſs, were any attempt made to expoſe their errors, nor is this the place : But let it not offend them, if it be obſerved, that their diſtinguiſhing marks are not very ornamental, nor their proper peculiarities extremely praiſe-worthy *.

Poor.

* So that I cannot adopt the ſentiment of one of the Statiſtical Wri-ters, viz. That " the exiſtence of Seceders, and of Seceding meeting-" houſes, has perhaps no bad effect upon the manners and ſentiments of " the people ; that they are in ſome degree ſpies and checks upon the " members of the Eſtabliſhed Church ; and the diſcourſes of their clergy " are often adapted, with ſingular felicity, to the capacity and the pre-" judices of the leaſt enlightened claſſes in the community."

Their manners, as they are ſeen in ſowing ſtrife and diviſion ; their ſpy-office, as it is glaringly invidious ; and their ſentiments, as they are

notoriouſly

their praise, it should be known, that in these times of
alarm and danger, their conduct is quiet, peaceable, and
loyal: in religion, serious, sober, moderate, charitable,
sympathising, observant of religious ordinances; and
chiefly of the Presbyterian persuasion. The parish-
church is the only place of worship in our bounds; but
we have some Episcopalians, and a few Seceders.

Poor.—Our poor roll varies, from 4 or 5 to 10 and upwards; and among these is distributed annually 17l. or
18l., arising from the kirk collections, and the interest of
a small sum in the management of the session, our only
funds for poor: and should these become insufficient, recourse must be had on the heritors, who are said to be liable in the last resort. Luckily, we do not feel our own
poor very burdensome; but we are oppressed with wan-
derers: I have known 2 dozen of them before 12 o'clock;
and, last summer, near twoscore of them called in the
course of one day. It was, indeed, a hard time; and it
would be a hard, nay, a bad thing, to send them hungry
away: for though many of them be extremely worthless,
most of them are extremely indigent; and they must not
be cast out to perish: " Whoso stoppeth his ears at the cry
of the poor, he also shall cry himself, and shall not be
heard."—It is to be wished, rather than expected, that
some general plan, of such efficacious benevolence as would
prevent strolling, not by hard restrictions, but by making
it needless, were established in the country; and, till this
be done, we must be doing. Perth usually furnishes out a
pretty

vent ſtrolling, not by hard reſtrictions, but by making it needleſs, were eſtabliſhed in the country ; and till this be done, we muſt be doing. Perth uſually furniſhes out a pretty large quota ; but there is no place ſends forth ſuch legions of thoſe itinerants, as Aberdeen, meaning the county as well as the town of that name. The county is extenſive, fertile, and populous; the town commercial and opulent : What harm would there be in giving Aberdeen a hint, that it would be both creditable and recommendable in them, to take meaſures, as they ought, to provide for their own poor at home, rather than ſet them off, like a flight of locuſts, to prey upon their neighbours, who are under no local obligation to receive or relieve them ?

Rent, Stipend, &c.—The valued rent of the pariſh is 2708l. Scotch. Lord Strathmore is patron. We have a good ſchool-houſe, with dwelling-houſe and garden for the maſter, and 100l. Scotch of ſalary.—The farmers of the pariſh give, beſides board, from 8l. to 12l. Sterling a-year to their ploughmen.—The manſe is in tolerable repair, and the offices good, being lately built, and covered with ſlate. The ſtipend conſiſts of 43l. money, 50 bolls 11 pecks meal, and 24 bolls of bear. There was a ſmall augmentation got, with the good will of the heritors, about 8 years ago ; and there yet remains a good ſtock of unexhauſted teinds. The glebe meaſures about 7 acres. It would contribute much to the convenience and comfort of the country clergy, if, inſtead of ſuch a trifling, pitiful ſpot of ground, glebes were enlarged to at leaſt 20 acres ; and if, in giving augmentations, a few acres of land could be added to the glebe, rather than as many pounds to the ſtipend, it would be found a beneficial exchange. The patrons of the new bill in favour of the clergy (with ſub-
miſſion)

miffion) fhould keep this in their eye. The church is pretty well as to the fabrick, but not large enough for the accommodation of the parifhioners, being only 50 by 20 feet within the walls, and not well feated. The prefent incumbent ferved the cure about $2\frac{1}{2}$ years, from 17th April 1774, as affiftant to his predeceffor, Mr. William M'Keay; after whofe deceafe he received, with the confent of the whole community, heritors and parifhioners, chiefly on the application of Mr. Hunter of Burnfide, a prefentation to the vacant charge.

In confequence of this prefentation, the prefentee was inftalled on the 3d of April 1777, and is ftill a bachelor. Bachelorifm is furely a pitiable, comfortlefs condition *; but unlefs the Court of Teinds (it is faid, to their praife, they are favourably difpofed at prefent; a rare thing!) fhall vouchfafe to deliver us from it, without the aid of a Pope's bull, it muft foon become more frequent.

Mifcellaneous Obfervations.—In a furvey of this fort, there is a circumftance that deferves to be particularly mentioned, as it contributes not a little to health and comfort; the dwelling-houfes are much better and more commodious, and neater and cleaner kept than formerly: even the cattle are now better lodged, than the people were wont to be. This is a moft fenfible improvement; and, befides giving an agreeable afpect to the face of the country, is no bad prognoftick of the wealth of the inhabitants. As to people, there can be no doubt that cleanlinefs and good air are to be ranked among the neceffaries of life; and as to cattle, they will be found always to thrive beft in free and pure air, and nothing can hurt them more than to pen them up in narrow hampered booths, where

the

---

* And they that are in, would fain be out on't.

the air foon becomes foul and naufeous : hence often
fhades are, in fome cafes, preferable to clofe ftalls ; and
the larger the ftalls, the purer will be the air, and the cattle in better condition. It muft be acknowledged, that
our fituation invites to thefe improvements, as the neighbourhood abounds in excellent materials, efpecially the
hills of Turin and Pitfcandbe (this laft is a continuation
of the other on the W. end), which contain inexhauftible
ftores of ftone of various kinds, and of every dimenfion fit
for ufe ; and where there are quarries now working, aftonifhing to look at, and affording ample fubject of contemplation and amufement to the naturalift and virtuofo.
Gentlemen of this caft would fometimes deign to come
and fee, if they knew what is to be feen. Befides the dif-
coveries to be made in the bowels of thefe hills, the ftu-
penduous rocks that rife upon them, in proud contempt
of human productions, may well be viewed as natural
prodigies, and muft ftrike with amazement the eye of the
ftranger.

There is nothing obfervable in the way of antiquity,
unlefs a ruin on the top of Turin-hill may be confidered
in that light. It has evidently been anciently a ftrong
hold, or place of defence, confifting of various extenfive
contiguous buildings, with a circular citadel of about 40
yards in diameter. The fituation has been well chofen,
being fecured by an impregnable rock in front, much like
the face of Salifbury Craigs, and of difficult accefs all a-
round. It is now called Kemp or Camp Caftle. Alfo, in
the E. end of the parifh, on the eftate of Balmadies, there
is a chapel-yard or burying-ground, in which it would
feem no grave has been opened a fecond time ; and the
tomb ftones are fo depofited, that a family hiftory might
be collected from them for a long period back : There are
particularly

particularly 2 large head-ftones, with 7 or 8 fmall ones, ftanding in a right line at the head of fo many parallel graves, which are faid to contain the afhes of the parents and their children. At or near this cemetery, there has probably been a chapel or place of worfhip ; but all tradition concerning it is loft.

We have no uncommon migratory birds ; and it is doubtful, whether all birds, ufually reckoned of this clafs, do really belong to it. The ground of this doubt well appears, from the following obfervations refpecting the fwallow : Owing to a hint given me by a neighbour, I have been, for fome feafons, pretty attentive to the firft appearance of this bird ; but not accurate enough to mark the dates, till laft fpring, when, on the 2d of May 1793, I faw them, for the firft time, pretty early in the morning, in confiderable numbers on the loch (about 18 yards from the bottom of the garden), from which they feemed to be juft then in the procefs of emerging ; though, as there was fome rippling on the water, it was difficult to difcern the breaking of the furface ; but the obferver is pofitive, they juft then arofe from the lake, and therefore muft have lodged or lain fomehow at the bottom, fince the time of their difappearing laft year. The weather, all day, continued as it began in the morning, moderate, with an eafy breeze from S. W. ; and the fwallows, fometimes in bodies, fometimes in detachments, enjoyed themfelves in fkimming along the furface, or foaring aloft in the air, or fluttering about the fhores, but went very little way off the water till evening, when they collected over the lake, and difappeared within obfervation. With anxious expectation, they were looked next morning, and all day through, but no appearance of them, nor for feveral days following ; and, therefore, there can be no doubt of their

descending

descending into their lodgings at the bottom, having, from that day's experiment, felt or judged the air not sufficiently encouraging for them to live in. Nor were they seen till the 11th of May, when they were again observed in the process of emerging from the lake, and continued playing their gambols, and fluttering about the shores of it, till evening, when they disappeared as formerly, and were seen no more till the morning of the 21st of May, when the manner of their appearing was exactly the same as before mentioned. This last experiment succeeded; they felt, it should seem, the temperature of the air encouraging, and in a few days began to prepare their summer dwellings. They have been known, some seasons, to show themselves sooner than last year; and to go away ten days or a fortnight : but till last summer, when, it may be remembered, there was some very cold, sharp, piercing weather, the narrator never observed them to disappear twice after their first coming : And he is now fully satisfied, that the swallow, instead of being classed with birds of passage, should be enrolled among the sleepers. But if any reader's scepticism shall suspend his belief of this narrative, let him consider, it is no theory, but matter of fact, which is here narrated : And the reporter must be excused for thinking it clearly decisive of a question in the natural history of this bird. If future observation shall afford sufficient reason for palinoding, it shall be candidly done.

PARISH OF RUTHVEN.

(County of Forfar, Synod of Angus, Presbytery of
Meigle.)

By the Rev. Mr. James Will.

Situation, Extent, Soil, and Produce.

THE parish of Ruthven is pleasantly situated on the N.
side of Strathmore, near the foot of the Grampian
mountains, sloping gently towards the S. Nearly of a square
form, it contains about 1700 acres, of which 63 are covered
with natural oaks, 240 with fir and hard wood, 40 of heath,
to be planted, 30 of marl-mires, and 16 of peat-moss : The
rest is partly arable, and partly to be improved during the
currency of the present leases. The soil, in general, is a light
hazel mould, with a gravelly bottom, producing excellent
grain, but liable to be parched in a dry summer. The present proprietor has been at great pains to introduce the modern improvements in agriculture, which he has accomplished
in

in a confiderable degree, by reftrictiag his tenants to a rotation of cropping the laft time their farms were let. The rotation is as follows : field, 1ft, grafs; 2d, ditto ; 3d, ditto ; 4th,
oats; 5th, barley; 6th, oats; 7th, fallow, or green crop; 8th,
barley with grafs-feeds. The tenants, from the prejudices of
education, came into thefe improvements rather reluctantly at
firft. They are now, however, as forward in them as their
neighbours, and begin to experience the advantages of them.
They are reftricted from raifing wheat or flax, in confiderable
quantities, becaufe thefe have been found to be rather exhauft-
ing crops for the foil. The parifh, however, was always remarkable for producing fine flax, but more fo, it is faid, before the introduction of marl. A greater quantity, indeed,
might be raifed now than formerly, but, in the opinion of experienced farmers, there is no comparifon as to the quality.
The foil is favourable for turnip and trees of every kind, fuited to the climate. The larix, in particular, grows with uncommon quicknefs, fome of them only 15 years old, having
meafured 46 inches root girth. Oaks grow naturally ; and
in a former period fome of them were of great fize, if we may
judge from two which have remained time immemorial in the
old courfe of the river Ifla, about a mile below the church.

Name and Proprietors.—The etymology of the name is
doubtful *. It was anciently expreffed in the plural, Ruthvens, having been divided into two parts, and belonged to two
different proprietors : That on the E. fide of the river Ifla was
termed Earls Ruthven, as having been the property of the
Earl

* It is pronounced Riven ; and, if a conjecture might be hazarded in a matter of fo much uncertainty, might be fuppofed to be compounded of the Gaelic
words *roy* (red), and *vean* (white), perhaps from the foil in general abounding
with fmall white ftones, or rather from the appearance of the rocks, on the
banks of the river in the N. fide of the parifh, which are of a red colour, but in
many places whitened over with age.

Earl of Crawford, who, at one period, poſſeſſed a great part
of the county of Forfar ; the other part was called Ruthvens
Davy, as having belonged to the laird of Kippen Davy. A-
bout 1380, both theſe eſtates came into the poſſeſſion of
a branch of the family of Crichton, who kept them until
1742 *. After the Frendraught family became extinct, and
the Dumfries family failed in the male line, the head of the
Ruthven family became chieftain of the ancient and illuſtrious name of Crichton. Upon the death of the late Thomas
Crichton, Eſq. of Millhill, and his brother William, the family of Crichton of Ruthven failed in the male line alſo. The
remaining part of their eſtates, which had been once very extenſive in this neighbourhood, was purchaſed 50 years ago by
Thomas Ogilvy, Eſq. of Coul, and is now in the poſſeſſion of
his ſon James Ogilvy, Eſq. of Iſlabank, who reſides in this
pariſh, and has built an excellent modern houſe, near the
much admired ſituation of the caſtle of Ruthven, which, being ruinous, was pulled down ſome years ago.

Hills, River, Black-fiſhing, Bridge.——There are no hills in
this

* The firſt of that family who held the barony of Ruthven was James, ſecond
ſon of Stephen Crichton of Cairns, brother to George Crichton, Earl of Caithneſs,
and couſin to Sir William Crichton of Crichton, Lord Chancellor of Scotland.
In the year 1477, James Crichton of Ruthven was Lord Provoſt of Edinburgh ;
another of the ſame name, who had the honour of knighthood, was maſter of
horſe to King Charles II. It is ſaid, that the haughty diſpoſition of Sir James
prevented him from enjoying long his elevated ſtation ; and that his merry mo-
narch having, on a particular occaſion, made him a preſent of 500 l., with a recommendation to " creiſh his boots" with it, alluding to his country and his
office, the knight took offence at the expreſſion, returned the money, reſigned
his office, and retired to Scotland. But, habituated to the extravagance of a
court he had abandoned, he diſſipated his fortune, and gave a blow to the family eſtate which it never recovered. There is a fine portrait of Sir James by
Vandyke, in the poſſeſſion of his deſcendant, in the female line, John Kinloch,
Eſq. of Kilrie.

this parish, though some rising grounds improperly retain that name. Upon one of these, called Candle-hill, the place is to be seen where the barons of Ruthven erected a gibbet in feudal times. Two of those eminences are distinguished by the name of Laws, upon one of which there was a large cairn some years ago. The only river in the parish is the Isla, which, after bounding it for upwards of a mile on the N. side, turns suddenly in the direction from N. W. to S. E., dividing the parish into two unequal parts, leaving the largest on the E. side. The upper part of its course is rocky and winding, with bold and steep banks, covered in many places with natural woods, and affording some very romantic scenery. After passing the Lin, which is a fall over several ridges of broken rock, the river resolves itself into a pool, called the Corral, probably a corruption of Quarry-hole, there appearing to have been a quarry on the E. side, at some remote period. This pool is deep and broad, but becomes more shallow toward the S., and ends in the broad ford, famous in the annals of black fishing. Upon leaving the ford, the river divides itself into two branches, forming a small island, called Stanner Island, containing about 6 acres : afterward, diversified with rapid streams and gentle meanderings, it continues to extend through level and fertile fields. In winter, the low grounds are greatly injured by the river shifting its course, carrying away the rich soil, and depositing barren sand and gravel in its place. It would be greatly to the advantage both of proprietors and tenants, that a straight channel was cut for this river, through its haughs or low grounds, for about 8 miles, from the S. side of this parish, where the river begins to take a direction to the westward, to the bridge of Cupar Angus. The river is well stocked with trout and salmon. In the months of October and November, the latter come here to spawn, at which time great havock is made a-

among

mong them by the black fishers. The practice of black-fishing is so called, because it is performed in the night time, or because the fish are then black or foul. At this season, they frequent the gravelly shallows, where the female digs considerable holes, in which she deposits the roe. During this operation, which usually continues for some weeks, the male attends her, and both are in a very torpid state. The black-fishers, provided with spears, composed of 5 barbed prongs, fixed upon a strong shaft, wade up and down upon the shallows, preceded by a great torch, or blaze, as it is called, consisting of dried broom, or fir tops, fastened round a pole. By this light the fish are soon discerned, and being then very dull, are easily transfixed. Formerly regular fish courts (as they were called), were held once a-year at least, before the justices of the district, where persons suspected of this practice were put upon oath, and if they refused to clear themselves in that manner, or if their guilt was proved by proper evidence, they were liable to fines and imprisonment. At present, no attention is paid to prevent a practice equally against the laws of the country, destructive of the health, and subversive of the morals of those who follow it. The fish, at this season, are very unwholesome food; the strongest constitutions often suffer from wading up to the middle in water for hours together in the dead of the night of all the year ; and a black-fishing match often ends in drunkenness and debauchery. There is a bridge of 2 arches over the river Isla in this parish, on the high road from Dunkeld and Blairgowrie to Kerriemuir and Brechin. It is not known when it was built, but, from its construction, being narrow, appears to be ancient. It was lately repaired, and is of great service to the country, there being only other 2, besides it, upon the river, from its source at Caentochan, in the head of Glenisla parish, to its junction with the Tay at Kinclaven, in a stretch upwards of 40 miles.

The

The many melancholy accidents which have happened at one of the fords of this river, might be expected to work upon the feelings of all concerned, fo far as to induce them to add one more at leaft to the number.

Ecclefiaftical Matters, Stipend, Poor, &c.—Tradition fays, that the church of Ruthven was erected by the Earl of Craw-ford, proprietor of the barony of Inverquiech, for the accom-modation of his tenants, feveral of them having been killed by the Rollos of Balloch, in going to their parifh church of Alyth. Afterward, when the turbulent neighbours were re-moved, and the church became of no further ufe to the te-nants of Inverquiech, the proprietor of Ruthven got that ba-rony erected into a feparate parifh, and obtained the Earl of Crawford's chapel, which lay convenient, to be the parifh church, and the lands mortified to its minifter to be a glebe. It does not appear how this tranfaction was brought about, probably it might have been through the interference of the abbot of Arbroath, who was both patron of the parifh, and titular of the tithes. Upon the forfeiture of the Panmuir fa-mily, in 1715, the right of patronage devolved to the Crown: the minifter is titular of the tithes by a gift in the year 1634, from the Marquis of Hamiltom, then proprietor of the Abbey-lands, to Mr. Patrick Crichton, minifter of Ruthven, and his fucceffors in office. The ftipend is below the minimum, and has never been augmented. The glebe, confifting of upwards of 20 acres of good foil, is pleafantly fituated on the W. bank of the river Ifla, with a gentle flope to the S. and E. The living, including, the glebe, may be reckoned rather better than 60 l. *communibus annis.*—There is a fund of upwards of 100 l. for the fupport of the poor, which was lately augmented by a legacy of 20 l. from Mr. Andrew Pitcairn, writer in Dundee, whofe father, Mr. Robert

bert Pitcairn, was the firſt miniſter here after the Revolution. The collections amount to about 5 l. yearly. There is at preſent only one poor family, confiſting of a mother and 3 children, who receive a weekly allowance from the fund.

Rent of the Pariſh, Population and Manners.—The preſent rent of the pariſh is 630 l. All the leaſes have 17 years to run, except one, which will expire in 3 years; and a conſiderable riſe of rent is expected from that farm. The above rent is excluſive of the oak, and other plantations, the moſs-marl, the annual value of which cannot eaſily be aſcertained. The oaks are ſold once in 20 years for the bark : the laſt time they were cut down, about 18 years ago, they gave nearly 200 l. From the increaſed value of oak-bark, a very great riſe is now expected. At the laſt cutting, between 3000 and 4000 of the beſt trees were reſerved, which have thriven remarkably.

According to Dr. Webſter's report, the population in 1755 was 280. The number of the pariſhioners in all, is now 220 : The medium number of births, for the laſt 7 years, is 7, and of deaths 4. The pariſh has been gradually on the decreaſe, owing to the enlarging of the farms. This has alſo contributed, in a great degree, to the removal of the cottagers *.

The

---

* The tenants being reſtricted from ſubſetting more or leſs, are effectually prevented from having cottagers upon the old eſtabliſhment. Until very lately, all of them had their proportion of theſe uſeful dependants. Every cottager family in this pariſh, poſſeſſed a houſe, garden, graſs for one cow, and one computed acre of good ground. The ground was laboured by the farmer, who alſo drove out their dung, brought home their corn and fuel, conſiſting of peat and turf. The one half of their acre was in oats, the other in barley. The rent was 1 l. a-man reaper in harveſt. The cottager and his family were ſubject to the call of the farmer, for what other work he might need, and were paid according to the rate of the country. With theſe advantages, and their own induſtry

at

The parishioners are all of the Established Church, except 2 of the Church of England, who attend public worship regularly in the parish church, while they reside here. The parishioners, for the most part, are employed in agriculture ; there are, however, a few manufacturers, tradesmen, millers, and day-labourers. They are, in general, honest, sober and industrious, living peaceably and comfortably. The ague was formerly very common among them, probably from their poor way of living ; but now it is scarcely ever heard of.

Antiquities.—On the S. and W. side of the parish, there is an enclosure of great antiquity, concerning the use of which tradition gives no account. It is nearly of a square form, and contains about an English acre of ground. The walls, which are of earth, as far as can be judged, have been originally of considerable height and breadth. A deep and wide ditch on the outside of the wall, filled with water from an adjoining morass, is still almost entire. This fort, now known by the name of Castledykes, was probably a place of retreat to the neighbourhood in times of turbulence and barbarism. The north part of this parish is said to have been the scene of engagement between the English and Scotch forces, under King Edward and Robert Bruce. Although there is no mention of this skirmish in history, yet it is confirmed by several monuments of antiquity and tradition: confirmed in this manner, it must ever be valuable in a country where authentic records have been destroyed by the barbarous policy of its invaders. The English army seems, at this time, to have been stationed

at home, the cottagers, in general, lived comfortably according to their station, and brought up a numerous and hardy offspring. For the most part they have emigrated to the manufacturing towns, and their removal has proved, in many respects, an essential loss to the interests of agriculture, particularly for one article, having rendered country servants and day-labourers very expensive, and difficult to be got.

stationed on the S. side of Strathmore, at Ingliston, (*i. e.* English town) where remains of their camp are still discernible; the Scotch forces, or a considerable part of them, at least, on the N. side of the strath, at the foot of the Grampian mountains, having their front covered by the river Isla. A conical mount in this parish, called Saddle-hillock, is said to have been made use of by the English, perhaps to command the ford at Dellavaird, whilst their troops marched over to attack the Scotch, and to have received its name from some circumstance which took place on that occasion, but which is not distinctly related. The hillock stands upon a very level field, is of considerable height, and has upon its top the remains of a small earthen fort, evidently artificial; and appears from an opening made in its side, to have been composed of large stones, some of which are smoothed, as if they had been taken from the bed of the river. Whether it was erected on this occasion, or whether it might not have been much more ancient, it is not easy to determine. It would appear that the English were repulsed in their attempt to ford the river, pursued by the Scotch, and brought to an engagement, to the S. of the river, and hillock above mentioned, where, under a huge cairn in the E. moor (heath) of Ruthven, their dead are said to be buried. On the S. side of the river, in the parish of Alyth, the place where the Scotch forces were stationed, still goes by the name of Brucetown; and 2 large standing stones are still to be seen erected in remembrance of this event. Upon one of these is a representation of a horseshoe, an emblem sufficiently expressive in the eventful history of the celebrated Scottish hero [*].

In

---

[*] This evidently alludes to Bruce's narrow escape from England, when Edward had resolved to murder him. " Brussius interea per comitem Gomeriæ astitum amicum certior de repentino periculo tactus; qui non ausus fugæ consilium

In the E. moor above mentioned, are two large granites, a species of stone rather uncommon in this neighbourhood, standing erect, between 5 and 6 feet above ground, at the distance of 12 feet from each other, and having each a flat side fronting due S. There are 2 smaller stones to the S. of the large ones, and 48 feet distant from them, and at right angles, but 12 feet distant from each other. The largest granite is on the W. side, and 20 feet in circumference. These stones might be considered as some Druidical monument; the more so, as the farm adjoining is called Draffan, which, according to some, is a corruption of Druidum Fanum, that is a temple, or place of worship of the Druids *.

Several stone coffins have been dug up in the parish, containing fragments of human bones, apparently of great size. Besides the cairns above mentioned, there is a number of smaller ones in this parish, one of which, known by the name of Crian's Gref, said to have been erected upon the grave of a noted robber, seems to indicate, that the sepulchral tumulus was not always raised in honour of the dead.

Minerals, Moss and Marl.—The parish abounds in mineral springs,

lium litteris committere, Bruffii exemplo monitus, ad eum calcaria inaurata, nummosque aliquot aureos misit, tanquam superiore hæc die mutuo ab eo accepisset. Robertus, ut in periculis homines sunt sagaciores, non ignarus quid eo manere significaretur, fabrum de nocte accersit, trium equorum soleas inversas ac preposteras equis affigere jubet, ne vestigia, velut abeuntium, per nivem fugam proderet.—Buch.

* Unfortunately for this conjecture, the following doubts occur:—1. It is doubtful if the Druids had any temples that were rectangular, or even circular, or any places of worship whatever, except groves. 2. It is doubtful if any Druids inhabited this part of the island. 3. Granting they did, it is doubtful if they or our forefathers, at that time, knew any thing of the Latin language. If the learned antiquary could sufficiently remove the two first of these, the latter might easily be got over, by supposing the name to have been of a later date.

springs, seemingly of different kinds, but their medicinal qualities have never as yet been ascertained. A steel spring was discovered lately near the manse. It is generally pure, but at times turbid, emitting periodically considerable quantities of reddish ochrey substance. There is a peat-moss in the parish, but it is difficult of access, except in a very dry summer. The principal dependence of the parishioners for fuel, is upon coal from Dundee, the nearest sea port. The parish contains shell marl, of very fine quality. It is found, for the most part, under peat-moss ; sometimes, however, under sand, and, what is remarkable, at one place, under a bed of pure clay, upwards of 3 feet thick. There is, indeed, a field of clay in the neighbourhood, but, as there is no running water near it, except small springs, it is not easy to conceive the length of time requisite for these, or the ordinary washing of rain-water, to have carried away and deposited such a tenacious substance as clay, to such a thickness above the marl, which, from its nature, must have been formed by degrees in the bottom of a lake. It is upwards of 50 years since this useful manure was discovered; but, such was the ignorance and obstinacy of the country people, that it was a long time before they would avail themselves of it. It is even told, that some of the neighbouring proprietors were under the necessity of binding their tenants under a penalty to make use of a certain quantity of it yearly. Afterward, however, when they began to perceive its effects upon the soil, from want of restriction, they overcropped some of their fields to such a degree, that they feel the effects of it to this day, and, in some places, are reduced to a *caput mortuum*. A darg of marl i. e. as much as could be cast up with one spade in one day, amounting often to 200 bolls, did not cost then above 18 d. or 2 s. ; it is now sold at 10 d. a-boll, at the neighbouring moss of Baikie, in the parish of Airly, their being none disposed of at present in

this

this parifh. A vein of clay marl, of a red and yellow colour, was obferved here feveral years ago, and found to anfwer well with the dry grounds. It was afterward difcovered to be a fpecies of fuller's earth ; but the difcovery came too late, as the vein by that time was nearly exhaufted.

Advantageous Situation for Machinery.—At Balbirnie, upon the E. fide of the river Ifla, there is a good fituation for a diftillery. Farther up the river, and on each fide of the Lin, where the corn and waulkmills ftand, there are excellent fituations for machinery, where, with little expenfe, a great body of water could be procured during the whole year, to any neceffary height. There are two other fituations for mills, at prefent unoccupied. The one at the bridge on the N. fide, where there was a waulk (or fulling) mill formerly ; the other at a little diftance on the S. fide of the bridge, where a lint-mill ftood fome years ago. It might be mentioned, that there would be a capital fituation for machinery on the water ridge of the glebe, with an excellent freeftone quarry, within 200 yards of it. What would be greatly in favour of this fituation, is, that the low glebe, confifting of about 10 acres of fine foil, lies directly above the water ridge, is very level, and might be watered, in every direction, for bleaching ground, by a fmall rivulet which never dries up, called the Kirkton burn. The abundance of freeftone in this parifh, its centrical fituation to the manufacturing villages of Cupar Angus, Alyth, and Kirriemuir, its moderate diftance from the flourifhing town of Dundee, being only 15 miles, and 12 of thefe upon a turnpike road ; the pleafantnefs and fertility of the country, and the reafonable price of provifions added to the water-falls above mentioned, feem to concur in pointing out this little parifh as a defirable fpot for machinery and manufacture. Something of this kind is much wanted to quicken

en the induſtry of the tenants, and give a ready market to
many articles at preſent of little value. It is to be hoped,
that theſe natural advantages will not always be overlooked,
and that an obſerving and induſtrious age will at length avail
itſelf of circumſtances ſo ſtrikingly favourable.

State of the Pariſh 50 years ago.—Agriculture was in the
ſame rude ſtate in this pariſh 50 years ago, that it had been
for time immemorial, without any improvement or alteration
whatever. A ſmall portion of the farm, called the infield,
which lay contiguous to the houſe, received all the dung, and
was kept conſtantly in crop with barley and oats, or ſometimes with flax, as the ground was in condition to bear it.
The reſt of the farm was called the outfield, and kept for
paſture, in ſuch natural graſs as it could produce. That
part of the outfield which was arable, after remaining three
years in graſs, was cropped for other three years ſuccef-
ſively with black oats, an inferior kind of grain, of which 2
bolls at leaſt were required to give 1 boll of meal. Unac-
quainted with the method of raiſing artificial graſſes, and unable to maintain their beſtial upon their ſcanty paſture, the
tenants were under the neceſſity of ſending the greater part of
them to the glens in the Highlands, from the concluſion of the
ſeed-time, about the beginning of June, until about the middle of September. From the want of turnip, and other green
food, their cattle were poorly fed in winter, and their cows
gave little or no milk. In place of milk, they were neceſſi-
tated to have recourſe to the wretched ſubſtitute of ſkrine, or
unboiled flummery, prepared from the refuſe of oatmeal ſoaked
in water. A cow was never known to have a calf oftener
than once in two years. Animal food was never ſeen in a
farmer's houſe above once or twice a-year. The rent was
trifling, but the tenant was inactive, perſiſting in the beaten
                                                      track

track of imperfect agriculture, and feldom feeking beyond daily fubfiftence. Yet thofe who have lived to experience the wonderful change which half a century has produced, do not fay that they were formerly unhappy ; fatisfied with little, if none of them were rich, neither were there any really poor. Their great dependence at that time was upon their fheep, of which they bred and maintained confiderable numbers. After the feparation of the crop from the ground, the fields became then a kind of common pafturage, until the enfuing feedtime ; but upon the introduction of fown grafs and turnip, it became neceffary to put away the fheep ; and there are now only a very few for private ufe. The whole of the wool was manufactured in the parifh into a kind of coarfe woollen cloth, with part of which the farmer clad himfelf and family ; the remainder was fold to help to pay the rent. All the flax which was then raifed, and which, like the wool, was confiderable in quantity, but more fo in quality, was manufactured in the parifh for home confumption, or fold in yarn. The following table, from good information, may ferve to give a comparative ftate of this parifh, and even throw fome light on the ftate of other parifhes, not only at the period alluded to, but for a long time back.—*Note :* 50 years are mentioned, becaufe fome authentic documents refer to that period. No alteration whatever was obferved here, until about 35 years ago. In the firft column in the article Servants Wages, there are fome perquifites called bounties, amounting from 5 s. to 10 s. yearly, not included ; in the fecond column all thefe perquifites are included.

Compa-

COMPARATIVE STATE of the PARISH for Years 1742 and 1792.

Those marked thus *, *are conversion prices, and may be reckoned a shilling at least below the market.*

	1742.			1792.		
Number of parishioners,	280			220		
———— of tenants, - -	40			12		
———— of ploughmen, -	31			37		
———— of work-horses, -	50			52		
———— of work-cattle, -	86			None		
———— of young cattle bred yearly, - - -	40			82		
———— of cattle maintained yearly, - - -	210			278		
———— of sheep, - -	1050					
———— of lbs. of wool, -	525					
———— of stones of hay, -	None			12,000		
———— of acres of turnip,	None			50		
Rent of the parish, - -	L. 280	0	0	L. 630	0	0
Wages of a man servant. -	2	0	0	10	0	0
———— of a halflin (between man and boy), - - -	0	11	8	5	0	0
———— of a herd, - - -	0	5	0	1	10	0
———— of a woman servant,	0	13	4	4	0	0
———— of a man reaper, -	0	11	1⅓	1	10	0
———— of a woman reaper,	0	8	10⅔	1	0	0
———— of a day labourer, with victuals, - - -	0	0	3	0	0	10
Price of a horse, - - -	5	0	0	25	0	0
——— of an ox, - - - -	2	10	0	8	0	0
——— of a calf, - - - -	0	4	0	0	16	0
——— of a sheep, - - - -	* 0	4	0	0	10	0
——— of a hog, - - - -	* 0	11	1⅔	2	0	0
——— of a cart, - - - -	0	15	0	9	0	0
——— of a plough, - - -	0	2	6	2	2	0
——— of wheat, the boll, -				1	1	0
——— of barley and oatmeal,	* 0	8	10⅔	0	16	0
——— of pease, - - - -				0	15	0
——— of seed oats, - - -	0	11	1⅓	0	16	0

Price

	1742.			1792.		
Price of malt, - - - -	L. 0	11	1⅔	L. 1	4	0
—— of corn with fodder, -	1	0	0	1	0	0
—— of hay the ſtone, - -				0	0	4
—— of flax, - - - - -	0	15	0	0	12	0
—— of butter, - - - -	0	5	0	0	12	0
—— of cheeſe, - - -	0	3	6	0	5	6
—— of wool the lib. - -	0	1	0	0	0	10
—— of beef, mutton and pork, - - - - - -	0	0	1	0	0	3½
—— of a hen, - - - -	0	0	4	0	1	0
—— of a chicken, - - -	0	0	2	0	0	4
—— of eggs the dozen, -	0	0	1	0	0	4

PARISH of St. VIGEANS.

(County of Forfar, Synod of Angus and Mearns, Presbytery of Aberbrothock.)

By the Rev. Mr. John Aitkin.

Name, Church.

THE parish of St. Vigeans has, according to tradition, received its name from a reputed Saint, who is said to have lived before, or during the 12th century; for, in that century the church was built, about the time, or soon after the erection of the abbey of Aberbrothock *. The church is

---

* The plan of the abbey and church of St. Vigeans, is said to have been drawn by the same architect, whose grave is shown to strangers in this churchyard. The above mentioned Saint, is said to have resided, for some time, about 3 miles from the place where the church stands, at a farm called Grange of Conan, where the vestiges of his chapel still remain, 23 feet long, by 15 broad. A few yards from the chapel, there are 3 or 4 acres of good land formerly belonging to it, but long since become the property of 1 of the heritors of the parish. The present proprietor, some years ago, enclosed a few falls of ground

is built in the form of a cathedral, 60 feet long, by 54 over walls, on a ſmall mount, the top of which is about 40 feet above the level of the circumjacent ground. The ſummit of the mount is of an elliptical form ; the greateſt diameter go-ing from S. to N., and the length of the church being from E. to W., there are only about 8 feet at each corner more than is ſufficient to contain the foundation of the fabric. The aſcent on the W. N. and E. ſides of the mount, is exceeding-ly ſteep *.

Extent, Surface, Produce, Rent, &c.—Formerly the ex-tent of this pariſh was conſiderably larger than it is at pre-ſent. The town and abbey of Arbroath belonged to it, till about the year 1560, when Arbroath became a diſtinct pa-riſh. But as no legal diviſion was ever made, the boundaries of the 2 pariſhes cannot be exactly aſcertained †. The boun-daries of what is now reckoned the pariſh, may be deſcribed

as

ground round the veſtiges of the chapel, with a ſtone fence, and planted it. Within a few yards of the chapel, there is 1 of the moſt copious ſprings, of ex-cellent water, in this country, called to this day St. Vigean's well.

* The mount ſeems to be partly natural and partly artificial ; for, on the S. ſide, when graves are digged, rock appears about 3 feet below the ſurface ; but on the N. ſide, there is fine mould for ſeveral feet deep. There is not, perhaps, in Scotland, a church ſo remarkably ſituated. The ſmall river Brothock, from which the neighbouring burgh has its name, runs within a few feet of the E. ſide of the church-yard, and is ſaid to ſignify the "muddy ſtream," as it runs a great part of its courſe on a muddy and clay bottom. The church is an Engliſh mile diſtant from Arbroath northward.

† Perhaps it may be proper to obſerve, as an uncommon thing, that the S. ſide of the church of Arbroath, for about 10 feet at the E. end, and a few feet on the W., ſtands in this pariſh, and not many years ago, the miniſter and ſchoolmaſter of Arbroath reſided in it. The eſtate of Guynd, in the pariſh of Carmylie, about 5 miles from St. Vigeans, belonged alſo to this pariſh, as ap-pears from writings belonging to that family, but when it was disjoined, is not now known.

as follows : The weft end of it borders on the fea for about 3 miles from the town of Arbroath, to about a quarter of a mile beyond the fifher town of Auchmithy. For about a mile eaft of Arbroath, the coaft is flat, with a fandy beach ; but within flood-mark, the bottom confifts of ribbed rocks, vifible only at low water. At the end of this extended plain, the coaft rifes abruptly, and becomes high, bold, and rocky, being the weftern extremity of the *rubrum promontorium*, or Red Head, which extends to about 3 miles beyond the limits of the parifh. From the point beyond Auchmithy, to the N. W. corner of the parifh, the length is about 7 miles, bordering for about 6 miles on the parifh of Inverkeillor, and 1 mile on the parifh of Carmylie. From the N. W. point to the S. W. corner, it is about 3 miles along the confines of the laft mentioned parifh. From the S. W. point to the E., the length is about 3 miles, lying on the N. fide of the parifh of Arbirlot, and a part of the country parifh of Arbroath. But this laft line is not fo regular as thofe on the other fides *.

The parifh, properly fo called, is divided into nearly 2 equal parts, E. and W., by the fmall river Brothock. The E. fide is by far the beft foil, and the moft favourable climate, and confequently the moft fruitful. From the river Brothock, the ground rifes gently for a mile towards the E., to the top of a hill called Dirkmountlaw, and afterward flopes in the fame gradual manner towards the fea, where the coaft is about 100 feet above the level of the water. On the
W. fide,

* Befides the extent comprehended within the above limits, there are 2 eftates entirely detached from this part of the parifh, and alfo from one another. One called Hofpitalfield, fo called from being the place where the hofpital for the fick of the Abbey of Arbroath ftood, lying a mile W. from the burgh, and divided from this parifh by the burgh roads of faid town. The other eftate, called Inverpeffor, lies about 4 miles from St. Vigeans, was formerly the feat of the Fletchers, now of Salton, and purchafed by the family of Panmuir fome time in the laft century.

W. fide, the ground rifes ftill more gradually for about 3 miles weftward, till it reaches the fummit of Grange of Conan hill, where the parifh borders on Carmylie. The reft of the parifh may be faid to be pretty flat, with a few gentle elevations in different places.

There is no map of the parifh ; but by a pretty exact inveftigation, aided by information from the proprietors and farmers, it is found to contain about 9385 Scotch acres, including the 2 detached eftates above mentioned ; 8355 acres of which are arable, of which 2334 acres are enclofed, the greater part with ditch, and the reft with hedge and ditch ; 1359 acres enclofed with ftone fences ; 250 acres planted, chiefly with Scotch firs ; 780 acres of moor, of which there are above 300 acres under improvement already, and more will foon be taken in for cultivation ; and, it is thought, that in a few years there will be no moor remaining in the parifh. The number of enclofed acres will appear more furprifing, when it is obferved, that in the year 1754, there were not 40 acres, gardens excepted, enclofed in the parifh.

There are, in the parifh, 138 carts, 300 horfes, 132 ploughs, 1633 black cattle, 510 fheep, a few of which are of Englifh breed, and 30 fwine. There are about 127 bolls of peafe fown yearly in the parifh ; 140 bolls wheat; 976 bolls barley and common bear ; 1578 bolls of oats. The yearly returns, at an average, may be 9 of wheat, 5 or 6 of oats, and 7 or 8 of barley. But perhaps this calculation may be rather high for the W. fide of the parifh ; but, it is thought, the E. fide will make up the deficiency. The valued rent of the parifh is 8299l. 6s. 8d. Scots, which is the higheft valuation of a country parifh in this county, and the real rent about 6000 guineas ; the number of proprietors about 40 ; the feuars fome hundreds. The higheft valuation of any heritor is 1200l. Scots, and the loweft 2l. Scots. Ten heritors refide

ſide in the pariſh. One heritor keeps a 2 wheeled carriage ; but there is not a 4 wheeled chaiſe belonging to any heritor reſiding. Moſt of the eſtates in this pariſh belonged former- ly to the Abbacy of Arbroath, and were ſold by Cardinal Beaton.

Soil, &c.——The ſoil, as may be ſuppoſed in ſuch an extent, varies very much. In ſome parts of the pariſn, it conſiſts of fine loam of a browniſh colour, many inches deep ; lying, in ſome places, on clay, in others, on a ſandy bottom, coarſe gravel, or ſand and clay intermixed. In others, it conſiſts of a black inſipid loam on clay ; and this clay, in ſome places, is ſo compact and impenetrable, that by the rain-water lying on or near the ſurface, a great part of the winter, the manure laid on it is much weakened, and, in ſome ſeaſons, fails con- ſiderably of its effect. This laſt, is the caſe with what has been formerly moor, and not ſo early brought into cultiva- tion as other parts of the pariſh. There is, in ſome places of the pariſh, very fine ſoil, and pretty deep, lying on extenſive beds of ſtone. There is, in general, a large extent of good ſoil, capable of producing any crop raiſed in Scotland ; and alſo, a conſiderable quantity of ground that will require no little attention and induſtry from the farmer, before it can repay the expenſe beſtowed upon it. But the ſpirit of in- duſtry that has of late pervaded almoſt the whole heritors and tenants here, has produced an amazing alteration upon the ſoil, ſurface, and appearance of the pariſh ; ſo that in many farms, there is not a ſingle acre uncultivated ; and if the ſame ſpirit ſhall continue, it is ſuppoſed, that in a few years the whole extent of the pariſh will be under cultiva- tion. It is generally allowed here, that the raiſing of the rents in this diſtrict, has, among other cauſes, contributed to the activity, attention, and induſtry of the farmers, who have

of

of late been roufed from that torpid ftate and infignificant
rank they formerly held in fociety, and are become, in this
part of the country, an acute, fenfible, and intelligent fet of
men, capable of converfing, and being in company with perfons of fuperior rank, and able to give advice and inftruction
to thofe who wifh to apply themfelves to the cultivation of
the country. Confidering the fmall advantages, which many
of them enjoy, for the improvement of their minds, it may
be queftioned, if there is any rank of men in fociety that
has fo rapidly emerged from ignorance, inattention to bufinefs, and rudenefs of manners, as they have done in a few
years ; and by confequence they have become entitled to all
the efteem and encouragement that is in the power of the
landed intereft to confer upon them ; for, on their fkill and
labour, under providence, the very exiftence of fociety depends.

In fome eftates in this parifh, a variety of fervices are required, fuch as ploughing, reaping, making hay, carrying
coals from Arbroath, kain fowls, &c. ; in other eftates no
kind of fervices are demanded. There are but a few farms
that are exempted from aftriction to mills; the multures payable to fome mills are high, to others moderate. There are
4 meal mills, 1 flour mill, 2 barley mills, 2 malt mills, 1
mill for wafhing yarn, 1 mill with 8 ftamps for beating yarn
when dry, and 1 waulk mill, all going by water. There is
a bleachfield, where about 1000 fpindles of yarn, and about
5500 yards of linen are bleached annually.

Village of Auchmithy.—Auchmithy is a fmall village fituated about 3 miles eaftward from the church, on ground elevated about 100 feet above the level of the fea, the defcent
to which is rough, fteep, and rocky. It contains 180 people of all ages. The men are generally employed in fifhing.
They

They have 6 boats, value about 120l., with 5 or 6 men to each boat. The people of that place are become fober and induftrious, and much civilized in their manners within 30 years paft. They find a ready market for their fifh in the neighbouring diftrict, but efpecially in the town of Arbroath, which alone would confume ten times the quantity they catch *. There is no harbour at Auchmithy, and from the number of rocks lying near the place where the boats land, it would be very difficult and expenfive to make one. When the boats come in from fifhing, they are drawn out on the beach above reach of high water. The value of what they call great lines, is about 1l. 5s. Sterling, and of the fmall lines half-a-guinea, and their creels for catching lobfters 2s. In 1792, there were about 16,000 lobfters taken there, at 3d. a-piece, the whole of which almoft were fent to London. The property of the village belongs to the Earl of Northefk, who allows ground to the fifhers for houfes, at the yearly rent of from 1s. 6d. to 3s. 6d. the houfe. The fifhers build their houfes on their own expenfes. His Lordfhip draws the tithes of the fifh, which are juft now let at 4l. 10s. Sterling a-year, and 7 years ago at 8l. The fifhing at that place appears to have been in a declining ftate for fome years paft. The Earl of Northefk has lately caufed a cart road to be made from the village down to the beach, about 12 or 14 feet wide, for the conveniency

---

* The fifh on this part of the coaft, are cod, ling, fkate, mackerel, hollybut, here called turbot, fea-dog, fome turbot, called bannakfluke, and haddocks, few of which have been got here for the laft 4 years; whitings and flounders are taken, lobfters alfo, and crabs in great plenty; vaft numbers of feals formerly frequented the rocks along this coaft, lying in hundreds together, but few of them have been obferved for fome time paft. For fome years, the price of fifh has rifen here very much. In 1754, and feveral years afterward, haddocks fold here for 2d. 3d. and 4d. the dozen, of late, they have coft 10d. and 1s. a-piece, and fometimes confiderably higher. The price of other kinds of fifh is ftill moderate.

conveniency of the inhabitants, though it is reckoned rather fteep for a carriage *. In Auchmithy, as perhaps in moft fifhing villages, the accent of the inhabitants differs remarkably from that of their neighbours, even to fuch a degree, that the writer of this can eafily diftinguifh the voice of any perfon belonging to that village, though fpeaking in a different room.

Stipend, School, &c.—The ftipend, by a decreet as old as the year 1635, is 11 bolls and 1 firlot of wheat, 47 bolls, 3 firlots, 1 peck, 3 lippies, and ⅓ of a lippie of bear, and 80 bolls and 1 firlot meal, at 7 ftones the boll, equal to 70 bolls, 3 firlots, and 2 lippies, at 8 ftones the boll, and 7l. 17s. 11½d. Sterling vicarage ; but there is no allowance in the decreet for the expenfes of communion elements †. The church contains

* This place was burnt down by fome fifhermen in the end of the laft century. In digging the floor of a houfe in Auchmithy, a few years ago, in order to erect a partition wall, 33 coins were found in a fmall earthen pitcher, fome of Henry IV. of France, others of feveral German Princes, the reft of Charles II. and William the III. Some of the pieces were of a fquare form. About 18 miles fouthward from Auchmithy, in the German ocean, there is a large rock about half an Englifh mile long, and one quarter broad, vifible at low water, where large cod are caught. Tradition relates, that in the laft century there was a bell erected there on pillars of wood, and a machine fo contrived, as to make the bell ring with little wind ; that a Dutch mafter of a fhip removed the bell, and that the next time he vifited the place, his fhip was wrecked.

† The decreet makes the teinds payable *ipfa corpora*, and it is not known when the above converfion was made. At the date of the decreet, James Marquis of Hamilton is mentioned as titular of the teinds of the faid parochine, and the ftipend is faid to be given in full contentment and fatisfaction to the faid minifter and his fucceffors, of any further provifion which they, or either of them, might claim thereafter, from Patrick Archbifhop of Glafgow, out of the penfion granted to him out of the rents of the Abbey of Aberbrothock. This was Patrick Lindfay, of the family of Edzell, in this county, who was fettled minifter

tains about 1000 people, but now not half fufficient for the accommodation of the greatly increafed number of parifhioners †. The glebe, of about 6 acres, is one of the worft in the county ; the manfe was built in 1663, has been feveral times

minifter of St. Vigeans in 1614, was depofed by the Affembly in 1638, and is faid to have died at Newcaftle in 1644. It may be proper to mention, as perhaps a fingular cafe, that a part of the ftipend, amounting to 36 bolls of victual of different kinds, out of an eftate in the parifh, is mentioned in the reddendo of the proprietor's charter from the Crown, as payable by him to the minifter of St. Vigeans.

† *Patronage of the Parifh.*—The patronage of the church belongs to the Crown, and is one of 34 that were in the gift of the Abbacy of Arbroath, All thefe devolved to the Crown at the Reformation, and, it is faid, were afterward gifted to the family of Dyfart, and were bought from that family in the laft century by Patrick firft Earl of Panmuir, and forfeited to the Crown, along with the eftate, in 1715, by James Earl of Panmuir; the eftate was fold by the Crown in 1717, to the York-building Company, but the Crown retained the patronages. In the times of Popery, public worfhip was generally performed in the church of St. Vigeans, by a Monk fent out from the Abbey, who was allowed the vicarage-tithes, which were then paid *ipfa corpora*, for his falary. The Abbots referved to themfelves the parfonage-tithes; and this cuftom, it is faid, prevailed in all the churches belonging to the Abbacy. Tradition relates, that the laft Monk who officiated here, was one of the name of Turnbull; and in the year 1754, part of the floors of 2 rooms in the fteeple, faid to be poffeffed by him, remained. He is faid to have been frightened from his chambers by the devil appearing to him in the fhape of a rat ; and no Monk after him would be perfuaded to refide in the fteeple. Such was the ignorance that prevailed in thefe times. But this foolifh conduct of the Monk will not, perhaps, appear in fuch a contemptible light, when the following more recent inftance of ignorance, credulity and fuperftition, is attended to. From the year 1699 to 1736, the Sacrament of the Lord's Supper had never been difpenfed in this church. A tradition had long prevailed here, that the water-kelpy (what Mr. Hume, in his tragedy of Douglas, calls " the angry fpirit of the water") carried the ftones for building the church ; that the foundation of it was fupported upon large bars of iron ; and that under the fabric there was a lake of great depth. As the adminiftration of the facrament had been fo long delayed, the people had brought themfelves to believe, that the firft time that ordinance fhould be difpenfed, the church would fink, and the whole people would be carried down and drowned

in

times repaired, and is now much decayed.—The fchoolmafter's houfe is flated, confifts of 4 rooms and 2 clofets; and there is alfo a fchool-houfe of 38 feet long, lately built by contribution. The falary is 100 l. Scots, which, with the dues a-rifing from his office of feffion-clerk, and from marriages, baptifms, &c. makes his living worth 30 l. Sterling. He has alfo a fmall garden. The fcholars are generally about 50 or 60, fome of whom are boarded in the fchoolmafter's houfe. The fees for reading Englifh are 1 s., for reading and writing 1 s. 6 d., for arithmetic 2 s., and for Latin 2 s. 6 d. the quarter.

Population.—According to Dr. Webfter's report, the population was 1592. Between the years 1770 and 1780, the commencement of the increafed population of this parifh may be dated. For fome years in that period, the increafe was flow; but fince the year 1780, it has been very rapid, generally above 50 perfons in a year. This increafe has been chiefly, if not entirely owing to the flourifhing ftate of manufactures in the town of Arbroath. An eftate, lying in detached parcels near that town, was fold very lately to feveral perfons, who immediately feued out **ground to** tradefmen, for houfes and fmall gardens. A number of houfes have been already

in the lake. The belief of this had taken fuch hold of the people's minds, that on the day the facrament was adminiftered, fome hundreds of the parifhioners fat on an eminence about 100 yards from the church, expecting every moment the dreadful cataftrophe. They were happily difappointed; and this fpirit of credulity "foon vanifhed, like the bafelefs fabric of a vifion." In the prefent times, it would prove a matter of great difficulty to make the people believe fuch abfurdities. Perhaps the local fituation of St. Vigeans, in the vicinity of the Abbey, might have difpofed the people to imbibe fuch principles as are not eafily rooted out. This much, however, may be faid in favour of credulity, that it generally flows from an honeft heart, though, on the other hand, it is feldom the offspring of a well informed head.

ready built; many are juft now building; and thefe are occupied moftly by weavers. In fome few farms, the number of people has decreafed, particularly in one, where the cottagers in 1754 were 18, and now there is only 1 family in that place. In April 1793, the houfes in this parifh were 730, and the number of people of all ages is 3336; and in that number there are 65 females more than males. In 1754, on the land contiguous to the town of Arbroath, there were but 12 families, by an exact lift taken by 3 elders, from houfe to houfe, 3 weeks ago, there are in this parifh, around the town, no lefs than 1369 perfons of all ages, 669 males and 700 females *.

In the parifh, there are 225 weavers, 40 wrights, 13 fmiths, 22 tailors, 17 mafons, 23 fhoemakers, 4 coopers, 2 dyers, 9 fhopkeepers, 16 public houfes, the moft part of thefe near Arbroath, 12 gardeners, 12 flaxdreffers, 2 flaters, 2 bakers, 8 wheelwrights, 2 midwives, 1 tan-yard and 2 tanners. In the above diftrict near Arbroath, there are 2 focieties, one of which takes the name of the St. Vigeans Weaver Society, inftituted

* *Baptifms.*				*Marriages.*		*Baptifms.*	
	Males.	Fem.	Total.				
1788	34	25	59	1788	33	1754	60
1789	50	35	85	1789	36	1755	47
1790	36	38	74	1790	24	1756	53
1791	26	39	65	1791	33	1757	40
1792	55	38	93	1792	33	1758	50
			376		159		250

The average number of baptifms for the laft 5 years, is 75; but it would have been greater, if the parents had been more regular in giving in the names of the children to the parifh-regifter. The baptifms for the year 1792, which were 93, may be depended on as the exact number adminiftered by the Eftablifhed minifter, as he baptized none during that period, which were not regiftered before baptifm. But there may have been about 4 or 5 more baptized laft year by minifters who are not of the Eftablifhment. The average number of baptifms from 1754 to 1758, both inclufive, is 50. There has never been any regifter of burials kept in this parifh.

ftituted in 1787, and governed by a prefes and counfellors, chofen annually. This fociety confifts at prefent of 87 members, all weavers; and they admit none but thofe who have been regularly bred to the bufinefs. The prefes buys from 800 to 1000 bolls of meal yearly, and from 400 to 500 bolls of coals, all which is given out to the members at 3 or 4 months credit; this fociety affords 2 s. a-weak to their poor, which is paid out of the general fund; and when the fund happens to be reduced to a certain fum, their poor are fupplied by a contribution among the members. The other is called the Townhead Society, is managed in much the fame manner as the former, but admits members of all occupations, and has no ftated allowance for their poor, but beftows as their funds will allow. The chief defign of the eftablifhment of thefe focieties was for providing coals and meal for the families concerned in them, which they are enabled to purchafe at a cheap rate, by laying in large quantities at proper feafons; and they find ample credit, by the whole members being bound for the payment. The members of both focieties fhow particular attention to the moral character of the perfons they admit.

It is but doing juftice to the inhabitants of thefe newly e-rected villages, to obferve, that they are generally fober, and remarkably induftrious; by which means the moft part of them are enabled to live comfortably. By their refidence in the vicinity of Arbroath, where manufactures are carried on to a very great extent, they enjoy every advantage for knowing the goodnefs and value of the materials they make ufe of, the method by which they may be beft manufactured, the character of the merchants with whom they deal, and when to embrace the fitteft opportunity for difpofing of their goods.

It is proper here to obferve, that the firft manufacturer of the cloths called Ofnaburghs, in this country, and perhaps in Scotland,

Scotland, was the late Mr. John Wallace, merchant, and some time provost of Arbroath, who began that business about the year 1740; and for many years after that period, all that kind of cloth manufactured in this part of the country centered in his shop. But now that business has been extended through almost every town, village, and parish in the county, and is now carried on to such an extent, that the very large sum of money brought into this county by that breach of business, cannot be estimated without an inspection of the custom-house books. By information sent the writer of this, from the master of the stamp-office in Arbroath, taken from his books, it appears, that from November 1791 to November 1792, there were stamped 1,055,303 yards of Osnaburgh and brown linen; and that one-fourth part of that quantity was manufactured in this parish. The value of the above cloth was 39,660 l. 6 s. 10$\frac{7}{4}$ d. Sterling. The bounty paid by government is 1 d. Sterling on each yard of Osnaburgh valued 6 d. and 1$\frac{1}{2}$ d. on each yard above 6 d. of price.

Rise in the value of land.——The property of many estates in this parish has been frequently transferred since the year 1754. One estate on the W. side of the parish, of about 300 acres, was sold about the above period for less than 600 l.; some years after that it gave 1300 l.; soon after 2300 l.; afterward for 2500 l.; it is just now in the market, and 6000 l. at least is expected for it. Another estate, on the W. side, but near Arbroath, consisting of 150 acres, was sold in 1765, for 2300 l. and 3 years ago it gave 5800 l. Another estate, on the east side, of 363 acres, was sold about 30 years ago for 1200 l., soon after for 1400 l.; about 3 years ago it gave 4000 guineas. A farm of about 800 acres on the W. side of the parish, a part of which is moor, was feued about 20 years ago, and divided by the proprietors into 2 farms; the whole

farm

farm paid of rent in 1754, and for several years after, about 70 l. One of the farms was let some years ago for above 200 l., and the other for 160 l. Another estate, lying near Arbroath, in detached parts, was sold about 43 years ago for 1750 l., several years after for 4750 l., and two years ago for 8000 l. in small parcels. Another estate in the E. side of the parish, was sold in 1765 for 850 l., and 2 years ago for 2000 l.

Crops, Ploughs, Farmers.——There are about 70 farmers in the parish, who pay of yearly rent from 2 l. to 200 l. Of 35 heritors, the number in 1754, only 2 are alive; and there is not one farmer alive in the parish, and now possessed of a farm, who was a farmer in 1754. Scots ploughs, very neatly made, and covered with yetling, are the only kind used in this parish. They are drawn by 2 horses, and worked by one man. The writer does not know of a plough drawn by oxen in the parish. In such variety of soil, difference of climate in the E. and W. sides of the parish, degrees of knowledge and taste of the farmers, power of habit, &c. the rotation of cropping must be very different. It is thought that the 2 following modes are the most common here. When a farmer breaks up ley ground, which has not been formerly improved, about 30 bolls of lime-shells are laid upon the acre ; the shells are delivered with the barley measure, the first crop oats, the second barley, without any manure, the 3d crop oats, the 4th a green crop, or, according to the condition of the ground, barley with grass seeds, and lies under grass generally 4 years. Or, they break up ley generally at Lammas, lay on lime and dung for wheat, 2d crop oats, 3d crop turnip, and 4th barley, with grass-seeds. There are raised here from 50 to 60 bolls of 16 stones Amsterdam weight of potatoes upon the acre, and of this useful root, great quantities are produced in the parish.
A con-

A considerable quantity of flax is also raised here, generally the 2d crop after breaking up ley ground, 9 or 10 pecks of Riga or Dutch lint-seed are sown on the acre, which produce from 25 to 30 stones avoirdupoise weight of dressed flax; rent of the acre about 5 l. About 200 stones of hay are raised on the acre. For threshing corns, the farmers allow their barn-men the 21st boll, without any victuals, or the 25th, with 1 meal a-day. There are now in the parish 4 or 5 threshing machines; but it will require some time and experience, before it is known whether or not they will prove advantageous to the farmers; they seem to think that the working of them is hurtful to their horses. It is supposed that the parish does not now produce meal sufficient for the consumption of the inhabitants; but there are about 1500 bolls of wheat, and between 2000 and 3000 bolls of barley sold yearly, the greater part of which is sent to Leith and Glasgow. Turnips are raised on almost every farm; and some black cattle are fed and sold to the butchers of Arbroath, from 10 l. to 14 l. the head *.

Poor, &c.—There are generally between 20 and 30 poor persons, who receive alms from the public fund of the parish, which consists of an annuity paid out of an estate in the parish amounting

* *Prices, Wages, &c.*—Day labourers have here from 1 s. to 1 s. 4 d., masons from 1 s. 8 d. to 2 s. and tailors from 6 d. to 8 d. a-day; these last have their victuals also. Ditchers for the rood 6 yards long, 5 feet broad, and 3 deep, 1 s. Dikers for 36 square yards, the stones laid down to them, from 9 s. to 10 s. Ploughmen having victuals in the farmer's house, from 7 l. to 9 l. and 10 l.; Ploughmen married, have a house from the farmer, the same wages, with 6½ bolls of meal in the year, with a Scotch pint of milk a-day. In place of milk, some have a cow maintained by the farmer, and have 5 l. wages. Beef from 4 d. to 4½ d. the Dutch pound, and veal 4 d., mutton 4½ d.; fowls 1 s., eggs 3 d. 4 d. 5 d. and 6 d. a dozen. Wages are more than double, and prices generally as 3 to 2, in 1754.

amounting to 2 l. 15 s. 6⅔ d. Sterling, mortified by George Chaplin, Efq. a native of this country, and fome time merchant in Jamaica ; alfo of the intereft of 83 l. 6 s. 8 d. Sterling, at 4⅞ per cent ; alfo of the intereft of 17 l. Sterling, of fome feat rents in the church, dues on mortcloths, proclamations, collections, and prefents, of which laft 15 l. Sterling has been given at 3 different times, within the laft 3 years, by an opulent farmer in the parifh. The whole fum arifing annually from the above articles, will amount to between 60 l. and 70 l. Sterling; all which is generally diftributed to the poor within the year ; and they receive their fhares on the laft Sabbath of every month, from 2 s. to 4 s according to their fituations and neceffities. The heritors contribute nothing to their fupport [*].

Curiofities, Antiquities, &c.—On the top of a mount of much the fame height with that on which the church is fituated, and about 180 yards directly eaft, there is heard a very remarkable echo, proceeding from the E. end of the church. It repeats very diftinctly 6, and in a calm evening 8 fyllables,

or

[*] When the poor are entered upon the roll, they are fuppofed to have given up their effects, in the event of their death, to the poor's fund ; but thefe feldom fall to the feffion, as there are generally claims offered by relations for attendance, occafional fupply, and the expenfe of burial. There are very few begging poor in the parifh.

In the parifh there are about 20 perfons of the Church of England, 70 of the Scotch Epifcopal church, 30 Independents, 35 Methodifts, 40 Seceders, 10 Bereans. The Eftablifhed Church is generally well attended, and the parifhioners contribute liberally for the fupport of the poor, to the amount of between 10 and 13 s. every Sabbath during the fummer. The difference that prevails here, and in Arbroath, in religious opinions, appears to have no difagreeable influence on the minds and manners of the people. However much they may differ in their fentiments, they affociate together, tranfact bufinefs, and meet in a focial and convivial manner, without an inftance almoft of any injury or perfonal abufe of one another.

or a line of our pfalms in metre, and does not begin to rever-
berate till the voice of the fpeaker has ceafed. When the
fpeaker moves a few yards from his firft ftation, 2 echoes are
heard, and, proceeding a little farther, in the fame direction,
3 echoes are repeated. The form of the ground from the
church to the ftation of the fpeaker is hollow, and nearly
in the fhape of a femicircle.—About 3 miles weftward
from the church, are feen the veftiges of Caftlegory, or
Caftlegregory, where it is faid that Gregory, king of Scotland, refided ; and the names of feveral places in the neighbourhood feem to fhow, that it had been once a royal refidence,
fuch as Grange of Conon, or Koning, Miltown of Conon, and
Park Conon. A proprietor in the parifh has informed the
writer of this, that his houfe was built of the ftones of this
caftle in the 16th century. Several ftone coffins have been
lately dug up in the parifh, above 5 feet long, and 3 broad,
and fome earthen jars with afhes in them. A deer's horns,
in high prefervation, were found a few years ago in a mofs,
fome feet below the furface, with mofs above and marl below.

There is a hill called Dick, or Dickmount-law, which is
faid, in one of the ftatiftical accounts, to fignify a rampart of
protection or peace. It is about a mile E. of the church, and
feems to have been very much adapted to both the above
mentioned purpofes. On the top of this hill there is a large
cairn, now covered with grafs, and hollow in the middle,
where the baron held his courts. From it there is one of the
moft extenfive profpects in this country. There is a view of
the Grampian hills, for more than 30 miles, the coaft of Fife
for about 18 miles, the Ifle of May, the Lowmonds of Fife,
Largo-law, and the German Ocean for above 50 miles.

For many years after 1754, agues were fo common in this
parifh, that the incumbent has often feen, in the months of
March,

March, April and May, and fometimes in autumn, from 15 to 25 perfons in that diftemper. He does not remember to have feen a fingle perfon in the ague for 20 years paft. There never feems to have been what could be called a lake in the parifh ; but as a great part of the ground lies on a clay bottom, and formerly muft have been very wet, it is thought that this muft have contributed to the prevalence of this diftemper. The climate muft, no doubt, now have become much more healthy by the great number of ditches lately made here.

There are feveral caves in the rocks, along the W. between Arbroath and Auchmithy, one of which can be entered only at low water. When feals abounded on this coaft, it was cuftomary to let people down to this cave with a rope round their body, to the depth of 40 feet, with ropes of ftraw rolled round their legs, and bludgeons in their hands, in order to kill feals. There is another, called the Maiden Caftle cave, the entry to which is about 10 feet above high water-mark. The mafon-lodge of Arbroath built a gate to it, and gave it a door many years ago. They walked in proceffion every year on St. John's day from Arbroath to this cave, where they admitted new members. It is about 231 feet long, and from 12 to 24 feet broad. At the farther end there is a fpring of fine water, but exceedingly cold. Above the cave are the veftiges of a fort, about 100 feet above the level of the fea, and on the land fide the remains of the foffe and rampart are ftill vifible. There is another cave, which appears as if it had been cut out of the face of the rock, the entry to which is about 40 feet above the fea. It is about 12 feet long, 10 broad, and 8 high. The accefs to it is difficult and dangerous *.

Mifcellaneous

* About a quarter of a mile weftward from Auchmithy, there is a curious phenomenon called the gayler, or gaylet-pot. It lies in an arable field, and is

distant

Miscellaneous Observations.—Upon the fide of the fmall river Brothock, and near the church, a brewery was erected in 1787, and in the fame place a diftillery in 1790, both belonging to one perfon. The ftill is 40 gallons, and pays 40 l. a-year to the Excife. The diftillery confumed 500 bolls of barley in 1792, when there were 2 (40 gallon) ftills; and the brewery,

diftant 100 yards from the front of the rocks that hang over the fea. The pot is of the fhape of an inverted urn, 50 yards in diameter, but towards the weft it lofes a part of its circular form, and the ground afcends in a gentler flop than the other parts of the circle, for 54 yards, till it terminates in an angular point, at the place where it reaches the level of the adjacent field. The entry to it from the fea is 130 feet below the top of the rock, and the depth of the pot is 120 feet, below the level of the ground round the edges of it. The opening from the fea is grand and awful, being about 70 feet high and 40 broad. The water from the fea runs into the pot by a fubterraneous paffage, which gradually contracts till it enters the bottom of the pot, where it does not exceed 10 or 12 feet in breadth and height. When the fea is rough, the wind eafterly, and high water, the boifterous element burfts in at the mouth of the pot, with amazing impetuofity, and roars, and boils, and froths, till the waves of the fea fall back, and allow it to retreat, which it does with great violence, and a loud noife, which, on account of the depth of the cavity, is not heard at any great diftance.

About half way between this place and Auchmithy, there is a large excavation in the rocks, in the form of a femicircle, and about 160 feet wide in the front towards the fea. It has a large pillar of rock in the middle of the entrance, almoft in a line with the rocks on each fide. The extent is fo large, that a fifhing boat with four oars can fail round the pillar, without being in danger of ftriking on the rock. There was a chapel dedicated to St. Ninians, fituated about 2 miles from the church on the fea-fide, near the place where the coaft begins to rife, between Arbroath and Auchmithy. No veftige of the chapel now appears, but a part of the burying ground remains, through the middle of which a road has been lately cut, and the ends of feveral coffins of ftone are vifible. St. Ninians well, near the church-yard, was in former times of great repute for the cure of feveral difeafes, but now totally neglected. One of the annual fairs of Arbroath was dedicated to this faint; it fhould be held on the firft Wednefday after Trinity Sunday, but it is fome time ago fixed the third Wednefday of June.

brewery, about 870 bolls the ſame year. The brewery pays between 300l. and 400l. a-year of exciſe duty.—There is nothing uncommon or remarkable in the ſtature, form, or appearance, or inhabitants of the pariſh. They are generally from 5 feet 6 inches, to 5 feet 9 inches high; their ſhape and ſize ſeem to indicate health and ſtrength, and in fact, they poſſeſs a conſiderable ſhare of both. There are few 6 feet high. Several young perſons betake themſelves to a ſeafaring life, and a few to the army. There are ſome people in the pariſh from 79 to 84 years of age, and 2 gentlemen died ſome years ago, each in his 86th year. One Alexander Burns died ſome time ſince in the 96th year of his age. On almoſt all the large farms in the pariſh, both young men and married cottagers are employed as ſervants. The farmers generally dreſs in a plain manner ; the common colour of their clothes is blue ; and many of them ſtill wear the Scotch broad bonnet. The dreſs of a number of the men ſervants is a little ſhowy, and rather ſuperior to that of the females of the ſame rank. Many of the farmers are now accommodated with good houſes, built of ſtone, and ſlated, and generally of the ſize of ordinary manſes *.

In the W. ſide of the pariſh, the farmers ſow earlier than thoſe in the E., yet the corns are generally earlier cut down

in

---

* Their mode of living is conſiderably altered ſince the year 1754, and yet few of them live up to what they could afford. Their attention to their buſineſs, and their finances, prevents them from going to any exceſs in their family expenſes. In 1754, there were not 3 farmers in the pariſh who had half a dozen knives and forks in their houſes, now theſe implements abound in almoſt all their houſes. Few of them at that time drank tea, it is now common among people of inferior ſtation. There were not then 6 watches among the farmers ; now many of the men ſervants have them, and there are above 100 watches and about 80 clocks in the pariſh. In 1754, it was common for the farmer and his wife to eat at the ſame table with the ſervants ; now they eat in a ſeparate room.

2

in the E. than in the W. fide.—The oldeft records belonging
to the church-feffion, commence in 1665, when Mr. Strachan
was ordained minifter here, by a mandate from the Arch-
bifhop of St. Andrew's, and they are continued down to the
year 1694. From that date, to the year 1727, there are no
records extant. Since that time they have been regularly
kept.—There are feveral quarries in the parifh of a reddifh
coarfe granite, but fcarcely any ftones found in the fields that
can be ufed in building. In confequence of an act of parliament 1789, 2 turnpike roads are making here, and toll-bars
have been erected about 3 years ago. The one from Arbroath to Forfar, paffes through a part of the parifh on the
W. fide, for about 4 miles. The other from Arbroath to
Montrofe, on the E. fide, for 3 miles. The act alfo enjoins
a commutation of the ftatute-labour at the rate of 24 s. Sterling for each 100 l. Scots of valued rent in the county, and
the fum arifing from the above affeffment, is appointed to be
laid out on private roads within each refpective parifh. The
fum collected out of this parifh for the above purpofe, a-
mounts to between 90 l. and 100 l. Sterling.—The writer of
this has been told, that in the year 1750, there were but 2
box carts, or, what is here called coup-carts, in the parifh,
but at prefent there is no other kind made ufe of here.—The
only eminent man that has appeared in this parifh, during
this and a part of the laft century, was Sir James Wood of
Bonnington, Colonel of the Scotch Fufileers, in the reign of
Queen Anne. He ferved in Flanders under the Duke of
Marlborough, and acquired confiderable reputation in his profeffion. Letham, once his feat, is half a mile diftant from the
church.

Advantages, &c.—The advantages which the people of
this parifh enjoy, are many ; and the difadvantages few or

none,

none, but ſuch as are in their own power to remedy. A
healthy climate, and, in general, a fruitful ſoil ; no epidemical diſtempers prevalent among them. Coals from Arbroath,
the common fuel, 70 ſtones Dutch weight, at 6s. and 6s. 6d.;
but laſt winter at 8s. 6d., when they were ſcarcer and dearer
than ever known. Every perſon who chooſes to work, finds
immediate encouragement, good wages, and ready payment
for his labour. Every perſon who has any of the neceſſaries
of life to diſpoſe of, finds a ready market. The farmers enjoy, in moderation, many of the conveniencies of life, and
their married ſervants, when they behave honeſtly and diſ-
creetly, find protection and ſupport from their maſters. Many
of the tradeſmen, particularly the weavers, are in comfortable circumſtances ; they appear to know their intereſt, and
to attend to it carefully. And people of all ranks ſeem to
aim at what is uſeful and ſubſtantial, rather than what is
ſhowy or ſuperfluous. Was the writer of this to expreſs
what he believes to be the general ſenſe of the people in this
pariſh, with reſpect to their ſituation and circumſtances as
members of ſociety, it might be comprehended in the following words : " May the bleſſings of providence we at preſent
enjoy, be continued to us ; may the preſent Britiſh conſtitution remain unſhaken, and may agriculture, manufactures,
and trade flouriſh. What remains to complete our temporal
proſperity, depends on our own activity, diligence, and induſtry. We want no more, we wiſh no leſs."

PARISH of STRATHMARTIN,

(COUTY OF FORFAR, SYNOD OF ANGUS AND MEARNS, PRESBYTERY OF DUNDEE).

By the Rev Mr ALEXANDER STRACHAN.

Situation, Extent and Soil.

THIS parish forms a part of that pleasant and delightful Strath, anciently called Srathdighty. The derivation of the name is uncertain. The parish is very small, being only about 2 miles square. The soil is light, partly gravel, partly clay bottom. The air is healthy, and the inhabitants in general long lived.

Proprietors, Improvements, Cattle and Produce.—There are 2 heritors in the parish, Captain David Laird of Strathmartin, and Walter Ogilvie of Tulledaph-hall. About 9 years ago, Captain Laird, who distinguished himself by his gallant behaviour in the service of Government, during the

the late American war, bought the eſtate of Strathmartin. His lands have been moſtly in his own poſſeſſion, ſince he purchaſed the eſtate. The greateſt part of them is encloſed with ſubſtantial ſtone fences, and in a high ſtate of cultivation. He has lately let one of his farms, at L. 2, 2 s. the acre, another at L. 1, 10 s. and a third at L. 1, 10 s. Captain Laird has erected a good dwelling-houſe, where the ancient fabric reared its head. The offices and garden are at a diſtance from the houſe. He has encloſed 200 acres of the moor, called Clatto, in the ſouth end of the pariſh, with an earthen fence: 50 acres of it have been planted with aſh, elm, &c. which will in a little time relieve the eye, that has been a long time hurt by the black heath. 150 acres of this moor are deſigned for a farm; and excellent offices have been erected on it. On a few acres of this farm, which were ploughed laſt ſeaſon, a good crop of turnips has been raiſed. Thirteen old houſes have been demoliſhed, on the eſtate of Strathmartin, ſince the year 1785. Eight ſubſtantial houſes have been built on or near their ſites, each of which might contain 2 ſmall families; they are covered with ſlate or tile. Several new houſes have been erected for tradeſmen, and a good houſe for a brewer, with a brewhouſe, malt-barn, kiln and bakehouſe. Mr Walter Ogilvie of Tulledaph-hall, has made very confiderable improvements on that eſtate. He has encloſed a great part of his lands, with excellent ſtone fences, and built ſome good houſes for his tenants. His farms are let from L. 1 to L. 2 the acre. People who underſtand the art of farming doubt if the produce of ſo light a ſoil, will enable farmers to pay ſo high a rent.

The valued rent of the pariſh is L. 1180 Scotch. The pariſh of Strathmartin was formerly very ill laid out, and

consequently

confequently not very famous for cattle ; what is called the runridge being common in every quarter of it ; but fince the runridge was abolifhed, improvements have gone on with fpirit. Oxen of a large fize have been introduced by the heritors, for the plough and wain. Horfes which were bought twenty years ago from L. 7 to L. 12, now coft from L. 15 to L. 25. A confiderable number of cattle, fince turnips began to be raifed, have been fed, and fold not only by the heritors, but alfo by the farmers. Calves have begun to be reared in abundance, for the market, and farmers ufe. No fheep are kept in the parifh, except a few for private ufe, though formerly almoft every farmer had a flock. The ground produces good oats, barley and peafe. The manure ufed here, is lime from Fife, brought to Dundee by water, marl from the mires of Auchterhoufe parifh, and compofts of dung and earth. There are fome excellent ftone quarries in the parifh.

Water, Bridges and Mills.—The rivulet, commonly called Dighty water, which has its fource in Lundie parifh, and runs into the frith of Tay, glides through the middle of this parifh. Some fine burn-trouts, and a few pikes and perches of a middle fize, are to be found in it ; they abound moft in fpring, but are never caught for fale. By the exertions of that public fpirited gentleman, David Laird of Strathmartin, 2 bridges have been thrown over Dighty, one on the road leading from Glammis to the Carfe of Gowry, and the other on the road from Sidlaw-hill to Dundee. A bridge has likewife been built of late over Dighty, to the eaftward, at the expenfe of the corporation of bakers in Dundee. There are 10 mills in the parifh ; 2 corn mills, 1 flour, 1 barley, and 1 fulling mill, in the intereft of Captain Laird. On Mr Ogilvies' eftate, there is 1 corn, 1 fulling, and 1 lint mill.

mill. In the eaſt end of the pariſh, are 2 flour-mills, on a piece of ground feued ſometime ago, by the town-council of Dundee, and commonly called the mills of Baldovan, and have been long held in tack by the baker corporation of Dundee.

Manſe, Stipend, Church, School, Poor, &c.—The manſe was built in 1775. It is a piece of good maſon work, but is too ſmall for the accommodation of a family. The offices were built in haſte, and have undergone a repair, although finiſhed only in the end of the year 1775. The ſtipend is 30 bolls of barley, 32 bolls of meal, and L. 26 : 14 : 7 in money, including L. 3 for communion-elements; which is too ſmall a living for a clergyman, who has a numerous family. The teinds are exhauſted. The church was re-built in 1779.—A new ſchool, and houſe for the ſchool-maſter, were lately built on a ſmall piece of ground, taken from the church-yard, with the conſent of the preſbytery. The ſchoolmaſter's ſalary is 100 merks Scots, and L. 1, 10 s. as ſeſſion-clerk. The number of ſcholars in ſummer is from 20 to 30, and in winter, from 30 to 40. The encouragement given to ſchoolmaſters in this pariſh and neighbourhood, being ſmall, they betake themſelves to land-meaſuring and marl gauging, or commence auctioneers, and thus the education of youth is neglected: a remedy for this evil has long been deſired.—The poor are maintained by the weekly collections, which amount to 2 s. or 3 s. each Sunday, and by the intereſt of L. 150.

Population.—According to Dr Webſter's report, the number of ſouls then was 368. The following liſt of births, marriages, and deaths, is extracted from the ſeſſion records.

Years.

Years.	Births.	Marriages.	Burials.
1775,	14	1	1
1776,	8	—	6
1777,	10	3	4
1778,	10	1	1
1779,	12	1	3
1780,	11	3	6
1790	16 }	The regifter of marriages and bu-	
1792	13 }	rials has been neglected.	

There are 340 fouls in the parifh. The people in general are quiet, peaceable, and well difpofed. In the parifh, are 2 Antiburghers, and 1 Epifcopalian. Since the year 1770, the wages of men-fervants, maid-fervants, and day labourers are nearly doubled, owing to the flourifhing ftate of manufactures and improvements in agriculture, in this neighbourhood. There is a remarkable alteration to the better, in the drefs of the parifhioners, fince the year 1780.

Antiquities.—On the weft fide of Clatto-moor, are the traces of a camp. It is generally believed to have been occupied by a part of Agricola's army, and afterward by Alpin, Wallace, and Monk. Tradition reports, that " Wal- " lace pitch'd his camp on Clatto-hill, and ground his corn " at Philaw's mill," which is about half a mile from the place where the traces of the camp are feen. To the eaft- ward of Strathmartin houfe, there is a hill, called the Gal- low-hill, on which the Lairds of Strathmartin, in the days of feudal tyranny, exercifed their power in hanging for petty offences. In the north end of the parifh is a large ftone, called Martin's ftone, of which Gordon takes notice in his Itinerary, (as belonging to the parifh of Tealing.)

Tradition

Tradition ſays, that at the place where the ſtone is erected, a dragon, which had devoured nine maidens, (who had gone out on a Sunday evening, one after another, to fetch ſpring water to their father), was killed by a perſon called Martin, and that hence it was named Martin's ſtone. There is alſo a ſtone on the weſt gate of the church-yard, which has the figures of 2 ſerpents upon it.

PARISH of STRICKATHROW,

(COUNTY OF FORFAR.)

By the Rev. Mr ROBERT HANNAH.

Name, Situation, Extent, Soil, Rivers, &c.

THIS diſtrict is compoſed of two pariſhes, Strickath-row and Dunlappie, united in 1618. The name, *Strickathrow,* according to ſome, is a Celtic compound, ſig-nifying the ' ſtrath or valley where the King fought.' This pariſh lies in the county of Forfar, preſbytery of Brechin, and Synod of Angus and Mearns, and is bounded by the pariſhes of Dun, Brechin, Menmuir, Lethnot, Edzell, Fettercairn, Marykirk, and Logie. It is about 7 miles in length, and 2 in breadth, lying S. E. and N. W.; is low in the middle, but riſes to each extremity, and compre-hends the whole breadth of Strathmore in this place. From the manſe, which is ſituated in the centre of the pariſh, the proſpect is every way extenſive, particularly towards the eaſt, extending in that direction upwards of 20 miles. The pariſh is not much incloſed, but the face of the coun-try is uncommonly pleaſant. The ſoil is various; on the S. it is clay, pretty deep; in the middle, black earth, ſharp, but not deep, with a channel bottom; on the N. it is

partly

partly clay, and partly loam, and the hills on either fide
are covered with heath. The air is generally dry, and
wholefome; though there are in feveral places, marfhes
and wafte grounds. The parifh is remarkably well watered. A large rivulet, called the Crook, enters it on the
W.; on the N. it is bounded by a confiderably larger
ftream, called the Weft-water, which, about half a mile
from the church, joins one ftill larger, called the Eaft-
water; and thefe foon joining the Crook, they form altogether the river Northefk. Thefe waters are well fupplied with trout, and in the Northefk there is a confiderable falmon-fifhing.

Agriculture, &c.—The productions of the parifh are
principally oats and bear, (commonly called Chefter), with
fome barley and wheat. Of this laft very little is raifed,
partly owing to the lightnefs of the foil, and partly to an
opinion that two crops of other grain are more profitable.
The return is various, according to the quality of the foil,
and the ftate of improvements, though it generally is from
6 to 10, and may be eftimated, at an average, 7 after 1.
In 1784, a field, containing $7\frac{1}{2}$ acres, yielded upwards of
90 bolls meal; it was indeed the firft crop after lime, and
that year the crop was good every where. Flax, for which
the foil feems to be generally adapted, is raifed to a confiderable extent, and is ufually the fecond crop after ley.
Eight pecks of feed are fown on each acre, and the return
is 32 ftones dreffed lint, but this depends on the ftate of the
ground. An acre of lint, fold on the foot, brings from
L. 10 to L. 14. The flax, which the farmer raifes and
fpins in his own family, brings him about L. 1, 2 s. the
ftone; when he gives it out to be fpun, he pays at the
rate of 1 s. 1 d. the fpindle. A farmer of this parifh has
attempted to raife white clover feed, and for 2 years paft
has

has furnished the country with feed, reckoned superior in quality, and better adapted to the climate than what is imported. The common mode of farming here, is half grafs and half crop, with a field of peas or turnips, but there are many exceptions. The rotation is, 1. oats; 2. bear or barley; 3. oats; 4. a green crop; 5. bear or barley, along with 12 pounds red, and 4 pounds white clover feed, and half a boll of rye-grafs feed the acre. As foon as harveft is got in, the ground is fallowed or ribbed; and March is generally well advanced, before any feed is fown, but this depends on the feafon. All hufbandry work that requires draught, is performed with horfes, and the ordinary fort of plough is ufed. Horfes, cows, fheep, fwine, &c. are generally of a middle fize, but the breed of horfes and cows is fenfibly improving. Black cattle, of a year old, will bring from L. 2 to L. 3 each; this article, and grain, form the two principal commodities of the parifh, and for thefe there is generally a ready market, the town of Brechin being at the diftance of 3 miles, and Montrofe 7 miles from this parifh. New leafed farms pay at the rate of L. 1, 1 s. the acre of arable land, but this is reckoned dear, the old leafes being confiderably lower. Tradefmen and others who choofe a fmall piece of ground for their convenience, pay from L. 1, 5 s. to L. 1, 10 s. an acre. The rent of land has advanced very confiderably fince 1751; in that year a farm was rented at 12 bolls of meal, 12 bolls of oats, and L. 4 : 13 : 6 in money, making altogether fomewhat lefs than L. 20; now the fame farm is divided into 2, one of which pays L. 86, and the other L. 44 a-year. The valued rent is L. 2614: 16: 11 Scots. The real rent cannot eafily be afcertained.

Minerals, Fuel, &c.—In the S. E. part of the parifh is a large bed of limeftone, which has been wrought for feveral

veral years, and ſells at the rate of 1 s. 10 d. the boll. The coal with which the lime is burnt, is imported at Montroſe from the frith of Forth; the uſual price of that neceſſary article is no leſs than 8 s. 6 d. the boll, or 72 ſtone, for Scotch coal, and 1 s. 6 d. the barrel for Engliſh coal. This pariſh producing ſcarcely any peats, the fuel chiefly uſed is turf and broom.—Stone abounds here, but it is of a red-diſh colour, and either very ſoft, or ſo hard as to reſiſt the chiſſel.—There are 2 mineral ſprings, impregnated with ſteel, but too weak to produce any effect.

Prices of Proviſions and Labour.—In 1751, ſeed-oats ſold at 13 s. 4 d. and meal at 12 s. 4 d. the boll, butter at 4 d. the pound, eggs 2 d. the dozen, an ox at L. 2. The wages of men ſervants were L. 1 : 13 : 4, and of women ſervants, L. 1 a-year, and a day-labourer got 2 d. a-day and victuals. In 1790, ſeed-oats and meal were ſold, the former at 15 s. and the latter at 13 s. 4 d. barley at 14 s. and bear at 12 s. the boll, butter at 7 d. a-pound, eggs at 4 d. a dozen, an ox at L. 6. The wages of men ſervants have advanced to L. 7, and of women ſervants to L. 3 a-year, and a day-labourer now has 9 d. and victuals. A girl that ſits at her wheel will earn $6\frac{1}{2}$ d. a-day, at the rate of 1 s. 1 d. the ſpindle.

Population.—According to Dr Webſter's returns, about the 1750, the numbers were 529. In 1790, they were 672; 269 males, and 403 females. The cauſes of this in-creaſe are ſaid to be improvements in agriculture, and the extenſion of trade. By the regiſter for 10 years preceding 1790, the births were 143, the burials 120, and the mar-riages 56. But there is reaſon to think that the births and marriages are not ſo fully inſerted as the burials, many chooſing rather to forego the advantage of having their mar-riages

riages and the births of their children regiftered, than pay
the tax; whereas, in the cafe of burials, the mortcloth is
always employed, for the hire of which the clerk muft account to the feffion. The number of children produced
from each marriage, at an average, is between 4 and 5.
In 1790, the number of deaths was confiderably greater
than ufual, occafioned by the ravages of a nervous fever,
and which raged moft in marfhy places. There are in the
parifh, 8 heritors, 3 of whom refide; 27 farmers, and 16
families of tradefmen.

Stipend, Church, Poor, &c.—The ftipend is L. 322, 17 s.
4 d. Scots, including L. 30 for communion elements, 13
bolls of oats, 23¾ bolls of meal, and 23¼ bolls of bear, the
whole not exceeding, at an average, L. 65 Sterling a-year.
Of the above, there is a part paid out of the neighbouring
parifh of Brechin. The manfe was built in 1748; and,
as this diftrict is compofed of two united parifhes, the minifter has two glebes, one of 5, and the other of 3 acres,
though, as the latter lies at the diftance of 2 miles from
the manfe, it is of little value. The church is little better
than a heap of ruins, and has all the marks of great antiquity. In Popifh and Epifcopal times, it was the church
of the Chantor of the Cathedral of Brechin. In the church-
yard are 3 graves, which, according to tradition, are the
burial places of 3 Danifh Generals.—Befides families who
receive occafional fupplies, there are 10 poor on the roll;
one of thefe is a lunatic, and for fome years coft the parifh
L. 10, but the expence is now reduced to L. 7 a-year; the
others are maintained in their own houfes. The funds a-
rife from the weekly collections, which, on an average,
are 4 s. 7 d. the profits of the mortcloth, and the intereft
of L. 187 capital ftock, amounting altogether to about L. 22
a-year.

Roads.

Roads.—The great roads from Brechin to Aberdeen, and from Brechin to Glenesk, pass through this parish, and are in tolerable repair; but the road from hence to Montrose, and the private roads, are a disgrace to the country. In 1789, an act of Parliament was obtained to repair the roads in this county, by which the statute-labour is converted into money, at the rate of L. 1, 4 s. for every L. 100 Scots of valued rent. The sense of the parishioners of Strickathrow, with respect to this act, is, that commutation of labour into money is an advantage both to them and to the roads, provided the sum is moderate; but in the present instance it is deemed too high.

Antiquities, and Miscellaneous Observations.—There is a place in the parish called Blackdikes, which is thought to be a corruption of Battle-dikes. This conjecture is strengthened by there being the remains of a camp of an oblong figure, 2 sides of which are still visible, lying in the neighbourhood, in the parish of Brechin. N. W. from this encampment, at the distance of about 3 miles, are 2 hills, forming a part of the Grampian Mountains, called Caterthun, or ' the East and West Cater,' the one surrounded with an immense assemblage of stones, the other with an earthen rampart, both being in a favourable situation for a camp. It is very strongly conjectured that this is the place mentioned by Tacitus, where the engagement between Agricola and Galgacus, General of the Caledonians, happened. Under this head, it may be mentioned that, according to some writers, the church-yard of Strickathrow was the scene of the abject surrender of the Crown of Scotland, by John Baliol, to King Edward I. in 1296.—Nature has denied coal to this parish, and that want is more sensibly felt by a tax of 2 s. the boll upon importation.

Coal,

Coal, however, is reckoned the cheapeſt fuel to be procured, peats being very dear.—The grain produced here
is of an inferior quality, and ſells lower than what is
raiſed in the more ſoutherly part of the county. Short
leaſes may alſo be ranked under this head, though they
are not peculiar to this pariſh.

PARISH OF TANNADICE,

(COUNTY OF FORFAR, SYNOD OF ANGUS AND MEARNS, PRESBYTERY OF FORFAR).

By JOHN JAMIESON, D. D. *Forfar.*

Name, Situation, &c.

THERE is no evidence that the name of this parish has been changed. The more ancient orthography is *Tannadys* or *Tannadyse*. This name is most probably of Gaelic origin.

It needs scarcely to be observed, that this parish is situated in the county of Forfar, in the presbytery of Forfar, and in the synod of Angus and Mearns. It extends about twelve English miles from E. to W.; in some places it is eight or ten miles broad; but, at an average, about four. It is bounded by the parish of Cortachie on the W.; by Outhlaw and Aberlemno on the S.; by Fern and Carraldstone on the E.; and by Fern and Lethnot on the N.

The

The greateſt part of the ground is hilly or mountainous. The ſoil, in the lower parts of the pariſh, is in general good. It is more inclined to clay than ſand, except on the brink of the river Eſk. The air is dry, pretty ſharp in winter, but in general wholeſome. In former times the ague prevailed much, eſpecially in one diſtrict, called the Glen of Ogil. But now the caſe is otherwiſe. The moſt common diſtemper is the low nervous fever, which may indeed be conſidered as the characteriſtic diſtemper of this county. Twenty or thirty years ago, what is commonly called the *louping ague* greatly prevailed. This diſeaſe, in its ſymptoms, has a conſiderable reſemblance to *St Vitus's dance.* Thoſe affected with it, when in a paroxyſm, often leap or ſpring in a very ſurpriſing manner, whence the diſeaſe has derived its vulgar name. They frequently leap from the floor to what, in cottages, are called the *baulks*, or thoſe beams by which the rafters are joined together. Sometimes they ſpring from one to another with the agility of a cat, or whirl round one of them with a motion reſembling the fly of a jack. At other times they run, with aſtoniſhing velocity, to ſome particular place out of doors, which they have fixed on in their minds before, and perhaps mentioned to thoſe in company with them, and then drop down quite exhauſted. It is ſaid, that the clattering of tongs, or any noiſe of a ſimilar kind, will bring on the fit. This melancholy diſorder ſtill makes its appearance; but it is far from being ſo common as formerly. Some conſider it as entirely a nervous affection; others as the effect of worms. In various inſtances, the latter opinion has been confirmed by facts.

There are ſeveral mineral ſprings within the bounds of this pariſh, but none of any conſequence. It contains no lake. But the want is amply ſupplied by the beautiful South Eſk, which in ſome places forms the boundary of the

pariſh,

pariſh, and in others runs through it; and by the limpid Noran, a ſtream which ſeeks its way from the hills to Eſk over a very clear and pebbly bed. The name of Eſk is common to a number of rivers in Britain; and the reaſon is obvious, as it literally ſignifies *water;* being the Celtic word *Uiſc* or *Iſc,* with very little variation. The manner in which the people of this country generally ſpeak of the North Eſk evidently reſpects the meaning of the name; for they call it *the North Water.* It is at leaſt highly probable that South Eſk may be viewed as a claſſical river, as the *Aeſica* of the Romans. In the Itinerary of Richard of Cirenceſter, *ad Aeſicum* is mentioned as one of the Roman ſtations in the province of Veſpaſiana; and it is marked as twenty-three miles diſtant from *ad Tavum,* or one of their ſtations on Tay. Now, although there are remains of a Roman camp at Kethick, near North Eſk, the diſtance does not anſwer; whereas there is a Roman camp at Battledikes, on the other ſide of the river from Tannadice *.

The banks of Eſk preſent a variety of delightful and romantic ſcenes. By far the greater part of this pariſh lies on the north ſide of the river. Here many ſalmon and ſeatrout uſed to be catched; but of late years their number is much diminiſhed. This is greatly owing to the height of the dam-dikes erected further down the river. It is alſo a general complaint with thoſe who are fond of fiſhing, that, where there are *cruives,* no regard is paid to the old equitable law concerning the Saturday's *Sloppe.*

Here, a good number of years ago, a conſiderable fiſhing was carried on in Eſk for the freſh water oyſter, in order to procure pearls. Some of theſe were ſo valuable, that L. 4 have been given for one at the firſt market. One was got
nearly

* This camp is deſcribed in No. 36 of the Bibliotheca Topographica Britannica; and in Gough's edition of Cambden's Britannia.

nearly as large as the ball of a pocket piftol. They were generally bought up, from thofe who fifhed for them, by people from Brechin ; and it is faid that this trade turned out to good account to fome individuals engaged in it. More than twenty years ago it was given up; fome fay, that there was not the fame demand for the pearls as formerly. It is afferted, however, that the fhells were nearly exhaufted, by reafon of the great number of hands employed in collecting them.

The only remarkable mountain in this parifh is St Arnold's feat ; on the top of which there is a large cairn. The hills are covered with heath, but are not rocky. The parifh exhibits no appearances which may be called volcanic, in the common fenfe of the term. But one natural phenomenon deferves to be mentioned. Near the eaftern extremity of the parifh is a fpot of ground, commonly called, the *Deil's Hows, i. e.* the *Devil's Hollows.* It has received this name from its being fuppofed that the devil has here given fome remarkable difplays of his prefence and power. It is a fmall hollow, furrounded with moorifh ground. At different times, within the memory of fome alive, pieces of earth, of 150 or 160 ftones weight, have been thrown out from the adjoining ground, without any vifible caufe. Upon examining the fpot, however, and digging to the depth of a foot and a half, or two feet, there appears a *ftratum* of a yellowifh colour, mixed with fmall ftones, thoroughly impregnated in the fame manner. At firft it feemed that the occafional eruptions might be partly owing to fome fulphureous fubftance confined here. But in confequence of fubjecting one of the ftones to a chemical procefs, it appears to contain no fulphur, nothing but argillaceous earth and iron. When calcined, the fubftance forms a good red ochre. I have been informed by one who has refided many years in the neighbourhood, that fuch eruptions

tions have taken place in this ſpot three or four times within his recollection, at the diſtance of twelve or ſixteen years
from each other.

I have heard of no figured ſtone but one, which was
lately found in the foundation of an old houſe; the back
of which houſe formed part of the wall of the church-yard.
It exhibits the figure of a man, very rudely cut, with his
head uncovered, and having a looſe garment, like a Highland *plaid*, thrown over his ſhoulders. With the one hand
he lays hold of the mouth of an animal, which has been
thought to be a lion, but has more appearance of a wild
boar. With the other, he brandiſhes a ſword or dagger,
with which he threatens deſtruction to his prey. There
has been an inſcription over the head of this figure, as
would ſeem, in Saxon characters. But only two or three
of theſe are now diſcernible; as the ſtone has not only been
broken into two pieces, but has been otherwiſe mutilated,
by the unſparing hands of ſome workmen employed to
repair the wall. It is not improbable, that this might be
an ancient grave-ſtone.

In a rock, at the weſtern extremity of the pariſh, exactly
on the north ſide of the bridge of Cortachie, a very coarſe
kind of marble is found, in ſmall veins. Not far from this,
in the pariſh of Cortachie, is a rock, the ſtones found in
which, from the deſcription given of them, ſeem to reſem-
ble quartz. They have ſomewhat the appearance of gold,
moſt probably in conſequence of metallic impregnation;
whence the rock itſelf is called the *Golden Craig*. The pariſh of Tannadice abounds with free-ſtone and moor-ſtone.
The large ſtones found in the field in detached pieces, are
here generally called *outliers*, to diſtinguiſh them from
thoſe found in beds. There is alſo abundance of the ſtone
vulgarly called *ſcurdie*, the ſame which is commonly known
by the name of *whin* in the weſtern parts of Scotland, and
uſed

used for paving streets. A bed of this kind of stone is said to extend to this parish, from the Milntown of Mather, a place in the county of Kincardine, between Montrose and John's-haven. Slate, of the grey kind, is found in the Glen of Ogil.

Inundations are not frequent here. About twenty years ago, however, all the houses in the farm-town of Justing-haugh were swept away by an inundation of the river Esk. Since that time a good deal of money has been expended in this quarter, in forming what are called *heads*, or angular banks of stone, for keeping off the water on the north side of the river.

This parish boasts of no remarkable quadrupeds. The land is infested with foxes, and the water with otters. Roes sometimes come down from the hills, and lodge in the woods; they are very common in the higher parts of the parish. There even the red deer abound. Besides partridge, grouse, the fieldfare, and other common birds, they have one called the *oswald*, or *oswat*, very much resembling a blackbird. This, I suppose, is what the English call the *ousel*, and describe as the very same with the blackbird. What is here called the *oswald*, however, passes for a different species. Various birds of passage make their appearance here, as wild-geese, swallows, lapwings, woodcocks, dottrels, &c.

Many cattle are bred in this parish. They are of an ordinary size. An ox fully grown often weighs 40 or 50 stones.

By reason of the parish being vacant, no exact account of the population can be obtained. By Dr Webster's account in 1755, it amounted to 1470. Fifty or sixty years ago there were 400 communicants; now there are generally between 500 and 600. At an average, there are annually 15 births, and 8 or 9 deaths. In the year 1794, however,

30 died. This was not the conſequence of any particular diſtemper; but this year proved fatal to a number of old people. Annually there are about 20 marriages. None have died, for a conſiderable time paſt, who have exceeded 86 years of age. But there is one perſon living in the pariſh, who is above 90.

As far as I can learn, the only Diſſenters are a few of the Epiſcopalian communion. The pariſh includes about 106 farms, but not the ſame number of farmers, as ſome of them poſſeſs more than one farm. There has, it is ſaid, been, of late years, a decreaſe as to population, in conſequence of the converſion of ſmall farms into larger, and the removal of a number of cottagers from their poſſeſſions. None, indeed, have been under the neceſſity of leaving the pariſh for want of employment. Thoſe who have left it have generally done ſo from the cauſes already mentioned, whence they have been obliged to remove into towns. It is ſuppoſed, that there may be about 200 ploughs in the pariſh. In the lower part of it, they are generally ſuch as are drawn by two horſes. In the higher, four are uſed. The ploughs are moſtly of the new conſtruction, with iron heads, and what are called metal boards. There are at leaſt between 200 and 300 carts. The beſt arable land is let at L. 1, or L. 1, 1 s.; inferior, at from 5 s. to 15 s. *per* acre. From what has been already ſaid, with reſpect to the converſion of ſmall into large farms, it muſt be evident that the number of farms is diminiſhing.

There is not much ground incloſed with ſtone fences. The farmers, indeed, are univerſally convinced of the advantages ariſing from proper incloſures. But they are unwilling to ſubmit to the expence; and ſome, even to pay the intereſt of the money which the proprietors might expend for this purpoſe. The old plan of incloſing with
earthen

arethen fences is generally given up, except for protecting young trees.

Not above one half of the land is laboured. The rest consists of mountains, moors, and plantations. The parish not only generally supplies itself with provisions, but spares a considerable overplus to other places. In the years 1782 and 1783 there was less scarcity than during last winter. The supply of meal, given by Government *anno* 1783, for assisting those parishes which were straitened for provisions, was found unnecessary here. Notwithstanding the general scarcity this year, little grain has been imported into the parish.

No hemp is raised here. But a considerable quantity of ground is employed in the culture of flax. Although this of necessity varies, it is supposed that, at an average, there may be 40 or 50 acres annually sown with flax-seed. Within the memory of some still living, no grass-seeds of any kind were sown. Now, a great deal of land is laid out in this manner.

A small quantity of marl was found, some years ago, in a pit on the farm of Deirachie. But it was all expended on that farm. Very little lime is used, because of the great length of carriage ; but a good deal of marl, which is brought from the Loch of Kinordie, in the parish of Kirrymuir. Some of the ground is very productive. This year, in a *haugh* on the estate of John Ogilvy, Esq; of Inshavan, I counted 21 stalks of oats growing from one root, the most of these from 5 feet 8 inches, to 6 feet high, and some of them carrying between 140 and 150 grains each.

A considerable part of the parish is employed in pasture. The hills afford excellent pasture for sheep. Wedders are sometimes brought down from the Glen of Ogil in the month of August, which weigh 10 lb. *per* quarter, and give 10 lb. of tallow.

Tenpence

Tenpence or 1 s. with meat, is the ordinary wages for a day-labourer in husbandry, whether male or female. 1 s. is the usual wages during harvest. A male-servant in husbandry, besides board, receives L. 10 or L. 12 *per* year; a female, between L. 4 and L. 5. Few carpenters, masons, &c. regularly labour in this parish. A tailor works for 10 d. a-day, with meat. The people are in general very industrious. There are a few weavers, some of whom are employed in the Osnaburgh trade; but the generality in what is called *country work*, for the use of families. There has been a great alteration in dress within the last twenty years. It is now far more expensive than formerly. A great many articles of dress are bought, which people used to manufacture for themselves.

The fuel used in the higher parts of the parish consists of peat and turf; in the lower, of coals, furze, and broom. The greatest disadvantage under which this parish labours, the lower part of it at least, is the want of fuel. Coals must be brought from Montrose or Arbroath, both about twenty miles distant.

The roads are greatly improved of late. This year, L. 105 have been expended in making and repairing private roads, leading to the turnpike-road newly formed between Forfar and Brechin, part of which lies in this parish. The general opinion is in favour of the turnpike-roads.

The prices of provision correspond to those of the neighbouring parishes. Butter, this year, (1796), sells at 1 s. *per* lb. The price of cheese is from 5 s. to 6 s. 8 d. *per* stone, according to the quality.

The *broad Scotch* is the only language spoken here. Some of the names of places are of Gaelic, and others of Gothic origin; although the former seems to abound most. To this class the following evidently belong: *Coul, Memus,* or *Memis, Ogil, Kinaltie, Balduckie, Balgillo, Quiech, Cairn, Inshavan,*

Infhavan, Achlouchrie. Infhavan is said to fignify *the ifland furrounded with water.* Befides the evident tautology of fuch a defignation, there is no reafon to fuppofe that it was ever defcriptive of the fituation of the place. The meaning given to *Achlouchrie*, which, it is faid, means the *cowhaugh*, is more natural, as it correfponds to the local fituation ; for a confiderable part of the grounds, which receive this name, lies low on the border of Efk. *Barn-yards, Jufting-haugh, Whitewall*, &c. are evidently Gothic. *Murthall* feems to acknowledge the fame origin.

The real rent of the parifh is between L. 3000 and L. 4000 Sterling. There are thirteen heritors, three of whom only are refident. The valued rent is divided in the following proportions, in Scotch money :

Cairn, Newmiln, and Quarriehill,		L. 256	0	0
Whitewall,	-	145	0	0
Infhewan and Eafter Memus,	-	533	6	0
Wefter Ogil,	-	700	0	0
Coul, the property of Mr Ogilvy of Iflabank,		1217	10	0
Findourie,	-	567	10	0
Glenquiech,	-	100	0	0
Forfechy, and the Miln of Cortachie,		230	13	4
Nethertown of Balgillo and Muirtown,		180	0	0
Wefter Memus,	-	166	13	4
Balgillo,	-	166	13	4
Eafter Ogil,	-	300	0	0
Kinaltie,	-	282	12	7
		L. 4845	19	3

The patronage of this parifh belongs to St Mary's College St Andrews. One of the Popes made a grant of the lands of Tannadice, for the erection of this College ; but in what year I have not been able to learn. In a feifin, dated

ted *anno* 1614, they are defigned *the ecclefiaftical lands of Tannadyfe.* The tithes are all exhaufted. The old ftipend confifted of one-third of the value of the tithes, amounting to 1000 merks *Scotch*, with 100 for providing elements. The ftipend has been lately augmented to L. 100 Sterling, exclufive of the glebe.

The oldeft regifter extant reaches no farther back than to the year 1693. Mr George Lyon, who feems to have been Epifcopalian minifter here for many years, was allowed to continue till the year 1715; when, on account of the ftate of public matters, many minifters of this perfuafion, who had been formerly fuffered to keep poffeffion of the parifh churches, and to enjoy the livings, were turned out. He was fucceeded by a Prefbyterian minifter of the name of Oliphant; and he, *anno* 1724, by Mr John Ogilvie, formerly minifter of Cortachie and Clova, Mr John Weath was fixed here, *anno* 1743; and was fucceeded by Mr John Buik, *anno* 1767. He died in March laft. The church is prefently vacant. During Mr Weath's incumbency both the church and manfe were repaired. The church is fuppofed to be pretty old; but it is not known when it was built.

Eleven or twelve perfons ufually receive alms. The contributions for the relief of the poor annually amount to about L. 30. A fmall fund, which produces L. 1 *per year*, was left, for their benefit, by Mr Ramfay of Kinaltie.

This parifh furnifhes very little to pleafe the tafte of an antiquary. On the north fide of Efk, very near the place where the bridge of Shealhill now ftands, formerly ftood the caftle of Quiech, the refidence of the Earls of Buchan, who, in ancient times, had an extenfive property in this county. The fituation is romantic; and was ftill more adapted for being the feat of a feudal chieftain, by the fecurity

rity which is promifed, than by its pleafantnefs. The caftle was built on a precipitous rock, immediately over-hanging the river. This rock appears as if infulated by na-ture. A ftream pours down through a deep chafm on each fide of it. Thus it fcarcely required any artificial means of defence. No veftiges of this ancient caftle are now dif-cernible. A humble cottage occupies its place. Within thefe few years, part of one of the walls of the chapel was ftanding. It was neatly built with hewn ftones. But they have been lately carried off, and applied fome other way.

A hill, in the neighbourhood of Achlouchrie, receives the name of *the Caftlehill.* Like the fite of the caftle of Quiech, it overhangs the river, which here runs in a deep bed, by reafon of the high rocks on either fide. A fofle, ftill twelve feet deep and thirty wide, forms a femicircle round this hill. This, it is fuppofed, had been dug with a defign to bring in water from the river for defending the place. It would feem, however, that there never has been any building here, as there are no marks of foundations.

Near the village of Tannadice, there is a place called *the Caftle of Barnyards.* According to the tradition of the country, a gentleman of the name of Lindfay began to erect a caftle here ; but having killed the proprietor of Finhaven, in a quarrel, near this place, was obliged to fly. Thus, it is faid, the building was never finifhed. Within thefe few years, feveral of the vaults were ftanding ; and fom eof the walls, from five to feven feet in height. But the ftones have been employed for building on the farm. Some cen-turies ago, great part of this county was in the poffeffion of the Lindfays, whofe chief, the Earl of Crawford, had his refidence at Findhaven, a little way from this, on the other fide of the river. The Lindfays, formerly of Glenquiech, pretended to be the proper heirs of the lands of Barnyards.

There

There are various *Laws* in this pariſh ; as the Law of Balgillo, the Law of Balduckie, the Law of Coul, and ſeveral others.

About twenty years ago, a conſiderable number of coins, both gold and ſilver, were found at Balgillo. But it is not known to what country, or to what age, they belonged.

PARISH OF TEALING.

(COUNTY OF FORFAR.)

By the Rev. Mr JOHN GELLATLY.

Name, Situation, Extent, Surface, Soil, &c.

THE name of the parifh, (fometimes corruptly fpelled *Telin*), is Gaelic, and fignifies " a country of brooks " or waters;" in which, indeed, this fmall diftrict a- bounds. It is fituated in the prefbytery of Dun- dee, and Synod of Angus and Mearns. It lies along the fouth fide of the Seidlaw hills, and is about 3 Eng- lifh miles from E. to W.; and from 2 to 1 N. and S. ex- clufive of two fmall farms which run out about 2 miles farther to the N.; and a third entirely detached from it on the W. It is is bounded on the W. by the parifh of Auch- terhoufe; by thofe of Glammis and Kinnettles on the N.; by Inverarity and Murrofe on the E.; and on the S. by Mains and Strathmartine. Its boundary on the N. is, for the greater part, a line running along the ridge of the hills juft mentioned; on the S. the little water of Fithie. The only hills in the parifh are thofe of Seidlaw, the moft con- fiderable range in this county next to the Grampians. Their tops are covered with heath; farther down, there is

a

a good deal of broom, interfperfed with patches of fhort grafs, affording good pafture for young black cattle. On the moft eafterly within this parifh, is a beautiful plantation of firs, containing not lefs than 150 acres. The fummit of the higheft, called Craig Owl, is found, by actual meafurement, to be 1100 feet above the plain; but the plain itfelf is full 500 feet above the level of the fea. There is fome grey flate, a good deal of moor-ftone, and plenty of free-ftone. The laft, however, lies rather deep, and is fome-what difficult to be got at.

The cultivated part of the parifh forms a plain gently declining towards the S.; of a foil light and gravelly towards the hill, rather fitter for pafture than tillage, black, deep and rich, fometimes inclining to clay in the middle; in the fouthern parts rather marfhy, and moftly ufed as pafture, or natural meadow. The great fault of the foil in general is an excefs of moifture, owing partly to the vicinity of the hill, but chiefly to a ftratum of clay, or rather clay and gravel, which runs immediately under the whole of it. The air is rather moift and cold, yet not, upon the whole, unhealthful. Sickly people from other quarters, fometimes find a fummer's refidence in it beneficial. The rheuma-tifm is the only diftemper remarkably prevalent. It may in part be owing to the nature of the air; but more pro-bably to the damp earthen floors, and infufficient doors and windows of the greater part of the houfes.

Population.—The population of this parifh, according to the return made to Dr Webfter, amounted to 735 fouls. At prefent the number of fouls is 802; of families 158, perfons to a family, 5. The people live all of them in fingle houfes, or in hamlets. The increafe in the popula-tion is to be afcribed to the erection of fome new farms. Several young people every year move to the fouthward,

to

to learn the handicraft trades. The annual average of births is 23; of marriages, 6; of burials, 18. A woman, about 20 years ago, died here, at the age of 102. There are 5 heritors, only one of whom refides. The number of confiderable farmers is 13. Befides thefe, there may be 15 or 16 who poffefs from 10 to 30 acres each, and 1 or 2 horfes. The other great clafs of inhabitants is weavers, of which there are about 90 employed in the manufacture of coarfe linens, which find a ready market at Dundee. The flax is moftly foreign, and brought from the town juft mentioned; but the far greater part of the yarn is fpun in the parifh. Two families of Independents are the only diffenters from the Eftablifhed Church.

Cultivation, Produce, &c.—Water has been long ufed as a manure in feveral parts of this county, and in other quarters of the kingdom; but as the fubject of watering in general, is either altogether omitted, or but flightly mentioned by feveral of our beft writers on hufbandry, the fubfequent account of the mode of watering land, adopted by Mr Scrymfoure of Tealing, may be of fome utility.

Mr Scrymfoure waters no lands but fuch as are of a dry black or loamy foil. Sand can receive but little benefit from water, as it cannot retain it for any time. Clay is rather chilled, and (efpecially if the following feafon prove remarkably dry) too much hardened by it. He does not water any field till it has been at leaft two years in grafs. Perhaps the year before it is broken up, is the moft proper for the operation. He finds the fpring and autumn to be the fitteft feafons for it. If it be done in the fpring, it fhould be before the grafs has made any confiderable advances, otherwife that crop will be apt to fuffer by it. If in autumn, it will be proper to draw off the water before the ftrong frofts fet in. Previous to the operation, it is neceffary to fpread the mole-hills

hills with great care; as also with the foot, to press down the run of moles, so far as it can be discerned, as it is very apt to draw off the water in an improper direction. The process commences with the drawing of water-furrows. First, one broad and deep furrow is drawn in the crown, and from end to end of the head-ridge, on the highest side of the field. This is to serve as a channel for the whole water you intend to make use of; and must be enlarged to a sufficient capacity with the spade, if it cannot be done with the plough. If the ridges be level, another furrow is drawn parallel to the first, of equal length to it, and a-bout 8 or 10 yards distant from it; and furrows in this manner are drawn down through the whole field. The more the ground slopes, the more numerous these furrows must be; and care must always be taken, that the sward turned up by the plough, be thrown upon the lower side.

The water is then brought in at the highest corner of the field, and allowed to run in the channel or great fur-row, for the breadth of 4, 5, or perhaps 6 ridges, ac-cording to the quantity of the stream. It is then dammed up, when upon a small opening being made in the lower side of the furrow, opposite to the crown of each ridge, it pours itself in an equal manner into the field be-low. It is soon intercepted by the next furrow, which serves not only as a channel for it, but as a dam-dike to make it spread itself over a considerable part of the ground immediately above : When it begins to overflow, let small apertures be made in the furrow opposite to those men-tioned before, and for the same purpose. In this manner is it sent from furrow to furrow, till it reaches the lowest side of the field. When the first 5 or 6 ridges are done suffi-ciently, (that is, when they are saturated with the water, which may be known by the soft swelling of the ground,

and

and the bright verdure of the grass), open the main furrow against other 5 or 6, and thus go along the whole.

When the ridges are much raised in the crown, as is still the case in many parts of the country, the furrows must be made in a different manner. One communicating with the first or great furrow must be drawn down the crown of every ridge, unless it was cloven when laid down in grass. From this again, at every 6 or 8 yards distance, others must be made, pointing obliquely down the sides of the ridge, till they meet and form an angle with others drawn in the same manner on the next ridge, taking care, as in the case above mentioned, that the plough throw the earth toward the lower side. The water is then let down into the crown-furrows, and stopped at proper distances, so as to make it spread over both sides of the ridge.

It would be vain to attempt to give directions for every particular situation or surface of ground. The great general rule is to draw your furrows in such a manner as to distribute the water equally and plentifully over every part. By attending to this, and taking a careful survey of the field, an intelligent ploughman will very soon see what he has to do. This also is to be attended to, after the water is brought upon the ground, and it will require a daily visit from a careful hand with a spade, to remove obstructions that may have dropt into the furrows; to place others properly; and to lead the water to such heights and dry spots as may have been overlooked. Mr S. sometimes employed a man for this sole purpose. It is ever to be kept in mind, that it is only when made to stand or stagnate on the ground, that water operates to advantage: But whether this be by depositing on the soil such rich particles, as make the immediate food of plants, or by dissolving and macerating it; or which is most probable,

bable, by both thefe means, it is not neceffary here to determine. Indeed Mr S. is inclined to think that it excites a proper fermentation, and the foftnefs which the foil thereby acquires and preferves for a confiderable time after, together with fome other circumftances, feems to favour the fuppofition.

While the ground is under water, and even for fome days after it is laid dry, no cattle of any kind fhould be allowed to fet foot on it. The water fhould be withdrawn rather gradually as otherwife, at leaft in a dry feafon, the grafs will be a little apt to decay. There is no ftriking difference between the effects of water which runs from pools, or foft water of any kind, and thofe of hard water immediately from the fpring. The former is, no doubt, preferable, but the latter will ferve the purpofe very well; and this feems to be agreeable to the experiments of Dr Home.—Such is the method of watering land, which Mr S. has followed with great fuccefs for nearly the fpace of fifty years. There is one inclofure of his which, by this management, was brought from an exhaufted ftate into good heart, and preferved an uncommon degree of fertility for a fucceffion of crops (one of them wheat) without fallow, lime or marl, and with very moderate affiftance from dung.

With refpect to the fubject in general, it may be obferved, that water not only ferves to enrich the land for future crops of corn, but alfo generally fecures an early and a large crop of grafs the year in which it is applied, a matter of confiderable importance, efpecially in a dry and backward fpring. Perhaps the only inconveniency attending it is its encouraging weeds of a certain kind, fuch as, thiftles, ragweed, &c.; but this appears to be fully balanced by the deftruction it occafions to weeds of another

kind,

kind, ſuch as commonly infeſt dry lands, but never thrive in water.

As to grain and other crops, it appears from ſeveral circumſtances, that wheat was cultivated long ago to a conſiderable extent. The culture of it was revived about 10 or 12 years ſince; when, after a very fair trial by a number of hands, it was entirely given up as unprofitable. It was found to ripen late and to impoveriſh the ſoil. Oats, barley, and a few haſting peaſe, are the only kinds of grain raiſed at preſent. About 20 acres may be employed in the culture of flax. Turnip and potatoes are raiſed on every farm, as are alſo clover and rye-graſs. Some yams have been planted within theſe few years, and the farmers ſeem to approve of them.

Of foreſt-trees the aſh, fir, elm and beech, thrive well. Oaks of a large ſize have been dug up in ſome moſſy parts of the plain, and ſome that have been planted of late are ſufficiently forward, Fruit-trees grow much to wood, and it muſt be owned difficult to raiſe fruit: The difficulty however is ſenſibly decreaſing, both the air and foil becoming more kindly by draining and planting the latter, particularly on the eaſt.

The number of horſes is about 200, about one third of which may be reared in the pariſh. Black cattle being uſed in labour now, there are about 30 kept for that purpoſe; cows about 300. With regard to ſheep, it is remarkable, that about 25 years ago there were 12 ſmall flocks in the pariſh, but that now there is not a ſingle animal of the kind, ſave a few kept by a gentleman moſtly for the uſe of his own family. They were found deſtructive to the ſown graſs, and liable to periſh for want of proper ſhelter. Young black cattle have been, with great advantage, put in their place.

The

The number of arable acres is about 3000. The parish does much more than supply itself with the articles of oat-meal, barley, beef, ale, whisky and potatoes. It may send to Dundee and other places,

Barley, 900 bolls, at 13 s. 4 d.	-		L. 600
Oat-meal, 500 ditto, at ditto,	-	-	330
Calves for the butchers, 150,		-	100
Coarse linens, to the value of	-	-	4000
Black cattle, 200,	-	-	1400
Hay, 10,000 stone,	-	-	330
Whisky,	-	-	200
Milk, butter and cheese,	-	-	500
			L. 7460

The people always sow as soon as the season and the condition of the land permit; it must, however, be owned that they reap rather later than some of their neighbours. Harvest commonly begins about the 10th September. There are about 280 acres in wood; arable inclosed, 550. The land-rent is about L. 1400.

Church and Stipend, School and Poor.—The church is of very ancient foundation, having been first built by Boniface, a legate or rather missionary from Rome, about A. D. 690. The present fabric, however, bears no marks of antiquity, and is but indifferent both as to style and condition. A few fragments of carved stones seem to indicate that the original church was an elegant Gothic structure. The stipend is about 2000 merks Scots, exclusive of the manse and garden; as to the glebe, it would be, as it generally is in the country, rather a disadvantage, if the incumbent had not been so lucky as to get a small farm. The Crown is patron.

The

The average number of scholars at the parochial school is only about 30, owing to the badness of the roads here in the winter-season, and the nearness of the skirts of the parish to the schools of the parishes around. The quarterly payments are, for English, 1 s. 6 d. ; for writing, 2 s. ; for arithmetic, 2 s. 6 d. The schoolmaster's salary is L. 6 Sterling, and as session-clerk he receives L. 2, with about L. 1 more in perquisites for baptisms and marriages. His whole emoluments, exclusive of a house, garden and small glebe of about an English acre, do not exceed L. 17 Sterling. The number of constant poor is 4 ; of those who receive occasional supplies, 5.

The collections weekly, amount in the year, to   L. 15
The rent of seats belonging to the kirk-session, to   -   6
The interest of L. 200 Sterling, to   -   10
At present there is not one beggar.

Wages, &c.—Common wages of a day-labourer in husbandry, 8 d. and victuals; in time of harvest, 1 s. a man, and 9 d. a woman, besides victuals. About 40 years ago, wages were 6 d. or 4 d. and victuals. As a child, in this part of the country, commonly finds employment at 8 or 9 years of age, a labourer has seldom, entirely at least, upon his hands above 3 children at once ; that number he brings up without assistance. The incumbent does not remember any man's asking assistance from the poors funds on account of the number of his children, however great, if he and they were in health. If they are all well, his wife, besides taking care of her family, may earn a shilling a-week by spinning ; nay, provided they have a cow, which is generally the case, she may earn other two shillings in the same space by the sale of butter for 3 months in the year. When a ploughman does not eat in the family, he is allowed for victuals 6 bolls and a half of oatmeal in the

year,

year, and a Scotch pint of milk a-day : Of the meal he
can eafily fell one boll after fupplying himfelf. The wages of a good ploughman, in general, are from L. 8 to
L. 9 Sterling, annually ; thofe of a maid-fervant, including
her bounties, as they are called, L. 3. The prices of moft
kinds of provifions are double of what they were 30 years
ago ; oat-meal, however, has rifen little more than one
fourth.

Antiquities.—On the farm of Prieftown, near the Glammis road, was difcovered fome years ago a fubterraneous
building of a very irregular conftruction It was compofed
of large flat ftones, without any cement, and confifted of
2 or 3 apartments, not above 5 feet wide, covered with
ftones of the fame kind. Some wood-afhes, feveral fragments of large earthen veffels, and one of the ancient hand-
mills called querns, were the only things found in it. It
was moftly filled up with rich black earth. A little weftward from the houfe of Tealing, about 60 or 70 years ago,
was difcovered an artificial cave or fubterraneous paffage,
fuch as is fometimes called by the country people a weem.
It was compofed of large loofe ftones; was about 4 feet
high, and as many wide, and was faid to be traced up to
a confiderable length. There were found in it a broad
earthen veffel, and an inftrument refembling an adze, both
of them formed very neatly. It ftill exifts, but is covered
up. On the farm of Balckembeck are feveral great round
ftones placed in a circle, evidently the remains of a Druidical temple. In two fandy hillocks, within thefe 20
years, were found ftone coffins, containing the fkull and
bones of a human body, with urns of earthen ware and
afhes in them. About 30 years ago there was found in
the mires, a veffel fomewhat refembling a kettle, about
2 feet in diameter, and 1 foot deep. Its materials (brafs
mixed

mixed with some other metal) and its elegant shape, gave it much the appearance of an antique vase. It was melted down, but its substance is still preserved in the form of 2 modern pots. It is pretty plain from *Tacit. in Vit. Agric.* that the Romans were well acquainted with the country between the Grampian mountains and the frith of Tay.

Miscellaneous Observations.—The people, in general, are of the middle size. They are exceedingly industrious, œconomical, rather plainer in dress than their neighbours, and not fond of a military life. Generally they are charitable and very helpful to one another. The condition of the people, for the most part, is rather more than tolerable, and they are apparently contented with it. It might, however, be, in some measure, improved at no great expence, by making their cottages more comfortable and convenient, by raising better fences round their gardens, and introducing among them the culture of a few more nourishing vegetables.

The roads, in general, are bad, and have been much neglected. An act, however, has been lately obtained for turnpikes throughout the county, and is already begun to be put in execution, but many people think they will prove too expensive.

The rent of the greater part of the open land is about 9s. the acre. Some, however, in the hands of the smaller tenants, gives from 15s. to 20s. Inclosed ground lets from 15s. to 25s. according to its quality. The farms are from about 100 to 150 acres; two farmers, however, possess considerably more. The number of farms is rather increasing, and many cottars and subtenants have, within these 20 years, been put immediately under their lairds.

About

About one fixth of the arable land is inclofed, and all the farmers, it is believed, are convinced of the advantages of inclofing. The fences are moftly of ftone.

The people have improved much in drefs and manners. Among the men, inftead of the bonnet and coarfe home-made woollens, the hat, Englifh cloth and cotton ftuffs, are much worn, and almoft every ploughman has his filver watch. The women ftill retain the plaid, but among the better fort it is now fometimes of filk or lined with filk, and numbers of them, on occafions, drefs in ribbons, printed cottons, white ftockings and lafting fhoes. The labouring fervants, formerly ignorant and lazy, are now generally fkilful and laborious. The wages both of men and women are doubled. The Sunday's collection, and all the poors funds, are doubled. The land-rent is more than doubled. The farmers live in a much more fociable manner, and entertain with great hofpitality. Their houfes, formerly covered with thatch, are now generally flated, and contain 2 floors. There are fome among them that ftill adhere to the old method of farming, yet a confiderable number are well acquainted with the principles of the new hufbandry, and practife accordingly. They fallow; they manure with compoft, marl and lime, fome of the laft brought even from England; and they crop judicioufly.

The heritors, notwithftanding the difadvantage moft of them lie under by refiding at a diftance, have all done fomething in the way of improvement. As Mr Scrymfoure of Tealing refides on the fpot, his improvements have been extenfive in proportion: He has, within thefe 30 years, planted about 260 acres of moor-ground with trees of different kinds; among which are many thoufand larches, (a tree which thrives here beyond moft others); inclofed and properly fubdivided upwards of 300 acres of arable with good ſtone fences, and near 100 acres of paſture and meadow ground with hedge and ditch; erected 3 conſiderable new farms; let a number of convenient poſſeſſions to the manufacturers at very reaſonable rents; doubled his rents upon the whole; and all without bringing any incumbrance upon his eſtate : He keeps a conſiderable farm in his own hand, and excites his tenants to the practice of good huſbandry by his own example.

The fuel commonly uſed is turf, which is brought from the neighbouring hills. Coal is likewiſe tranſported from Dundee, and its uſe is greatly increaſing. There are from 40 to 50 ploughs made after the beſt form.

In this pariſh there are ſtill ſome cottagers on almoſt every farm. Farmers differ ſomewhat in their notions about employing them. It is generally allowed, that turning off cottagers has an immediate tendency to make a ſcarcity of hands, and of conſequence to raiſe wages; and that where there are no people of this deſcription, it occaſions one conſiderable inconvenience in the time of harveſt, as then the corns muſt be cut down chiefly by ſtrangers, who, in tedious harveſts and rainy weather, are a heavy burden on the farmer. Cottagers, after all, are generally in a poor and dependent ſituation, and perhaps little villages of manufacturers and tradeſmen, immediately dependent on the land-owner, might anſwer the purpoſes of the farmer equally well, would be happier in themſelves, and of greater advantage to their country.

Parish of Tealing.

Additional Communications from the Rev. John Gellatly.

The deaths in the year 1792 encreafed about one fourth of our average number; but in the one immediately preceding, amounted even to more than double. This uncommon mortality was chiefly owing to an epidemical fore throat; the fatal iffue of which, I have reafon to believe, might, in feveral inftances, have been prevented by proper care.

On this occafion, I cannot help obferving, that one of the greateft evils under which the country people labour is, the want of proper medical affiftance. Though this, I believe, has been long and generally acknowledged, yet the only remedy for it I recollect ever to have heard propofed was, to oblige every ftudent of divinity to devote fome part of his time to the ftudy of furgery or phyfic. As fome ftrong objections may be made to this, I beg leave to afk, Would it be practicable to eftablifh in every three or four parifhes, fituated beyond a certain diftance from any town or confiderable village, a regular bred furgeon and man-midwife? I fhould be glad you found the query not altogether unworthy of your attention.

INDEX

Index

Index

Index

xl

Index

Index

Index